P9-APG-514

UITGAVEN VAN HET
NEDERLANDS HISTORISCH-ARCHAEOLOGISCH INSTITUUT TE ISTANBUL

Publications de l'Institut historique-archéologique néerlandais de Stamboul
sous la direction de
Machteld J. MELLINK, J.J. ROODENBERG
J. de ROOS et K.R. VEENHOF

LXXIV

STUDIO HISTORIAE ARDENS

Ancient Near Eastern Studies Presented to
Philo H.J. Houwink ten Cate
on the Occasion of his 65th Birthday

Philo H.J. Houwink ten Cate

STUDIO HISTORIAE ARDENS

Ancient Near Eastern Studies Presented to
Philo H.J. Houwink ten Cate
on the Occasion of his 65th Birthday

edited by

Theo P.J. van den Hout
and
Johan de Roos

Published with the financial support of

ALLARD PIERSON STICHTING,
STICHTING FRANK SCHOLTEN FONDS,
VAKGROEPSFONDS WEST-AZIE
(UNIVERSITEIT VAN AMSTERDAM)

NEDERLANDS HISTORISCH-ARCHAEOLOGISCH INSTITUUT
TE ISTANBUL
1995

CIP-GEGEVENS KONINKLIJKE BIBLIOTHEEK, DEN HAAG

Studio

Studio historiae ardens: ancient near eastern studies presented to Philo H.J. Houwink ten Cate on the occasion of his 65th birthday / ed. by Theo P.J. van den Hout and Johan de Roos.
Istanbul: Nederlands Historisch-Archaeologisch Instituut;
Leiden: Nederlands Instituut voor het Nabije Oosten [distr.]. — (Uitgaven van het Nederlands Historisch-Archaeologisch Instituut te Istanbul; ISSN 0926-9568; 74)
Met Duitse, Engelse en Italiaanse teksten.
ISBN 90-6258-075-0
NUGI 644
Trefw.: Anatolië, Hettitisch, Mesopotamië.

Printed in Holland

If we may borrow the phrase from Cicero in one of his letters to his friend Atticus, *studio historiae ardens*, "aflame with enthusiasm for history", that would adequately describe Philo Houwink ten Cate's characteristic attitude towards Anatolian Studies. Throughout the more than 35 years of his academic career at the University of Amsterdam he touched on almost every aspect of Hittitology and Anatolian languages but, whatever the subject, his primary goal has always been to further our knowledge of Anatolia and the Hittites in particular within the history of the Ancient Near East. It is with great pleasure that we, his colleagues and (former) students, whom he inspired so much with his teaching, as well as S. Alp, T.R. Bryce, A. Kammenhuber and G. Wilhelm, who were not able to contribute to the present volume, dedicate this book to him on the occasion of his 65th birthday!

Amsterdam, August 24th, 1995

Theo van den Hout
Johan de Roos

We wish to thank the following institutions for their financial support, which has made publication of this volume possible:

Allard Pierson Stichting, Amsterdam
Stichting Frank Scholten Fonds,
Vakgroepsfonds West-Azië, Universiteit van Amsterdam.

The editors are very grateful to Dr. Jin Jie for her help in preparing this publication.

Cover illustration: Cylinder seal (HMM 88-Z3) found at Tell Hammām et-Turkmān (Photograph M. Bootsman courtesy Dr. D.J.W. Meijer; see his contribution in this volume with Plate 21).

TABLE OF CONTENTS

Table of Contents vii
List of Plates ix
List of Abbreviations xi
Bibliography of Philo H.J. Houwink ten Cate xxiii
Jin Jie

Šalaš Consort of Dagan and Kumarbi 1
Alfonso Archi
Aḫḫiya e Aḫḫiyawā, la Grecia e l'Egeo 7
Onofrio Carruba
Die neuen Inschriften und beschriftete Bronzefunde aus den Ausgrabungen von den Urartäischen Burgen von Anzaf 23
Ali M. and Belkıs Dinçol
Reflections on the Musical Instruments *arkammi*, *galgalturi*, and *ḫuḫupal* in Hittite 57
Hans G. Güterbock
"Great Kings" and "Country Lords" at Malatya and Karkamiš 73
J. David Hawkins
About Questions 87
Harry A. Hoffner
Lycian Orthography and Some of its Consequences for Lycian Phonology 105
Theo P.J. van den Hout
Apology of Ḫattušili III or Designation of his Successor? 143
Fiorella Imparati
Historischer Kommentar zum Šaušgamuwa-Vertrag 159
Horst Klengel
The Palace Library "Building A" on Büyükkale 173
Silvin Košak
A Neo-Hittite Relief in Aleppo 181
Maurits N. van Loon
Comments on Continuity and Discontinuity in South Anatolian Coastal Toponymy 187
Machteld J. Mellink
A Cylinder Seal and Some Ramifications 195
Diederik J.W. Meijer
Bier und Wein bei den Hethitern 211
Giuseppe F. del Monte

Grammatische Skizze zum Text der althethitischen 'Palastchronik' 225
Erich Neu
Das Siegel B 229 von Ḫattušili III. - Puduḫepa 245
Heinrich Otten
Zur Geographie des nördlichen Zentralanatoliens in der Hethiterzeit 253
Maciej Popko
Early Travellers to Boğazköy 261
Johan de Roos
The Toponyms Tiwa and Tawa 271
Itamar Singer
Three Tablets from Tell Hammam et-Turkman 275
Wilfred H. van Soldt
Old Babylonian Corvée (*tupšikkum*) 293
Marten Stol
Old Assyrian *iṣurtum*, Akkadian *eṣērum* and Hittite GIŠ.ḪUR 311
Klaas R. Veenhof
Sigmatization and Thematization in Hittite 333
Jos J.S. Weitenberg

LIST OF PLATES

Philo H.J. Houwink ten Cate ii
Plate 1. Die Lage von Anzaf. 39
Plate 2a. Der Plan des Tempels und die Lage der Bauinschrift (schraffierter Block). 40
b. Der Gesamtansicht der Bauinschrift des Tempels.
c. Die lange Seite der Tempelinschrift.
Plate 3a. Die kurze Seite der Tempelinschrift. 41
b. Das Inschriftfragment a) aus dem Oberen Anzaf.
c. Das Inschriftfragment b) aus dem Oberen Anzaf.
d. Das Inschriftfragment im Haus von Özbey.
Plate 4a. Die Säulenbasis im Vorratskammer. 42
b. Die Bauinschrift a) im Niederen Anzaf.
c. Die Bauinschrift b) im Niederen Anzaf.
d. Das Inschriftfragment c) im Niederen Anzaf.
Plate 5. Der Gesamtplan des Tempelareals. 43
Plate 6. Ring Nr. 1, Zeile 1. 44
Plate 7. Ring Nr. 1, Zeilen 2 und 3. 45
Plate 8. Ring Nr. 2. 46
Plate 9. Ring Nr. 3. 47
Plate 10. Ring Nr. 4. 48
Plate 11a. Ring Nr. 1, Vorderseite. 49
b. Ring Nr. 1, Rückseite.
Plate 12a. Ring Nr. 2, Vorderseite. 50
b. Ring Nr. 2, Rückseite.
Plate 13a. Ring Nr. 3 und 4, Vorderseite. 51
b. Ring Nr. 3 und 4, Rückseite.
Plate 14a. Ring Nr. 5, Vorderseite. 52
b. Ring Nr. 5, Rückseite.
Plate 15. Ring Nr. 5, Zeilen 1, 2 und 3. 53
Plate 16a. Ring Nr. 5, Zeile 4. 54
b. Die Ringfragmente a) und b).
c. Die auf der Röntgenaufnahme erschienene Inschrift auf dem Köcher.
Plate 17. Die Rekonstruktion der Inschrift des Schildes. 55
Plate 18. Musicians in frieze on the Silver Fist in Boston. 72

Plate 19a. Basalt block from Aleppo citadel, 1.30 x 0.95 x 0.95 m.: genies flanking sunburst within moon crescent. After J.B. Pritchard, *The Ancient Near East in Pictures* (2nd ed. Princeton 1969), no. 652. 185
b. Detail of a. After H.Th. Bossert, *Altsyrien* (Tübingen 1951), no. 495.
Plate 20a. Basalt block in antecella of ʿAin Dara temple, 1.60 x 1.12 x 0.40 m.: false window? After ʿAli Abu ʿAssaf, *Der Tempel von ʿAin Dara* (Mainz 1990), Pl. 42b. 186
b. Limestone block left of the entrance to Great Mosque on Aleppo citadel: false window? Photograph by Mr. M.A.M. Kortenbout van der Sluijs.
Plate 21a, b. Photograph and drawing of cylinder seal HMM 88-Z3. 204
Plate 22a, b. Photograph and drawing of obverse of sealed bulla HMM 88-Z4. 205
Plate 23. Photograph of reverse of sealed bulla HMM 88-Z4. 206
Plate 24. Photograph of reverse of sealed bulla HMM 88-Z2. 207
Plate 25a, b. Photograph and drawing of sealing a on bulla HMM 88-Z2. 208
Plate 26a, b. Photograph and drawing of sealing b on bulla HMM 88-Z2. Cf. Plate 21. 209
Plate 27a. Siegelabdruck B 184, Umzeichnung. 250
b. Siegelabdruck Bo 90/491.
c. Siegelabdruck B 229, Umzeichnung.
Plate 28a. Siegelabdruck Bo 90/979. 251
b. Siegelabdruck Bo 90/1042.
Plate 29a. Siegelabdruck Bo 90/1018. 252
b. Rohumzeichnung der Keilschriftringe von a (= Bo 90/1018).
c. Siegelabdruck in kombinierter Umzeichnung (R.M. Boehmer - H.G. Güterbock, *BoHa* XIV Nr. 257).
Plate 30. HMM 86 - O8. 287
Plate 31. HMM 86 - O14. 288
Plate 32. HMM 86 - O6 side A. 289
Plate 33. HMM 86 - O6 side B. 290
Plate 34. HMM 86 - O6 side C. 291
Plate 35. YBC 10986. 309

LIST OF ABBREVIATIONS

/a, /b etc.	Inventory numbers of Boğazköy-tablets excavated 1931-1967
AA	Archäologischer Anzeiger, Berlin
AANL	Atti della Accademia Nazionale dei Lincei, Rendiconti della Classe di Scienze morali, storische e filologiche, Serie 8, Roma
AASOR	Annual of the American School of Oriental Research, New Haven
AbB	Altbabylonische Briefe in Umschrift und Übersetzung, Leiden
ABoT	K. Balkan, *Ankara Arkeoloji Müzesinde Bulunan Boğazköy Tabletleri*, İstanbul 1948
AEM	Archives épistolaires de Mari
AfO	Archiv für Orientforschung
AHw	W. von Soden, *Akkadisches Handwörterbuch*, Wiesbaden 1965-1981
AION	Annali dell'Istituto Universitario Orientale di Napoli, Napoli
Akkadica	Akkadica, Brussel/Bruxelles
Akten Lykien	J. Borchhardt - G. Dobesch (Hrsgb.), *Akten des II. internationalen Lykien-Symposions, Wien, 6-12. Mai 1990*, Wien 1993
AMI	Archäologische Mitteilungen aus Iran, Berlin
Anadolu Araştırmaları	see JKF
Anatolia (Anadolu)	Revue annuelle d'archéologie de l'Université d'Ankara, Ankara
Anatolica	Anatolica. Institut historique et archéologique néerlandais à İstanbul, Leiden
AnSt	Anatolian Studies, Cornwall Terrace
AOAT	Alter Orient und Altes Testament, Neukirchen-Vluyn
AoF	Altorientalische Forschungen, Berlin
AOS	American Oriental Series, New Haven
ARES	Archivi reali di Ebla. Studi, Roma
ARET	Archivi reali di Ebla. Testi, Roma
ARM(T)	Archives Royales de Mari (Textes), Paris
Arnaud, Emar VI	D. Arnaud, *Recherches au Pays d'Astata. Emar VI.1-3: Textes sumériens et accadiens*, Paris 1985-1986.

ArOr	Archiv Orientální - Prag
AS	Assyriological Studies, Chicago
ASJ	Acta Sumerologica - Hiroshima
ASNSP	Annali della Scuola Normale Superiore di Pisa, Pisa
AT	D.J. Wiseman, *The Alalakh Tablets*, London 1953
AttiAccTosc.	Atti dell'Accademia Toscana di Scienze e Lettere "La Colombaria", Firenze
AUCT	Andrews University Cuneiform Texts, Berrien Springs
BA	Beiträge zur Assyriologie und vergleichenden semitischen Sprachwissenschaft, Leipzig
BAM	F. Koecher, *Die babylonisch-assyrische Medizin in Texten und Untersuchungen 1-6*, Berlin 1963-1980
BaMi	Baghdader Mitteilungen, Berlin
BAP	B. Meissner, *Beiträge zum altbabylonischen Privatrecht*, Leipzig 1893
BE	The Babylonian Expedition of the University of Pennsylvania, Series A: Cuneiform Texts, Philadelphia
BIN	Babylonian Inscriptions in the Collection of J.B. Nies, New Haven
BiOr	Bibliotheca Orientalis, Leiden
Birot, TEBA	M. Birot, *Tablettes d'époque babylonienne ancienne*, Paris 1969
Bittel, Hethiter	K. Bittel, *Die Hethiter*, München 1976
BMECCJ	Bulletin of the Middle Eastern Culture Center in Japan, Wiesbaden
Bo	Inventory numbers of Boğazköy tablets
Bo 68/... ff.	Inventory numbers of Boğazköy tablets excavated 1968ff.
Boehmer-Güterbock, BoHa XIV	R.M. Boehmer - H.G. Güterbock, *Glyptik aus dem Stadtgebiet von Boğazköy*, Berlin 1987
Boğ.	K. Bittel, *Boğazköy I-VI. Funde aus den Grabungen*, Berlin 1935-1984
BoHa	Boğazköy-Ḫattuša. Ergebnisse der Ausgrabungen, Berlin
Boyer, CHJ	C. Boyer, *Contribution à l'Histoire Juridique de la 1re Dynastie Babylonienne*, Paris 1928
Bryce, The Lycians	T.R. Bryce, *The Lycians in Literary and Epigraphic Sources*, Copenhagen 1986
BSA	Bulletin on Sumerian Agriculture, Cambridge
BSL	Bulletin de la Société de Linguistique de Paris, Paris
CAD	*The Assyrian Dictionary of the Oriental Institute of the University of Chicago*, Chicago
Carchemish	L. Woolley et al., *Carchemish. Report on the Excavations at Djerablus (Jerablus) on behalf of the British Museum* I-III, London 1914-1952
CCT	Cuneiform Texts from Cappadocian Tablets, London

CHD	H.G. Güterbock -H.A. Hoffner (edd.), *The Hittite Dictionary of the Oriental Institute of the University of Chicago*, Chicago 1980ff.
ChS	Corpus der hurritischen Sprachdenkmäler, Rom
Collon, B.M. Cylinder Seals	D. Collon, *Catalogue of the Western Asiatic Seals in the British Museum. Cylinder Seals* II-III, London 1982-1986
CRRAI	Compte Rendu de la ... Rencontre Assyriologique Internationale
CT	Cuneiform Texts from Babylonian Tablets in the British Museum, London
CTH	E. Laroche, *Catalogue des Textes Hittites*, Paris 1971
CTMMA	Cuneiform Texts in the Metropolitan Museum of Modern Art, New York
DCS	D. Charpin - J.-M. Durand, *Documents cunéiformes de Strasbourg*, Paris 1981
DTCFD	Ankara Üniversitesi, Dil ve Tarih-Čoğrafya Fakültesi Dergisi, Ankara
DUS	G.A. Melikishvili, *Die urartäische Sprache*, Roma 1971
Edzard, ZZB	D.O. Edzard, *Die "zweite Zwischenzeit" Babyloniens*, Wiesbaden 1957
EL	G. Eisser - J. Lewy, *Die altassyrischen Rechtsurkunden vom Kültepe*, Leipzig 1930
Emar	see Arnaud
EVO	Egitto e Vicino Oriente, Pisa
Falkenstein, NSGU	A. Falkenstein, *Die neusumerischen Gerichtsurkunden*, München 1956-1957
FAOS	Freiburger altorientalische Studien, Wiesbaden
FdX	Fouilles de Xanthos, Paris
FHG	Fragments Hittites de Genève (*RA* 45, 183-194 and *RA* 46, 42-50), Paris 1951-1952
Friedrich, KlSpr.	J. Friedrich, *Kleinasiatische Sprachdenkmäler*, Berlin 1932
FsAlp	E. Akurgal - H. Ertem - H. Otten - A. Süel (edd.), *Hittite and Other Anatolian and Near Eastern Studies in Honour of Sedat Alp*, Ankara 1992
FsBittel	R.M. Boehmer und H. Hauptmann (edd.), *Beiträge zur Altertumskunde Kleinasiens. Festschrift für Kurt Bittel*, Mainz 1983
FsDiakonoff	M.A. Dandamayev et al. (edd.), *Societies and Languages of the Ancient Near East. Studies in Honour of I.M. Diakonoff*, Warminster 1982
FsGüterbock	K. Bittel et al. (edd.), *Anatolian Studies Presented to Hans Gustav Güterbock on the Occasion of his 65th Birthday*, İstanbul 1973

FsGüterbock^{2}	G.M. Beckman und H.A. Hoffner (edd.), *Kaniššuwar: A Tribute to Hans G. Güterbock on His Seventy-fifth Birthday May 27, 1983* (= AS 23), Chicago 1986
FsHallo	M. Cohen - D.C. Snell - D.B. Weisberg (edd.), *The Tablet and the Scroll. Near Eastern Studies in Honor of William W. Hallo*, Bethesda 1993
FsHirt	H. Arntz (ed.), *Germanen und Indogermanen. Volkstum, Sprache, Heimat, Kultur. Festschrift für Herman Hirt*, Heidelberg 1936
FsIvânescu	*Analele Ştiintifice ale Universitâtii 'Al.I. Cuza' din Iaşi (Serie Nouâ), Omagiu profesorului dr. doc. G. Ivânescu, Sectiunea II.e Lingvisticâ, tom xxviii/xxix*, 1982-1983
FsKraus	G. van Driel - Th.H.J. Krispijn - M. Stol - K.R. Veenhof, (edd.), *Zikir Šumim. Assyriological Studies Presented to F.R. Kraus on the Occasion of his Seventieth Birthday*, Leiden 1982
FsKupper	Ö. Tunca (ed.), *De la Babylonie à la Syrie, en passant par Mari*, Luik/Liège 1990
FsLaroche	*Florilegium Anatolicum. Mélanges offerts à Emmanuel Laroche*, Paris 1979
FsMeriggi^{2}	O. Carruba (ed.), *Studia Mediterranea Piero Meriggi dicata*, Pavia 1979
FsNeumann	J. Tischler (ed.), *Serta Indogermanica: Festschrift für Günter Neumann zum 60.Geburtstag*, Innsbruck 1982
FsOtten	E. Neu - Chr. Rüster (edd.), *Festschrift Heinrich Otten*, Wiesbaden 1973
FsOtten^{2}	E. Neu und Chr. Rüster (edd.), *Documentum Asiae Minoris Antiquae: Festschrift für Heinrich Otten zum 75.Geburtstag*, Wiesbaden 1988
FsNÖzgüç	K. Emre - B. Hrouda - M.J. Mellink - N. Özgüç (edd.), *Aspects of Art and Iconography. Anatolia and its Neighbors. Studies in Honor of Nimet Özgüç*, Ankara 1993
FsTÖzgüç	M.J. Mellink - E. Porada - T. Özgüç (edd.), *Anatolia and the Ancient Near East. Studies in Honor of Tahsin Özgüç*, Ankara 1989
FsPolomé	*Perspectives on Indo-European Language, Culture and Religion. Studies in Honor of Edgar C. Polomé*, McLean 1991
FsPugliese Carratelli	F. Imparati (ed.), *Studi di storia e di filologia anatolica dedicati a Giovanni Pugliese Carratelli* (= Eothen 1), Firenze 1988
Garstang - Gurney, Geogr.	J. Garstang - O.R. Gurney, *The Geography of the Hittite Empire*, London 1959

Götze, AM	A. Götze, *Die Annalen des Muršiliš* (= MVAeG 38), Leipzig 1933
~, Ḫatt.	~, *Ḫattušiliš. Der Bericht über seine Thronbesteigung nebst den Paralleltexten* (= MVAeG 29.3), Leipzig 1925
~, Madd.	~, *Madduwattaš* (= MVAeG 32.1), Leipzig 1928
~, NBr.	~, *Neue Bruchstücke zum grossen Text Hattušiliš und den Paralleltexten* (= MVAeG 34.2), Leipzig 1930
GsKronasser	E. Neu (ed.), *Investigationes Philologicae et Comparativae: Gedenkschrift für Heinz Kronasser*, Wiesbaden 1982
Gurney, Schweich	O.R. Gurney, *Some Aspects of Hittite Religion*, Oxford 1977
Haas, Gesch. d. heth. Relig.	V. Haas, *Geschichte der hethitischen Religion* (= HbOr I.Abt. Bd. 15), Leiden 1994
~, KN	~, *Der Kult von Nerik*, Roma 1970
HBM	S. Alp, *Hethitische Briefe aus Maşat-Höyük* - Ankara 1991
HbOr	Handbuch der Orientalistik, Leiden
HChI	W.F. König, *Handbuch der chaldischen Inschriften* I (= AfO Bh. 8), Graz 1955
HE I[2]	J. Friedrich, *Hethitisches Elementarbuch* I, Heidelberg 1960
HED	J. Puhvel, *Hittite Etymological Dictionary*, Berlin/New York/Amsterdam 1984ff.
HEG	J. Tischler, *Hethitisches etymologisches Glossar* (IBS), Innsbruck 1977ff.
Hethitica	Hethitica, Louvain-la-Neuve 1972ff.
HH	E. Laroche, *Les hiéroglyphes hittites* I, Paris 1960
HHL	J.D. Hawkins - A. Morpurgo Davies - G. Neumann, *Hittite Hieroglyphs and Luwian: New evidence for the connection*, Göttingen 1974
Hirsch, UAR	H. Hirsch, *Untersuchungen zur altassyrischen Religion* (= *AfO* Bh. 13-14), Graz 1961
HKM	S. Alp, *Maşat-Höyük'te Bulunan Çivi Yazılı Hitit Tabletleri/ Hethitische Keilschrifttafeln aus Maşat-Höyük*, Ankara 1991
HMM	inventory numbers of tablets and bullae found at Tell Hammām et-Turkmān
Hoffner, AlHeth.	H.A. Hoffner, *Alimenta Hethaeorum* (= AOS 55), New Haven 1974
Houwink ten Cate, LPG	Ph.H.J. Houwink ten Cate, *The Luwian Population Groups of Lycia and Cilicia Aspera during the Hellenistic Period*, Leiden 1965
~, Records	~, *The Records of the Early Hittite Empire (c. 1450-1380 B.C.)*, Leiden 1970
HSAO	Heidelberger Studien zum alten Orient, Heidelberg
HUCA	Hebrew Union College Annual, Cincinnati
HW	J. Friedrich, *Hethitisches Wörterbuch*, Heidelberg 1952

HW 1., 2., 3.Erg.	~, *Hethitisches Wörterbuch 1.-3. Ergänzungsheft*, Heidelberg 1957-1966
HW^2	J. Friedrich - A. Kammenhuber, *Hethitisches Wörterbuch*, Heidelberg 1975ff.
HZL	Chr. Rüster-E. Neu, *Hethitisches Zeichenlexikon. Inventar und Interpretation der Keilschriftzeichen aus den Boğazköy-Texten* (= *StBoT* Bh. 2), Wiesbaden 1989
IBoT	*Istanbul Arkeoloji Müzelerinde Bulunan Boğazköy Tabletleri* I-IV, İstanbul 1944, 1947, 1954, Ankara 1988
IBS	Innsbrucker Beiträge zur Sprachwissenschaft, Innsbruck
ICK	Inscriptions Cunéiformes de Kültépé, Praha
IF	Indogermanische Forschungen, Berlin
IM	Istanbuler Mitteilungen, Berlin
IPN	M. Mayrhofer (ed.), *Iranisches Personennamenbuch*, Wien 1977ff.
Iraq	Iraq, London
Izre'el, Amurru Akkadian	S. Izre'el, Amurru Akkadian: A linguistic study, vol.I-II (Appendix III: I. Singer, A Concise History of Amurru), Atlanta 1991
JANES(CU)	Journal of the Ancient Near Eastern Society (of Columbia University), New York
JAOS	Journal of the American Oriental Society, New Haven
JCS	Journal of Cuneiform Studies, Baltimore
JEOL	Jaarbericht van het Vooraziatisch-Egyptisch Genootschap Ex Oriente Lux, Leiden
JESHO	Journal of the Economic and Social History of the Orient, Leiden
JIES	Journal of Indo-European Studies, McLean
JKF	Jahrbuch für kleinasiatische Forschung/Anadolu Araştırmaları, Heidelberg - İstanbul
JNES	Journal of Near Eastern Studies, Chicago
JÖAI	Jahrbuch des Österreichischen Archäologischen Instituts, Wien
Kadmos	Kadmos. Zeitschrift für vor- und frühgriechische Epigraphik, Berlin - New York
KAR	E. Ebeling, *Keilschrifttexte aus Assur religiösen Inhalts*, Leipzig 1919-1920
KBo	Keilschrifttexte aus Boghazköy, Berlin 1916ff.
Kienast, ATHE	B. Kienast, *Die altassyrischen Texte des orientalischen Seminars der Universität Heidelberg und der Sammlung Erlenmeyer - Basel*, Berlin 1960
Klengel, Gesch. Syr.	H. Klengel, *Die Geschichte Syriens im 2.Jahrtausend* I-III, Berlin 1965, 1969, 1970
KlF	Kleinasiatische Forschungen, Weimar 1930

Kraus, Kön. Verfüg.	F.R. Kraus, *Königliche Verfügungen in altbabylonischer Zeit*, Leiden 1984
Kronasser, EHS	H. Kronasser, Etymologie der hethitischen Sprache. Bd.1-2, Wiesbaden 1963-66, 1987
~, Schw.Gotth.	~, *Die Umsiedelung der schwarzen Gottheit. Das hethitische Ritual KUB XXIX 4 (des Ulippi)*, Wien 1963
KTS	J. Lewy, *Keilschrifttexte in den Antiken-Museen zu Stambul. Die altassyrischen Texte vom Kültepe bei Kaisarīje*, Konstantinopel 1926
KUB	Keilschrifturkunden aus Boghazköy, Berlin 1921ff.
KUG	K. Hecker, Die Keilschrifttexte der Universitätsbibliothek Gießen, Gießen 1966
KZ	Kuhns Zeitschrift / Zeitschrift für vergleichende Sprachwissenschaft, Göttingen
Laroche, DLL	E. Laroche, *Dictionnaire de Langue Louvite*, Paris 1959
~, GLH	~, *Glossaire de la Langue Hourrite* (= *RHA* 34-35), Paris 1976-1977
Larsen, OACP	M.T. Larsen, *Old Assyrian Caravan Procedures*, Leiden 1967
Lebrun, Hymnes	R. Lebrun, *Hymnes et Prières Hittites*, Louvain-la-Neuve 1980
~, Samuha	~, *Samuha, foyer religieux de l'empire hittite*, Louvain-la-Neuve 1976
LKA	E. Ebeling, *Literarische Keilschrifttexte aus Assur*, Berlin 1953
LKU	A. Falkenstein, *Literarische Keilschrifttexte aus Uruk*, Berlin 1931
MAH	Inventory numbers of the Musée d'Art et d'Histoire de Genève
MARI	Mari. Annales de Recherches Interdisciplinaires
Materialien	A. kammenhuber et al., *Materialien zu einem hethitischen Thesaurus*, Heidelberg 1973ff.
MCT	O. Neugebauer - A. Sachs, *Mathematical Cuneiform Texts*, New Haven 1945
MDOG	Mitteilungen der deutschen Orientgesellschaft, Berlin
MDP	Mémoires de la Délégation Archéologique en Perse, Paris - Leiden - Nice
Meijer, Natural Phenomena	D.J.W. Meijer (ed.), *Natural Phenomena. Their Meaning, Depiction and Description in the Ancient Near East*, Amsterdam - Oxford - New York - Tokyo 1992
Melchert, AHP	H.C. Melchert, *Anatolian Historical Phonology*, Amsterdam 1994
~, CLL	~, Cuneiform Luvian Lexicon, Chapel Hill 1993
~, LL	~, Lycian Lexicon, Chapel Hill 1993^{2}

Meriggi, Manuale	P. Meriggi, *Manuale di eteo-geroglifico* I-II, Roma 1966-1975
~, Declinazione	~, La Declinazione del Licio I (= AANL VI 4, 410-450), II (= AANL XXXIII 5-6, 243-268), Roma 1928, 1978 [1979]
MHET	Mesopotamian History and Environment, Series 3. Texts, Gent/Ghent
MIO	Mitteilungen des Instituts für Orientforschung, Berlin
del Monte, RGTC 6(/2)	G. del Monte - J. Tischler, *Répertoire Géographique des Textes Cunéiformes, Bd. 6* and *6/2: Die Orts- und Gewässernamen der hethitischen Texte*, Wiesbaden 1978 and 1992
Mørkholm - Neumann, Münzlegenden	O. Mørkholm - G. Neumann, *Die lykischen Münzlegenden*, Göttingen 1978
MP	Inventory numbers of tablets in the Musée postal de Paris
MSL	B. Landsberger et al., *Materialien zum sumerischen Lexikon*, Roma
MSS	Münchener Studien zur Sprachwissenschaft, München
Mşt. ...	Inventory numbers of tablets from Maşat-Höyük
NABU	Nouvelles assyriologiques brèves et utilitaires, Paris
NATN	D.I. Owen, *Neo-Sumerian Archival Texts primarily from Nippur*, Winona Lake 1982
NBC	Nies Babylonian Collection, Yale University
Neumann, Neufunde	*Neufunde lykischer Inschriften seit 1901* (= TAM Erg. 7), Wien 1979
NH	E. Laroche, *Les Noms des Hittites*, Paris 1966
NPN	I.J. Gelb - P.A. Purves, A.A. MacRae, *Nuzi Personal Names*, Chicago 1943
Numen	Numen. International Review for the History of Religions, Leiden
OA	Oriens Antiquus, Roma
OAC	Orientis Antiqui Collectio, Roma
OECT	Oxford Editions of Cuneiform Texts, Oxford
Oettinger, Stammbildung	N. Oettinger, *Die Stammbildung des hethitischen Verbums*, Nürnberg 1979
OIP	Oriental Institute Communications, Chicago
OLA	Orientalia Lovaniensia Analecta, Louvain
OLP	Orientalia Lovaniensia Periodica, Louvain
OLZ	Orientalistische Literaturzeitung, Berlin
Or.	Orientalia, Rom
Oriens	Oriens. Journal of the International Society for Oriental Research, Leiden
Orthmann, Untersuchungen	W. Orthmann, *Untersuchungen zur späthethitischen Kunst*, Bonn 1971
Otten, Puduḫepa	H. Otten, *Puduḫepa. Eine hethitische Königin in ihren Textzeugnissen*, Wiesbaden 1975

Özgüç, İnandıktepe	T. Özgüç, *İnandıktepe. An Important Cult Center in the Old Hittite Period*, Ankara 1988
~, Kültepe - Kaniş	*~, Kültepe - Kaniş. New Researches at the (trading) Center of the Assyrian Trade Colonies (/of the Ancient Near East)* I-II, Ankara 1959, 1986
Pedersen, Hitt.	H. Pedersen, *Hittitisch und die anderen indoeuropäischen Sprachen*, Copenhagen 1938
~, LH	Lykisch und Hittitisch, Copenhagen 1949
PIHANS	Publications de l'Institut historique-archéologique néerlandais de Stamboul, Leiden
PRU	Le palais royal d'Ugarit, Paris 1955ff.
Quattro Studi Ittiti	F. Imparati (ed.), *Quattro Studi Ittiti*, Firenze 1991
RA	Revue d'Assyriologie et d'Archéologie orientale, Paris
RHA	Revue Hittite et Asianique, Paris
RIMA	Royal Inscriptions of Mesopotamia. Assyrian Periods, Toronto
RIME	Royal Inscriptions of Mesopotamia. Early Period, Toronto
RlA	Reallexikon der Assyriologie und Vorderasiatischen Archäologie, Berlin/New York
RS	Inventory numbers of tablets from Ras Shamra-Ugarit
RSO	Rivista degli Studi Orientali, Roma
SAA	State Archives of Assyria, Helsinki
SAAB	State Archives of Assyria. Bulletin, Padova
SBo	H.G. Güterbock, *Siegel aus Boğazköy* I-II (*AfO* Bh.5, 7), Berlin 1940, 1942
Schmitt, IPN V 4	R. Schmitt, *Iranische Namen in den indogermanischen Sprachen Kleinasiens (Lykisch, Lydisch, Phrygisch)* (= *IPN* Bd. V Fasz. 4), Wien 1982
Schrijvend Verleden	K.R. Veenhof (ed.), *Schrijvend Verleden. Documenten uit het Oude Nabije Oosten vertaald en toegelicht*, Leiden/Zutphen 1983
von Schuler, Heth. Dienstanw.	E. von Schuler, *Hethitische Dienstanweisungen für höhere Hof- und Staatsbeamte* (= AfO Bh.10), Graz 1957
~, Kaškäer	~, *Die Kaškäer*, Berlin 1965
SCT	C.H. Gordon, *Smith College Tablets. 110 Cuneiform Texts Selected from the College Collection*, Northampton, Mass. 1952
SD	Studia et Documenta ad Iura Orientis Antiqui Pertinentia, Leiden
SEb	Studi Eblaiti, Roma
SEL	Studi Epigrafici e Linguistici, Verona
SGDI	Collitz - Bechtel, Sammlung der griechischen Dialekt Inschriften, Göttingen 1884-1915

Siegelová, Verw.	J. Siegelová, *Hethitische Verwaltungspraxis im Lichte der Wirtschafts- und Inventardokumente*, Praha 1986
SLB	Studia ad Tabulas Cuneiformes Collectas a F.M.Th. de Liagre Böhl Pertinentia, Leiden
SMEA	Studi Micenei ed Egeo-Anatolici, Roma
von Soden, GAG	W. von Soden, *Grundriß der akkadischen Grammatik*, Roma 1952
Sommer, AS	F. Sommer, *Aḫḫijavāfrage und Sprachwissenschaft*, München 1934
~, AU	~, *Die Aḫḫiyavā-Urkunden*, München 1932
~, Heth.	~, *Hethitisches* 1, 2, Leipzig 1920, 1922
Speiser, Intr.	E.A. Speiser, *Introduction to Hurrian*, New Haven 1941
Speleers, Receuil	L. Speleers, *Receuil des inscriptions de l'Asie antérieure des Musées Royaux du Cinquantenaire à Bruxelles. Textes sumériens, babyloniens et assyriens*, Bruxelles/Brussel 1925
Sprache	Die Sprache, Wien
StBoT	Studien zu den Boğazköy-Texten, Wiesbaden
~ 3	H.M. Kümmel, *Ersatzrituale für den hethitischen König*, 1967
~ 5	E. Neu, *Interpretation der hethitischen mediopassiven Verbalformen*, 1968
~ 6	E. Neu, *Das hethitische Mediopassiv und seine indogermanischen Grundlagen*, 1968
~ 7	H. Otten - W. von Soden, *Das akkadisch-hethitische Vokabular KBo I.44+KBo XIII.1*, 1968
~ 8	H. Otten - V. Souček, *Ein althethitisches Ritual für das Königspaar*, 1969
~ 13	H. Otten, *Ein hethitisches Festritual (KBo XIX 128)*, 1971
~ 14	J. Siegelová, *Appu-Märchen und Ḫedammu-Mythos*, 1971
~ 16	C. Kühne - H. Otten, *Der Šaušgamuwa-Vertrag*, 1971
~ 17	H. Otten, *Eine althethitische Erzählung um die Stadt Zalpa*, 1973
~ 18	E. Neu, *Der Anitta-Text*, 1974
~ 23	F. Starke, *Die Funktionen der dimensionalen Kasus und Adverbien im Althethitischen*, 1977
~ 24	H. Otten, *Die Apologie Ḫattušiliš III. Das Bild der Überlieferung*, 1981
~ 25	E. Neu, *Althethitische Ritualtexte in Umschrift*, 1980
~ 27-28	I. Singer, *The Hittite* KI.LAM-*Festival. Part One - Two*, 1983-1984
~ 30	F. Starke, *Die keilschrift-luwischen Texte in Umschrift*, 1985
~ 31	F. Starke, *Untersuchung zur Stammbildung des keilschrift-luwischen Nomens*, 1990
~ 34	S. Košak, *Konkordanz der Keilschrifttafeln I. Die Texte der Grabung 1931. Mit einer Einleitung von Heinrich Otten*, 1992

~ 38	Th.P.J. van den Hout, *Der Ulmitešub-Vertrag. Eine prosopographische Untersuchung*, 1995
~ Bh.1	H. Otten, *Die Bronzetafel aus Boğazköy. Ein Staatsvertrag Tutḫalijas IV.*, 1988
~ Bh.2	see HZL
StMed	Studia Mediterranea, Pavia
~ 4	O. Carruba et al. (edd.), *Studi orientalistici in ricordo di Franco Pintore*, 1983
~ 7	O. Carruba (ed.), *Per una grammatica Ittita*, Pavia 1992
Sundwall, EN	J. Sundwall, *Die einheimischen Namen der Lykier nebst einem Verzeichnisse kleinasiatischer Namenstämme* (Klio Bh. 11), Leipzig 1913
SV	J. Friedrich, *Die Staatsverträge des Hatti-Reiches in hethitischer Sprache* (= MVAeG 31.1 and 34.1), Leipzig 1926-1930
Syria	Syria, Paris
Szlechter, TJAUB	E. Szlechter, *Tablettes Juridiques et Administratives de la IIe Dynastie d'Ur et de la Ire Dynastie de Babylone*, Paris 1963
TAM	Tituli Asiae Minoris (see TL)
TCL	Musée du Louvre, Département des antiquités orientales. Textes cunéiformes, Paris
TCS	Texts from Cuneiform Sources, Locust Valley NY
Tel Aviv	Tel Aviv. Journal of the Tel Aviv University Institute of Archaeology, Tel Aviv
THeth.	Texte der Hethiter, Heidelberg
~ 3, 4	A. Ünal, *Ḫattušili III. I. Teil: Ḫattušili bis zu seiner Thronbesteigung, 1. Historischer Abriß , 2. Quellen*, 1973
~ 11	I. Hoffmann, *Der Erlaß Telipinus*, 1984
~ 15, 16	A. Hagenbuchner, *Die Korrespondenz der Hethiter*, 1989
~ 21	M. Popko, *Zippalanda. Ein Kultzentrum im hethitischen Kleinasien*, 1994
ThWAT	G.W. Anderson - G.J. Botterweck (edd.), *Theologisches Wörterbuch zum Alten Testament*, Stuttgart
TIM	Texts in the Iraq Museum, Bagdad - Wiesbaden
TL	E. Kalinka, *Tituli Lyciae lingua Lycia conscripti* (= Tituli Asiae Minoris I), Wien 1901
TLB	Tabulae Cuneiformes a F.M.Th. de Liagre Böhl Collectae, Leiden
Troy&the Trojan War	M.J. Mellink (ed.), *Troy and the Trojan War. A Symposium held at Bryn Mawr College October 1984*, Bryn Mawr 1986
TuM	Texte und Materialien der Frau Professor Hilprecht *Collection of Babylonian Antiquities* in Eigentum der Universität Jena, Jena
TUAT	Texte aus der Umwelt des Alten Testaments, Gütersloh
UET	Ur Excavations. Texts, London - Philadelphia

UF	Ugarit-Forschungen, Neukirchen-Vluyn
UKN	G.A. Melikishvili, Urartskie klinoobraznye nadpisi, Moscow 1960
UM	The University of Pennsylvania. The University Museum, Publications of the Babylonian Section, Philadelphia
VAB	Vorderasiatische Bibliothek, Leipzig
VAT	Inventory numbers of tablets in the Vorderasiatischen Abteilung der staatlichen Museen in Berlin
VBoT	A. Götze, *Verstreute Boghazköy-Texte*, Marburg 1930
Veenhof, AOATT	K.R. Veenhof, *Aspects of Old Assyrian Trade and its Terminology*, Leiden 1972
Voix de l'Opposition	*La Voix de l'Opposition en Mésopotamie.* Colloque organisé par l'Institut des Hautes Études de Belgique. 19-et 20 mars 1973, Bruxelles s.a.
VS	Vorderasiatische Schriftdenkmäler der königlichen Museen zu Berlin, Leipzig - Berlin
Weidner, PD	E. Weidner, *Politische Dokumente aus Kleinasien*, Leipzig 1923
Weitenberg, U-Stämme	J.J.S. Weitenberg, *Die hethitischen U-Stämme*, Amsterdam 1984
WO	Welt des Orients, Göttingen
WZKM	Wiener Zeitschrift für die Kunde des Morgenlandes, Wien
Yaz[2]	K. Bittel et al., *Das hethitische Felsheiligtum Yazılıkaya* (*BoHa* 9), Berlin 1975
YOS	Yale Oriental Series. Babylonian Texts, New Haven - London
ZA	Zeitschrift für Assyriologie und verwandte Gebiete, Berlin/New York
Zgusta, KPN	L. Zgusta, Kleinasiatische Personennamen, Praha 1964

BIBLIOGRAPHY OF PHILO H.J. HOUWINK TEN CATE

JIN JIE

1. *Monographs and articles*

1960 "De Apologie van Ḫattusilis III als religieus document" *Handelingen van het Zesentwintigste Nederlands Filologencongres gehouden te Groningen*, Groningen, 224-226.

1961 *The Luwian Population Groups of Lycia and Cilicia Aspera during the Hellenistic Period*, Leiden.

1963 "De ontcijfering van de Hittitische hiëroglyphen" *Phoenix* 9, 11-20.

1964 "A Luwian connecting vowel *a* in composition and derivation" *JEOL* VI/16, 78-87.

~ Review of K.A. Kitchen's *Suppiluliuma and the Amarna Pharaohs: A Study in Relative Chronology* (Liverpool 1962), *BiOr* 20, 270-276.

1965 "Short Notes on Lycian Gram̧mar." *RHA* XXIII/76, 17-24.

1966 "A New Fragment of the 'Deeds of Suppiluliuma as Told by his Son, Mursili II.'" *JNES* 25, 27-31.

~ "Mursilis' Northwestern Campaigns — Additional Fragments of his Comprehensive Annals." *JNES* 25, 162-191.

~ *Mursilis II. De Bronnen voor een Karakterschets*, Leiden (inaugural speech University of Amsterdam).

~ "The Ending *-d* of the Hittite Possessive Pronoun" *RHA* XXIV/79, 123-132.

1967 "Mursilis' North-Western Campaigns. A Commentary" *Anatolica* 1, 44-61.

~ with F. Josephson "Muwatallis' Prayer to the Storm-God of Kummanni (KBo XI 1)" *RHA* XXV/81, 101-140.

~ "Kleinasien zwischen Hethitern und Persern" in E. Cassin, J. Bottéro, J. Vercoutter (Hrsgb.), *Fischer Weltgeschichte* 4 (= *Die Altorientalischen Reiche III*), Frankfurt 112-134.

1968 "Computer en Spijkerschrift" *Phoenix* 14, 159-165.

~ "Muwatallis' 'Prayer to be Spoken in an Emergency,' An Essay in Textual Criticism" *JNES* 27, 204-208.

1969 "Hittite Royal Prayers" *Numen* 16, 81-98.

1970 *The Records of the Early Hittite Empire (c. 1450-1380 B.C.),* İstanbul/Leiden.

1971 "The Hittite Computer Analysis Project" *Acta Orientalia Neerlandica. Proceedings of the Congress of the Dutch Orient Society held in Leiden on the occasion of its 50th anniversary, 8th-9th May 1970,* Leiden, 37-42.

1973 Review of E. Laroche's *Les Noms des Hittites* (Paris 1966), *BiOr* 30 (1973) 252-257.

~ Review of E. von Schuler's *Die Kaškäer* (Berlin 1965), *BiOr* 30, 77-79.

~ "Impersonal and Reflexive Constructions of the Predicative Participle in Hittite" in M.A. Beek, A.A. Kampman, C. Nijland, J. Ryckmans (edd.), *Symbolae Biblicae et Mesopotamicae F.M.Th. de Liagre Böhl Dedicatae* (Leiden), 199-210.

~ Review of V. Haas' *Der Kult von Nerik* (Roma), *ZA* 62, 277-281.

~ "The Particle *-a* and its Usage with respect to the Personal Pronoun" in E. Neu - Chr. Rüster (Hrsgb.), *Festschrift Heinrich Otten* 119-139.

1974 "Anatolian Evidence for Relations with the West in the Late Bronze Age" in R.A. Crossland, A. Birchall (eds.), *Bronze Age Migrations in the Aegean. Archaeological and Linguistic Problems in Greek Prehistory. Proceedings of the First International Colloquium on Aegean Prehistory*, Park Ridge, 141-161.

~ "The Early and Late Phases of Urhi-Tesub's Career" in K. Bittel, Ph.H.J. Houwink ten Cate and E. Reiner (eds.), *Anatolian Studies Presented to Hans Gustav Güterbock on the Occasion of his 65th Birthday* (İstanbul), 123-150.

~ De Hettitologie 1965-1975. Nieuwe tekstedities en nieuwe ontdekkingen op het terrein van de anatolische talen, *Phoenix* 20, 314-330.

~ the following articles in *The Encyclopaedia Britannica*, fifteenth edition, Vol. 1:
"Anatolia, Ancient" 819-825
"Anatolian Cultures" 825-830
"Anatolian Languages" 830-835.

1975 the following articles in de *Grote Winkler Prins Encyclopedie*, Amsterdam-Brussel 1966-1975^{8} vol. 11:
Hettieten 161-163, hettitologie 163, Hoerrieten 222.

1976 the following articles in J. Nuchelmans et al. (edd.), *Woordenboek der Oudheid*:
Bar-Rekub 445-446, Beycesultan 474, Halys 1307, Hantilis 1317-1318, Hattusas 1324-1325, Hattusilis, 1325-1326.

1979 "Mursilis' Northwestern Campaigns" in *Florilegium Anatolicum. Mélanges offerts à Emmanuel Laroche* (Paris), 157-167.

~ "The Mashuiluuas Affair" in O. Carruba (ed.) *Studia Mediterranea Piero Meriggi dicata* (Pavia), 267-292.

~ the following articles in J. Nuchelmans et al. (edd.), *Woordenboek der Oudheid*:
Hethieten 1396-1402, Hethitisch1402, Hilakku1411-1412, Hurrieten 1458-1460, Jamchad1551, Karatepe 1605-1606, Karkemis 1606-1607, Kaska 1612-1613, Kikkulli 1622-1623, Kis1624, Kizzuwatna 1625-1626, Kubaba(t) 1651-1652, Kumarbi 1653-1654, Kummanni 1654, Kunaxa 1654, Kussara 1655, Labarnas 1659, Luwisch 1755, Luwiya 1755, Madduwattas1779, Maras1803, Mazdeïsme 1844-1845, Midas (2) 1923, Mursilis 1958, Muski 1961, Muwatallis 1962, Naqsh-i Rustam 1979, Nerik 2005, Nesa 2008, Nuzu 2041, Pala 2104, Palaisch 2105, Pankus 2124, Perzisch 2209-2211.

1981 "Hurrieten en Hurritisch" *Phoenix* 27, 7-14.

1983 "The History of Warfare according to Hittite Sources: The Annals of Hattusilis I" *Anatolica* 10, 91-109.

~ "Instructies voor Hittitische Functionarissen. Aanwijzingen voor de 'Burgemeester' van Hattusa, de 'Lijfwacht' van de Hittitische koning en de 'Commandanten van de Grensdistricten', gevolgd door een eedsaflegging van locale 'bevelhebbers'" in K.R.

Veenhof (ed.), *Schrijvend Verleden. Documenten uit het Oude nabije Oosten vertaald en toegelicht*, Leiden/Zutphen, 160-181.

1983-1984 "Sidelights on the Ahhiyawa Question from Hittite Vassal and Royal Correspondence" *JEOL* 28, 33-79.

1984 "The History of Warfare according to Hittite Sources: The Annals of Hattusilis I (Part II)" *Anatolica* 11, 47-83.

1985 the following articles in J. Nuchelmans et al. (edd.), *Woordenboek der Oudheid*:
Puduhepa 2413, Quwe 2446, Sar(ru)mas 2636, Sauska 2647-48, Tabal 2917-2918, Tawagalawas 2950-2951, Tawan(n)anna(s) 2951, Tudhalias I-IV 3150-3163, Tusratta 3164-3166, Xanthus 3352-3353.

1986 "Brief Comments on the Hittite Cult Calender: The Outline of the AN.TAḪ.ŠUM Festival" in H.A. Hoffner, G.M. Beckman (edd.), *Kaniššuwar. A Tribute to Hans G. Güterbock on his Seventy-Fifth Birthday* (Chicago), 95-110

~ *De Hettieten. Geschiedenis en Cultuur* (brochure accompanying the Leiden exhibition "Schatten uit Turkije") Leiden, 24 pp. + 7 ill.

1987 "The Sun God of Heaven, the Assembly of Gods and the Hittite King" in D. van der Plas (ed.), *Studies in the History of Religion. Supplement to Numen* 51 (Leiden),13-34.

~ In Memoriam Prof. Dr. M.A. Beek, *Phoenix* 33, 3-5.

~ "De Hettitische wettenverzameling" *Phoenix* 33, 50-59.

1988 "Brief Comments on the Hittite Cult Calendar: The Main Recension of the Outline of the *nuntarriyašḫaš* Festival, especially Days 8-12 and 15′-22′" in E. Neu, Chr. Rüster (Hrsgb.), *Documentum Asiae Minoris Antiquae. Festschrift für Heinrich Otten zum 75. Geburtstag* (Wiesbaden), 167-194.

1992 "The Hittite Storm God: his Role and his Rule According to Hittite Cuneiform Sources" in D.J.W. Meijer (ed.), *Natural Phenomena. Their Meaning, Depiction and Description in the Ancient Near East* (Amsterdam), 83-148.

~ "The Bronze Tablet of Tudhaliyas IV and its Geographical and Historical Relations" *ZA* 82, 233-270.

~ "Hittite History" in *The Anchor Bible Dictionary* (New York), 219-229.

1994 "Urhi-Tessub revisited" *BiOr* 51, 233-259.

2. *Forthcoming articles*

~ "The Hurrian Birth Names of the Two Kings belonging to the Generation before Suppiluliumas I: Tasmisarri = Hattusilis II and Tulpi-Tessub (Senior) = Tudhaliyas III. The difference between a legalistic and a genealogical approach."

~ "The Hittite Dynastic Marriages of the Period between ca. 1258 and 1244 B.C."

3. *Editorial work*

1973 *Van beitel tot penseel. Schrift in het Nabije Oosten tentoongesteld in het Allard Pierson Museum bij het veertigjarig bestaan van het Vooraziatisch-Egyptisch Genootschap "Ex Oriente Lux"* (Leiden)

1974 *Travels in the World of the Old Testament. Studies presented to Professor M.A. Beek on the occasion of his 65th birthday* (Assen)

~ *Anatolian Studies Presented to Hans Gustav Güterbock on the Occasion of his 65th Birthday*: edd. K. Bittel, Ph.H.J. Houwink ten Cate, E. Reiner (İstanbul)

1976-1985 *Woordenboek der Oudheid*: edd. J. Nuchelmans, J.H. Brouwers, M.A. Beek, A. van den Born, Ph.H.J. Houwink ten Cate, J. Vergote, G. Bartelink and G. Bouwman (Bussum).

4. *Bibliography*:

1973 "Anatolian Languages" and "Hurrian" in J.H. Hospers, *A Basic Bibliography for the Study of the Semitic Languages* (Leiden), 84-109 and 110-113.

5. *Translation*:

1958 Dutch translation of Samuel Noah Kramer's *History Begins with Sumer*: *De geschiedenis begint met de Sumeriërs. 25 onderwerpen uit de vroegste geschiedenis*, Nederlandse bew. met een voorrede van P. van der Meer, Leiden.

ŠALAŠ CONSORT OF DAGAN AND KUMARBI

ALFONSO ARCHI

The further back in time written sources go and the more gaps are filled relating to particular areas, the greater is the number of elements which appear to have been transmitted from one culture to another throughout the history of the Ancient Near East.

Following certain cults through the centuries enables us to note which relationships were created between various populations, beyond the level of political events; which beliefs were received; which changes were provoked within cultural systems by the acceptance of external elements. The great cultural break with the past for Anatolia and Syria coincides with the advent of the Roman Empire.

In the Ebla texts (24th century B.C.) we find the divinity Šalaša, certainly a minor divinity as she only appears to be attested to four times, and never in the lists of offerings of sheep which reflect the official cult of the city. In three passages Šalaša is connected with ^{d}*Wa-da-'à-an*, who precedes her. Wada'an and Šalaša are the divine couple[1] of Gar(r)amu, a place which, according to the treaty with Abarsal, belonged to Ebla,[2] and which must have lain to the north-east, towards the valley of the Euphrates.[3] According to the fourth passage, given here below, Šalaša, represented by a female statue, was venerated also at Tuttul on the Baliḫ.

1) TM.75.G.2464 rev. V 4-10: tar bar_6 :kù šir-za ^{d}*Wa-da-'à-an wa* ^{d}*Ša-la-ša* lú *Ga-ra-mu*^{ki} "Thirty (shekels) of silver for a leaf for the gods Wada'an and Šalaša of Garamu."

2) TM.75.12505 rev. VII′ 8′-14′: 2 gín kù-gi kin_x-ak 4 $geštu_x$-lá ^{d}*Wa-*⌈*da*⌉-⌈*'à*⌉*-an wa* ^{d}*Ša-la-ša* dam$^{?}$-*sù* [... "Two shekels of gold to make four ear-rings for the gods Wada'an and Šalaša, his wife (?) [..."

[1] In the case of divine couples, the first name is that of the male god, which is followed by that of the female one preceded by the conjunction *wa* "and", cf. *ARET* VII 150 (2).

[2] E. Sollberger, *SEb* 3 (1980) 135, 67-70: *Ga-ra-mu*^{ki} *in* šu en *Ib-la*^{ki} "G. (is) in the hand of the king of Ebla."

[3] *Ga/Gàr-ra-mu*^{ki} cannot be identified with *Gàr-mu*^{ki}, *Gàr-me/mi-um*^{ki}, which was an independent town ruled by a king, see A. Archi - P. Piacentini - F. Pomponio, *I nomi di luogo dei testi di Ebla* (Roma 1993, = *ARES* II), 231-232, 242 and 239-242 respectively.

Gar(r)amu was a place belonging to the reign of Ebla; certain sons of the vizier Ibrium possessed lands there, TM.75.G.1452, *SEb* 3 (1980) 34-35, as well as certain sons of the judge Iram-damu, *ARET* VII 156.

3) ARET III 540 I 1′-6′: 2 mí[-TÚG] ^{d}*Wa-da-'à-an wa* ^{d}*Sa-a-sa* lú *Ga-ra-mu*^{ki} "2 m.-clothes for the gods Wada'an and Ša(l)aša of Garamu."

4) TM.75.G.1771 obv. X 1-15: ...] *Ib-rí-um* níg-ba ^{d}BE *Du-du-lu*^{ki} ša-pi gín DILMUN bar$_6$:kù šir-za 1 an-dùl mí ... 17 gín DILMUN kù-gi šir-za sag-*sù* 2 šu-*sù* DU-*sù* níg-ba ^{d}*Sa-a-ša si-in Du-du-lu*^{ki} *Ib-rí-um* šu-mu-"tak$_4$" "...] presented by (vizier) Ibrium to the god Lord of Tuttul. Forty shekels of silver for a leaf for a female statue, seventeen shekels of gold for a leaf for her head, her two hands and feet: gift for the goddess Ša(l)aša , brought by Ibrium to Tuttul."

Note the different ways of writing the name of the goddess: ^{d}*Ša-la-ša* (nos. 1, 2); ^{d}*Sa-a-ša* (no. 4); ^{d}*Sa-a-sa* (no. 3). At Ebla the sign *sa* expresses /š/, and *ša* is used for /d̠/ e /t̠/, a rule which is not, however, always respected.[4] Further, /l+V/ can be expressed simply by V.[5]

For the Eblaites, therefore, Šalaša was the consort of Wada'an(u), a god attested to in the administrative documents concerning cloth and metals as rarely as Šalaša, but who occurs eight times in the offering lists of sheep.[6] This means that Wada'an(u) had been included in the pantheon of Ebla. Another centre of the cult of Wada'anu was *A-dab*$_6$^{ki}, a minor locality belonging to the reign of Ebla, like Gar(r)amu, TM.75.G.1771 obv. I 1-14: níg-ba ^{d}*Wa-da-'à-nu* lú [*A-*]*dab*$_6$^{ki} *Ib-rí-um* in-na-sum. Of Wa-da'an(u), whose name would appear to be Semitic, there is no later trace.

At Tuttul, on the other hand, Šalaša was considered to be the consort of Dagan: passage no. 4 is sufficiently clear on this. Although only mentioned once for Tuttul, she is the only other divinity known of for that town, apart from Dagan.[7]

The name of Dagan is rarely used. In the texts, in general, the god is referred to by means of the epithet "lord of Tuttul", ^{d}BE *Du-du-lu*^{ki}(BE = *bēlu*), ^{d}Lugal *Du-du-lu*^{ki} (at Ebla lugal = *ba'al*, Akk. *bēlu*), or simply: "god (dingir) of Tuttul".[8] ^{d}BE/dingir kalam^{tim} "Lord/God of the country" is also to be identified with Dagan, as well as ^{d}BE *Ga-na-na*$^{(ki)}$, a locality of the Middle Euphrates, and probably some other ^{d}BE followed by a geographical name.[9] The frequency of -^{d}*Da-gan* as a theophoric element in the Eblaite personal names,

[4] M. Krebernik, *ZA* 72 (1982) 214-218. For the variants in the geographical names, see *ARES* II, 18.

[5] Krebernik, op.cit. 211. One finds *-a-* instead of *-la-* also in the name ^{d}*Ḫa-a-ba-du* /ḫalabājtu/, see Archi, *Or.* 63 (1994) 250, with further literature on the "L Reduktion." The name is not of Hurrian origin. The fem. PN Šalašu, borne by a ^{MUNUS}ŠU.GI from Kizzuwatna, KBo XIX iv 50, would, instead, appear to derive from the Hurrian *šali*, *šala* "daughter"; cf. V. Haas, *SMEA* 14 (1971) 139, who has pointed to a suffix *-šu*, which recurs in a number of fem. PNs.

[6] For the four lists already published, see G. Pettinato, *OA* 18 (1979) 111.

[7] See *ARES* II 203 section IV.

[8] *ARES* II, loc.cit.

[9] On Dagan at Ebla, see Pettinato, *Or.* 54 (1985) 234-244. It must, however, be borne in mind that the principal divinity of Ebla was Kura and not Dagan, as affirmed ibid. 244.

is analogous to that of -BE.[10] At pre-Sargonic Mari we have ᵈLugal *Ter₅*(BAN)-*ga*, and in an offering list of the šakkanakkus period ᵈLugal *Ter-ga* "Lord of Terqa"; from the oB documents from Mari it appears that "lord of Terqa", *bēl Terqa*, was Dagan.[11] The temple of Dagan at Tuttul was the most important sanctuary of the Middle Euphrates; it was there that the king of Nagar (Tell Brak) swore friendship to Ebla.[12] To the kings of Akkad the importance of this king was well-known: Sargon declares that he received as a gift "the upper land" (northern Syria) from Dagan, after having prostrated himself before the god at Tuttul.[13]

During the Third Ur dynasty, Dagan receives offerings at the court of Šu-Sin, three times alongside Išḫara, the great goddess of Syrian origin, and once alongside Ḫaburitum, the goddess of the river Ḫabur.[14]

The ancient tradition created at Tuttul, that Šalaš(a) was the consort of Dagan is received in the lists of gods of the second millennium.[15] In the documentation of Amorite Mari, Šalaš is not mentioned, possibly because the cult of Dagan of Terqa was more widely diffused at Mari,[16] and Šalaš does not appear to have been venerated at Terqa. The goddess only appears in a few theophoric feminine personal names, such as ᵈ*Ša-la-aš-tap-pí*, ARM XIII 1 III 26; ᵈ*Ša-la-aš-tu-ri-ja*, ARM XXII 10 IV 4.

A thousand years after Ebla, in the Hurrian-Hittite documents, Šalaš is connected with Kumarbi. The goddess has not passed on to new nuptials: more simply, her former spouse Dagan has been equated with Kumarbi through a syncretistic process.

In the work of systematization carried out in Babylonia and established in the great series An = *Anum* (Middle Assyrian copies), Dagan is equated with the ancient Enlil and Šalaš with Ninlil (CT 24: 6, 22-23; 22: 120). Dagan is seen as a god of primary importance, but somewhat in the shadow of Adad, the great Weather-god of the Amorites, which they had received from the Semitic peoples of the third millennium, when the principal centre of the cult of Adad was already Aleppo (Eblaite *Ḫa-lam*ᵏⁱ = Ḫalab).[17] The fact that in the series An = *Anum* the consort of Adad is Šala, a name similar to Šalaš, could mean

[10] Krebernik, *Die Personennamen der Ebla-Texte* (Berlin 1988) 150, 157-158.

[11] On the pantheon of Mari, see D.O. Edzard, in: *La civilisation de Mari* (*XVe Rencontre Assyriologique Internationale*, J.-R. Kupper (ed.), Liège 1967), 51-71 (in table 1, p. 69, *Da-gan* is to be cancelled); W.G. Lambert, *MARI* 4 (1985) 525-539. The pre-Sargonic texts from Mari have been published by D. Charpin, *MARI* 5 (1987) 65-127.

[12] A. Archi, *FsKupper* 198.

[13] Sargon b 2; H. Hirsch, *AfO* 20 (1963) 38.

[14] H. Waetzold, *Or.* 54 (1985) 248-249.

[15] A. Deimel, *Pantheon Babylonicum* (Romae 1914), 249.

[16] O. Rouault, *ARM* XVI/1, 254.

[17] See W. von Soden, in: *Ebla 1975-1985* (L. Cagni (ed.), Napoli 1987); Lambert, *MARI* 6 (1990) 641-643; Archi, *Or.* 63 (1994) 250.

that, in the Babylonian theological spheres, Dagan and Adad were perceived as gods with similar functions.[18]

In both versions of the treaty between Šuppiluliuma and Šattiwaza, in the pantheon of Mittani, only Šala appears among the goddesses. This could mean that, in Mittani, no distinction was made between Šala and Šalaš, and the form of the name closer to the Hurrian vocabulary was preferred. KBo I 1 rev. 57-58: (several Teššups) Nabarbi, Šurūḫi, Aššur MUL, ^{d}*Ša-la*, NIN.ÉGAL, Damkina, Išḫara. KBo I 3 rev. 25-26: (several Teššups) Nabarbi, Šuruḫi, Ištar DINGIR *ù* MUL, ^{d}*Ša-la*, NIN.É.GAL, NIN *ajakki*, Išḫara, Bardāḫi.[19]

As shown by the Emar texts, Dagan was still one of the principal deities of the Middle Euphrates in the 13th century.[20] He occupies an important position in the liturgical calendar, Emar VI.3 446: 8, 50′ (*be-el* numun^{meš} "lord of the seed"), 54′, 62′, 79′, 96′, 99′; 448: 4′, 5′, 18′. In an inventory of objects relating to the cult and in the *zukru*-festival, Dagan appears under various epithets, 274: 2: ^{d}Kur ^{uru}*Tu-ut-túl*; 9: ^{d}Kur *ša kara-ši* "of the camp"; 10: ^{d}Kur *ša ra-[qa-ti]* "of the bank-field"; 18′: ^{d}Kur en *ni-pi-ši* "lord of activity". 373 (*zukru*-festival): 156′: ^{d}Kur en *ṣa-lu-li pa-su-ri* "lord of protection and praise"; 157′: ^{d}Kur en *ma-aṣ-ṣa-ri* "lord of the guardian"; 161′: ^{d}Kur *iš-pa-a-at* "lord of the quiver"; 162′: ^{d}Kur en *ḫa-pa*-x; 175′, 176′, 185′, 192′: ^{d}Kur en *bu-qà-ri* "lord of cattle"; 195′: ^{d}Kur *a-bu-ma* "the father".

Šalas, on the other hand, appears only in a fragment of the "Anatolian Ritual", which harks back to the Hurrian-Hittite tradition, 480: 3: ^{d}*Ša-la-aš*.[21]

A central concept of Hurrian religious thought was that the gods had succeeded each other, generation after generation. For this reason, the Hurrians had no difficulty in equating Kumarbi, the predecessor of their Weather-god Teššup, with Enlil, as shown by the trilingual version of the series An = *Anum* (*Ugar.* 5 (1968) 137 35″-36″, p. 246, where also Ninlil is mentioned as "the consort of Kumarbi", *[aš-t]e Ku-mur-wi-ni-wi* = *A[širtum(?)]*). On this basis, Kumarbi comes to be equated with Dagan and, since in West Semitic *dagān* means "wheat", in the Hittite texts one can find NISABA instead of Kumarbi and, occasionally, also Ḫalki .[22]

In the Hurrian of the Hittite archives ^{d}*Ša-(a-)lu-uš* (variants: ^{d}*Ša-a-la-aš*; ^{d}*Ša-la* in the treaty with Mittanni) is generally associated with Kumarbi.

[18] Deimel, op.cit. 248-249; H. Schmökel, *RlA* II 100.

[19] E. Weidner, *PD* 32, ll. 57-58; 54 ll. 42-43.

[20] See D.E. Fleming, *The Installation of Baal's High Priestess at Emar* (Atlanta 1992), 240-248.

[21] On the pantheon of this ritual, see E. Laroche, in: *Fs Pugliese Carratelli* 111-117; R. Lebrun, *Hethitica* 9 (1988) 147-155.

[22] The documentation of Ugarit has been studied by Laroche, *Ugar.* 5 (1968) 453-454, 523-525. For Kumarbi = NISABA, see Laroche, *JCS* 2 (1948) 117. For Ḫalki, see the study by A. Kammenhuber, in: *BMECCJ* V, *Near Eastern Studies Dedicated to T. Mikasa*, ed. M. Mori, Wiesbaden 1991, 143-160. Kumarbi corresponds to Enlil also in the Akkadian-Hittite bilingual omen KUB IV 1 iv 22/24, see H.G. Güterbock, *RlA* VI 325.

In the 10th tablet of the *itkalzi* ritual (KUB XXIX 8 (= *ChS* I 1, 9; perhaps a later copy of a MH tablet) Kumarbi appears with Šalaš at third place (after Teššup and Šuwalijat = NIN.URTA); this reflects the fact that Kumarbi belonged to the preceding generation, i 12-20: Teššup - Ḫepat UTU of Arinna; Šuwalijat - Nabarbi; Kumarbi - ^{d}*Ša-a-lu-uš* ^{d}*Bi-ti-in-ḫi*; Ea; Šawuška - Damkina.

In other texts Šaluš appears in the circle, *kaluti*, of Ḫepat, constituted prevalently of goddesses; thus Šaluš precedes Kumarbi. The (*ḫ*)*išuwa*-festival, KUB XII 12 vi 20-25 (similarly v 33 ff., *ChS* I 4, 23; duplicates KBo XXXIII 194 vi 1-4, *ChS* I 4, 26; KUB XXVII 10 vi$^{!}$ 23-24, *ChS* I 4, 29, where the writing is ^{d}*Ša-lu-uš*) has: Ḫepat *mušuni*; ^{d}*Ša-a-lu-uš* - Kumarbi; Aa - Šimegi; Šawuška.[23] KBo XV 37 ii 17-23 (duplicates KUB XXXII 90 ii 3-9; IBoT I 24 i$^{!}$ 9-11), iv 14-22: Ḫepat's court; ^{d}*Ša-a-lu-uš* - Kumarbi; Aa - Šimegi; Šawuška; Išḫara. The same list appears in the fragment KBo XXXV 258. A different sequence is to be found in the ritual KBo XXIV 79, 2-4 (*ChS* I 2, 22): Šawuška; [...]; ^{d}*Ša-a-lu-uš* - Kumarbi; [...]; Aaiu - Šimegi. KBo XXXIII 121, 2-3: ^{d}]*Ša-lu-uš* Kum[arbi .....] Nupatik [... .

The epithet $^{(d)}$Pidenḫi, often attributed to Šalaš, is an ethnic from Piden, attested in the Alalaḫ Tablets.[24] In the ritual KBo V 2, Ḫepat is followed by certain goddesses such as Išḫara, Allani and Šawuška; there is then the sequence, iii 13-15 (duplicate KBo XXVII 131 iii 1-3): Nabarbi, Šūwala, Aiūn - Ekaldu,[25] ^{d}*Ša-a-lu-uš Bi-te-in-ḫi*, Adamma - Kupapa - Ḫašuntarḫi. The same sequence is found in the ritual (SISKUR) KUB XXVII 1+, dedicated to Šawuška by Muršili II, and reworked by Ḫattušili III. After many hypostases of Ḫepat and Šawuška (each followed by divinities closely connected with them) we have, ii 51-53: Nabarbi; Šūwala; x[..]; Ajan - Ekaldun; ^{d}*Ša-a-lu-uš B*[*i-ti-in-ḫi*]; Adamma - Kupapa - Ḫašuntarḫi.[26] KUB XLV 71, 1 ff. is parallel to this section. Similar (fragmentary) lists are KBo XX 29 rev. 3 ff. (l. 6: ^{d}*Ša-la*[*-aš*); KUB LX 51, 1 ff. (2-3: ^{d}]⌈*A*⌉*-i-u-un* - ^{d}*I-g*[*a-al-du*]; ^{d}*Ša-a-lu-uš* ^{d}[*Bi-ti-in-ḫi*]. Perhaps a ritual for Šawuška is KUB XLV 46, l. 4: ^{d}*Ša-a-la-aš Bi-*[*te-in-ḫi*].

Other lists give Uršui - Iškalli in the place of Aja - Ekaldu, such as KUB XXVII 8 obv.$^{?}$ 11-14, KBo XX 113 i 20-23, XXXIII 207 ii 8-11: Nābarwi Šūwala; Uršūi Iškalli ^{d}*Ša-a-la-aš* ^{d}*Bi-te-in-ḫi*; Adamma - Kupapa - Ḫašunta[rḫi].

KBo XIV 141 ii 2-4 is very fragmentary: ^{d}*Š*]*a-a-lu-uš Bi-t*[*e-in-ḫi*]; A[damma ... .

[23] Cf. Laroche, *JCS* 2 (1948) 131-133.

[24] Laroche, *GLH* 200; for the writings concerning Šaluš, see ibid. 213.

[25] Aja, consort of Šimegi, is a loan from the Akkadian pantheon, where Aja is the consort of Šamaš. $^{(d)}$*E-kal-du(-un)*/^{d}*I-kal-ti* is often connected to Aja in the Hurrian offering lists (see Laroche, *GLH* 39), and it is probably a loan-word too, from Akkadian *ikletu* "darkness"; Šamaš is said to be "who brightens the darkness", *munammir ikleti*, see *CAD* I-J 61.

[26] Cf. Lebrun, *Samuha*, 80.

The list of the gods of the "Rituel aux dieux antiques" stands alone, CTH 492, which for Šalas gives an entirely anomalous writing, an indication that this ritual belongs to a different tradition, KUB XVII 20 ii 4-6: Dauija; Kurwašu; Nekmi; ᵈ*Šal-lu-un*; Menkišuri.

In the pantheon of Yazilikaya, Kumarbi/NISABA (no. 40) is determinated by the head of grain, FRUMENTUM, and follows Tašmišu. Amongst the goddesses, the inscription (DEUS)*sa-lu-sa* identifies figure no. 52, which appears between Nabarbi and Damkina.[27]

27 See E. Masson, *Le panthéon de Yazilikaya* (Paris 1981) 38. Cf. V. Haas - M. Wäfler, *OA* 13 (1974) 220-222; Güterbock, *Les hiéroglyphes de Yazilikaya* (Paris 1982), 44.

AḪḪIYĀ E AḪḪIYAWĀ, LA GRECIA E L'EGEO

ONOFRIO CARRUBA

0.1 Uno sguardo alla situazione attuale delle ricerche sulla questione del rapporto fra *Aḫḫijawā* e 'Αχαιοί ci mostra qualche piccolo progresso su fatti marginali per l'aspetto filologico e storico, ma sostanzialmente uno stallo generale sull'interpretazione delle nostre conoscenze e dei fatti che se ne possono desumere. Nonostante la mancanza di prove concrete, tuttavia, è opinione diffusa che ci sia identità fra i due termini.[1]

Alcuni studiosi hanno riesaminato i documenti e le valutazioni che ne risultano sono da considerare al limite dell'inconcludenza, perché nella maggior parte dei casi si deve desumere che siamo rimasti fra Forrer, 1924[2], e Sommer, 1937[3], l'entusiasmo del ritrovamento e lo scetticismo profondo.

0.2 Per lo più gli autori mantengono o ripropongono l'originaria equazione di Aḫḫijawā con la Grecia e il Peloponneso in particolare, spesso ricorrendo al 'common sense' storico, come fa, sia pure con buoni motivi, il Güterbock[4], cui si deve peraltro il riconoscimento definitivo e ovviamente molto importante, di un 'gran re di Aḫḫijawā', 'fratello ed uguale' del gran re ittita, e di Tawagalawa come 'fratello del re di Aḫḫijawā'.

Per altri, come Marazzi (1989, 375), il problema dell'identificazione (e con ciò della localizzazione) sarebbe un falso problema ("Scheinproblem"), in quanto gli Ittiti considererebbero la presenza di Aḫḫijawā quale uno di quei gruppi di briganti e/o mercanti, strutturati come altri gruppi attivi nel Mediterraneo orientale (cfr. ad es. gli 'Amorrei' o i 'Ḫabiru'), e quindi interessante è per noi "die Erfassung der kulturelle Darstellungen, die seine Abstraktion erweckte"[5] Ciò può anche esser vero e utile dal punto di vista della

[1] La bibliografia fino al 1964 è valutata in modo critico e approfondito nella monografia di G. Steiner; cfr. anche idem, *UF* 21 (1989) 393-411, X. *Türk Tarih Kongresi* (Ankara 1990), II 523-530. Si veda anche fino al 1991, A. Ünal, *BMECCJ* 4 (1991) 16-44. L'ultima trattazione linguistica ampia del nome *Aḫḫiyawa* secondo i metodi consueti risale ad J. Harmatta, *Studia Mycenaea* (Proc. of the Mycenaean Symposium, Brno 1966) 1968, 117-124.

[2] *MDOG* 63 (1924) 1-22, *OLZ* 27 (1924) 113-118.

[3] *IF* 55 (1937) 169-297.

[4] *AJA* 87 (1983) 133-143, *PAPhS* 128 (1984) 114-122.

[5] Ci sembra tuttavia che, a parte la necessaria storicizzazione dei fatti, l'impressione che si ha

valutazione psicologica dei testi, ma schiva la realtà dei fatti e lascia intatto "das Geheimnis- und Reizvolle an Aḫḫijawā" con la conseguente necessità di scoprire comunque la verità storica.

0.3 Allo stato attuale delle ricerche in questo revival di studi su Aḫḫijawā ci sembra si siano verificati pochi reali progressi. In campo filologico, molto rilevante è quello su accennato di Güterbock circa la vera essenza del re di Aḫḫijawā e di Tawagalawa, fatto che pone questi personaggi, almeno dal punto di vista del sovrano ittito, al suo stesso livello, permettendo così di attribuire una precisa consistenza politica e storica di grande potenza ad Aḫḫijawā, già sospettata nel famoso passaggio, scritto e poi cancellato, del trattato con Šaušgamuwa d'Amurru (CTH 105; *StBoT* 16, Rs. IV 3, [23]), ma finora incerta e discussa.[6]

Un altro fatto storicamente rilevante è la conferma della datazione a Tutḫalija IV della 'lettera di Milawata' (CTH 182), già prospettata da Güterbock[7], argomentata da Singer[8], e ora provata anche dalla localizzazione nella Licia occidentale delle medesime città (fra l'altro *Pinata* e *Awarna*) là menzionate, nelle iscrizioni luvie geroglifiche di Yalburt e Emirgazi dello stesso sovrano (Poetto, *StMed* 8), che, seppure di minor rilievo per la questione di Aḫḫijawā, è importante per l'identificazione geografica di Wiluša[9], come si vedrà altrove.

1.1 E' tuttavia da un punto di vista linguistico, che mi sembra si possano registrare delle novità interessanti, operando sui nomi di luogo, la cui persistenza nel tempo è più tenace e duratura dei popoli che passano per la regione, nelle cui lingue essi entrano, seguendone le leggi di sviluppo soprattutto nelle derivazioni che si rendono via via necessarie.

Applicando criteri linguistici desunti da sviluppi pertinenti al lidio (di derivazione ittita) per le coste asianiche settentrionali (Eolia) e al luvio (e poi al licio) per quelle meridionali (Jonia), avevamo ricostruito molto tempo fa[10] i nomi locali che stanno dietro agli etnici Αἰολέες e' Ἰάονες, giungendo a quelli del II mill., rispettivamente itt.(-lid.) **Aḫḫijawāles* e luvio **(Aḫḫ)ija(wa)-wanes*, affermando così che la regione abitata da Eoli e Joni era stata

dai testi ittiti è ben diversa da quella che si ricava per i Ḫabiru o per i Lulaḫi nei testi orientali in genere.

6 E' ovvio che fatti già spesso rivisti e discussi, come quasi tutto su Aḫḫijawā, possono assumere particolare rilevanza alla luce di idee e interpretazioni nuove, come queste.

7 *AJA* 87 (1983) 133-143.

8 *AnSt* 33 (1983) 205-217.

9 Vd. H.A. Hoffner, *AfO* Beih. 19 (1982) 130-137, Ph.H.J. Houwink ten Cate, *JEOL* 28 (1983-1984) 33-79.

10 *Athenaeum* NS 42 (1964) 269-298.

l'*Aḫḫijawā* a noi nota, e che comunque gente di Aḫḫijawā l'aveva abitata.[11]

Con questo metodo procede praticamente M. Finkelberg, che in un recente articolo si propone: "to show that the ethnikon *Aḫḫijawā*, which repeatedly occurs in Hittite documents of the 14-13th centuries B.C., accurately reflects the contemporary Greek name whose development in accordance with the regular phonetic processes operative in Greek between the 14th and the 8th centuries B.C. terminated in the classical 'Ἀχαιοί."[12]

1.2 Considerando che le maggiori difficoltà prospettate nel confronto fra i due termini consistono nell'impossibilità della corrispondenza fra itt.-*ija*- e gr. -*ai*- e fra la velare spirante itt. -*ḫḫ*- e la palatale aspirata esplosiva gr. χ, specie se si pensa che si tratta di parole attestate a distanza di quattro secoli, in cui il greco ha avuto vari sviluppi, l'autrice mette in rilievo che Aḫḫijawā "looks like an extremely archaic form" per la semivocale *y* e per la velare spirante *x* e parte da questa per spiegare attraverso gli sviluppi greci la forma d'arrivo 'Ἀχαιοί/'Ἀχαία. Presupposto che *Aḫḫijawā* fosse una parola d'origine greca, il gruppo -*xiya*- diventava, tramite il processo di jodizzazione, -*xya*- e poi -*xa*-. La jodizzazione si accompagna ad un rafforzamento che nella maggior parte dei casi sfocia nella geminazione della consonante, com'è noto da sequenze quali **k(h)*- > *-*ty*- > *-*ts*- > -*ss*-/-*tt*- ecc., ma che per la spirante *x* deve essere stato un rafforzamento in un suono occlusivo aspirato. Si avrebbe così lo sviluppo **Ahhiyaw*- > **Ahhyaw*- > **Akhaw*-, da cui con il suffisso -*yo*-, > 'Ἀχαϝ-yός e infine attraverso * 'Ἀχαιϝός > 'Ἀχαιός. Da essi sarebbero derivati i più tardi 'Ἀχαΐα e 'Ἀχαιΐς.

La spiegazione con procedure linguistiche 'greche' degli etnici greci ci sembra in sostanza la sola metodologicamente corretta, pur partendo dal presupposto che il confronto fra i due termini sia legittimato dall'idea che Aḫḫijawā corrisponda storicamente ai Greci micenei, un'idea che, a tutt'oggi sembra basarsi solo sul 'common sense' e per la cui prova comunque non si ha al momento alcuna altra soluzione storicamente valida.

2.1 Ci sono tuttavia alcune objezioni e dei fatti nuovi che ci permettono di

[11] Oggi deriveremmo il nome direttamente da *(*Aḫḫ*)*ijawanes*, (cfr. §4.2.). Per Αἰολέες forse può restare l'etimo precedente da **Ahhijawales*, soprattutto a causa di -*o*- (< -*awa*- o -*au*-). Superfluo ricordare che la sparizione di *h* corrisponde alla psilosi di entrambi i dialetti asianici. Si tratta beninteso di designazioni dei Greci frequentatori o abitanti delle coste da parte di parlanti lingue anatoliche del NO e del SO, che furono poi utilizzate anche dagli abitanti della Grecia continentale.

E' chiaro che nella prospettiva qui delineata la tradizione delle migrazioni eoliche e joniche verso oriente va riesaminata a fondo.

[12] *Glotta* 66 (1988) 127.

andare oltre la constatazione della derivazione di 'Αχαιοί da *Aḫḫijawā*.

Innanzitutto, se il nome rappresenta un prototipo greco, come supposto, e c'è perfetta corrispondenza fra le sillabe itt. *-ija-* e *-wa* con quelle omofone ancora esistenti nel contemporaneo miceneo, non sappiamo invece che cosa possa corrispondere al suono ittito *-ḫḫ-*. In miceneo, dove esiste un *h* [*x*, ʾ, o ʿ ?] che è talvolta notato graficamente (per es. dal segno a_2, cfr. Lejeune, *Phonétique historique du mycénienne et du grec ancien* (Paris1972), §81; Doria, *Avviamento allo studio del miceneo* (Roma 1965), 55s.), esso proveniva, già allora, spesso da **s*: cioè *Aḫḫijawā* sarebbe derivata da un **As(s)iyawa*.

Non si può neppure pensare che l'itt. *-ḫḫ-* sia la spirantizzazione (straniera) di una occlusiva velare aspirata micenea -χ-, perché questo suono avrebbe certamente dato itt. *-kk-*.[13]

Di una laringale poi, cui potrebbe corrispondere itt. *-ḫḫ-*, non c'è più traccia in miceneo, se non andiamo errati, mentre l'ittito ne conserva sicuramente una e indizi di almeno un'altra. Il χ (*kh* dell'autrice) è quasi sicuramente un ripiego greco per la resa delle laringali (cfr. qui avanti §3.3 per i nomi luvi e lici), formalizzatosi molto presto, forse già in età micenea (cfr. *a-ka-wi-ja-de* ?).

2.2 Circa la determinazione del nome non sembra quindi che restino altre soluzioni che le seguenti:

1) si tratta di un nome pregreco e preittito (preanatolico) che aveva un suono adattato in modo diverso nelle due lingue: occlusiva velare aspirata in greco; spirante laringale in ittito.

In questo caso la lingua originaria è indeterminabile e gli sviluppi fonetici del nome (rappresentati, in questo caso, sia da *-x-* e *-ḫḫ-*, sia da *-iya-* e *-ai-*, così importante quest'ultimo nell'esame della Finkelberg), sfuggono certo ad ogni analisi nel periodo più antico, preistorico (neolitico o calcolitico), della sua esistenza. Ma dal momento dell'arrivo dei Greci indoeuropei gli sviluppi devono essersi adeguati a quelli della nuova lingua, sia pure eventualmente con qualche anomalia.[14]

Il problema è a quale regione attribuire il nome originario.

2) Si tratta di un nome indoeuropeo, ben conservato in ittito (e in

[13] Le occlusive aspirate indoeuropee corrispondono in ittita alle occlusive sorde, salvo che per le dentali, dove si distinguono [*d*] e [*t*], rappresentata questa graficamente con *-tt-* o *-dd-*, secondo la nota 'regola di Sturtevant' (*CGr.*, 65ss.) sulla distinzione grafica fra sonore e sorde.

[14] Il problema delle lingue di sostrato in Grecia è estremamente difficile, al di là delle discussioni da Kretschmer a Georgiev, che qui sono trascurate, ricordiamo, accanto all'indefinito (e crediamo indefinibile) 'pelasgico', come sicuri quello cosidetto 'anatolico', testimoniato dai nomi in *-ss-/-tt-* e *-nth-/-nd-*, per il Peloponneso e la Grecia centrale; e quello 'minoico' a Creta, ancora più dibattuto (una lingua a prefissi; lingua di tipo luvio; semitico; greco). Sarà da ristudiare con metodi nuovi.

anatolico), con consonante laringale sorda (segnalata dalla geminata), trasformatosi invece in greco mediante processi di sviluppo linguistico tipicamente greci.

Quest'ultima quindi potrebbe rappresentare la soluzione più ovvia, se si pensa che il nome dei 'Greci', 'Ἀχαιοί (e quindi *Aḫḫijawā*), dovrebbe essere di origine molto antica, 'greca' o indoeuropea, perchè Omero, che li ricorda spesso, non ha ancora una designazione per il paese, ma solo per il popolo, e d'altra parte in epoca storica ci sono terre chiamate dalla Tessaglia al Peloponneso, a Rodi come fossero resti di una designazione comune in un'area molto vasta, cioè tutta quella abitata in origine da 'Achei' ('Ἀχαιοί), frantumatasi per l'arrivo dei Dori e il formarsi di altri gruppi di popolazioni.

3) Ovviamente l'eventuale nome preindoeuropeo può essere stato assimilato nella subentrante lingua indoeuropea, greco o anatolico, e averne seguito le vicende.

Ritorneremo sulla questione più avanti.

3.1 Il fatto nuovo è costituito dalla constatazione che nel rapporto fra *Aḫḫijā*, il nome 'breve' e d'attestazione più antica, ed *Aḫḫijawā*, *-wā* costituisce un suffisso che designa il territorio intorno ad una città, la sua regione, forse la popolazione ed è attestato durante tutta la documentazione anatolica dal testo di Anitta del XVII sec., ma riferentesi a fatti del XIX (*Zalpa* vs *Zalpuwa*), fino al licio (*Pinale* vs *Pillewi*; *wedre* 'città' vs *wedrewi* 'paese').[15] Il suffisso, esclusivamente anatolico, sembra servisse a designare una collettività di terre, di regioni, forse anche di persone, come sembra mostrare anche la grafia con frequente scriptio plena della vocale finale (*A-ah-hi-ja-wa-a*), quale contrassegno del collettivo.[16]

Ciò significa che il nome originario è *Aḫḫiyā*, non *Aḫḫijawā*, una constatazione di fatto che contrasta con il ϝ ipotizzato nel termine greco, peraltro giustificato dal lat. *Achīvi*, e che ci costringe a postulare l'ipotesi che gli 'Ἀχαιϝοί (col ϝ!) siano venuti in Grecia con quel nome dall'Anatolia, non essendo rintracciabile, almeno finora un suffisso di funzione analoga nell'area più caratteristicamente greca.[17]

[15] O. Carruba, *FsMeriggi*² 94s.

[16] Il confronto fra *Arzawa*, la nota regione nell'Anatolia di SO, e *Arzija*, città della Siria, (M. Finkelberg, *Glotta* 66 (1988) 133 n. 18) non è ovviamente pertinente. *Aḫḫija* e *Aḫḫijawā* sono alternativi, in quanto derivati l'uno dall'altro con funzioni in parte differenti, come i nomi ittiti e lici citati.

[17] Si ricordi che per P. Wathelet, in *Actes du IXe Congrès International de Sciences Onomastiques* (Sofia 1975), 430ss. 'Ἀχαιϝός, è una forma inesplicabile. Ci domandiamo se il ϝ è veramente esistito e se nel nome latino non sia verosimile una mediazione etrusc(o-anatolic)a, come per altri elementi culturali (O. Carruba, in *Atti del VI Convegno internazionale dei Linguisti*

3.2 Ma è proprio la determinazione di *Aḫḫijā* come nome originario che ci permette di andare oltre nella ricerca, procedendo sempre con l'utilizzazione di regole di sviluppo fonetico continuatesi e rivelatesi nelle lingue dei luoghi che interessano i nomi.

Aḫḫijā infatti è usato dagli Ittiti nella stessa accezione storica e geografica del nome *Aḫḫijawā*, deve quindi verosimilmente avere valore storico e geografico identico o molto simile. E, fatto ancor più importante, appartiene alla stessa lingua e deve quindi essere analizzabile allo stesso modo.

A questo punto bisogna tener presente che itt. *-ḫḫ-* rappresenta una laringale spirante sorda (o l'eventuale assimilazione ad essa di un suono velare spirante straniero) e che le laringali indoeuropee sono dei suoni continui e dovrebbero quindi avere funzione sonantica, simile a quella delle liquide e delle nasali.[18]

Si può quindi postulare anche per il gruppo 'laringale + *y*', *-hy-*, uno sviluppo analogo a quello dei gruppi *-ly-*, *-ry-*, *-ny-*, (*-my-*) nei vari dialetti greci. Il processo morfofonologico è quello detto 'pendant inverse' della 'Legge di Sievers', consistente nel passaggio da *CiyV* a *CyV*, che nel miceneo era già avvenuto per es. per il gruppo *-tya* > *-sa*, non ancora per i gruppi del tipo *Cuwa* > *Cwa*, per i quali esistono segni speciali *dwe, dwo, nwa*, forse *swa* ecc.[19]

3.3 Qui sembra sorgere un problema di cronologia: il greco miceneo del XIV sec. ha già perso, forse da tempo, le laringali, anche se il nome comune del popolo, 'Αχαιοί, deve essere antico quanto la loro venuta in Grecia, sia che lo abbiano portato essi stessi sia che lo abbiano trovato in loco. Ma sulle coste asianiche gli Anatolici hanno ancora le laringali e i Greci che vi abiteranno devono in qualche modo tenerne conto, sia negli sviluppi fonetici, come quello postulato per *Aḫḫijawā* dalla Finkelberg, sia nella resa di nomi locali, in particolare per le laringali, come per es. Γύγης, anat. *ḫuḫḫaš* 'avo; nonno'.[20]

(Brescia 1977), 137-153). Ma vd. n. 29 per *-w* egizio.

[18] Quanto qui prospettato equivale all'ammissione di una funzione sonantica delle laringali, che noi vediamo proprio nella singolare ripartizione degli sviluppi: indoario *-i-*, tutte le altre lingue *-a-*, greco *-e-*, *-a-*, *-o-*. L'ipotesi, oggi più corrente, di una vocale anaptittica non spiega la regolarità di questi esiti nelle varie lingue. L'anaptissi è in genere condizionata dal contesto immediato e può essere sempre diversa nella medesima lingua. Per una breve esposizione dei fatti, cfr. O. Szemerényi, *Einführung in die vergleichende Sprachwissenschaft* (Darmstadt 1990), 127ss.; la discussione sul punto in questione in F. Lindeman, *Introduction to the 'Laryngeal Theory'* (Oslo 1987), 98ss.

[19] Cfr. C.J. Ruijgh, in A. Bammesberger (ed.), *Die Laryngaltheorie und die Rekonstruktion des indogermanischen Laut- und Formensystems* (Heidelberg 1988), 462s.

[20] Nei nomi propri il greco rende la laringale anatolica con *g* (cfr. ancora Πέργης vs itt. *Parḫaš*) e con *k* (cfr. Τροκονδας vs anat. *Tarḫuntaš*), ma una ratio è difficile da stabilire. Si

Quindi mentre nell'ittito del II mill. resta *Aḫḫijawā*, con le sua 'laringale', nel gr. miceneo esso passa ad **Akhawa*.

Lo stesso avviene, a nostro parere, per *Aḫḫijā*, che attraverso un originario **Ahya* (vd. avanti e n. 27) sarebbe divenuto **Ahha* o **Akha*, secondo un dialetto greco dove si ha geminazione o rafforzamento, come per es. può verificarsi da *κτέν-yω: in lesb. κτέννω vs jon. κτείνω ecc. Tuttavia il fenomeno più comune in greco, quando il gruppo *C+V* è preceduto da vocale, è l'interversione delle consonanti (o anticipo di -*y*- semivocalica: μοῖρα da *σμόρ-yα ecc.), cioè nel nostro caso si avrebbe **Ahhya* > **Aihha*, che doveva essere reso come *Αἶγα (cfr. Γύγης vs *ḫuḫḫaš*), perché non c'era 'rafforzamento' in questo caso.

Con questo termine, *Αἶγα, dunque i Greci delle coste e delle isole designavano forse il paese da essi abitato, ma esso non ci è rimasto in questa forma.

Tuttavia per indicare ciò che si riferiva ad *Αἶγα, se ne è formato col suffisso *-*yo*- l'aggettivo, che infatti troviamo in gr. *Αἰγαῖος/ν (πόντος/πέλαγος). Esso per la verità sarebbe derivato apparentemente, secondo la tradizione, da Αἰγαί (*W.Sp.* in *LFrGrE*, s.v.), nome di almeno quattro città, che tuttavia per la loro scarsa importanza e per la posizione eccentrica (e spesso lontane dalla costa) ben difficilmente possono aver dato il nome al mar '*Egeo*'.

Un breve commento è necessario per spiegare la differente notazione di -*ḫḫ*- nei due nomi mediante -γ- e -χ-, dovuta, come si è visto, a sviluppi che devono essere stati differenziati certamente anche dall'influsso dell'accento: fenomeni analoghi si verificano per es. in licio nella notazione della laringale nello stesso termine a seconda che l'accento precedesse o si spostasse in seguito a derivazione o composizione, come in *xugah*e (con -*á*-), da **ḫuḫḫaššaš* "dell'avo", ma *epñ xuxa* "proavo" (con *é*- o *ú*); *Zagaba* "la città di Lagbe" (con il secondo -*á*-), ma *Zaxabahe* "di Lagba" (con il terzo *á*) ecc.[21]

può eventualmente ipotizzare un criterio uguale o analogo a quello usato dal licio e basato almeno in parte anche sulla posizione dell'accento (cfr. bibl. qui sotto). Ricordiamo che la laringale ancora conservata nelle lingue anatoliche del II mill. sparisce nel lidio (cioè a NO = Eolia; O. Carruba, *MIO* 8 (1963) 383-408), si conserva nel licio, dove viene resa con quattro segni alfabetici diversi, che translitteriamo: *g*, *k* (*c*), x (*k*) e *q* (Carruba, *RIL* 108 (1974) 575-597).

[21] Quanto sopra presuppone che il licio utilizzasse i segni dell'alfabeto greco d'origine con lo stesso valore (cfr. Carruba, *Paleontologia linguistica, Atti del VI Convegno internazionale dei Linguisti*, (Milano 1974), Brescia 1977), ma che avesse una giustapposizione di *fortis*/*lenis*, piuttosto che quella di sorda/sonora, come si è supposto per l'ittito, dove si sta ristudiando questa tematica (cfr. H. Eichner, in M. Mayrhofer - M. Peters - O.E. Pfeiffer (edd.), *Lautgeschichte und Etymologie*, Wiesbaden 1980).

4.1 Il nome del mare Egeo Αἰγαῖον è dunque una derivazione di *Aḫḫijā*, che designava dapprima evidentemente tutte le regioni intorno all'Egeo. Queste poi a loro volta potevano essere riassunte nel 'collettivo' etnico di origine anatolica (ma attestato in itt.) *Aḫḫijawā*, col suffisso *-wa*.

Il fatto ci sembra comprovato dalla presenza in tutto il bacino dell'Egeo di nomi di regioni, città, isole che appaiono come i resti isolati e affioranti qua e là, spesso in zone marginali e periferiche, del nome originario di una grande area comune, frammentata e divisa dall'avvicendarsi delle popolazioni e dal rinnovarsi continuo delle culture in una tenace memoria storica e geografica.

Basta uno sguardo agli atlanti e ai repertori per convincersene. Ne diamo qui un rapido, incompleto sommario:

a) ci sono due 'Αχαΐα, nel Peloponneso del Nord e ai confini meridionali della Tessaglia, dove con gli *Achaici montes* si aveva forse il limite settentrionale della Grecia micenea; si ricordi anche l'"Αχαία πόλις a Rodi.

b) sotto il nome Αἰγαί sono note città in Achaia, nell'Eubea, in Jonia, in Macedonia, nella Penisola calcidica, nessuna delle quali avrebbe potuto dare il nome al mare Egeo, perché periferiche; si può aggiungere la tribù ateniese Αἰγηΐς;

c) ricordiamo alcuni temi in Αἰγι-, come Αἴγιον, città dell'Achaia; Αἰγίαλη, città di Amorgo; Αἰγιλία, isola vicino a Creta; o la stessa Αἴγινα, che ovviamente sono più difficili da ricollegare a quel tema, ma che difficilmente avranno tutti preso il nome dalle 'capre' (αἴξ, αἰγός), anche se si può postulare qualche etimologia popolare basata su di esso.[22]

4.2 Che siamo sulle orme di fatti concreti sembrano dimostrarlo altri toponimi ed etnici 'greci', che risalgono certamente ai due prototipi anatolici.

Alcuni potrebbero derivare da *Aḫḫijawā*, come 'Ιαωλκός 'porto degli Ioni', che sembra il corrispondente 'ionico' tardo di 'eol.' Αἰολέυς; o Χίος, la nota isola, col χ greco di 'Αχαΐα e l'aferesi ben attestata nei dialetti delle coste meridionali.

Altri derivano direttamente da *Aḫḫija* (con *í*!): 'Ιάς, 'Ιάδος, nome e agg. di 'Jonia', come 'Ιακός, entrambi con aferesi, frequente nelle lingue asianiche di S.-O., che sono stati creati con formanti tipici greci e difficilmente sono retroformazioni da 'Ιάων.

4.3.1 Un altro nome di un certo rilievo è "Ιασος, che rivela bene, se esaminato con i criteri surricordati, le sue origini 'ahhijawane', e ricorda ancora, tramite la sua accezione aggettivale, il toponimo asianico *Aḫḫijawā*.

22 Sui nomi del tipo Αἰγιαλ- e sull'assonante αἰγιαλός 'costiero' rinvio ai dizionari etimologici, H. Frisk, *GEW* e P. Chantraine, *DELG*, che mostrano i problemi senza essere soddisfacenti. Cfr. anche avanti.

Ἴασος è noto come il nome di una città, dove i ritrovamenti archeologici minoici risalgono al MM e TM (2000-1450 ca.), quelli micenei iniziano dal TE IIIA 1 (1450-1400 ca.). La città, così come Mileto (forse la nota *Millawanda*) e Müsgebi (a O. di Alicarnasso), che hanno le stesse tracce archeologiche per gli stessi periodi[23], è sita all'estremità meridionale della Jonia, in Caria, regione anch'essa di civilizzazione luvia.

Il suo nome deriva proprio dal toponimo *Aḫḫijawā* secondo il modello di analisi da noi proposto, ma con il suffisso dell'adjectivus genitivi *-aššali-*, tipico del luvio (come il suffisso etnico *-wanali* di cui sopra): **(Ahh)ijaw-assali-* cioè 'di Aḫḫijawā' > **ijawassa-* , attestato forse nel mic. *i-wa-so* (con *i-* da **-ija*), antroponimo masch. (cfr. Mader, *LFrGrE* s.v.; e Morpurgo Davies, *MGL* s.v.), ma certamente nel lic. *Ijaeusas*, e, infine, nel 'gr.' Ἴασος. Si tratta evidentemente della, o di una, 'città di/degli *Aḫḫijawā*' per eccellenza nella lingua degli indigeni che erano a contatto coi Greci.

4.3.2 L'aggettivo si ritrova sorprendentemente in una designazione, a prima vista strana, di Argo : τὸ Ἴασον Ἄργος "il Peloponneso 'iasico'", cioè abitato da Joni (Odys. XVIII 246; Mader RE s.v.).

E' questa una chiara spia linguistica di origine asianica della tradizione sul nome antico che vi sta dietro come per quello di Ἰάονες e conferma le notizie erodotee sull'esistenza di questi 'Ioni', pur venendo verosimilmente da una fonte diversa.

4.3.3 Dobbiamo accennare qui ai ben noti dati egiziani relativi ai Popoli del Mare nelle iscrizioni di Mernepta (Karnak, 5° anno; Athribis-stele) con la menzione degli *ʾj-qꜣ-(jj)-wꜣ-sꜣ*, letto *ʾáqajawasa* (*Ekweš*), che si è soliti far corrispondere ad *Aḫḫijawā* e quindi ad' Ἀχαιοί.

Se, come è chiaro da altri termini, per es. *Kꜣ-jn.jw-sꜣ,* cioè *Ku-nu-sa* 'Knossos'; *ʾj-m-ni-sꜣ*, *ʾá-m-ni-sa* 'Amnisos'; ma anche *Tw-rw-sꜣ, tu-ru-sa* (o *Turša*) 'Tyrsenoi' ecc., *-sa* (o, secondo altra lettura,*-ša*) fa parte del tema del nome in quanto suffisso (cioè, se non rappresenta la desinenza i.ea *-s* del nom. sing., con Barnett, *CAH* II 2, 367, il che è certo da escludere), è verosimile allora che *ʾáqajawasa* designi gli 'Aḫḫijawā' asianici, o di Iasos in particolare (**Aḫḫijawassa*), e non genericamente gli 'Achei', che come abitanti del continente greco sembrano essere distinti col termine di *Tj-nꜣ-jj(-w)*, *Ta-na-ju* o *Ta-na-ja*. Cfr. n. 29 su questo e altri nomi egiziani.[24]

23 M.J. Mellink, *AJA* 87 (1983) 138ss.

24 Naturalmente anche su questi nomi, sulla loro lettura e sulla loro interpretazione la letteratura è immensa sia da parte egittologica, sia da parte degli studiosi di anatolistica e dell'antichità classica. Essa è equilibratamente aggiornata in E. Cline, *Or.* 56 (1987) 1-35 (e *MINOS* 25-26 (1990-1991[1994] 7-36). Per il periodo dei 'Popoli del Mare' e per *ʾáqajawasa* in particolare, cfr. le pagine pertinenti di A. Strobel, *Der spätbronzezeitliche Seevölkersturm* (Berlin - New

5.1 Ma c'è un altro indizio che parla a favore dell'identificazione dei nomi *Aḫḫijā* e Αἰγα-(ῖον).

Nelle notizie sulla tradizione delle stirpi greche e straniere raccolta da Erodoto, VII 90ss., ai §§94 e 95 egli dice:

Ἴωνες δὲ ὅσον μὲν χρόνον ἐν Πελοποννήσῳ οἴκεον τὴν νῦν καλεομένην Ἀχαιίην καὶ πρὶν ἢ Δαναόν τε καὶ Ξοῦθον ἀπικέσθαι ἐς Πελοπόννησον, ὡς Ἕλληνες λέγουσι, ἐκαλέοντο Πελασγοὶ Αἰγιαλέες, ἐπὶ δὲ Ἴωνος τοῦ Ξούθου Ἴωνες. Νησιῶται δὲ ... · ... καὶ τοῦτο Πελασγικὸν ἔθνος, ὕστερον δὲ Ἰωνικὸν ἐκλήθη κατὰ τὸν αὐτὸν λόγον καὶ οἱ δυωδεκαπόλιες Ἴωνες οἱ ἀπ' Ἀθηνέων. Αἰολέες δὲ ... · ... καὶ τὸ πάλαι καλεόμενοι Πελασγοί, ὡς Ἑλλήνων λόγος.

These Ionians, as long as they were in the Peloponnese dwelling in what is now called Achaia, before Danaus and Xuthus came to the Peloponnese, as the Greeks say, were called Aegialian Pelasgians; they were named Ionians after Ion the son of Xuthus. §95 The islanders ...; they also were of Pelasgian stock, which was later called Ionian by the same right as were the Ionians of the twelve cities, who came from Athens. The Aeolians ...; in former days they were called Pelasgian, as the Greek story goes. (Testo e traduzione di A.D. Godley, *The Loeb Classical Library*, London 1971).

Si ricordi che nella tradizione greca e in particolare per Erodoto i Pelasgi sono i predecessori degli Elleni in Grecia.[25]

5.2 Queste notizie mostrano come restasse viva nella tradizione greca la nozione del fatto che le popolazioni precedenti del Peloponneso, delle isole, dell'Attica fossero ' 'Ιάονες.' Cioè, se è esatta la nostra etimologia del nome come derivato da **Aḫḫijawā-wana-* (che oggi, dopo la proposta fatta sopra, è da correggere piuttosto in un semplice **Aḫḫijā-wana-*), esso designa nella lingua degli abitanti luvi della futura Ionia le popolazioni di *Aḫḫijā*, a nostro parere, l'*Egeo* in genere, quindi anche quelle della Grecia ("as long as they were in the Peloponnese") e delle isole ("they also were of Pelasgian stock").

York 1976) e G.A. Lehmann, *Die mykenisch-frühgriechische Welt und der östliche Mittelmeerraum in der Zeit der 'Seevölker'-Invasionen um 1200 v. Chr.* (Vorträge der Rheinisch-Westfälische Akademie der Wissenschaften, G. 276, Opladen 1985). Per le letture seguiamo per lo più E. Edel, *Die Ortsnamenlisten aus dem Totentempel Amenophis III.* (Bonn 1966).

Sull'origine sostanzialmente anatolica occidentale dei movimenti dei 'Popoli del Mare' con motivazioni storiche, cfr. I. Singer, in M. Heltzer - E. Lipinski (eds.), *Society and Economy in the Eastern Mediterranean (c. 1500-1000 B.C.)*(Leuven 1988), 243ss.

[25] Cfr. F. Lochner-Hüttenbach, *Die Pelasger* (Wien 1960).

Lasciamo agli storici il commento dei dati della tradizione, ma dobbiamo segnalare come dietro quel Αἰγιαλέες (o *Αγιαλέες?) si tramandi il perfetto parallelo continentale dell'Αἰολέες del nord-ovest asianico.[26]

6.1 Secondo quanto detto qui sopra dunque *Aḫḫijā* risulta essere, all'epoca dei documenti ittiti, verosimilmente tutta l'Egeide, in quanto abitata da popolazioni 'achee' ed è esso stesso originariamente aggettivo in *-iya*, sostantivato, su un tema **ahha* (< **akʷ-a*, secondo sviluppo 'luvio'; vd. avanti e n. 27), *Aḫḫijawā* un sinonimo che indica collettivamente gli stessi paesi e/o quei popoli, da qui la sua estensione al continente greco (soprattutto?) nella sua componente culturale micenea ('achea').

I nomi *Aḫḫijā* e *Aḫḫijawā* hanno fonetica e struttura anatolica e sono pertanto originari con ogni verosimiglianza delle coste anatoliche in epoca molto antica.

I nomi' Αχαιός e Αἰγαῖον sono i corrispondenti nomi 'greci' (più propriamente 'achei') sorti essi stessi eventualmente sulle coste asianiche, ma con sviluppi fonetici, quali si riscontrano poi nei due dialetti greci della regione, l'eolico e lo jonico.

I nomi più importanti dei popoli e delle città della costa asianica sono invece degli etnici di origine anatolica Αἰολέες, 'Ιάονες, "Ιασος, derivati dai toponimi *Aḫḫijā* e *Aḫḫijawā*.

6.2 Il significato appena accennato di *Aḫḫijā* quale derivato dalla parola i.ea per 'acqua', **akʷ-ā*, in collegamento con la designazione dell'Egeo come 'mare', può sembrare troppo ovvio come significato e troppo lontano nel tempo per essere verificabile.

Ci sono tuttavia ovvie analogie con origini e sviluppi simili dallo stesso termine per 'acqua', per es. nelle lingue germaniche, che non solo comprovano quanto detto, ma ci permettono di precisare il significato proposto in modo sorprendente.

Il radicale i.eo **akʷ-ā*, lat. *aquā* ecc. corrisponde al got. *ahva* 'acqua', a.a.t. *aha*, a.isl. *á* ecc.; il suo derivato (dal radicale con *e-*; tralascio la notazione laringalistica) mediante suffisso **-yó*, **ekʷ-yó-s* 'quello dell'acqua', ha dato in a.isl. *áegir* 'mare'; il derivato in *-ya*, **akʷ-ya* 'pertinente all'acqua', significa 'isola', per es. in a.isl. *ey*, a.a.t. *ouwa* 'terra umida (ted. *Aue*); isola', a.ingl. *eig*, *ig-land* ecc.[27]

[26] Tralascio di menzionare qui *a-ka-wi-ja-de* 'verso l'Achaia' di KN C 914, e *]ja-wo-ne* di KN Ws 1707 perché troppo incerti (cfr. Finkelberg, *Glotta* 66 (1988) 129 n. 4) e perché, se hanno veramente a che fare con i nomi studiati, rientrano nelle tipologie analizzate, e, per loro forme 'moderne', sarebbero rilevanti solo per la cronologia alta dei mutamenti ricordati.

[27] E' verosimile che la forma sia derivata da **akʷ-ā* > **ahw-a* > **ah(w)ya* e infine **ahhiya* da una parte, **ahha* dall'altra con spirantizzazione luvia (ma anche palaica) di *k* davanti ad *-u*

E' verosimile quindi che anche nel nostro caso da **akw-a*, tramite 'luv.' **ahwa* si sia formato l'anat. *Aḫḫijā*, che, al collettivo o neutro plur., significava 'le isole', e da questo si sia avuto **ahha-* e **akha-* nel protogreco da cui infine Αἰγαῖον 'il mare delle isole'.

Con questa ricostruzione acquistano un senso concreto, sia i nomi di *Aḫḫijā* (la regione delle 'isole') e dell'*Egeo* (il mare), sia quello di *Aḫḫijawā* cioè, i paesi e/o i popoli della regione delle 'isole', questo quindi come designazione dei paesi che si affacciano sull'Egeo e sono abitati da popolazioni che hanno la stessa origine.

6.3 Superfluo ricordare qui che la designazione egiziana della Grecia, o comunque della regione egea, attestata almeno dal XV sec. *iww hryw-ib nw W3d-wr* suona proprio 'le isole in mezzo al Grande Verde (= mare/oceano)', si tratterebbe cioè di una interpretazione, quasi una 'traduzione' del termine originario locale, *Aḫḫija*, che designava appunto le 'Isole', come regione comune, mentre Αἰγαῖον era 'il mare delle isole.'

E' evidente allora che la definizione *iww hryw-ib nw W3d-wr* 'le isole in mezzo al Grande Verde/mare', collegata con *Keftiu* nelle iscrizioni di Rechmare (età di Tuthmosis III; Vercoutter 1954, 105ss.) non è un'espressione mitologica, come si tende a credere[28], ma un reale concetto geografico.[29]

(nella forma **akuwa*). Nella più tarda documentazione luvia infatti **ahw-a* si sarebbe sviluppato ulteriormente in **awa* e **uwa-* 'bere' (cfr. F. Starke, StBoT 30, 532ss.).

Ricordo ancora che anche in altre lingue il significato di 'mare' o 'isola' è basato sulla parola per 'acqua' mediante composti o sintagmi vari, per es. in scr. *dvipa-* significa 'isola', cioè 'con l'acqua (*apa-*) ai due (*dví-*) lati.'

In ittito la designazione dell''isola' viene fatta mediante l'espressione *arunaš anda*, esattamente come il lat. *insula* '(la terra) nel mare.'

[28] Cfr. W. Helck, in H.G. Buchholz (ed.), *Ägäische Bronzezeit* (Darmstadt 1987), 220s.

[29] Cfr. da ultimo, E. Cline, *MINOS* 25-26 (1990-1991 [1994]) 18s. In considerazione dei dati che risultano da quanto qui si viene dicendo, ci sia permesso di dare un suggerimento su un altra designazione egizia pertinente alla regione egea, *Tj-n3-jj-(w) (Tanaja)*, in cui si vogliono vedere i Δαναοί e il Peloponneso, che sarebbe stato abitato da essi (cfr. Helck, *Die Beziehungen Ägyptens und Vorderasiens zur Ägäis bis ins 7. Jh. v. Chr.* (Darmstadt 1979), 30).

Essendo già noti per la regione i nomi *K3ft(j)w (Keftiu)* 'Creta' e *Iww hryw-ib nw W3d-wr* 'le Isole nel mezzo del Grande Verde', cioè 'l'Egeo', è giusto ipotizzare che *Tanaja* sia un paese del continente (W. Helck, *op.cit.* 26ss.; E. Cline, *MINOS* 25-26 (1990-1991[1994]), 19; B. Sergent, *MINOS* 16 (1977) 126-173). Che il nome possa designare i Δαναοί ci sembra tuttavia poco credibile, perché in queste liste sono indicati non popoli, ma regioni, isole o città (cfr. G. Steiner, *LFrGrE*, s.v.). Ma di questi problemi tratteremo altrove.

Per il momento accenniamo solo alla possibilità che *Tj-n3-jj-w* della cosidetta 'Lista Egea' di Amenofis III (Kom el-Hetan; da ultimo E. Cline, Or. 56 (1987) 1-35) rispetto a *Tj-n3-jj* degli Annali di Tuthmosis III (cfr. W. Helck, *op.cit.* 28ss.) contenga quel suffisso di collettivo *-wa* egeo-anatolico che riscontriamo in *Ahhiya-wā*.

Si noti che ciò potrebbe valere pure per *K3-f-tj-w*, il cui *-w* appare per lo meno singolare

7.1 Le conseguenze storiche che se ne debbono desumere sono che i Greci nell'età micenea sono presenti sulle coste occidentali anatoliche, sia pure con una frequenza e un'intensità minori che nel I mill.[30] e, se è corretta la nostra interpretazione circa l'antichità dei termini *Aḫḫijā* e *Aḫḫijawā*, che essi sono passati per l'Anatolia nordoccidentale prima o intorno al 2000 anteriormente alla loro espansione nelle sedi più note e definitve, come si è proposto da parte degli studiosi della ceramica minia.[31] Ma il problema diventa a questo punto prevalentemente archeologico e non può essere affrontato in questa sede.

Le identificazioni evidenti dal confronto linguistico fra i nomi, *Aḫḫijā* e Αἰγαῖον; *Aḫḫijawā* e' Ἀχαιοί, e soprattutto la reale e stretta relazione che ne risulta fra paesi, popoli e il mare che li unisce, ci sembra risolvano positivamente e in modo definitivo (doch 'ein Ende'! Sommer, *IF* 55 (1937) 169-297) l'annosa questione della presenza dei Greci sulla costa asianica in età ittita, pur lasciandoci altri problemi archeologici, cronologici, storici, che possono comunque essere affrontati ora con maggiore certezza.[32]

Risulta ora ben comprensibile da un punto di vista storico, anche in base al parallelismo col I mill. di cui alla n. 30, la commistione di nomi quasi sicuramente 'greci', come i ben noti *Alakšanduš*/ 'Αλέξανδρος, *Tawagalawa*/ 'ΕτεϜοκλεϜης ed altri accanto a nomi anatolici come *Piyamaradu, Kukkunni* ecc. nelle vicende che riguardano Aḫḫijawā.

7.2 La soluzione del vecchio problema risulta tanto più reale, se si considera che abbiamo a che fare con designazioni etniche e toponomastiche concomitanti da lingue (o dialetti) differenti e in periodi differenti: ai nomi anatolici del II. mill. corrispondono nello stesso periodo, o poco dopo (nel 'medioevo ellenico'?), quelli 'greci' nei due dialetti asianici (Eoli e Joni) e quelli di 'Egeo' ed 'Achei' in greco ('acheo'). Senza dimenticare naturalmente la documentazione egiziana, ora concreta e diretta.

Gli storici sono giustamente severi nel ricostruire la storia di periodi oscuri o scarsamente documentati: chiedono fatti, e guardano con distacco le

(Helck, in H.G. Buchholz (ed.), *Ägäische Bronzezeit* (Darmstadt 1987), 264 n. 5) ed in cui, sulla base delle attestazioni orientali, accad. *Kaptaru*, ebr. *Kaftor* ecc. dovrebbe vedersi **Kaftar-wa* (cfr. la grafia micenea del toponimo *A-pa-ta-wa*, 'gr.*Απτα/ερα). Anche su questo, altrove.

30 Si consideri il perfetto parallelismo anche per quanto riguarda i rapporti con l'interno dell' Anatolia, tenendo presenti, in età storica, i rapporti e i contrasti fra Joni e Lidi e Persiani, e gli interventi militari degli Ateniesi.

31 Cfr. E. Vermeule, *Greece in the Bronze Age* (Chicago 1964), 72ss.; R.A. Crossland, in R.A. Crossland - A. Birchall (eds.), *Bronze Age Migrations in the Aegean. Archaeological and Linguistic Problems in Greek Prehistory* (London 1974), 5-16; e soprattutto R.J. Howell, ibid. 73-98.

32 Su questi nomi, cfr. F. Sommer, *AS*, per la fase antica della polemica; C. Watkins, in *Troy & the Trojan War*, per un tentativo di interpretazione basato su 'similarity' e 'contiguity.'

prove che possono venire dalle ricostruzioni linguistiche. Ma anche gli sviluppi linguistici sono dei fatti reali che ci permettono talvolta, come in questo caso, di andare oltre il 'common sense' per attingere la realtà storica.

Ogni studioso delle civiltà del II° millennio a.C. deve misurarsi col tema qui trattato, uno dei più affascinanti non solo della protostoria greca, ma anche dell'ittitologia.

Prof. Philo H.J. Houwink ten Cate, che ha subito anch'egli questo pericoloso fascino, voglia accettare di buon grado, come omaggio in questa felice occasione, la nostra rapida ricerca in un campo, che egli ha trattato da eccellente storico, filologo e linguista.

TAVOLA RIASSUNTIVA

Carruba, *Athenaeum* NS 42 (1964) 269-298:

Aḫḫiyawā

NO — etnico itt.-'lidio' ... 'greco'
**Aḫḫiyawa-li-* > **áiyawali-* > **áiyauli-* ... Αἰολέες

SO — etnico luvio ... 'greco'
**Aḫḫiya(wa)-wanni* > **(A)iyá(wa)unni-* > Ἰάονες

(qui) — con altro suffisso anat. e psilosi:
**Aḫḫiyaw-ašša-* > **(A)hhíyaussa-* > lic. *Ijaeusas*
> 'gr.' Ἴασος città della Caria; τὸ Ἴασον Ἄργος
il Peloponneso 'ionico'

Finkelberg, *Glotta* 66 (1988) 127-134:

Aḫḫiyawā > **Ahhyaw-* > **Akhaw-* > *Ἀχαϝ-yó-ς > Ἀχαι(ϝ)ός > Ἀχαι(ϝ)-ία
ecc.

Carruba (qui):

doppio etnico 'anatolico': *Aḫḫiya* e *Aḫḫiyawā* (suff. *-wa* coll.)

Aḫḫiya

svil. 'protoeolico':
> **áhhya* > **áhha-(/*akha-?)* > *Ἀγα- > ?

svil. 'protoionico':
> **áhhya* > **áihha-(*aikha-?)* > *Αἰγα- > *Αἰγα-yo-ν >
Αἰγαῖον

derivazioni possibili da un tema Αἰγι-:
Αἰγιαλέες (cfr. 'eolico' Αἰολέες); Αἴγινα ecc.

Aḫḫiya — spiega meglio Ἰάονες < **(A)ija-unni* < **Aḫḫiya-wanni*.

DIE NEUEN INSCHRIFTEN UND BESCHRIFTETEN BRONZEFUNDE AUS DEN AUSGRABUNGEN VON DEN URARTÄISCHEN BURGEN VON ANZAF

ALI M. DINÇOL - BELKIS DINÇOL

Die archäologischen Ausgrabungen an den bekannten urartäischen Burgen von Yukarı und Aşağı Anzaf Kalesi (= Obere und Niedere Burgen von Anzaf), die seit 1991 unter der Leitung von Herrn Dr. Oktay Belli, Dozent für Alte Geschichte an der Universität Istanbul, in jährlichen Kampagnen systematisch durchgeführt werden, tragen sehr zur Bereicherung des epigraphischen Repertoire von Urartu bei. Die Burgen von Anzaf stellten schon den Herkunftsort von fünf Steininschriften dar, die vor dem Beginn der Ausgrabungen in verschiedenen Daten von Wissenschaftlern gesehen und studiert worden waren (s. die Karte, Pl. 1).[1]

I. Die Inschriften auf Stein

1. Die Tempelinschrift

Schon während der ersten Kampagne der Ausgrabungen am Oberen Anzaf wurde ein typischer urartäischer *susi*-Tempel zu Tage gebracht, an dessen ziemlich gut erhaltenen Nord-Ost Ecke sich *in situ* eine Gründungsinschrift befand. Sie ist auf der langen Ost- und der kurzen Nordkante eines Kalksteinquaders geschrieben, dessen Maße 106 x 70 x 65 cm betragen. Die glattgemeißelten beschrifteten Flächen, die auf der Ostseite 90 x 51 cm und auf der Nordseite 51 x 50 cm groß sind, sind durch eine ca. 3 cm tiefen Bosse von dem Hintergrund herausgehauen. Die Zeilenabstände betragen auf der Langseite 3,5 und auf der Kurzseite 4,5 cm. Auch die Höhen der leeren Flächen über und unter den beschrifteten Oberflächen auf den Seiten unterscheiden sich: auf der Ostseite messen sie jeweils 3.5 und 6-7 cm, und auf der Nordseite jeweils

[1] Cf. HChI (= W.F. König, *Handbuch der chaldischen Inschriften* (AfO Beiheft 8), Graz 1955) 46, 55a, 72, und P. Hulin, *AnSt.* 10 (1960) 205-207.

6 cm und 13 cm. Wegen dieser Unterschiede entsprechen die Zeilen 2 und 10 der langen Seite jeweils der Zeilen 1 und 7 der kurzen Nordseite (s. Pl. 2a-c und 3a).

Auf diesem Eckstein wird derselbe Text dreimal wiederholt: einmal auf der schmalen Nordseite und zweimal auf seiner längeren Ostseite. Der Text auf der Kurzseite wird in sieben Zeilen und auf der Langseite in jeweils sechszeiligen Versionen wieder-gegeben.

Zwischen den Versionen auf den kürzeren und längeren Kanten des Steinblockes sind Schreibvarianten haplographischen Charakters anzutreffen, die wegen der unterschiedlichen Länge der Zeilen als eine Art Hiatustilger benutzt worden sind.

Nordseite	Ostseite
uš-ma-ši-ni	*uš-ma-a̲-ši-ni*
Me-i̲-nu-ú̲-a-še	*Me-nu-a-še*
i-ni su-si	*i-ni su-si-e̲*
ši-i-di-iš-tu-ni	*ši-i-di-iš-tu-ú̲-ni*

Umschrift der Nordseite

1 ^{d}*Ḫal-di-ni-ni uš-ma-ši-ni*
2 ^{m}*Me-i-nu-ú-a-še*
3 ^{m}*Iš-pu-u-i-ni-ḫi-ni-še*
4 ^{d}*Ḫal-di-e e-ú-ri-i-e*
5 *i-ni su-si ši-di-iš-tu-ni*
6 É.GAL *ši-i-di-iš-tu-ni*
7 *ba-a-du-ú-si-i-e*

Umschrift der Ostseite (2x)

1 ^{d}*Ḫal-di-ni-ni uš-ma-a-ši-ni*
2 ^{m}*Me-nu-a-še* ^{m}*Iš-pu-u-i-ni-ḫi-ni-še*
3 ^{d}*Ḫal-di-i-e e-ú-ri-i-e*
4 *i-ni su-si-e ši-di-iš-tu-ni*
5 É.GAL *ši-i-di-iš-tu-ú-ni*
6 *ba-a-du-ú-si-i-e*

Übersetzung
(Zeilenordnung nach der Ostseite)

1 Durch die Macht des Gottes Ḫaldi

2 hat Menua, Sohn des Ißpuini,
3 für den Gott Óaldi, den Herrn,
4 diesen Tempel(turm)
5 (und) diese Burg in perfektem Zustand(?)
6 erbaut.

Erklärungen

Z. 4. *susi*: Der in den älteren Wörterlisten als eine Art Kultanlage definierte Gebäudetypus (M. Salvini, *StMed* 1, 581 Fnt) wurde von Salvini mit dem charakteristischen Tempelturm gleichgesetzt (Salvini, "Der *susi*-Heiligtum von Karmir Blur und der urartäische Turmtempel", *AMI* 12 (1979) 249-269 passim), der aus einer einzigen Cella besteht und einen quadratischen Grundriß hat.
Z. 6. *badusie*: nach Melikishvili, *DUS* 81, bedeutet das Wort "erhaben, groß, majestätisch, hervorragend(?)". Salvini will darin die urartäische Entsprechung der assyrischen Form *libedi-ßu* sehen, die in dem quasi-Bilinguis von Kevenli vorkommt und im Sinne von "Volkommenheit, Perfektion" gebraucht wird (Salvini, *StMed* 1, 584-589). Es ist u.E. ein gutbegründeter Vorschlag, der aber noch weitere Belege zur Bestätigung braucht

2a-b. *Im Tempelareal gefundene Inschriftenfragmente*

In der unmittelbaren Nähe der Ostecke des Tempels wurden zwei kleinere Inschriftenfragmente gefunden, die wenige Keilschriftzeichen enthalten. Die Maße des ersten Fragments (a) betragen 13 x 9 x 6 cm. Darauf sind Reste von vier Zeilen (mit Abständen von je 4 cm) zu sehen (s. Pl. 3b). Wegen der Dünne der Steinplatten ist es anzunehmen, daß sie als Wandverkleidung benutzt worden waren. Die Rekonstruktion der vorhandenen Zeichen lautet:

µ*Me-nu-a-ße* µ*Iß*]-*pu-ú-*[*i-ni-_i-ni-ße*
_Óal-di-e] *e-ú-*[*ri-e*
]*ßi-d*[*i-iß-tu-ni*
ba-a-d]*u-*[*si-e*

Aus dem Vergleich mit der Inschrift an der Nordostecke des Tempels ergibt sich, daß es sich hier um ein Duplikat der Tempelinschrift handelt.

Die Untersuchung des anderen Fragments (b), dessen Maße 8 x 7 x 3,5 cm betragen, ergibt das gleiche Resultat. Der Text auf diesem kleineren Bruchstück kann analog zur Tempelinschrift wiederhergestellt werden (s. Pl. 3c):

ši-d]*i*-[*iš-tu-ni*
ba-du]-*s*[*i-e.*

Wegen der unterschiedlichen Dicke der beiden Fragmente ist ihre Zusammengehörigkeit unwahrscheinlich. Daher soll auch an der Westecke des Tempels mit der Wiederholung desselben Textes gerechnet werden. Leider ist dieser Teil des Tempels zu zerstört, um über die ursprüngliche Lage dieser Inschriften etwas Sicheres sagen zu können.

Ein weiterer Steinblock, worauf derselbe Text zu lesen ist, wurde schon vor siebenunddreißig Jahren in der Nähe der Oberen Burg gefunden.[2] Wegen seiner größeren Maße ist es anzunehmen, daß er als Baustein in den Mauern der Burg gebraucht worden war. Seine genaue Lage ist aber nicht bestimmbar.

3. *Die Inschrift im Haus von Ömer Özbey*

Eine Inschrift aus hartem Kalkstein wurde nach Aussage des heutigen Aufbewahrers Ö. Özbey vor Jahrzehnten beim Bau seines Hauses im Dorf vom Oberen Anzaf gefunden (s. Pl. 3d). Der Stein bildet den unteren Teil einer Wandplatte mit einer Dicke von 13.5 cm, deren erhaltene Höhe 58.5 cm und deren maximale Breite 43 cm betragen. Es sind auf dem Stein elf Zeilen zu sehen, deren Abstände alle 5.5 cm betragen. Entlang der linken Seite findet sich ein leerer Rand von 3 cm Breite.

Umschrift

1 É.G[AL
2 *su-ru-q*[*u*]-x[
3 É *bar-zu-di-b*[*i-du*
4 ^{NA4}*a-da-nu-sa*[
5 *e-ú-e pí-š*[*á*
6 *qu-ṭu-ḫu* x[
7 *e-ú-e* x[
8 *ta-ar-ma-ni*-[li
9 ^{NA4}*a-da-nu-ša*[
10 ^{m}*Me-nu-ú*-a-[
11 *a-lu-še i-n*[*i*

[2] Cf. P. Hulin, *AnSt.* 10 (1960) 205-207.

Über den Inhalt

Wegen der Vielzahl der ungedeuteten Wörter kann eine volle Übersetzung der Inschrift nicht erfolgen, es ist jedoch aus den vorkommenden Gebäude- und Steinnamen zu entnehmen, daß sie den Bebauungstätigkeiten des Menua gewidmet ist.

Der hier in der 3. Zeile vorkommende Gebäudename *barzudibidu* neben É.GAL ist in den Inschriften häufig belegt, aber seine genaue Deutung und die Bestimmung seiner Funktion stehen noch aus. Der Name *tarmanili* kann in Anlehnung an die hurritische Wortgleichung als "Quelle" übersetzt werden und paßt zu diesem Kontext (Salvini, "Anhang" zu *DUS* 91). Das Wort NA4*adanusa*[, das nach dem Determinativ der Name einer Steinsorte ist und mit den eben genannten Bauten in enger Beziehung zu stehen scheint, ist bisher nicht bezeugt. Ob das in der sogenannten Chorchor-Kronik des Argišti (s. *UKN* 127 I, 29), Sohn des Menua, einmal belegte NA4*a-x*[damit identifiziert werden kann, läßt sich nach jetzigem Stand des Wissens nicht entscheiden. Der Name kann auch nicht als akkadisch erklärt werden. Die anderen Steinsorten auf welcher urartäische Inschriften anzutreffen sind, namentlich NA4*gar-bi-e* (*UKN* 28, 7) und NA4*su-a-i*-e (*UKN* 153), harren noch einer näheren Definition. Es ist nicht unwahrscheinlich, daß das *pí-š[á-*, das der Kopula *eue* folgt, auch ein Bauterminus sein kann, aber auch diese Frage sei derzeit dahingestellt.

Neben den bekannten, aber undeutbaren Termini sind in der Inschrift zwei *hapax legomena* vorhanden (Z. 2 *suruqu*-x[und Z. 6 *qutuhu*-x[ ), die bisher weder im urartäischen noch im assyrischen Kontext gefunden worden sind. Das Wort *qutuhu-x*[weist eine gewisse Ähnlichkeit mit dem Verbum *kutia-/kutu-* "vorrücken, gehen, gelangen" auf, aber wir vermögen nicht, in der Beziehung die Existenz des Phonems *-hu* zu erklären.

Am Ende der Inschrift kommt die übliche Fluchformel, die mit der Phrase *aluše ini* [DUB-*te* = "wer diese Inschrift" anfängt.

4. *Der Säulenbasis im Özbey-Haus*

Das zweite schriftliche Dokument, das während der Bauarbeiten im Dorf Yukarı Anzaf ans Tageslicht gebracht worden ist und wieder in der Vorratskammer der Familie Özbey als Pfostenfundament aufbewahrt wird, ist die erhaltene Hälfte einer Säulenbasis, deren Durchmesser wegen des eingemauerten hinteren Teils nicht zu messen war, deren Dicke aber 23 cm beträgt. Darauf sind drei Zeilen zu sehen, alle mit Abständen von 3,5 cm, von denen die mittlere leer gelassen ist. Es sind wiederum leere Ränder über und unter den Zeilen, die jeweils eine Höhe von 5 cm und 7,5 cm haben (s. Pl. 4a). Auf den beiden Zeilen ist m]d*Sar*$_5$*-du-ri-ḫi-ni-*[= "Sohn des Sarduri"

zu lesen, was besagt, daß diese Säulenbasis zu einem vom Išpuini erbauten Gebäude gehörte. Die Bautätigkeit scheint also hier schon vor dem Bau des Ḫaldi-Tempels von Menua, in der Herrschaftsperiode seines Vaters Išpuini angefangen zu haben. Daß Išpuini der Bauherr der Anlagen in der Niederen Burg von Anzaf gewesen war, bezeugt der frühere Fund einer weiteren Säulenbasisinschrift ähnlichen Inhalts.[3]

5 a -c. *Die Inschriften von Aşağı (= Niederem) Anzaf*

Etwa vor zehn Jahren wurden die Südmauern der Burg vom Niederen Anzaf während des Baus der Landstraße Van-Özalp von Baumaschinen willkürlich zerstört und die zerstreuten Kalksteinblöcke wurden in der Umgebung als Baumaterial benutzt. Manche Inschriftenblöcke wurden sogar für diesen Zweck weiter zerschlagen. Glücklicherweise befinden sich zwei davon in fast unversehrtem Zustand, und die Inschrift auf einem Bruchstück erweist sich als ein Duplikat von diesen beiden.

Die Inschrift (a) ist auf die geglättete Oberfläche eines kyklopischen Kalkstein-blocks gemeißelt, dessen Maße 185 x 75 x 100 cm betragen (s. Pl. 4b). Der Stein lag mit seiner beschrifteten Seite auf der Erde in der Nähe der Burg von Aşağı Anzaf und wurde von den Ausgräbern, die nach den Bausteinen des zerstörten Eingangs suchten, wieder umgedreht. Der Text besteht aus 7 Zeilen, alle mit Abständen von 3,5 cm; darunter ist eine leere Fläche mit etwa 40 cm Höhe freigelassen, auch an der rechten Seite ist ein leerer Rand mit einer maximalen Breite von 18 cm vorhanden. Die Länge der Zeilen weicht voneinander etwas ab und mißt durchschnittlich 60 cm.

Umschrift der Inschrift (a)

1 d*Ḫal-d*[*i*]*-ni-n*[*i*] [*u*]*š-*[*ma*]*-a-ši-*[*ni*]
2 m*Iš-pu-ú-i-ni-še*
3 md*Sar*$_5$*-du-ri-ḫi-ni-še*
4 *i-ni* É.GAL *ši-di-iš-tu-ni*
5 *ba-a-du-si-*[*i*]*-e*
6 LUGÁL *DAN-NU* LUGÁL *al-su-i-ni*
7 LUGÁL KUR*Bi-i-a-i-na-*[*ú*]*-e*

[3] Cf. P. Hulin, *AnSt.* 10 (1960) 205.

Übersetzung der Inschrift (a)

1 Durch die Macht des Gottes Haldi
2 hat Išpuini, Sohn des
3 Sarduri
4 diese Burg
5 in perfektem Zustand erbaut.
6 Der mächtige König, der große König,
7 der König der Bia-Länder.

Die zweite Inschrift (b), die bis auf ein einziges Wort mit der vorigen Inschrift (a) identisch ist, findet sich auch auf einem Kalksteinblock, der in das Fundament eines Wohnhauses im Dorf Aşağı Anzaf eingemauert ist. Er ist 130 cm lang und hat eine maximale Höhe von 55 cm. Die beschriftete Oberfläche ist stark verwittert. Der Text ist auf sechs Zeilen verteilt, die etwa 75 cm lang sind. Von den Zeilenlinien ist nichts übriggeblieben; die Abstände sind durchschnittlich 3,5 cm. Im Mittelalter wurde ein Kreuz unter die Inschrift geritzt, das jedoch die Zeichen nicht zerstörte (s. Pl. 4c).

Umschrift der Inschrift (b)

1 ^{d}*Ḫal-di-ni-ni uš-ma-a-ši-ni*
2 ^{m}*Iš-pu-ú-i-ni-še* ^{md}*Sar*$_5$*-du-ri-ḫi-ni-še*
3 *i-ni* É.GAL *ši-di-iš-tu-*⸢*ú*⸣*-ni*
4 *ba-du-si-i-e* LUGÁL *DAN-NU*
5 LUGÁL *al-su-i-ni* LUGÁL *šú-*⸢*ú-ra-ú*⸣*-e*
6 LUGÁL ^{KUR}*Bi-i-a-i-na-ú-e*

Übersetzung der Inschrift (b)

1 Durch die Macht des Gottes Haldi
2 hat Išpuini, Sohn des Sarduri
3 diese Burg in perfektem Zustand
4 erbaut. Der mächtige König,
5 der große König, der König der Welt(?),
6 der König der Bia-Länder.

Bemerkungen

Z. 5 *šura*: Dieser Beleg stellt u.W. chronologisch den ersten Auftritt des Wortes dar. Im Gegensatz zu der von Melikishvili angenommenen Bedeutung "Universum, Welt, Reich, Königreich" (*DUS* 87), übersetzt Salvini die Phrase

LUGAL *šuraue* als "re dei paesi (?)."[4] Daß auf diesen Inschriften Titulatur die sonst übliche Aussage "Herr der Stadt Tušpa" nicht anzutreffen ist, sei hier auch bemerkt. Die längere Titulatur wird später während der Koregentschaft Išpuini-Menua eingeführt.[5]

An der Wasserquelle in der Nähe der Burgruine vom Niederen Anzaf befindet sich das Bruchstück (c) eines Kalksteinblockes, der für die Gewinnung von Bausteinen zerbrochen wurde (s. Pl. 4d). Der erhaltene Teil, dessen geglättete Oberfläche (50 x 22 cm) Reste einer ursprünglich siebenzeiligen Inschrift enthält, ist ziemlich groß (Maße: 70 x 54 x 58 cm). Darauf sind nur fünf Zeilenfragmente, alle mit Abständen von 3,5 cm, zu sehen; ein Vergleich mit der anderen Inschrift gleichen Inhalts zeigt, daß der Text mit der ersten völlig übereinstimmt.

Umschrift der Inschrift (c)

x+1 [mdSar5-du-r]i-[ḫi-ni-še]
2 [i-n]i [É.GAL ši-di-iš-tu-ni]
3 [ba]-a-[du]-si-i-[e]
4 [LUGÁL] DAN-NU LUGÁL al-su-[i-ni]
5 [LUGÁL] KURBi-i-a-i-na-[u-e]

Wegen der abgebrochenen ersten zwei Zeilen fehlt auch der Name des Herrschers, aber, wenn die Emendierung der ersten erhaltenen Zeilen zutrifft, soll er, wie auf den sonstigen Inschriften aus Niederem Anzaf, Išpuini sein.

II. Die beschrifteten Bronzefunde

1. *Die Votivringe* (s. Pl. 5)

In der ersten Kampagne der Ausgrabungen am Oberen Anzaf wurden dicht neben dem Eingang zum Tempelareal in einem durch starke Feuersbrunst sehr zerstörten Zustand bronzene Ringe gefunden, welche zu Restaurierungsarbeiten in das Labor der Universität zu Istanbul gebracht wurden.[6] Bei der Behandlung stellte sich heraus, daß die Ringe mit Inschriften versehen sind. Darauf wurden

[4] Cf. M. Salvini, *Or.* 62 (1993) 75.

[5] Cf. G. Wilhelm, "Urartu als Region der Keilschrift-Kultur" in *Das Reich Urartu* (ed. V. Haas), *Xenia* 17 (1986) 106-111.

[6] Zur Fundlage und archäologischen Besonderheiten der einzelnen Ringe, s. Belli, "Van Anzaf Urartu Kaleleri Kazısı" (Die Ausgrabungen an der urartäischen Festung Anzaf bei Van), *Arkeoloji ve Sanat* 54/55 (1992) 19-20, und id. "Aşaği ve Yukarı Anzaf Urartu Kaleleri Kazısı", *Arkeoloji ve Sanat* 58 (1993) 14-17.

die Verfasser dieser Zeilen benachrichtigt. Sie waren sehr tief korrodiert und hatten sich durch die (gegenseitige) chemische Reaktion mit den Bodensalzen teilweise bis zu ihren Kernen in eine Art Kreide verwandelt. Die Behandlung war ein sehr mühsamer Prozeß, der sich Schritt für Schritt in Zusammenarbeit der Restauratoren und Philologen entwickelte. Es ist leider zu fürchten, daß trotz aller Sorgfalt manche Keilschriftzeichen, besonders die auf den kreideartigen Zonen, mit der Zeit verlorengehen werden. Auf vier von diesen Ringen ist derselbe Text zu lesen, der auf Nr. 1 in drei, und auf Nr. 2, 3 und 4 in zwei Zeilen verteilt ist (s. Pls. 6-10).

Umschrift des rekonstruierten Textes

> ^{d}*Ḫal-di-e e-ú-ri-e* ^{m}*Iš-pu-ú-i-ni-še* ^{md}*Sar*$_{5}$*-du-ri-ḫi-ni-še* ^{m}*Me-nu-a-še* ^{m}*Iš-pu-ú-i-ni-ḫi-ni-še* ^{m}*I-nu-uš-pu-a-še* ^{m}*Me-nu-a-ḫi-ni-še uš-ṭi-tu i-ú* ^{URU}*A-mu-ša-ni* KUR*-ni-e ḫa-i-tu*

Übersetzung des rekonstruierten Textes

> Dem Gott Ḫaldi, dem Herrn, schenkten Išpuini, Sohn des Sarduri, Menua, Sohn des Išpuini (und) Inušpua, Sohn des Menua, als sie das Land der Stadt *Amuša* eroberten (s. Pls. 11-13).

Erklärungen

Die Existenz der verbalen Form *uštitu*, die hier zum ersten Mal bezeugt wird, kann dadurch erklärt werden, daß das Kennzeichen der Transitivität *u* vor den Dentalen *t* oder *d* ausfällt und daß die Verba wie *atu-, šidištu-* mit dem Suffix der 3. Person Plural der Vergangenheit regelmäßige Formen wie *atitu* und *šidištitu* bilden. Es sei hier am Rande bemerkt, daß die mittlere Silbe *-ti-* sehr schwer zu lesen war, und die ganze Form wegen des ersten Vorkommens nicht leicht emendiert werden konnte.

Bei der Rekonstruktion des Textes besteht nur das Problem, daß auf dem Ring Nr. 4 der Abstand zwischen den Silben *i-* und *-u* des Wortes *iu* größer als nötig ist, so daß wir den Verdacht haben, daß hier vielleicht die von König angenommene (*HChI* 9 Par. 13), aber von Melikishvili bezweifelte (*UKN* 128 Anm. 15) Form *iu iu* doch nicht in Frage kommen könnte; dadurch wäre die Lücke gefüllt. Leider haben wir keine Anhaltspunkte für die tatsächliche Existenz einer reduplizierten Form des temporalen Adverbs *iu*.

Der Ring Nr. 5 (s. Pl. 14a-b), der eine vierzeilige Inschrift enthält, befindet sich in einem gefährdeten Zustand wegen der tief eingedrungenen Korrosion und dadurch zustande gekommenen Oberflächenspannung. Trotz der sorgfältigen Behandlung kann leider von einer dauerhaften Rettung nicht gesprochen werden. Viele Keilschriftzeichen sind schon verlorengegangen und mit der Zeit fallen auch andere der Korrosion zum Opfer. Die Umschrift der lesbaren Zeilen ist wie folgt (s. Pl. 15-16a):

1 [ ]x *ma-si-ni i-ú ka-n*[*i*] U[R]U*A-mu-ša-ni* KUR-*n*[*i-e*
2 [URU*A-mu-š*]*a-ni* KUR-*ni-e* [-*d*]*i*(?) [
3 [ ] *uš-tu-li* m*Iš-pu-ú-*[*i-ni-ni* m*Sar*5*-d*]*u-ri-ḫe* m*Me-nu-a-ni* m*Iš-pu-ú-i-n*[*i*]*-ḫe* m*I-nu-uš-pu-a-ni*
4 [m*Me-nu*]*-a-ḫe* [d*Ḫal-di-e*] *e-ú-ri-e* [

Bemerkungen zum Inhalt der Inschrift

Obwohl die Komposition des Textes sich von dem der übrigen Ringe unterscheidet, ist es trotz der mangelhaften Überlieferung klar, daß auch hier von denselben Errungenschaften der Koregentschaft die Rede ist.

Da die bedeutenden Elemente des ersten Satzes fehlen, kann über die Funktion des Possessivpronomens der 3. Person Sg. wenig gesagt werden. In der Mehrzahl der Inschriften kommt *masini* im folgenden Satz vor: d*Haldini uštabi masini* GIŠ*šurie karuni*. Hier würde man etwas ähnliches – in anderer Satzordnung – erwarten, wenn es vor *masini* genügend Platz gegeben hätte. Hier wäre es anzunehmen, daß dieses Pronomen wahrscheinlich in dem Temporalsatz "als vor dem Land *Amuša* ... " (= *iu kani* URU*Amušani* KUR-*nie*) teilnimmt. In dem darauf folgenden Satz wird dieser Stadtname in sehr gebrochenem Kontext wieder erwähnt. Die verbale Form *uštuli* "sie schenkten sie (Akk. Pl.)" wird u.W. zum ersten Mal hier belegt und analog zum *šidištitu+li* > *šidištuli* gebaut. Zweifelsohne sind hier die als Votivgabe benutzten Ringe gemeint. Daß die genealogisch aufgezählten Namen der drei Herrscher im "Nominativ" stehen, ist ein Hinweis auf die Intransitivität des fehlenden Verbums, dessen Objekt wahrscheinlich von [d*Haldie*] *eurie* "dem Gotte Haldi, dem Herrn" vertreten wird.

Zu demselben Fundkomplex gehören noch zwei Fragmente, worauf einige Zeichen zu sehen sind, deren Lesung aber unsicher ist und deshalb weder in die zweizeilige noch in die vierzeilige Gruppe eingeordnet werden können. Deren provisorische Umschriften sind wie folgt (s. Pl. 16b).

Ringfragment (a)

1]*x ú lu še* (?) [
2 m*Me*]*-nu-a*[

Ringfragment (b)

1 *uš-tu-l*]*i* ^{m}*Iš-p*[*u-i-ni*
2 ^{d}*Ḫal-d*]*i-e e-ú-*[*ri-e*

Historische und Geographische Bemerkungen

Den einzigen Beleg über die Koregentschaft von drei Herrschern in der urartäischen Geschichte bildete bisher die Inschrift von Tebriz Kapı (*UKN* 18 = *HChI* 12) auf den Van Felsen. In dieser Inschrift, die aus einem dreimal wiederholten Text besteht, kommen die Namen von Išpuini, Sohn des Sarduri, Menua, Sohn des Išpuini und Inušpua, Sohn des Menua vor. Durch die singulären Endungen der konjugierten Verba wird es betont, daß die eigentliche handelnde Person oder der Autor Išpuini war. Dieselbe Eigenschaft ist auch auf den Inschriften aus der Koregentschaft von Išpuini und Menua anzutreffen (*HChI* 9= *UKN* 19; *HCh* 8= *UKN* 25), jedoch kann es nicht als eine feste Regel betrachtet werden (*HChI* 6 = *UKN* 20, *HChI* 7 = *UKN* 24, *HChI* 10 = *UKN* 27, *HChI* 11 = *UKN* 26). Auf den Inschriften von Karahan, die von den Verfassern dieser Zeilen veröffentlicht wurden (Karahan 14 in Dinçol-Kavaklı, *JKF* Bh. 1 (1978) 7-24; Karahan 58 in Dinçol-Kavaklı, *JKF* 6 (1978[1979]) 17-28), und alle in die Periode der Koregentschaft von Išpuini-Menua datieren, erscheint ein einzelner Herrscher als die handelnde Person, oder in diesem Fall der Bauherr aber in den Partien der Inschriften, wo ein Segenswunsch ausgesprochen wird, wird auch der Name des Koregenten erwähnt. Es ist auch bemerkenswert, daß in diesen Segenswünschen auf den Vorrang des älteren Herrschers geachtet wird:

Karahan 1

Handelnde Person: Menua, Sohn des Išpuini

Im Segenswunsch kommen vor: Išpuini, Sohn des Sarduri
Menua, Sohn des Išpuini

Datum: Die Koregentschaft von Išpuini und Menua

Karahan 2

Handelnde Person: Išpuini, Sohn des Sarduri

Im Segenswunsch kommen vor: Išpuini, Sohn des Sarduri
Menua, Sohn des Išpuini

Datum: Die Koregentschaft von Išpuini und Menua

Karahan 5

Handelnde Person Menua, Sohn des Išpuini

Im Segenswunsch
kommt vor: Išpuini, Sohn des Sarduri

Datum: Die Koregentschaft von Išpuini und Menua

Karahan 7

Handelnde Person: ?

Im Segenswunsch
kommt vor: Išpuini, Sohn des Sarduri

Datum: Die Koregentschaft von Išpuini und Menua

Karahan 8

Handelnde Person: Išpuini, Sohn des Sarduri

Im Segenswunsch Išpuini, Sohn des Sarduri
kommen vor: Menua, Sohn des Išpuini

Datum: Die Koregentschaft von Išpuini und Menua

Aus diesen Belegen ergibt sich, daß in einer Koregentschaft einer der Herrscher Tätigkeiten in seinem eigenen Namen durchführen konnte, daß er jedoch dabei die Erwähnung seines Koregenten nicht vernachlässigte. Es war natürlich durchaus möglich, daß Koregenten zusammenwirkten. Auf den Inschriften, die in die Periode der Koregentschaft von Menua und Inušpua datieren (*HChI* 13 = *UKN* 93, *HChI* 14 = *UKN* 94, *HChI* 15 = *UKN* 95) erscheint Menua als der eigentliche Täter, während sein Sohn nur in den Segenswünschen erwähnt wird. In keinem der Belege aus der Zeit der Koregentschaft von Menua und Inušpua bekleidet der Sohn die Position eines Täters. In der Inschrift von Tebriz Kapı ist wegen der umstrittenen Endung des Verbums *šidištu* "bauen" (Salvini, "Anhang m" in *DUS* 101-103) schwer zu entscheiden, ob als Erbauer des Haldi Tempels alle drei Herrscher in Frage kommen, oder, wie der Satz *Išpuiniše alie* schon am Anfang verrät, nur Išpuini dafür die Verantwortung trägt, was wegen seines Vorrangs als Vater und Großvater seiner Koregenten zu erwarten wäre. Auf den acht Bronzeobjekten finden sich zwar kurze Inschriften, in denen aber keine Tätigkeit erzählt wird, sondern nur die Zugehörigkeit der Gegenstände zu Inušpua ausgedrückt ist.[7] Auf den Ringen von Anzaf kommt zum ersten Mal eine Tätigkeit in Frage, deren Verantwortung von drei Koregenten gleichmäßig und zusammen getragen wird. Das bezeugen auch die zwei Verba, die in der 3. Person Pl. sind. Die Teilnahme Inušpuas an der militärischen Kampagne könnte, auf der anderen Seite, als ein Hinweis auf sein Alter betrachtet werden. Er sollte nicht ein kleines Kind sein, um mit seinem Vater und seinem Großvater ins Feld ziehen zu können. Ein weiteres Dokument, worauf sein Name vorkommt, ist eine silberne *Situla*. Die akkadische Inschrift lautet: "Išpuini, Sohn des Sarduri, gab (diese Situla) dem Inušpua, weil er seinen alten Mann (*kibaru* = hurr. *kewiru* = LÚŠU.GI = alter Mann, Großvater) gerne hat (Salvini, *SMEA* 29 (1992) 225; vgl. für seine frühere Interpretation Salvini, *Assur* I/8 (1978) 172). Die Interpretation dieser Inschrift als ein Beweisstück einer Koregentschaft zwischen dem Großvater und seinem Enkel unter Ausschaltung des Vaters Menua (V. Sevin, *JKF* 7 (1981) 45) scheint nicht zutreffend zu sein. Weil die Bedeutung des Wortes LÚ*kibaru* bis vor kurzem nicht bekannt war, wollte man darunter eine Verwandschaftsbezeichnung wie "Enkel" verstehen, aber da diese im Akkadischen nicht mit LÚ determiniert wird, wurde eine Amtbezeichnung wie "Thronfolger des Thronfolgers" vorgeschlagen (Salvini, *Assur* I/8 (1978) 174). Die Frage, wann dieses Geschenk dem Inušpua gegeben wurde, ist nicht leicht zu beantworten. Es ist anzunehmen, daß der Großvater Išpuini seinem Enkel zum Andenken an ein bestimmtes – vielleicht fröhliches – Ereignis diese Situla geschenkt hat, als Inušpua noch ein Kind war. Wir sind der Meinung, daß dieses Ereignis – was es immer sein mag – aus zweierlei Gründen nicht am Ende der Herrschaftsperiode Išpuinis stattgefunden hat (so Salvini, *Assur* I/8 (1978) 174). Erstens, weil die Benutzung des Akkadischen in der Hauptstadt eine ältere Anwendung war, die von Išpuini nicht fortgeführt wurde; und zweitens, weil wir im Licht der neugefundenen Votivringe jetzt wissen, daß Inušpua während seiner Partnerschaft mit seinem Großvater und Vater ein Erwachsener sein sollte. Deshalb kommt es uns angemessen vor, die Situla in die erste Hälfte Išpuinis Alleinherrschaft, also um 825 zu datieren. Als die Koregentschaft von Išpuini und Menua andauerte, wurde auch Inušpua als dritter König in die Herrschaft eingenommen, weil er wahrscheinlich ein bestimmtes Alter erreichte. Nach dem Tode Išpuinis, blieben erst Menua und Inušpua als Koregenten und nach dem vorzeitigen Tod seines Sohnes herrschte Menua allein auf dem urartäischen Thron. Warum er gleich nach dem Tode Inušpuas seinen jüngeren Sohn Argišti nicht als Mitherrscher ernannte, ist nicht mit Sicherheit zu beantworten. Einer der möglichen Gründen wäre es, daß Argišti während des Todes seines Bruders zu jung oder gar nicht

[7] Siehe O. Belli, "Inscribed Metal Objects" in *Urartu: a metalworking Center in the 1st Millennium B.C.* (ed. R. Merhav, Jerusalem 1991) 44-49.

geboren war. Eine andere Möglichkeit wäre die Abschaffung des Koregentsystems sein, das bis zum Ende des urartäischen Staates nicht wieder angewendet wurde.

Die bronzenen Votivringe aus Anzaf stellen das endgültige Beweismaterial für die Existenz der Koregentschaft von Išpuini-Menua-Inušpua dar, die wahrscheinlich nicht besonders lang dauerte, doch aber eine wichtige Phase der urartäischen Geschichte bildete und nicht wie bisher in manchen Studien unbeachtet gelassen werden darf.

Der Fundort der aus den beschrifteten Ringen bestehende Votivkette in einem Tempel, der in der Alleinherrschaft Menuas gebaut wurde, weist darauf hin, daß hier anstelle des von Menua erbauten, früher ein älteres Heiligtum vorhanden war. Nach dem Bau des Turmtempels(= *susi*) scheint auch diese Kette mit den anderen Kultgegenständen zu ihrem neuen Ort getragen worden zu sein, um dort bis zu einer Brandkatastrophe aufbewahrt zu werden.

Die Eroberung der Stadt *Amuša*, die diese Votivgabe veranlaßte, beweist, daß die Koregentschaft von Išpuini-Menua-Inušpua auch auf dem militärischen Feld nicht untätig blieb. Der Name *Amuša* wird bisher nur einmal auf einer Inschrift aus dem Dorfe Arevis in der Sisian Region von Armenien belegt. In der 22. Zeile eines 27-zeiligen Inschriften-fragments auf dem erhaltenen unteren Teil einer Stele kommt der Name im Direktiv Kasus mit der Endung *-di* vor.[8] Die Stadt *Amuša* wird von dem Verfasser südlich vom Sevan-See (Gökçe Göl) lokalisiert.[9] Dieser Vorschlag wird auch von I.M. Diakonoff - S.M. Kashkai angenommen[10]; sie wollen aber die Stadt südöstlich desselben Sees in die Region *Suluqu* lokalisieren, die dieselbe geographische Lage des modernen Nakhcevans hat. Wenn der leichte Verkehr von Anzaf, dessen urartäischen Namen wir leider nicht kennen, nach *Rusa-i* URU.TUR (= Bastam) über der heutigen Kreisstadt Özalp berücksichtigt wird, wäre es nicht falsch anzunehmen, daß das urartäische Territorium bis zu dieser Region schon so früh während der Koregentschaft von Išpuini-Menua-Inušpua expandieren konnte.

Eine ähnliche Votivgabe wegen einer Eroberung stellt die steinerne Keule aus der Zeit von Argišti I. dar, die der Herrscher nach der darüber geschriebenen dreizeiligen Inschrift aus dem Lande *Eriahi* mitbrachte und der Göttin 'A/Uarabani weihte.[11]

8 Cf. N. Harouthiounyan, "A new Urartian Inscription from Sisian", *Drevnei Vostok* 4 (1983) 305.

9 Cf. Harouthiounyan, op.cit. 308.

10 *RGTC* 9, 8; dort fälschlich in die Herrschaftsperiode von Argišti II. datiert, dieser Fehler wird aber unter "Erdua" berichtigt.

11 Siehe A. Dinçol - E. Kavaklì, *JKF* 8 (1980) 231-235.

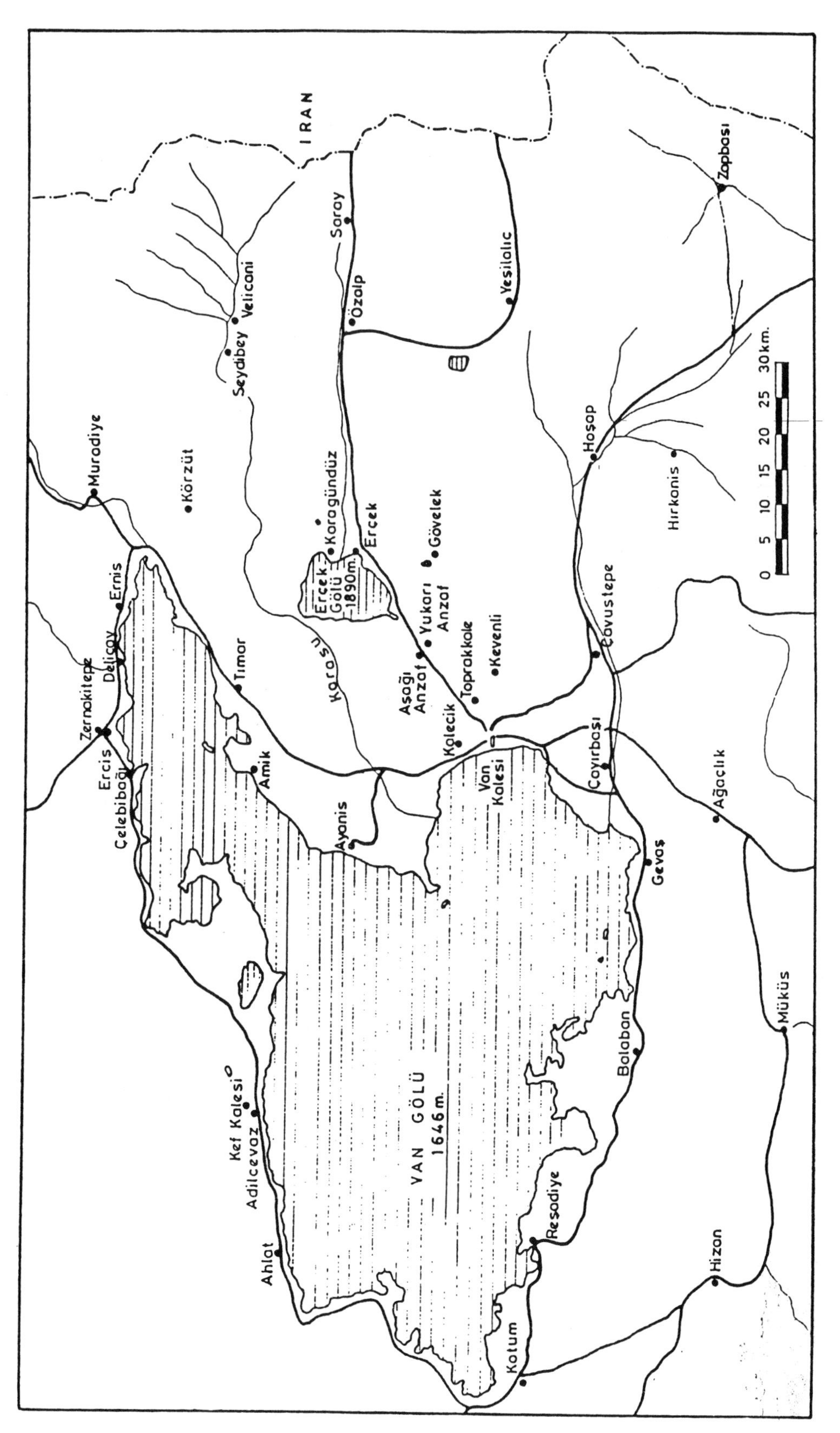

Plate 1. Die Lage von Anzaf.

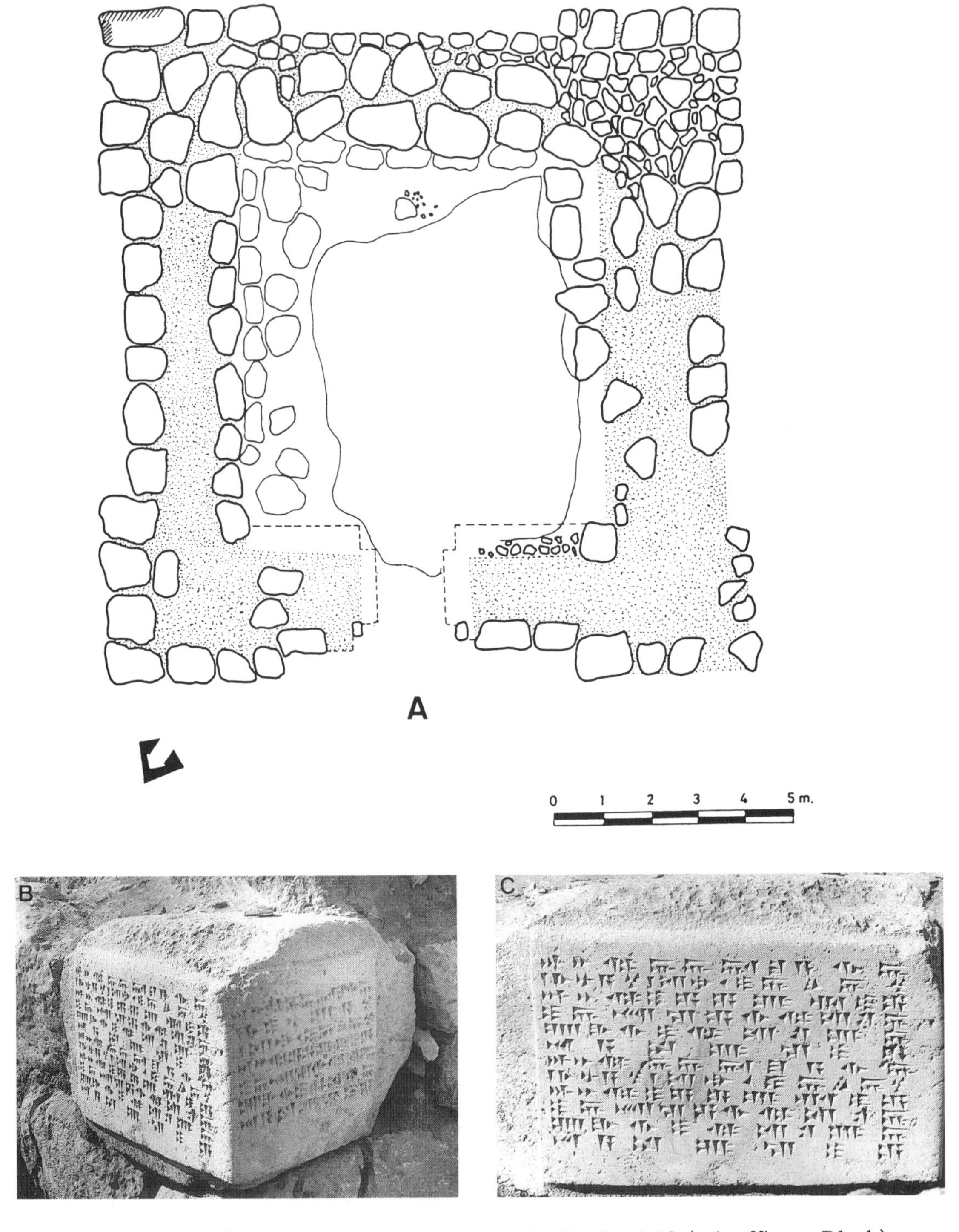

Plate 2a. Der Plan des Tempels und die Lage der Bauinschrift (schraffierter Block).
b. Der Gesamtansicht der Bauinschrift des Tempels.
c. Die lange Seite der Tempelinschrift.

Plate 3a. Die kurze Seite der Tempelinschrift.
b. Das Inschriftfragment a) aus dem Oberen Anzaf.
c. Das Inschriftfragment b) aus dem Oberen Anzaf.
d. Das Inschriftfragment im Haus von Özbey.

Plate 4a. Die Säulenbasis im Vorratskammer.
b. Die Bauinschrift a) im Niederen Anzaf.
c. Die Bauinschrift b) im Niederen Anzaf.
d. Das Inschriftfragment c) im Niederen Anzaf.

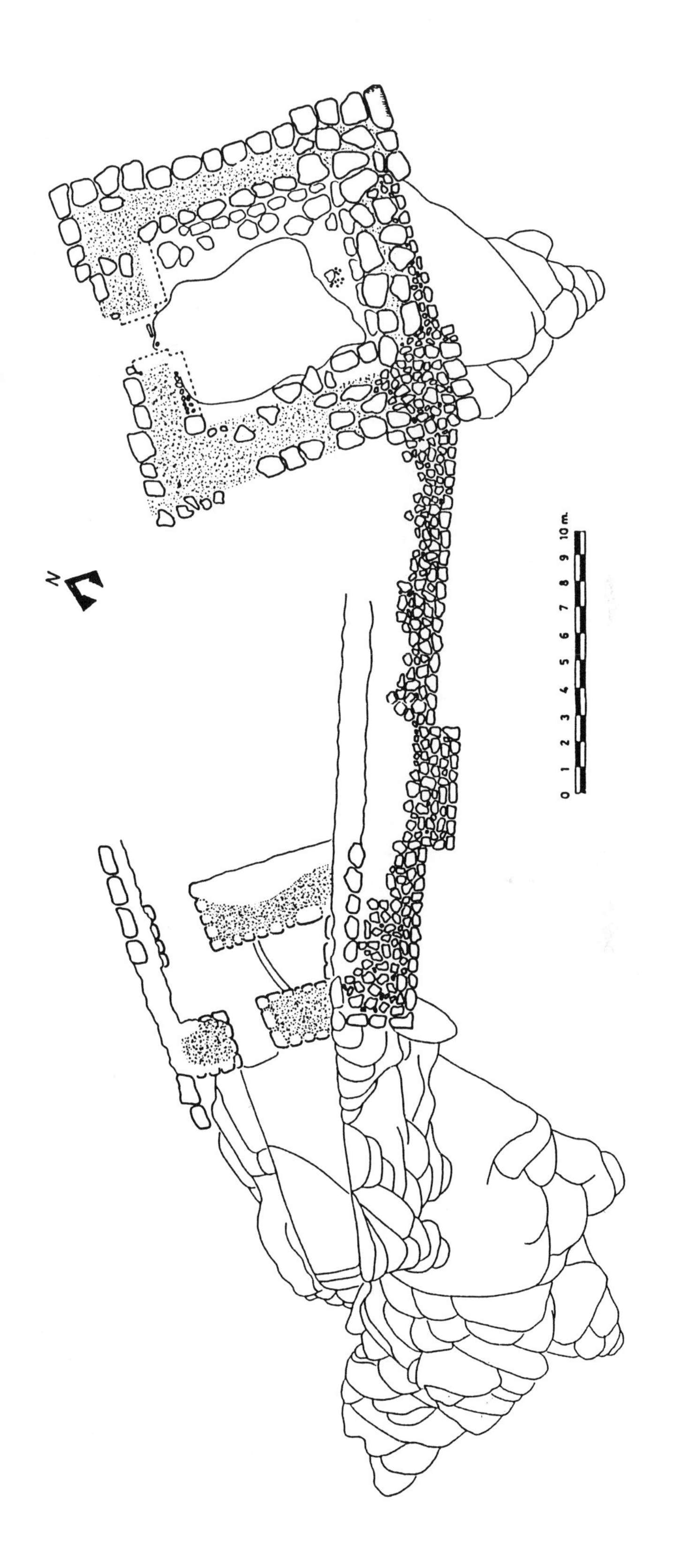

Plate 5. Der Gesamtplan des Tempelareals.

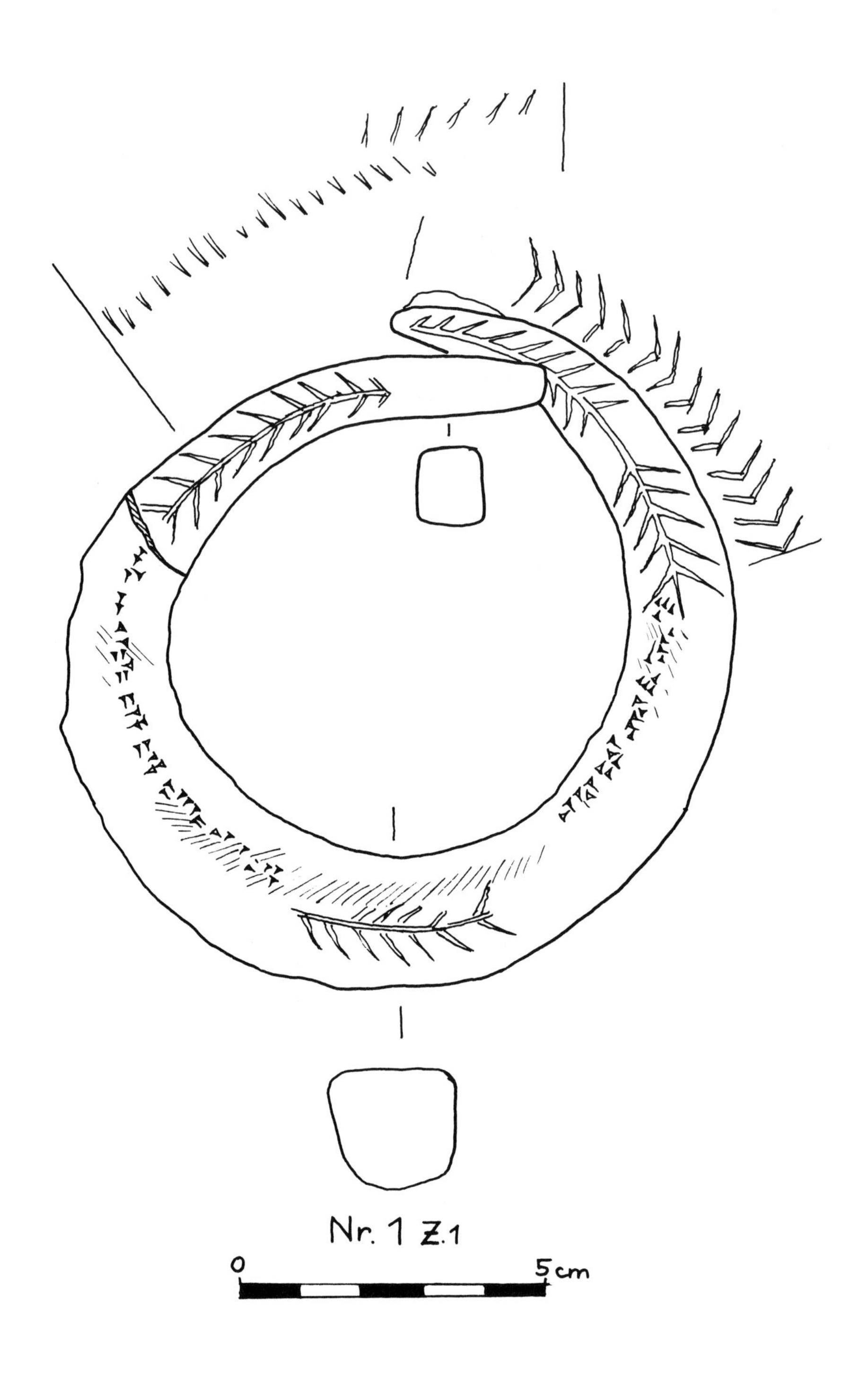

Plate 6. Ring Nr. 1, Zeile 1.

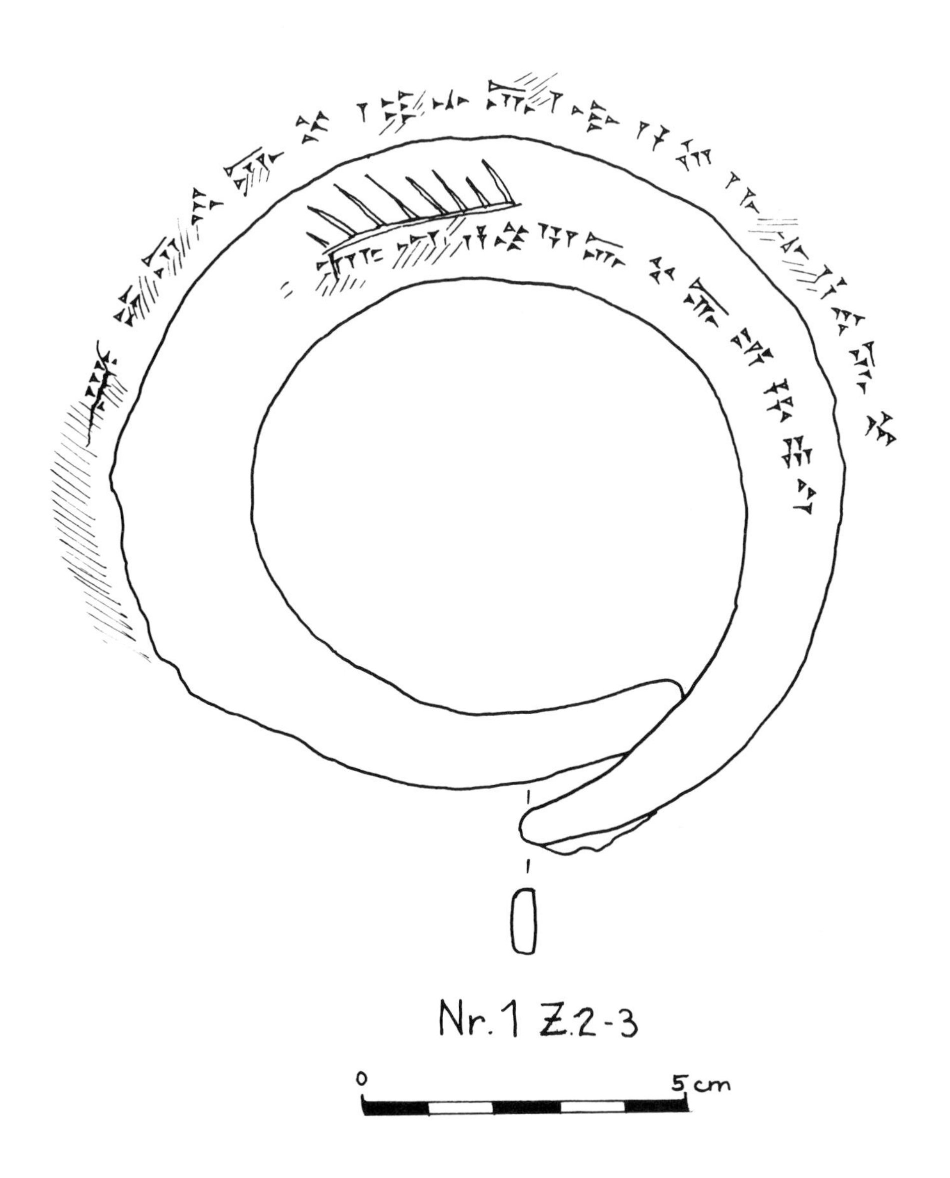

Plate 7. Ring Nr. 1, Zeilen 2 und 3.

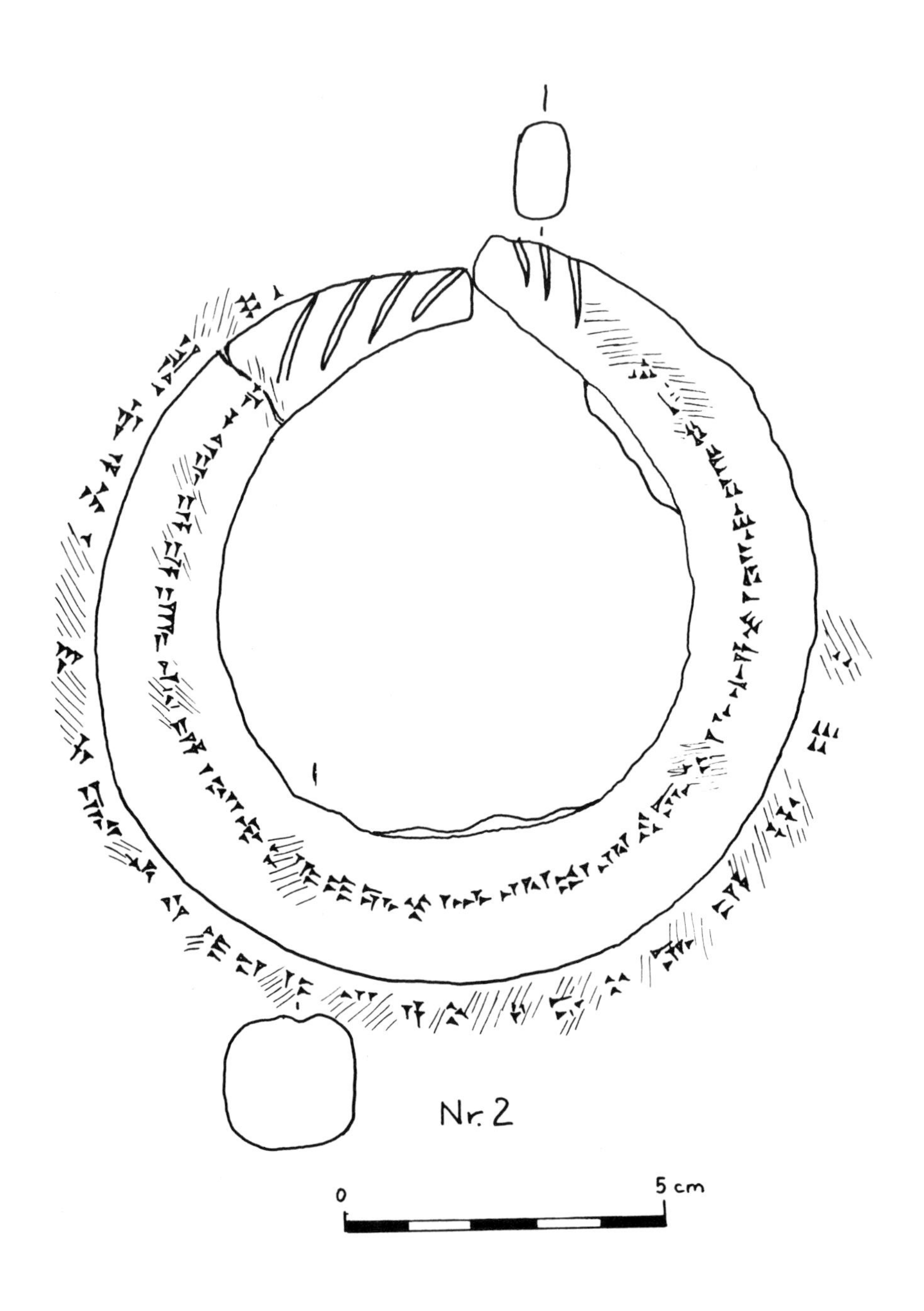

Plate 8. Ring Nr. 2.

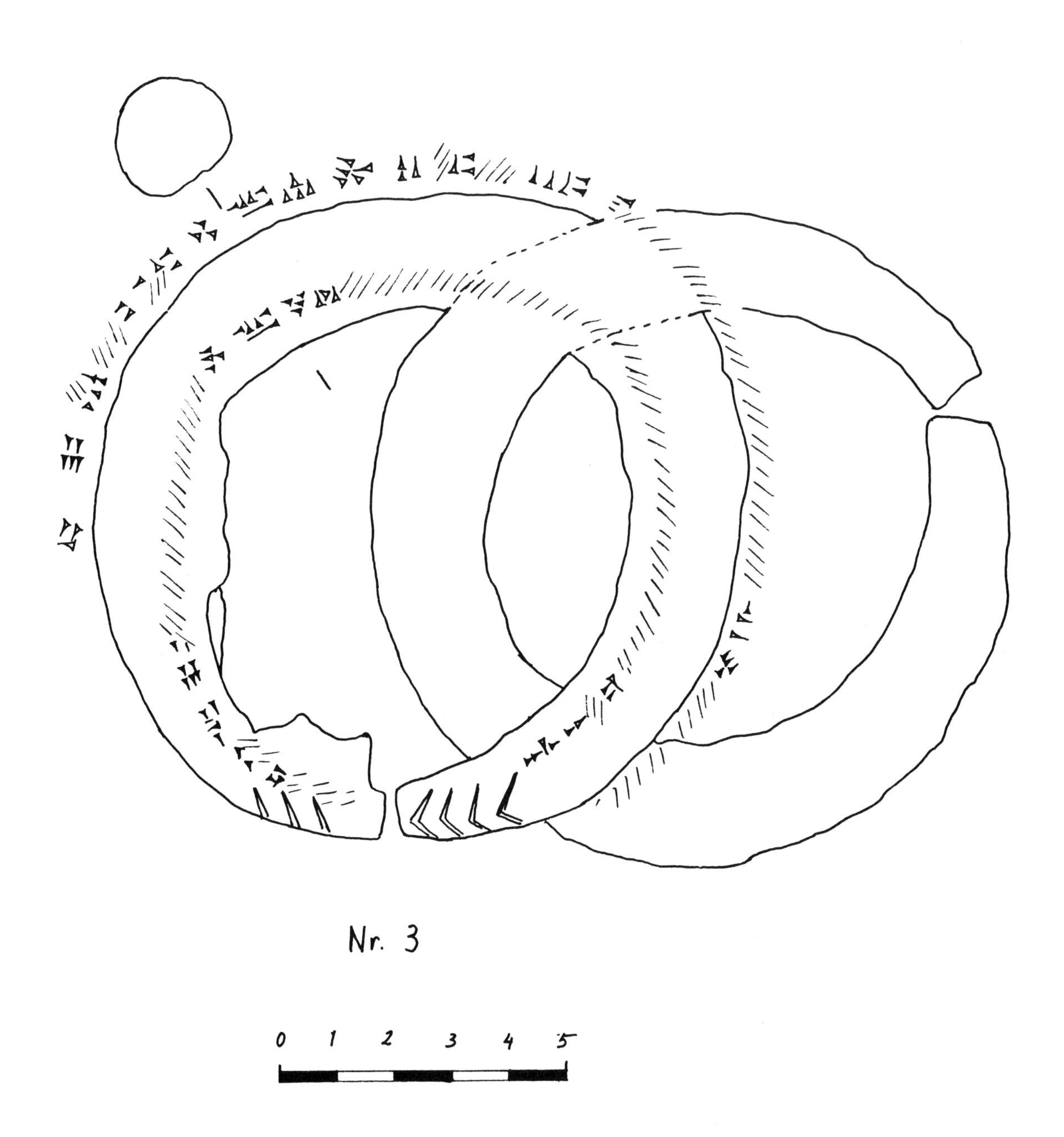

Plate 9. Ring Nr. 3.

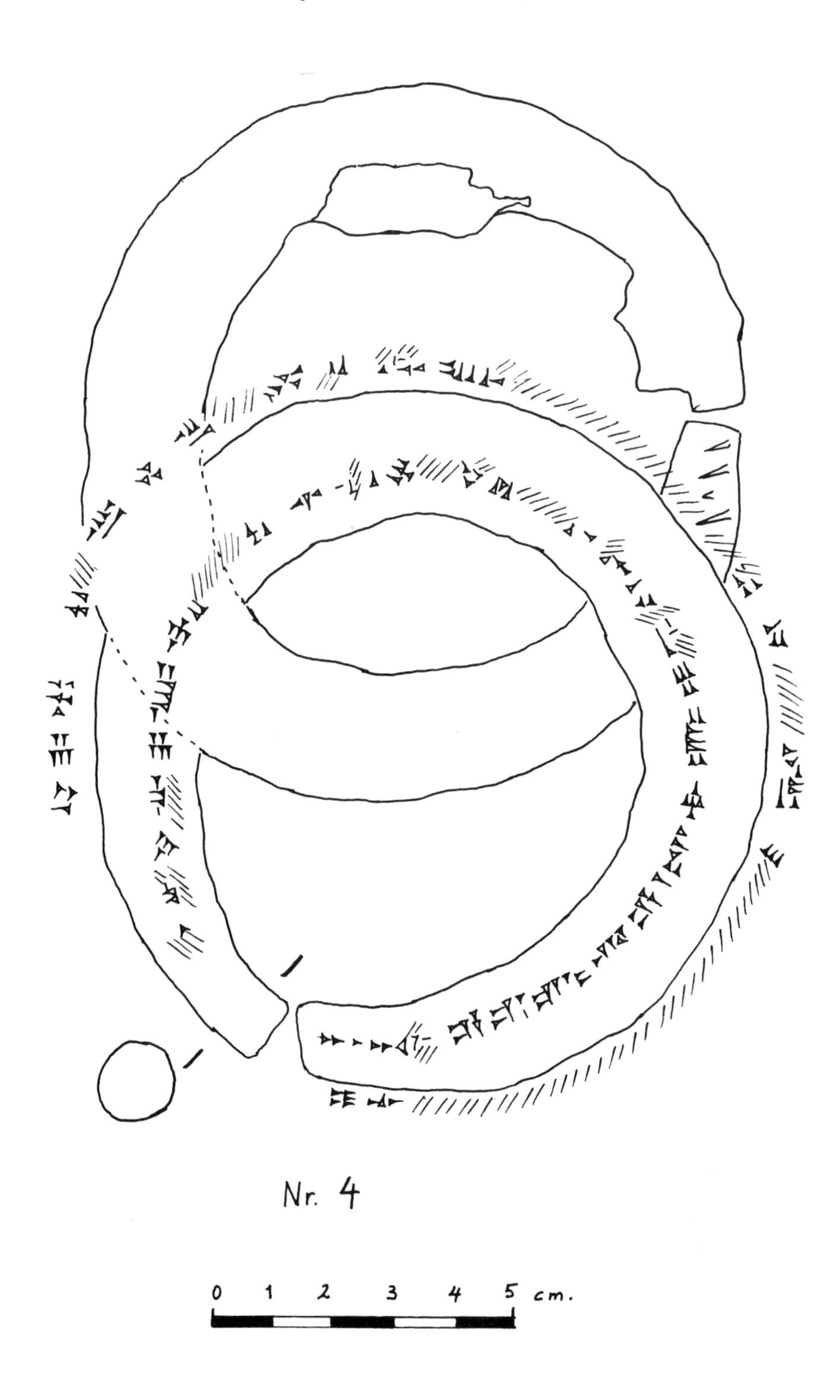

Plate 10. Ring Nr. 4.

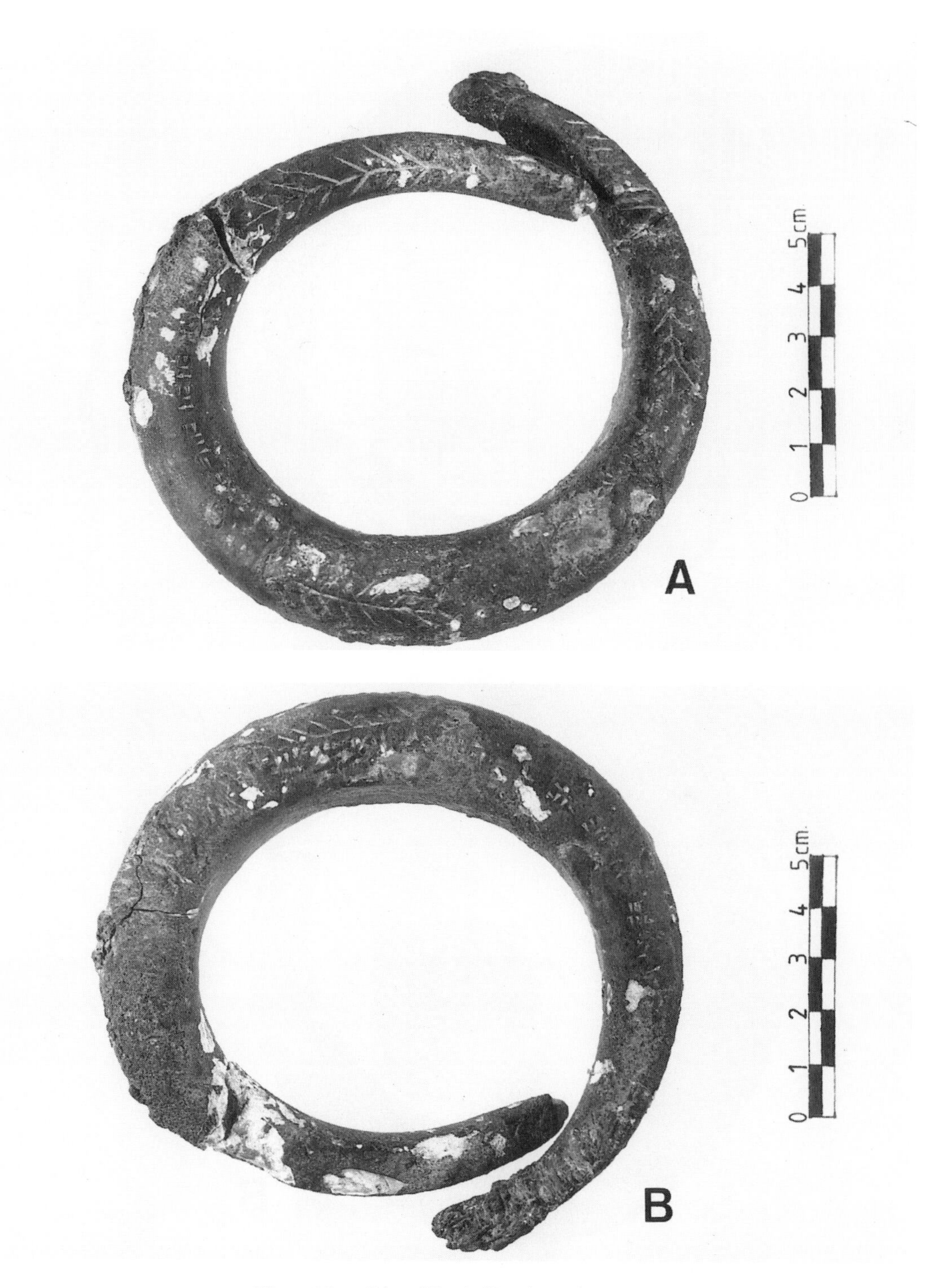

Plate 11a. Ring Nr. 1, Vorderseite.
b. Ring Nr. 1, Rückseite.

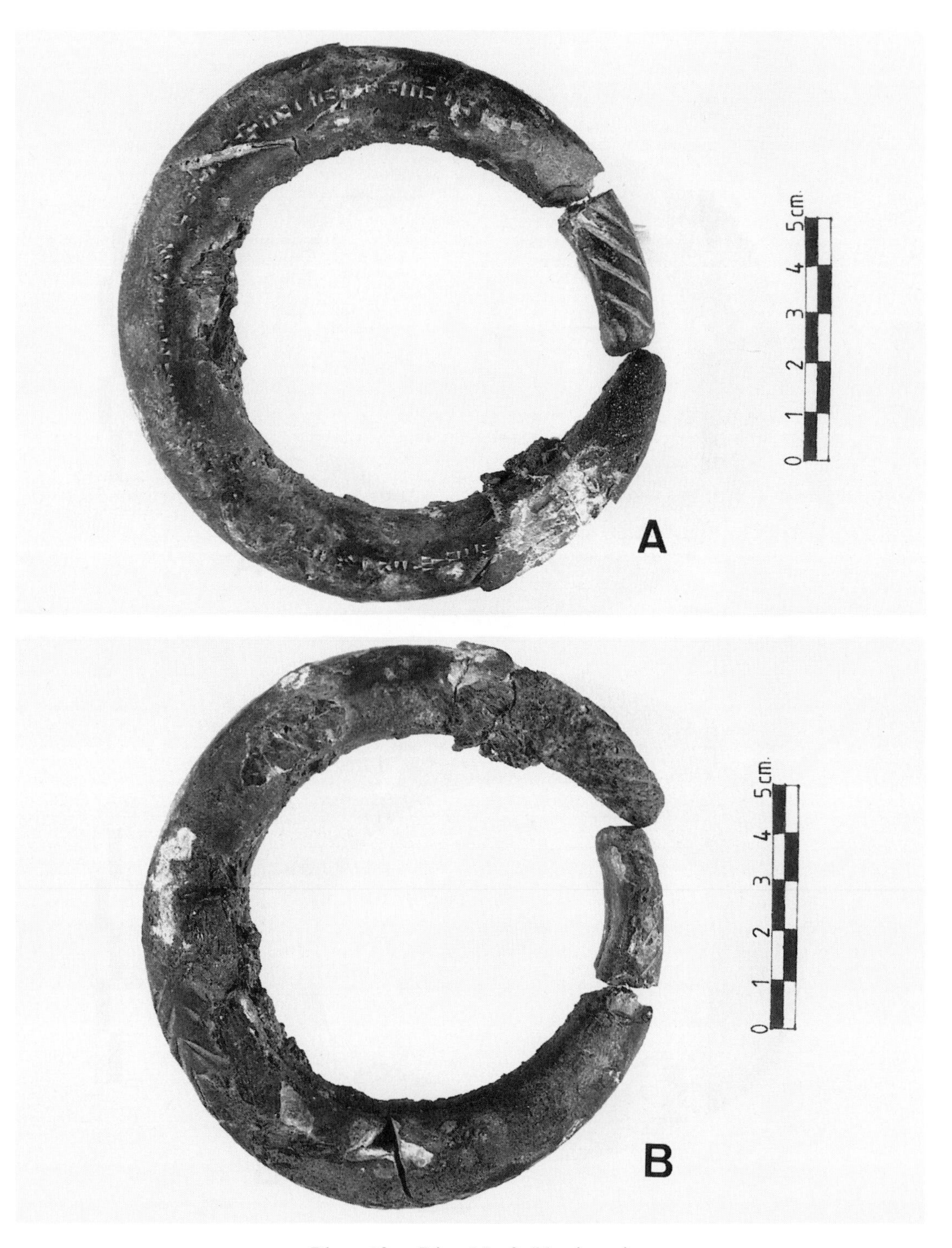

Plate 12a. Ring Nr. 2, Vorderseite.
b. Ring Nr. 2, Rückseite.

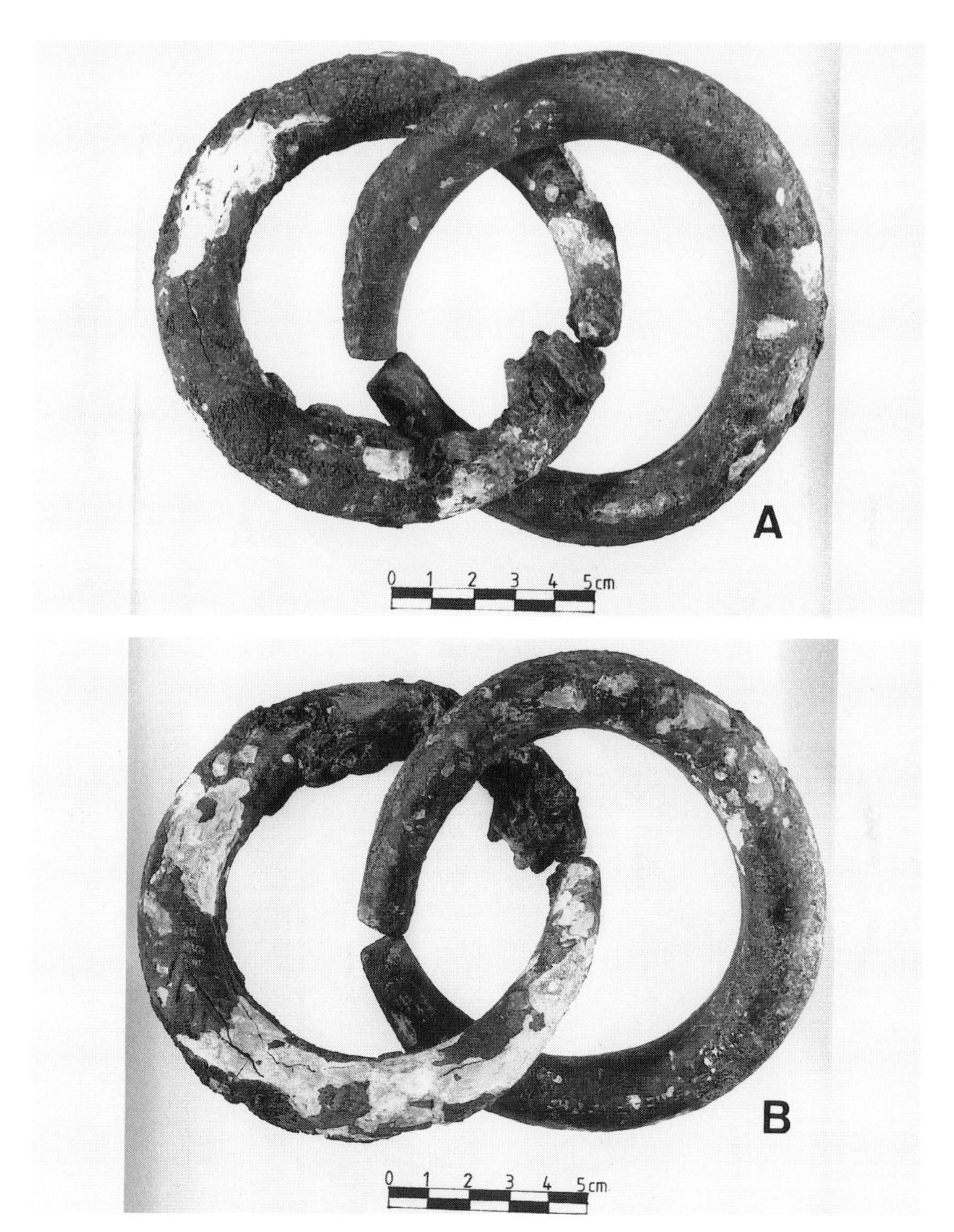

Plate 13a. Ring Nr. 3 und 4, Vorderseite.
b. Ring Nr. 3 und 4, Rückseite.

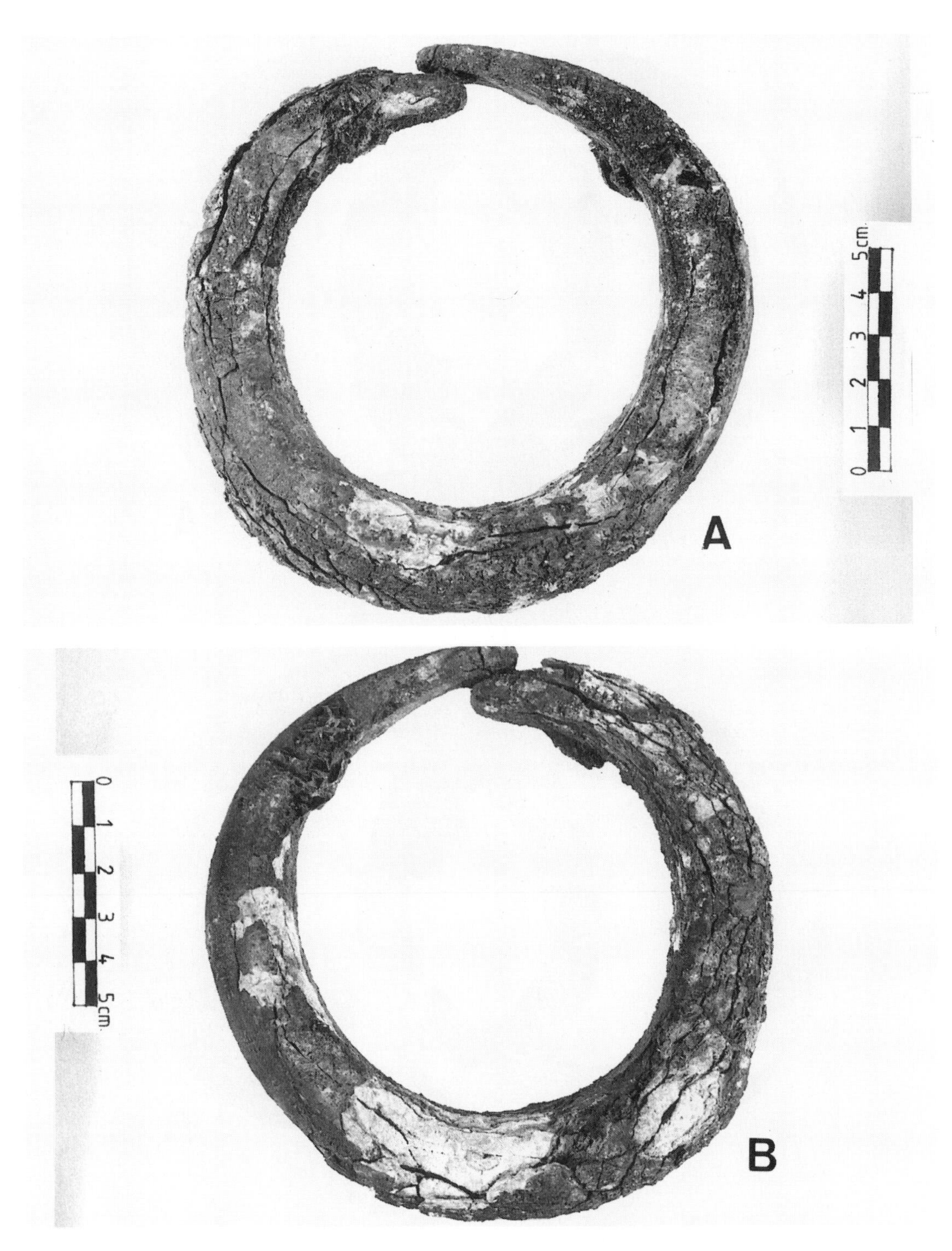

Plate 14a. Ring Nr. 5, Vorderseite.
b. Ring Nr. 5, Rückseite.

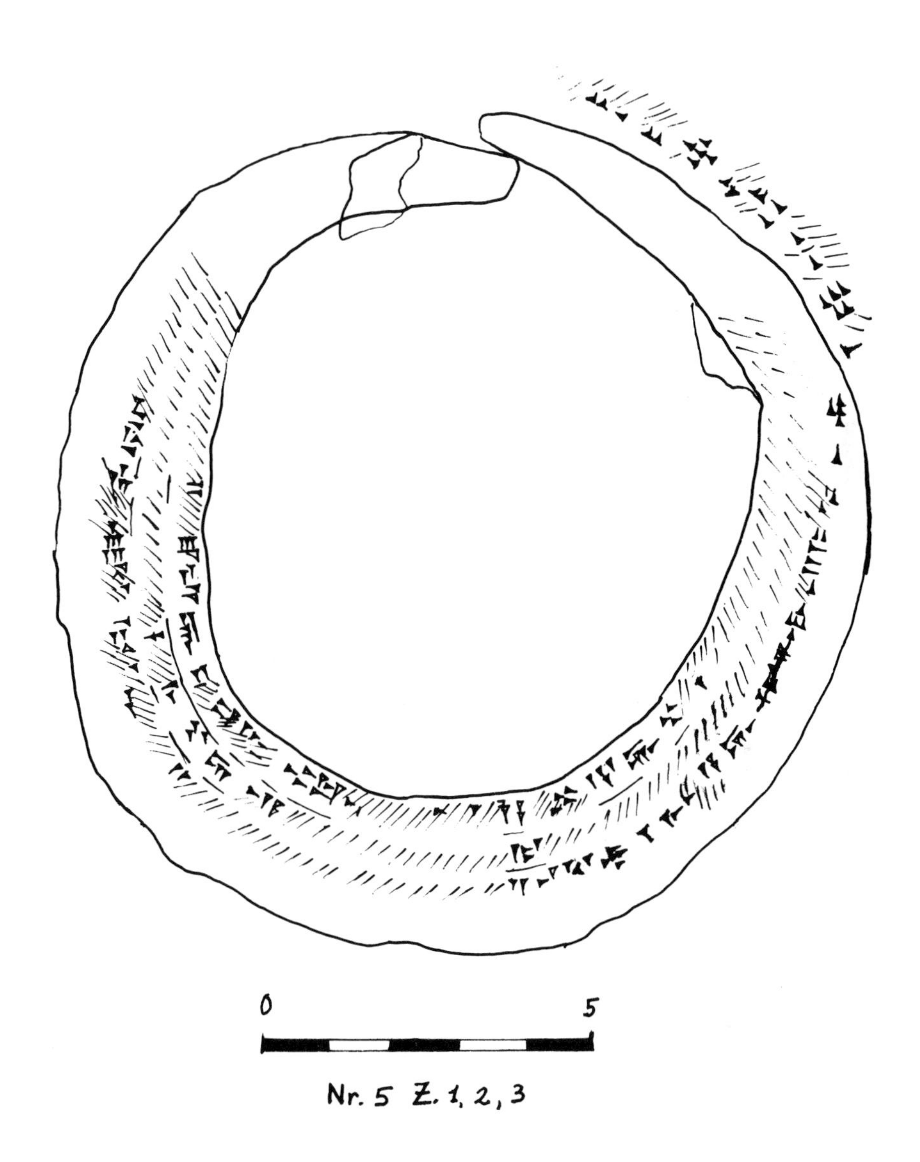

Plate 15. Ring Nr. 5, Zeilen 1, 2 und 3.

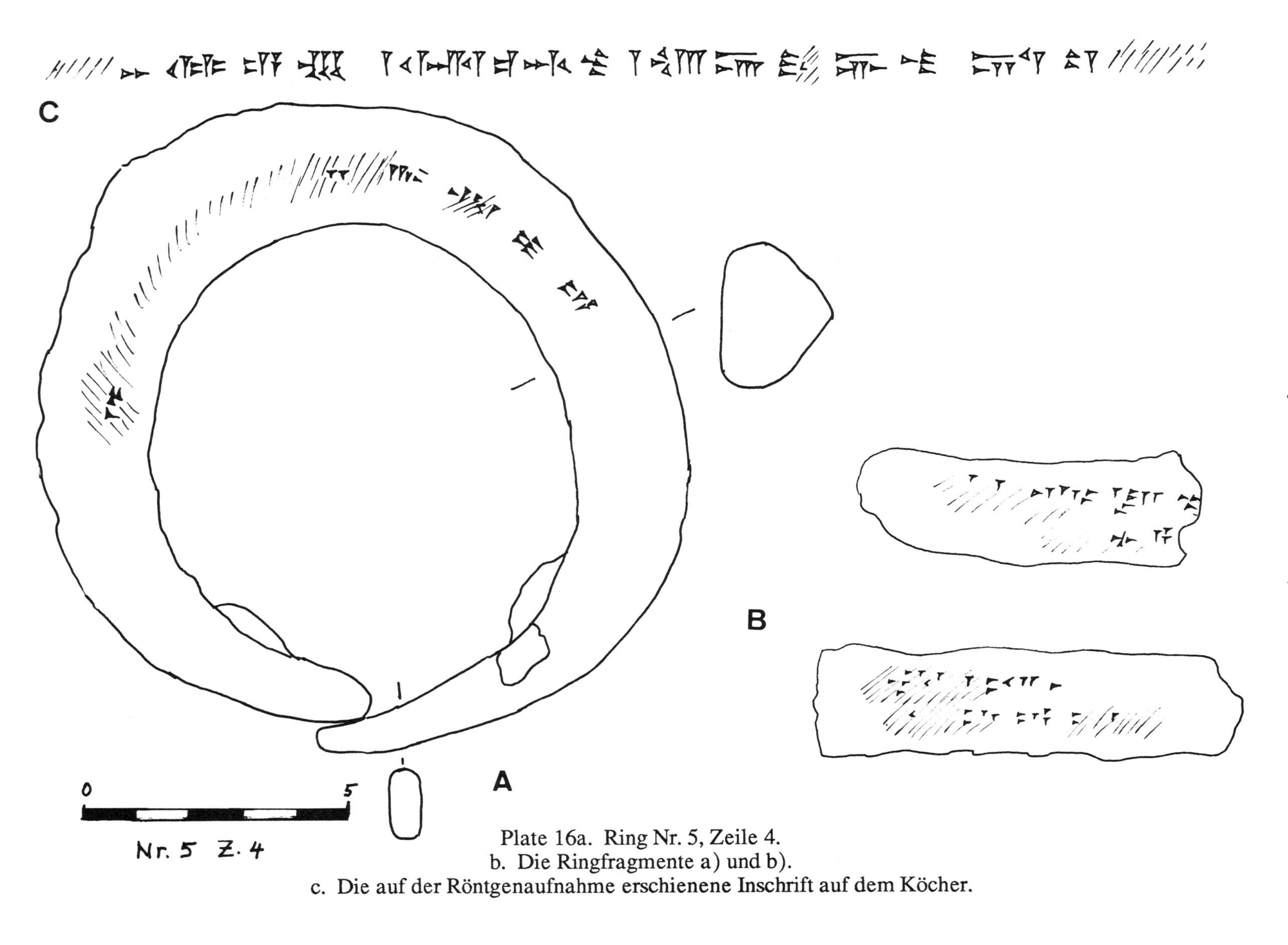

Plate 16a. Ring Nr. 5, Zeile 4.
b. Die Ringfragmente a) und b).
c. Die auf der Röntgenaufnahme erschienene Inschrift auf dem Köcher.

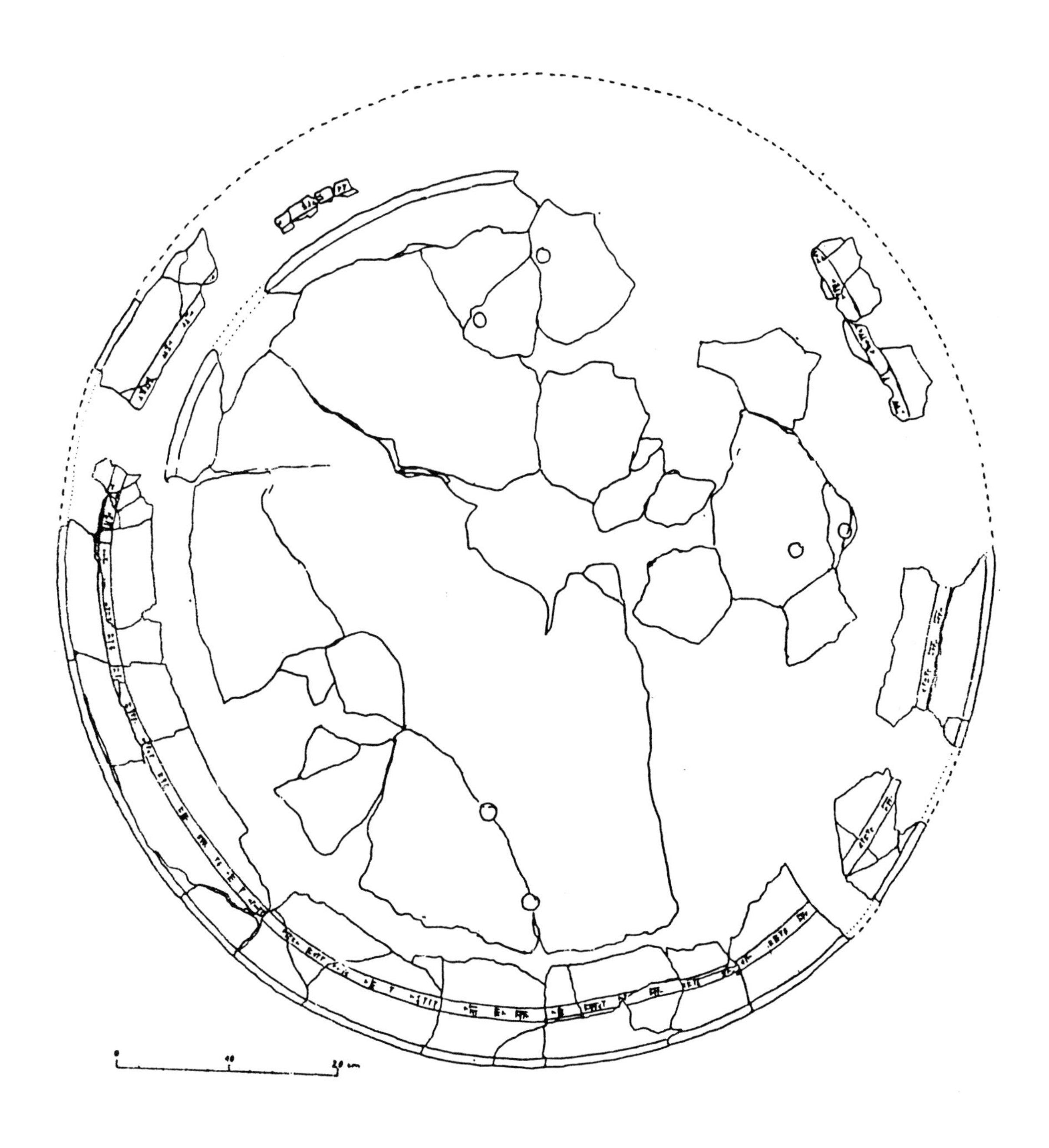

Plate 17. Die Rekonstruktion der Inschrift des Schildes.

REFLECTIONS ON THE MUSICAL INSTRUMENTS *arkammi*, *galgalturi*, AND *ḫuḫupal* IN HITTITE

HANS G. GÜTERBOCK

The Boston Museum of Fine Arts has on exhibit a unique Hittite vessel in the shape of a life-size human fist made of silver and decorated with a frieze depicting a cult scene.[1] In it a king pours a libation to the Stormgod who is shown with his bull. Behind the king there are three musicians, two playing the kithara, the third a pair of cymbals (see Pl. 18). The cymbals occur here for the first time in the art of the Hittite Empire. They are large disks whose size can be estimated by comparison with the man's arm as approximately 60 cm in diameter. They look rather shallow. One is shown slightly lower than the other, as if they had just been struck. A curved line hanging down from them may indicate a string connecting the two disks which served for carrying them over a shoulder when not played.

The kithara is now securely identified by the Inandık vase.[2] The cult scenes on that vase show two sizes of lyra-like instruments, one large, played by two standing men, and a small one carried on one arm. In the texts the most frequently mentioned instrument is the so-called Inanna-instrument: GIŠ dINANNA, Akkadian *zannaru* ; in Hittite the Hattic name *zinar* is used. It comes in two sizes, GAL "large"and TUR "small", identified by Laroche with Hattic *ḫunzinar* and *ippizinar*, respectively. The distinction of two sizes on the vase and in the texts cannot be accidental. This was recognized by everybody who saw the vase in the Ankara Museum before its publication, and is now accepted by practically everybody. [3]

I ask myself what instrument among those mentioned in the texts might have a chance of being the cymbals. The triad GIŠ*arkammi*, *galgalturi* ,GIŠ*ḫuḫupal* which frequently follows the Inanna-instrument came to mind. All three terms designate percussion instruments as is shown by the verb *walḫ*-"to beat" with its derivative forms *walḫannai*-, *walḫanniški*-. I agree with most

1 Hans G.Güterbock and Timothy Kendall, "A Hittite Silver Fist-Shaped Vessel" in J.B. Carter and S.P. Morris (eds.), *The Ages of Homer* (Austin, Texas 1995), 45-60.

2 T. Özgüç, *İnandıktepe* esp. fig. 64.

3 St. de Martino, "Il lessico musicale ittita II: GIŠ dINANNA = cetra", *OA* 26 (1987) 171-185.

scholars in thinking that this verb refers to the beating of percussion instruments, whereas *ḫazziki-*, the iterative form of *ḫatta* - "to hit", became the general term meaning "to play", said of string and percussion instruments.[4]

Of the three instruments mentioned together GIŠ*arkammi* is known to be a drum.[5] For GIŠ*ḫuḫupal* too I thought for many years that it could be some kind of drum. The determinative GIŠ implies that both *arkammi* and *ḫuḫupal* were at least partly made of wood. The only term of the three almost never written with GIŠ, *galgalturi*, thus offered itself as a candidate for the cymbals. The sound of the word *gl-gl- tr-* seemed to fit this idea. In making this proposal I intentionally set aside the growing literature on musical instruments. I am, of course, aware of the proposal that ḫuḫupal be the Hittite word for cymbals. [6]

In the following lines I shall discuss these two proposals. In dedicating them to my friend Philo Houwink ten Cate I must ask for indulgence for oversights and omissions caused by my visual handicap. I am deeply grateful to my wife Frances who read the literature in different languages and wrote as well as consolidated the text. My thanks also go to Richard Beal who consulted and excerpted the files of the Hittite Dictionary and prepared the transliteration of the text KUB XXV 37+. Both he and Harry Hoffner gave valuable help in interpreting this difficult text and looking up cuneiform copies. I also thank Steve Thurston for putting the manuscript on the computer.

The first of the three instruments frequently mentioned together is GIŠ*arkammi*, almost certainly a drum. Anna Maria Polvani devoted a special article to the discussion of this instrument.[7] In it she discusses the proposition made by several scholars that "*arkammi*" was the Hittite reading of the logogram GIŠBALAG.DI.[8] J. Friedrich[9] cites a communication by H. Otten based on an unpublished fragment. This is now KBo XXVI 64, part of the Ullikummi epic to which we shall return. O.R. Gurney, *Schweich* 34, cites Hans Martin Kümmel[10] who adduces examples for the combination GIŠBALAG.DI *galgalturi*, to which Polvani added more. In the frequent list of the three instruments *arkammi, galgalturi, ḫuḫupal*, the first word is never replaced by the logogram GIŠBALAG.DI.

4 St. de Martino, "Il lessico musicale ittita: usi e valori di alcuni verbi", *Hethitica* 9 (1988) 5-16.

5 O.R. Gurney, *Schweich* 34f.

6 A.M. Polvani, "Appunti per una storia della musica cultuale ittita: lo strumento HUHUPAL", *Hethitica* 9 (1988) 171-179.

7 A.M. Polvani, "Osservazioni sul termine ittita (giš)*arkammi*", *OA* 27 (1988) 211-219.

8 This is the Boğazköy spelling for simple BALAG, taken over from LÚBALAG.DI, the player of a BALAG. While BALAG originally designated the harp, it is now generally agreed that it later became the name of some kind of drum.

9 *HW* 3. Erg. (1966) 39.

10 H.M. Kümmel, "Gesang und Gesanglosigkeit in der hethitischen Kultmusik", *FsOtten* 174-176.

In the combination of ^{GIŠ}BALAG.DI with *galgalturi* alone, therefore, an instrument different from *arkammi* may be meant. In the passage from the Ullikummi epic,[11] Ištar takes a ^{GIŠ}BALAG.DI and a *galgalturi* in order to accompany her song at the seashore. Here the instruments must be rather small, the first probably a tambourine.[12] This translation was already suggested by Gurney and was applied by Franca Pecchioli Daddi and Anna Maria Polvani in their translation of Ulli-kummi.[13] In *O A* 27 (1988) 219, Polvani considers the possibility that ^{GIŠ}BALAG. DI and *arkammi* might be similar instruments without being identical. In KBo XXXIII 28, 4 we read [... *ar-g*]*a-mi-in* GIŠ-*aš* 3 *TA-PAL gal-g*[*al-tu-ri* ...] "an *argammi* of wood (and) 3 pairs of *galg*[*alturi*]". The reading of GAL in *StBoT* 15, 38 is contradicted by the hand copy which clearly has GIŠ-*aš*. If ^{GIŠ}BALAG.DI, at least in the hand of Ištar, is a tambourine, an "*arkammi* of wood" could be a drum with a wooden body. However, there was a large version of the ^{GIŠ}BALAG.DI, to judge from the phrase $^{\text{LÚ.MEŠ}}$BALAG.DI GAL *walḫanzi* "The men of the large BALAG.DI beat (scil. the large BALAG.DI)."[14] Nevertheless, the fact that ^{GIŠ}BALAG.DI and *arkammi* never occur side by side leaves open the possiblility that both terms refer to the same instrument so that the categorical rejection of the equation in HW^2 A 304 seems unwarranted. In any case ^{GIŠ}*arkammi* must be some kind of drum.

The second instrument, *galgalturi*, is the only one of the three whose name is almost never determined by GIŠ "wood". It occurs with the determinative "URUDU" (copper)[15] and is described as being made of bronze (ZABAR).[16] It also occasionally is said to occur in pairs or sets.[17] Of special interest is the passage KUB LIX 30 obv. 14: [X *TAPAL galgalt*]*ūri* AN.BAR ŠÀ.BA 2 *TAPAL* URUDU[...] "[x pairs of] *galgalturi*s of iron, including two pairs of copper". The lost first numeral must be more than twice the second, at least five. This strange mode of Hittite counting amounts to "five (or more) pairs of galgalturi, of which 3 (or more) pairs are of iron and two of copper".

It has been suggested that *ḪASKALLATUM* in 1-*NUTIM ḪASKALLATUM* ZABAR[18] might be the Akkadographic writing for *galgalturi*,[19] because *ḫuḫupal*

[11] KUB XXXVI 12 ii 1ff.+ KBo XXVI 64 ii 5 ff., in *JCS* 6 (1952) 14 f. still without the adjoining fragment.

[12] I follow other scholars in using this term for a hand-drum without jingles.

[13] *La mitologia ittita* (Brescia 1990), 157.

[14] KUB XX 78 iv 4, quoted by de Martino, *Hethitica* 9 (1988) 9.

[15] KUB X 89 i 27.

[16] KBo VII 46 iv 4; KUB LIX 17 obv. 18; and in the Myth of Ḫedammu KBo XXVI 70 i 12 (J. Siegelová, *StBoT* 14, 38f.).

[17] 1-*NUTUM galgalt*[*uri*] KBo XIX 131:4, HT 98:10. *TAPAL*: KBo XXV 190 rev. 1 (3 *TAPAL*), KUB LIX 30 obv. 14.

[18] KUB XXIX 4 i 24.

[19] J. Friedrich, *HW* 3. Erg. s.v. *galgalturi*, citing "Otten...brieflich" as his source.

and *arkammi* follow immediately. Even if this identification were correct it would not help for determining the meaning of *galgalturi*. The *CAD*, Ḫ 127 cites only this Boğazköy occurrence with its duplicate KUB XXIX 5 i 8. A similar word *ḫasḫallatu* (*ḫasḫaltu*) (ibid. 125) has a completely different meaning, "foliage, ... green leaves." Von Soden, *AHw* 330 lists both words under one lemma, with the translation "Blatt?".

The evidence adduced so far would be in favor of the proposed meaning "cymbals" for *galgalturi*. More difficult is the occurrence of GIŠ*galgalturi ŠA* GIR4, a *galgalturi* made of baked clay.[20] This *galgalturi* of an unusual material is the only example for the determination with GIŠ which I can only understand as the use of the common determinative of implements. A thin plate or platter of baked clay could produce a tone when struck, but it could hardly be used like cymbals. In the myth of Ḫedammu we read, "[Šaušga] began to speak [to Ninatta and] Kulitta, 'Take [a *galgaltu*]*ri* to the border of the sea[...] but with the left beat the *galgalturi*'".[21] E. Laroche used this passage for his identification of the reliefs Nos. 36-38 in Yazılıkaya.[22] In no. 36 Kulitta holds in her hand an object that looks like a disk with a straight handle which we used to take for a mirror. In no. 37 Ninatta clearly holds a horn; which we thought was a container for ointment. These two objects would be easily understood in the hands of Šaušga's handmaidens. Laroche thinks of "une sorte de tambourin" for the object in no. 36; this implies that the horn also would be the musical instrument *šawatar*.[23] "Tambourine" is not likely here, because of the shape with the straight handle and because there are other candidates for tambourine. One might think of some kind of castanets (see below for such instruments of the Early Bronze Age). I still prefer the old interpretation as mirror. At the beginning of column II of the Song of Ullikummi, we read: "Šaušga beat the BALAG.DI and the *galgalturi*", to accompany her song by the seashore.[24] Later, when she is told that the monster is blind and deaf she throws both instruments away. Since she alone has to handle two instruments each of them must be small. This ruled out the cymbals of the size depicted on the fist. In any case it is clear that a *galgalturi* is usually made of metal. There is nothing that shows it to be a membranophone.[25] E. Neu[26] cites V.V. Ivanov for the translation:

20 IBoT IV 145:3.

21 KUB XXXIII 88 rev.? 12-14 etc. with dupl. KBo XXII 51:1-4 (Siegelová , *StBoT* 14, 54f.).

22 *JCS* 6 (1952) 117.

23 A.M. Polvani, "A proposito del termine ittita *šawatar* 'corno'" *SEL* 6 (1989) 15-21.

24 KUB XXXVI 12 ii 1′ + KBo XXVI 64 ii 9′ -10′ (*JCS* 6 (1952) 14f. without the join).

25 Thus H. Roszkowska, "Musical Terminology in Hittite Cuneiform Texts", *Orientalia Varsoviensia* 1 (1987) 23-30, esp. 24.

26 *StBoT* 26, 89.

"Zymbeln" for *galgalturi*.[27] Especially suggestive is the passage from the *ḫišuwa* festival edited by Polvani[28] where we read in lines 7'-8' *nu za-aḫ-ḫi-i̯a-aš* SÌR-*RU* GIŠBALAG.DI-*i̯a gal-gal-tu-u-ri u̯[a-a]l-ḫa-an-ni-i̯a-an-zi* "They sing (a song) of battle and beat the BALAG.DI and the *galgalturi*", where "drum" and "cymbals" would go well with a battle song. For the playing of *galgalturi* both verbs, *u̯alḫ-* (e.g. Ḫedammu KUB XXXIII 88 rev. 14, *StBoT* 14, 54f. line 14) and *ḫazziki-* (e.g. KBo IV 9 i 40-41) are used.

The above observations make it highly probable that *galgalturi* is the name of the cymbals. We now have to turn to the term GIŠ*ḫuḫupal* which has been claimed for cymbals by other scholars.[29] This identification is based on the fact that the *ḫuḫupal* is occasionally filled with beer or wine which is then drunk by the participants in the ceremony. This was compared with the observation that in the Phrygian cult of Cybele wine was drunk from cymbals.[30] While this analogy is suggestive, it does not, of course, prove that the Hittite *ḫuḫupal* must be the same as the kymbalon of the Phrygians.

When I saw the picture of the cymbal player on the Fist my first reaction was that these huge shallow disks were not suited for drinking. For the Hittite Empire period this representation is so far the only example of cymbals. A pair of cymbals belonging to the Phrygian period was found in Boğazköy.[31] Bittel devoted a special article to these cymbals.[32] They are shaped like bowls 1.17 cm deep with a wide, slightly upward slanted rim and a hole in the center. The diameter is 10.2 cm. The hole must have served for the insertion of a leather thong secured by a knot on the inside. If that knot was pulled tight the bowl could hold a liquid. According to Bittel these cymbals, now in the Ankara Museum, still produced a lasting sound when struck together. Bittel dates the find to the 7th century B.C. on the basis of the pottery found with it. He also adduces comparable examples of the Archaic Greek period. This find of actual Phrygian cymbals is a welcome illustration of the Cult of Cybele, but it does not tell us much about other regions and periods.

From the Middle Bronze Age come two pairs of similar objects found at Kültepe and datable to the period Karum Ib (18th century B.C.).[33] They are bowls with wide, flat rims and have a round hole in the middle. One pair (12.8

27 V.V. Ivanov, *Etimologija* 1978 (1980), 176f.; 1979 (1981) 132.

28 KBo XV 52 + KUB XXXIV 116 v 3'-8', A.M. Polvani *OA* 27:218.

29 A.M. Polvani in *Hethitica* 9 (1988) 171-179; Jaan Puhvel, *HED* s.v.

30 H. Thiemer, *Der Einfluss der Phryger auf die altgriechische Musik* (Bonn-Bad Godesberg 1979 - Band 29 der Orpheus-Schriftenreihe) 39, quoting Julius Firmicus Maternus: *De Errore Profanarum Religionum* 18, written A.D. 335-337, cf. *Der Kleine Pauly* vol. 2 p. 554 s.v. Firmicus Maternus for editions and translations of the text.

31 P. Neve, in Kurt Bittel et al, *Boğazköy* IV, 34 with plate 21 a and b.

32 K. Bittel, "Cymbeln für Kybele", in *FsWasmuth* 79-82.

33 T. Özgüç, *Kültepe-Kaniş* II 74 pl. 128 1-2, 3-4.

and 13 cm in diameter) was found in the house of Peruwa. The other pair was found in a grave (6.4 and 6.2 cm respectively). In shape and size these objects are very close to the Phrygian cymbals just mentioned. Like them they could have held a liquid if the hole was securely closed. Since these cymbals of the Colony Age are so similar to those of the Phrygian period we have to assume that this shape existed also through the Hittite period. However, compared to the cymbals depicted on the Fist they would be 1/4 smaller in diameter. Assuming for the moment that the cymbals were called *galgalturi*, the "large" variety, *galgalturi* GAL, might refer to the size depicted on the Fist.[34] Less relevant for our problem are the pairs of instruments found in tombs of the late phase of the Early Bronze Age, which have been adduced by some scholars as cymbals or castanets.[35] They come from Horoztepe[36] and Höyük near Alaca.[37] They were all found in pairs at Pompeiopolis as well.[38] They consist of small metal disks to which a vertical handle was soldered in the center. The average diameter of the disks is 7-8 cm. The length of the handle differs. The player needed both hands to strike the disks together. It is clear that these instruments could not hold a liquid.

Concerning representations in art, Polvani[39] correctly states that "in iconography it is difficult to decide whether cymbals or tambourines are depicted". Most prominent among pictorial representations of such instruments is the relief vase found at İnandıktepe.[40] Several figures in its four friezes carry disk-shaped instruments whose color, off-white or cream, point to membranes rather than metal plates. Speaking of fragments of such vases from Bitik[41] and Alishar, Bittel already called these instruments "tambourines".[42] However, Rainer Michael Boehmer defines similar representations as cymbals,[43] as does T. Özgüç for those on the Inandık vase. The large disks shown in the Banquet Scene from

34 KUB XXV 49 iii 25, KUB LI 19 obv 8.

35 K. Bittel, *FsWasmuth* 80f., T. Özgüç, *İnandıktepe* 96.

36 T. Özgüç and M. Akok, "Horoztepe Eserleri", *Belleten* XXI/82 (1957) 201-219, esp. 205 with figs. 12 and 36; T. Özgüç and M. Akok, *Horoztepe* 45.

37 R. Oğuz Arık, *Les Fouilles d'Alaca Höyük ...* 1935, *TTKY* V/1a (Ankara 1937) 81 and pl. 276; H. Zübeyr Koşay, *Ausgrabungen von Alaca Höyük ...* 1936, *TTKY* V/2a (Ankara 1944); idem, *Les Fouilles d'Alaca Höyük ...* 1937-39, *TTKY* V/5 (Ankara 1951) p. 160 and pl. 126.

38 K. Bittel, "Der Depotfund von Soloi-Pompeiopolis", *ZA* 46 (1942) 183-205 esp. 198 and pl. VI.

39 *Hethitica* 9 (1988) 176.

40 T.Özgüç, *İnandıktepe*, esp. fig. 64 and color plates.

41 T. Özgüç, "The Bitik Vase", *Anatolia* 2 (1957) 57-78, esp. pl. IVb.

42 *FsWasmuth* 81.

43 Die Reliefkeramik von Boğazköy, *BoHa* 13, 28, fig. 16 (Alishar) and no. 25 on pls. IX - X.

the South Gate at Karatepe[44] and on a relief from Zincirli[45] have been defined by Orthmann p. 393 as frame drums (Rahmentrommeln). This is evidenced by the narrow rim and the position of the hand of the player, which is beating, not holding, the object.

To summarize, we found no pictorial representation of cymbals apart from the Fist. Among actual finds the existence of small, bowl-shaped cymbals at Kültepe and at Phrygian Boğazköy led us to the conclusion that this shape existed throughout the Hittite period.

We now turn to the textual evidence for *ḫuḫupal*. As mentioned before the only determinative used with *ḫuḫupal* is GIŠ. Although this could be taken as the general determinative of implements, it would still be surprising if it designated objects made entirely of metal. In one text a *ḫuḫupal* is said to be made either of boxwood or of ivory:[46]

(24) 1-*NU-TIM ḪA-AS-KAL-LA-TUM* ZABAR 1-*NU-TIM* GIŠ*ḫu-u-ḫu-pa-al* (25) *ma-a-an ŠA* GIŠTÚG *ma-a-an ŠA* ZU$_9$ AM.SI 1-EN GIŠ*ar-kam-mi-iš*

"One set (or pair) of *ḪASKALLATUM* of bronze, one set (or pair) of *ḫuḫupal*s, either of boxwood or of ivory, and one *arkammi*".

As mentioned earlier, *ḪASKALLATUM* may or may not be the Akkadogram for *galgalturi*. As for *ḫuḫupal*, the fact that it is counted by sets (*ištenutu*) might be taken in favor of the meaning "cymbals", but the materials, boxwood and ivory, do not fit this interpretation. Polvani[47] tries to avoid the difficulty by assuming that these are miniature models which could be made of any material. However, the entire passage is an enumeration of materials and real objects, not models. 2 *TAPAL ḫuḫupal* occurs in the cult inventory KBo XIII 235 i 2, but this seems to be the only other example. What may be meant by such "sets"or "pairs" will be discussed in connection with the "Lallupiya Ritual".

We now turn to the text which gave rise to the whole discussion. This is KUB XXV 37 with adjoining fragments.[48] This is a ritual performed by the "men of Lallupiya" for the king and queen. It contains songs sung in Luwian. A full edition of this text cannot be undertaken here. We shall limit our investigation to those sections which deal with the ḫuḫupal. KUB XXV 37 i:

1' [o o o o o o o o -*i*]*š*? *ku-iš* LÚx[o o o o o o o o?]
2' ⌈ x x x x⌉ *me-na-aḫ-ḫa-an-da e-ep-zi ša-ra-*⌈*a*⌉ x[

44 K. Bittel, *Hethiter* 271, fig. 309 and in E. Akurgal, *Die Kunst der Hethiter* (Munich 1961), pl. 142.

45 W. Orthmann, *Untersuchungen*, pl. 63. F/8a, 7.

46 KUB XXIX 4 i 24-25, ed. H. Kronasser, *Schw.Gotth.* 8f.

47 *Hethitica* 9 (1988) 173 with footnote 17.

48 CTH 771: KUB XXV 37 +KUB XXXV 131 + 132 + KUB LI 9 transliterated by F. Starke, *StBoT* 30, 342-352.

3' *IŠ*-⸢*TU*⸣ 2 ŠU.ḪI.A-*ŠU* *e-ep - zi*

It seems from these fragmentary lines that somebody holds something out to somebody. And that someone "holds up"something "with both hands". Whether the object of these actions is the *ḫuḫupal* first mentioned below in line 10' cannot be decided.

4' *nu ŠA* LÚ.MEŠ ⸢^{URU}*La*⸣-*al-lu-pí-i̯a* LÚ.GAL-*ŠU-NU A-NA* ^{LÚ}SAGI.A *ki*-⸢*iš-ša-an*⸣
5' *ḫal-za-a-i u̯a-a[-ri-i̯]a-ti ḫa-pa-nu-ša* ^{LÚ}SAGI.A-*ma tar-u̯i*$_5$-*iš-ki-u-an*
6' [*d*]*a-a-i* ^{LÚ}MUḪALDIM [*m*]*a-aḫ-ḫa-an tar-u̯i*$_5$-*iš-ki-it nu a-pa-a-aš-ša QA-TAM-MA*
7' [*tar*]-⸢*u̯i*$_5$-*iš*⸣-*ki-u-an da-a-i pé-di-i̯a-aš-ša-an u̯a-aḫ-nu-uš-ki-iz-zi*
8' ⸢*ta-ma-iš*⸣-*ma-an* LÚ ^{URU}⸢*La*⸣-*al-lu-pí-i̯a iš-ki-ša* EGIR-*an* ^{TÚG}*ši-ik-nu-un*
9' *ḫar-zi nu-uš*-⸢*ša*⸣-*an ták-ša-an pé-di u̯a-aḫ-nu-uš-kán-zi* ^{LÚ}SAGI.A-*ma*
10' $^{[GI]Š}$⸢*ḫu*⸣-*ḫu-pa-al ḫar-zi-pát Ú-UL-at* GUL-*aḫ-ḫi-iš-ki-iz-zi*

(4'-10') The leader of the men of Lallupiya calls out to the cupbearer as follows: "*wāriyati ḫapanuša*".
The cupbearer begins to dance. Just as the cook danced, he too begins to dance in the same way. And he turns on the spot. Another man from Lallupiya holds him from the back by his cloak. And they turn on the spot together. The cupbearer only holds the *ḫuḫupal*; he does not beat it.

11' ⸢LÚ.MEŠ ^{URU}⸣*La-al*-⸢*lu-pí*⸣-*i̯a-ma* LÚ.GAL-*ŠU-NU ku-e* ^{GIŠ}*ḫu*-[*ḫ*]*u-pa-al ḫar-kán-zi*
12' *na-at* GUL-*aḫ-ḫi*-[*i*]*š-kán-zi* ^{LÚ}SAGI.A-*ma-aš*-⸢*ma-aš*⸣-*kán*
13' *ki-i* SÌR *pé-ra-an* *da-a*[*š-ki-iz*]-*zi*

14' ⸢x⸣ [o o] x x x x x [o o o *ma-aš-ša-ni-i̯*]*a-aš-ši-in u̯a-al-za-me-en*
15' [ ]x-*zi*
16' [ ]x-*iz-zi*

(11'-13') The *ḫuḫupal*s which the men of Lallupiya (and) their leader hold, they beat. The cupbearer be[gin]s[?] the following song in front of them.

(14'-16') [... *maššaniy*]*aššin walzamen* [...] he [...]-s [...] he [...]-s.

17' [LÚ.MEŠ $^{UR]U}$*La*-[*al-lu-p*]*í-i̯a*
18' [ ]x [o]-⸢*e*⸣-*da-ni še-er*
19' [-*z*]*i*

Lines 15'-19' do not yield any intelligible text. One may ask whether [o]-*edani šer* [...] in line 18' is to be restored according to lines 29'-30'. If so it would mean that the action of putting one *ḫuḫupal* on top of the other was introduced in line 18'.

20' [*nu?* LÚ.ME]Š URU*L*[*a-al-lu-pí-i̯a* o o o o o o o o?]x *kar-pa-an-zi*

21' .... GIŠ*ḫu-ḫ*[*u-pa-al* o o o o o o o o o?]x *ku-it*

22' [*mar?*]-*nu-an kat-t*[*a la-a-ḫu*]-⸢*u*⸣-*an*

23' [*n*]*a-at-kán Ú-U*[*L* *na-at a-pád-da*] *pa-aḫ-ḫa-aš-ša-nu-ma-an-zi*

24' [*a*]*n??-ku ḫa-an-da* [*i*]-⸢*i̯a*⸣-[*an*]

(20'-24') The men of Lallupiya lift [o o o]. [when they fill(?)] a *ḫuḫupal*, what [*mar*]*nuwan* [is pour]ed down that is not [to be lost(?)]. [It is there]fore certainly(?) [m]a[de] to be preserved.

25' *na*!-*aš-ta ma-a-an ša-ra-a-az-zi-i̯a-az* [GIŠ*ḫu-ḫu-pa-l*]*a-az ar-ḫa-i̯a*

26' *la-ḫu-u-u̯a-a-ri na-at-kán kat-ta a-pé-e*[*z kat-*]*te-er-ri*

27' GIŠ*ḫu-ḫu-pa-li la-ḫu-u-u̯a-a-ri na-at-kán* DINGIR-*L*[*UM*] *a-pé-ez ar-ḫa*

28' *e-ku-zi da-ga-a-an-ma-at-kán Ú-UL la-ḫu-u-u̯*[*a-a-r*]*i na-at a-pád-da ḫa-an-da*

29' *pa-aḫ-ḫa-aš-ša-nu-ma-an-zi i-i̯a-an nu* GIŠ*ḫu-ḫu-pa-al* 1-*a*[*n* 1-*e-d*]*a-ni*

30' *še-er* *a-pa-a-*⸢*at*⸣-*ta* *ḫu-i-nu-an-z*[*i*]

(25'-30') Then if (it) flows out of the upper [*ḫuḫ*]*upal*, then it flows from that down into the lower *ḫuḫupal*. And the god drinks it from that one. But it does not flow to the ground. For that reason it is made to be preserved. It is for that reason they arrange(??) one *ḫuḫupal* above the other.

31' *ma-an-ma-kán da-ga-a-an-ma ku-iš-ki ar-ḫa la-ḫu-u-u̯a-a-i* [o o o]x

32' *na-at-kán a-pí-i̯a-pát* [*u̯a*]-*ar-ši-ni-i̯a-az* ZABAR *ḫa-ap*[-*pu?-ša?-an-z*]*i*

33' *nam-ma-ma* NU.GÁL *ku-it-ki*

(31'-33') But if someone pours (it) out on the ground, they re[trieve?] it right there with a bronze *waršini*-. There is nothing more.

(KUB XXV 37 i + KUB LI 9 obv.)

34' [*m*]*a-aḫ-ḫa-an-ma-kán* GIŠ*ḫu-ḫu-pa-al IŠ-TU* GEŠTIN *šu-un-na-an-z*[*i*]

35'+1 *na-at-kán ḫa-an-te-ez-zi pal-ši* LÚSAGI.A-*pát u̯a-ar-šu*!-*li ar-ḫa*

36'+2 *e-ku-zi* ⸢LÚ⸣.MEŠ URU*La-al-lu-pí-i̯a-ma ki-iš-ša-an* ⸢*iš*⸣*-ḫa-mi-iš-ki-u-an*

37'+3 ⸢*ti-an*⸣*-z[i ú]-i-in-tar ú-i-in-tar tar-u-u̯a-a-li-i̯[a-a]n ú-i-in-tar*

38'+4 ⸢*nu ku-it-ma-an ak*⸣*-ku-uš-kán-zi ku-it-ma-an a-[ku-an-]na ḫu-u-ma-an-te-eš*

39'+5 ⸢*ir-ḫa-a-an-zi iš-ḫa-mi-iš-kán-ma a-pa-a-a[t*]SÌR

40'+6 *[n]a-at iš-ḫa-mi-i̯a-u-an-zi* EGIR-⸢*pa*⸣ *u̯[a-aḫ?-nu?-u]š-kán-zi*

(34'-40') When they fill the *ḫuḫupal* with wine. The first time only the cupbearer drinks it up, sniffing (? lit. in the smell). The men of Lallupiya sing as follows: *"wintar, wintar taruwaliyan wintar"* while they drink and while they finish drinking that song is sung. They reply(??) singing.

KUB XXV 37 i 41'ff. + KUB XXXV 131 i 1'ff.+ KUB LI 9 obv. 8ff.

41'+1+8 ⸢*na-aš-ta*⸣ GIŠ*ḫu-ḫu-pa-al ḫ[a-a]n-[ti]* LÚSAGI.A*-pát ku-it*

42'+2+9 ⸢*u̯a*⸣*-ar-*⸢*šu*⸣*-ú-*⸢*li*⸣ *e-k[u-z]i ma-an[-ká]n ku-it-ki* GIŠ*ḫu-ḫu-pa-li*

43'+3+10 *kat-ta a-aš-zi [na-a]t-za-kán* x *i*?[ ]x x [ ] ⸢*na*⸣*-an-kán ar-ḫa*

44'+4+11 *e-ku-zi* GEŠTIN ⸢x x⸣ *pa-an-ku-un-pát ak-ku[-uš-kán-zi ar-ḫa-ma-an-ká]n [Ú-UL]*

45'+5 *la-a-ḫu-u-an-zi Ú-UL a-*⸢*a-ra*⸣ [

(41'-45') If something remains in the *ḫuḫupal* which only the cupbearer separately drinks sniffing(?), [he tak]es it (the ḫuḫupal) [up] and drinks it up (the wine). they drink all the wine. [They do not] pour [it] out; it is not right.

46'+ 6' *[n]a-aš-ta ma-aḫ-ḫa-an* GIŠ*ḫu-ḫu-pa-al* LÚSAG[I.A o o o]

7' *[n]a-at šu-un-na-i-pát ša-an-ḫa-zi-ma-at-k[án? Ú-UL]*

8' *[Š]A* LÚ.MEŠ URU*La-al-lu-pí-i̯a ku-iš* LÚ.GAL-*ŠU[-NU]*

9' *[nu]* ⸢*a*⸣*-pé-e-da-ni pa-a-i nu-uš-ši* GIM*-an* L[Ú...]

10' [o o o?]x *šu-u-u̯[a-a]n(?)-[n]a(?) me-na-aḫ-ḫa-an-da e-e[p-zi]*

11' *[nu-uš-ši me-n]a-aḫ[-ḫa-an-da Q]A-TAM-MA* MUNUS*-ni-li i[š-ḫa-ma-a-i]*

(46'+ 6'-11') When the cupbearer [...-s] the *ḫuḫupal*, he just fills it, but [does not] wipe it out. [...] He gives it to him who is the leader of the men of Lallupiya. When a man of Lallupiya holds out to him [...] and a full one, he s[ings] opposite [him] like a woman in the same way.

KUB XXV 37 + KUB XXXV 132 ii

1’ *iš-ḫa-m[i-i̯a-an-zi* o o o *ú-i-in-tar]*
2’ *ú-i-in-tar [tar-ú-u̯a-a-li-i̯a-an ú-i-in-tar]*

(ii 1’-2’) [The men of Lallupiya] sing [as follows: “ ... *wintar*] *wintar* [*taruwalian wintar*”].

3’ *ma-aḫ-ḫa-an-ma*[
4’ *a-ku-an-na* x[
5’ *ku-i-e-eš-qa* x[
6’ ^{GIŠ}*ḫu-ḫu-pa-li* x - x[
7’ *ša-ra-a Ú-UL ap*[*-pa-an-zi*
8’ *iš-ḫu-na-u-i-i̯a* ZAG-*a*[*n*
9’ *Ú-UL ku-u̯a-aš-š*[*a-an-zi*]

(3’-9’) But when [...] to drink [...] some people [...] in the *ḫuḫupal*(s) do not hold up [...] and on the upper arm [...] the right [...] [They] do not kiss [...]

10’ *ma-aḫ-ḫa-an-ma a-ku-an-na* ⸢*ḫu-u*⸣*-ma-a*[*n*?
11’ *nu* ^{LÚ}SAGI.A *nam-ma QA-TAM-MA* ^{GIŠ}*ḫu*[*-ḫu-pa-al*]
12’ *u̯a-ar-šu-li e-ku-zi ma-aḫ-ḫa-an-ma* x[
13’ *nu* ^{LÚ}SAGI.A ^{GIŠ}*ḫu-ḫu-pa-al ša-ra-a* x[o o o]
14’ *na-at ḫa*$^{!?}$*-<az>-zi-ki-u̯a-an* *da-a-i*

(10’-14’) When they all [finish?] drinking the cupbearer drinks the *ḫuḫupal* sniffing(?) in the same way. When [...], the cupbearer [takes] the *ḫuḫupal* up and begins to play it.

15’ *nam-ma tar-u̯i*$_{5}$*-iš-ki*$^{!}$*-u-an da-a-i pé-e-di-iš-š*[*a-a*]*n ma-*⸢*aḫ-ḫa*⸣*-an*
16’ *u̯a-aḫ-nu-uš-ki-iz-zi* EGIR*-an-da-ma-an ta-ma-iš*
17’ LÚ ^{URU}*La-al-lu-pí-i̯a iš-ki-ša* ^{TÚG}*ši-ik-nu-un ḫar-zi*
18’ *nu ták-ša-an tar-u̯i*$_{5}$*-iš-kán-zi pé-di-i̯a-aš-ša-an u̯a-aḫ-nu-uš-kán-zi*

(15’-18’) Then he begins to dance. As he turns in place, behind him another man of Lallupiya holds him by the cloak on his back. They dance together and turn in place.

19’ *iš-ḫa-mi-iš-kán-zi-ma* [*ki-i*] ⸢SÌR⸣ *tar-u-u̯a-li-ya* [o]
20’ *tar-pa-at-ta-ti a-aš-ta* [o]x *an-da ma-aš-ša-ni-i̯a pa-i-*⸢*ú*⸣
21’ [*k*]*at-ta-an-ma pa-an-ku-uš* [*ḫal-*]*zi-iš-ša-a-i*

(19'-21') They sing [this] song: "*taruwaliya tarpattati āšta* [...] *anda maššaniya paiu*". The crowd calls out with (them).

22' [*m*]*a-aḫ-ḫa-an-ma* 3-*ŠU ú-e-*[*ḫ*]*a-an-zi nu* ^{LU}SAGI.A *kat-ta*
23' *pár-ša-na-a-iz-zi iš-ki-ša-ma-an ku-iš* EGIR-*an ḫar-zi*
24' *na-an-kán* ^{TÚG}*ši-ik-nu-az-pát an-da* SAG.DU-*ŠÚ ka-ri-i̯a-zi*
25' ^{LÚ}SAG[I].⸢A⸣-[*ma*]-*kán* ^{GIŠ}*ḫu-ḫu-pa-al A-NA* GÌR.MEŠ-*ŠU*
26' [o o o o -*z*]*i*

27' [LÚ.MEŠ ^{URU}*L*]*a-al-lu-pí-i̯a-ma ki-i* SÌR *iš-ḫa-mi-iš-kán-zi*

(22'-26') When they have turned three times, the cupbearer squats down. The one who holds him from the back, covers his head with the cloak. The cupbearer [...]-s the *ḫuḫupal* to/at his feet.

(27'-35')The men of Lallupiya sing this song:

There follows a long, but fragmentary Luwian song partly preserved on the adjoining fragment KUB XXXV 132 obv.

On the reverse of KUB XXXV 132 which belongs to the upper part of col. iii we read, among other things, the following: (3'-5') [LÚ.MEŠ ^{URU}*La-al-lu*]-*pí-i̯a-i̯a A-NA* ^{LÚ}SAGI.A [...] *ḫal-zi-iš-ša-an-zi* [*nu* ^{LÚ}SAGI.A] *ša-ra-a ti-i̯a-zi*: "[The men of Lallu]piya call [...] to the cupbearer. [The cupbearer] gets up". After four further lines there is a gap of 7-8 lines before col. iii of KUB XXV 37 sets in with five fragmentary lines:

6' [-*z*]*i nu A-NA* LÚ.MEŠ ^{URU}*La-lu-pí-i̯a*
7' [*ú-i-ni-i̯a-an-da-a*]*n*$^{!?}$ *a-ku-an-na IŠ-TU* GAL *pí-an-zi*
8' [o o o o o o o] *ki-iš-ša-an ma-al-ti*

(6'-8') [...] then they give [wine?] to the men of Lallupiya to drink from a cup. [...] recites as follows.

9' [*ḫu-u-ma-an-da-an-u̯a*] *ku-i-e-eš ša-aš-nu-uš-kán-*[*z*]*i*
10' [*a-ra-nu*(??)-*an-z*]*i-i̯a-u̯a-ra-an ku-i-e-eš ša-ra-a-u̯a-*⸢*ra*⸣-*an*
11' [*ku-i-e-eš* SIG$_5$-]*in da-a-er*$^{!}$ *kat-ta-u̯a-ra-an-kán*
12' [*ku-i-e-eš* SIG$_5$-*i*]*n da-a-er*$^{!}$ *nu-u̯a a-pé-e-pát*
13' [*ak-ku-uš-kán-du*] NINDA.GUR$_4$.RA-*ma* NU.GÁL SÌR-*i̯a*
14' [NU.GÁ]L *nam-ma ḫu-u-ma-an-ti-i̯a*
15' [*a-ku-an-na pí-an-z*]*i nu ḫu-u-ma-an-za e-ku-zi*

(9'-15') Those who put [each person] to bed, those who [arouse?] him, [those who] took (or: put?) him up well, [those who] took (or: put?) him down well, those also [should drink]. There is no (offering of) thick bread. There is no singing [...] Then to everyone they give to drink and everyone drinks.

16' [*nu* GAL.ḪI.A(?) *a-ku-*]*an-na ḫa-an-da ir*$^{!}$*-ḫa-it-ta-ri*
17' ⸢*nu I-NA*(?) x⸣ [o *ú-*]*i-ni-i̯a-an-da-an a-ku-an-zi*
18' *nu-kán* ^{SI}*š*[*a-u̯a-tar*]*-ša a-ku-an-zi ḫal-zi-iš-ša-an-zi-ma*
19' *ki-iš-ša-an* ⸢*ú*⸣-[*i*]*-ni-i̯a-an-da-an ú-i-ni-i̯a-an-da-an e-ku-zi*
20' *nu ma-aḫ-ḫa-an ša-*⸢*u̯a*⸣-[*tar*] *ša-ra-a da-an-zi*
21' *na-at-kán ú-e-te-na-*⸢*az*⸣ *ar-ḫa ša-an-ḫa-an-zi*
22' *nam-ma-kán u̯a-a-tar* ^{NA4}*ḫu-u-*[*u̯*]*a-ši-i̯a pé-ra-an ar-ḫa*
23' *da-lu-ga-aš-ti la-a-*⸢*ḫu-u*⸣*-an-zi*

(16'-23') The [cups(?) are] lined up for drinking. They drink wine in(?) [...]. They drink (from) the (drinking-)horn. They call out as follows: "Wine, wine he drinks!" When they pick up the (drinking) horn, they clean it out with water. Then they pour out the water in a line along the front of a *ḫuwaši*-stela.

24' LÚ.MEŠ ^{URU}⸢*La*⸣*-al-lu-pí-i̯a-ma-za* LÚ.GAL-*ŠU-NU-i̯a* $^{[GI]Š}$*ḫu-*⸢*ḫu*⸣*-pa-al*
25' *da-an-zi na-at ḫa-az-zi-ki-u-an ti-an-zi*
26' ^{LÚ}SAGI.A*-ma-kán ma-aḫ-ḫa-an ša-a-ú-u̯a-tar-ša ar-ḫa*
27' ⸢*ša-an-ḫa*⸣*-zi na-at-kán A-NA* LU.MEŠ ^{URU}*La-al-lu-pí-i̯a*
28' *A-NA* LÚ.GAL-*ŠU*<*-NU*> *me-na-aḫ-ḫa-an-da e-ep-zi*
29' LÚ.GAL ^{URU}*La-al-lu-pí-i̯a-ma A-NA* ^{LÚ}SAGI.A
30' *me-na-aḫ-ḫa-an-da ki-iš-ša-an ḫal-za-a-i u̯a-ri-i̯a-ti ḫa-pa-nu-ša*

31' *nu* ^{LÚ}SAGI.A *tar-u̯i*$_5$*-iš-ki-u-an da-a-*⸢*i*⸣ [*nu ki-i*]
32' SÌR *iš-ḫa-mi-iš-kán-zi* x -x [
33' *ma-aš-ša-ni-i̯a-aš-ši u̯a-al-*⸢*za*⸣-[*me-en*

(24'-30') The men of Lallupiya and their leader take the *ḫuḫupal*(s?), and begin to play it/them. When the cupbearer cleans the (drinking-)horn, he holds it out to the men of Lallupiya, namely to their leader. The leader of Lallupiya calls back to the cupbearer as follows: "*wariyati ḫapanuša*".

(31'-33') The cupbearer begins to dance. They begin to sing [the following] song: [...] *massaniyašši walza*[*men* ...]

After two mutilated lines col. iii breaks off. In col. iv no mention of *ḫuḫupal* is preserved. The fourth column contains a description of the ritual performance to which the first three columns are introductory. Apparently the king and queen are to lie down in a tent in which "the men of Lallupiya" have made the necessary preparations. The formulae pronounced in col. iii 9'-13', the only speech quoted in Hittite (apart from *winiyandan winiyandan ekuzi* col. iii 19'), recur in col. iv (KUB XXXV 131 rev. 8'ff). "Those who make everyone lie down and get up" must be divine beings as shown by the fact that the formulae are introduced by *malti* in the first instance and preceded by a libation in the second.

What do we learn from this text for *ḫuḫupal*? I think it is fair to say that it does not contain any compelling reason why *ḫuḫupal* should be cymbals. It is not easy to understand the course of actions. In the section (col. i line 20'-24') the liquid used seems to be "*marnuwan*". At least we could not find another restoration for [x]-*nu-an* of line 22'. The precautions taken in order to avoid loss of the liquid are not easy to understand. As part of these precautions one *ḫuḫupal* is apparently put on top of the other so that the lower can catch any overflow from the upper. If these were two cymbals one wonders how the central hole could have been closed permanently enough. The hole left for the insertion of the leather thong is essential in cymbals even to the present day.

It is hard to understand why these precautions are taken in order to preserve the liquid called *marnuwan* which is a kind of beer (*CHD* s.v.). Beginning with the next paragraph only wine is mentioned as contained in a *ḫuḫupal*. In these sections it is only one *ḫuḫupal*. In col. iii line 24'-25' where the men of Lallupiya and their chief take and play *ḫuḫupal*, it is reasonable to assume that there are many such instruments rather than one (^{GIŠ}*ḫuḫupali* in col. ii 6; probably the plural form, it is without context.). While it is possible that each man played a pair of cymbals, there is nothing in the text necessitating this interpretation. On the other hand the *ḫuḫupal* in which some wine is left after the cupbearer has drunk from it (col. i line 41'-45') seems to be a relatively large vessel fit for holding the liquid which is then drunk by several people (*akkuškanzi* 45').

In col. ii line 11'-14' the cupbearer, having drunk wine from the *ḫuḫupal*, begins to play it (if our emendation *ḫazzikiwan* after col. iii 25' is correct). He then dances together with the man who holds him by his cloak, then squats down. His partner covers his head with the cloak and he puts the *ḫuḫupal* at his feet. It seems that he held it all the time while dancing (as in col. i 5'-10').

In col. iii lines 3', 4'-8' the men of Lallupiya get something to drink from cups, (GAL). The object here is *winiyandan*, restored after col. iii line 19'. This seems to be another word for "wine" beside the better known "*wiyana-*". Why are cups used here? Were they filled from the *ḫuḫupal*? I am thinking of the comparable cases where cups are prepared for drinking from a *bibru*. The cupbearer, however, drinks directly from the *ḫuḫupal*. What then is a *ḫuḫupal*? The idea that *ḫuḫupal* could be the lute[49] is hardly compatible with our text.[50] Gurney cites Alp, *Beamt.* 70 n. 2, for the definition "ein hohles Schlaginstrument". Because of this frequent association with *arkammi* and *galgalturi* and with the verb *walḫ-* I originally thought of some kind of drum, influenced also by the sound of the verb. A drum open at one end could, I thought, be filled with liquid. I was encouraged in this assumption by a note in Riemann's music dictionary[51] according to which tubular drums with only one membrane were widespread in ancient times. Since no fragments of pottery of roughly cylindrical shape have been found we would have to assume that the body of such a drum was made of wood. Hans Hickmann[52] describes Egyptian "Röhrentrommeln" as having either barrel or hour-glass shape. Although the Egyptian examples described by him have membranes on both sides, it is conceivable that there was a variety with only one membrane. The bulge of the barrel or the tapering of the hour-glass shape would make it possible to secure the strings which keep the membrane tight. A possible connection of *ḫuḫupal* with drums may be found in the verb *ḫuppiya-*, *ḫuppiški-*, discussed by de Martino in *Hethitica* 9 pp. 8-10. On the one hand we find the sentence *nu-za ú-uk* GIŠ*ḫu-ḫu-pa-al-li da-a-a*[*ḫ-ḫ*]*é nu ḫu-up-pí-e-mi*, in an old Hittite text,[53] on the other hand the phrase LÚ.MEŠBALAG.DI *ḫuppiškanzi* (reference de Martino loc.cit.). As de Martino has seen the object is not expressed, but must be understood: the *ḫuḫupal* in the first example, the GIŠBALAG.DI in the others. Of great importance for determining the meaning of the verb is KBo XV 69 i 10'-12' (l.c. p. 8) according to which the players of the BALAG.DI blow the horn and *ḫuppiškanzi*, but do not beat the BALAG.DI.

It seems to me that the verb *ḫup(p)-/ḫup(p)ai-* discussed by H. Hoffner and others is a different word. For *ḫuppiya-* I propose the meaning "to tap(lightly)". I would translate: "Then I shall take *ḫuḫupal*-instruments and tap (them)" in the first text, and "they tap but do not beat the BALAG.DI" in the second.

I know full well that I have not proven that *galgalturi* must be cymbals or that *ḫuḫupal* is a drum, but I hope that my observations will cause some rethinking and provoke new discussion.

49 J. Friedrich *HW* s.v. 2. Erg. 13, O.R. Gurney, *Schweich* 35.

50 Cf. A.M. Polvani, *Hethitica* 9 (1988) 172.

51 H. Riemann, *Musik Lexikon: Sachteil* (Mainz 1967), 991.

52 "Die altägyptischen Röhrentrommeln", *Oriens* 17 (1964) 172-181.

53 KUB XXXII 117 rev.! 8-9 + KUB XXXV 93 rev.! 13'-14' + KBo XIX 156 rev 1-2 (E. Neu, *StBoT* 25, no. 137).

Plate 18. Musicians in frieze on the Silver Fist in Boston .

"GREAT KINGS" AND "COUNTRY-LORDS" AT MALATYA AND KARKAMIŠ

DAVID HAWKINS

The existence at Karkamiš in the period following the fall of the Hittite Empire of kings claiming the title "Great King" has long been observed[1], but has only begun to be recognized in its full significance, following recent discoveries. These are first, that Talmi-Tešub, hitherto the last known king of the Empire dynasty at Karkamiš, was in fact succeeded by his son Kuzi-Tešub, as is shown by the discovery of impressions of the latter's seal at Lidar Höyük in 1985[2]; and second, that the name of Kuzi-Tešub is found as that of the grandfather in genealogies of two kings of Malatya, where he is entitled "Great King, Hero of Karkamiš."[3] The significance of these discoveries resides in a number of connecting points: a member of the Hittite Empire dynasty of Karkamiš, in direct descent of five generations from Suppiluliuma I, is seen to be the ancestor of the post-Empire dynasty of Malatya, and is moreever given the title "Great King", borne by none of his predecessors on the throne of Karkamiš, not even the great Ini-Tešub.[4] I have inferred from this that at the destruction of Hattusa and the disappearance of its dynasty, Kuzi-Tešub in Karkamiš was left holding the line of the Euphrates from Malatya perhaps to Emar[5], from which another fragment impression of his seal may come[6], and that as a surviving descendant of Suppiluliuma I, he assumed the vacant title of "Great King".

If this were indeed the situation from which the post-Empire political system of North Syria and the Euphrates developed, it should be of interest to

[1] Cf. for example the remarks of R. Barnett, apud L. Woolley, *Carchemish* III 259; H.G. Güterbock, *JNES* 13 (1954) 105.

[2] See D. Sürenhagen, *MDOG* 118 (1986) 183-190; for the reading of the seal's legend, J.D. Hawkins, *AnSt* 28 (1988) 99f.

[3] Hawkins, ibid. 101f.

[4] Ibid. 104 and nn. 27-28.

[5] Ibid. 104 and n. 32.

[6] This impression was circulating on the antiquities market, and a photograph of it was seen by me in the British Museum in 1981: see Hawkins, ibid. 99 n. 1. The bulla is now in the Rosen Collection, and will be published by Dr. Gary Beckman, to whose courtesy I owe this information.

review the evidence of the Neo-Hittite inscriptions for indications as to how this came about.[7] I have pleasure in dedicating this study to Philo Houwink ten Cate.

The Malatya dynasty or dynasties, together with their inscriptions and sculpture, are probably, by this genealogical link, to be pulled back to a 12th-11th century dating from the rather later one envisaged by Orthmann.[8] The inscriptions provide evidence for the reconstruction of three dynastic sequences, A, B and C[9]:

A (GÜRÜN+KÖTÜKALE, İSPEKÇÜR+DARENDE)

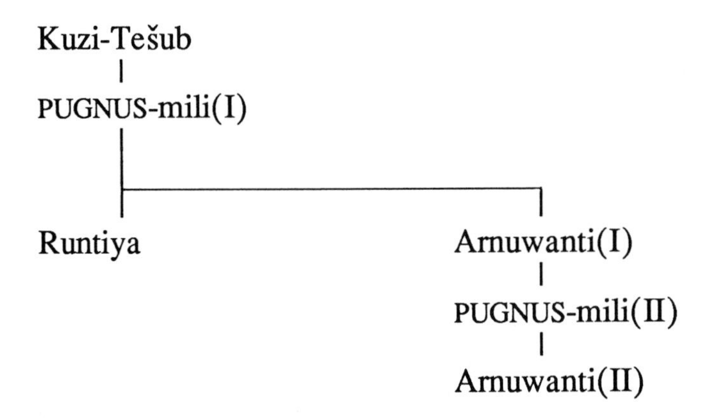

B (IZGIN, MALATYA 1, and MALATYA 4)

CRUS+*RA/I*
|
Wasu(?)-Rutiya
|
Halpa-sulupi()

[7] I and others have already covered this ground in contributions cited below. But the new evidence, and new interpretations offered for the relevant inscriptions do I think shed new light on historical processes.

[8] *Untersuchungen* 140-142, 148.

[9] See recently my entry Melid. A. Historisch, in *RlA* VIII/1-2 (1993), especially §§3-4. This was written at about the time that I identified Kuzi-Tešub in the Malatya inscriptions, and my conclusions were somewhat tentatively expressed. In the time which elapsed since, reflection suggests that these may be stated more positively. For the problems of reading the Malatya rulers' names, see loc.cit., §3. f.

C (MALATYA 3)

Suwarimi
|
Mariti

Dynasty A seems certain to be the earliest, by reason of its descent from Kuzi-Tešub. A link between Dynasties A and B is possible, even probable, but not attested. Dynasty C's Stag Hunt relief with inscription MALATYA 3 is stylistically so close to Dynasty B's lion Hunt with inscription MALATYA 1 that they can hardly be too widely separated in time, but again no links are attested between the two dynasties. The ruler PUGNUS-mili of the Lion Gate sculpture could be either PUGNUS-mili I, though this might seem rather early, or II, or a third of that name.

Though the members of Dynasty A at least were descended from Kuzi-Tešub, king of Karkamiš, there is nothing in their inscriptions to indicate that they remained subordinate to Karkamiš. Indeed they appear to be rulers in their own right,[10] though by no means all have the title "king".[11] One has the title "Hero", with its grandiose and Empire pretensions.[12] The regular title which they all bear is "Country-Lord of the city Malatya",[13] and this thus appears to be the regular Malatya dynasty title. In origin this may have been a rather subordinate title: the Empire period has Cun. EN KUR[14] and its Hier. equivalent no seals, REGIO.DOMINUS,[15] which seem to designate no more than a provincial governor or local magnate.

10 Cf. the statement of the author of IZGIN 1 (§2) that he seated himself on his father's throne.

11 Arnuwanti I on DARENDE, §1, and İSPEKÇÜR, B§1; Halpasulupi(?) on MALATYA 4, and PUGNUS-mili of the lion Gate (MALATYA 5, 8, 9, 10, 11, 14) have the title "potent(?) king" (REX.*462).

12 Author of IZGIN 1 (§1), and the same man named as grandfather on MALATYA 1.

13 Written MA_x.LI_x-*zi* (URBS) REGIO.DOMINUS. In the name "Malatya", the signs transliterated MA_x.LI_x, a calf's head and leg (HH nos. 109+125), are not known to have phonetic values and may simply be logograms. The *zi* appears to be a phonetic complement as in the writting of the name TONITRUS. *HALPA-pa* "Halab". The probability is that behind this writing lies the name *Malizi* . On MALATYA 3 it is uncertain whether to restore the title as REGIO. [DOMINUS]-*sa* or to emend REGIO to REX-*sa* .

14 See F. Pecchioli Daddi, *Mestieri* 451 f.

15 *SBo* II 140; *Boğazköy* III Taf. 29 no. 13; *CIH* Taf. XL, 12; Tell Açana (see Woolley, *Alalakh* (Oxford, 1955), pl. LXVII no. 155); and several new examples among the bullae from Nişantepe excavated in 1990-91.

In summary we may say that apparently the Malatya dynasty, originating as a branch of the Karkamiš royal house, perhaps at a time when in the immediate aftermath of the fall of the Hittite Empire Malatya itself was under the authority of Karkamiš, endured through a considerable number of generations and bequeathed a style of sculpture showing close links with the iconography of the Empire period. But there is no evidence that the dominion of Karkamiš over Malatya lasted for a significant period. A sizeable territory lies between the two cities. On the Euphrates was the land of Kummuh, which at least by the 9th century was under its own dynasty[16], and to the west of Kummuh, the land of Gurgum was under a dynasty which originated well back in 10th century B.C.[17]

Kuzi-Tešub, as noted, is known from impressions of his seal found at Cider Höyük and elsewhere, and from the genealogies of the Malatya inscriptions. His name is also found in fragmentary contexts in Boğazköy texts.[18] No trace of his presence has been found at Karkamiš itself, but this is hardly surprising since no trace of the entire Hittite Empire dynasty has been found there. The earliest identifiable inscriptions from Karkamiš are the two similar stelae, one well preserved (KARKAMIŠ A4b), the other fragmentary and now almost all lost (KARKAMIŠ A16c). Both are surmounted by elaborate winged discs and the latter additionally with another disc and crescent, and both are the work of rulers entitled "Great King, Hero, King of the Land of Karkamiš", almost the same titles as those given to Kuzi-Tešub on GÜRÜN.[19]

The fragmentary KARKAMIŠ A16c appears to give on its only surviving fragment (the upper part, frag. 1) the name of the Great King as Tudhaliya written in the usual Empire way.[20] On KARKAMIŠ A4b, the Great King's name is

16 See Hawkins, *RlA* VI/5-6 (1983) s.v. Kummuh.

17 See Hawkins, *RlA* VII/5-6 (1989) s.v. Maraş.

18 Sürenhagen, *MDOG* 118 (1986) 189.

19 Note that "land of Karkamiš", like "Hero", appears to hark back to the Empire period, where it is normal on the seals of Ini-Tešub, Talmi-Tešub and Kuzi-Tešub. Neo-Hittite inscriptions normally refer to "the city Karkamiš", the only exception besides the two stelae under discussion being the lion inscription of Astuwatamanza, KARKAMIŠ A14*b*, which also has "land".

20 MONS+*tu*. H.Th. Bossert's reading of this name (*Asia* 74), doubted by Barnett (*Carchemish* III 259) and P. Meriggi in his edition of the piece (*Manuale* II/3, no. 186, p. 327 and Tav. XVI), is supported by my collation of the piece in Ankara Museum in 1987. Note also the fragment Ankara 10.948, naming a Great King Tudhaliya, reported by Meriggi as seen in Ankara and represented by a squeeze in the British Museum: *Manuale* II/3, no. 266p, p. 329 and Tav. XVI; and cf. Barnett, apud Woolley, *Carchemish* III, addendum slip inserted following p. 264. Working in Ankara and the British Museums, I have not been able to locate either the fragment or the squeeze.

given as MAGNUS.TONITRUS, (i.e. logographically written),[21] son of x-pa-ziti,[22] also entitled "Great King, Hero". The name MAGNUS.TONITRUS could be read in Luwian or conceivably Hurrian: reasons are given below for Luwian reading like the name of the father, thus Ura-Tarhunza.[23]

The Fragmentary stele yields no more than the name and title of the Great King Tudhaliya. Even the fully preserved stele is very difficult to read, being faintly incised on poor stone, and now in the Ankara Museum, it is also difficult to light and photograph. Nevertheless, having spent some time working on it in the Museum, and having taken latex and paper squeezes,[24] I am now confident of being able to offer a fairly complete text and interpretation. The full transliteration and commentary will appear in my forthcoming *Corpus of Hieroglyphic Luwian Inscriptions*. Here for the purpose of discussion a translation with explanatory notes should suffice.

KARKAMIŠ A4b
§1. Ura-Tarhunza, Great King, Hero, King of the land of Karkamiš, son of x-pa- ziti, Great King, Hero.
§2. Against him from the land . . . [25] a dispute[26] came[27] forth,
§3. and (one) put the army against.
§4. (To) King Ura-Tarhunza the mighty Storm God (and) Kubaba gave a mighty courage,[28]
§5. and by (his) mighty [courage] he resolved[29] the dispute.

[21] Reading by Bossert, *Belleten* 16 (1952[1953]) 523, 542f., pl. CXXVI, fig. 19, correcting Barnett, apud Woolley, *Carchemish* III 259.
[22] Reading of name by Bossert (*Belleten* 16 (1952[1953] 523) and Güterbock (*JNES* 13 (1954) 105), correcting Barnett, loc. cit. The first sign is damaged and uncertain: Meriggi in his edition (*Manuale* II/3, no. 163, p. 325 f. and Tav. XVI), considers *sara/i*, but collation hardly supports this.
[23] See below n. 59: the MAGNUS+*ra/i*-TONITRUS-*ta*- (KARKAMIŠ A11*b*+*c*) is identified as the same individual, and the phonetic complements indicate the Luwian reading.
[24] I am most grateful to the Director of Ankara Museum, Dr. İlhan Temizsöy, for permission to do this work.
[25] Written CORNU+*RA/I*-*ti* (REGIO), presumed reading *surati*; uncertain whether -*ti* is part of the stem, or abl. sing. ending.
[26] Logogram HH no. 24 (facing profiles across seal), formerly interpreted as "anger" (IRA), now as "dispute, quarrel" (LIS).
[27] Written SPHINX (HH no.121). Itamar Singer ingeniously interprets *awiti*-, "sphinx" as rebus-writing of verb *awi*-, "come" (personal communication).
[28] Written logographically FORTIS *273 DARE, which is exactly paralleled by the phonetic writing in SULTANHAN (+ new fragment), §8, . . . [*muw*]*atalin warpin piyata*: see J.D. Hawkins and A. Morpurgo Davies, *FsGüterbock*[2] 76.
[29] Written DELERE-*wa/i*-*ta*: cf. Melchert, *AnSt* 38 (1988) 34-38.

§6. This stele ... [30]erected, son of Suhi the ruler, the priest of Kubaba.[31]

This stele appears to commemorate the victory of the Great King over an uncertainly identified country. For our present enquiry the interest however lies more in the final clause with the newly recognized information that the stele was set up by the priest of Kubaba, a son of a "ruler". We are not told whether the erection of the stele was contemporary with the military event, or whether it commemorated an event in the more or less distant past. The mention of Suhi the ruler does however link this inscription to the main group of early Karkamiš inscriptions, those of the "house of Suhi".

This four-generation dynasty, reconstructable from the genealogies in the inscriptions of its members, has long been recognized,[32] running father to son: Suhi I[33]-Astuwatamanza[34]-Suhi II[35]-Katuwa.[36] These dynasts have two titles, tarwani- and "Country-Lord of the city Karkamiš". The former title, conventionally translated "judge" or "ruler", is of rather uncertain connotations.[37] Elsewhere it is used by the rulers of Tell Ahmar,[38] Maraş,[39] Commagene,[40] and

30 Apparently personal name written AVIS2-*nu*(-) *466, possible reading *Arnu* ... .

31 Written I(DEUS)*ku*+AVIS I *355-*sa*. A combination of this context, and KARKAMIŠ A2+3, §14*a-c* (quoted below p. 79 and n. 43), also SUVASA, B, shows that the sign HH no. 355 is a title of an office attached to gods, i.e. "priest". The sign is perhaps a late version of the Empire HH no. 372 (the "ear"), commonly found on seals and representing "priest".

32 See Meriggi, *ZA* NF 5 (1930) 201.

33 Known only as father of Astuwatamanza, on inscription cited in following note.

34 Known from own inscription on lion fragment KARKAMIŠ A14*b*; also in genealogies of Suhi II (KELEKLİ), and Katuwa (KARKAMIŠ A11*a*, A11*b*).

35 Known from own inscription KELEKLİ, lion fragment KARKAMIŠ A14*a*, and own and wife's inscriptions KARKAMIŠ A1*a*+*b*; also in genealogies of Katuwa KARKAMIŠ A11*a*, A11*b*, A2, A12.

36 Own inscriptions KARKAMIŠ A2+3, A11*a*, A11*b*+*c*, A12, A13*d*, A23, and other attributable fragments.

37 Translation "judge" by Laroche, following the Karatepe equivalent Hier. *tarwana-* = Phoen. *ṣdq*, "justice." See the study of F. Pintore in *StMed.* 4, 474-494; also the remarks of R. Stefanini, ibid. 595-602 esp. 600f. with nn. 10, 11. Recently I have suggested that the logogram determining *tarwani-*, HH no. 371, may be derived from the Empire sign HH no. 277, which determines the title Labarna/Tabarna: see *StBoT* Beiheft 3 (forthcoming), 107-109.

38 Title applied to father in the genealogy on TELL AHMAR 1, §1; but the kings of Til-Barsip normally call themselves "king": TELL AHMAR 1, §1; 2, §1; BOROWSKI 3, §1.

39 Halparuntiyas II (MARAŞ4, §1) and Halparuntiyas III MARAŞ1, §1) combine the title with "Gurgumean king".

40 Suppiluliuma (BOYBEYPINARI 1, §§1; 2, §1) and Hattusili (MALPINAR, §§1, 2).

Tuwana,[41] but not Malatya. But it is the title "Country-Lord" which seems to serve as the main dynastic title at Karkamiš[42] as at Malatya. Its status at Karkamiš seems to be expressed in the topos "whether he (be) a King, or he (be) a Country-Lord, or he (be) a Priest".[43]

Subsequent rulers of Karkamiš whose inscriptions preserve their titularies follow a similar pattern. In the house of Astiruwa,[44] Kamani, who was apparently a legitimate ruler, has the title "*tarwani*-, Country-Lord", significantly "of the cities Karkamiš (and) Malatya".[45] He also appears to be entitled "King" in an inscription set up by someone else.[46] Yariri, whose position has been identified simply as that of regent and guardian of Kamani,[47] takes only the titles *tarwani*- and "prince" (CAPUT-*ti* -). Of Kamani's father Astiruwa no inscriptions, thus no full titularies survive. He is referred to by Yariri as "Lord",[48] and by a subordinate as "King".[49] Also on a fragmentary genealogy probably to be attributed to Kamani we read: "[Kamani . . . Karkamišean] Country-Lord, the Hero Astiruwa's son".[50] The title "Hero" at Karkamiš is certainly archaic, going back to Kuzi-Tešub and the other "Great Kings", thus here representing the revival of archaic claims visible in the inscriptions of Kamani and later. Finally we have the genealogy of Kamani's vizier Sastura's son, author of KARKAMIŠ

41 Warpalawa combines it with "King" and "Hero" (BOR, §1; BULGARMADEN, §1); Kiyakiya with "King" (AKSARAY, §9); Saruwani with "City-Lord" (ANDAVAL, §1). Subordinate rulers have the title (BULGARMADEN, §1; KULULU 3, §1(?); KULULU 4, §1).

42 Used by Astuwatamanza, Suhi II and Katuwa in their inscriptions with or without *tarwani*-; also without *tarwani*- of their fathers in their genealogies.

43 *was man* REX-*tis mapas* REGIO.DOMINUS-*s mapas* *355-*lis* (KARKAMIŠ A2+3, §14*a-c*; cf. ibid., §19a-b). It is this context which places *355-*lis* as a title of authority, while KARKAMIŠ A4*b*, §6, and SUVASA, B, linking it to the gods Kubaba and Sarruma, establish it as a religious office: see above, n. 31. For "King" as against "Country-Lord", see also MARAŞ 8, §§13-16.

44 See in general Hawkins, *TTK*, Ankara 1981, Kongreye sunulan bildiriler, I. Cilt (Ankara, 1986) 259-271. Since writing this paper I have examined all the inscriptions preserved in Ankara Museum and corrected a number of readings.

45 CEKKE, §6. "Malatya" is written MA$_x$-*zá* (URBS). Laroche reports the doubts in identifying this as Malatya, HH no. 109.2, notes, but the view taken in this article on the political developments after the end of the Hittite Empire inclines one to accept it; see further below.

46 The house-sale record KARKAMIŠ A4*a*, §1: see Hawkins and Morpurgo Davies, *FsNeumann* 94.

47 Hawkins, *AnSt* 29 (1979) 157-160.

48 KARKAMIŠ A15*b*, §17; references to the "lord", ibid., §§4, 21, seem likely to refer also to Astiruwa, as also on KARKAMIŠ A6, §8 ("Kamani my lord's son").

49 KÖRKÜN, S4.

50 KARKAMIŠ A27*e* 1+2: ...] REGIO.DOMINUS *á-sa-ti-ru-si-sá* ⌈HEROS⌉ (INFANS) *ni-za-sa* [... ; attribution to Kamani argued in my *Corpus of Hier. Luwian Inscriptions*.

A21, from which his own name is lost,[51] who has the titles "Hero, Country-Lord of the city Karkamiš and the land Malatya",[52] i.e. a titulary very similar to that of Kamani on CEKKE, but replacing *tarwani-* with "Hero".

Having reviewed the Karkamiš titularies, we may ask why the rulers, who clearly were effectively kings and occasionally acknowledged as such in the inscriptions of others,[53] never used the title but instead the inferior one of "Country-Lord". Consideration suggests that the usage goes back to the period of the "Great Kings",[54] which forms the focus of enquiry in this paper.

We return to the KARKAMIŠ A4b, recording a victory of a "Great King, Hero, King of the land of Karkamiš", but set up by a priest, son of Suhi the *tarwani-*. This Suhi has long been identified as Suhi I, father of Astuwatamanza,[55] and facts presented below serve to corroborate this probability.[56] The Ura-Tarhunza, the Great King of the stele, has also been identified with the Ura-Tarhunza twice mentioned in an inscription of Katuwa in the context of a dynastic struggle against "the grandsons of Ura-Tarhunza", who include one named individual.[57] The relevant passages translate as follows:

KARKAMIŠ A11b+c.

§2. This city of my father and grandfather was of Ni(?)nuwi,[58]

[51] Restored by Meriggi as *Astiru* from a fragment with this name (*Manuale* II/2 147f.). I preferred the attribution on stylistic grounds to Pisiri, last king of Karkamiš mentioned in Assyrian sources, 738-717 B.C. (*AnSt* 29 (1979) 162). I now feel the question is open and that Meriggi might be right, thus Sastura's son would be Astiru II. This would however necessitate the dating of the associated sculpture to before 738 B.C., the latest date for the beginning of the reign of Pisiri. The matter is further discussed in my forthcoming *Corpus*.
[52] Written MA_X(REGIO); Meriggi in his edition supported the Malatya identification (*Manuale* II/2 147f.).
[53] Astiruwa and Kamani, above p. 79 and nn. 45, 48.
[54] The question was raised and an answer outlined by Stefanini, loc.cit., n. 37 above. But I believe the new translations of the relevant texts offered here permit our understanding of the situation to go further.
[55] E.g. by Barnett, *Carchemish* III 260. Bossert incorrectly identified Suhi the ruler as son of Ura-Tarhunza: *Belleten* 16 (1952[1953]) 523, and see his genealogical chart, lev. CXXXIII abb. 40. Cf. the remarks of Stefanini, loc.cit. n. 37 above 600 with n. 9.
[56] See pp. 82f.: the further evidence for the connections of the house of Suhi with the Great Kings.
[57] Bossert, *Belleten* 16 (1952) 539; cf. Meriggi, *Manuale* II/1 62.
[58] Written [m]*447-*nu-wa/i-ia-si*, certainly a personal name gen. sing. The only evidence for a phonetic reading of the sign HH no. 447 occurs on TOPADA, where it alternates with *ni* in the

§3. but he extended (sc. the hand) in vain,[59]
§4. Him together with Ura-Tarhunza's grandsons[60] I exiled(?),[61]
§5. and from them my . . . [62]city Ipani, also my . . . . .s[63] of Muziki [I . . . ed],
§6. and I (re)built it (sc. the city).
. . .
§30. Since[64] I took away this city from the grandsons of Ura-Tarhunza by force,[65]
§31. and since I did not exile(?) it,[66]
§32. let these gods be heard![67]

The same incidents may also be referred to in another Katuwa inscription:

KARKAMIŠ A11a.
§3. [and to me the gods . .] gave [my] father's power,[68]
§4. me they raised in strength because of my justice.
§5. But my kinsmen(?)[69] revolted[70] against me,
§6. wherefore they caused the lands to . . .[71] from under me . . .[72]

"Ura-Tarhunza's grandsons" may well mean simply descendants; we could hardly rely on it to mean specifically "descendants of the second

writing of the ethnic adj. *parzutawani-* (§§13, 23), but this is very dubious evidence for a syllabic reading here.

[59] For (*245) *danati-*, "empty, vain", see J.D. Hawkins and A. Morpurgo Davies, *FsGüterbock*² 74f.; for an alternative interpretation of the clause, see Melchert, *AnSt* 38 (1988) 32 ("it (the city) stretched out empty/desolate").

[60] Written ᵐMAGNUS+*ra/i*-TONITRUS-*ta-sa-za* INFANS.NEPOS-*sa-za*. The phonetic complements +*ra/i*- and -*ta*- establish the reading of the name as *Ura-Tarhunta-*, i.e. Luwian, as against a Hurrian reading *Talmi-Tešub*.

[61] Written (LOCUS) *pi-ta-ha-li-ia-ha*, perhaps a compound or derivative of LOCUS /*pita-, "place"; also §31.

[62] Word (adj.) of unknown meaning, *sá-pa-ta₄-li*.

[63] Written TERRA.PONERE-*ru-tà*, acc.plur. N, probably indicating "estates" or the like.

[64] REL+*ra/i-i*; "since" seems most appropriate translation of the conjunction.

[65] Written ("*314") *ha-sá-ti-i*, abl. sing.; see Starke, *StBoT* 31, 123 and n. 370, identifying the word as Luw. *has-*, "bone; force".

[66] "Exiling it (the city)" may be understood as its inhabitants, as in Hittite usage.

[67] Written AUDIRE+MI-*ta-ra/i-ru*, apparently a Med.-Pass. imperative.

[68] Cf. below, n. 73.

[69] Written 20-*tá-ti-zi*: for identification of 20-*tá-ti-* as representing probably some degree of kinsman (uncle, cousin), see Hawkins, *AnSt* 30 (1980) 148, citing also this passage.

[70] Written *ARHA* CRUS+*RA/I*, literally "stood away, seceded".

[71] Written (PES₂) *tara/i-za-nu-wa/i-tá*.

[72] Unknown word in unidentified grammatical form, *314(-) *sá-pa-za*.

generations". Thus all that we may understand from the passages cited, beyond the setting up by a *tarwani* 's priest-son of a stele commemorating a Great King's military encounter, is that that *tarwani* 's great-grandson had to contest the city, which had been held by his father and grandfather, with that Great King's descendants, who may perhaps have been his kinsmen. The statement that the city had belonged to his father and grandfather is reliterated by Katuwa with the statement that the gods gave him his father's power, and by identical statement made by his father Suhi II.[73]

But other evidence may well take us further. The KELEKLİ stele of Suhi II,[74] after his introductory statement of genealogy, makes the following remarkable statement(§2):

"When King Tudhaliya shall take for himself (i.e. marry) . . . my dear daughter".[75]

Unfortunately the text breaks off at this point.

Who then could King Tudhaliya be, and what would be his status in relation to the Country-Lord of Karkamiš? One naturally thinks of the Great King Tudhaliya attested on the fragmentary stele KARKAMIŠ A16c and another fragment.[76] But the implications of this would be extraordinary, namely that there would be both a Great King and a Country-Lord in Karkamiš at the same time, and that the former was of the same generation as the latter or even as his daughter, thus the same generation as the Country-Lord's son Katuwa. Furthermore the Tudhaliya stele KARKAMIŠ A16c is so similar to the Ura-Tarhunza stele KARKAMIŠ A4b, that Great King Tudhaliya must have been in some way connected with the two Great Kings, father and son, of the latter. He could hardly have preceded them, because his contemporary Suhi II's uncle, the priest of Kubaba, is not likely to have set up a stele for the Great King Ura-Tarhunza, perhaps three generations his junior. If thus Tudhaliya represents the

73 More fully preserved: *wamu amanza tatiyanza* (LIGNUM) *salahaza piyata*, "he/they (god(s)) gave me my father's power" (KARKAMIŠ A14*a*, §3). Hier. *salahaza* is recognized as being the equivalent of Hitt. **šallatar*, "greatness, succession": see Gurney, *AnSt* 33 (1983) 101.

74 My text of KELEKLİ is based on work which I did on the stele in September 1985 in the Near Eastern Section of the Berlin Museum, and will be treated in detail in my forthcoming *Corpus*. I am most grateful to the Museum authorities, in particular to the then Director of the Near Eastern Section, Dr. Liane Jakob-Rost, for permission to carry out this work.

75 *wati kuman* (MONS)TÚ-*s* ⸢REX⸣-*tis* ⸢... -*n*⸣ *ami*n BONUS-*mi*n FILIA-*trin tai*; the missing word is probably the daughter's name. (MONS)TÚ is taken as a writing of the name Tudhaliya almost exactly in Empire style except that *tú* instead of Empire *tu* is used.

76 See above p. 76 and n. 20.

generation following Ura-Tarhunza, we would have to reckon Ura-Tarhunza and his father corresponding in generation to the first two generations of the house of Suhi. Thus not only would the lines of Great Kings and Country-Lords overlap completely, but the priest-son of Suhi I who set up the stele KARKAMIŠ A4b would have been the contemporary of the Great King. Schematically this may be presented as follows:

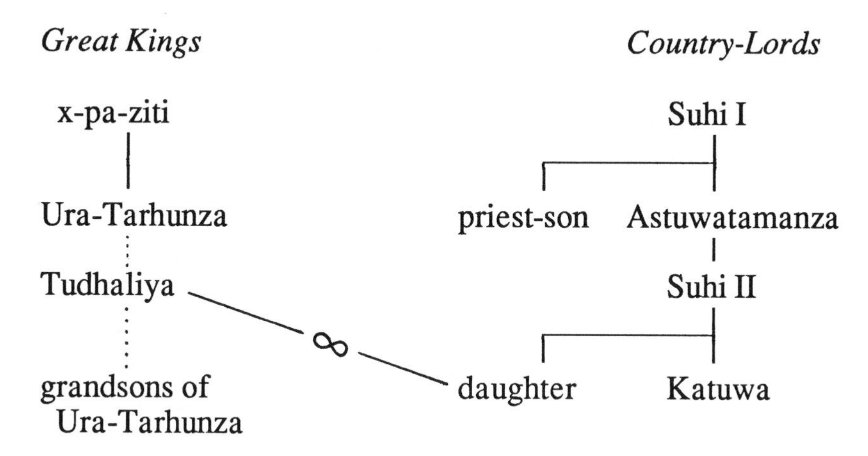

While this formulation may be excessively neat, some such degree of co-existence does undoubtedly seem to be implied by the evidence cited. Is this credible and might it be understood? We conclude with a somewhat speculative attempt at explanation.

The Great Kings of Karkamiš may well have been descended from Kuzi-Tešub. If Katuwa's statement about the revolt of his *kinsmen* (?) is correctly identified with the incident involving the grandsons of Ura-Tarhunza, and if the word *kinsmen* is correctly interpreted, the family of Country-Lords of Karkamiš might also be descended from Kuzi-Tešub, as were the Country-Lords of Malatya.

The four-generation house of Suhi is dated approximately to the period 1000-900 B.C.[77], and the three generations of Great Kings would belong to a similar period. Kuzi-Tešub himself must belong to the period spanning the fall of the Hittite Empire, thus before and after c. 1200 B.C. The four generations of Country-Lords of Malatya descended from him would extend from the early 12th to early 11th centuries B.C., and there are of course a probable further five

[77] It has been generally agreed that they must have preceded Sangara of Karkamiš, who is first attested in Assyrian records c. 870 B.C.

generations of Country-Lords of Malatya[78] to accomodate. It is hard to suppose that these dynasts would not have stretched down into the 10th century B.C. and so overlapped with those of Karkamiš.

In Malatya we have supposed that the Country-Lords were originally under the authority of a Great King of Karkamiš but broke free as the power of Karkamiš declined. Tiglath-pileser I, c. 1100 B.C., recorded contact both with Hatti (i.e. Karkamiš[79]) under a king Ini-Tešub,[80] and with Malatya under a ruler Allumari,[81] without implying any political links between the two. The Malatya rulers appear to have maintained their originally subordinate title, seldom supplementing it with "king".[82]

In Karkamiš the surviving evidence does not stretch back as far as in Malatya, not apparently beyond the house of Suhi and their contemporary Great Kings, i.e. not much before c. 1000 B.C., almost two centuries after the time of Kuzi-Tešub. An unattested line of Great Kings may have occupied this blank period: the Ini-Tešub named by Tiglath-pileser I should have been one of them. They may have had subordinates with the title Country-Lord as at Malatya. At a certain date, not necessarily earlier than Suhi I, a line of Country-Lords seems to have split off from that of the Great Kings, and to have assumed political power in the city without either appropriating the title Great King or removing its hereditary holders. These Country-Lords, while never at this date called "king", certainly behaved like kings, if we may judge from their surviving building, sculpture and inscriptions. Finally the descendants of the Great Kings in the person of one Ni(?)nuwi succeeded temporarily in recovering control of Karkamiš, only to be extruded by Katuwa, the most active of the line of Country-Lords.

The sequel is not clearly known. The later house of Astiruwa, attested in at least three generations, ruling from the later 8th century to the later 7th century B.C., still adhered to the dynastic title "Country-Lord", but began to adopt archaic titles and claims. The title "Hero" first replaced *tarwani-* for

78 Dynasties B (3 generations) and C (2 generations).

79 See Hawkins, *RlA* IV 2-3 (1973), s.v. Hatti, §§3, 4.1.

80 Ibid.; also now K. Grayson, *RIMA* 2, A.O. 87.3, ll. 26-28. The Assyrian writing ^{m}NI.NI-^{d}*te-šub* seems in the context certain to represent Ini-Tešub. This king at this date could perhaps be the grandson of Kuzi-Tešub and would have borne the name of the latter's famous grandfather.

81 Hawkins, *RlA* VIII/1-2 (1993), s.v. Melid. A. Historisch. §2.1; also now Grayson, *RIMA* 2, A.O. 87.4, ll. 31-33; A.O. 87.4, ll. 28-30; A.O. 87.10, ll. 33-35. Note that the name Allumari is reconstructed from two different broken texts, being fully preserved on neither.

82 See above p. 75 and n. 11.

Astiruwa, while his son Kamani claimed the Country-Lordship of Malatya as well as Karkamiš. In both of these presentations they were followed by Sastura's son, probably the last king of Karkamiš, whose inscriptions also show a markedly archaizing style of sign-forms and orthography. Urartian and Assyrian referen-ces throughout the 8th century B.C. to independent kings of Malatya, Kummuh, Gurgum and Samʾal show up this claim as anachronistic and hollow. But it would be very interesting to discover the unattested antecedents of the house of Astiruwa.

ABOUT QUESTIONS

HARRY A. HOFFNER

> "I keep six honest serving men
> They taught me all I knew:
> Their names are What and Why and When
> And How and Where and Who"
>
> – *Rudyard Kipling*

> Whether life lasts for ten years or a
> hundred or a thousand, there are no
> questions asked in Hades.
>
> – *ben Sirach* 41:4

Introductory

A few words of explanation need to be made at the outset. Interrogative sentences have, of course, been treated generally in J. Friedrich, *HE* §§284-286 (pp. 146f.). L. Mascheroni, *SMEA* 22 (1980) 53-62, also dealt with aspects of the subject. Negative questions, both rhetorical and not, were studied by H.A. Hoffner in *FsGüterbock*2 89-91.[1] What does this new essay attempt to add?

First, the first large collection of examples of Hittite questions is presented here. It is not easy to identify questions in Hittite texts. Sentence questions are not marked by any interrogative word. And even questions containing interrogative words can easily be mistaken for relative clauses, since many interrogative words (*kui-, kuwapi, maḫḫan*) are identical with the relatives. For this reason, many questions go undetected even by good Hittitologists. Since no complete collection is available elsewhere in print, all known examples will be included here, either in full transcription and translation or at least by text

[1] A collection of examples of rhetorical questions was assembled by Güterbock and presented as a "handout" at one of the annual meetings of the Midwest Branch of the American Oriental Society, but this collection was never published.

reference. The only exceptions will be those already published in the dictionary articles, such as *CHD maḫḫan*, *mān*, etc.

Secondly, although the *CHD* has now covered the question words *maḫḫan* and *mān*, none of the newer dictionaries has published the K entries, where most of the others are found. It is important to make available at this time most of the examples of questions, with and without interrogative words, which exist in well-preserved contexts.

Thirdly, even after the good work which has been done on varieties of interrogative questions by Sommer, Friedrich, and others, there remain aspects which are insufficiently studied. For this reason, having been collecting and studying examples for the past thirty years, I have decided to present this analysis as a tribute to my good friend, Philo Houwink ten Cate, from whose ideas and published works I have learned so much.

Marking Questions

In the spoken language, questions were probably marked in two ways: (1) by voice intonation (which is normally not indicated in the writing, but see next paragraph for an exception), and (2) with interrogative words. Sentence questions were marked only by voice intonation (Friedrich, *HE* §284 and Mascheroni, *SMEA* 22 (1980) 53f.). Marking sentence questions by inverted word order, as in English "Are you going?" versus "You are going", is not a feature of Hittite.

Scribes in Assyria and Babylonia who wrote Akkadian in cuneiform script sometimes indicated the interrogative intonation by a plene spelling of the final vowel of the central word in the interrogative clause.[2] Since the Hittite cuneiform writing system was initially derived from scribes who used it to write Akkadian, it is no surprise that in one of the oldest Hittite tablets, KBo 22.1, an instruction text written in the Old Hittite ductus, one finds the same phenomenon in writing Hittite questions. *nu ki-iš-ša-an A-WA-A-AT A-BI-IA ar-ḫa-a-an ḫar-te-**ni-i*** "Is this the way you hold my father's word (as) a limitation?" (lines 30-31). But this phenomenon is found to date only in this text. It did not become a regular scribal method of indicating interrogative stress.

2 W. von Soden, *GAG* §153 d.

Sentence Questions

Sentence questions are those containing no interrogative word (who, which, what, why, where, etc.). Some sentence questions are what we would call "yes-or-no" questions:

(1) ŠEŠ-*YA⸗za malāši* "Are you agreed, my brother?" KUB XIV 3 iii 62 (Tawagalawa letter);

All of the questions in the oracular texts are of this type:

(2) DINGIR-*LUM⸗za kīdaš waškuwaš šēr* TUKU.TUKU-*wanza* "O deity, are you angry on account of this offence?" KUB V 10 i 12 (oracle question, NH);

(3) DINGIR-*LUM⸗za apaddan šer* TUKU.TUKU-*uwanza* "Are you, O god, angry on that account?" ibid. 23.

(4) DINGIR-*LIM⸗za QATAMMA malan ḫarti* "Have you agreed in the same way, O god?" KBo XXIV 118 + ABoT 14 ii 15 (oracular inquiry). Many other examples of this exist.

In Hittite, as in many other languages, one answered such a question not with a "yes" or "no" word, but with a statement: *UL⸗an šakti* "Do you not know it?" is answered with *šaggaḫḫi⸗an* "I know it" or with *UL⸗an šaggaḫḫi* "I do not know it".

Rhetorical sentence questions

Some sentence questions are also rhetorical questions, that is, the speaker knows the answer in advance and expects it to be the opposite to the situation stated in his query:

(5) *kiššan AWAT ABI⸗YA / paḫšanutten* "Is this the way you (pl.) have kept my father's word (i.e., command)?" KBo XXII 1:4-5 (instructions for magistrates, OS); here the *kiššan* has been fronted for emphasis; compare the unmarked position of *kiššan* in *ANA* ^{d}UTU-*ŠI BELI-NI / QIBI-MA UMMA* ^{m}*Mariya / U* ^{m}*Hapiri* ÌR.MEŠ-*KA-MA* / ^{d}UTU-*ŠI=m[u] kuit BELI-YA / ammuk* ^{m}*Hapirin / kiššan watarnaḫta* "Say to His Majesty, my lord: Thus says Mariya and Hapiri, your servants: 'Concerning that which Your Majesty, my lord, instructed me and Hapiri, as follows'" HKM 48:1-6 (letter, MH/MS); or in NH: *nu=za maḫḫan kun memian* ZI-*ni* EGIR-*pa kiššan AQBI* KBo IV 4 ii 49 (detailed annals of Murš. II);

(6) LUGAL-*š⸗an idalu k[uitki iyanun]* "[Did I,] the king, [treat] him badly s[omehow]?" KUB I 16 ii 16 (OH/NS);

(7) *peḫḫi⸗wa<r>⸗at⸗ši mān⸗wa⸗ši UL pe[ḫḫi]* "Shall I give it to him? (What) if I do not give it to him?" KUB XII 60 i 21 (myth, OH/NS);

(8) *nu ammel* / *dammešḫaš ŠA DAM-YA ḫinkan* SIG$_5$-*yattat* "My punishment is the death of my wife. Has (this) gotten any better?" KBo IV 8 ii 20-21 (prayer of Murš. II), ed. Hoffner, *JAOS* 103 (1983) 188;

(9) *zik=za=kan ammuk=a* / 1-*edani* AMA-*ni ḫaššanteš* "Were you and I perhaps born of one mother?" KUB XXIII 102 i 14-15 (letter to Adad-nirari of Assyria), CREF **[73]**;

(10) *n=an=kan ANA* ^{GIŠ}GIGIR *waggariyanun našma=an=kan* ŠÀ É-*TI* / *waggariyanun* "Did I rebel against him in the chariot, or did I rebel against him in the house?" Ḫattušili iii 67-68;

(11) *nu zikka kuwatqa* / *ŠA* ^{m}*Mašturi iwar iyaši* "Will you perhaps also act like Mašturi?" KUB XXIII 1+ ii 29-30 (treaty, Tudḫ. IV), ed. *StBoT* 16:10f.

(12) ("I said to Mr. Lilawanta: '(If) I go somewhere to His Majesty, what can Ḫešni do to me? He certainly won't strike me!'") ^{d}UTU-*ŠI=ma=wa=mu=kan UL* SAG.DU-*an=pat kuerzi mān=wa UL paimi* "'But won't His Majesty cut my head off, if I don't go?' So L., and I and the grandees went to His Majesty in Ḫattina" KUB XXXI 68:13-14 (letter or inquest), ed. Stefanini, *Athenaeum* NS 40 (1962) 23-26;

(13) [(KUR.KUR.ḪI.A)=*m*]*a ḫūman kuiš ḫarzi* "Who holds all the lands?" KUB XXXI 4 + KBo III 41:12; [...]-*ma ḫūman kuiš ḫarzi natta uk* ÍD.MEŠ-*uš* ḪUR.SAG.MEŠ-*uš* ... [... EGIR-*p*]*a tarmaiškimi* "Who holds everything [...]? Do not I fix the rivers, mountains (and) ...?" KUB XXXI 4 + KBo III 41 obv. 12-13, ed. Otten, *ZA* 55 (1963)158ff.; for another example see **[101]**.

Some rhetorical sentence questions serve as the apodosis of a contrary to fact conditional clause:

(14) [DUMU.LUGAL]=*ma*[*n=wa*]=*naš kuwapi ēšta anzaš=man=wa* / [*da*]*medani* KUR-*e uwawen mān=wa=naš* / [*an*]*zel BELI wekiškiwen* "If we had [a prince] anywhere, would we have come into a foreign land and kept requesting a lord for ourselves?" KBo XIV 12 iv 15-17 (Deeds of Šuppiluliuma, frag. 28), ed. *JCS* 10 (1956) 97f.;

(15) *mān=war=aš=mu=kan šulliyat kuwapi UL* / *mān ḫandan* LUGAL.GAL *ANA* LUGAL.TUR *katterraḫḫir* "If he (Urḫitešub) had not picked a quarrel with me, would (the gods) have truly subjected a Great King to a minor king?" Ḫattušili iii 76-77.

Others introduce a clause giving the grounds:

(16) *kinuna apel* TI-*tar idalawešta* TI-*anza kuit* / *nu nepišaš* ^{d}UTU-*un* IGI.ḪI.A-*it uškizzi* "Has her (i.e., Tawannanna's) life now become bad, just because she is (still) living and sees with her eyes the Sungod of Heaven?" KBo IV 8 ii 18-19 (prayer of Murš. II), ed. Hoffner, *JAOS* 103 (1983)188;

(17) ^{LÚ}ŠÀ.TAM[-x ḪUL]-*luš* [^{GIŠ}ŠÚ.A-*an*] / [*kui*]*š dāiš nu=za UL ešat* LÚ.BANŠUR-*aš* ḪUL-*luš* [^{GIŠ}BANŠUR-*un kuiš*] / [*d*]*āiš nu=za UL ezatta* ^{LÚ}SAGI.A-*aš* ḪUL-*l*[*uš* GAL-*in*] / *kuiš pāiš nu UL ekutt*[*a*] "Is the chamberlain who set [the chair] in place [bad], that you didn't sit down? Is the table man [who] placed [the] table bad, that you did not eat? Is the cupbearer who gave [the cup] bad, that you did not drink?" KUB XXXIII 96 iv 18-21 (= Ullikummi Tabl. I A iv 55-58, *JCS* 5 (1951)160f.).

Negated sentence questions

Negated sentence questions are usually rhetorical questions, which expect a positive answer. Although these are often marked by fronted negation, this is not always the case (contra HE §282c, see Hoffner in *FsGüterbock*^{2} 83-94).

Fronted examples:

(18) *natta=šamaš* $^{\text{LÚ.MEŠ}}$DUGUD *tuppi ḫazzian ḫarzi* "Has (my father) not inscribed a tablet for you dignitaries?" KBo XXII 1 obv. 23 (instructions, OS);

(19) *UL=war=an=kan tuetaza memiyanaz kuennir* "Was it not at your word that they killed it (the Bull of Heaven)?" KUB VIII 48 i 12 (Gilgamesh, NH); the marked (fronted) element in this clause is *UL tuetaza memiyanaz*, which is only interrupted by the sentence enclitic chain;

(20) *UL=an šakti* "Do you not know him ...?" KUB XXXIII 106 iii 36 (Ullikummi);

(21) *UL=kan* ^{LÚ}*TARTENU pariyan uiyanun* "Did I not send the *TARTENU* over there?" KUB XIV 3 i 67 (Tawagalawa letter);

(22) *UL=aš šarkuš* LUGAL-*uš ešta* "Was he not a mighty king?" ibid. i 74.

Non-fronted examples:

(23) *memiyan=w*[*a*]*=tta UL kuiški udaš* "Has no one brought word to you?" KUB XXXIII 106 iii 31 (Ullikummi);

(24) (If a mortal were to live forever, the unpleasant illness of such a man would also continue;) "If I got well," *nu tuel šiunaš uddanta natta lazziyaḫḫat* "did I not get well through your word, O god?" KUB XXX 10 obv. 17-18 (prayer, OH/MS);

(25) *man=at=ši natta kattawatar* "Wouldn't it (then) be a grievance for him?" ibid. obv. 23;

(26) *man zik UL aršanieše* "Wouldn't you be upset?" ABoT 65 rev. 6 (letter, MH/MS);

(27) "Since I heard this affair," *man=an ANA* ŠEŠ-*YA UL AŠPUR* "should I not have written it to My Brother?" ibid. rev. 10;

(28) "But now My Brother, the Great King, my equal, has written to me;" *nu=wa annauliyaš memian UL ištamašmi* "shall I not listen to the word of my equal?" KUB XIV 3 ii 16-16 (Tawagalawa letter).

Neither *UL kuiški* **[23]** nor *UL imma* **[29-31]** are usually fronted.

Because of their emotional content, rhetorical questions often (but not always) employ *imma* "actually, really, indeed" (see Otten apud L. Rost, *MIO* 4 (1956) 332f. and Melchert, *KZ* 98 (1985) 184-205) or *kuwatka* "perhaps" (see KUB XXIII 1+ ii 29-30 cited above):

(29) *n=at=mu ANA* LÚ.MEŠ KUR URU*Ḫatti piran UL imma walliyatar UL kuit ešta* "Was this perhaps not something for me to be proud of in front of the Hittites?" KUB XXI 38 obv. 48 (letter of Puduḫepa);

(30) "If a person brings up a child for the parents," *nu=šši attaš annaš ŠA* UMMEDA *UL imma pai* "will the parents perhaps not give him a nurse's fee?" KUB XIV 7 iv 11-13 (prayer of Ḫattušili III);

(31) *nu=wa=ta UL imma peḫḫi peḫḫi=ta* "Will I indeed not give it to you? I will (certainly) give (it) to you!" VBoT 2:8-9 (letter). For another example of *imma* in a question see **[135]**. for other negative rhetorical questions see **[56, 57, 65, 116, 123, 129, 131, 132, 137]**.

Some **negative** questions do not necessarily assume either a positive or negative answer, but strongly suggest a positive one. This type of question in Hittite is expressed with *nekku*:

(32) *ūk=za neku* DINGIR-*YA tuk kuit iy*[(*anu*)]*n nu kuit waštāḫḫun* "I haven't done something against you, my god, have I? Or sinned in some way, have I?" KUB XXXVI 75 ii 13-14 (prayer, OH/MS) with dupl. 1698/u (+) 221/w ii 12-14, ed. Eichner, *MSS* 29 (1971) 33f.;

(33) KUR-*e=wa nikku kuwapikki ḫarkan man=wa* URU.DIDLI.ḪI.A / *nikku kuwapikki dannateššanteš* / *mān=wa* LÚÉRIN.MEŠ *nikku kuwapikki ḫullanteš* "The land is not destroyed somewhere, is it? The cities wouldn't be devastated somewhere, would they? The troops wouldn't be defeated somewhere, would they?" (If they aren't, then why has this deity come to me?) KUB XXIV 8 + KUB XXXVI 60 ii 16-18 (Appu), ed. *StBoT* 14, 8f. I take both the plene *ma-a-an* and the non-plene *ma-an* in this sequence to be the irrealis *man*.

With interrogative words

The following are some examples of Hittite questions employing interrogative pronouns, adjectives and adverbs. L. Mascheroni (*SMEA* 22 (1980) 60f.) calls these "domande complende" (German "Ergänzungsfragen"), because the reply cannot be merely "yes" or "no", but must supply the information requested ("where, how, why, when").

With maḫḫan *"how?":*

Clause initial:

(34) dIM-*aš* dNIN.TU-*ni tet maḫḫan iyaweni / kištantit ḫarkweni* "The Stormgod said to Ḫannaḫanna, 'What shall we do (lit. how shall we act)? We will die of starvation!'" KUB XVII 10 i 29-30 (Telipinu myth, OH/MS);

Not clause initial:

(35) *nu=wa wattaru māḫḫan iyan* "How is the fountain made?" KBo XXI 22:41-42 (blessings for the Labarna, OH/MS);

(36) *n=an=ši=kan* EGIR-*an* GAM GIM-*an karšmi* "How shall I cut him (the ghost) off from him?" KUB XXXIX 61 i 6-7 (ritual, NS); cf. *CHD maḫḫan* 4 for further examples.

With interrogative pronoun or adjective kui- *"who?" or "what?":*

Clause initial:

kuiš as subject of finite verbal predicate:

(37) *kuiš=war=aš=kan ku*[*enta*] "(King Ḫanteli said:) Who kil[led] them (i.e., his wife and children)?" KBo III 67 ii 4 (Telipinu procl.);

(38) *kuiš=war=an ḫaran* ... URU*Ḫaššuwaz uwatez*[*zi*] "Who will bring the eagle ... from Ḫaššuwa?" KUB XLVIII 99:6-7;

kuiš=war=aš [*namma*] *uškizzi šallayaš* DINGIR.MEŠ-*aš / daššaweš zaḫḫau*[*š*] "Who will [any longer] endure them, the great gods' strong battles?" KUB XXXIII 95 + KUB XXXVI 7b iv 15-16 (Ullikummi), ed. *JCS* 5 (1951) 156f.;

(39) *UMMA ABI ABI-YA=MA* [*kuiš=wa p*]*aizzi UMMA ABU-YA=MA ammuk=wa paimi* "My grandfather said: '[Who] will go?' My father said: 'I will go" KBo XIV 3 iii 9-10 (Deeds of Šuppiluliuma, frag. 14);

(40) *kuiš waštaš* "Who sinned?" (i.e., "Who is at fault?") KUB XXXIII 24 i 31;

(41) [(*kuiš=w*)]*a=kan* DINGIR-*LUM nutarriyaš aruni anda* [*artari*] "What swift god stands there in the sea?" KUB XXXIII 93 iv 30-31 (Ullikummi), ed. *JCS* 5 (1951) 158f.;

kuiš as subject of "to be" clause:

(42) *kuiš=war=aš aši* DUMU-*aš ku*[*in*] *namma šallanuer* ᵈ*Gulšuš* / DINGIR.MAḪ.MEŠ-*uš* "Who is he, this child, whom they raised again, the Fate-Goddesses and Mother-Goddesses?" KUB XXXIII 95 + KUB XXXVI 7b iv 14-15 (Ullikummi), ed. *JCS* 5 (1951) 156f.;

(43) *nu=za kuiš* x[...] / [*anz*]*el* Ú.MUNUS *arḫa wešiškiši* "What kind of [a ...] are you, that you are ruining our meadow by (over) grazing?" KUB XXIV 7 ii 56-57 (Cow and Fisherman story);

(44) (When the barber approaches the gate, the gateman says:) *zik=za kuiš* "Who are you?" KBo V 11 iv 24 (MH?/NS);

(45) [...] / *punušzi kuiš=wa=z zik* [...] '[...] asks: 'Who are you [...]?'" KBo XII 118:12-13 (rit. frag.);

(46) *kuiš=za* MUNUS-*naš zik* "Who among women are you?" KUB XXXIII 86 + KUB VIII 66 iii 3 (Ḫedammu);

kuin as direct object of finite verb:

(47) [*tue*]*ll=a* DUMU.MEŠ-*KA kuin šagain iyanzi* "And what miracle do (i.e., can) your sons perform?" VBoT 58 i 7;

kuit as direct object of finite verb:

(48) *UMMA ŠI=MA* / [*k*]*ī=wa kuit walkuwan ḫašḫun* "Thus she said: 'What mob is this that I have borne?'" KBo XXII 2 obv. 1-2 (Zalpa text, OS), ed. *StBoT* 17;

(49) *kuit=ta memaḫḫi* "What can I say to you?" KBo XXVI 65 iv 23, 25 (Ullikummi);

(50) *kuit iyanun kuit* "What have I done? What?" KUB 31.4 + KBo 3.41 obv. 3 (OH/NS); *takku natta=ma* [(*kuwatqa pai*)]*mi uga kuīt dāḫ*[(*ḫi*)] "If I don't go anywhere, what will I get?" KUB XLIII 25:7-8 (myth) restored from KUB XXXIII 60 and KUB XXXIII 61;

(51) *kuit=wa=šši=kan ŠUM-an* [*teḫḫi*] "What name shall [I put on] him?" KUB XXXIII 93 iii 16 (Ullikummi), ed. *JCS* 5 (1951) 152f.;

(52) ("My father, you built a house for yourself, and you made it a *marnan* high and nine 'bones' wide;") *arḫa=ma=kan kuit datti* "But what will you take away (when you die)?" KBo XII 70 rev.! 12 (proverbs or wisdom text);

(53) [*mān* ᵈUTU]-*un epmi n=an munnami nu kuit iezzi* ᵈIM-*aš* "If I seize the Sungod and hide him, then what can the Stormgod do?" KUB XXXVI 44 i 5-6.

kuit as subject of "to be" clause:

(54) *ini=wa kuit* "What is that?" KBo IX 127 + KUB XXXVI 41 i 12; *eni=ma=wa kuit* KUB XLIV 4 rev. 9;

(55) *uk=uš punuškimi [kī=wa k]uit walkuwan* "I ask them, 'What is this mob?'" KBo III 40:15;

(56) *kī=wa kuit UL=wa ḫarnammar* "What is this? (Is it) not yeast?" KBo VI 34 i 30 (soldier's oath);

(57) *kī=wa kuit UL=wa ŠA* MUNUS TÚG.NÍG.LÁM.MEŠ "What is this? (Are they) not the fine garments of a woman?" ibid. ii 44-45;

(58) *kuit=wa waštul=tit* "What is your problem (lit. sin)?" KUB XXIV 8 i 45 (Appu);

kuit and its noun as subject of finite verb:

(59) *apaš=a pait* dIM-*ni tet kī kuit kišat* "He proceeded to say to the Stormgod, 'What is this that has occurred?'" VBoT 58 i 16 (myth of disappearance and return of the Sungod, OH/NS);

(60) *nu=tta mān* DINGIR.MEŠ *kiššan punuššanzi kī=wa kuit ieššir* dLAMMA KUŠ*kuršaš=wa* dIMIN.IMIN.BI=*ya mukiškir* "And if the gods ask you as follows: 'What is this they have been doing?' They have been invoking the Patron Deity of the *kuršaš* and the Heptad" KBo XVII 105 ii 17-17 (incantation);

(61) *[kui]t=naš=kan* DI-*eššar ištarna kišat* / *kuit=pat* DI-*za arḫa tiyawen nu=tta ḫatreššar kue ḫatreškimi* "What legal dispute has occurred between us? Why have we stepped away from the dispute? And what kind of messages should I keep sending to you?" KBo XVIII 24 i 3-5 (letter to Šalmanezer I), ed. Otten, *AfO* 22 (1968-1969) 112f.;

(62) *kuit=wa ēššatti* "What are you doing?" KBo 2.11 rev. 6 (letter fragment);

(63) *paiši kuit iyaši* "What are you going to do?" KUB 28.4 ii 25 (Moon that Fell from Heaven myth);

(64) *nu* MUNUS.LUGAL GAŠAN-*YA kuit iyaši* "O queen, my lady, what will you do?" KBo VIII 23:17 (letter to the queen).

kuel with noun as subject or predicate (CREF **[131]**):

(65) *nu=za kuel walliyatar UL=za ŠA* dU *piḫaššašši* / EN=*YA walliyatar* "Then whose glory am I? Am I not the glory of the Stormgod *piḫaššašši*?" KUB VI 45+ iii 48-49 (prayer of Muw. II), note that *-za* excludes the translation "Then whose is the glory? Is it not the glory of the Stormgod *p*." found in *ANET* 397f.;

(66) *kuel=wa=kan* ZI-*anza uriš dandukeš=wa=kan* / ZI-*anza uriš* "Whose soul is great? The mortal soul is great." KUB XLIII 60 i 27-28.

kuedani (CREF **[132-133]**):

(67) *kuedani=wa=za menaḫḫanda išḫamiškiši kuedani=ma=wa=za menaḫḫanda* KAxU-*iš IŠTU* I[M.MEŠ] *šunneškiši* "Before whom are you singing? Before whom are you filling your mouth with w[ind(?)]?" KUB XXXVI 12 ii 9-10 (Ullikummi II B), cf. *MGK* 22 for interrogative interpretation; interpretation as relative clauses is also possible;

(68) [*kued*]*ani=war=an peḫḫi aši* DUMU-*an kuiš=war=an=za=an* [*dai*] ... *nu=war=an=ka*[*n* GE_6-*i*] KI-*pi=ya anda* [*kuiš ped*]*ai* "To whom shall I give him, that child? Who will take him ...? Who will carry him off to the Dark Netherworld?" KUB XXXIII 93 (+) KUB XVII 7 iii 27-30 (Ullikummi), ed. *JCS* 5 (1951) 152f.

kuez See below **[145]** for KBo XXI 22:22-26.

With *kuit ḫanda* "why?" (not clause initial):

(69) [d]IM-*š=a tezzi nu=war=an kuit ḫanda UL wemiya*[*tten*] "The Stormgod says: 'So why didn't you (pl.) find him?'" VBoT 58 i 23;

(70) [*uk=uš*] *punuškimi karawar=šet kuit ḫanda lipšan* "I ask [them]: 'Why is its (i.e. the bull's) horn bent/cracked?'" KUB XXXI 4 + KBo III 41:16 (OH/NS), ed. Otten, *ZA* 55 (1963) 156-168.

kuwatta(*n*) and *kuwattan šer*:

Clause initial:

(71) *kuwatta šer* / [... Ḫ]UL-*aḫḫun* "Why should I have harmed [...]?" KUB XXIII 95 iii 16-17 (letter frag.);

(72) *kuwattan šer ḫarnikt*[*eni* DUMU.LÚ.U_{11}.LU-*UTT*]*I* "Why do you destroy [mankind]?" KUB XXXIII 100 + 36 16 iii 10 (Hedammu), ed. *StBoT* 14, 46f.

Not clause initial:

(73) *tuk=ma* ŠEŠ-*tar kuwatta šer* / [*ḫ*]*atrāmi* "Why should I write 'brotherhood' to you?" KUB XXIII 102 i 13 (letter to Adad-nirari I) CREF **[9]**;

(74) *n=aš kuw*[*a*]*tta šer* SIxSÁ-*ri* "Why is (it) determined?" KUB LII 79 iii 18 (oracular inquiry);

(75) [*n*]*u=tta=kkan kuwattan šer* [...] / [...]-*kunuškimi* "Why should I keep [...]-ing you?" KBo XVIII 24 i 17-18 (letter to Šalmanezer);

(76) *eni=za* IZKIM.MEŠ ḪUL.MEŠ *ku-wa-at-tén šer kikkištari* "Why are unfavorable omens occurring?" IBoT I 33:95 (snake oracles).

With kuedani šer *"on what account? why?"*

(77) DUMU.MEŠ LUGAL=*ma kuedani* / [*še*]*r ḫarkiškantari* "Why are the princes dying (i.e., being put to death)?" KBo III 1+ ii 56-58.

With kuwat, kuit *"why?"*

Clause initial:

(78) (The king asked him:) *kuit ueš* "Why have you come?" KBo VIII 42 obv. 4;

(79) *kuit=wa uw*[(*aš*)] "Why have you come?" KBo XXVI 124 (+) KUB XXXIII 24 (+) KUB XXXIII 28 i 38 (myth, OH);

(80) *kuit uwanun* / *kuit tariyanun* "Why have I come? Why have I exerted myself?" KUB XXX 36 ii 2-5;

(81) [*UMMA ŠI=MA ku*]*wat=mu kī tepu paitta* "[She said: 'W]hy have you given me this little bit?'" (KUB XL 65 +) KUB I 16 iii 10;

(82) LUGAL-*uš=a memaḫḫun* / [*kuwa*]*t=war=e akkanzi* "And I, the king, said: '[Wh]y should they die?'" KBo III 1 ii 28-29 (OH/NS);

(83) (The Egyptian queen wrote back to Suppiluliuma I:) *kuwat=wa apeniššan TAQBI appaleškanzi=wa=mu* "Why do you speak that way: 'They are deceiving me'?" KBo V 6 iii 52-53 (Deeds of Šuppiluliuma, fragm. 28 A);

(84) (Pharaoh Ramses II writes to Puduḫepa:) *kuwat=war=an=mu kinun UL pešta* "Why have you not given her (sc. the bride) to me now?" KUB XXI 38 i 8;

(85) *kuwat šara=mu kiššan iyatten nu=mu=šan kī yugan išḫaišt*[*en*] "Why did you (pl.) do thus over me and bind this yoke upon me?" KUB XXXI 4 obv. + KBo III 41:7 (OH/NS); see also [143-144];

(86) *kuwat uwateši* "Why will you bring (them then)?" HKM 37:12 (MH/MS);

(87) *kuwat=wa=du=za attaš=ti*[*n* ...] / *piran markiškanz*[*i*] "Why are they continually finding fault with your father in your presence?" KUB XXXI 66 ii 25-26 (prayer of Ḫattušili III);

(88) *nu īt ANA* [d]*Kumarbi* [(*memi*)] *kuwat=wa* / É-*ri* IGI-*anda ka*[*rtimmiy*]*awanza uit* "Go say to Kumarbi: 'Why have you come against the house in anger?'" KUB XXXIII 102 ii 7-8 (Ullikummi), *JCS* 5 (1951) 148f.;

(89) *kuwa*[*t=wa*] / [*tu*]*ḫḫait* DUMU-*annaza=wa=za tuḫḫiman UL šakti* "Why did you gasp? Gasping in childbirth you do not know" KUB XXXIII 118 left col. 16-17;

(90) *UMMA* [d]*Gilgameš kuwat=wa=mu / kartimmiyattan iyaši* "Gilgamesh said: "Why are you angry with me?'" KUB XXXIII 124 iv 4-5 (Gilg.);

(91) *kuwat=za UL ez*[*atti*] / [*kuwat*] *UL ekutti ammel išḫa=mi* [.. "Why are you not eating? [Why] are you not drinking, my lord?" KBo XIX 112 rev.(?) 8-9 (Ḫedammu);

(92) *kuwat=wa* URUDU-*an kuin laḫun nu=wa=mu appa / ḫurzakizi* "Why is the copper which I cast cursing me?" KBo XXXII 14 ii 53-54;

(93) *kuwat wetenun kuin kuttan nu=mu ḫurzakizi* "Why is the wall which I built cursing me?" KBo XXXII 14 rev. 45; note how the interrogative, which properly belongs to the *nu=mu ḫurzakizi* clause, precedes the relative clause and how the sequence of direct object and finite verb is reversed in these two otherwise parallel relative clauses;

(94) *kuwat ḫaliyatar memiš*[*ta*] "Why did you speak *ḫaliyatar*?" KBo XXXII 16 ii 12.

Not clause initial:

(95) LÚ.MEŠ *ṬEMI-YA=mu kuwat UL uieškittani* "Why are you not sending my envoys (back) to me?" HKM 53:29-30 (letter, MH/MS);

(96) *zik=wa=kan apūn anda kuwat aušta* "Why did you look at that (woman)?" KBo V 3+ iii 71 (Ḫukkana);

(97) *nu kūn memiyan kuwat iyatten* "Why did you do this thing?" KBo III 3 iii 3-4;

(98) *annišan=war=an* / [LUGA]L-*eznanni kuwat tittanut kinun=ma=wa=šši kururiyaḫḫuwanzi* [*k*]*uwat ḫatriškiši* "Why did you previously put him on the throne, and why now are you writing to him to declare war?" KUB I 4 + KBo III 6 + iii 40-42 (Ḫattušili iii 75-76);

(99) *uk=ma=šmaš* / [IGI-*a*]*nda zaḫḫiya kuwat UL paimi* "Why should I go against them in battle?" KUB XXXI 1 + KBo III 16 ii 16-17 (OH/NS);

(100) [*šešu*]*n šumeš=a=wa=mu šašandan* [*kuwat aranutten*] / [*nu=wa=mu š*]*antan ku*[!]*wat memanutten* "I was asleep. [Why did you awaken] me when I was sleeping? [And] why did you make [me] talk when I was sulking?" KUB XXXIII 10 ii 7-8;

(101) *ANA* [LÚ.MEŠ]DUB.SAR.MEŠ *šaḫḫan luzzi / apiya=ma=at kuwat iššai* "Do scribes owe *šaḫḫan* and *luzzi*? Then why is he peforming them there?" HKM 52:13-14;

(102) ŠEŠ.DÙG.GA=*YA=ma=mu / aššul kuwat UL / ḫatraeš / nu=du=za=kan kāša / šanza* "Why did you, my dear brother, not write me your greeting? I am angry with you!" HKM 56:8-12; cf. HKM 56:26-27;

(103) *n=an* EGIR-*pa* / [*k*]*uwat UL pišteni* "Why don't you give him back?" HKM 58:21-22;

(104) KUR ^{URU}*Ḫapalla=wa ŠA* ^{d}UTU-*ŠI kuit* KUR[-*e zi*]*g=a=war=at kuwat datta kinuna=war=at=mu appa* [*pai*] KUB XIV 1 rev. 56 (Madd., MH/MS);

(105) *kuš=kan* / [*ANA*] ^{d}UTU-*ŠI kuwat kuent*[*a* ...] ibid. rev. 81-82;

(106) [*IN*]*A* URU-*ŠUNU* / EGIR-*pa ašišanuškanzi nu kun memiyan* / *kuwat iyatten QATAMMA* "They resettled (them) in their city, and why have you treated this matter in the same way?" KBo III 3 + KUB XXIII 126 + KUB XXXIII 36 (+) 1459/u iii 2-4;

(107) *mān=aš* ^{d}UTU=*ŠI* EGIR-*an šanḫun mān=aš=za* / ^{d}UTU-*ŠI daḫḫun šumeš=ma=aš=za* ZI-*az kuwat* / *daškatteni* ibid. iii 23-25;

(108) *addu=man=ma=za* DAM=*YA ANA* MUNUS.LUGAL *išiyaḫḫiškattallaš* ...[...] / *nu idalu kuitki iyat* MUNUS.LUGAL *apun memian ANA* [....] / EGIR-*pa waštul kuwat iyat* KUB XIV 4 iii 16-18 (prayer of Murš. II about Tawannanna);

(109) *nu* DINGIR.MEŠ EN.MEŠ=*YA* ḪUL-*waš* / *memian kuwat ištamašten* "O gods, my lords, why do you listen to the word of an evil (person)?" ibid. iii 20-21;

(110) *nu=šmaš=aš* ^{LÚ}*EMI-ŠUNU kuit* / [*nu*]*wa memian kuwat šannanzi* "Because he is their father-in-law, why is he still concealing (it)?" KUB XIV 3 i 64-65 (Tawagalawa letter);

(111) [(^{GU4}*Šeriš* ^{d}IM-*ni* E)GIR-*pa memišta* (EN=*m*)]*i kuwat=aš* / [(*ḫurzak*)*iši*] [(DINGIR.MEŠ-*i*)]*š* E N=*mi* / [(*kuwat=aš*) *ḫurzakiši* (^{d}EN.K)]I-*an=a kuwat* / [(*ḫurzakiš*)*i*] "The bull Šeriš spoke back to the Stormgod: 'My lord, why are you cursing them, (namely) the gods? My lord, why [are you cursing] them? Why are you cursing Enki?'" KUB XXXIII 120 iii 30-33 (Song of Kumarbi);

(112) KÙ.BABBAR-*ya kuwat=w*[*a=naš* GUL-*aḫḫiškiši*] / *nu=wa=naš=kan kuwat kuwaškiši* "My Silver, why [are you striking us]? Why are you (trying to) kill us?" KUB XVII 4: 4-5 (Song of Silver);

(113) *ammuk=wa=za duddu :ḫalziḫḫi ŠA* AMAR=*mu=šan* / 4 GÌR.MEŠ-*ŠU kun=ma=wa=za ŠA* 2 GÌR.MEŠ-*ŠU kuwat* / *ḫašun* "I have a complaint! My calf should have four legs! Why have I borne this two-legged thing?" KUB XXIV 7 iii 22-24 (Tale of Cow and Fisherman);

(114) *nu kiššan memai taknaš* ^{d}UTU-*i ki u*[*ttar* ..] / *daškiwani kī* É-*er kuwat tuḫḫaitt*[*a*...] / *šara nepiši kuwat šakueškiz*[*zi*] "Thus s/he says: We take this word/thing from the Sungoddess of the Netherworld. Why is this house gasping? Why does it look up into the sky?" KUB VII 41 i 9-11 (rit. to purify house);

(115) *šumeš=a* TI$_8$.MUŠEN *kuwat UL ḫuškitten* "But you – why did you not await the eagle?" KUB XXXI 101:15.

With *kuwapi* "Where?"

(116) *ŠA* LÚ.GAL.GAL-*TIM* É-*ŠUNU kuwapi UL=at ḫarker* "Where are the houses/estates of the grandees? Have they not perished?" KUB I 16 iii 45 (Political Testament of Ḫattušili I);

(117) *nu kuwapi* [d]UTU-*uš mumiezzi* / [...]-*i=ku ḫappeni=kku* GIŠ-*i=kku ḫaḫḫali=kku mumiezzi* "So where will the Sungod fall? Will he fall into the [...], or the flame(?), or the tree(s), or the brush?" KUB XXXVI 44 iv 8-9 (myth);

(118) EME-*aš* EN-*aš kuwapi pāši* "Where are you going, O lord of the tongue?" KUB XII 62 obv. 10, cf. rev. 3;

(119) EME.ḪI.A EME.ḪI.A *kuwapi=wa paitte[ni]* "Tongues, tongues, where are you going?" KUB XLIV 4 + KBo XIII 241 rev. 22 (rit.);

(120) *kuwapi=war=at andan piddaiškanzi* / [LÚ.MEŠ]*ATḪUTIM* "Where are they running to, (these) brothers?" Ullikummi Tablet II B i 19.

With *kuwapit* "Where? To what place?"

(121) *kuwapit arumen nu* ANŠE-*iš arkatta* "What have we come to, that a donkey will climb? (Expressing incredulity.)" KBo XXII 2 obv. 10 (Zalpa text, OS);

(122) *mān=wa ANA* [d]IM [URU]*Nerik* / *paiwani nu=wa=šan kuwapit* (variant: *kuwapi*) / *ešwaštati* "When we go to the Stormgod of Nerik, where shall we sit down?" KBo III 7 iv 6-7 (Illuyanka myth, OH/NS).

kuenzumna-: only in the lexical entry (Sum.) [ŠU.UŠ.ŠA] = (Akkad.) *MA-AN-NA-ŠU* = (Hitt.) *ku-en-zu-um-na-aš* KBo 1.35+ iv 7 and the broken context [...]-*ši ku-en-zu-um-na-aš-za* / [...] KUB XXIII 95 iii 9 (letter frag.).

maši- and *mašiyant-/mašiwant-*: *CHD* s.v.

Passages with a mixture of interrogative words:

(123) *nu mašieš* MU.ḪI.A *pair* / [*mašieš*]=*a=kan ḫuwair ŠA* LÚ.GAL.GAL-*TIM* É-*ŠUNU kuwapi UL=at ḫarker* "How many years have passed? [How many] have run (by)? And where (are) the houses of the great men? Have they not perished?" KUB I 16 iii 44-45 (Political Testament of Ḫattušili I, OH/NS).

From these examples it is clear that Hittite – unlike English – does not always place the interrogative word first in the clause. On the contrary, the interrogative word sometimes precedes the finite verb as closely as possible. And since the finite verb is usually clause final, the interrogative word gravitates to the end of the clause. In very short clauses, it is usually initial: **[58]** and **[78-80]** and *[kuw]at≈war≈e akkanzi* "why should they die?" KBo III 1 ii 29 (Telipinu procl., OH/NS), ed. *THeth.* 11:30f.; and *[UMMA ŠI≈MA kuw]at≈mu kī tepu paitta* "[Thus she said: Wh]y have you given me this little bit?" (KUB XL 65 +) KUB I 16 iii 10-11 (Political Test. of Hatt. I, OH/NS). If a demonstrative (e.g., *ka-, eni-*,etc.) is in the clause, it will take clause initial position instead of the interrogative: **[56, 57, 59, 60, 76, 105, 106]** but exceptionally **[81]**.

Questions which pose alternatives take a special form in Hittite (Sommer, AU 77f.). The second question of the pair frequently has the form *nu ... ≈ma ...* (but see CHD sub *-ma* a 1' b' 4", where it was shown that the initial *nu* is only optional):

(124) BAL *andurza kuiški* DÙ-*zi* ... *nu* BAL *araḫza≈ma kuiški* DÙ-*zi* "Will someone revolt from inside (the kingdom), or will someone revolt from outside?" KUB V 4 i 33-35;

(125) *nu≈war≈at* ŠEŠ-*YA IDI nu≈war≈at UL≈ma IDI* "Does my 'brother' know it or not?" KUB XIV 3 i 5 (Tawagalawa letter);.

(126) *kuit≈at* ŠEŠ-*UTTA n≈at kuit≈ma / ŠA* ḪUR.SAG*Ammana uwawar* "What is it, (this) 'brotherhood'? Or what is it, (this) 'seeing the Amanus Mountains'?" KUB XXIII 102 i 7-8 (letter to Adad-nirari of Assyria), cf. *AU* 78 and *CHD negnatar*. For indirect alternative questions see **[139-140]**.

A special kind of alternative question is that which is also rhetorical in nature, implying a denial of the stated situation:

(127) DAM-*YA* MUNUS.LUGAL *idalawaḫta kuitki / n≈an tepnutta≈ma kuitki nu≈kan* f*Tawannannaš* DAM-*YA kuendu* "Did my wife harm the queen (Tawannanna) in some way, or did she demote her, so that Tawannanna should kill my wife?" KUB XIV 4 iii 21-22 (prayer of Murš. II).

Indirect questions (*SMEA* 22 (1980) 58ff.) are often formed in conjunction with clauses containing the verb *šak-* "to know" or *auš-/uški-* "to see" or *ḫatrai-* "to write":

Using a form of *kui-* "who? what?":

kuiš as subject:

(128) *UL ša-*[*a*]*q-qa-a*[*ḫ-ḫ*]*i kuiš=aš aši* DINGIR-*LIM-iš* "I don't know who that god is" KUB XXXIII 106 iii 44 (Ullikummi); ed. Güterbock, JCS 6 (1952) 28f.;

(129) *šumeš=wa* [D]INGIR.MEŠ *UL uškatteni* / *kiššan=wa=mu kuiš iyan ḫarzi* "Don't you gods see who has done this (literally 'thus') to me?" KUB LIV 1 i 20-21 (deposition, NH).

kuit as direct object of finite verb (CREF **[59-64]**):

(130) *nu kāš kui*[*t*] *memai n=at zik šakti ziga kuit* [*mema*]*tti n=at kāš šakki*(!) (text *-ti*) "You know what this one says, and this one knows what you say" KUB XXXV 148 iii 12-13 (rit. of Zuwi, NS), cf. *CHD* s.v. *maniyaḫḫa-*.

kuel (CREF **[65-66]**):

(131) *nu* DINGIR.MEŠ *UL* / [*šekteni k*]*uel=aš dammešḫaš* "O gods, don't [you know] whose is the injury?" KBo IV 8 iii 3-4, ed. Hoffner, *JAOS* 103 (1983) 188.

kuedani:

Clause initial (CREF **[67-68]**):

(132) *nu=za* ŠEŠ-*YA* KUR URU*Karanduniyaš UL IDI kuedani=*(*y*)*at ilišni* "Does my brother not know Babylonia, in which rank it is?" KUB XXI 38 i 56 (letter of Pud. to Ramses II), ed. Stefanini, *AttiAccTosc* 29 (1964) 13 and W. Helck, *JCS* 17 (1963) 91f.

Not clause initial:

(133) KUR URU*Wiluša=ma ANA* KUR URU*Ḫatti kuedani* LUGAL-*i awan arḫa tiyat nu memiyaš kui*[*t*] *ištantanza n=an UL šagga*[*ḫḫi*] "Since the incident occurred long ago, I don't know from which Hittite king Wiluša defected" KUB XXI 2 + KUB XLVIII 95 i 6-9 (Alakš. treaty), ed. *SV* 2:50f. (without join piece).

kuit maḫḫan in indirect questions has been treated in *CHD* sub *maḫḫan*, and the formula in letters has been discussed by Hagenbuchner in *THeth.* 15: 71. Example:

(134) *MAḪAR* dUTU-*ŠI* / *MAḪAR* MUNUS.LUGAL *aššul* / *kuit* GIM-*an* / *nu=mu ABI* DÙG.GA-*YA* / EGIR-*pa ŠUPUR* "Write back to me, my dear father, how it is with His Majesty and with the queen" KBo XVIII 4:8-12 (letter of King of Išuwa).

Using *kuwapi* "where?":

(135) *kišan=mu kuit ḫatrāeš* / *kāša=wa* LÚ.KÚR *uit* / *nu=wa=za=kan* URU*Ḫaparan iniššan* / *tamašta* URU*Kašipuran=ma=wa=kan* / *kez tamašta apāš=wa=kan* / *ištarna arḫa uit* / *namma=ma=wa<r>=aš kuwapi pait* / *nu=war=aš UL IDI* / *nu apāš* LÚ.KUR / *alwanzaḫḫanza imma* / *ešta n=an UL* / *šākta<<-aš>>* "(Concerning) what you wrote me as follows: 'The enemy has come and has besieged the city Ḫapara on that side, and has besieged the city Kašipura on this side; and he has passed through (and gotten away). But I do not know (text: 'he does/did not

know') where he was going.' Was that enemy perhaps bewitched, that you did not know him?" HKM 6:3-14 (MH/MS), ed. *HBM* 126-129;

(136) *kuwapi=wa paiši ammuk=ma=wa=tta le šaggaḫḫi* "Wherever you may go, I don't want to know about you (*-ta* lit. you)" KBo V 9 ii 44-45 (Dupp. treaty), ed. SV 1:18f.

Using *maḫḫan* "how?" CREF *maḫḫan* mng. 3:

(137) *zik* ᵈ*IŠTAR* ᵁᴿᵁ*Nenuwa* GAŠAN-*NI UL šak-ti* KUR ᵁᴿᵁ*Ḫatti* GIM-*an dammešḫan* "Don't you know, *IŠTAR* of Nineveh, our Lady, how the country of Hatti has been oppressed?" KBo II 9 i 38-39 (prayer in a rit., NH);

(138) *ḫantezziuš=ma=at* LUGAL.MEŠ *maḫḫan arḫa pittalair n=at* ᵈUTU ᵁᴿᵁPÚ-*na* GAŠAN-*YA šakti* "How the earlier kings neglected it (i.e., Nerik), you, Sun Goddess of Arinna, my Lady, know it" KUB XXI 27 + 676/v + 546/u i 16-18 (prayer, NH), ed. Sürenhagen, *AoF* 8 (1981) 108ff.; cf. ibid. i 43.

Indirect questions which pose alternatives take the form *mān* ... *mān* ... (HE §333, Mascheroni, *SMEA* 22 (1980) 58 and *CHD* sub *mān*):

(139) (Since Urḫi-Teššup is there,) *n=an punuš mān kišan mān UL kišan* "just ask him if (it is) so or not" KUB XXI 38 i 11-12 (letter of Puduḫepa to Ramesses II);

(140) *nu UL šagga[ḫḫun] mān=za* LUGAL KUR ᵁᴿᵁ*Mizri ANA* [*ABI*]-*YA edaš ANA* KUR.KUR.MEŠ *šer ar*[*kamma*]*n iyat mān=za UL kuitki* [*iyat*] "I don't know if the King of Egypt has rendered tribute to my father for those lands or if he has rendered nothing" KUB XXXI 121a ii 9-12; cf also KUB XXXI 121 iii 12-15.

The following are examples of short, abrupt questions (*AU* 122, 174):

(141) *nu namma kuit* "So now what?" KUB XIV 3 iv 20 (Tawagalawa letter);

(142) *nu kuit iššanzi* "And what are they doing?" KUB XXIX 1 ii 5; *kuit apāt* "What is that?" ibid. ii 37.

As negated statements which continue through more than one clause omit the negation after the first clause (Sommer, Heth. 2:8 note 3; Götze, Hatt. 93; e.g., "(As malt has no ability to germinate,) *UL=an* AŠÀ-*ni pedanzi n=an* NUMUN-*an* / *ienzi* "they don't carry it into the field and use it as seed" KBo VI 34 ii 33-33), so interrogative words which continue their force in succeeding clauses may be discontinued:

(143) *n=ašta* DINGIR-*LIM-ni* [*:zuwan kuw*]*at* KAxU-*it parā ḫuittiyatteni* / *n=an=za* [*arḫa*] *datteni* "Why are you drawing out [food] from the mouth of the god and taking it [away] for yourselves?" KUB XIII 4 ii 16-17 (instructions for priests, pre-NH/NS);

(144) *kuwat=wa / weškiši nu=wa=ta=kan šuppayaza / [ša]kuwaza išḫaḫru para arš[zi]* "Why are you weeping, and tears flow out of your holy eyes?" KUB XVII 9 i 20-22 (Gurparanzaḫu story). See also example **[85]**.

Finally, it may be helpful to cite a few passages where a series of questions and answers are given, to show how questions worked in dialogue:

(145) *ḫāš nu kuez uwaši šuppaz=wa uwami / nu=wa kuez šuppayaz zaḫanittennaz=wa / nu=wa kuez zaḫanittennaz* ᵈUTU-*waš=wa* É-*az / nu=wa kuez* ᵈUTU-*az ešri=šet=wa* GIBIL-*an* GAB-*ŠU* GIBIL / [...]-*ZU=wa* GIBIL-*an* LÚ-*tar=šet=wa nēwan* "Soap, where are you coming from? From the holy (place)! From what holy (place)? From the cult room (*zaḫanittenna-*)! From what cult room? From the Sungod's house! From what Sungod? The one whose form is new, whose chest is new, whose [...] is new, (and) whose penis (lit. manhood) is new!" KBo XXI 22:22-26 (blessings for the Labarna); a parallel passage in KUB XX 54 + KBo XIII 122:1-10 has an Old Woman asking the questions, and a DUMU É.GAL answering with "we" forms of the verbs. The change of speakers is also indicated by the insertion of *UMMA* ... formulas.

Questions enliven discourse, and Hittite texts are richly seasoned with them. This brief study is presented with the hope that it will help Hittitologists to more readily recognize them in texts, and comparative linguists to see how the Hittites formed them.

LYCIAN CONSONANTAL ORTHOGRAPHY AND SOME OF ITS CONSEQUENCES FOR LYCIAN PHONOLOGY

THEO P.J. VAN DEN HOUT

1.1 The importance of Hieroglyphic Luwian and Lycian among the 'minor' Anatolian languages has enormously increased over the years.* The often painstaking struggle of several generations of scholars, boosted by extraordinary finds like the Karatepe bilingual and the Xanthos trilingual, has resulted in a situation where these languages can now be studied in their own right and where they are of invaluable help to further our understanding of the still less well known members of the Anatolian branch: cuneiform Luwian and Lydian. Founded on the work of such eminent scholars as Pedersen, Meriggi and Laroche, one of the pillars of Lycian studies most certainly is Philo Houwink ten Cate's *The Luwian Population Groups of Lycia and Cilicia Aspera during the Hellenistic Period* (Leiden). Treading in the footsteps of Jan Six and going far beyond the confines of an onomastic study, he offered in this, his originally 1961 dissertation at the University of Amsterdam, reprinted already in 1965, the first full-fledged Lycian Grammar. Today, almost 35 years later, it is still the most comprehensive description of the Lycian language.

The evidence of an alphabetically written language like Lycian can be of particular importance for the historical phonology of the Anatolian languages where the inadequacy of the cuneiform and hieroglyphic writing systems is clearly felt. The more so, since Lycian was embedded in the Hellenistic Greek and Persian world of that time, so that we find many Lycian names transposed into Greek or Old Persian and vice versa, thus providing us with invaluable information on how Lycian must have 'sounded.' The Lycian script and ortho-

* Research for this article was made possible through a fellowship of the Royal Dutch Academy of Arts and Sciences. I would like to thank Profs. H. Craig Melchert and C.J. Ruijgh for their stimulating criticism and valuable remarks. As became even more clear when Melchert's *Anatolian Historical Phonology* (Amsterdam/Atlanta, GA 1994) appeared, in many cases we independently reached the same conclusions. As far as was still possible, references to this important book have been worked into the text of this contribution. When the manuscript for the present contribution had already been finished, Dr. I. Hajnal (Zürich) very kindly sent me the chapter on Lycian consonantism from his important forthcoming book *Der lykische Vokalismus*. I am happy to say that his conclusions, too, largely coincide with Melchert's and mine.

graphical system, however, still pose problems. Although a standard transliteration seems to have been reached by now (with *k* for K and *x* for Ɣ) the orthography still looks puzzling. Spelling matters are often only mentioned in passing, if at all, and some authors explicitly question the reliability of Lycian orthography, thereby implicitly undermining any conclusion one might want to draw from Lycian for the Anatolian language group as a whole. R. Schmitt, for instance, in his excellent study on Iranian names in Lycian, writes: "allerdings sind ... die orthographischen Normen des Lykischen, soweit solche überhaupt anzunehmen sind, zu wenig bekannt."[1] Making a virtue of necessity, G. Neumann admits there is no orthographical norm thus opening the way to use variant spellings within Lycian for the study of its phonetics.[2] This question, whether there was an orthographical norm in the Lycian writing system and, if so, what it means for our understanding of Lycian phonology, can only be answered through a detailed and primarily internal analysis of all extant material. Such an analysis will be undertaken here. In order not to exceed the limits of a Festschrift contribution I will restrict myself to consonants, i.e. stops and obstruents (fricatives, sibilants and resonants). It is with immense gratitude that I dedicate this small study to my teacher, colleague and friend Philo Houwink ten Cate.

1.2 "Elision and the doubling of consonants lend Lycian its characteristic appearance" Philo Houwink ten Cate wrote.[3] Anyone, who ever glanced in E. Kalinka's corpus of Lycian inscriptions, *Tituli Lyciae*,[4] or in J. Friedrich's transliterations in his *Kleinasiatische Sprachdenkmäler*, must have been struck by such spellings as *prñnawate, hlm̃mi, Xzzbãseh* or *Trqqñti*. Two almost contradictory tendencies seem to be fighting for precedence here, vowel reduction and doubling of consonants. It is clear from within Lycian itself that such consonant clusters mostly involve some resonant (*m/m̃, n/ñ, r, l*) and that those resonants must have had a strong sonantic value. But still, to a Greek or Persian ear, it may have seemed as if "the vowel sounds of Lycian were dominated by the consonants to the point where they were strongly muted or virtually indistinguishable as separate sounds, and took what shade and colour they had from the particular consonantal contexts in which they appeared."[5] However, to attribute sonantic value to certain consonants like *k* or *t* because of such correspondences as *Katamlah* = Ἑκατόμνω or *Tẽnegure* = Ἀθηναγόρας,[6] is

1 *FsNeumann* 372.
2 *HbOr*. 375.
3 *LPG* 110.
4 In the following all references to this work will be to text numbers unless explicitly ("p.") marked as a page number.
5 T.R. Bryce, *Kadmos* 26 (1987) 94.
6 So T.R. Bryce, *Kadmos* 26 (1987) 93.

unnecessary as well as phonologically unlikely. To explain the most difficult among these consonant clusters, i.e. the geminated consonants in Anlaut (*tteri*, *ppuweti* etc.), A. Heubeck reconstructed for some of them reduplicated presents which had subsequently lost their vowel by vowel reduction.[7] For #*dd*-, however, he considered the possibility of a sound separate from a single written *d*[8], as had done H. Pedersen before him.[9] Parallel to Sturtevant's law for Hittite and Cuneiform Luwian, Laroche suggested that *zz* might be a voiceless phoneme, *z* a voiced one.[10]

The question of these consonant clusters in both An- and Inlaut has been addressed for the first time, it seems, by Moriz Schmidt in 1868[11] followed by Pedersen in 1899, who formulated the main rule that a consonant after a consonant is always written double except for after nasals.[12] A summary of Pedersen's findings was given and somewhat elaborated upon by Kalinka, TL p. 4-5 ("*De consonantibus duplicatis*"). At the outset it is stated there that in the doubling of consonants not so much a law as a certain pattern (*norma quaedam*) can be observed. Whereas in Anlaut and between vowels consonants are sometimes geminated and sometimes not, *nulla causa aperta*, a consonant following another consonant is almost always (*semper fere*) geminated. Exception is made for nasals that are never geminated themselves, unless to *ñn* and *m̃m*, and after which consonants never geminate. The letters *b* and *l* are almost never (*fere non*) doubled either, except after *r*. The letter *h* is written double only once by mistake; *k*, ◇, τ, *j*, *w* and *r* are never geminated either. Kalinka concludes his summary by saying that, although this 'norm' is most often neglected in the Milyan or Lycian B inscriptions (*in titulis non vere Lyciis* (44. et 55.)), it was generally applied even where more consonants come together like in *Ddapssm̃ma*.

Apart from the obvious question whether all this still holds good after more than 90 years and almost 30 new inscriptions and graffiti[13], the description of this alleged 'norm' lacks precision (witness the repeated *fere*) and leaves room for several uncertainties (e.g. are *bss* and *dpp* as much possible as *zxx* and *pdd*?). More importantly, the system is only described but no attempt at explaining is undertaken. In the following paragraphs we will pass in review all clusters of consonants including liquids, nasals, sibilants and the pharyngeal(?) *h*. Only *j*

[7] *KZ* 98 (1985) 44.

[8] *KZ* 98 (1985) 37-38.

[9] *LH* 42: "Einen anderen Laut muss *dd*- ausdrücken; ein langes *d*?"

[10] *FdX* 6, 100.

[11] *The Lycian Inscriptions after the Accurate Copies of the Late Augustus Schoenborn with a critical commentary and an essay on the alphabet and language of the Lycians*, Jena-London-Paris 1868.

[12] *Nordisk Tidsskrift for Filologi*, 3. Raekke, 8 (1899) 85-87.

[13] Numismatic inscriptions not included.

and *w* are left out of consideration because they do not figure in any cluster at all. A distinction is made between clusters containing a resonant (§ 2; *r, l, m/m̃, n/ñ*) and those without (§3). Then, 'simple' geminates either in Anlaut or in intervocalic position will be discussed. The results of this internal Lycian evidence will then be confronted with the phonological information provided by Aramaic, Greek and Persian correspondences. We will conclude with general remarks on the Lycian consonantal system. The corpus used for the present phonemic-graphemic relational study[14] is the same as the one that served as a basis for H.C. Melchert's invaluable *Lycian Lexicon* (second fully revised edition) supplemented only by some readings from O. Mørkholm - G. Neumann, *Die lykischen Münzlegenden* and the additional coin legends as given by O. Carruba in the *Akten des II. internationalen Lykien-Symposions*, 21. The distinction between non-onomastic and onomastic material will be maintained more rigorously, though, than in the said *Lycian Lexicon*. This analysis is thus based on the entire extant Lycian (A) material. Although Lycian B (Milyan) is not taken into consideration here, a survey of the material as given in Melchert's *Lycian Lexicon*[15] reveals that it roughly adheres to the same orthographic system.

1.3 The Lycian script offers for labial, dental and dorsal consonants twelve graphemes which are nowadays mostly transliterated following the system of Pedersen and Laroche (in brackets the transliteration according to the Arkwright-Kalinka system):

labial	*p*	*b*			
dental	*t*	*d*	*θ*	*ᴛ*	
dorsal	*k* (*c*)	*g*	*q*	*x* (*k*)	*β*, ◇ (*κ*)

Of these we may leave aside the graphemes ᴛ, β, and ◇ as rare (and possibly chronologically and/or locally conditioned) variants of *t*, Greek κ/Lyc.B *b*, and *k* respectively.[16] The grapheme *g* is an allophone of *x* and is relatively rare as

14 From the viewpoint of methodology S.-T. Teodorsson's *The Phonetic System of the Attic Dialect 400-340 B.C.* (Lund 1974), 46-66, has been very helpful. For a critical assessment of his results see C.J. Ruijgh, *Mnemosyne* 31 (1978) 79-89 (= C.J. Ruijgh, *Scripta minora ad linguam graecam pertinentia*, edd. J.M. Bremer, A. Rijksbaron, F.M.J. Waanders (Amsterdam 1991), 651-661).

15 Appendix 2: Milyan Word List, 115-130.

16 The grapheme ◇ is found in five inscriptions (54, 69, 106, 128 and 149). Apart from *ᴛezi* (72) and the name *Mñneᴛeide* (36,5) all instances of ᴛ come from the Xanthian pillar TL 44; the alleged **ᴛezi* (so Melchert, LL 63, 72) is an emendation of *sieti* as read by Kalinka, TL p. 16, and Friedrich, *KlSpr.* 55. It is important to note that TL 44 belongs to the oldest datable inscriptions, viz. ca. 400, cf. Houwink ten Cate, *LPG* 5 n. 9, Demargne, *FdX* 5, 113, Laroche, *FdX* 6, 54, and Bryce, *The Lycians* 46; Carruba, *ASNSP* 8 (1978) 849-850, characterizes both

well.[17] The remaining graphemes can be arranged in their transliterated form as follows:

liquids	*r*	*l*		
nasals	*m*	*n*	*m̃*	*ñ*
sibilants	*s*	*z*		
pharyngeal?	*h*			

The nasal graphemes transliterated as *m̃* and *ñ* have strong sonantic value as is immediately apparent from such variants like *Lusñtre*/*Lusãñtre*/ *Lusãtre* = Λύσανδρος.

2. *Consonant clusters involving resonants*

2.1 If we consider that writing to be the norm which is found most frequently[18], we can set up the following basic rules. Clusters with two, three or four consonants mostly involve either a nasal (/N/) or a liquid (/R/). For two- or three-consonant clusters (e.g. *ml* or *rbb*) these combinations can be divided into two pairs, either the resonant preceding the consonant (/NC/ or /RC/) or the resonant following the consonant (/CN/ or /CR/):

— the nasal preceding the consonant is always written with its allograph </Ñ/>: </ÑC/>
— the consonant in /RC/ is doubled to </RC_1C_1/>
— the nasal in /CN/ is 'doubled' resulting in the graphemic sequence </CÑN/>
— the liquid following a consonant is written single: </CR/>.

Clusters of three or more consonants (e.g. *qñt* or *hrpp*) occur mostly with the resonant in the middle: /CNC/ or /CRC/:

— in case of a nasal (/N/), its allograph </Ñ/> appears, and the consonant following this nasal is always written single: </CÑC/>
— in case of a liquid (/R/), the consonant following the liquid is always written double: </CRC_1C_1/>.

In the following we will review the non-onomastic and onomastic material for these clusters and their exceptions.

◇ and τ as "segni arcaici per suoni non più esistenti o in via di sparizione." β is attested on the same pillar TL 44 as well as on the new Xanthian trilingual N 320; according to Laroche, *FdX* 6, 57, its appearance may be due to foreign, that is, Carian influence.

[17] Cf. Carruba, *ASNSP* 8 (1978) 860, 864-865 and Schmitt, *FsNeumann* 386 with n. 73; see also Melchert, *HS* 105 (1992) 189-191.

[18] Cf. S.-T. Teodorsson, *The Phonetic System*, 49-50.

Two- or three-consonant clusters in non-onomastic material

2.2 In the cluster /NC/ we virtually only encounter (-)*ñt-*, either at the beginning of a word (e.g. *ñtata* "grave, sarcophagus") or within (e.g. *qãñti* "they (will) destroy"); only once *-m̃t-* is attested in *zẽm̃tija* (44a,41) and *ñk* in (*me=*)*ñke* "(and) when". The nasal is always written single with its allograph </Ñ/>: </ÑC/>. Anomalous seems to be only *ñzzijaha* in 29,8 where **ñzi*° is expected. The "odd phonology" is already recognized by Melchert, *LL* 50; it is not even sure whether it is an appellative or a name.

Mention should be made also of those cases where the nasal is graphically expressed by way of the nasalized vowels *ã* and *ẽ* (</ṼC/>). Except for such vowels preceding dentals (frequent in 3. plur. verb forms)[19] and nasals, we may add for *ẽ* the combinations *ẽk* in *ẽke* "when" and *ẽz* in *telẽzije-* "headquarters." Both *ã* and *ẽ* are once attested before *h* in *ebãhã* (148) and *ebẽhẽ* (44a,18). A real deviation seems to be *hãxxati* 84,4 (3. sing. pres.) with the geminate *xx* after the nasalized vowel.

2.3 In the cluster </RC_1C_1/> we find both *r* and *l*, and as a rule the consonant following that liquid is written double, e.g. *erbbe* "battle(?)", *xultti* "?" (3 sg.pres.). Three exceptions are known to me:

— *arsez*.[..] 35,19 "?" in broken context; the possibility of a personal name cannot be altogether excluded. A spelling **arssez*° is expected.

— *t[a]rb⸢i⸣de* 44a,46-47 "?"; this is the reading as given by Kalinka and Friedrich but the passage is heavily damaged as indicated. The traces, however, do not favor a restoration to **tarbb*°.

— *xalte* 29,12 "?" (3 sg.pret.); the expected double writing of the consonant following the *l* can be seen in this same inscription (29,5) in the 1 sg.pret. of the same verb, *xalxxa*. Compare also *xultti* 84,5.

For].*partai*(-)*sedi* 44b,33 see below among the names. The reading of the combination *-rn-* in *sernitẽ*, given by Kalinka and Friedrich for the inscription 20,1, is too dubious to be considered here. The room between individual letters in the first line of this inscription even makes the assumption of two letters to be restored uncertain. Equally uncertain in its reading is the combination *rt* in *xñtaibañazrtum*[N 323a,2, a graffito on a phiale.[20]

2.4 In the combination consonant + nasal (/CN/), the nasal is written double with its allograph </Ñ/>: </CÑN/>; e.g. *asñne* "to do" (inf. of *as-* "to do, make"), *tupm̃me* "two(fold), pair". Such a double nasal is excluded, however, at the end

19 For occasional denasalization of such vowels before dentals see A. Garrett, *HS* 105 (1992) 203.

20 Cf. Neumann, *Neufunde* 50-52, Carruba, *FsMeriggi*^{2}, 92.

of a word. Here the second nasal element is dropped; compare, for instance, the acc.sg. of *s*-stems (*arusñ*, *tuhesñ*), the acc.sg. of the indefinite pronoun *tise* "whoever, anyone" (*tisñ*), *qehñ* (next to the abl. *qehñnedi*) and *terñ*.

2.5 In the combination consonant + liquid (/CR/) both elements are written single, e.g. *atla-/atra-* "self, person". The same rule applies in case the consonant is a nasal, e.g. *mluhidaza-* (some profession) or *esẽ]nemladi* "?" (abl.). The only exceptions here are the nouns *tllaxñta* "payment, salary"[21] and *hruttla* "?". The former is found in the Xanthos trilingual N 320,19-20, derived according to Laroche, *FdX* 6, 69, from the verb *ttlei-* "to pay", always attested with *ttl*Vº; this writing, therefore, is best taken as a mistake for **ttlaxñta*. For the geminate *tt-* in Anlaut see below 4. The latter, *hruttla* (131,3), is isolated and obscure.

Two- or three consonant clusters in onomastic material

2.6 Clusters of the type /NC/, graphically expressed as </ÑC/>, are most frequently represented by (-)*ñt-*, either word initial (e.g. *Ñtarijeus*(*e*/*i*) = Darius, cf. R. Schmitt, *IPN* V 4, 24 s.v.) or in Inlaut (cf. *Xexxebẽñti*). There is one instance of *-ñz-* in *Xsseñzija*; for *-ñp-* see the following remarks on *Arttum̃para*. The labial nasal *m̃* is attested in combination with *p* in *A m̃pu*[.]*eu* and *Arttum̃para-* (='Αρτεμβάρης, cf. R. Schmitt, *IPN* V 4, 18-19) with twice the variant spelling *Artuñpara*/*i-* (for the *-rt-* see below 2.7) on the coins M 302, M 231c. This cluster *m̃p* is also attested word initially in *M̃parahe* 104b,3 (gen.sg.). According to a suggestion originally made by A. Torp[22] and recently again put forward by A. Keen apud Melchert, *LL* 100, this could be an abbreviated form of *Arttum̃para*/*i-*. Although this cannot be ruled out from a contextual point of view (104b,2-4 *Gasabala* : *ẽke* : *ese* : *Perikle* :/ *tebete* : *Arttum̃parã* : *se M̃parahe* :/ *telẽzijẽ* "When Gasabala with? Perikles besieged? Artumbara and Mpara's headquarters"), this would be an isolated example of an abbreviated name outside the numismatic material. Moreover, this type of abbreviation would be unusual within Lycian, since abbreviations always run from right to left: compare the name *Kuprlli* where each abbreviated variant between *Kuprll* and *Ku* is actually attested. The occasional dropping of a vowel in Anlaut (e.g. (*E*)*seimija*, (*E*)*katamla*) is probably not to be interpreted as a form of abbreviation. For *Mpara-* = Ιμβρης as a Carian name see Houwink ten Cate, *LPG* 14, 104 and 222.

[21] Erroneously cited as *ttlaxñta* by A. Heubeck, *KZ* 98 (1985) 40.

[22] *Lykische Beiträge* 2, 10.

The anomalous writing to be found in this group is in the name *Winbẽte* (26,15): instead of *n* one would have expected at least *ñ* (if not *m̃*).[23] Moreover, it is the sole example for *b* in this position.

For the group of names where the sequence /NC/ is spelled </ṼC/> the following combinations can be cited as not being found written </VÑC/>: *ãs/ẽs* in *Ahamãsi* and *Mẽsewe, ãz* in *Asawãzala* and *Murãzah, ãk* in *Ãke,* and *ẽl* in *Ebẽla.* These writings are all conform to the rule of a consonant being written single after N. Exceptional are the names *Idãb* (or *Idẽb*) M 26[24] and *Q/ñtbẽddi* 5,2-3[25]: not only because of the geminate after the nasal *ẽ* in the latter but also because after a nasal the only labial and dental used are *p* and *t.*

2.7 Besides the numerous clusters of the type /RC/ with doubling of the consonant to </RC$_1$C$_1$/> (cf. *rbb, rKK, rll, rm̃m, rñn, rpp, rss, rtt*; </*l*CC/> does not seem to be attested, for a possible example see below), there are some rare examples of *rs* and *rz*:

— *Ursejetẽ* 29,13; although the handcopy by Heberdey given in TL seems to leave no doubt as to the reading of this name, the previous copies of Arkwright and Kalinka and the latter's transliteration (cf. TL p. 27) clearly attest to the uncertainties, especially at the beginning of the word.

— *Erzesinube* 111,1 (a priest).

— *Parza* 44c,14 "Persian"; in the same inscription the correct spelling *Parzza* (44c,2) occurs as well. The restoration of *Pa*[ ]*a* (40d,1-2) to either *Pa*[*rzz*]/*a* or *Pa*[*rz*]/*a* is debated, cf. the remarks by Kalinka, TL p. 36; Laroche, *FdX* 5, 139, reads *Pa*[*rz*]/*a*.[26]

The alleged *A*]*rmaxutaw*[.] (63,1) can be read *A*]*rm̃maxutaw*[, as is clear from the handcopy on TL p. 58. There seems to be too much space between the

23 It should be reminded at this point, that the Lycian script lacks a nasal variant for the vowel *i* as opposed to the pairs *a/ã* and *e/ẽ* Apart from few exceptions (see below) the vowel *i* seems to appear before a written nasal only in an open syllable (e.g. *seine, tideimi, Tuminehi*), in a closed syllable the nasal is usually not expressed in the script, which accounts for the 3. plur. verb forms in *-iti/e* = /*-inti/e*/; cf. Morpurgo Davies, KZ 96 (1982-1983) 253. In this respect, the consistent spelling (for *mitti* 42,4 see Laroche, FdX 5, 134) of the word *miñti-* with *-iñ-* is quite surprising. The names *Uwiñte* (120,2) and *Uwitahñ* (28,4) might thus be forms of the same name (but not necessarily of the same person).

24 Apud O. Carruba, Akten Lykien 21, cf. ibidem 15.

25 Theoretically, this name might also be read **Qñtbãddi*, the signs *ã* and *ẽ* having merged in this inscription; for this merger in younger inscriptions see Laroche, FdX 6, 56.

26 A similar case is the restoration of *Wat*[ ]*ata* 40d,1 to either *Wat*[*aprdd*]*ata* (thus Imbert, cf. Kalinka TL p. 36, followed by Melchert, *LL* 111) or *Wat*[*aprd*]*ata* (thus Friedrich, *KlSpr.* 62, followed by Schmitt, *FsNeumann* 382, und *IPN* V 4, 26 n. ***). According to the drawing in A.H. Smith, *The Nereid Monument and Later Lycian Sculptures in the British Museum. Catalogue of Sculpture in the Department of Greek and Roman Antiquities* IV,2 (London 1900) Plate XI, there seems sufficient space to accomodate the expected spelling *-aprdd-*.

r and *m* for the reading given in Kalinka, TL, and repeated since, while there is enough for the reading proposed here. Traces of the two lower 'legs' of the X (= *m̃*) can still be discerned with the right one pulled up higher than the one on the left, as can be observed more often; cf., for instance, the graph X in 68,1 in the name *Arm̃palitxa.*

There is one possible example of a sequence *lp* in the name that is read as *E[lp]eti* by Kalinka, TL 23,2, and Friedrich, KlSpr. 57. G. Neumann, *Or.* 52 (1983 = *FsKammenhuber*) 131, reads *El[puw]eti*, followed by Melchert, LL 100. As Kalinka remarks, the traces between the first *E*- and -*eti* at the end are highly dubious with, at least theoretically, more room than for just two letters. The inscription, on the other hand, sometimes shows large spaces in, what seems to be, the middle of words. Of course, the restoration by Neumann (op.cit. 131 n. 5) is based on the Greek name Ελποα(τ)τις. Because of its fragmentary state and because of the fact that the signs are lost exactly after the *l*, this name is best left out of the discussion.

Only once a stonemason made the mistake of writing a consonant three times after *r*, viz. in the dat.sing. of the genitival adjective of the Persian name *Arpppaxuhe* (77,2b).

Contrary to what was said about the combinations </RC$_1$C$_1$/>, the cluster -*rt*- behaves quite differently. As opposed to the rare exceptions, just discussed, to the general rule stated above, there is among the onomastic material a clear majority of spellings -*rt*- versus -*rtt*-. Next to *Arttum̃para*- (four times), *Erttimeli*, *Hurttuweti*- (twice), *Parttulaj*[.]*mi*, and *Xawartta*-, we find the following names with -*rt*-:

— *Artum̃/ñpara-* M 231a-c
Ãmartite M 13
Ddawãpartah 101,1
Ertaxssirazahe 44b,59-60
Ertelijeseh 120,1[27]
Ertelẽmeli- 44c,8, N 311,1
Pertinah 82
Pertinamuwa 66,1
Spparta° 44b,27 and 44, c 2-3?[28]
Urtaqijahñ 25,6 (= Ορτακια)
Xertubi 108,2.

To the attestations for *Spparta*° we may tentatively add the hapax]*epartai*(-)*sedi* attested only once in the same inscription 44b,33, where the reading (*e*) of the first sign immediately after the break is not assured. I propose to read *S*]*p*?*partai*(-)*sedi* instead. Friedrich, *KlSpr.* 65, took it as two words with *sedi* as

27 For this name cf. Neumann, *Or.* 52 (1983 = *FsKammenhuber*) 130.

28 *Sp/*[*par*]*talijahe*, or is the break at the beginning of line 3 long enough for *Sp/*[*part*]*talijahe*?

the conjunction (*se=*) followed by enclitics (*=d=i*): "and it/them to him"(?). Melchert's interpretation of this sequence as one word in the abl. might find support in the immediately following abl. *truwepeijadi*, but would imply the assumption of a Lyc. B/Milyan genitival adjective form at this point.

2.8 In the cluster formed by a consonant + nasal (/CN/) realized as </CÑN/>, the onomastic material offers no real surprises. Sometimes, the consonant preceding the nasal is a nasal itself as in *Erimñnuha*. Doubling of the nasal is the rule, e.g. in *Ddepñnewe* or *Erm̃menẽni*. Here, too, we see the dropping of the second nasal only in Auslaut: *Lusãñtrahñ*, *M̃ẽmrezñ*.

The only real deviation from the rule seems to be the name read by Friedrich as *Abaqmˀãme* in 29,10. The main copy given by Kalinka gives *Abiqmˀãme*, but the additional copies (as of line 10), reproduced there, by Arkwright and Kalinka himself read *Abaˀ.mãme* (Arkwright) and *Abaqmm̃me* (Kalinka). If the latter reading were correct, one could see in the cluster *-qmm̃me* the scribe's attempt to correct himself after writing the wrong *m* following the *q*: in that case, the name should have been spelled *_Abaqm̃me_. In view of the uncertainties surrounding this particular name as well as TL 29 as a whole, it seems better to refrain from further speculation.

For the apparent exception *A]rmaxutaw[* see the remarks already made above sub 2.7. The restoration in 112,2 to *Ada[m̃]mñnaje* by Kalinka, TL p. 79, and Friedrich, *KlSpr*. 82, is likely to be incorrect, because one would expect *_Adamñnaje_ (compare *Erimñnuha*); only a vowel would seem to fit in the gap. Slightly deviating is *Padrñma* 49, next to *Padrm̃ma* (three times) and *Padrãma* (once). Uncertain, finally, in its reading seems to be [.]*xnahetub*/[(= gen. in *-he* of a name followed by a form of the verb *tub(e)i-* "to strike") in N 325,7' apud Bousquet, *FdX* 9, 186; according to the photo[29] both the *n* and the *a* cannot be considered as secured readings.

2.9 Finally, there is the cluster of a consonant + liquid (/CR/) with the two phonemes being expressed each by a single graph, e.g. *(H)erikle* = Ηρακλῆς, *Pigrẽi*. The place of the consonant can be taken by a nasal as seen in *(E)katamla*. The only real deviation seems to be *Eppleme* (16,1) with dittography of the first element of this cluster. Twice we encounter a sequence (-)*pll-*; one of these, *Kuplli* M 124b, is an obvious mistake (rather than a numismatic abbreviation) for *Kuprlli* with regular doubling of the *-ll-* after *-r-*. The other example, *Pllewih<e>*, also found on a coin[30], is regarded by Neumann

29 Bousquet, *FdX* 9, vol. 2, Pl. 76.1.

30 Cf. O. Mørkholm apud Neumann, *KZ* 92 (1978) 129-130.

and Mørkholm as a syncopated form of *Pillewi*, derived from the city name *Pille*.[31]

Three- and four-consonant clusters in non-onomastic material

2.10 As was already stated shortly above (2.1), in case of a nasal (/N/) in a sequence /CNC/, its allograph </Ñ/> appears, and the consonant following this nasal is always written single: e.g. *xñtawata-* "kingship", *tisñke* "whoever", *tm̃peri* "?".

2.11 In case of a liquid (/R/) in a sequence /CRC/, the consonant following the liquid is always written double: e.g. *hrppi* "on, for", *plqqa* "?".

There are few exceptions to this rule which in most cases can be explained as scribal mistakes in view of the overwhelming amount of examples constituting the norm:

— *ãxrhi* "?" 29,4; because of *ãxrahis*, acc.pl. of the same word (N 318,4), an *a* (**ãxrahi*) may have been left out by mistake. Double written *hh*, moreover, is not attested after consonants nor after liquids but only between vowels (see below 4). As we observe time and again, this same inscription TL 29 shows a number of orthographic peculiarities, which, apart from the fragmentary state of preservation, suggest that a stonemason not too familiar with Lycian orthography worked on this sarcophagus.

— *hrmazaxa* "?" 29,8 (1 sg.pret.); although the letters involved (⸢*rm*⸣) are damaged, there is no need to doubt Kalinka's copy of this inscription at this point (see the remarks on the preceding word). The correct spelling would have been **hrm̃mazaxa*, as found in the noun which served as the basis for this derived verb, *hrm̃ma(n)-* "land section, temenos", attested four times. Because of the incorrect spelling Meriggi, *Declinazione* 1, 439, suggested to read *hamazaxa*.

— *hrpi* "on, for" 4,2, 88,2; twice written with single *p* instead of *hrppi* which occurs over 90 times.

— *przis* "front-, foremost" 26,10 (acc.pl.c.); the other forms of the stem *przze/i-* are all written *przz°*.

— *trbẽtadrazata* "?" 134,3 (nom.-acc.pl.n.?); probably compound with first part *trbbe/i-* "counter-, against". All other attestations of this stem and its derivatives show a spelling *trbb°*. The same inscription 134 has one obvious mistake in line 1, where instead of **meñne* we find *meñje*.

The transliteration]*laxrti* "?" of Xanthos inv. 6244+5606, 2 apud Bousquet, *FdX* 9, 194 with Pl. 82.1, seems doubtful, Melchert, *LL* 38, reads]*laxati*.

[31] Cf. Mørkholm - Neumann, *Münzlegenden* 26.

Three- and four-consonant clusters in onomastic material

2.12 The onomastic material adds four more exceptions to the combinations dealt with in 2.10-11:
— *Kuprli* M 125 rev., name of the ruling dynast at Xanthos during the first half of the fifth century B.C., outside the Xanthos stela (TL 44) and N 324 attested on numerous coins either written in full or in various abbreviations. Apart from the abbreviation *Kuprl* (M 204c) and the obvious mistake *Kup<r>lli* (M 124b; cf. 2.9) all non-abbreviated forms have the spelling *Kuprll*°.
— *Pñntreñni* 102,3, left unchanged by Kalinka, TL p. 75, but emended by Friedrich, *KlSpr.* 80. Normally we find this name spelled as *Pñtre/ẽñni.*
— *Trqas* "Tarḫunt, the Stormgod" 93,3; in view of the other attestations of this name (five times nom.sg. *Trqqas*, five times dat.sg. *Trqqñti*) most probably a mistake for regular *Trqqas*. Melchert, *LL* s.v. *Trqqñt-* lists 80,3 as a possible example for the spelling with single *q* as well, but the restoration in the curse formula in the latter inscription is not entirely certain:

80,2 ... *me ne* / (3) [ ]*as tubidi*
"and [ ]as shall strike him!"

Judging by the handcopy in TL, there seems to be room for two letters or two and a very short letter in the break, but hardly for *[*Trqq*]*as*, *q* occupying relatively much space. So, in spite of the parallel passage 83,15-16 (*mene* : *tubidi* : *Trqqa* / *s*) and 93,3 (*mẽne Trqas tubidi*), discussed here, this attestation must remain inconclusive.
— *Zabrxah<>* "of/belonging to Zabrxa" N 313c (gen.sg.); graffito on bottom of a scyphos dated to the second half of the fifth century BC. The fact that it was probably not written by a professional scribe may account for the defective spelling.

Three- and four-consonant clusters involving resonants other than </CÑC/> or </CRC_1C_1/>

2.13 The exceptions to the observation that all clusters of three and four consonants are of the type /CNC/ or /CRCC/, i.e. having the resonant in second position, are *ñxr*-and *sttr*- in the non-onomastic material. The relevant forms are: *ñxrahidijẽ* and *sttrat*[...]. The latter combination conforms to the rule by which *t* geminates after a number of consonants (see below 3). Although not violating any 'rule', the cluster *ñxr*- in the hapax *ñxrahidijẽ* "?" 29,2 is surprising. The first three signs are damaged, but the reading — judging by the handcopy — seems sufficiently certain to take it serious. Unfortunately, the context admits of no clear interpretation; the possibility of a name does not seem likely, though. Melchert, *LL* s.v., suggests a loanword ("old woman") from Greek γραΐδιον.

Formally, the latter is a diminutive of the much later (first centuries AD) attested γραίς, whereas γραΐδιον itself is found from the fifth to the third century BC, predominantly in the language of the comedy, so that the translation "old hag" (*LSJ*) seems quite suitable. This, among other things, may have prompted A. Keen (apud Melchert, *LL*) to take the word as referring not to any old woman but to "female spirits of death." However this may be, foreign influence, because of the strange sound combination, may be appropriate.

As in 2.1 above, we have to consider here also those cases where the nasal is expressed by way of a nasalized vowel (*ã* or *ẽ*). Here, too, we encounter Ṽ*x* in *pddẽxba*.[32] The combination *ãkb* is attested in *qñnãkba* "?".

2.14 Among the consonant clusters in the onomastic material involving either a nasal, liquid or both, but not in middle position surrounded by consonants or other resonants, there is, first of all, a group of personal names with a cluster *ñtr*, all of Greek origin: *Ala/ixssañtra-* ('Αλέξανδρος), *Lusañtra-* (Λύσανδρος), and *Milasãñtra-* (Μελήσανδρος). To this we may add the five attestations of the ethnic adjective *Pñtre/ẽñni-* "from the Pandaros deme(?)."[33] Interesting are the variant spellings of *Lusañtra-*: *Lusñtra-* and *Lusãtra-*, both conform to Lycian orthographic rules. Although the cluster *ñtr* does not violate any such rule either, we may conclude that such a sequence, not being found in the non-onomastic material, was apparently strange to the Lycian language.

The same may be true for the other clusters that, however, do not conform to Lycian orthography. These are attested in the following personal names: *Arm̃pa-/Arm̃palitxa-, Ddẽñtmi-, Ertllẽni-* and *Tettm̃pe.*

— The first two, *Arm̃pa-* (69,1) and *Arm̃pa!litxa-* (68,1) must have been a real dilemma to the Lycian scribe or stonemason. On the one hand, the *-m̃-* might have been expected to be written *-m̃m-* after *-r-*, but this convention seems to be overruled by the fact that *-m̃m-* can only be followed by a vowel. Thus, both *-rm̃p-* and the not attested **-rm̃mp-* run counter to Lycian spelling rules.[34] It is interesting to note that the actual confusion of the scribe might indeed be tangible in the emended reading *Arm̃pa!litxa-*: in spite of the apparently damaged surface of the stone the handcopy clearly shows *Arm̃pplitxa*![35]

— For *Ddẽñtmi-* M 234a one would have expected **Ddẽñtm̃mi-*, with characteristic 'doubling' of the *-m-* to *-m̃m-* after a consonant and before a

[32] For the possible meaning of this word ("local Ḫebat"?) and its analysis as a compound with the divine name *Xba-* = Ḫebat, see the remarks by E. Laroche, *FdX* 6, 115 n. 11 with literature.

[33] See, however, the sceptic remarks of E, Laroche, *FdX* 6, 75-76, whose main objection is that the suffix -(*ẽ*)*ñni-* is added only to toponyms and not to personal names.

[34] Neumann, *Or.* 52 (1983 = *FsKammenhuber*) 129, tentatively compares 'Greek' Αρυνβασις; so already J. Sundwall, *EN* 55.

[35] For this name see also below 8.

vowel.[36] However, another coin of the same weight (M 234b) bears the variant writing *Ddẽñtim* (cf. also M 234c *Ddẽñt*), which Melchert, *LL* 100, convincingly interprets as abbreviations for a name **Ddẽñtimi-*.
— The name *Ertllẽni*[37] also occurs on a coin (M 211), for which one would expect a writing **Erttlẽni*. The spelling of the double *-tt-* in *Tettm̃pe* in 75,1 only makes sense if a vowel has been left out, e.g. **Tettẽm̃pe*.[38] So in both cases a mistake has to be assumed.

In conclusion we can state that, while *Ddẽñtmi* is an abbreviated form for **Ddẽñtimi-*, the other words contain clusters of consonants which were not common to the Lycian language and that as such they caused the stonemasons trouble. Sometimes they do conform to the rules (*-ñtr-*), more often they do not (*-rm̃p-*, *-rtll-*, *-ttm̃p-*).

For those words where a nasalized vowel (</ṼC/>) is found instead of a nasal itself, we add *ãkb* in *Xãkbi-*, the city of Κάνδυβα, and *ãxr* in the personal name *Idãxre* = Ιδαγρος.

2.15 At this point we may briefly discuss the name read by both Kalinka, TL 113, and Friedrich, *KlSpr*. 82, no. 113, as *Urssm̃m*[..]. This spelling would be correct with the regular doubling of the *-ss-* after *-r-*, and the doubling of *-m̃m-* before the vowel that is likely to be restored (cf. Friedrich: "*urssm̃*[*mah*?]"). Kalinka's handcopy, however, shows a completely different spelling: *Urrsm̃e*?[..] as was already noted by Zgusta, *KPN* 383 (§1113 with n. 67[39]). Arkwright, according to Kalinka's comments to the inscription, apparently first thought of reading *Uras-*, but then changed to *Urss-*. The letter *a* in this inscription has a characteristic form with its horizontal bar protruding to the right[40], which is not seen in the third letter of this name; this looks more like another *-r-*: *Urrs-*. Finally, the last letter before the break is drawn as a regular *-e*[but emended into *-m̃*[. Note that the stonemason making this inscription probably at first left out the name of the grave owner, Pttarazi, but then added it right above *Urrsm̃e*[, as if to insert it there; cf. Friedrich who transliterated it between the verb *prñnawatẽ* "built" and the restored gen. "*Urssm̃*[*mah*?]" "(son/descendant) of U."

36 **Ddẽñtm̃mi* was actually read by E. Babelon, *Traité des Monnaies Grecques et Romaines* 2, 303 no. 421 (Paris 1910), and repeated by Friedrich, *KlSpr*. 90 under no. 188. This reading is corrected by O. Mørkholm - G. Neumann, *Münzlegenden* 28, who explicitly state that there is no trace of *-m-*.

37 Not "*Erttlẽni*" as read by Neumann, *Or*. 52 (1983 = *FsKammenhuber*) 130.

38 For this name cf. Neumann, *Or*. 52 (1983 = *FsKammenhuber*) 128.

39 See also R. Schmitt, *FsNeumann* 375.

40 For the form see the table given by Laroche, *FdX* 6, 54, under "Formes rares" second variant.

3. *Consonant clusters not involving a resonant*

3.1 Besides the two-, three- and four-consonant clusters discussed up to now (</(C)ÑC/>, </(C)RC_1C_1/>, </CÑN/>, </(C)CR/>), there are other combinations as well. It is here that we encounter such spellings as *eb/ptte, kbatra, pzziti, tdi* and *zxxa-*. Within the non-onomastic material there seems to be a fairly clear cut distribution of graphemes appearing in second position in such a cluster, either written double, single or not figuring at all in that position.

The following graphemes are written double after a consonant: *p, q, t*, θ, *x* and *z*. The following combinations can be observed:

hpp	*hqq*	*btt*	*xθθ*	*hxx*	*pzz*
		htt		*zxx*	*xzz*
		ptt			
		stt			
		xtt			

All the above combinations are followed by a vowel, except for *stt-* and *xtt-* which are found before a consonant as well. The sequence *hpp-* is attested before *ñ* only (see below); *hppi* 111,2 is an obvious mistake for **hrppi* "for", already emended since Thomsen.[41] A cluster *sttr-* occurs in *sttrat*[44b,18, possibly a Lycian rendering of Greek στρατηγός; for *xttb-* we have the four attestations of the nominal stem *xttba-* "harm(?)." Although both damaged, the attestations for *hppñterus* "?" (58,5 *hp*⌜*p*⌝*ñterus* and 139,4 *h*[*p*]*pñter*[) support each other mutually. All three spellings (*hpp-*, *sttr-*, *xttb-*) can be regarded as regular according to the norm, with geminated *tt* and *pp* after a preceding consonant and the single written *r* and *b*; for the latter see below 3.3. Just for the sake of completeness *sttq* in the graffito on the phiale N 323a,1 should be mentioned; its reading and interpretation (name?) are not assured however.[42]

The hapax "*hqqadijedi*" 44a,37-38 (Kalinka, TL p. 42: "hqq[ad]i ..- / d]i", Friedrich, *KlSpr*. 64: "hqq*adi*[je-] 38 [d]i") must be read *hqqda*⌜*i*⌝[..] / [*d*]*i* according to the handcopy. Meriggi[43] took it as a name, (*A*)*hqqadi*, where the *a* and *d* had inadvertently changed places. The cluster *hxx* is attested only in the compound *aladehxxãne* 57,5.[44]

41 Cf. Kalinka, TL p. 78 ad 111.

42 See Neumann, *Neufunde* 50-52; Carruba, *FsMeriggi*[2], 93 takes it as a name.

43 *FsHirt* 2, 278.

44 The alleged second attestation 112,4 (cf. Melchert, *LL* 4 s.v. *alaha-*) is extremely dubious. Kalinka, TL p. 79, following Arkwright, read *alade*[*hãne*, Friedrich, *KlSpr*. 82, had *alade*[*h*]*x*[*ãne*, Melchert, *LL* 4, *aladehxxãne*; as far as the handcopy allows, the word can be read with reasonable certainty up to *alade*[.?]*x*, with traces of three more signs following before a complete break of several signs. The first of these cannot be either *ã* or *x*, but rather

One might add *s* to the letters being doubled, because of the repeated writing *xss-*, but this combination only occurs in the Persian loanword *xssaθ/drapa-* "satrap' and its derived verb *xssaθrapaza-* "to be a satrap" (cf. Old Persian *xšaçapāvan-* "satrap" < Iranian **xšaθra-pā-van-* "Reichs- oder Herrschaftsschützer", see Schmitt, *FsPalmer* 373-390). For this apparent non-Lycian combination see below in the onomastic section (3.2).

The *b* in first position only occurs in the adjectival gen. *ebttehi-* "their" of the demonstrative *ebe-* "that" as a variant spelling of *epttehi-*, and once (*ebtte* 107a,2) in the paradigm of *ebe-* itself; on this combination see below 6.

Sole exceptions to the situation described here are *xpã* 108,1 and *xzuna* "?", 35,14. The former is evidently a mistake for *x<u>pã*.[45] Concerning the latter, we see the word recurring in line 18 of this same inscription, written *xzzuna* with the expected double *-zz-*. The cluster *xs* in *axsãtaza* 149,3 may not be a scribal error: the word was already emended by Kalinka, TL p. 92 into *axãtaza* (cf. *axãti-* "?"), because he suspected that the alleged *s* was in fact a crack in the rock surface. Correct in its second part but mistaken in the first is the cluster *pptt* in *apptte* "he took" 29,9; consequently, this should be emended into *ap<<p>>tte*.[46] The same may be true for [*q*]*a*[*ss*]*tt*(*ebi*) 84,3 (so read by Kalinka and Friedrich; but Melchert, *LL qastt°*), if read correctly.

3.2 In the onomastic material *p, q, t, x* and *z* are geminated after a consonant as well (e.g. *Ixtta*, *Musxxa-* and *Xzzubeze-*); double *θθ* is not attested. Double *ss*, like in *xssaθrapa-* (see above 3.1), is found several times after *x*: *Ertaxssiraza-* (cf. R. Schmitt, *IPN* V 4, 21-22), *Turaxssi-*, *Wa/exssere-* and maybe *Waxssepddimi-* (cf. R. Schmitt, op.cit. 26 with n.*, 27; see also below 3.4), *Xelijãnaxssa-* and *Xssẽñzija-*. It seems to represent either Old Persian *xš* (*xssaθrapa-*, *Ertaxssiraza-*, *Wa/exssere-*) or Greek ξ (*Xelijãnaxssa-* = Καλλιάναξ). Three times we encounter *-ss-* after *p* in *Krupsse-*, *Pssure-* and *Ddaps*[!]*sm̃ma*. The first *s* in the latter word has an irregular form if compared to the one immediately following and the other examples of this graph in the same inscription. No likely, alternative reading seems to present itself, however.

looks like *t* inspite of the strange sequence resulting from it. The sign now read as *x* cannot be *ã* (thus Arkwright-Kalinka): compare the *ã* in *alahãti* ibid. 5.

45 Emended already in Kalinka, TL p. 77, and Friedrich, *KlSpr.* 81.

46 The restoration of *tijap*[.]*di* in 94,3 remains problematic. Melchert, *LL* 4 s.v. *app-* suggests either *ap*[*p*]*di* or *ap*[*d*]*di* "he takes/will take", the traces in Kalinka's handcopy TL p. 72, however, seem to allow of neither. A spelling **appdi* is, at any rate, not to be expected; **apddi* or **ap*V*di* might be possible, although a 3. sing. pres. **apddi* next to the preterite *a<<p>>ptte* instead of **aptti* would require explanation. The lemma in the *LL* should therefore better read *ap-*.

Double *pp* is found in the derivations *Sppartali-, Sppartazi* of the name **Spparta-* (for the spelling *-rt-* here see above 2.7), in the Persian name *Wizttasppa-*, and in *Xpparama*; double *qq* is attested in *Zisqqa.*

Most of these combinations are followed by a vowel; followed by a consonant as well we encounter *ptt-, spp-, -stt-, xss-*, (-)*xtt-* and *xzz-*. A cluster *pttl-* occurs twice in the names *Pttlezẽi* (10) and its dative *Pttlezeje* (143,4). Like in the non-onomastic material *stt* is found followed by *r* in *Zimasttrah* (59,2); besides this *Sppñtaza* is attested, mainly on coins, the linguistic origin of which – either Persian or Anatolian – is debated.[47] The combinations with *x* (*xss-*, (-)*xtt-* and *xzz-*) all involve *b*: *Hrixttbili* (22,1), *Xssbezẽ* (25,2) and *Xzzbãseh* (sic[48], 19,2). In all these cases the orthographical norm is upheld; for the single *b* after </*x*C_1C_1/> see below 3.3.

Deviations from the orthographical norm in this category are *Arm̃pa!litxa* (for which see above 2.14 and below 8) instead of *-*txxa*, as well as *Stemaha* (127,1)[49] and *Xisterija* (19,2) with *st* instead *stt*. Completely enigmatic is the coin legend *z-a-xxh* M 14.[50] Whether or not it is read as one word or more, the sequence *xxh* would only make sense in its reversed order **hxx*.

3.3 Of the other letters seen in second position, we are only left with *b* and *d*. The former of these seems to be written single as a rule; the following combinations are found:

hb *kb* *sb* *xb* *zb*.

The only exception is *kbbidã* 147,4 in completely damaged context, which in view of the numerous examples for *kb-* (cf. the attestations for *kbatra-* "daughter", and *kbi-* "other"), can be considered anomalous.

The difference in behavior between *b* on the one hand and the geminated *t, q, x* and *z* on the other is not conditioned by the preceding consonants: with the exception of *k* and *p*, the same consonants (*h, s, x* and *z*) for both groups occur in first position.

Confusing, however, are the combinations involving *d* in second position. Here we find:

47 See the discussion in R. Schmitt, *IPN* V 4, 25 s.v. with literature.

48 So according to handcopy, erroneously read **xzzbãzeh* by Kalinka, TL 19, and so listed in *LL* with a gen. in *-ah*.

49 Kalinka, TL p. 85, followed, it seems, by all subsequent scholars, read *Stamaha*; Melchert, *LL* 109, however, reads *Stemaha* which seems better according to the handcopy.

50 This reading seems to be missing in *LL*.

kd	*pd*	*sd*	*td*	
	pdd		*tdd*	*xdd.*

Whereas the writings *esde* "?" 118,4, and *kduñ* "?" 90,3[51], both hapax, stand isolated, the combination *td-* occurs four times in the dat.-loc.sg. *tdi* and *tdike* of the relative pronoun *ti-* "who, which" and the indefinite pronoun *tike* "some, anyone" respectively. The once occurring *tdeime* 42,4 is an obvious lapsus scribae for *tideime* "for (his) children" and was already emended by Kalinka, TL p. 36, and Friedrich, *KlSpr*. 62.[52] Of the two examples for *tdd-* one is *tddi* (apud E. Laroche, *FdX* 6, 117 line 2, with Planche XV), most probably to be interpreted as the 3 sg.pres. of *ta-* "put, place", for which we usually find *tadi*. The resemblance of the letters Α and Δ may plead for *tddi* as a mistake for *tadi*. The other example is *tddẽñta* "?" 29,11.

The one occurrence of *pd-* in *pdẽxba* 102,3-4 (*pd / ẽxba*), on the other hand, seems an exception because of *pddẽxba* in N 309c,6 and the numerous attestations of other words derived from *pddẽn-* "place" (*pddẽn-*, *pddãt-*, *pddãti-*), all written with initial *pdd°*. The division of the word over two lines (*pd / ẽxba*) may be held responsible for what seems a defective spelling. The cluster *xdd-*, finally, is attested in the hapax *xddazas* acc.pl.c. "slaves" in the Lycian trilingual from Xanthos N 320,20.

We thus end up with a possible opposition of *kd, sd* and *td* versus *pdd* and *xdd.*

3.4 For single written *b* in names compare the above (3.2) discussed clusters *xssb, xttb* and *xzzb*. No double written *b* after consonant is found. Geminated *-dd-* is, again, only found after *p*: *Pddalãxñta* and *Waxssepddimi*[53].

4. *Geminates in Anlaut and between vowels*

4.1 Now that we have seen the various types of consonant clusters involving two or more different consonants, we finally should take a closer look at the smallest clusters, i.e. the intervocalic geminates and those in Anlaut: </VC_1C_1V/> and </#C_1C_1V/>. We will refer to them with an, admittedly, somewhat contradictory term as 'simple' geminates.

[51] The irregular sonantic nasal *ñ* at the end of the word after a vowel may be due to the — without word divider (:) — immediately following *tijãi*: *kduñtijãi*.

[52] Laroche, *FdX* 5, 134, also takes into account the possibility of a mistake by the modern copyist.

[53] For the last name cf. R. Schmitt, *IPN* V 4, 26 n.*; according to Carruba, *Akten Lykien* 12 (with lit.) this name should be read *Waxsserddimi*.

It can be observed immediately that, as opposed to the vast majority of single written consonants including sibilants, resonants and glides (compare intervocalically e.g. the many verbforms 3 sing. and plur. in -V*ti/e* or -V*di/e*, all the ablatives in -V*di* etc.), only a limited number of such geminates occur. Below a list of all such geminates in the non-onomastic as well as in the onomastic material known to me is given. The number of attestations is indicated and distinction is made between Anlaut (<#C_1C_1->[54]) and Inlaut (<-C_1C_1->). References will only be given if considered necessary, in most cases the reader is referred to Melchert's *Lycian Lexicon*.

4.2 'Simple' geminates in the non-onomastic material:

		-bb-	1x: *ebbehi* 124,6-7[55]
#dd-	10x: see LL	*-dd-*	5x:]*taddi plm̃maddi*, *se=dde* 44b,47, 51, c,9[56]
#hh-	1x: (*meij=eseri-/*)*hhati* N320,40-41[57]	*-hh-*	2x: *alahhãti* 11,3, *ala⌜h⌝?ha*[*di*] 134,2[58],
		-ll-	1x:]*xalle* 44a,11[59]
#m̃m-	10x: see LL and one occurrence s.v. *ẽmi-* "my".	*-m̃m-*	14x: *a/ãm̃mãman-* (6x), *zum̃m°* (8x).
#ñn-	1x: *ñnemle* as variant of *ñtemle*.	*-ñn-*	114x: *ebẽñnẽ*, *esede/ẽñnewe-*
#pp-	4x: *ppuwe/ẽti*		

[54] For most of these see already the article by Heubeck, *KZ* 98 (1985) 36-46.

[55] Emended to *e/«b»behi* in Kalinka, TL p. 84, and Friedrich, *KlSpr.* 84.

[56] The attestations 44b,29 (*señnahijedi dde*), c,6 (*pddãti / ddewẽ*) and 9 (*se ddewe*) have not been included here because it cannot be ruled out that we are dealing here with separate words (cf. *ddewezehi–*, *ddewi-*) instead of particles. If so, they belong to the left column of the above table.

[57] Heubeck, *KZ* 98 (1985) 43-44, and Laroche, *FdX* 6, 76, take *=eseri-hhati* as a compound of the verb normally known as (-)*ha-*, because of the unique writing (-)*hh-*, however, Morpurgo Davies, *KZ* 96 (1982-1983) 253 n. 23, considers the possibility of a different verb.

[58] The traditional emendation of *alahhãti* to *alahãti* with Kalinka, TL p. 5 ("++ perperam scriptum esse omnes consentiunt", cf. also ibid. pp. 19, 20 and Friedrich, *KlSpr.* 56), was questioned by Heubeck, *KZ* 95 (1981) 160, and *KZ* 98 (1985) 43. Compare also the isolated]*hh*[without word divider on fragment 6072, 3 of N 325 (Bousquet, *FdX* 9, 187).

[59] For the restoration to *erixalle* combining 44a,5-6 and 11 see Laroche, *FdX* 5, 144 and 146; although the reading of the first part of this word may not be absolutely certain, the double intervocalic *-ll-* seems assured.

#tt-	17x: *ttãna/e* (3x), *ttaraha, ttazi, tteri-, tti-* (2x), *tt*[!]*laxñta, ttl*(*e*)*i*-(8x)[60]	*-tt-*	12x: *ebette* (8x), *ebettehi, epatte, epenẽtijatte,* (*sede*)*≈tti*
#θθ-	2x: *θθe-*	*-θθ-*	3x: *laθθi-* (2x), *punamaθθi*
#zz-	4x: *zzati* (2x), *zzimaza-* (2x)	*-zz-*	2x: *azzala-*

'Simple' geminates in the onomastic material:

#dd-	18x: see LL.	*-dd-*	1x: *]addeh* 95.1
		-ll-	2x: *Mullijeseh, Urebillaha*
#m̃m-	1x: *Mmije*	*-m̃m-*	2x: *Un*[.?]*ab*[.?]*ãm̃me* 44c,11[61], *Mam̃mahaje*
		-ñn-	5x: *Mlããnazi, Qañnuw*[!]*ili, Uñna, Xuñnejẽi* (2x[62])
#pp-	1x: *Ppebẽñti*		
		-qq-	1x: *Meqqese[*
#ss-	4x: *Ssepije, Ssewa/e* (3x)		
		-θθ-	9x: *Leθθi, Teθθiweibi* (w. var., 7x), *Tiwiθθeimija*
		-xx-?	1x: *Xexxebẽñti*[63]
#zz-	5x: *Zzajaa, Zzala* (4x)	*-zz-*	9x: *Idazzala* (2x), *Kizzaprñna* (3x), *Pizzi, Plezzijeheje, Wazzije, Wezzeimi*

4.3 As already stated above, these 'simple' geminates are relatively rare, and where larger figures are attested, these occur — in the case of intervocalic 'simple' geminates — in very few lemmata: compare e.g. the fourteen occurrences for -V*m̃m*V- in only two words (*a/ãm̃mãman-* "fine, penalty(?)"and *zum̃m*° "?"), the hundred and fourteen occurrences for -V*ñn*V- in the two words *ebẽñnẽ* (93x not counting the emended attestations) and *esede/ẽnnewe-* "descendancy" or the nine out of twelve attestations for -V*tt*V- in the lemma *ebe-* "that". These same words, on the other hand, show that within one lemma such spellings were apparently very consistent. In fact, only in the case of *]taddi*

60 The alleged **ttadi* (see LL 66 s.v. *ta-* with question mark) can be restored to [*x*]*ttadi* with Neumann, *Neufunde* 26.

61 Since Kalinka the word has been given as *unabãmme*, and the breaks in the inscription are supposed to have never been filled in. Note, however, that Arkwright's remarks (apud Kalinka, TL p. 45a) to that effect only concerned the lines 12ff.

62 118.1, the second attestation in this line seems to have -*]ñmijeje*.

63 Reading by Friedrich, *KlSpr*. 59, uncertain.

plm̃maddi, -dde and *alahhãti* (/*alahhadi*) variant writings can be observed: e.g. *alahat/di* is the more frequent variant of the latter, and if the sequence]*taddi plm̃maddi* indeed contains two ablatives, one may question the correctness of these spellings in view of the overwhelming majority of ablatives with single *-d-*. In the case of *-dde*, on the other hand, Melchert, *LL* s.v., rightly asks whether this is the same particle *-de* with single written *d*. Among the intervocalic 'simple' geminates within the onomastic material variation with single consonants can only be seen in *Mula* and *Mulese* versus *Mullijeseh*, the three occurrences of *Teθi-* versus *Teθθi-* in *Teθθiweibi*, and *Wazijeje* versus *Wazzije*.

The same applies mutatis mutandis for the 'simple' geminates in Anlaut: these, too, are relatively rare although less consistent. Variant writings are attested for *hhati*, if this is the same verb as in *alaha-*, for *ttãna/e* versus *ta/ãne* "to put" (inf. of *ta-*), *ttaraha/tteri* versus *teteri-* "city" and *ppuwe/ẽti* versus *puweti* from the verb *puwe-* "to inscribe". It is important in this respect to stress the fact, that in contrast to what is sometimes stated[64], *#*d*V- is not attested: all instances of initial single #*d-* in Kalinka's index I (TL p. 98 middle column) have to be analyzed differently as clearly emerges from Melchert's *LL*.

Initial 'simple' geminates were studied by Heubeck, who on the sole evidence of the variant spelling *tteri-* of the noun(!) *teteri-* posited a present reduplication for all verbal forms with initial 'simple' geminates. No apparent semantic difference, however, could be established in case of pairs like *puweti/ppuweti*. Moreover, commonly accepted examples of reduplicated presents, like *pibi-* "to give" and *tideimi-* "child" (from **tide-* "to nurse")[65], never show a similar syncope[66], whereas for verbal forms like *ppuwe/ẽti* and *ttãne* no precursors such as **pipuwe-* or **tita-* are attested. These facts, supported by the general consistency of such geminates within one lemma, strongly invalidate this hypothesis. Although in cases like *tteri-* this explanation is plausible, it fails to convince as an overall solution.

5. It seems useful to present at this point a short catalogue of the various types of deviations from the orthographical norm as defined above.[67] We will leave out of consideration the cluster *rm̃p* in *Arm̃pa*° (cf. 2.14) as well as the 'simple' geminates in Anlaut. A distinction can be made between deviations from the norm which may be phonetic in origin and those that probably have

[64] Cf. recently Heubeck, *KZ* 98 (1985) 36; Morpurgo Davies, *KZ* 96 (1982-1983) 252, comes close by calling initial #*d*V- "practically non existent."

[65] Compare also the list of other possible examples of reduplicated presents given by Heubeck, o.c. 45.

[66] The once occurring *tdeime* is a clear scribal mistake, cf. above 3.3.

[67] Cf. S.-T. Teodorsson, *The Phonetic System*, 56-63.

nothing to do with the phonetics of a language. In the latter category belong obvious mistakes resulting from haplography, dittography, etc. The following tentative list of deviations may be drawn up:

haplography: *arsez*.[, *t*[*a*]*rb*[*i*]*de*, *xalte* (2.3), *Erzesinube*, *Parza*, *Ursejetẽ*, and the group of foreign names with *rt* (2.7), *hrmazaxa*, *hrpi*, *przis*, *trbẽtadrazata* (2.11) *Kuprli*, *Trqas*, *Zabrxa<>* (2.12), *Urrsm̃e*[(2.15), *xzuna* (3.1), *Arm̃p*ˡ*alitxa*, *Stemaha*, *Xisterija* (3.2), *pdẽxba* (3.3)

dittography: *hãxxati* (2.2), *hruttla* (2.5), *Idãb*, *Qñtbẽddi* (2.6), *Eppleme* (2.9), *Arm̃p*ˡ*alitxa* (2.14), *apptte*, *qassttebi*(?) (3.1), *kbbidã* (3.3), *ebbehi* (4.2)

inversion: *tllaxñta* (2.5), *Ertll̃eni* (2.14), *Urrsm̃e*[(2.15)

zero graph: *ñzzijaha*(?) (2.2), *Kuplli*, *Pllewih<e>* (2.9), *ãxrhi* (2.11), *Ddẽñtmi*, *Tettm̃pe*(?) (2.14), *hppi*, *xpã* (3.1), *tdeime* (3.3), *xãhb*[68]

similar graph: *tddi* (3.3)

similar phoneme: *Artuñpara*-, *Winbẽte* (2.6)

By 'inversion' we mean the doubling of the 'wrong' consonant, e.g. *tll* instead of *ttl*; the term 'zero graph' designates those cases where a graph is clearly left out by the stonemason, e.g. in *Kuplli* for *Kuprlli*; 'similar graph', means the stonemason inadvertently cut a graph very similar to the one he was supposed to cut, e.g. the confusion between A and Δ in *tddi* for *tadi*.[69] The examples under 'similar phoneme' balance on the edge between non-phonetic and phonetic deviations: the occasionally surprising choice of a nasal before a consonant may not have much value as an indicator for phonetic changes or tell us more about the phonetic status of the expected nasal graphemes, but the deviation is certainly conditioned by its belonging to the general class of nasal graphemes <M/M̃/N/Ñ>.

68 Although not treated in any section here since it only violates the rule that words normally do not end in consonants except for *n* and *s*, the spelling of *xãhb* (44a,31) is also odd because of the *ã* instead of *a*. Contextually (*Ku*]/*prlleh* : *xãhb* : *Xezigah* : *tuhes* "grandson of Kuprli, nephew of Xeziga") the nominative sing. of the word for "grandchild" *xahba*- is expected; cf. Meriggi, *Declinazione* 1, 436.

69 Cf. similarly the confusion between *e* (ⱯΛ with stroke)and *l* (Λ) in *eadi* (for **ladi* 149,6), *i* (E) and *w* (F) in *prñnaii* (for **prñnawi* 57,6), *prñnaiatẽ* (for **prñnawatẽ* 112,1), and *xadaitihe* (for **xadawãtihe* M 245 with the *ã* left out as well, cf. Mørkholm-Neumann, *Münzlegenden* 30), *w* (F) and *i* (E) in *twdeimi* (for **tideimi* N 316,2), *ñ* (Ξ)and *z* (I)in *punemedeñi* (for **punemedezi* 149,11); double mistake in *hrm̃miei* (for **trmmili* 118,3) with *h*(+) for *t* (T) and *e* (ⱯΛ with stroke) for *l* (Λ).

As far as the words from the epichoric language are concerned, all these deviations may be taken to fall in the category of 'careless writing' including insufficient knowledge on the part of the stone carver, and they constitute an extremely small number compared to the entire corpus of Lycian texts and graffiti. Taking into account the restricted part that names constitute in the entire lexicon, it is striking – although not surprising – that almost half of the above deviations come from the onomastic material. Apart from the uncertainties scribes experienced in rendering foreign names, the onomasticon often reflects archaic and/or local spelling variants. The script thus shows an advanced degree of orthographical standardization[70] as far as the handling of consonant clusters is concerned, which may stand in relation to the relatively short period, in which it was used. It is interesting to note that the majority of deviations concern haplography: geminates obviously represent the marked feature as opposed to the unmarkedness of single consonants. The doubling of consonants required the attention of the stonemason as well as specialized knowledge of the orthographic system. For 'hypercorrect' dittography much less examples are attested. The fact, moreover, that the deviations seem mostly due to carelesness, may lead to the conclusion that the resulting orthographical variations, which we have observed, have little or no value for the phonetics of Lycian consonants. This is not to say, that spelling variation in general does not occur: Morpurgo Davies, for instance, has convincingly shown the phonetic relevance of the variation between *t* and *d* in the verbal endings, and, apart from the very important comparison with Greek representations of names, certain spelling variations within the onomastic material turn out to be most valuable in this respect. In this category may also belong some of the variations between 'simple' geminates and single consonants, whether in An- or Inlaut.

In general we may say, that in view of the tendency of orthographic systems to be conservative and the fact that discrepancy between orthography and the phonetics of a language is proportional to the length of time over which a system is in use, the observed 'standardization' of Lycian orthography and the limited period of attestation may imply a still relatively close relation between orthography and phonology of the Lycian language in general.

6. Summarizing the behavior of consonants in Lycian orthography we can discern the following positions:

— in Anlaut:	#-
— intervocalic:	V-V
— after consonant:	C-

[70] Cf. similarly but with different arguments Carruba, *ASNSP* 8 (1978) 856.

— after liquid: R-
— after nasal: N-
— before double consonant -CC
— before resonant: -R/N.

A position in Auslaut for consonants, other than nasals or sibilants, is normally excluded; a position before a single consonant (-C), other than a resonant, is not relevant (see below). The following table summarizes for the above consonants except for τ, β and <>, how and where they occur (between brackets those spellings which occur less frequently or only rarely):

	#-[71]	V-V[72]	C-	R-	N-	-CC	-R/N
t	*t-* (*tt-*)	*-t-* (*-tt-*)	*-tt-*	*-tt-*	*-t-*	—	*-t-*
d	*dd-*	*-d-* (*-dd-*)	*-dd-*/*-d-*	—	—	—	*-d-*
θ	*θ-* (*θθ-*)	*-θθ-*	*-θθ-*	—	—	—	*-θ-*
p	*p-* (*pp-*)	*-p-*	*-pp-*	*-pp-*	*-p-*	*-p-*	*-p-*
b	—	*-b-* (*-bb-*)	*-b-*	*-bb-*	(*-b-*)[73]	(*-b-*)[74]	*-b-*
k	*k-*	*-k-*	—	(*-kk-*)[75]	*-k-*[76]	—	*-k-*
q	*q-*	(*-q-*/ *-qq-*)	*-qq-*	*-qq-*	—	—	*-q-*
x	*x-*	*-x-* (*-xx-*)	*-xx-*	*-xx-*	*-x-*	*-x-*	*-x-*
g	(*g-*)[77]	(*-g-*)	—	—	—	—	(*-g-*)

If we remove those variants which are rare, we get the following picture:

[71] For the less often or even rare writings between brackets see above the material collected in 4.2.
[72] For the less often or even rare writings between brackets see above the material collected in 4.2.
[73] Only once in the name *Winbẽte*, cf. above 2.5.
[74] Only five times (in two inscriptions: TL 83 and 107) in the paradigm of *ebe-* "this,that/he, she, it" and its gen. adj. *eb/pttehi-* "their".
[75] In the hapax *hrkkeledi*.
[76] Only after nasalized vowels (*ã, ẽ*).
[77] Attested only three times in names, cf. Melchert, *LL* 101.

	#-	V-V	C-	R-	N-	-CC	-R/N
t	*t-* (*tt-*)	*-t-*	*-tt-*	*-tt-*	*-t-*	—	*-t-*
d	*dd-*	*-d-*	*-dd-/-d-*	—	—	—	*-d-*
θ	*θ-*	*-θθ-*	*-θθ-*	—	—	—	*-θ-*
p	*p-* (*pp-*)	*-p-*	*-pp-*	*-pp-*	*-p-*	*-p-*	*-p-*
b	—	*-b-*	*-b-*	*-bb-*	—	—	*-b-*
k	*k-*	*-k-*	—	—	*-k-*	—	*-k-*
q	*q-*	—	*-qq-*	*-qq-*	—	—	*-q-*
x	*x-*	*-x-*	*-xx-*	*-xx-*	*-x-*	*-x-*	*-x-*

This table clearly shows that — except for a position in Anlaut — the double or single writing of consonants is subject to specific rules, that is, restricted to specific phonetic environments. It also emerges that single writing of consonants is the rule: geminates are found only following liquids and certain consonants. The writing of double consonants after liquids is automatic disregarding the quality of the following consonant. It may be significant, though, that *d*, *θ* and *k* are never or hardly ever found in that position. The doubling of consonants after another consonant, however, does not seem to be similarly automatic: *b* and *d* seem to resist such doubling, that is, *b* is never found geminated after a consonant, *d* only sometimes. Moreover, not every consonant is found followed by a geminate: among the above listed consonants only *p* and *x* appear as such, to which we may add *h, s* and *z* (cf. above 3.1-3). Actually, only combinations of tenuis or voiceless obstruent+tenuis (e.g. *ptt, spp*), tenuis or voiceless obstruent+ media (e.g. *pdd, sb, td*) regularly occur.[78] A combination media+tenuis is attested only for *bt* in the *ebttehi-* and *ebtte* (see above 3.1). The latter two are either examples of etymological spelling retaining the original *-b-* still visible in the rest of the paradigm (*ebe-*) as opposed to *epttehi* with assimilation of the labial before the dental *-tt-*, or they may represent intermediate stages in a development *ebette* > *ebtte* > *eptte*.[79] The combination media+media is not

[78] The terms tenuis and media are used here as a general indication of graphemes that normally represent such sounds; it is, however, not said that this is necessarily true for Lycian from a phonological point of view as well.

[79] Meriggi, *FsHirt* 269, opted for this last possibility. It is, unfortunately, still largely impossible to date most of the Lycian inscriptions. However, of those where *eb*° occurs, i.e. TL 83, 107 and N 324, the inscriptions 83 and N 324 are roughly datable in the period 400-360 BC (cf. Bryce, *The Lycians* 46-47) on historical grounds; of those where *ep*° is attested, i.e. TL 6, 39 and 121, number 39 was dated relatively late by Laroche, *FdX* 6, 55-56 (for criticism on Laroche's paleographic approach see Bryce, o.c. 59-60). On the same priciple TL 6 might stem from the same general period as TL 39; TL 121 seems paleographically non-committal. The chronology of some of the texts in which these spellings occur may thus be in favor of the simple chronological development.

attested in the non-onomastic material and just once among the names: *Medbijahe* 44a,48.[80] So it may safely be stated that the latter two combinations were strange to the Lycian phonological system.[81]

As a result, geminates can be considered as allophones of their single counterparts, and the double writing may be supposed to reflect a phonetic reality. This observation makes it hard to explain the gemination of Lycian consonants as generally dependent on, for instance, accent, vowel reduction — a feature otherwise well known in this language — or syllabification rules. The latter is offered as explanation for the similar but inconsistently attested phenomenon found in a number of Greek inscriptions and referred to by Neumann[82], i.e. the gemination stresses the hetero- or rather ambisyllabic status of the cluster (e.g. αρισστος = αρισ|στος or the only rarely attested οκττω = οκτ|τω).[83] However attractive, the fact that Lycian geminates are systematically written in all positions, including in Anlaut (e.g. *httemi-*, *xddaza-*) where the cluster is necessarily tautosyllabic, renders this explanation less likely. Elaborating upon a theory of Bernabé Pajares, H.C. Melchert has recently put forward a similar suggestion that gemination might reflect the spreading of the consonant cluster over two syllables assuming an anaptyctic vowel in all clusters with geminated consonants.[84] A form like *astti* "he/she is" is thus said to contain three syllables: [a|s^{e}t|ti]. In this case it seems strange that virtually no trace of this anaptyxis can be found in the Lycian material in Greek or Iranian. On the other hand, the apparent complete syntactic and semantic identity of pairs like *puweti/ppuweti* and *tane/ttãne* shows that *pp* and *tt* were phonetically similar to single *p* and *t*, differring only in length or intensivity.[85] The fact that Lycian geminates are always matched by single written consonants in Greek[86] and Iranian strongly suggests the same.[87] We may thus tentatively conclude that in Lycian the sounds graphically represented by *p, x, h, s, z* as well as *r* and *l* generally caused lengthening (e.g. [t:]), or some kind of strengthening or fortition ([T]) of the following consonant, except for *b* and with restrictions for *d* as we just saw. This

80 Another example might be the name *Pagda* 26,14 but since we do not know the phonetic value of Lycian *g* we should not be misled by the convention of transliterating it with a voiced dorsal.

81 For the rarity of the cluster *db* see already Meriggi, *Declinazione* 1, 417.

82 *HbOr.* 372.

83 Cf. M. Lejeune, *Phonétique Historique du Mycénien et du Grec Ancien*, 285-286. For the 6th century inscription from Ephesus with spellings like εκ ττων, οκττω and ηνειχτθησαν see Collitz-Bechtel, *SGDI* IV 870-871.

84 *AHP* 295-296.

85 For some equally rare variations in the onomastic material see above 4.3; the same argument for phonetic similarity was used by Heubeck, *KZ* 98 (1985) 38.

86 Cf. Houwink ten Cate, *LPG* 111.

87 Cf. the lists of correspondences in Schmitt, *FsNeumann* 377 and 383-384.

lengthening or fortition was graphically expressed by gemination. This is, in fact, the same explanation both Pedersen and Heubeck already suggested for *#dd–*.[88]

7. Having summarized the results of our orthographical findings, it seems expedient to see what we know of Lycian pronunciation from an external point of view by looking at the handling of foreign, i.e. mostly Greek and Persian, names and words in Lycian and vice versa. This has been done most systematically by Houwink ten Cate, *LPG* 101-112 and 197-201, for the Greek, and by Schmitt, *FsNeumann* 373-388, for the Iranian material. For the proper distinction between Greek names in Lycian disguise and the other way around the reader is referred to the work of Houwink ten Cate. Taking into account the most recently found material and supplementing some of the Aramaic correspondences from the Xanthos trilingual, their findings for dental, labial and dorsal consonants may be summarized as follows (between brackets some examples are given):

Lycian	*Greek and Aramaic*	*Persian* (unless otherwise indicated, Old Persian)
t/tt	τ in all positions[89], except for after nasal, δ (NB. the correspondence Lycian *t* with Aramaic *ṣ* in KNDWṢ - KNDWS/*xñtawati*[90])	*t* in all positions (*Vištāspa/ Wizttasppa, Utāna/Utāna, Rta-xš-/ Erttaxssiraza*), no correspondence for position after nasal
d/dd	λ in Anlaut and intervocalically (Λαπαρας/*Dapara*, Κεσινδηλις/ *Xesñtedi*), but intervocalically also δ; no correspondence for C*dd* seems available; *dr* = δρ (Κυδρῆλος/*Kudrehila*)	intervocalically *d* (Iran. **Māda- /Mede*), *d* after R (Iran. **Vāta- fradāta-/Wataprddata*), *č*, Med. θ before R (*xšaθrapa-/ xssad/θrapa-*), but also *d* (*Vidrna- /Widrñna*)

[88] Pedersen, *LH* 42, Heubeck, *KZ* 98 (1985) 37-38. M. Schmidt put forward a similar suggestion for *ss* versus *s*, cf. Arkwright, *JÖAI* 2 (1899) 68.
[89] That is, where according to the orthographic rules of Lycian we find either *t* or *tt*, there we find it rendered by Greek τ.
[90] Cf. A. Dupont-Sommer, *FdX* 6, 145.

p/pp	π in all positions, except for after nasal, β	*p* in all positions (*Pārsa/Parzza*, *Vištāspa/ Wizttasppa*), except for after nasal and liquid, *b* (Iran. **Rtambara-/Arttum̃para*, Iran. **Arbaka-/Arppaxu*) and before R, *f* (**Vāta-fradāta-/Wataprddata*, **Čiçafarna-/(Kizza/Zisa-)prñna*)
b/bb	β and μ intervocalically (Τυβερισσός/*Tubure<>*, Τελμησσός/*Telebehi*); π after *s* (Σπιγασα/*Sbikaza*)	intervocalically *p* (only Iran. **Bagapāta-/Magabata*), after R, β/b (Αρβιν(ν)ας/Ir. **Arb-ina /Erbbina*)
k	κ in Anlaut and before R (Κοπριλις/*Kuprlli*, Ἑκατόμνω/*Katamlah*/KTMNW, Περικλῆς/ *Perikle*; but cf. also below -κλῆς= *-xle*); σ (before front vowel) and γ (after front vowel) intervocalically (Τισευσεμβραν/ *Tikeukẽprẽ*, Σπιγασα/ *Sbikaza/Sbi<>aza*), δυ after nasal (Ενδυομις/*Ekuwemi*)	*č* in Anlaut (**Čiçafarna-/ Kizza/Zisa-*(*prñna*))
q/qq	in Anlaut (Κονδορασιος/ *Qñturahahñ*/KDWRS), intervocalically (Ορτακια/*Urtaqija*) after consonant (Σεσκως/*Zisqqa*) and liquid (Ταρκ°, Τροκ°/*Trqq*°) κ	
x	in Anlaut κ, once γ (Κπαραμω/ *Xpparama*, KNDWṢ - KNDWS/*xñtawati*, Γεργις/*Xeriga*), intervocalically κ, γ or ξ (Ερμακοτασ/*Arm̃maxutaw*, Μεγιστῆς/*Mexistte*, Πιξε/ωδαρος/*Pixedere*/PGSWDR[91]) after a nasal γ (Ιδαγρος/*Idãxre*), before ρ, γ (Πιγρης/*Pixre*), before λ, κ (κλης/ *-xle*), before consonant κ (Ικτας/*Ixtta*), after σ, χ (Μοσχᾶς/*Musxxa-*).	in An- and Inlaut before *s* Iran. *x* (*xšaθrapa-/ xssadθrapa-*), intervocalically *k* (Iran. **Arbaka- /Arppaxu*)

91 Cf. Dupont-Sommer, *FdX* 6, 140.

For both dentals and labials the situation seems relatively clear:[92] on the one hand, Lycian *t*/*tt* and *p*/*pp* are consistently matched by the Greek and Iranian voiceless τ/*t* and π/*p* except for the position after a nasal, where they correspond to voiced δ/d and β/b respectively. From this we may infer, as is well known[93], that Lycian *d* and *b* themselves apparently were not mere voiced stops. This is confirmed at least partly by the correspondence of Lycian *d* with Greek λ and Median θ, and Lycian *b* with Greek μ. Note also the inner-Lycian change *b*/*w* in the name *Teθθiweibi*/*Teθθiwewe*. The initial *m* of Lycian *Magabata-* representing Iranian **Bagapāta-* and the use of the combination *ñt* in Lycian for foreign /d/ (cf. *Ñtarijeuse* = Darius, *Ñtemuxlida* = Δημοκλείδης) lead to the same conclusion. The fact that we find also Greek δ and β as corresponding to Lycian *d* and *b* does not have to contradict this because by this time the Greek mediae were in the process of becoming or had already become voiced fricatives themselves in intervocalic position.[94] The wavering representation of Lycian *d* and *b* also shows that the phonetic quality had no exact counterpart in either Greek or Iranian. The evidence for *d* and *b* thus points to some sort of a fricative in most cases which, moreover, may not have been simply voiced as Median θ and the π in Σπιγασα = *Sbikaza* seem to indicate. Greek τ and π not having been subject to fricativization, Lycian *t* and *p* are most likely to be voiceless stops.

The situation for the dorsals is complicated because of the extra member in the series as opposed to the dentals and labials and is less unequivocal on the whole.[95] Nevertheless, parallel to the main opposition between fricative *d*/*b* and tenuis *t*/*p*, there seems to be at least a partial opposition between fricative *k* and tenuis *x* and *q*, in the sense that *k* is the only member of the three to be subject to real fricativization in certain positions: compare Τισευσεμβραν and Σπιγασα. The variant *Sbi◇aza* in 106,1 with the sign ◇ which otherwise seems to vary with *h*(*e*),[96] strongly supports this. For the latter we may, moreover, refer to Brixhe who states that in the Pamphylian dialect γ remained a stable voiced dorsal except in intervocalic position after /e/ and possibly /i/ where it developed into a yod.[97] If so, neither the correspondences Greek γ = Lycian *x* in *Maxa, Pixm̃ma, Pixre* (the latter two not being intervocalic; the *x* in *Idãxre* corresponding with γ is, of course, completely in keeping with the use of *t* and *p*

92 For this section now also compare H.C. Melchert, *AHP* 40-41.

93 See already Pedersen, *LH* 41-42, 44, cf. also Morpurgo Davies, *KZ* 96 (1982-1983) 252.

94 Cf. in general Schwyzer, *GG* 1, 207-210, for Asia minor especially see Hauser, *Grammatik der griechischen Inschriften Lykiens* 55-57, Brixhe, *Le dialecte grec de Pamphylie* 81-88, id., *Essai sur le Grec Anatolien au debut de notre ère* 37-42.

95 Cf. recently Laroche, *FdX* 6, 83-84.

96 See Pedersen, *LH* 12, and Carruba, *ASNSP* 8 (1978) 854.

97 *Le dialecte grec de Pamphylie* 86 (with n. 3)-88; cf. also Hauser, *Grammatik der griechischen Inschriften Lykiens* 57.

after a nasal) nor the overlap between *k* and *x* by Greek γ in the suffix -κλῆς (*Herikle, Perikle* versus *Ijetruxle, Terssixle*) or the correspondence *k* = κ in Anlaut need to worry us too much.[98] On the contrary, the latter two justify the choice in the Lycian alphabet to use the grapheme <K> for a dorsal stop. It may very well be that the apparent fricativization of Lycian *k* in some positions was relatively late and posterior to the introduction of the alphabet. Note that the oldest evidence for the Lycian script dates from around 500 BC but the oldest stone inscriptions do not start until in the late 5th century.[99] The *-xle*/*-kle* variants show that the opposition between *k* and *x* must have been neutralized before a following consonant. The correspondences for Lycian *x* above prove Arkwright right in his conclusion: "The normal and only true representative of κ is V."[100] It should be noted also that Lycian *x* is the only dorsal matching *t* and *p* in its distribution over all positions. Greek χ, at this time, was still a genuine aspirated dorsal stop: /kʰ/. The choice for the grapheme <V> is therefore fully justified as well and even highly significant in view of its almost consistent etymological connection to Hittite-Luwian *ḫ*. This, as is well known, prompted Pedersen[101] to suggest the transliteration of Lycian <K> by *x*, understandable from his etymological point of view but highly questionable from an internal and synchronic one. One can only conclude that the second millennium fricative guttural *ḫ*, if such it was, had in Lycian in the second half of the first millennium developed into a dorsal stop of some sort: only the extra feature of aspiration, which led to the choice for the Greek aspirated dorsal stop χ instead of the non-aspirated κ, reminds of its origin. This is not to say that Lycian x was an aspirated voiceless dorsal stop, but the pronunciation of Greek χ may have been felt a more appropriate candidate to represent the Lycian sound than was Greek κ. Note that in one case Lycian *x* matches Greek χ: Μοσχᾶς/*Musxxa*-.[102] Problematic, however, is the name Μεγιστῆς/*Mexisttẽ* (as opposed to Σπιγασα/*Sbikaza*). The internal evidence, as we saw (6), supports the partial parallellism of Lycian *k* with *b*/*d*.

8. Combining our findings on Lycian orthography (6) and its correspondences in Aramaic, Greek and Iranian (7), it is significant that all the phonemes (*p, x, h, s, z*) that preceed a doubled consonant, seem to have been voiceless. It should

[98] Cf. Houwink ten Cate, *LPG* 111-112.

[99] See Bryce, *The Lycians* 45-46, and *Kadmos* 26 (1987) 84. For the oldest inscription, the name *Pinike* incised on an olpe, see Neumann, *Neufunde* 30, who suggests to equate the name with Greek Ἐπίνικος.

[100] *JÖAI* 2 (1899) 65; H.C. Melchert, *AHP* 40, has come to the same conclusion.

[101] *LH* 9-11.

[102] Pace H.C. Melchert, *AHP* 40.

be kept in mind that Lycian *z* always matches Greek σ[103] and Iranian *s, š, ç* or θ.[104] Lycian *h* with **s* as its primary source is usually not graphically represented in Greek[105] and may have been some fricative pharyngeal sound. For *x* it is, again, important that it is the only dorsal sound to match *p* and *t* in its distribution over all positions as opposed to *k* and *q*; on this see further below. The surprising absence of *t* in this series must be due to chance: except for *tr, tl, td*(*d*) and *tb* no other combinations (e.g. **tpp*, **tqq*, **tss*, **txx*) are attested so far within the non-onomastic material. The sole counter example is found among the names in *Arm̃pa¦litxa-* (instead of *-*txxa*), a problematic case in many respects (see above 2.14 and 3.2). Lycian B, on the other hand, offers one instance of *tss*: *kitssel/*[.]*m̃* 44d,69-70.

We should now turn again to those cases where gemination did not seem to be automatic but incidental, i.e. the striking amount of *rt* spellings instead of the much less attested *rtt* in foreign names (2.7), the 'simple' geminates in Anlaut (4) and the variation of *d* and *dd* after *t* and *p* (3.3). Given the status of allophones for the geminated consonants and their phonetic similarity to single consonants as just described, these phenomena require a purely phonological rather than morpho(-phono)logical explanation. This, however, brings along a certain degree of uncertainty and sometimes, admittedly, ad-hoc reasoning.

As far as names in general are concerned, the fact that the Lycian sounds did not have exact counterparts in the other languages readily explains the apparent uncertainty scribes display in representing foreign names as opposed to the — relatively speaking — fairly limited amount of deviations from the norm in writing their own language (cf. above 5). The *rt* spellings have to be seen in that perspective as well: their high amount is simply the result of the cluster /*rt*/ being the most attested one.

As to the 'simple' geminates in Anlaut, a position in Anlaut for any given phoneme is different from one in Inlaut in intervocalic position and likely to be more prone to phonological strengthening. Note that word-initial *#*b*- and *#*d*- do not exist at all, only #*dd*- where the gemination can only be explained, it seems, out of a phonetic reluctance to start a word with a (voiced) fricative. The onset of the word caused a fortition which finds its graphic expression in the geminate. Although the automatically conditioning environment (preceding R, *p, h, x, s, z*) is absent, such 'incidental' factors like sentence phonetics and prosody may also have played an important role here.

103 Cf. Houwink ten Cate, *LPG* 112.

104 Cf. Schmitt, *FsNeumann* 377 and 384-385.

105 Cf. Houwink ten Cate, *LPG* 112. For Iranian there is only the name *Humrxxa* reconstructed by Schmitt, *FsNeumann* 379-380 and *IPN* V 4, 22, as **Humarga-* "schöne Wiesen/Fluren besitzend" which is likely to be the same name as Greek Ἀμοργης.

Concerning the variation between *d* and *dd* after consonant we saw that we are dealing with a contrast of *kd, sd* and *td* as against *pdd* and *xdd*. Leaving the cluster *td* aside for the moment, this means an opposition of fricatives (*k, s*; for *k* as a possible fricative see above) versus tenues (*p, x*). One could hypothesize that in the combination of two fricatives (*kd, sd*) the condition to either lengthen or strengthen the second fricative was lost, whereas the stops *p* and *x* could have caused the fricative *d* to become less fricative *dd*. For *td* one would have to take recourse to something like dissimilation of the two dentals which might have prevented the same development. Such an explanation seems to be warranted because historically both (*p*)*dd* in *pddãt-* "place, spot" and (*t*)*d* in *tdi* "cui" go back to the same voiced dental. For the former we must reconstruct on the basis of Hittite *pedan* "id." a development **ped-* > (with vowel reduction) */pd-/*, written *pdd-*; for *tdi* on the basis of Hittite *kued*(*ani* etc.) a development **kued-* > **ted-* > (with vowel reduction) */td-/*, written *td-*.[106] Disadvantage of such a hypothesis is that in a similar way we would at least expect spellings like **xbb*: however, while *xb* is well attested,we lack any examples for **xbb*. The phonemes *b* and *d*, on the other hand, may not have been completely parallel. Whereas *dd* was apparently admitted in Anlaut, after a liquid and after consonant, *bb* was restricted to the position after liquid. Thus, we may not have to expect entirely parallel developments for *b* and *d*.

106 If we compare *tdi* to *ebtte* it is interesting to note that both forms seem to use a different dental root extension as Laroche, *FdX* 6, 65 observed (thus revising his earlier view in *BSL* 55 (1960) 182). The deictic *eptte* is demonstrably the result of *ebet-* > *ebt-* > */ept-/*, written *eptt-*. This seems to be confirmed by *apatti* , the regular dat.-loc. of *apa-* "that; he, she, it" in Cuneiform Luwian (cf. Melchert, *CLL* 20), where the double written dental reflects an original voiceless dental. This *t*-extension, however, is probably the same as the one found in adverbial derivatives of the deictic and relative stems in Hittite like *apadda*(*n*) "therefore" and *kuu̯atta*(*n*) "where." The *d*-extension of Lycian *tdi* matches the voiced dental in the oblique cases of the Hittite *kui-* (*kued-*) and *apā*-paradigm (*apēd-*) but is, in its turn, used in Cuneiform and, it seems, in Hieroglyphic Luwian for adverbial derivates, cf. Cluw. *apati*(*n*) "thus" (cf. Melchert, *CLL* 22) and Hluw. *apati*/*apari* "there" (cf. KARATEPE XXXI). Although no oblique cases of the Cuneiform Luwian relative pronoun seem to be attested (cf. Melchert, *CLL* 119), the adverbial *kuu̯ati* "where" (and not dat.-loc. "for/to whom") runs parallel to *apati*(*n*). Only in Lycian would we find both *t*- and *d*-extensions in one function, i.e. forming the oblique cases of the deictic and relative stem. This poses a problem for Laroche's idea in *BSL* 55 (1960) 181 to see in *ebeli* "here" the regular outcome of **ebedi*. Apart from the problem of an alleged regular inner-Lycian development **d* > *l* (the correspondences of Lycian *d* with Greek λ do not prove anything in this respect, pace Carruba, *Die Sprache* 24 (1978) 178), the parallel *teli* "where" formed on the relative stem would have the same preform as *tdi* < **tedi* < **kuedi*.

9. Finally, we may posit for Lycian dentals and labials the following phonetic approximations:

graph	phonetic approximation	condition
<*t*>	[t]	#-, V-V, -R/N
	[d]	N-
<*tt*>	[t:] or [T]	C/R-
<*d*>	[δ] vel sim.	V-V, C-(not being *p*-, *x*-), -R/N
<*dd*>	[δ:] or [Δ] vel sim.	#-, *p*-, *x*-
<*p*>	[p]	#-, V-V, -CC, -R/N
	[b]	N-
<*pp*>	[p:] or [P]	C/R-
<*b*>	[β] vel sim.	V-V, C-, -R/N
<*bb*>	[β:] or [B] vel sim.	R-

Judging by its distribution over all phonetic environments, *x* is the only one among the dorsal phonemes (*x*, *q* and *k*) completely matching *t* and *p*. Moreover, where correspondences with Greek and/or Iranian are available, we saw it matching a non-fricative dorsal. So we may tentatively set up a similar series for *x*:

graph	phonetic approximation	condition
<*x*>	[k]	#-, V-V, -CC, -R/N
	[g]	N-
<*xx*>	[k:] or [K]	C/R-

Of the remaining dorsals *q* almost certainly represents a voiceless phoneme, too, according to its systematic representation by Greek κ. Its distribution, however, is restricted in comparison to that of *x*. The fact that *q* as opposed to *x* does not seem to be attested before *u* or *b*, might mean, as Arkwright[107] already suggested, that "the sound of -u was already inherent in the letter", whence the transliteration *q*. This leaves us with *k* to take up the position of a fricative parallel to *d* and *b*.[108] This appears to be the case inasmuch as *k* sometimes corresponds, as we saw, with Greek σ and γ (having become a sort of yod-sound

107 *JÖAI* 2 (1899) 66.

108 Laroche, *FdX* 6, 84, sees between *k* and *q* an opposition of palatal versus velar: "*k* devant voyelle antérieure *e, i*; *q* devant voyelle postérieure et nasalisée, ou devant consonne: *qñt-*, *ql-*, *qr-*." Examples like *kumaza-* "priest" and derivatives, *kñme-* "how(ever) many" and several words in *qe*° contradict this.

in Greek in intervocalic position parallel to the fricativization of β and δ), and Iranian *č*. Its correspondence with Greek κ (e.g. *Kuprlli*/Κοπριλις, *Perikle*/Περικλῆς), on the other hand, attests to the fact that this proces was not extended to all positions. Both these correspondences and the fact that *k* is frequently combined with *b* (*kb*) and once with *d* (*kd*), however, do not render it likely that *k* was a *voiced* fricative/stop; as for the latter, we already saw that the cluster media+media seems to be avoided in Lycian. This again shows that the parallelism with Lycian *b* and *d* is only partial.

The Lycian consonantal phoneme system can thus be schematized as follows:

	tenuis	fricative
labial	*p*	*b*
dental	*t*	*d*
dorsal	*x*/*q*/*k*	*k*

nasal	*m n*
sonantic nasal	*m̃ ñ*
liquid	*l r*
sibilant	*s z*

INDEX OF LYCIAN WORDS DISCUSSED (numbers refer to paragraphs):

a) non-onomastic

aladehxxãne	3.1, n. 44
alahati	4.3
ala[h]ha[di]	4.2, 4.3
alahhãti	4.2, 4.3
a/ãm̃mãman-	4.2, 4.3
ap[.]di	n. 38
apptte	3.1, 5, n. 46
arsez.[	2.3, 5
arusñ	2.4
asñne	2.4
atla/atra	2.5
ax(s)ãtaza	3.1
azzala	4.2
ãxrhi	2.11, 5
-dde	4.3, n. 56
ddewezehi-	n. 56
ddewi-	n. 56
ebãhã	2.2
ebbehi	4.2, 5
ebẽhẽ	2.2
ebẽñne	4.1, 4.3
ebette(-)	4.1, 6
eb/ptte	3.1, 6
]epartaisedi	2.7, 8
epatte	4.2
epenẽtijatte	4.2
erbbe	2.3
esde	3.3
esedẽñnewe-	4.1, 4.3
esẽ]nemladi	2.5
ẽke	2.2
ẽmi-	4.1
hãxxati	2.2, 5
(-)hhati	4.1, 4.3
hppñterus	3.1
hqqdai[	3.1
hrkkeledi	n. 75
hrmazaxa	2.11, 5
hrppi/hppi/hrpi	2.11, 3.1, 5
hruttla	2.5, 5
kbatra-	3.1, 3.3
kbbidã	3.3, 5
kbi-	3.3
kduñ	3.3
kitssel[.]m̃ (Lyc.B)	8
la/eθθi	4.2
]laxati	2.11
mẽmrezn	2.8
miñti/mitti	n. 23
ñke	2.2
ñnemle/ñtemle	4.1
ñxrahidijẽ	2.13
ñzzijaha	2.2, 5
pddãt-	8
pddẽn-	3.3
pibi-	4.3
plm̃maddi	4.2, 4.3
przzi-/przi-	2.11, 5
punamaθθi	4.2
puwe-/ppuwe-	1.2, 4.2, 4.3, 6
pzziti	3.1
qassttebi	3.1, 5
qehñ(nedi)	2.4
qñnãkba	2.13
seine	n. 23
sernitẽ	2.3
sieti	n. 16
sttrat[	2.13, 3.1
]taddi	4.2, 4.3
tadi	3.3
ttãna/e	4.2, 4.3, 6
ttaraha	4.2, 4.3, 6
tarbide	2.3, 5
ttazi	4.2
tddẽñta	3.3
tddi	3.3, 5
tdi(ke)	3.1, 3.3, 8
telẽzije-	2.2
tteri-	1.2, 4.2, 4.3, 6
terñ	2.4
teteri-	4.3, 6
ᴛezi	n. 16
(-)tti-	4.2
tideimi-/tdeime	3.3, 4.3, 5, n. 23
tijap[.]di	n. 46
tise/tisñke	2.4, 2.10
ttlaxñta	2.5, 4.2, 5
trbẽtadrazata	2.11, 5
tuhesñ	2.4
tupm̃me	2.4

θθe-	4.1
xãhb	5
]xalle	4.2
xalte	2.3, 5
xddaza-	3.3
xñtaibãnazrtum[	2.3
xñtawata-	2.10, 7
xpã	3.1, 5
[x]ttadi	n. 60
xttba-	3.1
xultti	2.3
xzzuna/xzuna	3.1, 5
zzati	4.1
zzimaza-	4.2
zum̃mã/ẽn-	4.2, 4.3
zxxa-	3.1

b) onomastic

Aba/iqmãme	2.8
Ada[.]mñnaje	2.8
]addeh	4.2
Ahamãsi	2.6
Ala/ixssañtra-	2.14
Añpu[.]eu	2.6
Arm̃maxutaw[	2.7, 2.8
Arm̃palitxa	2.7, 2.14, 3.2, 5, 8
Arppaxu	2.7, 7
Arttum̃para-	2.6, 2.7, 5, 7, 8
Asawãzaa	2.6
Ãke	2.6
Ãmartite	2.7, 5, 8
Dapara	7
Ddapssmma	1.2, 3.2
Ddawãpartah	2.7, 5, 8
Ddẽñtmi-	2.14, 5
Ddepñnewe	2.8
Ebẽla	2.6
Ekuwemi	7
E[lp]eti	2.7
El[pu]weti	2.7
Eppleme	2.9, 5
Erbbina	7
Erimñnuha	2.8
Erm̃menẽni	2.8
Ertaxssirazahe	2.7, 3.2, 5, 8
Ertelijese	2.7, 5, 8
Erte/ẽmi	2.7, 5, 8
Ertllẽni	2.14, 5
Erzesinube	2.7, 5
Herikle	2.9, 7
Hrixttbili	3.2
Humrxxa	n. 104
Idã/ẽb	2.6, 5
Idãxre	2.14, 7
Idazzala	4.2
Ijetruxle	7
Ixtta	3.2, 7
Katamlah	1.2, 2.6, 7
Kizzaprñna	4.2, 7
Krupsse	3.2
Kudrehila	7
Kuprlli	2.6, 2.9, 2.12, 5, 7, 9
Lusãñtre	1.3, 2.8, 2.14
Magabata	7
Mam̃mahaje	4.2
Maxa	7
Medbijahe	6
Meqqese[	4.2
Mexistte	7
Milasãñtra-	2.14
Mlãñnazi	4.2
Mluhidaza	2.5
Mñneτeide	n. 15
Mula	4.3
Mulese	4.3
Mullijeseh	4.2, 4.3
Murãzah	2.6
Musxxa	3.2
M̃mije	4.2
M̃para	2.6
Ñtarijeuse/i-	2.6, 7
Ñtemuxlida	7
Padrñma	2.8
Pagda	n. 80
Parza/Parzza	2.7, 5
Pdda/ãxñta	3.4
Pddẽxba	2.13, 3.3, 5
Ppebẽñti	4.2
Perikle	7, 9
Pertinah	2.7, 5, 8

Pertinamuwa 2.7, 5, 8
Pigrẽi 2.9
Pillewi-/Pllewi- 2.9, 5
Pixedere 7
Pixm̃ma 7
Pixre 7
Pizzi 4.2
Plezzijeheje 4.2
Plqqa 2.11
Pñntrenni 2.12, 2.14
Pssure 3.2
Pttlezẽi 3.2
Qañnuwili 4.2
Qñtbã/ẽddi 2.6, 5, n. 25
Qñturahahñ 7
Sbik/<>aza 7
Spparta° 2.7, 3.2, 5, 8, n. 28
Sppñtaza 3.2
Ssepije 4.2
Ssewa/e 4.2
Stemaha 3.2, 5
Telebehi 7
Tẽnegure 1.2
Terssixle 7
Tettm̃pe 2.14, 5
Teθθiweibi 4.2, 4.3, 7
Tikeukẽprẽ 7
Tiwiθθeimija 4.2
Tm̃peri 2.10
Trqqa- 2.12, 5, 7
Truwepeijadi 2.7
Tubure<> 7
Tuminehi n. 23
Turaxssi 3.2
Uñna 4.2
Urebillaha 4.2
Urrsm̃e[2.15, 5
Ursejetẽ 2.7, 5
Urtaqija- 2.7, 5, 7, 8
Uwiñte n. 23
Uwitahñ n. 23
Wataprddata 7, n. 19
Waxssere 3.2
Waxsser/pddimi 3.2, 3.4
Wazzijeje 4.2, 4.3
Wezzeimi 4.2
Winbẽte 2.6, 5
Xãkbi- 2.14
Xba- n. 32
Xelijãnaxssa 3.2
Xertubi 2.7, 5, 8
Xesñtedi 7
Xexxebẽñti 2.6, 4.2
Xisterija 3.2, 5
]*xnahe*(*tub*) 2.8
Xpparama 3.2, 7
xssad/θrapa- 3.1
Xssbãseh 3.2
Xssbezẽ 3.2
Xsseñzija 2.6, 3.2
Xuñnejẽi 4.2
Xzzubeze 3.2
Zabrxa 2.12
zaxxh(?) 3.2
Zẽm̃tija 2.2
Zimasttrah 3.2
Zisaprñna 7
Zisqqa 3.2, 7
Zzajaa 4.2
Zzala 4.2

APOLOGY OF ḪATTUŠILI III OR DESIGNATION OF HIS SUCCESSOR?[1]

FIORELLA IMPARATI

1. *The Purpose of the Document*

As I have already had occasion to express elsewhere[2] after the discovery and publication of the Bronze Tablet[3] with the information it contained (ii 35 ff., 43 ff.) that Tutḫaliya succeeded his older brother to the position of *tuḫkanti*, it seemed to me that the so-called Apology or Autobiography of Ḫattušili III[4] was drawn up for a different motive than has been understood up to now.[5]

In my opinion in fact, already at the beginning of this text, in §2, there is presented the purpose for which it was drawn up, and this purpose is repeated more specifically and concretely at the end of the document.

As a matter of fact, immediately following the preamble, which contains the name and titles of the king who drew it up (§1), Ḫattušili declares that he intends to speak of "solicitous will" of Ištar, which everyone must heed, and that in the future the son of My Sun, his grandson, and all his descendants will owe particular respect and devotion to Ištar among all the gods (§2).

And in the concluding paragraphs (§§12b, 13, 14, *infra*) Ḫattušili, after stating that he has placed Kurunta on the throne of Tarḫuntašša[6], bestows gifts on Ištar and names his son Tutḫaliya priest of the goddess and administrator of her property. The text ends with a reminder to his son, grandson, and the "progeny of Ḫattušili (and) Puduḫepa" of their duty to honor the goddess, thus repeating the concept expressed in the first part of the document and completing the symmetry of the text.

The name of Ḫattušili's son is not specified in §2, but it is plausible that

[1] Among his far-ranging research on problems of Hittite history, Ph.H.J. Houwink ten Cate has done important work on the epoch of kings Ḫattušili III and Tutḫaliya IV. I would like, therefore, to dedicate to him these brief remarks on some aspects of the reigns of these two sovereigns, as evidence of my profound esteem.

[2] *Seminari dell'Istituto per gli Studi Micenei ed Egeo-Anatolici* 1991 (= *Seminari* 1991), Rome 1992, 76-78.

[3] See H. Otten, *StBoT* Beih. 1.

[4] CTH 81; see most recently H. Otten, *StBoT* 24, which I have followed also in the numbering of the paragraphs.

[5] I now see that the observations of Ph.H.J. Houwink ten Cate, *ZA* 82 (1992) 265 ff., also tend in this direction.

[6] On the importance of the use here of verbs in the past tense, see below.

the allusion is to the only one of Ḫattušili's sons mentioned in the text, right at its conclusion (iv 77, 78): Tutḫaliya, on whom is bestowed the priesthood of Ištar.[7]

Then, from §3 to the concluding paragraphs, Ḫattušili tells the story of his life[8] and his ascension to the throne, emphasizing constantly the invaluable assistance given him by Ištar in his achievement of his goal.

As is known, a large part of the documents drawn up by this king contain long prologues in which he narrates extensively the events leading up to his ascension to the throne, always presenting his power as the legitimate expression of divine will. Since he usurped the throne, this practice is particularly useful for attributing validity not only to his past actions but also to every initiative he would take, present and future.

It seems important, in fact, to recall here that such documents were prepared with a precise purpose, usually stated at their conclusion, and not only with an apologetic aim in favor of the person drawing them up:[9] thus the narration of preceding events – even when extensive and in great detail – appears aimed at furthering the achievement of this goal.

We can cite here as examples KBo VI 29+[10], a text whose contents are close to the Autobiography – albeit with some differences – in which property and privileges are conferred on Ištar and the priesthood of this goddess on an unnamed son of the king and on this son's descendants; KBo VI 28+[11], in which certain benefits are granted to a sacred foundation indicated as ^{NA4}*ḫekur Pirwa*[12]; KBo IV 12[13], a decree in favor of the family of Mittannamuwa; KUB

[7] On the king's mention of Kurunta in this text as, most plausibly, "[son of m]y [brother]", see below.

[8] Ḫattušili's statement that he was the youngest of Muwattalli's four children could be a literary topos (see F. Imparati, *FsAlp* 307 with notes 9 and 10); we must keep in mind, however, that this was a case of a recent fact, easily verifiable by Ḫattušili's audience.

[9] This is true also of other documents issued by other kings, as for example the so-called "Testament of Ḫattušili I", drawn up to name Muršili I as successor to the throne, etc.

[10] CTH 85; see A. Goetze, *Ḫatt.* 44 ff.; *NBr.* 46 ff.; F. Imparati, *RHA* 32 (1974) (= *Šaḫur.*) 155 ff.

[11] CTH 88; see F. Imparati, *Šaḫur.* 154 f. and *SMEA* 18 (1977) 38-49. This document and the one cited in the preceding note – as well as KUB XXVI 58, also drawn up by this king, but in which the bestowal of a benefit on a high personage in the Hittite court appears very near the beginning of the text (see note 14) – have been designated "Freibriefe"; see my observations on this topic in *Šaḫur.* 148 ff.

[12] In this text the narration of the preceding events (obviously quite different from the narrations in KBo VI 29 + and in the Autobiography) goes back quite far in time, perhaps to point out the very old link between this sanctuary and the Hittite dynasty, and the merits it could have earned with regard to the dynasty from the remote reaches of time, with the purpose of justifying the benefits which were now being granted (see *Šaḫur.* 154 f.). Furthermore, if we accept the proposal of H. Otten, *ZA* 58 (1967) 233, to recognize this sanctuary as the *ḫešti* building, which remained standing when a large part of Ḫatti's kingdom and even the capital itself had been destroyed (obv. 14-15), this historical narration is justified even more; cf. my observations in *SMEA* 18 (1977) 47 and 60 with bibliographical notes. On the *ḫešti* building see V. Haas - M. Wafler, *UF* 8 (1976) 65-99; 9 (1977) 87-122; H. Otten, *RlA* IV 369; J. Puhvel,

XXVI 58[14], which bestows certain benefits on someone named Ura-Tarḫunta, who had earned Ḫattušili's esteem and gratitude.

2. *The Presence of Puduḫepa in KBo VI 29 + and the Autobiography*

In the preamble of most of the documents mentioned above, we can note some discrepancies in the titles of the kings.[15] Furthermore, as opposed to the case in these documents[16], we do find the name of the queen Puduḫepa in the preamble to KBo VI 29 + i 5, precisely the text, as we have seen, whose contents are close to the Autobiography.

Earlier[17], I tried to justify the mention of this queen along with her consort in the preamble to KBo VI 29 + by her close tie with the goddess Ištar, whose glorification permeates the entire text; this observation, however, would be true also for the Autobiography, where, instead, the queen's name does not occur in the preamble.

HED 3, 319-323.

13 CTH 87; see A. Goetze, *Ḫatt.* 41 ff.

14 CTH 224; see also *Šaḫur.* 152 f. In this text the narration of preceding events is brief, as it concerns only a person, albeit important, whom Ḫattušili presumably wished to reward for his devotion and his assistance with the king's undertakings.

15 For example, the absence in the titles of Ḫattušili and his predecessors of the title UR.SAG "hero" in the Autobiography and in KBo VI 29+, as opposed to KBo IV 12 obv. 2-4, KBo VI 28+ obv. 1, 3, 4[, KUB XXVI 58 obv. 4[; or the presence of the title Tabarna before Ḫattušili's name in the Autobiography i 1, in KBo VI 28 + obv. 1, in KUB XXVI 58 obv. 1, where in KBo VI 29 + i 1 and in KBo IV 12 obv. 1 we find ^{d}UTU^{ŠI}, etc. It should also be noted that in KBo VI 28+ obv. 2 the name of Ḫattušili is accompanied not only by his usual appellations but also by "beloved of the Sun goddess of Ari[nna], the Storm god of Ḫatti and Ištar of Šamuḫa", a way of highlighting the favor Ḫattušili enjoyed in the sight of the major divinities of Ḫatti, that is the divine couple who reigned over the Hittite pantheon and its divine protectress. We recall here that also in KUB XXI 11 (CTH 90) obv. 1 Ḫattušili III bears the appellation of "beloved of the Stormgod of Nerik" and that also Tutḫaliya IV in the treaty with Šaušgamuwa of Amurru, CTH 105 i 2, is presented as "[beloved of] the Sun goddess of Arin[na]." On the royal titles in the preambles to some documents issued by these two kings, see F. Imparati, *Šaḫur.* 40-43, with relevant notes; cf. also H. Gonnet, *Hethitica* 3 (1979) 56-63, 71-73, obviously taking into account in both cases some modifications resulting from the most recent discoveries.

16 This is the case only with the preambles of these documents, since within their texts and also other texts the queen is often mentioned along with her husband or named specifically or by her title of MUNUS.LUGAL. She does not appear, instead, alongside Tutḫaliya IV in the "political" texts issued by this king; she is mentioned with Tutḫaliya in the preamble of a document of an administrative nature concerning the assignment of the property of Šaḫurunuwa, KUB XXVI 43 obv. 3 and rev. 15. The queen's presence in this text can be explained either by the fact that this document reproduced, at least in part, a decree issued by Ḫattušili III with his wife (referring furthermore to a preceding decree issued by Muwattalli; see F. Imparati, *Šaḫur.* 21 f.; cf. also below, note 35) or even because Tutḫaliya could have taken his father's place in the drawing up of the document, perhaps due to Ḫattušili's death before this was completed; see F. Imparati - F. Pecchioli Daddi, *Quattro studi ittiti* 60 and cf. 48 f.

17 See *Šaḫur.* 156.

Therefore, I wonder if this discrepancy between the two documents might not be due to political reasons.[18] Perhaps in the case of the text that seems to come first chronologically, KBo VI 29+, in which the process of establishing Tutḫaliya in the priesthood of this goddess was still *in fieri*[19], it could have been beneficial to show from the very beginning of the text how the queen participated actively in the operation, also in order to highlight the fact that this priest had to be a son not only of the king, but of Puduḫepa as well.

A reason, instead, for the absence of the queen in the preamble to the Autobiography, where the operation was already practically concluded, could be due to the fact that this was a state document, whose nature was essentially political, and whose purpose was not only the conferring of property on Ištar but mainly the explicit nomination of Tutḫaliya to the priesthood of the goddess, which functioned implicitly as his designation as successor to the throne:[20] in fact it should be recalled that in Ḫattušili III's official political documents known to date, only the king appears in the preamble as issuer of the act.[21]

It should be further noted that in KBo VI 29 + iii *infra*, it is Ḫattušili alone who confers property and privileges on Ištar and the priesthood of this goddess on his son, unnamed in the text, and this son's descendants; to safeguard their rights, the request is made that everything established in the act be respected.

In the Autobiography instead, even if it is Ḫattušili alone who grants the priesthod of Ištar to Tutḫaliya (iv 76-79), nonetheless when mention is made of the future safeguard of the rights conferred on this son and his descendants, the text specifies that these are in effect the "progeny of Ḫattušili (and) Puduḫepa" (iv 81, 86 f.).[22] It seems almost as though in this text, despite the fact that

18 Unless the reason was much more casual, such as an insertion or omission on the part of the scribes writing the two documents; but this seems to me highly improbable, since these were royal acts.

19 In effect, this text does not yet give the name of the son of Ḫattušili and Puduḫepa who was proposed as priest of Ištar; see below.

20 The reason for the fact that, since this document was in its definitive phase, there was by then no longer any need for the presence of the queen for further confirmations or indications, is contradicted by the fact that she appears in the two concluding paragraphs of the act (iv 81, 87); see above in the text.

21 Cf., for example, the international treaties stipulated by Ḫattušili III. Puduḫepa instead is mentioned with her husband also in the preamble to KUB XXI 17 (CTH 86) i 1-2, containing the so-called "case against Arma-Tarḫunta." We could thus presume that the queen appeared with her husband in the preambles to decrees whose nature was administrative (such as KBo VI 29+), juridical or religious, but not those concerning the domestic or foreign policy of the kingdom.

22 Besides, the queen – certainly Puduḫepa – appears alongside the king in the clauses for the dynasty's protection with regard to the royal power in KBo IV 10+ rev. 5-6, 8-9, and in the treaty between Ḫattušili III and Bentešina of Amurru, CTH 92 obv. 38, 39[; see G.F. Del Monte, *OAC* 18, 182 f., *EVO* 14 (1991) 139 f., and O.R. Gurney, *AnSt* 43 (1993) 19; see also the observations contained in F. Imparati - F. Pecchioli Daddi, locc. citt. in note 16, regarding the implications of the queen's presence in the above passages from KBo IV 10+ for assigning a date to this text.

Puduḫepa does not appear in the preamble, Ḫattušili wants in this way to head off from the beginning any claims which might be made in future by other members of the royal family, and more precisely by other sons of the king, specifying that in this instance the text speaks specifically of the son of this queen and his descendants. It should be recalled here that Puduḫepa was the mother of Tutḫaliya – whose success she had worked actively to attain – and also of other sons of Ḫattušili, but not of all the king's children.[23]

3. *Comparison between the two above-mentioned documents*

In the preceding paragraph we have noted certain discrepancies in the preambles to these two acts and in the mention of Puduḫepa at different points in them.

Furthermore, even if the bestowal of the priesthood of Ištar on the king's son and his descendants is placed in both acts at their conclusion, we see that in the Autobiography mention is made of this in the beginning as well, in §2.

Both texts contain the observation that Ḫattušili was the youngest of his brothers (see note 8), whose names however are specified only in the Autobiography.

Further, despite the fact that the two texts speak at different points of the marriage between Ḫattušili and Puduḫepa[24], in both an important element is highlighted: that this marriage was the will of Ištar, of whom Puduḫepa was the "servant."[25]

In both documents another important fact is remembered, that Muwattalli, once he had succeeded his father to the throne, had entrusted to his brother Ḫattušili the administration of certain countries and had bestowed on him the priesthood of the Storm god of Nerik in Ḫakpiš. Rather, even more in the Autobiography, after stating that Ḫattušili had been named by his brother

23 At any rate, also in the documents where it is spoken about the bestowal of the kingship over Tarḫuntašša on Kurunta (cited apud F. Imparati - F. Pecchioli Daddi, op.cit. 24), we usually find also the "queen", obviously Puduḫepa, mentioned along with Ḫattušili. This confirms yet again her influential participation in the whole process. We should note, however, that she is not mentioned at the point concerning Kurunta's enthronement in the Autobiography (iv 62-64).

It should be recalled in this instance that in KBo IV 12, which we have already mentioned, Puduḫepa, even if she does not appear in the preamble, does appear (rev. ⌈5'⌉) with the title of "great queen" alongside her husband in a passage concerning the concession of their benevolence to the family of Mittannamuwa; furthermore, the promise is made that this benevolence will be maintained by "our sons, our grandchildren, the son of My Sun, the grandson of My Sun, the progeny of Puduḫepa, Great Queen" (rev. 8'-9'): see most recently on this passage Ph.H.J. Houwink ten Cate, op.cit. 261 f. with note 43.

24 It is spoken of almost immediately in KBo VI 29+ i 16-20, while in the Autobiography, iii 1-8 it appears only after the narration of other events, including the war against Egypt, which is not mentioned in KBo VI 29+.

25 Cf. KBo VI 29+ i 20 (cf. also note 17) and Autobiography iii 2.

lord of the army (EN KARAŠ) and later chief of the royal bodyguards (GAL *MEŠEDI*)[26] it is specified that he and his wife had been named king and queen of Ḫakpiš (ii 62 f. and iii 12 f.).[27] It should be noted, instead, that the fact that Ḫattušili held the position of GAL *MEŠEDI* is not recorded in KBo VI 29+; it is mentioned, though, in KBo IV 12 obv. 14.

In the Autobiography (*infra*) extensive attention is paid to the plots against Ḫattušili on the part of Arma-Tarḫunta and Ḫattušili's subsequent expropriation, once he had become king, of Arma-Tarḫunta's property as well as that of his son Šippaziti, in order to donate it to Ištar, while this is not mentioned in KBo VI 29+. Could this, too, depend on the more official nature of the Autobiography and thus on the more propagandistic tone used in the document?

Both texts remark – albeit with able nonchalance – on Ḫattušili's installation on the Hittite throne of Urḫi-Teššup, son of Muwattalli and a *woman from his harem*, as this king had no *legitimate* sons.[28] This statement, among other things, leads one to think that also Kurunta was not a legitimate son of Muwattalli.

Urḫi-Teššup's illegitimacy, besides, is skilfully recalled, although indirectly, also by Tutḫaliya IV in his treaty with Šaušgamuwa of Amurru.[29]

The Autobiography highlights everything that Ḫattušili had to endure at the hand of his nephew, king of Ḫatti; in KBo VI 29+ we find a large lacuna in this context which prevents our making a comparison on this point.

The two texts go on to speak with great emphasis of the continuing, solicitous intervention of Ištar of Šamuḫa in favor of her protegé.[30]

It is interesting to examine the passage in the Autobiography, iii 73 ff., where Ḫattušili answers, before it is formulated, an accusation which might be raised against him, evidently with the purpose of preventing it: "Now if

[26] On the meaning of the attribution of this position also to Tutḫaliya IV, see below.

[27] This position too had probably been held by Tutḫaliya; see below.

[28] See KBo VI 29+ i ⸢34⸣ and Autobiography iii ⸢40'⸣.

[29] See my observations in *Seminari* 1991, 66, concerning Tutḫaliya's deploration of the behavior of Mašduri with regard to the son of Muwattalli; this deploration, to my mind, is done solely with a specific purpose, to warn Šaušgamuwa not to do to Tutḫaliya's direct descendants anything like what Mašduri had done. Nonetheless Tutḫaliya seems to want to point out – while attributing the statement to Mašduri – that Urḫi-Teššup was a "bastard" (KUB XXIII 1 + ii 29). It appears significant, besides, that in the paragraph preceding this one (ii 13) Tutḫaliya urges Šaušgamuwa to consider his own (= of Tutḫaliya) brothers as "bastards", which shows that the use of this term with regard to Urḫi-Teššup, even though its use is attributed to Mašduri, was not casual. Still in this article, loc.cit., I observed also that Tutḫaliya, in the same treaty, continues to refer to Urḫi-Teššup using his personal name and not his dynastic appellation of Muršili (III), highlighting in this way the fact that he did not recognize the legitimacy of the royal power being exercised by Urḫi-Teššup. Besides, we must remember that Tutḫaliya ascended to the throne both by usurping it from his father and by taking over from one of his brothers the position of *tuḫkanti*.

[30] In the Autobiography (iii 71 f.) we find Ḫattušili appealing to divine justice to solve this dispute: "now may Ištar of Šamuḫa and the Storm god of Nerik decide the suit for us!"

someone says the following: <<Why did you earlier place him in the royal function, why do you now write to him of enmity?>>", a question which Ḫattušili answers by attributing the responsibility for this conflict to Urḫi-Teššup, who began it, and by citing the divine verdict in Ḫattušili's favor.[31]

From what we have observed up to now, as well as other elements which it would take too long to discuss here, we can see that in the Autobiography the narration of preceding events appears to be more extensive and detailed, even considering that in KBo VI 29 + there are many lacunae. Furthermore, greater emphasis seems to have been given in the Autobiography to the military endeavors entrusted to Ḫattušili by Muwattalli[32], which Ḫattušili carried out successfully (see *infra*), to the expulsion of the Kaškeans[33] from Ḫakpiš (iii 11) and the fact that he had been named king of this country (iii 12-13, 45', iv 42), to the reconstruction of Nerik, destroyed as early as the time of Ḫantili (iii 46'-48'). This too was perhaps due to the more official nature and greater importance of this document as compared to KBo VI 29+ (cf. above), since in the Autobiography not only is Tutḫaliya granted the priesthood of Ištar, but also the path is opened for him to succeed to the throne. It could therefore have been important to highlight certain offices held by Ḫattušili and certain tasks he had performed, especially when they could be seen as relating in some way to offices held or operations carried out at a later date by Tutḫaliya (see below).

Both texts speak of the king's gift of property to the goddess Ištar and the bestowal of benefits connected to the ownership of this property, consisting in exemption from a number of duties.

We can note that these exemptions are spelled out in detail in KBo VI 29 + iii 19'-28', and that in their formulation they present numerous analogies with other exemptions[34] granted by Ḫattušili in other texts mentioned above, such as KBo VI 28 + rev. 22-27 and KUB XXVI 58 obv. 8-13. It is interesting to see that the formula granting these exemptions corresponds to the one used for the exemptions concerning the patrimony bequeathed to the children of a daughter of a high official in the Hittite court, named Šaḫurunuwa (KUB XXVI 43 rev. 10-14). In fact, even if this last document was drawn up by Tutḫaliya IV, it

[31] We should note the use in this two texts of two different images to describe Ištar's capture of Urḫi-Teššup: "but Ištar of Šamuḫa, my Lady, caught him like a fish with a net" (KBo VI 29+ ii 33-34) and "she (= Ištar) shut him up at Šamuḫa like a pig in a sty" (Autobiography iv 26): see most recently J. Puhvel, *HED* 2, 472.

[32] One wonders at this point if Muwattalli did not send his brother – whom he must have already recognized as dangerous to the royal dynasty, as far as we can infer, for example, also from the fact that he had called him to answer for his actions (see Autobiography i 36), even though he later recognized his innocence – to perform all these feats of war in order to distance him from the court and the kingdom, even if this could in the end yield the opposite result, that is giving Ḫattušili the opportunity to acquire too much prestige and even to make in this way alliances; cf. my observations in *Hethitica* 8 (1987) 188.

[33] Who, as Ḫattušili points out still in the Autobiography, were on his side in the dispute with Urhi-Teššub, as was also the case for all of Ḫattuša (iv 26-29).

[34] See A. Goetze, *NBr.* 55-59 and F. Imparati, *Šaḫur.* 105-112; cf. here also 55-75; cf. also *SMEA* 18 (1977) 40-47.

reproduced, at least in part, a decree pronounced by Ḫattušili III.[35]

The Autobiography (iv 85), instead, regarding the exemptions given to the property offered to Ištar, speaks only of the *šaḫḫan* and the *luzzi*, as though it were not deemed necessary to specify once again what had already been stated in KBo VI 29 +; this could confirm the earlier date of this document with respect to the Autobiography.[36]

Nonetheless, the absence in the Autobiography of a detailed description of these exemptions could be caused also by the fact that the primary purpose of this document was to grant the priesthood of Ištar to Tutḫaliya, thus designating him successor to the throne. KBo VI 29+, on the contrary, has the nature more of an administative than a political act.

In this document[37] appears a clause regarding the possibility that this son might not have direct descendants in the male line. In that case the priesthood would fall to the family, that is the descendants, of the daughter of the king and of *Ḫa*[....], most plausibly the husband of this daughter: the priesthood must not pass to another's descendants (iii 13'-19').[38] A similarly formulated clause does not appear in the Autobiography.

Finally, at the conclusion of the two acts[39], we find clauses inserted as a safeguard, also for the future, of what is established in the documents.[40]

In light of the interpretation which I proposed concerning the motive for drawing up the Autobiography (to designate Tutḫaliya as successor to the throne), the last paragraph of this text (iv 86-89) seems particularly interesting, if we accept the meaning given by A. Goetze to the expression *šara išparzazi* (lines 87-88): "zur Regierung kommt."[41] That is, this paragraph would treat of the respect that also in the future would be owed to Ištar of Šamuḫa by that son or grandson or descendant of Ḫattušili and Puduḫepa who ascends (to the kingship). Could this be an implicit reference to Tutḫaliya – invested a few lines earlier (iv 76-79) with the priesthood of Ištar of Šamuḫa and the task of administrating her patrimony – and to his descendants?

35 And in it reference was even made to an earlier exemption granted by Muwattalli: see above note 16 infra.

36 Unless the Autobiography refers to the concession of other property to Ištar, that is that belonging to Arma-Tarḫunta and Šippaziti (iv 66, 71 ff.), not mentioned in KBo VI 29+, but this seems to me quite improbable.

37 Where Ḫattušili repeats that his son (unnamed in the text) nominated to the priesthood of Ištar, and his son, grandson, and great-grandson ("*my* progeny", summarizes Ḫattušili) must preserve this priesthood (iii 9'-13').

38 See F. Imparati, *Šaḫur*. 16 note 46. See also the Bronze Tablet §20 iii 10-11, 17-20, and KBo IV 10+ obv. 12-14.

39 KBo VI 29+ iii 32'-43', iv 1'-2'; B iv 1'-18'; Autobiography iv 81-89.

40 A safeguard, that is, of the maintenance of the priesthood of Ištar in the hands of the son of Ḫattušili and his descendants (in the Autobiography: "to the progeny of Ḫattušili <and> Puduḫepa") and of the benefits – exemption from the *šaḫḫan* and the *luzzi* – granted to the property donated to this goddess.

41 *Ḫatt*. 41 and 105; see most recently J. Puhvel, *HED* 447.

4. *Who was the tuḫkanti who preceded Tutḫaliya?*

As is known, the Bronze Tablet has informed us that Ḫattušili had earlier named to the position of *tuḫkanti* an older brother of Tutḫaliya, whose identity is still disputed by scholars.

The proposal to identify him as Kurunta himself[42], who would have been adopted as a son by his uncle Ḫattušili, even if in some ways plausible, does not however conform to the way in which Kurunta formulates his vow of loyalty to Tutḫaliya, who had not yet been named *tuḫkanti* (Bronze Tablet ii 37-41). The formulation in lines 40-41, in fact, appears improbable if attributed to someone bearing the title of heir to the throne[43], especially when we compare it to the much less servile formula which Tutḫaliya in his turn uses to express his loyalty to Kurunta in the next line 42.

Besides, in the Autobiography (iv 62) Ḫattušili – if we accept the plausible integration of the lacuna at the beginning of this line with [*nu* DUMU.ŠEŠ-*Y*]*A*[44] – speaks of Kurunta specifically as the son of his brother. This precise designation could have been included not only in order to justify the nomination of Kurunta as king of Tarḫuntašša, but also to exclude completely – and openly – any possible claims he might make to be a direct descendant of the reigning king. In any case, this does not seem to me to constitute evidence that Kurunta was adopted by Ḫattušili.

I have already written elsewhere[45] about the other proposal to identify the *tuḫkanti* Tutḫaliya's predecessor[46] as Neriqqaili, most probably an older stepbrother of Tutḫaliya[47], who appears in the Bronze Tablet (iv 30) simply with the title of "son of the king," in the act for Šaḫurunuwa (rev. 28) with the titles of "son of the king" and *tuḫkanti*, and in the treaty with Ulmi-Teššup of Tarḫuntašša (rev. 28) only with the title of *tuḫkanti*.[48] Since much has been said[49] about the person mentioned with this name also in other Hittite texts,

[42] See most recently Ph.H.J. Houwink ten Cate, op. cit. 259 ff.; this hypothesis is based also on two passages from the so-called "letter of Tawagalawa": see however R. Beal, *AnSt* 43 (1993) 31 f. note 10.

[43] Cf. R. Beal, loc. cit.

[44] See A. Goetze, *NBr*. 32-34, and most recently H. Otten, *StBoT* 24, 28.

[45] *Seminari* 1991, 71-73.

[46] Proposal advanced by H. Klengel in *AoF* 16 (1989) 186 and *AoF* 18 (1991) 228 and 230 f. This is also the opinion of G.F. Del Monte, op. cit. 134 f.; R. Beal, loc. cit.; O.R. Gurney, op. cit. 22 f.; see instead Ph.H.J. Houwink ten Cate, loc. cit.; cf. also A. Hagenbuchner, *SMEA* 29 (1992) 111-126 infra.

[47] See H. Klengel, *AoF* 16, 187 note 8, and *AoF* 18, 228.

[48] For this chronological sequence of these documents, see my observations in *Seminari* 1991, 63 and infra; cf. also H. Otten, *StBoT* Beih. 1, 7 ff.

[49] For a more extended treatment, see J. Lorenz, *Der Vertrag mit Ulmi-Tešub von* ᵈU-*ašša* (CTH 106): *Sprachliche und historische Würdigung und Einordnung innerhalb der hethitischen Staatsvertragstradition.* Hausarbeit vorgelegt am Fachbereich 11 - Aussereuropäische Sprachen

here I shall only report some observations I made in the article cited in note 45.

Firstly, we note in the Bronze Tablet the absence of the title *tuḫkanti* next to the name of this personage. Now, if we accept the opinion that this title designated, at least in that period, the Hittite crown prince[50], we must presume that, at the time of the treaty with Kurunta, Neriqqaili did not hold that position[51], otherwise, since this was the most important position in the Hittite court, it would certainly have been mentioned in a political document of such great significance.

As we have seen, in the political act for Šaḫurunuwa, which also can be dated in the early years of Tutḫaliya IV's reign, when he probably did not yet have children, Neriqqaili's name is accompanied by the titles "son of the king" and *tuḫkanti*, perhaps in order to highlight more effectively the legitimacy of his nomination to that position, that is, to specify that the designated heir, although not the son (but rather the brother) of the reigning king, was nonetheless a member of the royal family. This observation, of course, is more sustainable if we do not identify Neriqqaili as the *tuḫkanti* who was Tutḫaliya's predecessor.

The designation "son of the king" does not appear to have been necessary any longer by the time, albeit not long thereafter, of the treaty with Ulmi-Teššup – in my opinion stipulated by Tutḫaliya IV after the date of the Bronze Tablet[52] – since the internal political situation of Ḫatti in all likelihood had changed, perhaps also because of Kurunta's disappearance from the scene.

As I have observed in the same article, I believe that Tutḫaliya, since at the time of his ascension to the throne he had no direct heirs, found himself forced, even if *obtorto collo*, to name a brother as *tuḫkanti*. But it does not seem truly plausible to me to think that he could have chosen for such a position that very brother whom he had earlier replaced as heir to the throne. Thus, he chose Neriqqaili for this office, even if he feared him – as he certainly feared also his other brothers and close relatives[53] – but judging perhaps that Neriqqaili was less dangerous than the preceding *tuḫkanti*, whom Tutḫaliya had

und Kulturen - der Philipps-Universität Marburg, 1986, 71-75; Th. van den Hout, KBo IV 10+ (CTH 106): *Studien zum Spätjunghethitischen. Texte der Zeit Tuthalijas IV.*, Academisch Proefschrift, Universiteit van Amsterdam 1989, 106-112; H. Klengel, *AoF* 16, 185-188; A. Hagenbuchner, op.cit. 111-126.

[50] Which seems to be confirmed also by the Bronze Tablet, ii 35, 43; see instead H. Klengel, *AoF* 18, 226 f. note 21.

[51] Even if one could think that he held it already *in pectore*, given his prominent place in the list of witnesses to the document.

[52] See F. Imparati - F. Pecchioli Daddi, op.cit. 58-68; contrary to what appeared on page 66, it is now felt, after the publication of Peter Neve, *Ḫattuša - Stadt der Götter und Tempel*, Mainz am Rhein 1993, 19 ff. and 55, that Kurunta's *coup d'etat* was successful, even if for a short period of time.

[53] It is known that Tutḫaliya IV considered Neriqqaili very dangerous to the succession of his direct descendants to the Hittite throne, in the same way that he considered dangerous his many brothers or his relatives who descended from Muwattalli; see my observations on this topic in *Seminari* 1991, 71 f.

succeeded and who could at any moment have pretended to the throne with greater credibility.

Furthermore, concerning the proposal to identify Neriqqaili as Tutḫaliya's predecessor as *tuḫkanti*, I spoke in the same article of a text of inventories attributed either to Ḫattušili III or to Tutḫaliya IV – KUB XLII 51 (CTH 250) – where in obv. 2' a *tuḫkanti* is mentioned, whose name either was not indicated, or else was in the lacuna preceding this title. In this same text, in rev. 5', there appears, along with EN-LUGAL-ma[54], the anthroponym *Nerik*[, properly completed by J. Siegelová[55] as *Nerik*[*kaili* and identified as the son of Ḫattušili III and brother of Tutḫaliya IV. Now, even if we do not know the name of the *tuḫkanti* to whom this text refers, it seems difficult to me to presume that this was the Neriqqaili in question, because in the same document this latter is mentioned after EN-LUGAL-ma, an improbable position if he were the current *tuḫkanti*.

Therefore, at the time of this document, this position could have been held either by Tutḫaliya himself or by the brother designated before him as successor to the throne of Ḫatti.[56] Thus the document in question would be from the time of Ḫattušili III rather than Tutḫaliya IV, which would find a correspondence also in the mention in obv. 6' of a queen, in all likelihood Puduḫepa.[57]

To my mind the problem of the identification of Tutḫaliya's older brother who was removed by his father from his position as *tuḫkanti* is still an open question; it is understandable that Tutḫaliya, as a political tactic, did not want to mention his name in the Bronze Tablet, and it is also possible that he did not speak of him in later documents or that at the least he tried to gloss over his existence.

It seems also significant to me that Ḫattušili did not refer to this son in his Autobiography, perhaps because he had already deposed him from the position of *tuḫkanti*, or because mentioning him in that context did not further his plans.

5. *Conclusions*

As I have already observed elsewhere[58], I therefore feel it is reasonable to hypothesize in this context that Ḫattušili did not compile his Autobiography soon after he seized power in Ḫatti, in order to justify his usurpation, but at a later date, with the purpose of creating a favorable climate for his decision to

[54] = Ewri/Ibri-Šarruma, who in all likelihood is the same person present in the list on the Bronze Tablet iv 35; see my observations in *FsAlp* 314 f.; see also Th. van den Hout, op. cit. 150 f.

[55] *Verw.* II 344 f.

[56] See the Bronze Tablet ii 34 f., 43 f.

[57] Even if we know that Puduḫepa continued to be active in political life also during the early years of her son Tutḫaliya's reign; see H. Klengel, *AoF* 18, 233.

[58] *Seminari* 1991, 76.

name Tutḫaliya as his successor to the throne in place of an older son who had earlier been placed in that position.[59]

In effect, between Ḫattušili's assumption of power and the writing of his Autobiography enough time must have passed to allow him to designate his first heir to the throne; to allow Puduḫepa to weave her plots to prepare the ground for her son Tutḫaliya's nomination as crown prince; to allow Tutḫaliya to work toward this goal, with Kurunta as accomplice in a certain sense during that period, in exchange for which the latter would be given the throne of Tarḫuntašša, even if only for his accepting to withdraw from the race for power; and finally to allow Ḫattušili to change in Tutḫaliya's favor, albeit not yet officially, his earlier decision concerning his successor[60] and thus to place Kurunta on the throne of Tarḫuntašša. This last act took place before the Autobiography was compiled, as demonstrated in iv 62-64, where the use of the past tense for the verbs shows that this was something that had already happened.

I do not feel that Ḫattušili gave Kurunta the throne of Tarḫuntašša solely to reward him for his loyalty on the occasion of the former's usurpation of the throne, as has sometimes been believed.[61] In effect, even if I do not exclude that this could also have been a motive, I nonetheless think that the Hittite king, by mentioning this nomination in his Autobiography before naming Tutḫaliya as priest of Ištar, wanted to point out to Kurunta and any of his followers that he had already been well taken care of and that now he must leave the way free for Tutḫaliya.

It truly must not have been easy for Ḫattušili to make not only his enemies, but also his supporters, accept without protest such a substitution in the position of *tuḫkanti*[62], and there was the further danger that in this fluid situation around the question of succession, Kurunta too could enter into the power struggle and pretend to the throne, a stand that would not have been without a certain legitimacy.

It was therefore of fundamental importance for the king both to reaffirm in this instance the "legitimacy" of his assumption of power, which was the consequence of Ištar's divine will – in order thus to consolidate the stability of his hold on the throne and at the same time to validate every decision of his –

59 The fact that Ḫattušili had drawn up this document about ten years after his ascent to the throne has been rightly observed also by H. Otten (*StBoT* 24, 27, note to line 58 f.) on the basis of the passage in rev. IV 58 f. From this he deduces that the issue of the legitimacy of Ḫattušili's assumption of power had remained questionable throughout the king's entire reign; as confirmation, he cites §10c of the Autobiography and KUB XXIII 1 ii 15 ff. To support this we can add that doubts as to this legitimacy could arise even more forcefully above all in those circumstances in which the king wished his decisions of fundamental importance to the country, like the designation of his successor to the throne, to be accepted, in particular when it was the case of a decision replacing one he had made earlier.

60 As a result of the pressure brought to bear on him by Puduḫepa and by Tutḫaliya himself.

61 See H. Klengel, *AoF* 18, 232 with note 19.

62 Also because his other son whom he named to this position was older than Tutḫaliya, and furthermore this son too could also have had supporters in the court.

and to take care of Kurunta by placing him on the throne of Tarḫuntašša.

In this way, it seems particularly significant that Ḫattušili, right in the conclusion of his Autobiography, that is, in the most crucial part of the document, recalls both that he has settled Kurunta and also that he has placed his son Tutḫaliya at the service of this very goddess whom the Hittite king has throughout his entire text presented repeatedly and emphatically as his guide in his conquest of power.

The placement of Tutḫaliya in the goddess' service – as had been the case for Ḫattušili himself when he was still a boy (Autobiography i 13-21)[63] – thus takes on a clear political significance, that is, an investiture with the succession to the throne. Ḫattušili says in fact (Autobiography iv 78 f.): "I (am) a servant of the goddess, and may he (=Tutḫaliya) too be a servant of the goddess."

It is known, besides, that Ḫattušili tends in both his Autobiography and other documents to emphasize certain aspects of his life which show analogies with the life of his son Tutḫaliya[64], presumably with the purpose of preparing the way for him to attain the same goal: royal power.

Both of them had in fact held the position of GAL *MEŠEDI*, which was the highest in the Hittite kingdom after that of *tuḫkanti*, and in that position had performed deeds of great importance.[65] Both of them had held the priesthood of the Stormgod of Nerik and the "vice-kingship" in Ḫakpiš[66]; Tutḫaliya IV was most likely the DUMU.LUGAL who took part in cult ceremonies in Nerik in his father's place[67]; and finally, like his father Ḫattušili III, Tutḫaliya had also been placed in Ištar's service.[68]

In this context, then, §12a of the Autobiography is particularly interesting. There Ḫattušili, summarizing his career, reiterates twice that he had been prince and GAL *MEŠEDI*, and that as GAL *MEŠEDI* he had become king of Ḫakpiš, and finally that as king of Ḫakpiš he had become Great King. Dominion over the kingdom of Ḫatti, granted him by Ištar (iv 47-48), is thus presented almost as the natural conclusion of such a path.

I have spoken above, at the end of section 3, of the particular significance that the concluding paragraph of the Autobiography takes on in this light.

63 The statement that Ištar had taken care of Ḫattušili ever since his boyhood tends to underscore the fact that, even as a child, he was already predestined to become king.

64 Cf. most recently Ph.H.J. Houwink ten Cate, op. cit. 263 note 45 infra and the observations of Th.P.J. van den Hout, *ZA* 81 (1991) 298 ff.

65 I would like in this context to recall the acute essay by K.K. Riemschneider, *JCS* 16 (1962) 110-121, especially 119 ff., concerning the evident emphasis which Ḫattušili had wanted to give to certain deeds done by a Tutḫaliya GAL *MEŠEDI*, whom he properly identified as Tutḫaliya IV. At our current state of knowledge, this intention to glorify the prince clearly appears to be a function of furthering of his father's projects. It is particularly interesting to examine this GAL *MEŠEDI*'s zone of operation in the fragments studied by Riemschneider in the same article.

66 Certainly Ḫattušili and in all likelihood Tutḫaliya; see V. Haas, *KN* 13 f., 15, 24, 175 ff.

67 See V. Haas, op. cit., 42, cf. also 41.

68 With this investiture Ḫattušili seems to have wanted to pass on to his son his own fortunate connection with the goddess in order to have the same successful result: the kingship.

As I already hinted at in note 29, Tutḫaliya's political acts, once he was on the throne, were forced to fluctuate dramatically between severely distancing from his father's misdeeds and supporters[69] – necessary so as not to place in question or in danger the rights of his descendants to succeed to the throne – and at the same time an inevitable recognition of the legitimacy of his father's operations in order not to weaken his own hold on power, a power he had attained precisely as a result of his father's workings and also of other intrigues, which are in large part unknown to us but were certainly familiar to those living at court at that time.

I also wonder if Tutḫaliya's concession to Kurunta in §19 of the Bronze Tablet of freedom of choice in his successor to the throne and the commitment made by this Hittite king to respect that choice might not have been influenced by what had happened in the past in the naming of Tutḫaliya as heir to the throne in place of his older brother, a fact recalled by the king in that same text. In this manner Tutḫaliya may perhaps have tried to prevent any future claims on the throne on the part of anyone who could in some way have had any rights to it.[70] Furthermore, he thus established also his liberty to choose his successor in the future, with the proviso, however, that this choice always remained with the king and had to be from among his descendants.

Summing up what I have observed up to now, I ask, if Ḫattušili had only wanted to present an apology for himself, with the sole purpose of reconfirming the legitimacy of his power, why would he have spoken in the concluding part of this text of Kurunta and Tutḫaliya?

And if this document was drawn up only for the purpose of granting the priesthood of Ištar to Tutḫaliya, as a public act of devotion and gratitude to the goddess on Ḫattušili's part and as a visible remembrance of what she had done to bring him to royal power, why would he have mentioned there also Kurunta along with Tutḫaliya? It does not seem to me enough to say that it was with the sole purpose of recalling to everyone that he had behaved correctly in connection with his brother's progeny or to reward Kurunta for his loyalty, since Ḫattušili had drawn up various other documents in this sense. It would also be surprising to find the two cousins mentioned in such close context without there being some precise reason, while the current *tuḫkanti* and other children of Ḫattušili were not named at all.

In my opinion, finally, it is possible that the Autobiography, which, we know from Ḫattušili himself, was drawn up after the establishment of Kurunta on the throne of Tarḫuntašša – and therefore after Ḫattušili's first treaty with Kurunta – preceded however the second treaty between Ḫattušili and Kurunta, a treaty less favorable to the latter than the earlier one. In fact, the reduced

69 Cf. his judgement concerning Mašduri, recalled in note 29.

70 Houwink ten Cate, op.cit. 242 note 44, instead harks back to H. Otten, *StBoT* Beih. 1, 7 and 9 with note 30, who sees in the brother of Kurunta mentioned in this passage "a veiled allusion to Ulmi-Teššub, Kurunta's successor after the two treaty partners eventually fell out with one another." This hypothesis, however, seems to me to be premature at the time of the drawing up of the Bronze Tablet and not in agreement with the context.

concessions given to Kurunta in this document seem evidence of the stability of Ḫattušili's hold on power[71] and the acceptance, at this point well-established at court and throughout the kingdom, of Tutḫaliya as his successor to the throne, so that there was no longer any need for Ḫattušili to appease Kurunta to keep him from opposing the king's plans. Ḫattušili, rather, had more reason to reduce Kurunta's position so that he could not obtain too much power. KBo VI 29+ could be dated either before Kurunta was placed on the throne of Tarḫuntašša or between this event and the compilation of the Autobiography.

[71] Cf. F. Imparati - F. Pecchioli Daddi, op. cit. 64.

HISTORISCHER KOMMENTAR ZUM ŠAUŠGAMUWA-VERTRAG

HORST KLENGEL

Der als Vertrag zwischen dem hethitischen Großkönig Tutḫalija IV. und Šaušgamuwa von Amurru bezeichnete Text ist bislang in zwei Exemplaren überliefert (CTH 105).[1] Beide wurden offenbar in den Ostmagazinen des Großen Tempels von Ḫattuša aufbewahrt; zwar fehlen für die wesentlichen Textfragmente von Tafel A (VAT 7421, Bo 4062 und 4193) ebenso wie für das Fragment Bo 4372 der Tafel B entsprechende Hinweise der Ausgräber, doch lassen die bei späteren Grabungen dort entdeckten Anschlußfragmente darauf schließen, daß beide Tafeln an dieser Stelle deponiert wurden. Das ist auch deshalb bemerkenswert, als es sich, wie schon von F. Sommer[2] bemerkt wurde, bei Exemplar A um eine "Kladde" handelt, worauf die häufigen Tilgungen und – meist in kleinerer Schrift vorgenommenen – Zusätze weisen dürften. Die zweikolumnige Tafel A bietet den größten Teil des Textes[3], während B eine einkolumnige Tafel darstellt, von der nach dem Zusammenfügen mehrerer kleiner Fragmente nur noch der rechte obere Teil der Vs. und der rechte untere Teil der Rs. erhalten sind.[4] Tilgungen und Zusätze sind auf B nicht erkennbar[5], und die auf der Rs. noch teilweise erhaltene (und nach KBo XII 31 ergänzbare) Liste der Eidgottheiten deutet wohl darauf, daß es sich hier um ein abgeschlossenes Vertragsexemplar handelt.

Seit der Bearbeitung beider Tafeln durch C. Kühne und H. Otten (StBoT 16, 1971) sind m.W. keine weiteren Fragmente als zugehörig identifiziert worden. Bewußt wurde bei der Textbearbeitung in StBoT 16 auf einen historischen Kommentar verzichtet.[6] In der Hoffnung, das Interesse des verehrten Jubilars zu

[1] Bearbeitung durch C. Kühne und H. Otten, *Der Šaušgamuwa-Vertrag* (*StBoT* 16), Wiesbaden 1971. Im folgenden nur noch abgekürzt *StBoT* 16.

[2] F. Sommer, *AU* 322, s. auch *StBoT* 16, 1.

[3] Vgl. die Joinskizze in *StBoT* 16, 2 f.

[4] *StBoT* 16, 4.

[5] So nach Kollation des Fotos von Bo 4372 (KUB VIII 82) und den in *StBoT* 16, 80 gebotenen Kopien der weiteren Anschlußfragmente.

[6] Siehe die Bemerkungen in *StBoT* 16, 5. Ein solcher Kommentar hätte im Hinblick auf das für diese Periode vor allem aus Ḫattuša und Ugarit verfügbare umfangreiche epigraphische Material und die damit verbundenen historischen Probleme das Anliegen der Textbearbeitung weit überschritten. Auch im folgenden können nicht alle in einem Zusammenhang mit dem

finden, sei im folgenden versucht, den Šaušgamuwa-Vertrag im Hinblick auf seinen historischen Hintergrund zu interpretieren. Neue Textfunde in Ugarit, die Entdeckung der Bronzetafel mit dem Vertrag Tutḫalijas IV. mit Kurunta von Tarhuntašša[7] sowie die an diesen Text und archäologische Neufunde[8] anschließende Diskussion der Herrschaftszeit dieses hethitischen Großkönigs[9] bieten dafür eine gegenüber dem älteren Forschungsstand erweiterte Grundlage. Nicht zuletzt haben auch die weiteren Untersuchungen zur Geschichte Syriens und insbesondere von Amurru neue Erkenntnisse erbracht.[10] Von besonderer Relevanz ist dabei Tafel A, die gerade durch ihren Charakter als ein Entwurf, der sich um eine dem Anliegen gerecht werdende Formulierung bemüht und während der Niederschrift "aktualisiert" wurde, aufschlußreich für die Sicht des großköniglichen Hofes auf vergangene und zeitgenössische politische Verhältnisse ist.

In Kol. I 1-7 wird zunächst die Genealogie des Tutḫalija IV. geboten, der als Nachfahre eines Tutḫalija (I./II.) bezeichnet wird.[11] Das geschieht wohl im Hinblick auf die Namensgleichheit sowie auf die Rolle, die dieser Großkönig bei

Šaušgamuwa-Vertrag stehenden Fragen diskutiert werden; es geht lediglich um eine historische Bewertung des Vertragstextes selbst. Ältere Literatur wird in *StBoT* 16, 1 Anm.1 und 2 genannt; die Textvorlage und der zugleich gebotene historische Kommentar von I. Sugi, *Orient. The Reports of the Society for Near Eastern Studies in Japan* 1 (Tokyo 1960) 1 ff., sind inzwischen weitgehend überholt.

[7] H. Otten, *StBoT* Beih. 1.

[8] Gemeint ist vor allem die Auffindung von Tausenden von gesiegelten Tonbullen im Archivgebäude am Nişantepe in den Jahren 1990/91, darunter vor allem Siegeln der hethitischen Großkönige, dazu vorläufig P. Neve, *AA* 1991, 325 ff. und *AA* 1992, 307 ff. sowie H. Otten, *Zu einigen Neufunden hethitischer Königssiegel* (Akad.d.Wiss.und der Lit., Abhandl. der geistes-und sozialwiss.Klasse, Jahrgang 1993, Nr.13, Mainz - Stuttgart 1993).

[9] Zur Diskussion vgl. Th.P.J. van den Hout, *JCS* 41 (1989) 100 ff.; G. Beckman, *WO* 20/21 (1989/90) 289 ff.; H. Klengel, *AoF* 18 (1991) 224 ff.; F. Imparati - F. Pecchioli Daddi, *Quattro studi ittiti*, 23 ff.; G.F. Del Monte, *EVO* 14/15 (1991/92) 123 ff.; S. Heinhold-Krahmer, *AfO* 38/39 (1991/92) 138 ff.; Ph.H.J. Houwink ten Cate, *ZA* 82 (1992) 233 ff.; D. Sürenhagen, *OLZ* 87 (1992) 341 ff.; H.A. Hoffner, in: W.A.Ward - M.Sh.Joukowsky (eds.), *The Crisis Years: The 12th Century B.C.. From Beyond the Danube to the Tigris* (Dubuque/Iowa 1992), 46 ff., sowie O.R. Gurney, *AnSt* 43 (1993) 13 ff. An dieser Stelle soll auf die dort vor allem behandelte Problematik der chronologischen Einordnung der Tarḫuntašša-Verträge (dazu siehe jetzt Th.P.J. van den Hout, *StBoT* 38) sowie der Identifikation des abgesetzten *tuḫkanti* nicht noch einmal zurückgekommen werden.

[10] Vgl. zusammenfassend I. Singer, in: Sh. Izre'el, *Amurru Akkadian: A Linguistic Study*, II (Atlanta 1991), 135 ff. (im folgenden abgek. I. Singer, *Amurru*) sowie H. Klengel, *Syria 3000 to 300 B.C.. A Handbook of Political History* (Berlin 1992), 160 ff. (im folgenden H. Klengel, *Syria 3000 to 300 B.C.*).

[11] Vgl. seine Genealogie in anderen Urkunden sowie auf den Königssiegeln; siehe dazu zuletzt die Literatur bei H. Klengel, *AoF* 18 (1991) 224 f. – Die Streichung in Kol. I 5 erfolgte offenbar wegen einer versehentlichen Doppelung des Titels "König von Ḫatti"? Dem Vorderasiatischen Museum Berlin danke ich für die Erlaubnis, die Tafel VAT 7421 für diesen Beitrag einzusehen.

der erneuten Stabilisierung und Expansion des hethitischen Reiches spielte.[12] Der Vertragspartner Šaušgamuwa wird nicht mit seiner Stellung und Genealogie genannt, was bei Vasallenverträgen, durch die der Vertragspartner nach hethitischer Auffassung erst ein rechtmäßig regierender Fürst wurde, gebräuchlich war.[13] Als maßgeblich für die nachfolgende Darstellung werden in Kol. I 8-12 die Verschwägerung des Tutḫalija mit Šaušgamuwa, der eine Schwester des Tutḫalija zur Ehefrau erhielt, sowie die Ausfertigung einer Vertragstafel (*išḫiulaš tuppi*) genannt. Der Hinweis auf die Verschwägerung wird in Kol. II 1-3 zunächst wiederholt und zugleich erweitert mit der Erwähnung der Investitur des Šaušgamuwa in Amurru durch Tutḫalija, die damit Vertrag und Erlangung der Königswürde gleichsetzt, ohne daß eine gleichzeitige Abfassung des vorliegenden Textes (Tafel A) impliziert wird. Daß Šaušgamuwa als Sohn und Nachfolger des Bentešina König von Amurru wurde, wird an beiden Stellen nicht erwähnt; die Sohnschaft des Šaušgamuwa gegenüber Bentešina wird nur in Kol. I 44 in einem anderem Kontext, der diesen Hinweis notwendig machte, genannt. Die familiäre Beziehung zum hethitischen Großkönig wird hier als wesentliches Argument für die im weiteren Text gestellte Forderung benutzt, daß Šaušgamuwa Tutḫalija und das großkönigliche Haus gegen innere und äußere Bedrohung schützen solle – das Hauptthema des gesamten Textes zumindest der Tafel A.

Von besonderem historiographischem Interesse ist die hethitische Wiedergabe (Kol. I 13-48) des Verhältnisses zwischen Ḫatti und Amurru bis zur Niederschrift des auf Tafel A vorliegenden Textes. Dabei konzentriert sich die Darstellung auf Aspekte, die aus hethitischer Sicht für die Forderung unbedingter Treue als von besonderem Belang erschienen: Das Verhältnis des Azira/Aziru zu Šuppiluliuma I. und Muršili II. sowie des – hier nicht mit Namen genannten - Bentešina zu Muwattalli II. und Ḫattusili III. Eine "Geschichte" von Amurru bis zur Zeit des Šaušgamuwa zu bieten war nicht die Absicht des Verfassers des Šaušgamuwa-Vertrages.

In Kol. I 13-27 wird unter den o.g. Gesichtspunkten die Zeit behandelt, in der sich im mittelsyrischen Raum, dem strategisch und ökonomisch wichtigen Grenzbereich zwischen Mittani und Ägypten bzw. dann Ḫatti und Ägypten, das Fürstentum Amurru herausbildete. Die Situation wird am ausführlichsten, wenngleich nicht immer zuverlässig in den Amarna-Texten reflektiert.[14] Der Name

[12] Vgl. *StBoT* 16, 22 sowie H. Klengel, *AoF* 18 (1991) 224 f. – Die Zählung der hethitischen Großkönige dürfte nach neueren Forschungen, die die Existenz eines Tutḫalija I. sowie des Ḫattušili II. in Frage stellen, wohl zu verändern sein: Ḫattušili II. (statt III.) und Tutḫalija III. (statt IV.). Bis diese Frage eindeutig entschieden werden kann, sollte bei den bislang üblichen Zählungen geblieben werden, insbesondere in der historischen Literatur.

[13] Vgl. etwa die übrigen Amurru-Verträge, in Umschrift und Übersetzung zuletzt vorgelegt von G.F. Del Monte, *OAC* 18, 116 ff.

[14] Dazu zuletzt siehe mit früherer Literatur, H. Klengel, *Syria 3000 to 300 B.C.* 160 ff.

des neuen Fürstentums nimmt eine eher geographisch determinierte Bezeichnung (Amurru/MAR.TU) für den mittel- und nordsyrischen Raum auf, d.h. den Bereich, der zur Regierungszeit Šuppiluliumas zunächst von Mittani kontrolliert wurde.[15] Neben dem Namen für das Fürstentum, das sich von der mittelsyrischen Ebene bis zur Mittelmeerküste erstreckte[16], ist die weiter gefaßte Bedeutung von "Amurru" offensichtlich erhalten geblieben; sie wurde später auch von Tiglath-pilesar I. in diesem erweiterten Sinne benutzt. Im vorliegenden Text geht es vor allem um die Unterwerfung und nachfolgende Treue des Aziru, der zuvor – wie andere Fürsten des nördlichen Syrien auch – die Oberhoheit des Königs von Ḫurri-Mittani anerkannt hatte[17]; daß er zugleich in einem engen Verhältnis zum ägyptischen Pharao stand, wird offenbar mit Absicht nicht erwähnt. Die genealogische Beziehung des Tutḫalija IV. zu Šuppiluliuma I. sowie die des Šaušgamuwa zu Aziru (*ABI ABI*) wird mit "Ahnherr" wiederzugeben sein; die wörtliche Übersetzung mit "Großvater" wäre in beiden Fällen nicht zutreffend: Tutḫalija war Urenkel des Šuppiluliuma, Šaušgamuwa sogar Ur-Urenkel des Aziru.[18]

Der geographische Bereich, in dem Aziru aktiv war, wird in Kol. I 18 f. zur Einflußsphäre von Ḫurri-Mittani gerechnet, doch verweist der Text darauf, daß die Unterordnung unter Mittani nicht Ergebnis eines bewaffneten Eingreifens von Mittani gewesen sei (Z. 20 f.). Wahrscheinlich hätte sich Mittani, das ein enges, durch dynastische Ehen gefestigtes Verhältnis zu Ägypten aufgebaut hatte, ohnehin nicht zu einem militärischen Konflikt mit dem auch mit Ägypten verbundenen Amurru entschlossen. Weder die Aktionen Azirus im ägyptisch kontrollierten Küstengebiet um Ṣumur, Sitz eines Beamten des Pharaos, noch seine engen Beziehungen zum ägyptischen König werden erwähnt, da dieses Doppelspiel Azirus[19] für den Vertragsschluß Šaušgamuwa nicht nur unerheblich schien, sondern auch der Absicht des Textes nicht entsprochen hätte. Wenn in Kol. I 24-26 dem Aziru Treue gegenüber Ḫatti bescheinigt wird, so ist offenbar auch seine Rolle während des Aufstandes nordsyrischer Fürsten gegen die hethitische Oberherrschaft nicht negativ bewertet worden.[20] Die Erhebung

15 Vgl. I. Singer, *Iraq* 53 (1991) 69 ff., der insbesondere auf die oft parallele Verwendung des Begriffes Amurru in einem weiterem und einem engerem Sinne hinweist.

16 Dazu bereits H. Klengel, *Gesch.Syr.* 178 ff., vgl. auch die Karte bei I. Singer, *Amurru* 134.

17 Nach *Ḫurriat* folgt in Kol. I 18 ein Tafelbruch, vielleicht mit Resten eines Zeichens.

18 Siehe dazu auch *StBoT* 16, 29 f. *A-BA-A-BI-KA* in Kol. I 21 über Rasur, doch sind noch Spuren des getilgten Textes zu erkennen.

19 Vgl. dazu H. Klengel, *MIO* 10 (1964) 57 ff. und zuletzt in: *Syria 3000 to 300 B.C.* 161 ff., ferner M. Liverani, *StMed* 4, 93 ff. sowie I. Singer, *Amurru* 148 ff.

20 Vgl. dazu die Darstellung im Duppi-Tešup-Vertrag (CTH 62), der dem Fürsten von Amurru gegenüber eine sehr positive Einschätzung der Haltung des Aziru gibt (Akkad. Vs. 2 ff., Hethit. I 3 ff.). Seinem Nachfolger DU-Tešup (SUM-Tešup/Ari-Tešup?) wird ebendort gleichfalls Treue gegenüber Ḫatti bestätigt, doch war das für die Einleitung des Šaušgamuwa-Vertrages

konnte erst durch Muršili II. in seinem 9. Regierungsjahr durch persönliches Eingreifen beendet werden. Der Vertragsschluß Muršilis mit Duppi-Tešup von Amurru (CTH 62), einem Enkel des Aziru, sowie dessen Verhältnis zu Ḫatti werden ebenfalls übergangen, da sie für die historisch-didaktische Absicht des Textes wohl ohne besondere Relevanz waren. Ein Passus im Duppi-Tešup-Vertrag fordert den Amurru Fürsten auf, künftig nicht mehr eine Abgabe (*arkamma-*) an Ägypten zu senden, wie das seine "Väter" getan hätten; denn Ägypten sei nun mit Ḫatti verfeindet.[21]

Vs. I 28-39 widmet sich dem Verhältnis zwischen Ḫatti und Amurru während der kritischen Phase der ägyptisch-hethitischen Beziehungen, die von erneuten militärischen Aktivitäten Ägyptens im Bereich Mittelsyriens geprägt war und in der Schlacht von Qadeš zwischen Muwattalli II. von Ḫatti und seinen Verbündeten sowie Ramses II. gipfelte. Die bewaffnete Präsenz Ägyptens nahe Amurru, die wohl mit den militärischen Unternehmungen des Sethos I. in Verbindung gebracht werden kann,[22] veranlaßte offenbar Bentešina, sich auf die Seite Ägyptens zu schlagen. Im Text wird dies in Kol. I 29 ohne Nennung des Namens des Bentešina erwähnt; der Vorgang wird vielmehr als eine Aktion der "Leute des Landes Amurru" (LÚ^{MEŠ} KUR ^{URU}*A-mur-ra*) dargestellt.[23] Der mit dem hethitischen großköniglichen Haus und wohl auch Tutḫalija eng verbundene Bentešina wird damit nicht mit der Affäre belastet; der Text konnte also weiterhin im Sinne eines vorbildhaften Verhaltens der Amurru-Dynastie formuliert werden.[24] Die im Wortlaut zitierte (I 31 f.) Freiwilligkeit der Unter-

offenbar ohne Belang; der Aziru-Vertrag hatte zu seiner Zeit noch Gültigkeit, ein Vertrag mit DU-Tešup ist nicht überliefert und wurde wohl auch nicht abgeschlossen. Im Bentešina-Vertrag (CTH 92) wird sowohl von DU-Tešup als auch Duppi-Tešup gesagt, sie hätten sich an den Wortlaut des Šuppiluliuma - Aziru - Vertrages gehalten (Vs. 7 ff.), der demnach seit Aziru die Grundlage für das Verhältnis Amurrus zu Ḫatti bildete und nach dessen Vorbild dann auch der Duppi-Tešup-Vertrag formuliert wurde.

[21] Heth. I 33 ff.; in der akkad. Fassung nicht überliefert. Im Duppi-Tešup-Vertrag spielte offenbar die Problematik einer Auslieferung von Flüchtlingen und Überstellung von Deportierten eine besondere Rolle, was wohl in einem Zusammenhang mit der voraufgehenden politischen Situation in Nordsyrien, d.h. einer Rebellion gegen Ḫatti, gesehen werden darf.

[22] Vgl. dazu H. Klengel, *Syria 3000 to 300 B.C.* 116 f., ferner I. Singer, *Amurru* 165; eine Stele des Sethos I. wurde in Tell Nebi Mend/Qadeš entdeckt, siehe M. Pézard, *Syria* 3 (1922) 108 ff. Zu den militärischen Unternehmungen des Sethos I. in Syrien siehe A. Spalinger, *Bulletin of the Egyptological Seminary* (of New York) 1 (1979) 68 ff. sowie W.J. Murnane, *The Road to Kadesh* (Chicago 1985), 53 ff.

[23] Vgl. schon den Hinweis von A. Götze, *OLZ* 32 (1929) 834 f. I. Singer, *Amurru* 165 f. bemerkt, daß es sich bei dem Šaušgamuwa-Vertrag nicht um eine so "objektive" Quelle handele, daß daraus auf innere Auseinandersetzungen in Amurru geschlossen werden müsse.

[24] Die Beziehungen des Bentešina zu Ḫattušili III., dessen Gemahlin Puduḫepa sowie den Prinzen spiegeln sich in einer Reihe von Texten wider; vgl. seine Briefe bei A. Hagenbuchner, THeth 16, Nrn. 260-266 und 334. sowie H. Klengel, *Syria 3000 to 300 B.C.* 172. Zur Ehe des Bentešina mit Gaššulijawija, Tochter von Ḫattušili III. und Puduḫepa, siehe

stellung Amurrus unter Ḫatti, die nun zugunsten eines Anschlusses an Ägypten aufgekündigt wurde, deutet sogar einen gewissen politischen Handlungsspielraum Amurrus an, d.h. seine Möglichkeit, trotz vertraglicher Bindungen der Dynastie einen anderen Oberherrn zu wählen, was der Realität kaum entsprochen haben dürfte. Bei Qadeš hat Amurru offenbar auf ägyptischer Seite gestanden; es wird jedenfalls nicht unter den hethitischen Bundesgenossen erwähnt. In Kol. I 35 f. wird die hethitisch-ägyptische Auseinandersetzung ausdrücklich als Kampf um Amurru bezeichnet.[25] Diese Wertung dürfte nicht nur der Tendenz des Vertragstextes entsprochen haben, sondern vermied zugleich den Eindruck, als habe es sich um einen Eroberungskrieg gegen Ägypten selbst gehandelt. Das hätte weder den Absichten Ḫattis entsprochen noch wäre es aus Rücksicht auf Ägypten zur Zeit des Tutḫalija IV. opportun gewesen. Während Šuppiluliuma die Unterwerfung von Amurru mittels militärischer Gewalt vermeiden konnte, hat Muwattalli die (erneute) Unterwerfung von Amurru erst durch die Schlacht von Qadeš erreicht. Die Absetzung des Bentešina wird in diesem Zusammenhang nicht erwähnt; sie hätte ihn als Schuldigen am Abfall von Ḫatti dargestellt. Im Bentešina-Vertrag selbst (CTH 92) wird darauf verwiesen (Vs. 11 ff.), daß Bentešina von Amurru (politisch) "tot" gewesen, von Muwattalli abgesetzt und nach Ḫatti deportiert worden sei. Die Darstellung Ḫattušilis III. zielte darauf ab, den Kontrast seiner Handlungsweise gegenüber der seines Bruders deutlich zu machen; hier ging es um die Sicherung der hethitischen Position in Amurru, nach wie vor wichtiger Grenzbereich zur ägyptischen Sphäre Syriens. Im Hinblick auf die Zielstellung, Amurru wieder an Ḫatti zu binden, hatte die Schlacht von Qadeš jedenfalls zum Erfolg der Hethiter geführt, die einen sonst wenig bezeugten Šapili in Amurru einsetzten. Ramses II. hat auch nach der Schlacht von Qadeš versucht, Ägyptens Macht im zentralen Syrien militärisch zur Geltung zu bringen, wobei er vielleicht von der inneren Situation in Ḫatti (Auseinandersetzung Ḫattušilis mit Muršili III./Urḫi-Tešup) profitieren konnte.[26]

Kol. I 40-48 wird die Vorgeschichte des Vertrages mit der Einsetzung des Bentešina durch Ḫattušili III. und der Absetzung des von Muwattalli II. nach der Qadeš-Schlacht installierten Šapili (I 39) abgeschlossen; Bentešina sei Ḫatti gegenüber treu geblieben. Im Šaušgamuwa-Vertrag konnte somit der Eindruck erweckt werden, daß Bentešina erst jetzt König von Amurru geworden sei. Unerwähnt bleibt die Regierung des Muršili III., von Tutḫalija entsprechend der von seinem Vater getroffenen "Sprachregelung" stets Urḫi-Tešup, d.h. nicht mit

den Bentešina-Vertrag (CTH 92) Vs. 18 ff. sowie den Puduḫepa-Brief KUB XXI 38 (CTH 176).

[25] Vgl. schon den Hinweis von A. Götze, *OLZ* 32 (1929) 833 f., daß Amurru der Maßstab für die Macht Ägyptens bzw. Ḫattis gewesen sei.

[26] Vgl. dazu I. Singer, *Amurru* 167 sowie H. Klengel, *Syria 3000 to 300 B.C.* 118.

seinem Thronnamen als Großkönig, bezeichnet. Dadurch scheint Ḫattušili III. dem Wortlaut des Textes nach als direkter Nachfolger des Muwattalli auf den Thron gelangt zu sein, was dem syrischen Vertragspartner wohl kaum suggeriert werden sollte, sondern einfach durch das Weglassen eines im gegebenen Zusammenhang nicht relevanten Kapitels bedingt war.[27] Bentešina, dereinst von Ḫattušili aufgenommen und über längere Zeit in der Umgebung dieses immer mehr an Macht gewinnenden Onkels des Muršili III. lebend, wobei sich ein enges Verhältnis zu Ḫattušili, dessen Gemahlin Puduḫepa und gewiß auch zum Prinzen Tutḫalija entwickelte,[28] ist dann in Amurru offenbar ein treuer, den mit ihm geschlossenen Vertrag achtender Vasall geblieben, der das großkönigliche Haus "geschützt" habe (*paḫḫašta*).

Mit Kol. II 1 ff. werden die unter Gotteseid gestellten Festlegungen für Šaušgamuwa eingeleitet, wobei zunächst die Kol. I 8-12 erwähnte Verschwägerung erneut hervorgehoben und danach darauf verwiesen wird, daß es Tutḫalija (IV.) gewesen sei, der Šaušgamuwa im Lande Amurru zum König gemacht habe (II 1-3).[29] Danach folgen ausführliche Darlegungen zu den sich daraus ergebenden Schutz- und Hilfeverpflichtungen des Šaušgamuwa, die den größten Teil des Textes von Tafel A einnehmen.[30] Vielleicht darf hier nicht nur auf die Bedrohung der hethitischen Herrschaft in Syrien durch die bis in Euphratnähe vorgestoßenen Assyrer hingewiesen werden, sondern auch auf eine für den hethitischen Großkönig offenbar verunsicherte innere Situation in Ḫatti selbst.[31]

27 Vgl. die Selbstdarstellung des Weges zum großköniglichen Thron durch Ḫattušili III.: H.Otten, *StBoT* 24. Die Darstellung wäre allerdings korrekt, wenn man Ph.H.J. Houwink ten Cate, *BiOr* 51 (1994) 242f. und 247, folgt, der jetzt annimmt, daß die Wiedereinsetzung des Bentešina in Amurru durch Muršili III./Urḫitešup auf Anraten des Ḫattušili (III.) erfolgte und Muwattalli II. der Vorgänger des Ḫattušili III. gewesen sei.

28 Bentešina erscheint als noch in Amurru regierender Fürst auch unter den Zeugen des Kurunta-Vertrages, siehe die Bronzetafel Bo 86/299 Kol. IV 36; außer ihm wird aus Syrien nur noch Ini-Tešup genannt, Angehöriger des großköniglichen Hauses und hethitischer Vizekönig, Inhaber einer "großen Stelle" (*šalli peda-*) und von Tuthalija IV. selbst wohl als "großer König" (= Großkönig?) bezeichnet (RS 18.06+17.365 = PRU IV 137 f.). Die Aufnahme des Bentešina unter die Vertragszeugen ist hier wohl weniger durch sein enges Verhältnis zu Tutḫalija zu erklären, sondern deutet eher auf die besondere Rolle von Amurru unter den syrischen Vasallen Ḫattis; in diesem Sinne auch I. Singer, *Amurru* 169.

29 Am Anfang von Kol. II 1 ist eine Überschreibung des Textes erfolgt, wohl ohne Rasur.

30 In Kol. II 6 ist *ta-ma-i* NUMUN, "ein anderer Nachkomme" ersatzlos getilgt worden. Die Lesung *ka-a-aš-ta* kann nach Autopsie des Originals bestätigt werden.

31 Vgl. dazu bereits H. Klengel, *AoF* 18 (1991) 230 ff. Inzwischen hat Th.P.J. van den Hout, *ZA* 81 (1991) 274 ff. weitere Argumente für die Annahme beigebracht, daß Tuthalija von Ḫattušili nicht nur zum Koregenten gemacht wurde, sondern auch Anzeichen einer "Nervosität" im Hinblick auf die alleinige Machtübernahme durch Tuthalija zu erkennen sind. Offensichtlich wollten Ḫattušili und seine Gemahlin Puduḫepa, die Tutḫalija auf seinem Weg zum Kronprinzen tatkräftig unterstützt hatte, mittels ihrer Autorität einen problemlosen

Auch der Kurunta-Vertrag der Bronzetafel (Bo 86/299) läßt eine besondere "Befindlichkeit" des Tutḫalija erkennen, die gewiß nicht nur von der Art der Machtergreifung durch seinen Vater Ḫattušili herrührte, sondern auch seine eigne Bestellung zum Thronfolger unter Ausschaltung des bisherigen *tuḫkanti*.[32] Legitime Nachkommen und Brüder des Großkönigs, aber ebenso die Söhne von Nebenfrauen des Ḫattušili sowie andere Söhne königlicher Abkunft sollten von Šaušgamuwa nicht in einem Streben nach dem Thron unterstützt werden.[33] Um das zu erläutern, wird in Kol. II 15-30 das Beispiel eines gewissen Mašturi eingefügt, der – ebenso wie Šaušgamuwa – Schwager eines Großkönigs (Muwattalli II.) und von diesem zum König (im Šeḫaflußland) gemacht worden war und in diesem Amt auch unter den Zeugen des Kurunta-Vertrages der Bronzetafel erscheint.[34] Gerade aber dieses Exempel bereitete bei der Formulierung beträchtliche Probleme, wie die mehrfachen Tilgungen und Zusätze in diesem Abschnitt zeigen; vielleicht ist in das endgültige Vertragsexemplar dieses Beispiel nicht aufgenommen worden? Ein Vergleich des Textumfangs von Tafel A und B dürfte anzeigen, daß der vollständige Text von A auf B, das außerdem noch die Liste der göttlichen Zeugen bietet, nicht enthalten sein kann.

Die Veränderungen in Kol. II 16-38, d.h. bei der Darstellung der Mašturi-Episode und den daraus gezogenen Folgerungen, resultieren zweifellos daher,

Übergang zur Regierung des Tutḫalija gewährleisten; vgl. dazu die Bemerkungen von H. Otten, *FsNeve* 113 ff.

32 Verf. hatte Nerikkaili für die Person dieses *tuḫkanti* in Betracht gezogen, siehe *AoF* 18 (1991) 224 ff.; Ph.H.J. Houwink ten Cate, *ZA* 82 (1992) 233 ff. (insbes. 240 ff.) plädiert dagegen im Anschluß an H.G. Güterbock, *Or* 59 (1990) 162 für Kurunta, der damit zugleich einen zusätzlichen Grund dafür erhalten haben würde, gegen Tutḫalija zu rebellieren (vgl. ebd., 269 Anm. 50, Addendum). Siehe zur Diskussion jetzt auch S. Heinhold-Krahmer, *AfO* 38/39 (1991/92) 142 ff.

33 Vgl. dazu die ähnlichen und ebenfalls sehr ausführlichen Formulierungen Tutḫalijas IV. in seinen "Dienstanweiseungen" für 'Obere" (LÚ^MEŠ^SAG) sowie für "Prinzen" (DUMU^MEŠ^.LUGAL) und "Herren" (*BELŪ*^MEŠ^): E.von Schuler, *Heth.Dienstanw.* 8 ff. und 22 ff. (CTH 255). Vgl. auch KUB XXVI 18 (CTH 275) Vs. 9' ff.

34 Bo 86/299 IV 32, siehe H. Otten, *StBoT* Beih. 1, 26 f. Zu Mašturi vgl. auch S. Heinhold-Krahmer, *AfO* 38/39 (1991/92) 154 ff. Sein Name wird in der gleichen Zeile gefolgt von dem des ebenfalls mit dem großköniglichen Haus verschwägerten Šaušgamuwa. Es ist bemerkenswert, daß Šaušgamuwa hier seine Position unter den Zeugen offenbar seiner Rolle als "Schwager des Königs" (^LÚ^*ḪA-DA-AN* LUGAL, Kol. IV 32) verdankt. Es ist zwar nicht *a priori* davon auszugehen, daß die Positionierung in einer Zeugenfolge ein sicherer Hinweis auf Stellung bzw. Ansehen einer Person sein muß, doch fällt hier die spätere Nennung des Bentešina auf. Zusammen mit Šaušgamuwa wird Mašturi, König des Šeḫaflußlandes, genannt, wobei wohl die (gewachsene?) Rolle dieses westkleinasiatisches Landes von Belang gewesen sein könnte; vgl. dazu auch F. Imparati - F. Pecchioli Daddi, *Quattro studi ittiti* 62 Anm.79. Da die im Šaušgamuwa-Vertrag erhobene Schutzforderung zunächst aus der Verschwägerung der Partner abgeleitet wird, dürfte diese auch schon bestanden haben, als Šaušgamuwa noch nicht auf dem Thron von Amurru saß.

daß sich nun doch die Notwendigkeit ergab, Muršili III./Urḫi-Tešup mit ins Spiel zu bringen (II 20-23) und die Handlungsweise des Mašturi zu erläutern (II 24-30). Mašturi hatte zunächst Muwattalli II. und Muršili III. gedient, bis dann Ḫattušili dem letzteren den Thron "wegnahm" (*arḫa* ME-*aš* II 22). Letztere Formulierung[35] ist insofern von Interesse, als sie bei Tutḫalija einen Zweifel an der Legitimität des Handelns seines Vaters erkennen läßt.[36] Die Tilgung der Zeilen II 22 und 28 dürfte, da mit Z. 24 das Mašturi-Beispiel eingeleitet wird, sich wohl auf die Probleme bei der Wiedergabe des nicht korrekten Thronwechsels bezogen haben; die ursprüngliche Fassung hatte den Sachverhalt wahrscheinlich in einer Weise formuliert, die sich bei der weiteren Niederschrift des Textes als ungeeignet erwies und daher nachträglich eliminiert wurde. Die Neufassung war offensichtlich kürzer als die ursprüngliche, so daß Z. 23 frei blieb. Mašturis "Verrat" erfolgte durch seine Parteinahme für Ḫattušili; die Formulierung (*kupijatin kupta*[37]) ist in II 28 noch einmal – diesmal mit "Glossenkeilen", wie sie gerade in hethitischen Texten der Spätzeit häufig auftreten – wiederholt und dann als Doppelung getilgt worden (Zeichenspuren sind noch vorhanden).[38] Als Begründung für diesen Seitenwechsel wird Mašturi selbst zitiert (II 29): Er wolle nicht einen "Bastard" (LÚ*paḫḫurši-*) schützen.[39] Es wird deutlich, daß während der Niederschrift dem Verfasser offenbar selbst bewußt wurde, daß das Beispiel eigentlich nicht ganz glücklich gewählt war: Einserseits sollten Vasallen, wie das Tutḫalija IV. auch von Šaušgamuwa forderte, unbedingt dem rechtmäßigen Herrscher die Treue halten; andererseits wird das Verhalten des Mašturi mißbilligt, der sich in die Gefolgschaft des gewiß mächtigsten Großen des Landes begab. Da Tutḫalija von seinen Vasallen selbst unbedingte Treue erwartete, mußte er Mašturis Tat verurteilen, obgleich dieser sich seinem Vater, d.h. dem Vater des regierenden Großkönigs, angeschlossen hatte.

35 Sie wurde in kleinerer Schrift über Rasur geschrieben! Das Anschlußfragment Bo 4062 zeigt, daß nach ME-*aš* das Überschreiben des früheren Textes beendet war; die ursprüngliche Zeile ging noch bis unter das Ende von Z. 21 und schloß mit einem senkrechten Keil. Die Z. 23 wurde – wohl mit dem Griffel – breit weggestrichen; nur wenige Zeichenspuren verblieben an den Rändern der Tilgung, die ein Erkennen der früheren Formulierung nicht mehr möglich machte.

36 Vgl. I. Singer, *Amurru* 173, sowie – zur sonst üblichen Terminologie hinsichtlich der Übernahme des Thrones – zuletzt Th.P.J. van den Hout, *ZA* 81 (1991) 274 ff.

37 Zur Bedeutung und luwischen Herkunft vgl. J. Tischler, *HEG* I, 638 ff.

38 Daß die Durchstreichung mit dem Griffel den getilgten Text noch lesbar ließ (s. *StBoT* 16, 10), spielte wegen der fehlenden inhaltlichen Brisanz des ursprünglichen Wortlauts offenbar keine Rolle.

39 Zur Problematik der Einordnung des Nachtrags in den Text sowie der möglichen Interpretation, den Kommentar in *StBoT* 16, 39. Das -*ḫi* sowie die Lesung DÙ-*mi* sind nach Kollation des Originals gesichert.

In Kol. II 31-38 wird dann die Schutz- und Hilfepflicht des Šaušgamuwa wieder erneut thematisiert. Hier gab es bei der Formulierung des Textes offenbar kaum Probleme; die Tilgung in II 32 löschte nur eine Wortwiederholung, und auch in Zeile II 38 , die ersatzlos gestrichen wurde, muß nicht von einer inhaltlichen Korrektur ausgegangen werden.[40] Auffällig ist jedoch eine Steigerung des üblichen Schutzgebots durch die Forderung, Šaušgamuwa solle gegebenenfalls mit Frauen, Söhnen und Truppen zu Hilfe kommen, in aufrichtiger Gesinnung und bereit, für den großköniglichen Herrn zu sterben.[41] Die Formulierung, wörtlich genommen, dürfte ebenfalls den Eindruck einer Verunsicherung und besonderen Bedrängnis des Tuthalija IV. verstärken.[42] Die Schutzforderung wird im nächsten, nicht mehr vollständig erhaltenen Abschnitt fortgesetzt (Kol. II 39-49) und in Kol. III weiter behandelt; sie nimmt in diesem Textentwurf einen ungewöhnlich breiten Raum ein.[43] Auch Angehörige des großköniglichen Hauses werden als potentielle Verschwörer oder Verleumder erwähnt.[44] Zur Zeit des Tutḫalija, als die Position Ḫattis in Syrien durch die

[40] Am Anfang der Z. 38 ist wohl noch ein INIM zu lesen, vielleicht in Verbindung mit der Aufforderung, den Wortlaut des Textes zu beachten.

[41] Vgl. zum Passus *StBoT* 16, 40 und Anm. 78 den Hinweis auf eine ähnliche Formulierung in einem anderen Text der hethitischen Spätzeit, KBo IV 14 (+) KUB XL 38; als Imperativ erscheint die Forderung noch einmal in einem wohl ähnlichen Kontext in Rs. III 25. R. Stefanini, *AANL* XX, fasc. 1-2 (1965) 51 Anm. 38, verweist in diesem Zusammenhang auf die Verwendung von "tot" im Sinne einer Absetzung bzw. eines politischen "Totseins" (Benteŝina-Vertrag), doch ist nicht sicher, ob sich diese Interpretation auf den Passus im Šausgamuwa-Vertrag anwenden läßt. Vielmehr findet sich diese Aufforderung jetzt auch im Kurunta-Vertrag Tutḫalijas IV. auf der Bronzetafel, diesmal bezogen auf die Nachkommen des Vertragspartners (Kol. III 21 ff.); für die Bereitschaft des Kurunta selbst, für Tutḫalija zu sterben, siehe ebenda Kol. II 54 f.

[42] Vgl. den Hinweis auf andere Texte der hethitischen Spätzeit, die eine verunsicherte Situation widerspiegeln könnten, in *StBoT* 16, 40.

[43] Vgl. die "Dienstanweisungen" Tutḫalijas (CTH 255), ferner die Forderung nach Loyalität sowie die Eidesleistungen der hethitischen Spätzeit; siehe dazu bereits H. Otten, *MDOG* 94 (1963) 1 ff. – In Kol. II 48 sind Rasuren überschrieben worden, in II 49 wohl keine Rasur. In III 16 steht der Zeilenanfang über einer Rasur.

[44] Inwieweit dabei auch an Kurunta von Tarḫuntašsa gedacht wurde, läßt sich nicht sagen. Die Rolle Kuruntas als thronberechtigter Verwandter ist bereits des öfteren hervorgehoben worden, und der Fund von Abdrücken eines Siegels am Nişantepe in Boğazköy, in dem sich ein Kurunta als "Großkönig (und) Labarna" bezeichnet (s. dazu P. Neve und H. Otten, *AA* 1987, 403 und 410 ff. sowie H. Otten, *Die 1986 in Boğazköy gefundene Bronzetafel. Zwei Vorträge,* Innbruck 1989, 14 f. und Abb. 4) hat dazu geführt, daß ein – zeitlich allerdings noch nicht sicher zu positionierender – "Putsch" des Kurunta angenommen wird (vgl. dazu demnächst J. Börker-Klähn, *AoF* 21). Der Titel eines Labarna, den Kurunta auf dem Siegel (angemaßt oder vielleicht konzediert?) trägt, kann hierbei eher als Argument dienen als der Gebrauch des Titels "Großkönig" (bzw. "großer König"), der seitens Tutḫalijas offenbar auch dem Ini-Tešup von Karkamiš zugestanden wurde, siehe PRU IV, 137 f. (RS 18.06+17.365, 21') und dazu P. Artzi - A. Malamat, *FsHallo* 31. Die Rolle des Fundorts Ḫattuša für die

assyrische Expansion schwieriger geworden war, was auch zu einem selbstbewußteren Auftreten einiger Vasallen führte[45], zudem sich wohl bereits Vorboten der Veränderungen im ägäischen Raum und Westkleinasien ankündigten[46], dürfte den beiden wichtigsten, mit der Dynastie eng verbundenen (Vize-)Königtümern besondere Bedeutung zugefallen sein – Karkamiš in Syrien[47] sowie Tarhuntašša im südlichen Anatolien[48], das bis zum Mittelmeer reichte und den Weg von der Küste zum zentralanatolischen Raum kontrollierte. Wie dem auch sei: Selbst Brüder des Großkönigs blieben nicht über einen Verdacht des Strebens nach der großköniglichen Krone erhaben, und Šaušgamuwa wird dringlich dazu aufgefordert, in dieser Hinsicht niemanden zu unterstützen.[49]

In der Textlücke Rs. III 30 ff. (Abbruch von KUB XXXI 43 und Beginn XXIII 37) ist dann inhaltlich der Übergang von der Innen- zur Außenpolitik erfolgt. Soweit erhalten, ging es zunächst um Ägypten, dem keine unzulässige Nachricht übermittelt werden sollte und das offensichtlich auch als potentieller

Interpretation des Siegels wird dadurch relativiert, als sich unter den Siegeln auch ein solches von Ini-Tešup von Karkamiš fand, das offenbar an einer Holztafel angebracht war, die aus Syrien nach Ḫatti gesandt wurde; siehe zu letzerem H. Otten, *Zu einigen Neufunden hethitischer Königssiegel* (Mainz - Stuttgart 1993), 41 (Bo 91/1899). Bislang ist jedenfalls dieses Siegel der einzige Hinweis auf einen Großkönig dieses Namens.

45 Vgl. etwa die Säumigkeit des Ibiranu von Ugarit bei der Befolgung seiner Verpflichtungen als Vasall des Großkönigs, siehe RS 17.247 = PRU IV 191 und vgl. H. Klengel, *Syria 3000 to 300 B.C.* 145. Zum Verhältnis Ḫatti - Assyrien während der Herrschaft des Tutḫalija IV., siehe S. Heinhold-Krahmer, *AfO* 35 (1988) 94 ff., ferner auch C. Zaccagnini, *FsPugliese Carratelli* 299. Von besonderem Interesse ist in diesem Zusammenhang der in Ugarit entdeckte assyrische Königsbrief, siehe S. Lackenbacher, *RA* 76 (1982) 141, und dazu den historischen Kommentar von I. Singer, *ZA* 75 (1985) 100 ff.

46 Vgl. zur Situation in Ḫatti H.A. Hoffner, in: W.A.Ward - M. Sharp Joukowsky (Eds.), *The Crisis Years: The 12th Century B.C.* (Dubuque 1992), 46 ff. sowie H. Klengel, *Syria 3000 to 300 B.C.* 182 ff.

47 Vgl. dann auch den paritätischen Vertrag zwischen Šuppiluliuma II. und Talmi-Tešup von Karkamiš (CTH 122).

48 Zur Bedeutung und Lage von Tarḫuntašša siehe Ph.H.J. Houwink ten Cate, *ZA* 82 (1992) 249 ff.; vgl. die Angaben auf den Karten bei M. Forlanini - M. Marazzi, *Atlante storico del Vicino Oriente antico* (Rom 1986), sowie bei H. Otten, *Die 1986 in Boğazköy gefundene Bronzetafel. Zwei Vorträge* (Innsbruck 1989), 17, ferner O.R. Gurney, *AnSt* 43 (1993) 26 ff. Daß Tarḫuntašša bis zum Meer reichte, wird auch durch einen Text aus Ugarit nahegelegt, siehe den neuen Ugarit-Text bei P. Bordreuil (Ed.), *Une bibliothèque au sud de la ville* (*Ras Shamra-Ougarit* VII, Paris 1991), Nr. 14, der zugleich die Existenz eines Königtums Tarḫuntašša noch zur Zeit des ugaritischen Königs Ammurapi (bzw. Šuppiluliumas II.) anzeigt.

49 Zu Kol. III 19 ff. mit dem noch erhaltenen " ... sei du König von Ḫatti", *StBoT* 16, 44. – In Kol. III 20 sind in der Rasur noch Zeichenspuren stehengeblieben (urspr. LUGAL-*iz-za-na-an-ni*??) sowie ein auf den Tafelrand übergreifender Nagel- (oder Griffel-)Abdruck, der wohl bei der Tilgung entstand. In III 26 (Bo 4062) ist am Ende der Rasur noch ein -*ti* erhalten, in III 27 blieb in der sehr flachen Tilgung ein *ḫu* statt des DINGIR (^{d}UTU^{ŠI}) stehen.

Gegner betrachtet wurde (vgl. auch Kol. IV 4-7). Der "ewige" Friedensschluß zwischen Ḫattušili III. und Ramses II. war offenbar nicht mehr eine zuverlässige Grundlage für ein freundliches Verhalten des Pharao, vielleicht auch im Hinblick auf die politische Situation im Hethiterreich und an dessen westlichen und östlichen Grenzen [50]

Rs. IV beginnt mit der Aufzählung gleichberechtigter Herrscher, wobei neben dem König von Ägypten auch die Könige von Babylonien und Assyrien genannt werden, letzterer trotz einer inzwischen ausgebrochenen offenen Feindschaft.[51] Die Erwähnung des Königs von Aḫḫijawa wurde getilgt.[52] Der vorliegende Entwurf weist deutliche Anzeichen einer während der Niederschrift erfolgten "Aktualisierung" auf; es scheint daher nicht ganz auszuschließen sein, daß die ursprüngliche Nennung des Herrschers von Aḫḫijawa nicht ein einfacher Fehler des Verfassers war, sondern die Tilgung erfolgte, da dem Verfasser bewußt wurde, daß Aḫḫijawa nicht mehr als "Großmacht" existierte? Die Ursache dafür könnte dann in den grundlegenden Veränderungen zu suchen sein, die zu dieser Zeit im ägäischen Raum vor sich gingen und dann auch auf Kleinasien übergriffen. Da Aḫḫijawa zweifellos in diesem Raum zu suchen ist[53], könnte es zur Zeit des Tutḫalija bereits seine politische Bedeutung eingebüßt haben; mangels relevanter Quellen über das Vorrücken von "Seevölker"-Gruppen in Kleinasien[54] sind hier noch keine gesicherten Aussagen zu treffen. Die aktuelle Situation zur Zeit der Niederschrift von Tafel A wird auch in Kol. IV 12 ff. reflektiert[55]: Eine Freundschaft mit dem König von Assyrien wird hier

[50] Vgl. dazu schon E. Forrer, *MDOG* 61 (1921) 33.

[51] In Kol. IV 1 wurde zunächst ein anderes Wort getilgt und durch (LÚ)*MIḪRŪTI* ersetzt, das offenbar nicht ein freundschaftliches Verhältnis implizierte; vgl. auch für Rs. IV das Foto bei F. Sommer, *AU* Taf. VIII, 1.

[52] Dazu bereits E. Forrer, *MDOG* 63 (1924) 16 f. – Auf die Erwähnung des Königs von Assyrien folgt ein getilgtes Zeichen; danach wurde mit zwei Griffelstrichen LUGAL KUR *Aḫ-ḫi-i̯a-u-wa-i̯a* getilgt, blieb aber lesbar. G. Steiner, *UF* 21 (1989) 409 f. vermutet die Tilgung einer "mechanischen Einreihung des Herrschers von Aḫḫijawa unter die gleichberechtigten Könige bzw. die Löschung wegen fehlender Relevanz für den Vertragstext."

[53] Zur Diskussion siehe vor allem H.G. Güterbock, *Troy & the Trojan War* 33 ff. sowie in *FsAlp* 235 ff.

[54] Vgl. dazu demnächst den in Pavia auf dem Internationalen Hethitologen-Kongreß (Juni 1993) gehaltenen Vortrag von J. Yakar, in dem auf Zerstörungsschichten in west- und zentralanatolischer Fundstätten hingewiesen wird, die als Anzeichen für feindliche Aktivitäten verstanden werden.

[55] Der Verfasser des Textes sah sich hier erneut der Aufgabe gegenüber, einen problematischen Sachverhalt zu berücksichtigen und in den bereits niedergeschriebenen Text – wie zuvor schon im Falle von Urḫi-Tešup und Mašturi – einzugreifen. Das ging nicht ohne Korrekturen sowie Nachträge, die aus Platzgründen zwischen die Absätze bzw. Kolumnen eingeschoben wurden. In IV 12 f. wird der Text zwischen LUGAL KUR *Aššur* und *ešdu* umgearbeitet und im Hinblick auf die nunmehr bestehende Feindschaft zwischen Ḫatti und Assur neu formuliert.

nicht mehr in Erwägung gezogen, und die feindliche Haltung Assyriens führte sogar zu der - für einen Staatsvertrag ungewöhnlichen - Beschränkung des assyrischen Handels mit Amurru und dem ostmediterranen Raum (Kol. III 14 ff.): Der Handel Amurrus mit Assyrien sollte eingestellt werden, Amurru sollte nicht mehr den Durchgang zu den Seehäfen gewähren, und ein in kleinerer Schrift auf dem Intercolumnium nachgetragener Text fordert überdies, daß assyrische Kaufleute, die dennoch kamen, auszuliefern seien. Offenbar war dem Verfasser deutlich geworden, daß eine unmittelbare Wirkung dieser "Handelsblockade" sich nicht so rasch durchsetzen ließ. In IV 23 f. scheint [*Aḫḫ*]*ijawa* dann noch einmal in einem nicht mehr vollständig erhaltenen Kontext genannt zu werden, der als Hinweis auf direkte Handelsbeziehungen zwischen Aḫḫijawa und Amurru verstanden wurde. Die von G. Steiner vorgeschlagene Ergänzung [*laḫḫ*]*ijawaš*(*-ši*) GIŠMÁ in Kol. IV 23, d.h. "Kriegsschiff" statt "(Handels)schiff des Landes Aḫḫijawa", würde sich auch mit der politischen Situation in Einklang bringen lassen, läßt sich jedoch noch nicht sichern.[56] Der Krieg mit Assyrien, der offen ausgebrochen war, wird in IV 19-22, einem wiederum in kleinerer Schrift vorgenommenen Nachtrag als eigner Abschnitt und einer darauf folgenden getilgten Zeile, als ein Ereignis gewertet, das die Hilfe Amurrus dringlich machte; es bedeutete *de facto* den Eintritt des im Vertrag geforderten Hilfefalles, womit der Text nicht mehr den Charakter eines Vertrages, sondern eher eines Memorandums annimmt. Tafel A weist Rs. IV eine Lücke auf, die auch durch die späteren Zusatzfragmente 720/v und 670/v nicht geschlossen werden kann (Umschrift in StBoT 16, 16). Es bleibt dabei auch offen, wessen Frau und Sohn in 670/v gemeint sind, das in Z. 5' ebenfalls kleinere Schrift aufweist; zu denken wäre wiederum an Šaušgamuwa, doch wiederspricht dem die Verwendung des Possessivsuffixes der 3. statt 2. Sg. Auf dem linken Rand ist – auch das weist auf den Entwurfcharakter von Tafel A - noch ein zweizeiliger Zusatz in kleiner Schrift erhalten, der selbst die Möglichkeit des Vordringens eines Feindes bis Ḫattuša nicht ausschließt.

Die sonst in den offiziellen Exemplaren von Staatsverträgen üblichen Eidgottheiten finden sich auf Tafel A nicht; statt dessen sind sie auf dem einkolumnigen Exemplar B teilweise erhalten, wobei sich ihre Namen aufgrund des parallelen Textes KBo XII 31 IV 2' ff.[57] ergänzen lassen. Es fehlen auch die Zeugen des Vertrages, die Forderung nach seiner Einhaltung sowie ein Hinterle-

Der vor dem – noch zum ursprünglichen Text gehörenden – *ešdu* stehengebliebene senkrechte Keil wurde mittels des Griffels eliminiert.

[56] G. Steiner, *UF* 21 (1989) 393 ff.; vgl. ders., in: *Akten Lykien* 134.

[57] CTH 132 (Kizzuwatna-Vertrag); zur Datierung in das 13. Jh. vgl. J. Klinger - E. Neu, *Hethitica* 10 (1990) 139 f.

gungsvermerk, anders etwa als auf der Bronzetafel, die ein vollständiges und ausformuliertes Vertragswerk bietet.[58]

Insgesamt verstärkt sich hinsichtlich der Tafel A somit der Eindruck, daß die Bezeichnung als Vasallenvertrag des Tutḫalija IV. mit Šaušgamuwa von Amurru nur unter gewissen Vorbehalten verwendet werden kann. Die Deckungsgleichheit des Textes mit Teilen des Exemplars B läßt A zwar dem "Dossier Šaušgamuwa-Abkommen" zuordnen, doch dürfte sicher sein, daß der Entwurf in dieser Form nicht dem endgültigen Vertragstext entsprochen hat, für den vielleicht ebenfalls auch eine Übertragung auf eine Bronzetafel vorgesehen war. Seine Konzentration auf die Frage der Schutz- und Hilfeverpflichtung Šaušgamuwas, das Fehlen wesentlicher Bestandteile der Staatsverträge mit Amurru (wie Tributfestlegung, Erscheinungspflicht bei Hofe, Schutzerklärung des Großkönigs) und die mit zahlreichen Korrekturen vorgenommene Niederschrift erwecken eher den Eindruck einer unter bestimmten politischen Bedingungen entstandenen *ad-hoc*-Abmachung bzw. eines Memorandums. Die Vertragsurkunde des Šaušgamuwa wird in Kol. I 10 f. von Tafel A erwähnt, ohne daß darin notwendigerweise ein Verweis auf den auf dieser Tafel niedergeschriebenen Text gesehen werden muß. Hier stellen sich weitere Fragen, die noch einer Klärung bedürfen.

58 Vgl. zur Frage der Vertragstypen (formalen Verträgen und *ad hoc* -Vereinbarungen) siehe jetzt Ph.H.J. Houwink ten Cate, *ZA* 82 (1992) 236 ff.

THE PALACE LIBRARY "BUILDING A" ON BÜYÜKKALE

SILVIN KOŠAK

In Ḫattuša, several archives and libraries were discovered. Among them those in the Temple I, the House on the Slope and the buildings A, D, E, and K on Büyükkale, the "Great Fortress", housed the larger collections of tablets.[1] A systematic study of these, as well as several minor caches of tablets, such as was done in an exemplary fashion for Assur,[2] is still lacking. When a handbook mentions a building throughout which clay tablets have been scattered,[3] there is no convenient way to check this statement and see whether the contents of the texts[4] might indicate what the function of the building in question was, or even who might have been its owner.

A while ago, I began a systematic investigation of the building A on Büyükkale. Originally, a choice of a smaller archive seemed to be more appropriate for such a long term project because a limited amount of data would have been more manageable. But since Kurt Bittel reassumed the excavations in Boğazköy in 1931 with the building A, and the texts could be traced back to their findspots from this time onwards, it turned out to be more expedient to take the plunge and start from the beginning.[5] By now, a preliminary survey of the texts with the siglum /b and /c has been accomplished which represents by far the greatest part of the tablets in the building A. It is my pleasure to offer a summary of this investigation to our esteemed colleague.

[1] See in general H. Otten, *Das Altertum* 1 (1955) 73ff.; K. Bittel, *Hattusa: The Capital of the Hittites* (New York 1970), 84f.

[2] O. Pedersén, *Archives and Libraries in the City of Assur I-II*, (Uppsala 1985-86), id., apud *Keilschriftliche Literaturen* (32. *CRRAI*, 1985; *BBVO* 6), Berlin 1986, 143ff.

[3] R. Naumann, *Architektur Kleinasiens* (Tübingen 1971²), 432 (on the building D on Büyükkale), cf. P. Neve, *Büyükkale, die Bauwerke: Grabungen 1954-66* (*BoHa* 12, Berlin 1982), 99f. and Table 9 on 138f.

[4] One such tool is the preliminary list of text compositions arranged according to the CTH and their respective findspots: P. Cornil, *Hethitica* 7 (1987) 5-72. If, e.g. Naumann (n. 3) 433 defines the House on the Slope as "Archiv für religiöse Texte", a glance at the Cornil's list reveals many historical texts from that building and thus helps to modify the original statement.

[5] The pilot sample is S. Košak, *Konkordanz der Keilschrifttafeln. 1. Die Texte der Grabung 1931*, mit einer Einleitung von H. Otten (*StBoT* 34).

The tablet collection was studied by several scholars, most extensively by E. Laroche,[6] H. Otten,[7] and H.G. Güterbock.[8] For all of them, Hittite library catalogues or shelf lists serve as a point of departure. These list various titles of text compositions which can in turn be identified with the actual texts found in the library.

It was H. Otten who first brought the diachronic view into the understanding of the tablet collection of the building A. The whole complex on the Büyükkale was completely rebuilt during the Late Hittite Empire, probably during the reign of Tutḫaliya IV,[9] replacing some old derelict buildings from the earlier periods. Otten was able to demonstrate on palaeographical grounds that some library catalogues date from the early Empire and are written in the Middle Hittite Script. He also pointed out that one Middle Hittite tablet (KBo XXI 82 = 441/c++, CTH 734.9) corresponded to a title in the library catalogue, and concluded that both the catalogue and the tablet were transferred from an older to the new tablet collection.

We can now, after each fragment was identified and dated reinforce some earlier impressions and draw a more complete picture.

The tablet collection of the building A contained some 5000 fragments. It cannot be far wrong if we allowed an average of 10 fragments to a tablet. This would amount to a library of some 400-600 tablets, which is a fair sized collection in comparison with other libraries in the Ancient Near East.

From this bulk we first have to eliminate those pieces which were not found in the building A although they bear the sigla .../a - .../c. Fragments with the inventory siglum .../a are listed by H. Otten;[10]; during the excavations in 1932 (.../b) there were no fragments found outside the building A, while for the following year 1933 (.../c) several caches, mainly from in and around the building E, but also D, H, N do not belong here.[11] With these fragments eliminated and all the joins known to date taken into consideration, we are left with some 2500 entries.[12] Ideally, we can expect 500 entries corresponding to the

[6] E. Laroche, CTH, pp. 154ff.

[7] H. Otten, in *Cuneiform Archives and Libraries* (30. *CRRAI* 1983, Leiden 1986), 184ff.

[8] H.G. Güterbock, *AfO* 38/39 (1991/92) 132ff.

[9] P. Neve (n. 3), 90, 104ff.

[10] Apud S. Košak (n. 5) 4-6.

[11] 1/c-10/c, 15/c-18/c, 20/c-22/c, 47/c-48/c, 81/c-84/c, 93/c-99/c, 105/c-108/c, 546/c-551/c, 585/c-593/c, 1113/c-1131/c, 1598/c-1601/c, 1750/c, 1761/c-1771/c, 1865/c-1866/c, 2139/c-2234/c, 2258/c-2301/c, 2344/c-2347/c, 2625/c-2629/c, 2769/c-2777/c, 2791/c-2794/c, 2797/c-2809/c.

[12] An "entry" is the largest possible part of a tablet to which a CTH number can be assigned. This could be either a complete tablet, a tablet or part of it joined from several fragments, or a single fragment. In my Concordances (n. 5) an entry corresponds to a box with a CTH number.

postulated 500 tablets of the library. In other words, some 2000 entries are waiting to be distributed and joined with the 500 remaining ones. Of course, this can never be achieved. Too many fragments have been lost, destroyed, or have perished. To judge by the contemporary remarks jotted down during the stock-taking of the library holdings on the so called "shelf lists",[13] such as "one half(?) of the tablet: of the *zintuḫi*-women. - Ancient"[14], some tablets stood on the shelf in a fragmentary state.

The dispersion of fragments, at times puzzling and unpredictable, poses an additional problem, so that it is difficult to determine their original findspots. This can best be illustrated with direct joins of widely scattered fragments, e.g. KBo XXI 60 (= 693/b) + KUB XXXIII 64 (= 30/g): the first fragment comes from the room 4 of the building A, whereas the second one was found in the section 1/13-14 which lies between the buildings E and D.[15] A similar problem arises with the tablet KBo XVII 1 (= 717/b++) written in the Old Script:[16] eleven fragments come from the building A, the fragment 315/w from the section p-q/10-11,[17] 2801/c even from the building E. The list of such and similar cases is considerably longer. Conversely, KUB XXX 43 comes from the section s/12, and KUB XXX 66 even from the building C, yet H.G. Güterbock very plausibly assumes that they were originally deposited in the building A.[18]

With these caveats in mind we can now turn to the contents of the library. It has to be emphasized that the figures are only given in order to indicate approximate ratios but they are of no statistical value: because of the different sizes of the entries the items cannot be compared. The texts written in the Old Script and the Middle Script are listed according to their genres.[19]

Texts in the Old Script

CTH	Entries	CTH	Entries	CTH	Entries
25	*1*	627	*4*	677	2
39	*1*	631	*4*	733	*1*

13 For this term, see H.G. Güterbock, (n. 8), 134.

14 KUB XXX 62+, 8-9, ed. E. Laroche, CTH 168. Could this refer to a fragmentary tablet in an older script?

15 According to the field notes, "im Schutt über der Lehmschüttung der Magazine, oben".

16 E. Neu, *StBoT* 25, 5ff. (Nr. 3).

17 Described in the field notes as "unter Fußboden des phryg. 'Pfeilerhofes' ... aus steinigem Schuttstratum".

18 H.G. Güterbock (n. 8), 135 (on nos. 12 and 13).

19 An enumeration by the inventory numbers is superfluous since they will be available in the forthcoming volumes of my concordances (cf. n. 5).

238	1	645	2	735[20]	1
292	1	648	6	744	3
335	1	649	8	745	1
412	1	660[20]	1	750	1
416	2	665	7	752	3
470	1	669	4	772	1
530	1	670	39	832	6
547	1				

Total: *105* entries

Although this group of texts is small it reflects a variety of texts typical of a library, containing among others Hittite, Luwian, Palaic and Hattic rituals and festivals, some mythology, the treaty between Zidanza of Ḫatti and Pilliya of Kizzuwatna, a tablet of the second series of the Laws, and a liver model. Were these texts brought into the newly built library from one single site or were they collected in more than one place? The same question can, of course, be asked for the collection of the Middle Hittite texts:

CTH	Entry	CTH	Entry	CTH	Entry
28	1	417	1	670	45
41	1	430	3	675	1
137	1	433	2	677	2
138	1	448	1	692	13
209	3	449	1	693	5
212	4	458	4	694	20
214	1	459	1	701	2
216	1	470	25	704	7
222	1	478	1	705	3
251	1	479	1	706	4
270	1	480	1	710	1
271	8	489	1	713	2
278	2	495	1	714	3
282	1	500	7	734	1
283	1	571	3	735	1
285	1	591	1	738	10
286	6	608	3	743	1
287	1	609	1	744	3
295	2	621	2	745	1

20 Dating uncertain.

324	*5*	625	*1*	751	*1*
325	*1*	626	2	752	*1*
327	*1*	627	*8*	757	2
329	*1*	630	2	760	2
330	*5*	631	2	763	2
331	2	634	*1*	766	*1*
332	*1*	638	*1*	767	*1*
335	*3*	644	*1*	770	*5*
370	*3*	645	2	771	*1*
371	2	646	*1*	772	2
373	*1*	647	*6*	773	*1*
374	2	649	*7*	777	*6*
385	*1*	650	2	778	*4*
389	*1*	652	*3*	780	*1*
396	*1*	656	*1*	781	*1*
402	*1*	660	*1*	787	*1*
404	5	662	*1*	790	*9*
412	*1*	663	*4*	820	2
415	*1*	669	*6*	832	*13*

Total: *272* entries

In this collection, again nearly all literary genres typical for a library are represented: Hittite rituals and festivals, prayers, mythology, Palaic, Luwian, and Hurrian texts or compositions stemming from these cultural backgrounds. New are some letter fragments, the horse training manual, fragments of protocols and treaties, notably treaties with the Kaškeans and with Šunaššura of Kizzuwatna, as well as two fragments of library catalogues mentioned above.

The remaining over 2000 entries are written in the New Script, and contain all the genres represented in both older sections in great variety and quantity, and in addition, Sumerian and Akkadian scholarly texts, omens, instructions, laws, Hittite and Akkadian letters, including the correspondence with Egypt, a good dozen each of fragments belonging to the annals of Šuppiluliuma I and of Muršili II, as well as library labels and catalogues or shelf lists. In short, the tablet collection of the building A contains virtually all the genres known in Hittite literature. Scarcely represented are treaties, the only exceptions being those with Kizzuwatna and the Kaškeans. There can be little doubt that this was a palace library.[21]

21 H. Otten apud Košak (n. 5), 8.

The paucity of archival material is also conspicuous. There is one single fragment of a Middle Hittite land grant deed (806/b) found in the room 5 of the building A.

Inventory texts are by their very nature ephemeral and not at all suited to be preserved in a library. We only have five entries for this group: 1042/c (= KBo XVIII 190) and 2505/c (= KBo XVIII 191) are no genuine inventories although registered as CTH 241. The same is true of 312/a (CTH 242). The classification of 46/c as CTH 250 is highly tentative. The only remaining text, 995/c (= KBo XVIII 184, CTH 250) from the room 6, is so typical for this genre in its vocabulary that it is difficult to be explained away.

Another genre not typical for a library are the oracles. Our list shows some two dozen entries for this group. Some are without a findspot (161/a, 261/a), some do certainly (310/a) or probably (295/a, 302/a) not stem from the building A, some are unclear, e.g. 582/b (= KBo XXXIV 142, Bk. A4) + 143/m (= KBo VIII 55, x/12 i.e. building G), or, 396/c (= KBo XVI 97) where the fragment 828/f comes from the area of the building D, and the fragment 166/m from the area of the building M. Nevertheless, there are several fragments which come without any doubt from the building A (e.g. 416/b, 72/c, 640/c, 432/c, 2360/c, etc), and they obviously belonged to the library holdings of this building.[22]

A more detailed analysis of the library of the building A is in my view still premature because a large part of the texts has yet to be defined with a greater precision. Every Hittitologist knows the "universal dustbins", the most prolific being CTH 470 "Fragments de rituels", CTH 500 "Fragments de rituels' (ou de fêtes) du Kizzuwatna", CTH 669-670 "Grands fragments de fêtes" and "Fragments divers", CTH 790-791 "Fragments de rituels et conjurations hourro-hittites" and "Fragments en langue hourrite de nature inconnue", and CTH 832 "Fragments en langue hittite de nature inconnue". Actually, very few texts listed under CTH 832 are really of unknown nature, the bulk belongs either to CTH 470, or to CTH 670. Of the 2500 entries we have at present in our liberary, almost one half belongs into the category of the "universal dustbins". Only further joins will enable a more precise identification of the texts, which in turn will allow a closer definition of the entire library. These shortcomings notwithstanding, the general impression that the library contained all the genres will only be modified but not radically changed.[23]

To sum up: the building A was constructed towards the end of the Hittite Empire, probably under Tutḫaliya IV, and it housed a collection of tablets from

[22] For the presence of archival texts in royal libraries, cf. S. Parpola, in 30. *CRRAI* (n. 7), 231ff.

[23] In spite of this general statement, it is my personal impression that Kizzuwatna with its Luwian-Hurrian background is somewhat overrepresented, see especially CTH 25, 26, 41, 475, 479, as well as CTH 404, 471-477, 500, 628, 701-706, 774-791.

the Old Kingdom, as well as from the Early and Late Empire periods. The vast majority stems from the Late Empire, but there do not seem to be many tablets written in the latest ductus typical for the time of Tutḫaliya IV and his successors. This means that most tablets have been brought into the new library from other locations. We cannot know whether they were brought in as complete collections, or whether they were haphazardly gathered together from various caches. The latter view cannot be dismissed lightly. We simply do not know in what state the archives and libraries in Ḫattuša were left after repeated upheavals. What has survived after the sack of Ḫattuša at the end of the Early Empire?[24] The Middle Hittite library catalogue studied by H. Otten[25] might have been compiled for a library which has long ago ceased to exist. We also do not know what the transfer of the capital[26] from Ḫattuša to Tarḫuntašša has entailed. We are only told that Muwatalli II took with him the Hittite gods and the Manes (GIDIM$^{ḪI.A}$) but it is hard to imagine that the administration could function if all the files were left behind. A generation later, there followed an armed civil strife between Urḫi-Tešub/Mursili III and Ḫattušili III, and when the latter firmly held the reins of power in the old capital Ḫattuša again, not many libraries might have remained intact. The foundation of the new libraries on Büyükkale can be seen within the framework of general stabilisation and renewal under Tutḫaliya IV. It would be attractive to think that the shelf lists written in the New Script reflect the stocktaking of library holdings by the scribes of Tutḫaliya IV after the inauguration of the new library in the building A. But even this cannot be said with any certainty yet. They could just as plausibly reflect the holdings of some other earlier collections. This may also help to explain why so many text compositions quoted in the shelf lists have not been found in this library. Only a meticulous palaeographical investigation could show that the New Hittite catalogues are indeed the shelf lists made for the newly assembled tablet collection in the building A and that they are compiled by the scribes of Tutḫaliya IV.

24 "And Ḫattušaš, the city, was burned down", see O.R. Gurney, *The Hittites*, 21f.

25 H. Otten (n. 7).

26 Ph.H.J. Houwink ten Cate, *JEOL* 28 (1983-84) 68f. (with lit.).

A NEO-HITTITE RELIEF IN ALEPPO

MAURITS VAN LOON

With the discussion of a Neo-Hittite relief on the citadel of Aleppo I hope I may contribute, however modestly, to the celebration of Philo Houwink ten Cate's 65th birthday.

He and others have often stressed the importance of Aleppo as a political and religious center in the middle Bronze to Early Iron Ages as revealed by the texts.[1] Here are some of the facts that are relevant to this article:[2] around 1350 B.C. the Hittite great king Šuppiluliuma I appointed his son Telipinu as high priest of the Stormgod of Aleppo, Tešub, of the latter's wife Ḫepa and of their son Šarruma. In a hieroglyphic Hittite inscription built into the "Mosque of the Crows" (Jamiᶜ el-Qiqan) at Aleppo, Telipinu's son and successor Talmišarruma records having built a temple for Ḫepašarruma (Ḫepa and Šarruma?), presumably near the pre-existing temple of the Stormgod. It is likely that Aleppo suffered the same desolation at the hands of the Sea Peoples as Hatti and Carchemish about 1185 B.C.

It has always seemed strange to the present writer that apart from one Late Bronze Age and four Early Iron Age inscriptions nothing was left of this great center but one basalt orthostat, first published in 1931.[3] This block was found reused in a later wall on the citadel of Aleppo and is now in the Aleppo Museum (Inv. 53, here Pl. 19a-b.). Winfried Orthmann has discussed it at length,[4] coming to the conclusion that it is probably not Neo-Hittite in style.[5] The religious subject matter – two winged genies worshiping sun and moon – does relate this

1 For short summaries, see Dietz O. Edzard in Elena Cassin et al. (eds.), *Fischer Weltgeschichte* 2 (Frankfurt am Main 1965) 190; Heinrich Otten in *Fischer Weltgeschichte* 3 (Frankfurt am Main 1966) 119-120; Philo H. J. Houwink ten Cate in *Fischer Weltgeschichte* 4 (Frankfurt am Main 1967) 116-120.

2 Horst Klengel, "Halab", *RlA* IV 50-53; J. David Hawkins, "Halab: The 1st millennium", ibid. 53.

3 Ploix de Rotrou, *Revue Archéologique Syrienne* 1 (1931) 8ff., René Dussaud, *Syria* 12 (1931) 95f.

4 *Untersuchungen* 54.

5 Ibid. 479.

relief to the orthostat groups *Späthethitisch* I (1150-950) and II (950-850 B.C.).[6] The genies' crowns, with horns forming a horizontal line turning up into vertical points in front and behind, are a feature also seen for instance at *Späthethitisch* II Malatya.[7] The fists clenched in reverence or greeting are a Hittite gesture taken over by the Assyrians from the time of Tukulti-Ninurta I (1244-1208).[8] The motif of touching or supporting celestial symbols has Mitannian prototypes, as Orthmann has pointed out.[9] Despite the lively modeling of the genies' faces (Pl. 19b.), which is reminiscent of 9th-century B.C. Assyrian sculpture, one is struck by their awkward *Knielauf* posture and by the asymmetry of the composition. The sculptor obviously started from the left, not leaving enough space for the right-hand figure's wing and foot. Some *Späthethitisch* I-II reliefs like Zincirli A/2, A/7, Tell Halaf A3/167, A3/49[10] display the same lack of solid verticality.[11] The new evidence to be presented below tends to confirm Orthmann's dating of this relief to the 10th century B.C.[12]

A short while ago the writer had occasion to review ʿAli Abu ʿAssaf's fine publication of the temple at ʿAin Dara in north Syria.[13] Among the mostly figurative orthostats revetting the walls in the temple's second phase are two basalt reliefs with geometric ornament apparently simulating windows with grills (Pl. 20a.).[14] Curiously, the rectangular blocks stand on their long sides, with the cylindrical mullion placed horizontally. It divides the window into two panels, each filled with three joined figures "eight". At the central intersection of each figure eight, one diagonal clearly passes over the other. The two blocks stood in the side walls of the antecella, each one between a mountain god relief and a corner of the antecella. There is nothing in the architectural remains to suggest why it was thought necessary to have a false window or door at these spots. A third similar block formed part of the balustrade of the ambulatory which was

[6] Ibid. 465-466. See also my *Iconography of Religions* XV, 13: *Anatolia in the Earlier First Millennium B.C.* (Leiden 1990) 1-2.

[7] Orthmann, *Untersuchungen* pls. 39-41.

[8] Margarete Falkner, "Gebetsgebärden und Gebetsgesten", *RlA* III 176; Maurits N. van Loon, *Iconography of Religions* XV, 12: *Anatolia in the Second Millennium B.C.*, pls. XVd (Alaca Höyük), XXIV (Boğazköy), XXX (Yazılıkaya) and passim; Henri Frankfort, *The Art and Architecture of the Ancient Orient* (Harmondsworth 1954), pl. 73B. In the Assyrian gesture, the forefinger, not the thumb is stretched out. Note that the Akkadian verb *karābu* means both "to bless" and "to greet or adore".

[9] Edith Porada, *Seal Impressions of Nuzi* (*AASOR* 24, New Haven 1947), nos. 726-727.

[10] Orthmann, *Untersuchungen*, pls. 8b, 10c, 55a, 56b.

[11] This term was coined by Edith Porada, *Ancient Iran* (London 1965) 50, to describe seals of the early first millennium B.C.

[12] *Untersuchungen* 54.

[13] *BiOr* 51 (1994) 157-159.

[14] ʿAli Abu ʿAssaf, *Der Tempel von ʿAin Dara* (*Damaszener Forschungen* 3, Mainz 1990) pl. 42.

added along the outside of the temple in its third phase.[15] As such it was meant to be seen from the ambulatory and from the outside. One side carried a scene, now damaged, including a bull, probably brought to sacrifice. The other side displays the familiar "figure-eight" grill pattern. Perhaps these blocks simulated openwork balustrades rather than windows.

In my review of Abu ʿAssaf's publication I compared the "false-window" blocks to the fragmentary grills that were found in the great destruction level at Hama immediately north and next to the entrance of the palace.[16] Wall foundations, paving slabs, cedar beams and lion sculptures were all that was left of a small but important structure, possibly a sanctuary, at this spot. Inscriptional evidence mentions Baʿalat, "the Lady", which brings to mind a similarly flimsy structure beside the entrance of the Late Bronze Age palace at Qatna in Syria, dedicated to "the Lady of the Palace".[17] At Hama the basalt grills, reconstructed as vertical screens by Fugmann, are probably the remains of a horizontal balustrade like the one simulated in the ambulatory at ʿAin Dara. The rounded openings alternate with triangular openings in the same way. Why similar grills should have been placed in the antecella at ʿAin Dara remains unclear, unless they were surmounted by real windows.

Recently I visited both ʿAin Dara and the citadel of Aleppo. I was immediately struck by the likeness between the "false-window" blocks at ʿAin Dara and a block in Aleppo of which the significance had previously eluded me (Pl. 20b.). It is incorporated into a presumably medieval wall to the immediate left of the entrance to the Great Mosque on the citadel of Aleppo.

Apparently it is made of limestone. Each of the recessed panels contains four raised "figure-eight" motifs. Like the ʿAin Dara blocks and unlike the Hama grill fragments the design merely simulates openwork grills. The openings have not been carved all the way through the stone.

The resemblance between the Aleppo and the ʿAin Dara "false-window" reliefs is so close – including the way one set of diagonal bands passes over the other – that there can be no doubt they belong to the same period and culture. A 10th-century B.C. date was proposed by Abu ʿAssaf for Phase II at ʿAin Dara. I concur with this dating, although I would not extend the entire Phase I-III range beyond 1150-850 B.C.[18] A 10th-century B.C. date was also assigned to the Aleppo relief with the two genies by Orthmann.[19]

[15] Ibid., pl. 62a-d.

[16] Ejnar Fugmann, *Hama* II 1: *L'architecture des périodes pré-hellénistiques* (Copenhagen 1958) figs. 257-258. The palace was probably built ca. 850 and destroyed in 720 B.C., ibid., pp. 268-269.

[17] Comte du Mesnil du Buisson, *Le site archéologique de Mishrifé-Qatna* (Paris 1935) pls. 15, 16.

[18] Abu ʿAssaf gives 1300-740 B.C. as the limits for this range, op.cit. in note 14, pp. 39-41.

[19] Ibid., p. 54.

This brings us to the question: do the "false-window" block and the "two-genies" block, both found on the Aleppo citadel, come from the same building, perhaps the famous temple of the Stormgod of Aleppo? In my opinion this is quite likely, although hard to prove. The fact that the "false-window" block is made of limestone and the "two-genies" block of basalt does not preclude their use in the same building. The temple at ʿAin Dara has basalt sculptures but limestone paving slabs and other elements. In some of the *Späthethitisch* II relief series at Carchemish there was a regular alternation of basalt and limestone orthostats.[20]

After the upheavals at the end of the Late Bronze Age Aleppo's political role lapsed. In due course it was taken over by Arpad, the capital of Bit-Agusi, founded some time before 883 B.C. by the Aramaean Agusi or Gusi. The temple of the Stormgod of Aleppo, however, must have been rebuilt, perhaps by this Agusi, since Aleppo continued to function as a center of the Stormgod cult. The Assyrian king Shalmaneser III brought him offerings in 853 B.C. before engaging in the battle of Qarqar. It seems quite possible that both the "two-genies" block and the "false-window" block formed part of the Stormgod's temple as rebuilt around 950 and still standing in about 850 B.C.

20 Orthmann, *Untersuchungen* 31 (Herald's Wall), 505-509 (Processional Entry).

Plate 19a. Basalt block from Aleppo citadel, 1.30 x 0.95 x 0.95 m.: genies flanking sunburst within moon crescent. After J.B. Pritchard, *The Ancient Near East in Pictures* (2nd ed. Princeton 1969), no. 652.
b. Detail of a. After H.Th. Bossert, *Altsyrien* (Tübingen 1951), no. 495.

Plate 20a. Basalt block in antecella of ʿAin Dara temple, 1.60 x 1.12 x 0.40 m.: false window? After ʿAli Abu ʿAssaf, *Der Tempel von ʿAin Dara* (Mainz 1990), Pl. 42b.
b. Limestone block left of the entrance to Great Mosque on Aleppo citadel: false window? Photograph by Mr. M.A.M. Kortenbout van der Sluijs.

COMMENTS ON CONTINUITY AND DISCONTINUITY IN SOUTH ANATOLIAN COASTAL TOPONYMY

MACHTELD J. MELLINK

Philo Houwink ten Cate gave archaeologists a great tool of research in the book resulting from his dissertation: *The Luwian Population Groups of Lycia and Cilicia Aspera during the Hellenistic Period* (Leiden 1961). The archaeologist and cultural historian find ample evidence here for the quality of Anatolian conservatism and continuity observed by linguistic and especially onomastic analysis. The basic tenet of the 1961 book is still valid after remarkable new discoveries such as the bronze tablet with the Tarḫuntašša treaty found at Boğazköy in 1986.[1]

The linguistic and historical discoveries in Lycia and Cilicia Aspera challenge the archeologist to uncover material evidence of cultural continuity exemplified in the records from the Hittite to the Hellenistic period, even if, admittedly, Anatolian coastal populations did not remain of identical composition from the days of Tutḫaliya IV to Alexander.

One aspect facilitating analysis of cultural continuity is the persistence not just of personal names, names of deitites, cults and geographical features, but specifically of identifiable habitation sites which maintain their names from the Bronze Age to Iron Age and late Hellenistic-Roman periods.

Toponymic continuity provides a challenge to the field archaeologist. The durability of place names in Anatolia is remarkable for its positive aspects and raises questions of onomastic survival from pre-Luwian as well as Luwian contexts to the Hellenistic, Roman and later eras. We know that discontinuity in place names can be caused by historical circumstance and authoritative decisions. The change of names of Byzantium-Constantinople-Istanbul was the result of historical-cultural intent and manifestation; on the other hand, the name of Ankyra-Ankara has weathered major political developments and retained the historical respect of many authorities, most prominently Atatürk. Old names of less prominent sites, especially of villages in many areas, were in many instances replaced by Turkish names, although the local residents often remember and use the pre-Turkish names which are a direct link to linguistic history and prehistory.[2]

[1] H. Otten, *StBoT* Beih. 1.

[2] Louis Robert lamented about the arbitrary abolition of old village names in *La Toponymie Antique* (Colloque de Strasbourg 1975), 61-62.

The task of the archaeologist and historian is to analyze the material and recorded circumstances favoring or disfavoring continuity in toponymy. In the region of CILICIA PEDIAS, which offers great resources to early farmers and traders, instances of tenacious place names stand out, first and foremost Tarsus, whose name is attested (Tarša) in Hittite texts,[3] in Assyrian annals of Shalmaneser III and Sennaherib (Tarzi), and amply in classical authors.[4] The entire range of these toponymic references is confirmed by archaeological evidence brought to light by the excavations of Gözlü Kule,[5] with their yield of Hittite and Assyrian tablets and bullae.[6]

Adana-Adaniya, though not as famous as Tarsus, presents a parallel case of continuity from Hittite times to the present. We are less well informed on its status in the early Iron Age than on its role under Hellenistic and Roman auspices, principally because the large mound containing oldest Adana, now built over in the Tepebağ district by a school, a mosque and medrese and houses of the town (once also the American hospital), has never been excavated but just probed superficially;[7] but an Egyptian Middle Kingdom statuette of a nurse Sit-Snefru was found in this mound[8] during building operations, perhaps attesting some prominent status of Adana in the early centuries of the second millennium B.C.

In any case, both Tarsus and Adana had acquired enough status and identity to maintain their names from at least Hittite times through the Dark Ages of the Sea Peoples' wars into the period when Assyrian and neo-Babylonian kings developed an interest in Cilicia, and through the Persian, Hellenistic and Roman era into Byzantine, Armenian, Selcuk and Ottoman periods to the modern age. Archaeologically the Middle-Late Bronze-Iron Age sequence has been tested and found continuous by excavation at Gözlü Kule-Tarsus, where little doubt can be raised about the past viability of this ancient town. The antiquity of the name of Tarsus may well go back to the Early Bronze Age, when the site had urban traits and developed its fortification system, or to Late Chalcolthic, and one may repeat E. Laroche's question: "qui a nommé Tarse, et dans quelle langue?"[9]

At Adana, limitation of archaeological testing leaves the possibility of some troubles in the Dark Ages, but one expects that the forthcoming new publication of Karatepe and the interpretation of its bilingual texts will clarify the relationship of Danunim and ʾdn/Adanawa, the old city of Adana.

3 A. Goetze, *Kizz.* 54-56, fn. 3, J. Garstang - O .R .Gurney, *Geogr.* 61.

4 D. Magie, *Roman Rule in Asia Minor* (Princeton 1950) II, 1146-1148.

5 H. Goldman, *Excavations at Gözlü Kule, Tarsus* I-III (Princeton 1950-1963).

6 A. Goetze, *JAOS* 59 (1939) 1-16.

7 M. V. Seton-Williams, "Cilician Survey", *AnSt* 4 (1954) 148.

8 H. E. Winlock in *Bulletin of the Metropolitan Museum of Art,* September 1921, 209. W. C. Hayes, *The Scepter of Egypt* I (Harvard University Press 1953), 215, fig. 132. W. Stevenson Smith, *Interconnections in the Ancient Near East* (New Haven 1965), 14, fig. 23.

9 *La Toponomie Antique* (supra n. 2) 215.

In Cilicia Pedias, there are other mounds and other historical toponyms which cannot be linked this far back. The substantial mound of Misis-Mopsouhestia must be a prominent Bronze Age site renamed in the Dark Ages and associated with the history and legend of Mopsos, whose fame reaches from Kolophon to Karatepe via Greek and Anatolian dynastic mythology presumably in the Dark Ages resulting from the Sea Peoples' wars stranding victors and victims along the Anatolian coasts.[10] Special circumstances will interfere with persistence of toponyms. The archaeology of the early Iron Age at Misis may reveal the motivation of this change.

In many coastal sites survivors of the Sea peoples' wars, especially Mycenaean refugees, settled among local residents. Tarsus manifests a LH. IIIC contingent in its ceramic evidence, but ceramic and ethnic elements are gradually submerged in a new koine.

The results of Achaean linguistic penetration in PAMPHYLIA have been analyzed by Claude Brixhe.[11] The placename of Aspendos, as its survives numismatically ΕΣΤϜΕΔΙΙΥΣ, links it with the name of Azatiwatas of Karatepe, pointing to early links with the Karatepe developments.

The discovery of the Tarḫuntašša treaty revealed that the western boundary fortress of the Tarḫuntašša land was Parḫa on the Kastaraya river.[12] The survival of these names in classical Greek Perge and the Kestros river is evident, as is the modern loss of these second millennium names. In the case of Perge we see a good instance of continuity through the Dark Ages, from the 13th century B.C. to the Hellenistic-Roman-Byzantine era, with later gradual abandonment of the site and change of the river name (now Aksu). We do not know the chronological origin of the name Parḫa-Perge.

Archaeological soundings have not been made to determine the age of the site of Perge, which has yielded a splendid harvest of Hellenistic and Roman architecture, sculpture and inscriptions with respects paid to Mopsos. The importance of Perge-Parḫa as the western border fortress of Tarḫuntašša came as a surprise in the text of the bronze tablet. Archaeologists will now have to probe for strata at Perge representing its 13th century B.C. role; perhaps most likely to be found on the citadel which hitherto has just yielded some Byzantine deposits.

As we move west to LYCIA, the toponymic situation is similar to that of Parḫa-Perge in its river valley. The principal Lycian river is named Xanthos by the Greeks and by the Lycians in the Iliad.[13] In its valley lies the capital known by the Greek name of Xanthos, whose Hittite-Luwian name is Awarna-Arñna-Arinna.[14] The durability of Hittite and Luwian place names in the Xanthos valley is remarkable: Arñna-Xanthos, Pina-Pinale-Pinara, Dalawa-Tlos and

[10] *LPG* 44-50.

[11] *Le dialecte grec de Pamphylie* (Paris 1976) 147-150.

[12] H. Otten, *StBoT* Beih. 1, 12-13, 37-38, text I, 60-61.

[13] It is conceivably identical with the Šiyanta river of Hittite texts, *RGTC* 6/1, 548-549; Garstang-Gurney, *Geogr.* 91.

[14] *RGTC* 6/1, 32; L. Zgusta, *Kleinasiatische Ortsnamen* (Heidelberg 1984), 97:1.

Wiyanawanda-Oinoanda.[15] The harbor of the capital was on the coast at Patara, Lycian Pttara, the mountain of which occurs as Patar in the Yalburt inscription of Tutḫaliya IV.[16] The series of Luwian hieroglyphic references to these sites in the second millennium B.C. has recently become better known by the publications of Yalburt and the south citadel vault at Boğazköy, soon to be followed by J. D. Hawkins's reading of the Nişantepe inscription.

The Xanthos river valley, famous in the Greek tradition and in the Iron Age, and tied into Greek Bronze Age mythology via the Bellerophon legend, has the clearest record of continuity in toponymy, facilitated by the survival of Luwian speech from Lukka to Lycia. The contacts of the Hittite kings date to the 14th and 13th centuries, with Hittite cuneiform and Hieroglyphic Luwian attestation. Archaeologically the task of identifying the second millennium substance of Lukka history is still waiting for focused research and excavation.[17]

If we expect the historical framework of other Lukka citadels and harbors to emerge from local and Hittite records, the continuity will probably again run from the later second millennium into the classical period, reflected by Greek poets and historians. Candidates are coastal towns with harbors, such as Kaş-Antiphellos-Habessos, Demre-Myra, Finike-Limyra-Zemuri. The shipwreck near Uluburun is a signal of active 14th-13th century international sea-trade along the Lycian coast.

NORTHERN LYCIA. Inland Lycia is less well known archaeologically because of its mountainous nature; but like Cilicia Aspera it may have had important stations along mountain passes in its highlands. The upland plain of Elmalı shows that prehistoric sites from the Neolithic period on were settled in this fertile region.[18] The Elmalı plain was clearly connected with coastal Lycian communities by seasonal transhumance to and from cooler upland sites. Toponymy in modern times shows that upper (summer) and lower (winter) villages have the same names; language and customs must have connected the transhumants and permanent upland residents.

Names of sites in the Elmalı plain in general have been adjusted to the speech of later residents, although here too nomenclature and cultural roots must have been long maintained by conservatism. The phenomenon of durable toponymy can be discerned for several villages, although many have recently had to accept new Turkish names, e.g. Mügren (now Gölova), Gilevgi (Karaköy), Söğle, Diruna-Tirune, and in the mountainous fringe Gömbe, Dont, Dirmil, or Zivint in the Korkuteli plain.[19]

The principal archaeological landmarks are mounds of substance, witnesses to prehistoric use of mud and mudbrick as building materials along with timber, which is the predominant substance of coastal Lycian (and 2nd

15 M. Poetto, *StMed* 8, 79-82. J. D. Hawkins, *AA* 1990, 306, 313, and *FsAlp* 264.

16 M. Poetto, *StMed* 8, 33 and 80.

17 M.J. Mellink, in *FsVermeule*.

18 Christine Eslick, *Elmalı-Karataş I: The Neolithic and Chalcolithic Periods* (Bryn Mawr 1992).

19 G.E. Bean, *AnSt* 10 (1960) 68-73.

millennium Lukka?) architecture. The high mounds invariably show relics of third millennium habitation, without clear surface scatter of second millennium pottery. This can be misleading, but the sequence of short-lived, numerous Chalcolithic habitation sites followed by durable Early Bronze Age centers (presumably citadels with lower settlements) is clear from surface exploration.

The one excavated site in the Elmalı plain, the small mound of Karataş with its fortified central complex and sizeable surrounding village of the third millennium B.C., did not yield surface signals of second millennium habitation, but in excavation several pithos burials of the mid-second millennium came to light, as did remnants of habitation with domestic pottery of local "Hittite" type, probably once belonging to the inventory of timber houses.[20] Here at Karataş we have no ancient names for the site, although the nearby village of Semayük-Bozüyük has an older name of Samun.

Relatively large mounds are found in all three main parts of the Elmalı plain: to the East and Northeast, Gilevgi and Söğle; in the northwest plain, the twin mounds of Sivri- and Yassıtepe south of Eskihisar, all three turkicized in nomenclature; and to the South and Southwest, Akçay (Neolithic and later) and Hacımusalar-Beyler, the largest of all mounds in the Elmalı plain, c. 300 x 350m, now under excavation by a team from Bilkent University under İlknur Özgen, with a first campaign in 1994. At Hacımusalar Early Bronze Age habitation is evident and can be held responsible for the initial prominence and size of the mound along the upland roads from the coast near Kaş and Finike.

The search for continuity encounters a true hiatus in the case of Hacımusalar. Martin Harrison in 1963 discovered a series of inscriptions which identify the Roman city on top of the mound as Choma.[21] The date of most of these inscriptions of the Χωματεῖται is Roman imperial.[22] As Harrison and Bean pointed out, the name of Χῶμα was given to the late Hellenistic or Roman site by the Greek-speaking newcomers, descriptively, to indicate the nature of the site as a mound of earth, somewhat in the manner of modern Turkish villages established on old mounds designated as Höyük, e.g. the once famous Hattic site of Alaca Höyük and other sites less well endowed with spectacular prehistory.

If the ancient name of Lycian Choma had survived, the later inhabitants would have used it, to judge by other sites nearby such as Podalia and Gömbe-Comba. The hiatus which made the new (and somewhat alienated) name necessary can only be measured by the new excavations. Accumulation of building residue and mound substance was evidently strong in the plain of Elmali with its many other mounds. None of them became as solid as Hacımusalar-Choma and excavation will reveal how high the mound had risen in the Early Bronze I-II period, which in general is well represented in this area. Early Bronze III, the stage of intensive contact along the west and south coast of Anatolia from Troy to Cilicia, is likely to emerge as an articulate phase; the

20 *AJA* 73, (1969) 329, figs. 41-45.

21 *AnSt* 14 (1964) 10; *Journal of Roman Studies* 57 (1967) 40-44.

22 G.E. Bean, *Lycian Turkey* (1978) 156.

second millennium remains elusive on the basis of preliminary surface surveys. The hiatus may therefore lie in the second millennium. Some Iron Age habitation is in evidence. The break in nomenclature is evident and may have occurred more than once.

It is difficult to assign the origin of oid names to specific prehistoric periods, and we can be sure that several North Lycian sites of the third millennium B.C. were prominent and known by their own names. Without excavation we cannot make a chronological and geographical chart of names.

G. Bean, who knew the North Lycian area from intensive exploration, suggested that the site of a citadel northwest of the former Avlan Lake should not be identified as Podalia, a site name known from Pliny and other authors and from coins.[23] The site near the lake was first identified by Eugen Petersen,[24] who was told by spokesmen in Elmalı that its name was Podalia or Podamia; these names are still current with variants of Bodamia and Buralye. The site itself has Lycian classical and later features with a fortress on a rocky hill, remnants of fortifications and two rockcut tombs. It is strategically located to control access to the plain from the direction of Arycanda. Bean rejected the identification with Podalia because of a lack of inscriptions and major buildings; yet the grid plan of a well laid-out lower city is visible in the fields to the north, as Petersen observed in 1882 and we still noticed recently. It is remarkable that the old name of Podalia still clings to the spot and survives in phonetic adaptation to modern village speech.

Bean suggested that Podalia should be located at Söğle, a site with many inscriptions and a solid prehistoric mound southeast of Elmalı.[25] There are no references to the ancient name of Söğle in the many Greek inscriptions from this village. It is more likely that Söğle has preserved its own ancient name perhaps with affinity to names like Sagalassos-Ağlasun and Poğla-Fiğla-Fuğla (now Çomaklı) in Pisidia.[26] The mound and cemeteries of Söğle remain unexcavated but the modern villagers have searched for building stones and treasure.

Sites along the main roads in the southern part of the Elmalı plain are Choma, Podalia, Akçay and Gömbe. The latter site has preserved its old name (Comba, Kombe) to the present day[27] and is remarkable for its local cult of twelve gods whose votive reliefs date to the second and third century of our era.

The contribution archaeology can make to the analysis of continuity and change of place names remains potential in the plain of Elmalı and elsewhere in Anatolia. The archaeological stratification of the oldest mounds in the Elmalı

[23] G.E. Bean, *Anzeiger der Österreichischen Akademie der Wissenschaften*, 1968, No. 8, and *Lycian Turkey* (1978) 153-156.

[24] E. Petersen and F. von Luschan, *Reisen in Lykien, Milyas und Kibyratis* II (Vienna 1889) 161-162.

[25] G.E. Bean, *Journeys in Northern Lycia* 1965-1967, Supplement to *Tituli Asiae Minoris* 4 (Vienna 1971) 28-32.

[26] G.E. Bean, *AnSt* 10 (1960) 55.

[27] D. Magie, *Roman Rule in Asia Minor* (Princeton 1950), II 1391; G.E. Bean, *Lycian Turkey* (1978) 158-160.

plain may reveal circumstances of linguistic changes which may have affected toponymy. The transition from Neolithic and Chalcolithic to Early Bronze is a matter of speculation linguistically; the presence of Luwian-speakers is archaeologically as well as historically probable for coastal and northern Lycia in the second millennium B.C. One clear change is the introduction of Greek place names in Hellenistic times, some of which did not permanently supersede the old names (cf., in Cilicia, the transient name of Antiochia for both Tarsus and Adana). The case of Choma is special because it signifies a gap in transmission.

Survival of old names, the origin of which cannot be pinpointed in the archaeological sequence, is a sign of stability of at least a significant contingent of inhabitants and management, as it must have been in the case of Tarsus in the plain of Cilicia, a prosperous center with Mediterranean links via the Kydnos river and with overland trade routes east-west as well as north-south through the Taurus mountains.

Philo Houwink ten Cate's 1961 work on survival of indigenous Luwian personal names into Hellenistic times, yielded an ample harvest in this category. The book also presented a series of Lycian place names in north Taurus sites with their Greek equivalents, and instances of continuity of place names in north Taurus sites (Cybistra, Tyana, Tuna-Tynna).[28] French archaeologists have begun investigations of the site of Porsuk-Tunna-Atuna(?), which has good Bronze Age substance and evidence for fortification of Hittite date.[29] The continuity of this key site for Cilician traffic to and from the plateau is therefore being tested.

Hittite and Luwian scholars have presented their most recent challenges in the texts of the Tarḫuntašša treaty, the Šuppiluliuma vault at Boğazköy, and the Yalburt basin. The negative statements about a lack of Bronze Age habitation in Lycian-Luwian and Pamphylian territory must be revised by field action.

Investigation of linguistic stratification might also benefit from a study of local speech and phonetic peculiarities of the regions in question, such as the l/r confusion in modern village speech of the Elmalı plain (e.g. Burdur/Buldur, Lengebi/Rengebi for place names).

Regional speech patterns may reveal symptoms of continuity, but this aspect will have to be investigated by experts in phonetic and dialect studies. Other aspects are closer to the archaeologist's craft: continuity in material culture: building traditions, timber architecture, methods of food preparation and storage, bee-keeping, hunting apparatus and lore, sports such as wrestling, still annually celebrated in Elmalı at a public festival with wide-ranging post-Luwian ritual and loyal attendance (yağlı güreş or güleş). There is much room for ethno-archaeological studies which may reveal the persistence of cultural traits as language, religion and political rule change. Anatolia is a land of stratified cultures which accumulate elements of tradition to enrich and enliven a

28 *LPG* 106-108, 194.

29 O. Pelon, *La Cappadoce méridionale jusqu'à la fin de l'époque romaine* (Paris 1991) 15-18.

continuum to which anonymous prehistory and early history, with toponymy as an articulate element, have made their contributions.

A CYLINDER SEAL AND SOME RAMIFICATIONS.

DIEDERIK J. W. MEIJER

There are teachers who give examples, and there are those who are examples. Philo Houwink ten Cate has always been one of erudition, acute critical sense, but above all of a very humane approach to human beings and their actions, in the past as in the present. It is an honor to dedicate the next few lines to him. They touch upon a subject that has caught his interest since his own student days: the relations between ancient Anatolia and Syria.[1]

During the 1988 excavation season at Tell Hammam al-Turkman on the Balikh in Northern Syria, unique finds were made in the western wing of a large building complex provisorily named "the administrative complex."[2] In square K 22 we uncovered a baked clay cylinder seal, and a fortnight later, in the adjacent square J 22, an ancient impression on a lump of clay, which proved to have been made with that very cylinder.[3] Thirdly, at the very beginning of the season, a bulla had been found with the impressions of two cylinder seals. One of these impressions is almost certainly from the same cylinder.

The exact find spots will be described in the excavation report (D.J.W. Meijer (ed.), *Hammam al Turkman* II, forthc.); suffice it here to note that all three finds occurred in dirt fill deposited in connection with the process of rebuilding the complex. They may be taken to belong to one and the same general situation. It is clear that the find spots represent non-primary contexts (as indeed is the case with almost all parallels, see below); this unfortunately precludes a precise archaeological dating (difficult with seals in any situation) and forces us to concentrate upon stylistic arguments.

The seal cylinder

The cylinder in question (find no. HMM 88-Z3, see Pl. 21a-b) measures 1.7 cm in height, has a diameter of 1.0 cm, and is dark orange in color; medium

[1] I am grateful to E. van Driel for the drawings, and to M. Bootsman, J. Pauptit and W. Vreeburg for the photography.

[2] The excavations began in 1981, directed by M.N. van Loon and the writer up to 1986, by the latter thereafter. For reports on the earlier campaigns, see Van Loon (ed.), *Hammam et-Turkman* I (*PIHANS* 63; Istanbul 1988); for the MBA administrative complex, D.J.W. Meijer, *Akkadica* 64/65 (1989) 1-12, and idem, *forthcoming*.

[3] Cf. Meijer, *Akkadica* 64/65 (1989) 2 and figs. 6, 7.

coarse inclusions (< 0.5 mm) of the levigation of the clay are clearly visible. It is perfectly cylindrical with evenly rounded (slightly worn) edges and a well-executed perforation not showing excessive wear.

The representation is bordered by a relatively clear incised line at the top, and one at the bottom that only remains in faint traces. A vertical plant-like motif, consisting of stacked V-shaped incisions, is encased between two vertical lines and can be taken as the image divider. A row of three walking male figures is depicted next to it, the figures separated by two further plant-like motifs, one consisting of a straight stalk with leaves beginning slightly above mid-height, the other being a narrower version of the image divider.

Of the three male figures, the first and the third wear identical long mantles incised in small horizontal lines; the middle figure's mantle suggests the well-known so-called "kaunakes" type. All three garments are probably intended to leave the leg stepping forward partially uncovered, as is found ubiquitously in Old Syrian seals of the more carefully cut genres. The men all have one hand raised.[4] A deep excision in the cylinder, resulting in a heavy blob on the impression, represents one shoulder covered by the long mantle, which leaves the other shoulder (not indicated) free.

The men's heads and faces have received very little care, but the execution of their heads suggest they wore caps. The object in front of the middle figure's foot is the result of damage to the cylinder.

The sealings

a. The unbaked piece of clay HMM 88-Z4 was found some 10 cm under the surface, i.e. in surface dirt in what remained of the western part of the administrative complex, near faint traces of a doorpost-hole. The surface there sloped down to the west due to erosion of the side of the tell. The surface mentioned can be said to be roughly contemporary with the find spot of seal Z3, and it is thought that both objects became deposited in their respective secondary contexts at the same time. This deposition must have occurred sometime during the earlier Middle Bronze II period.

The object measures 4.8 x 3.3 x 2.8 cm, and has an obverse with a cylinder-seal impression (Pl. 22a-b). The reverse shows two slightly curving impressions with faint imprints of rope, to which there are two perpendicular straight and straight-sided impressions (of slats? – see Pl. 23). The nature of the object that was sealed by the bulla is difficult to determine. We are probably dealing with a sealed door bolt-arrangement, or, less probably, with the closing of a sack with the aid of a rope knotted around slats or sticks; a jar sealing is even less probable.

[4] In this class of simple seals (where the figures persistently seem to walk to the left on the impression) only one arm is indicated; in other seals and impressions showing this or related motifs, either the left or the right arm can be raised.

The impression shows the upper left third of the tree-like motif between vertical lines visible on the seal, and two of the male figures to the left of it.[5] The bottom of the sealing is broken away; in the lower right a 90° turn of the clay slab suggests that the rolling was never complete, and that the clay had been pressed into a corner – supporting the suggestion of a bolt arrangement on a door.

b. The sealed bulla HMM 88-Z2 was found on a sloping surface that was heavily disturbed by subsequent rebuilding activity. It lay some 3 m distant from the seal HMM 88-Z3. There is no doubt that also this object came to be deposited at the same time as the others discussed here.

The object measures 3.4 x 3.4 x 1.5 cm, and had been lightly burned.[6] The obverse shows the impressions of probably two cylinder seals (α and β). The bulla's reverse is gently concave and round in plan (Pl. 24); it also carries the impression of a slightly curved object, perhaps the rim of a vessel.[7] In this case a door bolt arrangement seems less probable.

The impression α on the right side of fig. 4 (cf. Pl. 25a-b) constitutes the object's least incomplete rolling and shows an inverted male figure in a long mantle possibly sporting a tassel. The shoulder shows the familiar bulge. He faces left and stands in front of a vertical line, which may well represent the encasement of a plant-like motif found on the seal Z3. At this point, however, the clay surface falls away and the rolling stops. The figure's right hand is raised. It should be noted that his feet extend through the upper borderline. This must have been the intent of the seal cutter: this figure belongs on the seal together with the other figures; it is not a secondary addition to the seal, judging by the depth of the figures' relief, which is about equal.[8]

To the left of the inverted figure we see a similar figure with raised hand and shoulder bulge, whose lower half is missing. He confronts a vertical line, one of two encasing a simple zigzag motif. To the left of this, the bulla's surface curves away, and unclear blobs separate the scene from the second cylinder seal impression.

Inverting figures is a well-known phenomenon in Old Babylonian glyptic, and needs no comment here. It must be noted, however, that it most often occurs on seals of a slightly more elaborate character.

The impression β (Pl. 26) shows the upper half of the familiar standing figure with raised hand and shoulder bulge. He confronts the same encased plant motif as on seal Z3, made of stacked V-shapes. It is *extremely probable*

[5] On the second figure, the treatment of the head seems to be more detailed than on the photograph of the modern rolling, but careful measurements and inspection confirmed that seal and sealing belong together: the "tilde" above the figure's head is a stray piece of clay.

[6] This must have occurred when someone connected with the rebuilding made a small fire, which resulted in a spot of ash at the rim of which the sealing was found.

[7] There are no clear impressions of fibres, so reed or rope seem to be excluded.

[8] The thought of two abutting rollings presents itself, but careful scrutiny shows this to be extremely improbable.

that this impression was made with cylinder HMM 88-Z3. Although a third change of direction of the surface occurs to the left of the encased motif, we have all reason to believe that also the next figure with shoulder bulge is part of the same scene, that is to say, made with the same cylinder.

Classification and typology

Originally H. el Safadi grouped together some seals from Alishar, Karahöyük, Kültepe and Sukas[9] noting that they originated in the period of Kanesh Ib rather than earlier; S. Mazzoni shortly thereafter published an article discussing seals with similar and related designs and at later stages added various pieces[10], and also R.M. Boehmer commented on the group.[11] The general impression is that many of these seals indeed form a relatively closely-knit group in design and style, as well as in size.[12] Their chronological distribution may eventually have to be condensed if more precise information about find spots and sub-groupings becomes available, but at the present state of our knowledge it seems to run from Kültepe - Kanesh Ib through Early Hittite, i.e. the Middle Bronze II period, altogether perhaps some 200 years.

The *motif* is ultimately derived from the Mesopotamian presentation scene, i.e. a scene of audience with a higher placed person, be it human or divine (or a *symbol* of a deity), to whom hands are raised in devotion, or to whom a gift is presented. The motif's origin goes back to the Mesopotamian Early Dynastic period, although the present composition rather derives from the Akkad-period styles; however, its Mesopotamian forebears will not be discussed here. Suffice it to note that the motif of a row of "audience-grantees" has a considerable Cappadocian pedigree also, which was clearly established already in Karum II times.[13]

[9] *UF* 6 (1974) 351.
[10] *AION* 35 (1975) 21-43, *SE* 1 (1979) 49-64, and in M. Kelly-Bucellati et al. (eds.), *Insight through Images. Studies in Honor of Edith Porada* (Malibu 1986), 171-182.
[11] *FsTÖzgüç* 42f.
[12] Their height is always ca. 2 cm, their diameter ca. 1 cm. Although it is understandable that Mazzoni includes her nos. 8 and 21 in her group because of their cursory execution, their subject matter and style are rather different from those of the walking men-seals (see also our note 17). Mazzoni's nos. 8 and 21 have recently published parallels in, e.g., Ugarit (P. Amiet, *Sceaux-cylindres en hématite et pierres diverses* (Corpus des cylindres de Ras-Shamra-Ougarit II, Paris 1992), no. 6); cf. also B. Teissier, *Ancient Near Eastern Seals from the Marcopoli Collection* (Berkeley/London 1984), no.378. In general one can say that on closer scrutiny, the group as defined by Mazzoni incorporates various styles as well as motifs. See also note 20.
[13] See, for instance, B. Hrouda, *Or.* 52 (1983) 102-106 pl. I, A; P. Garelli - D. Collon, *Cuneiform Texts from Cappadocian Tablets in the British Museum, Part* VI (London 1975), pl. 48 no. 3, 5 and pl. 49 nos. 11, 12, 14 etc.; K.R. Veenhof - E. Klengel-Brandt, *Altassyrische Tontafeln aus Kültepe. Texte und Siegelabrollungen* (Vorderasiatische Schriftdenkmäler, Berlin 1992), pl. 41 no. 25; Teissier, *Sealing and Seals on Texts from Kültepe Karum Level 2* (*PIHANS* 70, İstanbul 1994), nos. 1-14, and many others.

Initially this theme is to be distinguished iconographically from the well-known Old (West) Syrian "Indian File" of men, often clad in short skirts and interpreted as a row of soldiers or, preferably, servants.[14] These figures usually clasp their hands in front of their breast or at the belt, or hold a weapon.[15] The theme of this row of men lives on into the Late Bronze Age.[16] It must be noted, however, that a mixture of the two classes of representations does occur.[17]

Since Boehmer adduces Elamite examples for comparison with our main theme of the audience[18], it is worth noting that also the row of soldiers/servants has clear reflections in Elam: cf. P. Amiet, *Glyptique Susienne* (Paris 1972) nos. 1999 and 2000. Boehmer's comparisons are not without foundation if one concentrates on the motif alone; the style of execution of Susa 2001 etc. differs considerably from that of the group under discussion.

In this context one wonders, with Mazzoni[19], if Amiet is not being too cautious with his remark that the " ... *ressemblance avec la glyptique cappadocienne nous paraît trop fortuite pour être significative*" (Amiet, *Glyptique Susienne* 239): Amiet's no. 2009 is another example of an almost certainly Syro-Cappadocian-inspired seal.[20] In view of the known Elamite political

[14] E.g., Collon, *The Seal Impressions from Tell Atchana/Alalakh* (Neukirchen-Vluyn 1975), 13 no. 12; C.F.A. Schaeffer, *Corpus I des Cylindres-sceaux de Ras-Shamra-Ugarit et d'Enkomi-Alasia* (Paris 1983), p.68 no. A23; Teissier, *Sealing and Seals on Texts from Kültepe Karum Level* 2, nos. 117, 126, cf. 116. Perhaps identifiable as soldiers: e.g. VA 2721 = A. Moortgat, *Vorderasiatische Rollsiegel* (Berlin 1940), pl. 63 no. 530. It is less probable that they are dancers, as Porada and Collon suggest (cf. Collon, *The Seal Impressions from Tell Atchana/Alalakh* 140f. and pl. 34): dancers would presumably hold hands or each other's shoulders or middle. In the extant scenes, the suggestion is rather one of guards or servants in attendance in the wings on an important occasion. This might even be true of a scene like Collon, *The Alalakh Cylinder Seals* (Oxford 1982), 51 no. 17, where the slanted incisions at the three figures' right shoulders suggest (to this viewer at least) only an upper arm, not specifically a whole arm resting on the preceding figures' shoulder, as Collon suggests. The Indian File might ultimately derive from Egypt.

[15] This Syrian Indian File probably is the forebear of the soldier-gods in Yazılıkaya. Such a derivation seems attractive iconographically, although of course the soldier gods in Yazılıkaya are in fact depicted as received in audience by the main gods, and could hence be classed in the other group.

[16] E.g., Amiet, *Sceaux-cylindres en hématite et pierres diverses* 111ff. for the "Défilés de personnages", representing a number of examples of the motif's Late Bronze *Weiterleben*; or Collon, *The Alalakh Cylinder Seals* 103 no. 87.

[17] E.g., when the little men are depicted with raised hands: Veenhof - Klengel-Brandt, *Altassyrische Tontafeln aus Kültepe. Texte und Siegelabrollungen* pl. 41 no. 19; Teissier, *Sealing and Seals on Texts from Kültepe Karum Level* 2 no. 609, and many others.

[18] *FsTÖzgüç* 43.

[19] *AION* 35 (1975) 40 n. 79.

[20] Here Mazzoni's inclusion in her group of seals like her nos. 8 and 21, from Kültepe and Klavdia, Cyprus respectively, gave rise to some unnecessary confusion: Teissier, *Ancient Near Eastern Seals from the Marcopoli Collection*, rightly compares her no. 378 (cf. p. 62) to these two seals, but unjustly comments that 'the group' has also been found in Elam, thus drawing rather acerbic criticism from Amiet (*Sceaux-cylindres en hématite et pierres diverses*, 14 n. 7).

interest in Syria at this time[21], contacts between the regions are feasible, and glyptic correlates would not be amazing.[22]

The *style*, i.e. the manner in which the seals are cut, can be characterized as linear and quick, with a marked emphasis on small horizontal incisions. In all of the seals, little attention has been paid to the execution of the heads, and also the plant-motifs are stylized.

A sub-group

The in- or exclusion of specific seals in a defined group is basically a subjective procedure. In the following table we concentrate on the direct parallels of the Hammam seal. Only *excavated* seals of the group under discussion are included which show the shoulder bulge and the long mantle, since it is this specific motif and stylistic idiom that seem to set this new sub-group apart from the rest of the "linear-cursive" (thus Mazzoni, *SE* 1 (1979) 49-64) style. The latter as a whole incorporates many motifs and ranges wider in time.

SEAL	SITE	LOCATION	MATERIAL	PUBLISHED
TM67F142	Ebla	above pavement	brownish stone	Mazzoni, AION 35, 21
TM70B232	Ebla	?	id.	ibid.:22
TM70E505	Ebla	palace refuse	id.	ibid.
TM70E542	Ebla	palace refuse	id.	ibid.
Karahüyük 26	Karahüyük	refuse pit	black st.	Alp 1972[23]
id. 27	Karahüyük	id.	id.	ibid.
id. 28	Karahüyük	id.	id.	ibid.
id. 29	Karahüyük	id.	brown st.	ibid.
id. 30	Karahüyük	id.	black st.	ibid.
id. 31	Karahüyük	id.	id.	ibid.
id. 32	Karahüyük	id.	id.	ibid.
Kt. r/k 107	Kanesh Ib	?	serpentine	Özgüç 1968:48[24]

21 E.g. M.W. Stolper, in E. Carter - M.W. Stolper, *Elam. Surveys of Political History and Archaeology* (Berkeley 1984), 28-30.

22 There was diplomatic contact between, e.g., the kingdoms of Mari and Elam which had ramifications, at least in occasional exchanges of tin, toward northwestern Syria (F. Joannès, *CRRAI* 1989 (Ghent 1991), 67-76). This predated the Elamite presence in the region of Shubat Enlil (Stolper, loc.cit.). And although no straight parallels can be adduced from the Diyala, a stylistically not unrelated seal may perhaps be recognized in H. Frankfort, *Stratified Cylinder Seals from the Diyala Region* (Chicago 1954), no. 943 from Isçali, and be used in this argument. It is somewhat similar to Alishar 1535 (H.H. von der Osten, *The Alishar Höyük Seasons of 1930-1932, Part* II (Chicago 1937), 207 fig. 246 = S. Mazzoni, *AION* 35 (1975) 21-43 no. 14).

23 = S. Alp, *Konya Civarında Karahöyük Kazılarında Bulunan Silindir ve Damga Mühürleri* (Ankara 1972).

24 = N. Özgüç, *Seals and Seal Impressions of Level 1b from Karum Kanish* (Ankara 1968).

Alishar 3362	Alishar	refuse pit	serpentine	vdOsten 1937:207[25]
Sukas 2011	Sukas	tomb	'steatite'	Riis 1960:129[26]
HMM 88-Z3	Hammam al Turkman	dirt fill	baked clay	(here)
HMM 88-Z4	Hammam al Turkman	id.	id.	id.
HMM 88-Z2 α	Hammam al Turkman	id.	unbaked clay	id.
id. β	Hammam al Turkman	id.	id.	id.

From this list, which is a derivate of Mazzoni's, several things become apparent.

First, the simple cutting style as well as the modest outlay necessary for the material of which most of these seals were made suggest a relatively low price for these cylinders because of the little demand on craftsmanship, and thus a comparatively lowly position for the owners/users of these seals. In the Hammam case this suggestion is underlined by the cheap material of which the seal was made.[27] Possibly the fact that the Sukas seal, which is said to be made of steatite, was found in a tomb in which more than thirty individuals had been collected (presumably over a longer period of time) also reflects a lowly position of the seal owner: richer owners might have preferred to be buried in more serene and less crowded surroundings.

Furthermore, although the number of seals and impressions belonging to this group is too small for any sort of statistical significance, it is striking that notably the seals are found, and only few impressions.[28] This fact may partly be due to the perhaps somewhat lowly function the seal owners performed: if the Hammam example is anything to go by, that function may primarily have been that of guard of a store room. Broken door sealings probably were discarded and recycled into other uses of clay quicker than, e.g., sealed contracts or accounts, since there was no need to refer to them repeatedly or over long periods in view of possible litigation; and the seals themselves were prized possessions unless they were made for use at specific occasions.

Thirdly, the location of the excavated pieces is striking. All seals except

[25] = H.H. von der Osten, *The Alishar Höyük. Seasons of 1930-1932. Part* II (Chicago 1937).

[26] = P. Riis, *Annales Archéologiques Syriennes* 10 (1960) 111-132.

[27] The Hammam cylinder must have been the cheapest by far. The material of the other stones is described as simply "stone" or "(variously colored) stone", serpentine, steatite or haematite, of which the latter may have been the most expensive – and exactly that seal (Mazzoni's no. 21, from Klavdia, Cyprus) shows a different, more complex motif. It is not included in our discussion here.

[28] I.e. the Hammam impressions. Although Mazzoni includes her no. 13 (= TC XXI pl. 235 no. 79, an impression from Kültepe) in the group, it is cut in quite a different style (as are her 11 and 12), and on that count it is not included in our discussion.

the one from Sukas were found in refuse soil (as were the impressions) and this at places very distant from each other.[29] Is this consistently careless disposal of these seals also an indication of their relative inexpensiveness?

Lastly, their geographical distribution over sites such as Kültepe, Karahüyük, Mardikh and Hammam easily suggests a connection of the use of these seals with the international trade networks known to have existed at that time and involving these places.[30] It is clear that one should not only think of the Assur-Kanesh axis, but of several co-existing networks that intertwined. Although the role of sites like Sukas in this context cannot be ascertained as yet, traces of contact should not surprise us in this period of increasing internationalisation.

Conclusion

The fifteen listed seals together with the sealed bullae form a closely-knit group both in subject matter and in cutting style. We might call this group the "Simplified Audience Group."[31]

Within the tradition of "linear cursive" seals isolated by el-Safadi and Mazzoni, they constitute a clear sub-grouping of which it would not surprise this author if they were made over a short period of time by, or by order of, people who were closely connected with, and had underlings functioning in, the wide-ranging international trade networks spanning the ancient Near East during the Middle Bronze Age. Although the greatest concentration of these seals has been found at Karahöyük, both motif and style remind one more of Syrian/North Mesopotamian genres than of purely Anatolian styles. This would be understandable at a period when archaeologically the Syrian imports in a place like Kültepe/Kanesh seem to increase from those of Karum level II [32]

Seals of this class have not yet been excavated at sites like Mari, and although this line of reasoning is highly suspect, it may support the idea that we are dealing with a principally North Syrian group. Sheer weight of numbers cannot be used to pinpoint a site of origin for this group. However, at Hammam both the seal and its ancient impression probably sealing an immovable object (a door) have been found, together with impressions of seals

29 No information is available as to the exact find spot of the Kültepe seal.

30 For the role Hammam may have played in this respect, cf. Van Loon, *Hammam et-Turkman* I (İstanbul 1988), xxvf., and Meijer, *Akkadica* 64/65 (1989) 3-4.

31 Simplified in two ways: the figure being greeted is almost always lacking, and the style of the cylinders is extremely simple. Concerning the first aspect a long discussion would be possible regarding the plant-like motifs as objects of adoration, in the way of symbols of divine figures. This will not be attempted here.

32 Cf. T. Özgüç, *Kültepe-Kanis II. New Researches at the Trading Center of the Ancient Near East* (Ankara 1986), 53: "*Level Ib has a much higher percentage of imported North Syrian ware than level II. Also, there are more, although infrequent, imitations of North Syrian shapes in native ware.*"

that are at least very similar (if not partly made by the same seal, see above); this strongly suggests a local origin for at least HMM 88-Z3, Z2 and Z-4.

The role played by sites like Hammam al Turkman within the political and economic framework of Northern Syria and adjacent regions cannot be treated here. We note, however, that finds such as the ones described above emphasize the node-function of Hammam al Turkman in a larger network. The site is thought to have been a regional center with a considerable degree of political independence, albeit subject to temporary unifying tendencies by energetic overlords; at such times, the economic structure is thought to have remained largely unimpaired. In this view politics and economy can be intertwined relatively loosely. At the demise of these overlords, city-states like Hammam could revert quite easily to their former status of relative independence.[33]

Summarizing, we may call this Simplified Audience Group a North Syrian invention in the context of Syro-Anatolian trade ventures. The group forms part of the larger group discussed by el-Safadi and Mazzoni, characterized by quick, relatively deep linear incisions; this larger group seems to have had a longer life span than the sub-group discussed here.

Allowing some time, perhaps a generation, for the simplified group to have been used before they were discarded, a dating at the very beginning of the Middle Bronze II period would seem to be in order.[34] It must be repeated that the dates of disposal and of deposition of the Hammam finds may differ considerably, but they do fall well within the Middle Bronze age.

[33] For a lengthier treatment of these ideas on the politics and economy of North Syrian "city-states" in the Middle Bronze Age, see Meijer, in O. Rouault - M. Wäfler, *La Ǧazīra et l'Euphrate Syriens. Actes du colloque international* (Paris 1995) forthcoming.

[34] The only slight traces of wear on the Hammam seal would seem to support a limited period of usage.

Plate 21a-b. Photograph and drawing of cylinder seal HMM 88-Z3.

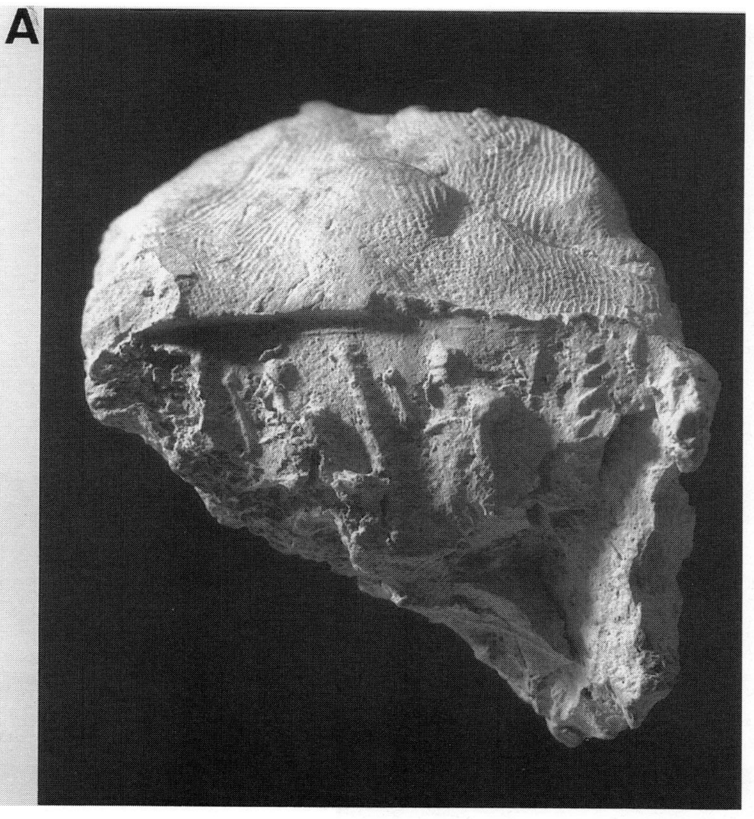

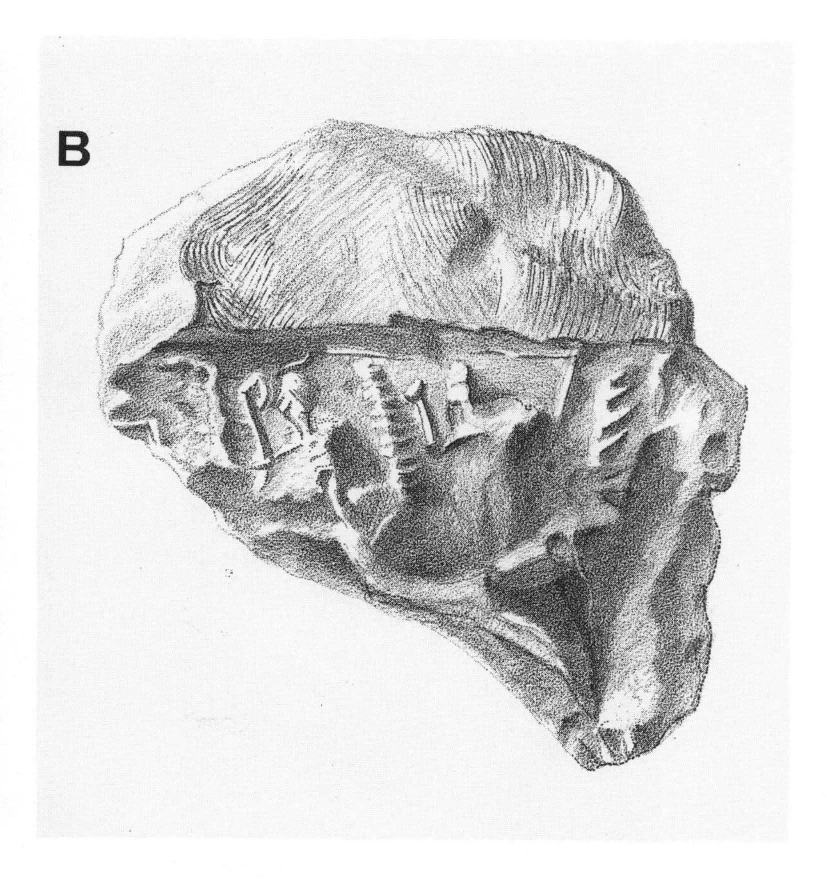

Plate 22a-b. Photograph and drawing of obverse of sealed bulla HMM 88-Z4.

Plate 23. Photograph of reverse of sealed bulla HMM 88-Z4.

Plate 24. Photograph of reverse of sealed bulla HMM 88-Z2.

Plate 25a-b. Photograph and drawing of sealing α on bulla HMM 88-Z2.

Plate 26a-b. Photograph and drawing of sealing β on bulla HMM 88-Z2; cf. Pl. 21.

BIER UND WEIN BEI DEN HETHITERN

GIUSEPPE F. DEL MONTE

Das sumerische Wort k a š bezeichnet irgendein vergorenes Getränk im allgemeinen, unabhängig vom Rohstoff und den benützten Zutaten; im südlichen Mesopotamien freilich zuerst die Produkte der Gärung von Gerste und Emmer, primäre Erzeugung des Landes, kurz, das "Bier"[1]. Die allgemeinere Bedeutung des Wortes jedoch verschwand nicht bei den anderen Kulturen, dabei auch die hethitische Kultur, die die Keilschrift benutzten. Ein gutes Beispiel ist die Nebeneinanderstellung in den *Rituels anatoliens* aus der hethitischen Stadt Emar[2] von den Logogrammen KAŠ.GEŠTIN und KAŠ.ŠE, eigentlich "aus der Gärung der Trauben (GEŠTIN) hergestelltes Getränk" bzw. "aus der Gärung der Gerste (ŠE) hergestelltes Getränk."

In der Schreibertradition von Ḫattuša scheint das Logogramm KAŠ.ŠE nicht im Gebrauch zu sein, und das einfache Zeichen KAŠ genügt, das Gerstenbier näher zu bezeichnen; häufig begegnet man dagegen in den hethitischen Texten dem Logogramm KAŠ.GEŠTIN. Die Fachgelehrten sind noch heute verschiedener Meinung über das Wesen dieses Getränkes, obwohl es schon lange bekannt ist.[3] In der früheren hethitologischen Literatur wurde es lediglich als die Nebeneinanderstellung zweier Wörter, "Bier (und) Wein", betrachtet. E. Neu[4] sieht es als "eine besondere Art Bier" an, gestützt auf die Gleichung KAŠ.GEŠTIN = akk. *kurunnum* in *AHw* 513b, das W. von Soden als "ein Feinbier" deutet. Diese Deutung geht indirekt auf F. Hrozný, *Das Getreide im alten Babylonien,* (Wien 1913), 142 zurück. *Kurunnum* aber, aus sumerisch k u r u n / m entlehnt, ist manchmal nicht Gerstenbier: in Hh XXIV = MSL 11 (1974) 81:89 wird es aus Sesam hergestellt. Im Kommentar HAR-g u d zu Hh XXIII, MSL 11 (1974) 88:74 gilt *šikāru* "Gerstenbier" als Synonym für *kurunnu*, aber Aa = MSL 14 (1979) 410 f.:127-131 übersetzt sumerisch k u - r u - u m mit *ṭābu* , "das Süße", *dāmu*, "das Blut", *kurunnu*, *šikārum*, "Gerstenbier", *karānu*, "Wein": vergleichbar dem Wort k a š ist auch k u r u m /*kurunnum* vieldeutig. Nach M.

1 Vgl. J. Bottéro, *RlA* III 303; G. Steiner, ebd., 307.

2 Vgl. D. Arnaud, *Emar* VI/3, 455 ff.

3 Vgl. nur G. Steiner, *RlA* III 307; I. Singer, *StBoT* 27, 157 mit Anm. 25.

4 *HZL* 163; *StBoT* 26, 246 Anm. 32b mit Verweis auf W. von Soden, W. Röllig, G. Steiner und I. Singer. Der Verweis auf die letzten zwei Gelehrte ist aber irreführend, weil sie das KAŠ.GEŠTIN als eine Art "Wein" ansehen.

Stol "*Kurunnu* is primarily a literary word originally standing for a sweet red alcoholic beverage of high quality."[5]

Das Wesen des KAŠ.GEŠTIN-Getränkes, wenn nicht einfach Nebeneinanderstellung "Bier (und) Wein"[6], hellt sich auf, wie von G. Steiner und I. Singer hervorgehoben, erstens aus dem Umstand, daß es vom ZABAR.DAB, dem "Kellermeister", verwaltet und zugeteilt wurde, anders als die übrigen, von dem AGRIG, dem "Verwalter", zugeteilten Getränke: es steht außer Zweifel, daß KAŠ.GEŠTIN ein "aus der Gärung der Trauben hergestelltes Getränk" war, kurz und gut: "(eine Art) Wein." Ferner, KAŠ.GEŠTIN wird oft von den Schreibern als GEŠTIN abgekürzt; das heißt, daß die Logogramme KAŠ.GEŠTIN und GEŠTIN, wenn auch manchmal unterschieden, oftmals ein einziges Getränk ("Wein") bezeichnen und daß beide nicht immer als zwei Sonderqualitäten Wein betrachtet werden sollen. Denn man liest in dem Ritual KUB XXXIII 70 Vs. ii 3'-9' // KUB XLVI 52 Vs? ii 3'-8'[7]:

3' ... *nu-uš-ša-an A-NA* DINGIR*lim*
4' [(NINDA.Ì.E.DÉ.A EGIR-*pa*)] *da-a-i nu* KAŠ.GEŠTIN *ši-pa-an-ti nu te-iz-zi*
5' [(dUTU-*i e-it-za :m*)]*i-i-ú-un a-a-an-ta-an ša-ku-wa-an-ta-an*
6' [Ì-*nu-an-ta-a*(*n nu* Z)]I-*KA mi-i-e-eš-tu e-ku-ma* GEŠTIN-*an*
7' [*nu-uš*]-*ša-an ša-ra-az-zi* KASKAL-*ši ti-i̯a*
8' [(*nu* LUGAL MÍ.LUGAL)] DUMUMEŠ LUGAL *šar-la-a-i nu* NINDA.Ì.E.DÉ.A *a-da-an-zi*
9' [(*nu* dUTU-*un* 3-*š*)]*u a-ku-wa-an-zi*

"Man legt einen fetthaltigen Kuchen vor der Gottheit nieder, spendet Wein (KAŠ.GEŠTIN) und sagt: Iß, Ištanu, die angenehme, warme, ..., [ölhaltig]e? Speise und werde deine Seele angenehm! Trink den Wein (GEŠTIN) [...]! Trete auf die obere Straße und erhebe den König, die Königin (und) die Königssöhne!. Sie essen den fetthaltigen Kuchen und trinken dreimal dem Ištanu."[8]

GEŠTIN als Abkürzung von KAŠ.GEŠTIN begegnet man in der Schilderung des Verlaufs einer Feier in manchen Ritualtexten, wo eine einzige, wiederholte rituelle Handlung uns nicht erlaubt, sie als zwei verschiedene gespendete Getränke zu betrachten. In KUB XXXII 84 (= CTH 704.1B) Vs? i, z.B., der ersten erhaltenen Spendung von GEŠTIN folgen zwei Spendungen von KAŠ.GEŠTIN, dann wird die ganze rituelle Handlung mittels des Logogramms

5 M. Stol, "*Beer in Neo-Babylonian Times*", in: L. Milano (Hrsg.), *Drinking in Ancient Societies* (Padova 1994), 165.

6 Vgl. z.B. KBo XXI 1 Vs. ii 5-6: 5 30 DUG*taḫ-ga-pí-ša IŠ-TU* KAŠ 6 GEŠTIN *ta-wa-al-az wa-al-aḫ-ḫi-i̯a-az šu-un-an-zi* "Man füllt 30 *t.*-Gefässe mit KAŠ, GEŠTIN-Wein, *tawal*-Bier (und) *walḫi*-Bier».

7 Es handelt sich um eine anthologische Tafel; diesem Ritual folgt ein Ritual der Mallidunna von Turmita.

8 Vgl. *CHD* L-N 307a *sub* a2', wo man von "wine-beer" redet.

KI.MIN "ditto" zusammengefaßt, doch handelt es sich immer wohl um eine Spendung desselben Getränkes, d.h. "Wein":

2' [EGIR-*a*]*n-da-ma A-NA* [dGN 1 NINDA.SIG]
3' [*pár-ši*]-*ịa še-ra-aš-ša-an* UZUNÍG.GIG UZUŠÀ *ku-r*[*a-a-an*]
4' [*da-a-i*] UZUNÍG.GIG-*ma-aš-ša-an še-ir* 1 UZUTI *za-nu-an-d*[*a-an da-a-i*]
5' *n*[*a-a*]*t-ša-an* EGIR-*pa* GIŠ*la-aḫ-ḫu-u-ra da-a-i*
6' *nu* GEŠTIN *PA-NI ḫu-up-ru-uš-ḫi ši-pa-an-ti*
7' EGIR-*an-da-ma A-NA* dIŠKUR 1 NINDA.SIG *pár-ši-ịa*
8' *še-ra-aš-ša-an* UZUNÍG.GIG UZUŠÀ *ku-ra-a-an da-a-*[*i*]
9' [ ] UZUNÍG.GIG-*ma-aš-ša-an še-ir* 1 UZUTI *za-n*[*u-an-da-an da-a-i*]
10' [*na-a*]*t-ša-an* EGIR-*pa* GIŠ*la-aḫ-ḫu-u-ra da-a-i*
11' [*nu*] KAŠ.GEŠTIN *PA-NI ḫu-up-ru-uš-ḫi ši-pa-an-ti*

12' [UZUNÍG].GIG-*ma* UZUŠÀ *hu-u-ma-an ku-ra-a-an-na*
13' [ ]-*a-an*[-*zi*?]

14' [EGI]R-*an-da-ma A-NA* d*šu-wa-li-ia-at-ti*
15' [1 NINDA.S]IG *pár-ši-ịa še-ra-aš-ša-an* UZUNÍG.GIG UZUŠÀ
16' [*ku-r*]*a-a-an da-a-i na-at-ša-an* EGIR-*pa* GIŠ*la-aḫ*-[*ḫu-u-ra*]
17' [*da*]-*a-i nu* KAŠ.GEŠTIN *PA-NI ḫu-up-ru-uš-ḫi ši-pa-an-*[*ti*]

18' [EGI]R-*an-da-ma A-NA* dNIDABA 1 NINDA.SIG *pár-ši-ịa*
19' KI.MIN

20' EGIR-*an-da-ma A-NA* dÉ.A 1 NINDA.SIG *pár-ši-ịa*
21' KI.MIN

22' EGIR-*an-da-ma A-NA* dUTU 1 NINDA.SIG *p*[*ár-ši-ịa*
(Abgebrochen)

"Dann [zerbrich]t man [ein Fladenbrot] der [Gottheit GN], darauf [legt man] Leber (und) geschnitt[ene] Eingeweide, auf die Leber [legt man] eine gebraten[e] Rippe [und] legt sie auf den Opfertisch? zurück; man spendet Wein (GEŠTIN) in dem Weihrauchfaß.
Dann zerbricht man ein Fladenbrot dem Tešub, darauf leg[t] man Leber (und) geschnittene Eingeweide, auf die Leber [legt man] eine gebr[atene] Rippe [und] legt sie auf den Opfertisch? zurück; man spendet Wein (KAŠ.GEŠTIN) in dem Weihrauchfaß.
Jedes Stück Leber aber und jedes Stück gebratener Eingeweide [...] man.
Dann zerbricht man [ein Fladenbrot] dem Šuwalijat, darauf legt man Leber (und) ge[schn]ittene Eingeweide und [le]gt sie auf den Opf[ertisch?] zurück; man spend[et] Wein (KAŠ.GEŠTIN) in dem Weihrauchfaß.
Dann zerbricht man ein Fladenbrot der Getreidegottheit - ditto.

Dann zerbricht man ein Fladenbrot dem Ea - ditto.
Dann z[erbricht] man ein Fladenbrot dem Šimigi - ditto."

Daß GEŠTIN, wenn es ein Getränk bezeichnet, oft lediglich Abkürzung von KAŠ.GEŠTIN ist, scheint uns außer Zweifel stehen[9]. Abkürzungen aber, die keine Schwierigkeit für den alte Schreiber und die in dem Kult Beschäftigten darstellten, können dagegen uns wirkliche Rätsel aufgeben. Dazu betrachte man das zweite Ritual der anthologischen Ritualsammlung KUB XVII 28 Vs. ii 33 - Rs. iii 17:

33 [*ma*]-*a-an an-tu-uḫ-ši* ^{LÚ}*TAP-PU-ŠU la-a-la-an kar-ap-zi*
34 *na-aš-ma-aš-ši-iš-ša-an* DINGIR^{MEŠ}-*uš ú-e-ri-i̯a-az-zi*
35 *nu ki-i* SISKUR.SISKUR-*ŠU* 1 NINDA.GUR$_4$.RA 1 ^{DUG}ḪAB.ḪAB GEŠTIN
36 *a-ra-aḫ-za ka-ri-ta-aš-ḫi pí-e-da-an-zi*
37 *nu* NINDA.GUR$_4$.RA GÙB-*la-az pár-ši-i̯a na-an da-ga-a-an*
38 *da-a-i* KAŠ.GEŠTIN GÙB-*la-az* BAL-*an-ti*
39 *n*[*u k*]*i-iš-ša-an me-im-ma-i*

"Wenn gegen einen Menschen sein Gefährte eine böse Zunge hebt oder anruft die Götter gegen ihn, ist dies das Ritual dafür: Man bringt ein dickes Brot und eine Kanne Wein (GEŠTIN) nach draußen auf einem *karitašḫa*-[10], links bricht man das dicke Brot und legt es auf den Boden, links spendet man den Wein (KAŠ.GEŠTIN) und sagt: ..."

Die folgende Beschwörung hat keine Bedeutung in diesem Zusammenhang. Die Gleichung GEŠTIN = KAŠ.GEŠTIN ist an dieser Stelle naheliegend, im Folgenden aber wird die Angelegenheit ziemlich problematisch:

48 *nu* NINDA.GUR$_4$.RA *pí-e-di-eš-ši da-a-i* ^{DUG}ḪAB.ḪAB-*ma*
49 *ar-ha du-wa-ar-ni-i̯a-zi nu-za-kán QA-TI-ŠU*
50 *a-ar-ri na-aš ar-ḫa ú-iz-zi*
51 *nu* ^{GIŠ}BANŠUR TUR ^{d}UTU-*i me-na-aḫ-ḫa-an-da da-a-i*
52 *nu-uš-ša-an* NINDA-*an da-a-i še-ir-ra-aš-ša-an*
53 3 NINDA.GUR$_4$.RA *da-a-i na-aš-ta* 1 UDU.NÍTA ^{d}UTU-*i* BAL-*an-ti*
54 *na-an ḫu-u-kán-zi nu* KAŠ *ši-ip-pa-an-ti*
55 *nu ki-iš-ša-an me-im-ma-i*
...
III 4 UDU-*kán ar-kán-zi nu šu-up-pa* ^{UZU}NÍG.GIG ^{UZU}GAB
5 SAG.DU [Ú]R GÌR^{MEŠ} *PA-NI* ^{GIŠ}BANŠUR *da-a-i*
6 ^{UZU}NÍG.G[I]G$^{\text{ḪI.A}}$ *za-nu-an-zi* NINDA.GUR$_4$.RA$^{\text{ḪI.A}}$ *pár-ši-ia-an-da*

9 Indirekte Beweisführungen auch durch Duplikatstellen, vgl. z.B. in CTH *621: KBo XXI 80+KBo XX 44+FHG 7(+)KUB XXXIV 122 Vs. i 15 KAŠ.GEŠTIN-*an* gegen KBo XX 71+76+KBo XXIII 99+KBo XXIV 87 Vs 17' GEŠTIN-*an*.

10 Vgl. F. Starke, *KZ* 93 (1979) 258: "Hapax ... Unsicherer Bedeutung." Es handelt sich jedenfalls um einen Raum, wo man hinein- und heraustreten kann.

7 *nu* 1 NINDA.GUR$_4$.RA *da-ga-an da-a-i nu ma-al-ti*
8 ^{d}UTU-*i ku-iš pí-ra-an ar-ta*
9 *nu-wa-kán* ^{d}UTU-*i pár-ra-an-da* SIG$_5$-*in me-mi-iš-ki*
10 2 NINDA.GUR$_4$.RA$^{HI.A}$ *pár-ši-ia na-aš-kán A-NA* ^{GIŠ}BANŠUR TUR
11 *da-a-i še-ir-ra-aš-ša-an* ^{UZU}NÍG.GIG *da-a-i*
12 KAŠ.GEŠTIN BAL-[*a*]*n-ti* ^{UZU}Ì-*ma za-nu-wa-an-zi*
13 *na-at ar-ḫ*[*a*] *a-da-an-zi nu* 3-*šu a-ku-wa-an-zi*
14 *nu* ^{GIŠ}BANŠUR *ša-ra-a da-an-zi*

"Man legt das dicke Brot an die gleiche Stelle, die Kanne aber zerbricht man. Man wäscht sich die Hände und kommt heraus. Man stellt einen kleinen Tisch vor die Sonnengottheit, man legt das Brot darauf, dann legt man drei dicke Brote darauf. Dann opfert man ein Schaf der Sonnengottheit, schlägt es nieder, spendet das Bier/den Wein (KAŠ) und sagt folgendermaßen: ... Man schlachtet das Schaf. Man legt das reine Fleisch, Leber, Brust, Kopf, Lende, Fuß auf dem Tisch, man brät die Fleischstücke. Man bricht die dicken Brote, legt ein dickes Brot auf den Boden und sagt: Wer vor der Sonnengottheit steht: rede immer wieder günstig vor der Sonnengottheit!. Man bricht die zwei (übrigen) dicken Brote und legt sie auf den kleinen Tisch, darauf legt man die Leber (und) spendet den Wein (KAŠ.GEŠTIN). Man brät das Fett, ißt es auf, dreimal trinkt man. Den Tisch hebt man dann auf."

Freilich ist wohl denkbar, wenn man sich an den Buchstaben klammert, daß eine erste Spendung Wein im *karitašḫa-* stattfindet, dann eine zweite Spendung Bier außerhalb und wieder eine dritte Spendung Wein, doch scheint uns der Ritus vielmehr einfach und einheitlich: es gibt einen Widder (UDU.NÍTA ii 53, UDU iii 4: man denkt wohl nicht an zwei verschiedene Tiere), drei Brotlaibe und Wein, um die Opfergabe zu begleiten. Der Schreiber bezeichnete den Wein durch den Zeichen KAŠ.GEŠTIN, GEŠTIN und sogar einfaches KAŠ, "alkoholisches Getränk (allgemein)", das kontextuell dem zeitgenössischen Leser keinen Anlaß zu Mißverständnissen geben sollte.

Der beibehaltene Gebrauch des Zeichens KAŠ als allgemeine Bezeichnung für "alkoholisches Getränk", nicht immer spezifisch für "Gerstenbier", wird allerdings durch die Stelle KBo XXIX 93+KUB XXXII 126 (= CTH 692, 7B) Rs. iv 7-9 bewiesen: [7][^{LÚ}SÌL]A.ŠU.DU$_8$-*aš* ^{MÍ}*ḫu-wa-aš-ša-an-na-al-li* GAL KAŠ. GEŠTIN *pa-a-*[*i*] [8][*na-a*]*n pa-iz-zi A-NA* DINGIR^{lim} *pa-ra-a e-ip-zi* [9][*na-a*]*š ti-i̯a-zi* GAL KAŠ-*i̯a ḫar-zi* "Der Mundschenk gibt der Ḫuwaššanna-Priesterin einen Becher Wein (KAŠ.GEŠTIN); sie geht und hält ihn der Göttin hin. Sie tritt hin und hält den Becher Wein (KAŠ)." Indirekter Beweis auch in der Beschreibung einer in zwei Exemplaren erhaltenen Handlung: die erste, KUB XXXII 125+KBo XXIX 100 (= CTH 692,13) Rs. iv, bietet aufeinanderfolgend: "[Man gibt] der *alḫuitra*-Priesterin [und dem Opfermandanten zu trinken und sie trinken sitzend] der Ḫuwaššanna ... Der Mundschenk [gibt der] Ḫuwaššanna-Priesterin [einen Becher KAŠ]; sie geht und h[ält] ihn der

Göttin hin. [Sie tritt hin] und hält den Becher KAŠ ... Sie trinken sitzend der Sonnengottheit ... Der Mundschenk gibt einen Becher KAŠ ... [Sie trinken sitzend dem Wettergott] ... [Der Mundschenk] gi[bt] der [Ḫuwaššanna-Priesterin] einen Becher GEŠTIN [...].” Dem entspricht KUB LIV 9 Vs. ii: “Sie trinken sitzend Ḫuwaššanna] ... Der Mundschenk [gibt] der Ḫuwaššanna-Priesterin einen Becher K[AŠ; sie geht und] hält [ihn] der Göttin hin. Sie tritt hin [und hält] den Becher K[AŠ] ... Sie trinken sitzend der Sonnengottheit ... [Der] Mundschenk gi[bt] der Ḫuwaššanna-Priesterin einen Becher KAŠ; [sie geht und] hält [ihn] der Göttin hin. Sie tritt hin [und hält den Becher KAŠ] ... Sie trinken sitzend dem Wettergott ... Der Mundschenk gibt der Ḫuwaššanna-Priesterin einen Becher KAŠ (dagegen GAL GEŠTIN in der parallelen Stelle); [sie geht und] hält [ihn] dem Gott hin. Sie tritt hin [und hält den Becher ...].”[11] Es ist anzunehmen, daß auch an anderen Stellen der den Kult der Ḫuwaššanna betreffenden Bruchstücke mit KAŠ tatsächlich der Wein gemeint ist, selbst wenn der Gebrauch von Gerstenbier in diesem Kult durch das Vorkommen von *ši-i-e-eš-šar* in KBo XXIX 102: 2’ bewiesen wird.

Wir führen ein letztes Beispiel an, um diese Problematik kurz zu umreißen: das Ritual für die uralten Götter CTH 446, herausgegeben von H. Otten, *ZA* 54 (1961) 114 ff. In KBo X 45 Vs. i 32’-35’ (B) // KUB XLI 8 Vs. i 16’-19’ (C) // IBoT II 128 Vs. ii 7-9 (E) geht der Zelebrant (LÚAZU) zu dem Flußufer *nu* Ì-*an da-a-i* (C om. *da-a-i*) KAŠ.GEŠTIN (E: GEŠTIN-*i̯a*) *wa-al-ḫi mar-nu-wa-an ku-it-ta pa-r*[*a*]*-a* GAL GIR4 NINDA.Í.E.DÉ.A *me-ma-al* TU7.BA.BA.ZA *da-a-i* SILA4-*i̯a ḫar-zi nu-uš-ša-an pát-te-eš-ni* GAM-*an-ta ḫu-u-u*[*k*]*-zi nu kiš-an me-ma-i* “er nimmt Öl, nimmt Wein (KAŠ.GEŠTIN, Var. GEŠTIN), *walḫi*-Bier, *marnuan*-Bier, jedes gesondert in einem Tonbecher, einen fetthaltigen Kuchen, Grütze, Gerstenbrei und hält einen Lamm. Er spricht die Beschwörung in die Grube hinunter (oder, mit Otten: (das Lamm) schlachtet er in die Grube hinab) und sagt folgendermaßen ...” Am Ende der langen Beschwörung, in Vs. ii 9 ff. // KUB XLI 8 Vs. i 39 ff. legt er in der Grube den fetthaltigen Kuchen, die Grütze und den Gerstenbrei nieder, spendet den KAŠ.GEŠTIN-Wein, [das *walḫi*-Bier] und das *marnuan*-Bier, nimmt Lehm aus dem Flußufer und mischt ihn mit Öl und Honig (LÀL), um daraus göttliche Figürchen zu kneten – Honig wird nicht erwähnt in der vom Zelebranten mitgenommenen Opferausrüstung, vgl. aber passim im Verlauf der Ritualhandlungen. Für diese Gottheiten aus Lehm, Öl und Honig wird eine weitere Spende zubereitet, KBo X 45 Vs. ii 21-22: 4 DUGḪAB.ḪAB GEŠTIN NINDA.GUR4.RA *me-ma-al* TU7.BA.BA.ZA TU7.*kán-kán-ti da-a-i na-aš ú-i-te-ni pa-iz-zi nu ki-iš-ša-an me-ma-i* “Er nimmt 4 Kannen Wein (GEŠTIN), dickes Brot, Grütze, Gerstenbrei, *kankanti*-Brei, geht zum Wasser und spricht folgendermaßen.” Selbstverständlich können wir wohl annehmen, daß

[11] Parallelstellen: mit GAL GEŠTIN: KUB XXVII 49 Rs. iii 1-3; KUB XXVII 62 Rs. iii 4-5; KBo XIV 92 Vs. 1′, 6′; KBo XXIX 98: 7′-9′; mit GAL KAŠ: KUB XXVII 57+KBo XXIX 139 Vs. ii 3 (vgl. in verschiedenem Zusammenhang 16-18 DUG KAŠ und GAL GEŠTIN); KUB XXVII 51: 3’; KBo XXIX 94 Vs. i 4’ (in Ras.), 13’-16’ (erste Stelle in Ras.; wechselnd mit GAL GIR4 GEŠTIN Vs. ii 2’-4’); KBo XXIX 95: 3’, 11’; IBoT III 74: 9’-11’. Über die Kulthandlung vgl. auch A. Archi - A. Kammenhuber, *Materialien* 7 (1976) Nr. 5, 362 ff.

einem ersten Trankopfer von KAŠ.GEŠTIN-Wein ein zweites Trankopfer von GEŠTIN-Wein folgt; am Ende aber der Beschwörung, Vs. ii 57, wird das Trankopfer mit den Worten beschrieben: NINDA.GUR$_4$.RA *pár-ši-ia* GIŠ.GEŠTIN BAL-[*ti*], "Er bricht das dicke Brot und libiert GIŠ.GEŠTIN", wo GIŠ.GEŠTIN keinesfalls Weinrebe oder Weintraube meinen kann: unserer Meinung nach kann GIŠ.GEŠTIN nur als Hörfehler für KAŠ.GEŠTIN erklärt werden. Ähnlich in KBo X 45 Rs. iv 45-49: **nu* DINGIR^{MEŠ}* *a-ša-ši a-ni-i̯a-ad-du-uš-ša-aš-ma-aš pí-ra-an-mi-it da-a-i* GIŠ.GEŠTIN-*i̯a* BAL-*an-ti nu-kán* 1 SILA$_4$ 8 MUŠEN *A-NA* ^{d}A.NUN.NA.KE$_4$ BAL-*an-ti nu A-NA* 3 GUNNI^{MEŠ} *QA-DU* NINDA.SIG^{MEŠ} ^{GIŠ}ERIN Ì LÀL *wa-ar-nu-zi nu* GEŠTIN BAL-*an-ti nu kiš-an me-ma-i* "Die Gottheiten läßt er sitzen, legt vor ihnen die Opferausrüstung nieder und libiert GIŠ.GEŠTIN; er spendet den Anunna ein Lamm (und) 8 Vögel und verbrennt Fladenbrote, Zeder, Öl (und) Honig auf drei Herden, libiert Wein (GEŠTIN) und spricht folgendermaßen." In den übrigen Ritualhandlungen wird immer GEŠTIN geschrieben, doch müssen wir annehmen, daß unter verschiedenen Schreib-weisen stets KAŠ.GEŠTIN-Wein gemeint ist.

Ein Anzeichen für die Qualität des als KAŠ.GEŠTIN bezeichneten Weines bietet uns eine Kulthandlung des Rituals CTH 415. In KBo XIII 114 Vs. ii 16'-18' = KBo XV 24+KBo XXIV 109+KUB XXXII 137 Vs. ii 67-69 nimmt der Zelebrant, außer Brot, 1 DUG KAŠ 1 ^{DUG}ḪAB.ḪAB GEŠTIN 1 ^{DUG}*KU-KU-UB* GEŠTIN 1 ^{DUG}*KU-KU-UB* KAŠ 1 ^{DUG}*KU-KU-UB mar-nu-an* 1 ^{DUG}*KU-KU-UB ta-wa-al* 1 ^{DUG}*KU-KU-UB wa-al-ḫi*. Das erste Trankopfer vor dem Opfertisch des Gottes Ea wird in KBo XIII 114 Vs. ii 28'-29' folgendermaßen beschrieben:

28' [(*nam-ma PA*)]-*NI* ^{GIŠ}BANŠUR GEŠTIN KAŠ.GEŠTIN *mar-nu-an A-NA* ^{d}É.A
29' [*ku-it-t*(*a*)] 3-*šu ši-pa-an-ti*
"Dann libiert er dem Ea GEŠTIN-Wein, KAŠ.GEŠTIN-Wein (und) *marnuan*-Bier vor dem Opfertisch, [jede]s (Getränk) dreimal."

Dagegen in KBo XV 24+KBo XXIV 109+KUB XXXII 137 Rs. iii 10-11:

10 *nam-ma PA-NI* ^{GIŠ}BANŠUR [(GEŠTIN)] KAŠ.LÀL *mar-nu-an A-NA* ^{d}É.A
11 [*ku-it-t*]*a* 3-*šu ši-pa-an-ti*

"Dann libiert er dem Ea GEŠTIN-Wein, KAŠ.LÀL (und) *marnuan*-Bier vor dem Opfertisch, [jede]s (Getränk) dreimal».

Hier werden KAŠ.GEŠTIN und KAŠ.LÀL als Synonyme betrachtet, was uns gleich die in Aa angeführten Übersetzungen des sumerischen k u r u n / m ins Gedächtnis zurückführt: *karānu* «Wein», *kurunnu* und *ṭābu* "süß", das heißt, wie von M. Stol erläutert, "a sweet ... alcoholic beverage."

KAŠ.LÀL, mit KAŠ.GEŠTIN in der Bildung gleich, heißt nicht notwendig "honighaltiges Bier"[12], auch nicht notwendig "Met." LÀL heišt *ṭābu*, "süß", in MSL 3 (1955) 71:33' (S^a), *dišpu* in MSL 3, 138:103 (S^b); in der Boğazköy-Fassung von S^a KUB III 105:12'-14' = MSL 3, 72 heißt *dišpu*, *ṭābu* und *matqu*. Hh XXIV = MSL 11 (1974), 78:1-11 verzeichnet verschiedene Arten von LÀL, unter denen l à l . z ú . l u m . m a = *dišip suluppi*, "Dattelsirup" (auch in den altbabylonischen Fassungen)[13]. LÀL, wie *dišpu*, heißt "Honig", in erweitertem Sinne aber auch jeder Süßstoff. In der angeführten Stelle KAŠ.LÀL ist Synonym zu KAŠ.GEŠTIN, "Süßwein" (ob künstlich oder natürlich versüßt, wissen wir nicht), aber in einem anderen Ritualtext wird es als Synonym zu das *marnuan*-Bier betrachtet, KBo XXV 178 (CTH 630, Tafel 2) Vs. i 5-15:

5 [UG]ULA $^{\text{LÚ.MEŠ}}$MUḪALDIM *mar-nu-wa*$^{!}$*-an-da-aš ta-pí-*[*ša-n*]*a-an šu-*[*un-na-i*
6 LUGAL-*uš-ša*$^{!}$*-an tu-u-wa-az QA-TAM da-a-i nu-uš-š*[*a-an*
7 ^{NINDA}*ḫar-ša-i̯a-az-kán še-ir ar-ḫa ḫa-aš-ši-i* x [
8 UGULA $^{\text{LÚ.MEŠ GIŠ}}$BANŠUR-*ma-aš-ši tu-u-wa-az an-da* [
9 ^{KUŠ}*kur-ši* 1-*šu ši-pa-an-ti* ^{GIŠ}DAG-*ti* 1-*šu* ^{GIŠ} *l*[*u-ut-ti-i̯a* 1-*šu*]
10 *ḫa-at-tal-wa-aš* GIŠ-*ru-i* 1-*šu nam-ma* *x* *ḫa-aš-š*[*i-i ta-pu-uš-za*]
11 ZAG-*az* 1-*šu ši-pa-an-*[*ti*]
12 UGULA $^{\text{LÚ.MEŠ}}$MUḪALDIM KAŠ.LÀL *ta-pí-ša-ni-it ši-pa-an-du-a*[*n-zi zi-in-na-i*]

---

13 *nu* 2 UDU$^{\text{ḪI.A}}$ *ku-i-e-eš ḫa-aš-ši-i ta-pu-uš-za* ZAG-*az* [
14 *na-aš-kán* UGULA $^{\text{LÚ.MEŠ}}$MUḪALDIM GEŠTIN-*it ši-pa-an-ti na-aš-kán* [*pa-ra-a pí-e-da-an-zi*]
15 LUGAL-*uš UŠ-KE-EN* ^{LÚ} *ki-i-ta-aš ḫal-za-a-i*

"Der Aufseher der Köche fü[llt] ein *tapišana*-Gefäß mit *marnuan*-Bier, der König legt von ferne die Hand daran, [...] und [man zerbricht] die dicken Brote auf dem Herd. Der Aufseher der Tafeldecker aber [...] ihm von Ferne. [Der Aufseher der Köche] libiert einmal auf dem Jagdsack, einmal auf dem Thron, [einmal am] F[enster], einmal auf dem Riegelholz, dann libiert er einmal rechts [seitwärts] des Herdes.
Der Aufseher der Köche bringt [das] Spenden mit dem *tapišana*-Gefäß voll KAŠ.LÀL [zu Ende]. Die zwei Schafe, die rechts seitwärts des Herdes [stehen], die spendet der Aufseher der Köche mit Wein (GEŠTIN). [Man schafft] sie [hinaus]. Der König neigt sich; der *kita*- ruft."

[12] Vgl. aB *MSL* 11, 153: 66 k a š . š à . l à l.
[13] Vgl. *MSL* 11, 156: 271, 163: vi 22, ii 1.

Die allgemeine Bedeutung von KAŠ.LÀL, "süßes oder versüßtes alkoholisches Getränk", wird nicht nur dadurch betont, daß es sowohl den KAŠ.GEŠTIN-Wein wie auch das *marnuan* -Bier bezeichnen kann, sondern auch dadurch, daß nach KAŠ.LÀL noch andere, aus dem Zusammenhang unbestimmbare, aber von den genannten verschiedene Getränke benannt werden. Vgl. z.B. VBoT 58 = CTH 323 Rs. iv 21: 1 DUG GEŠTIN 1 DUG *mar-nu-wa-an* 1 DUG KAŠ.LÀL 1 DUG GEŠTIN.L[ÀL] "Wein, *marnuan*-Bier, KAŠ.LÀL (= honighaltiges Bier?), Süßwein (= honighaltiger Wein?)"; ebd. Rs. iv 32 = KUB LIII 20 Rs. 7': 3 DUGḪI.A GEŠTIN-*n*[*a*] *mar-nu-an* KAŠ.LÀL "drei Becher: (ein Becher voll) Wein, (ein Becher voll) *marnuan*-Bier (und ein Becher voll) KAŠ.LÀL"[14]; ebd. Rs. iv 42-43 = KUB LIII 20 Rs. 16': *nu mar*-[(*nu-an* KAŠ. LÀL)] GEŠTIN-*an* *A-NA* dUTU *ši-pa-an-ti* "er libiert der Sonnengottheit *marnuan*-Bier, KAŠ.LÀL (und) Wein."[15] In einem Programm des KI.LAM-Festes, ABoT 5+KBo XVII 9+20+KBo XX 5+KBo XXV 12 = *StBoT* 28, 34 Vs. ii 8'-9', werden auch bestimmte Angestellte für KAŠ.LÀL genannt: LÚ.MEŠKAŠ.LÀL KAŠ.LÀL *ša*[*r*]-*ra*-*a*[(*n-zi*)] "Die Angestellte dem KAŠ.LÀL teilen das KAŠ.LÀL zu"; in einem anderen Programm, KBo XX 33+KBo XVII 46+21+KBo XXV 19+KBo XXXIV 2 = *StBoT* 28, 89 Vs. 8, liest man: [LÚ.M]EŠKAŠ.LÀL KAB?.KA.GA KÙ.BABBAR KAŠ.LÀL *pí-iš-kán-zi* "Die Angestellte dem KAŠ.LÀL verteilen ein silbernes K.-Gefäß[16] voll KAŠ.LÀL."

Als eine besondere, minderwertige, Bierart sieht man das Logogramm DUG.KA.GAG(.A) an; im einzelnen, wäre DUG das Gefäß, das das KA.GAG-Bier enthält. Das Logogramm bezeichnet an sich ein Gefäß, dessen akkadische Name *pīhu* ist: als solches wird in Hh X, in der eben den Gefäßen gewidmete Gliederung, gebucht, MSL 7, 79 f.:75-78: d u g . KAŠ.ÚS.SA = *hi-it-tum*/[*ha*]-*at-t*[*u*], d u g . KAŠ.ÚS.SA.KA.GAG = *pi-hu*; d u g . KA.GAG = MIN (i.e., *pi-hu*); d u g. p i . h u = MIN. KA.GAG qualifiziert seinerseits das d i d a -Bier (KAŠ.Ú.SA/ KAŠ.US.SA = *billatu*), und der Komplex gewinnt die akkadische Bedeutung *pīhu* (in diesem Falle offenbar eine Art *billatu*) in Hh XXIII = MSL 11, 69 f.:1'-2': [KAŠ.Ú.SA.x.x] = *p*[*i-hu*], [KAŠ.Ú.S]A.KA.GAG = MIN. Die altbabylonische Vorläufer bieten dafür verschiedene Schreibweisen: Nippur Forerunner MSL 11,

[14] G. Beckman, *StBoT* 29, 82 übersetzt: "And three wine vessels (one each of) *marnuwan*, beer (and) honey." Weil es aber kein Anzeichen dafür gibt, daß auch das Zeichen GEŠTIN, wie das Zeichen KAŠ, für alkoholische Getränke im allgemeinen, auch für Bier also, verwendet werden konnte, und weil *marnuan*- sicher eine Art Bier war (vgl. *CHD* L-N 194b), so ziehen wir, trotz des Enklitikons -*a*, unsere Deutung vor. Vgl. auch die folgende Stelle.

[15] Ähnlich ebd. 44-45 = KUB LIII 20 Rs. 18', dem Telipinu, und KUB LIII 20 Rs. 24'. In dem unveröffentlichten Bruchstück Bo 3752 Vs.? ii 8' liest man nach der Transliteration von E. Neu, *StBoT* 25, 179: 1 *mar-nu-wa-aš* 1 KAŠ.LÀ[L. Weil aber das Zeichen LÀL ist offenbar auf dem Bruch, und mit Rücksicht auf der Beschreibung des Bruchstückes in *StBoT* 25, 179 Anm. 599, so fragen wir uns, ob eine Lesung KAŠ.GE[ŠTIN] nicht möglich sei. Selbst wenn die Lesung LÀL sich bewahrheiten sollte, scheint uns das Bruchstück nicht so streng parallel zu KUB LV 39 (Bo 2372) Vs. i und damit die Gleichung KAŠ.LÀL = *walḫi*- so nicht beweisbar (vgl. noch *HZL* 163). Auf Grund der bisherigen Ergebnisse jedoch sollte man sich nicht wundern, wenn man ein KAŠ.LÀL als versüßtes *walḫi*-Bier irgendwo finden sollte.

[16] Über den Namen des Gefäßes vgl. infra.

115:10-11 KAŠ.ÚS.SA.KA.GAG.A, KAŠ.ÚS.SA KA.GI.GAG; Forerunner 13 BM 15279 = MSL 11, 150:176-177: KAŠ.Ú.SA.KA.GAG.A, KAŠ.Ú.SA.GI.GAG.A. In Diri V 231 f., angeführt in MSL 7, 79 Anmerkung ad 76-78 lesen wir noch: p i . h u = KAŠ.Ú.SA.KA.GAG = *pi-hu*, p i . h u = DUG.NUNUZ+ÁBxKAŠ = MIN.[17] Vgl. noch KAŠ.Ú.SA (ohne DUG) zur Bezeichnung eines Gefäßes in M. Birot, TEBA 75 Nr. 35:21 und in den ebd. S. 76 erwähnten Stellen.

DUG.KA.GAG ist also vor allem Abkürzung von DUG.KAŠ.Ú/ÚS.SA.KA.GAG, akkadisch *pīhu*; das Logogramm bezeichnet zuerst ein Gefäß, und in erweitertem Sinn den *üblichen* Inhalt dieses Gefäßes.[18] Bei den Hethitern, auf denen wir unsere Überlegungen hier einschränken, ist der Gebrauch des Logogramms keinesfalls verschieden: ein Gefäß, das *gewöhnlich* Bier enthält; das Logogramm aber sagt uns nicht, was für ein Bier dieses Gefäß enthielt - und auch nichts über die Qualität des Bieres.

Als Gefäß hatte das DUG.KA.GAG freilich eine eigene Kapazität, sogar eine Vielzahl, wie aus der 8. Tafel des Rituals für das *ḫišuwa*-Fest hervorgeht. Der aus einer Anzahl von Bruchstücken[19] wiederhergestellte Text lautet:

> *nam-ma* 4 DUG.KA.GAG *da-an-zi* ŠÀ.BA 1 DUG.KA.GAG *ŠA* 1 *PA A-NA* dIŠKUR URU*ma-nu-zi-i̯a ti-an-zi* 1 DUG.KA.GAG *ŠA* 3 *ŠA-A-TI A-NA* GUNNI ZAG-*az A-NA* DINGIRMEŠ LÚMEŠ *ti-i̯a-*[*an-zi*] 1 DUG.KA.GAG *ŠA* 3 *ŠA-A-TI A-NA* GUNNI [GUB-*za*] *A-NA* DINGIRMEŠ MÍMEŠ *ti-an-zi* 1 DUG.KA.GAG *ŠA* 3 *ŠA-A-TI* EGIR GUNNI *A-NA* ḪUR.SAGMEŠ ÍDMEŠ *ti-an-zi* / *ku-u-uš-kán* DUG.KA.GAG.A *an-na-al-la-*[*aš*] *A-NA ṬUP-PA*ḪI.A [*Ú-UL e-šir*] *na-aš-kán* mNIR.G[ÁL LUGAL.GAL EGIR-*an-da ne-i̯a-at*]

"Dann nimmt man 4 DUG.KA.GAG-Gefäße, darunter: 1 DUG.KA.GAG-Gefäß von 1 *parisu* legt man dem Tešub von Manuzija, 1 DUG.KA.GAG-Gefäß von 3 *sūtu* legt man den männlichen Göttern rechts des Herdes, 1 DUG.KA.GAG-Gefäß von 3 *sūtu* legt man den weiblichen Göttinnen [links] des Herdes, 1 DUG.KA.GAG-Gefäß von 3 *sūtu* legt man den Bergen (und) Flüssen hinter dem Herde. Diese DUG.KA.GAG-Gefäße [wurden nicht] in

[17] Außer dem Gebiet der Getränke ist KA.GAG ein "Luftloch" und ähnliches, vgl.*Hh* X = *MSL* 7, 95: 343-344 KA.GAG. i m . š u . n í g i n . n a, KA.GAG = *pikallulu* "Ofenloch" (*AHw* 863a), 345 KA.GAG = *nappašu* "Luftloch" (*AHw* 740a).

[18] Vgl. den gleichen Gebrauch des Zeichens DUG in den Verwaltungstexten aus Nippur in kassitischer Zeit, dazu G.F. del Monte, "Recipienti enigmatici", in: L. Milano (Hrsg.), *Drinking in Ancient Societies* (Padova 1994), 187-208. Daß auch in Anatolien das DUG.KA.GAG-Gefäß als Behälter für aus gegorenem Getreide hergestellte Getränke verwendet wurde, geht aus der Tatsache hervor, daß es, gleich dem *marnuan*-Bier, von dem AGRIG verwaltet wurde, vgl. KBo XXI 82 (CTH 734.9) Rs. iv 13'-15': 1 DUG*ḫu-u-pár mar-nu-an* [1] DUG.KA.GAG 1 ŠAḪ 1 UR.TUR LÚA[GRIG UR]U*ḫa-at-ti pa-a-i* [1] DUG*ḫu-up-pár* KAŠ.GEŠTIN 1 DUG*ta-pí-ša-n*[*a-an* G]EŠTIN LÚ.GEŠTIN *pa-a-i*, vgl. G. Steiner und I. Singer (Anm. 3).

[19] KUB XL 102 Rs. v 8'-10'; KUB LI 21 Rs.? 10'-15'; KBo XX 116+117+KBo XXIV 14 Rs. v 1'-4'; KBo XXXIV 181 Rs. v 2'-9'; KBo XXXV 249: 1'-6'; IBoT II 52: 8'-12'.

die alten Tafeln (eingetragen): [der Großkönig] Muwatalli [hat] sie [eingeführt]."

Also gab es DUG.KA.GAG-Gefäße von 1 *parisu* und DUG.KA.GAG-Gefäße von ein halben *parisu*, d.h. 3 *sūtu*[20]. Von 3 *sūtu* ist auch das DUG.KA.GAG-Gefäß in KBo II 7 (CTH 505.1) Vs. 13'-14' (analog ebd. 21'): 2 BÁN ZÍD.DA 1 DUG.KA.GAG *ŠA* 3 BÁN 1 ^DUG^*ḫu-u-up-pár-aš* KAŠ ^GIŠ^ZAG.GAR.RA "2 *sūtu* Mehl, 1 DUG.KA.GAG-Gefäß von 3 *sūtu*, 1 *ḫuppara*-Gefäß Bier für den Opfertisch." Obwohl wir die Größenordnung des hethitischen *sūtu*, jedenfalls unterschiedlich, nicht kennen, war das DUG.KA.GAG ein größeres Gefäß, und es wird oft für das der Kultversammlung zuzuteilende Getränk benutzt.

In KBo XIV 142 (CTH 698.1A) Vs. i 37-41[21] hat 1 DUG.KA.GAG-Gefäß die Kapazität von 30 DUG, allgemeiner Ausdruck für "Gefäß", der in den parallelen Stellen KUB XXVII 13 Vs. i 29 und KUB XXVII 15 Vs. i 13' als ^DUG^*wa-lu-ta-aš-ši-ia-an* präzisiert zu sein scheint:

37 [U]D-*ti-li-ma-aš-ši* 3 NINDA.GUR$_4$.RA ZÍD.DA.DUR$_5$ *UP-NI* 4! NINDA.
GUR$_4$.RA ZÍD.DA.DUR$_5$ *tar-na-aš*
38 [14 NINDA ZÍ]D.DA.DUR$_5$ *tar-na-aš* 80 NINDA.SIG^MEŠ^ ZÍD.DA-*ma-at* $\frac{1}{2}$
BAN 1 *UP-NI-ia*
39 [x ^DUG^*PUR*]-*SÍ-TUM* GA 3 ŠU.GÁN^SAR^ 1 DUG (ras.) KAŠ

---

40 [*I-NA* ITU 10+]2.KAM-*ma-aš-ši* 2 *PA* 4 BAN (ras.) 1 ZÍD.DA 1 DUG.KA.
GAG.A

---

41 [MU-*ti me-i*]*a-ni-ma-aš-ši* *I-NA* ITU.12.KAM NINDA.GUR$_4$.RA *U$_4$-MI kiš-an*
42 [32 *PA* 2+]1 BAN ZÍD.DA.DUR$_5$ 12 DUG.KA.GAG.A

"Für ihn (d.h., für Tešub, Ḫebat und Šarruma) täglich: 3 dicke Brote aus feuchtem Mehl von 1 *upnu*, 4! dicke Brote aus feuchtem Mehl von 1 *tarna*-, [14 Brote aus] feuchtem Mehl von 1 *tarna*-, 80 Fladenbrote. Gesamtgewicht des Mehls: $\frac{1}{2}$ *sūtu* 1 *upnu*. [x *pur*]*sītu*-Gefäße Milch, 3 ŠU.GÁN-Gemüse, 1 DUG-Gefäß Bier.
[In jedem der 12 Monate] für ihn: 2 *parisu* 4 *sūtu* 1 (*ḫazil*-) Mehl, 1 DUG.KA.GAG.A.
[Im Laufe des] Jahres, in zwölf Monaten, ist das tägliche Brotopfer für ihn folgendermaßen: [32 *parisu*] 3 *sūtu* feuchtes Mehl, 12 DUG.KA.GAG.A."

20 Über die hethitischen Hohlmasse vgl. zuletzt Th.P.J. van den Hout, *RlA* VII s.v. "Maße und Gewichte. Bei den Hethitern",. 522 ff. Vgl. die DUG verschiedener Größe - 1, 3, 10 *sūtu* bei G.F. del Monte, a.a.O. Anm. 16, 187 f.

21 Vgl. G.F. del Monte, "Le misure di capacità per aridi": *OA* 19 (1980), 220, 222.

Es braucht nicht besonders betont werden, daß DUG.KA.GAG an dieser Stelle als Hohlmaß für ein Getränk verwendet wird, und daß das Getränk einfach KAŠ, eigentlich "Bier", genannt wird. Wir sind der Meinung, daß auch alle Buchungen der *Administration religieuse* (CTH *Chap.* VIII), die die Gliederung x DUG.KA.GAG x DUG KAŠ x *ḫuppar* KAŠ zeigen, in derselben Weise interpretiert werden müssen[22]. Auch in Mari enthielt das Gefäß *pīhu* (von 20-24 *qa*) k a š-Bier, vgl. *ARM* 23 (1984), 286-290. In Larsa zur Zeit des Rīm-Sîn war das k a š . ú . s a . k a . g a g mehr wert als das k a š . ú s-Bier: 1 k a š . ú . s a . k a .g a g von 2 *sūtu* war nach TCL 10 45 Vs. 6 (15.iii RS 16, vgl. YOS 5 95: 5, 30.xii RS 32) 30 Korn Silber wert, 1 *sūtu* k a š . ú s-Bier nur 9 Korn Silber (TCL 10 39 Vs. 22, Rs. 2, -.xii RS 14).[23]

Das Logogramm DUG.KA.GAG bezeichnete vor allem ein Gefäß, dessen Inhalt man näher zu bezeichnen nicht brauchte, weil es üblicherweise aus KAŠ bestand, im Gegensatz z.B. zu dem DUG-Gefäß. Besonders bedeutend scheint uns in diesem Zusammenhang das Ištanuwa-Ritual KUB XXXII 123+KBo XXIX 206 (CTH 772,3A)[24] zu sein. In der Aufzählung der Opferausrüstung (*ḫalkueš-šar)* werden in Vs. ii 18' verzeichnet: 3 DUG.KA.GAG NAG[25] 3 DUG KAŠ 3 DUG GEŠTIN 1 *pu-ú-ti-iš* GEŠTIN die in Vs. ii 40' den Teilnehmern zugeteilt werden (DUG.KA.GAG NAG DUG KAŠ DUG GEŠTIN *pu-u-ti-iš*, wo man auch den Inhalt des *puti*-Gefäßes, "Wein", nicht näher zu bezeichnen braucht). In Rs. iii 41-47 wird ein kompliziertes Gußopfer beschrieben:

41 *nam-ma* EGIR-*an-da IŠ-TU* GAL KAŠ 3-*šu ši-pa-an-ti*
42 *ši-pa-an-za-ki-iz-zi-ma* dU URU*iš-ta-nu-wa-pát*
43 dUTU-*un* «DUG» DUG.KA.GAG NAG-*i̯a-kán dam-mi-i-li-in*
44 NA4*ḫu-wa-ši-i̯a pí-ra-an la-ḫu-wa-an-zi*
45 *nu* GIA.DA.GURḪI.A *tar-na-an-zi nu A-NA* DUG.KA.GAG NAG-*i̯a*
46 «*nu*» *ŠA* dIŠKUR URU*iš-ta-nu-wa* dUTU-*un*
47 dU URU*iš-ta-nu-wa-i̯a ši-pa-an-da-zi*

"Dann libiert er wieder dreimal mit einem Becher Bier (KAŠ) und jedesmal libiert er dem Ištanu eben des Wettergottes von Ištanuwa. Man

[22] Daß auch das *ḫuppar*-Gefäß als Hohlmaß benutzt werden konnte, wird durch Stellen bewiesen, wie KBo XVI 49 (CTH 635.10) Rs. iv 7'-8': 1 DUG GEŠTIN *ŠA* 2 *ḫu-u-up-*[*pár*] 1 DUG *mar-nu-an ŠA* 2 *ḫu-u-up-pár*, oder KBo XVI 78 (CTH 662.6) Rs. iv 6: [1 D]UG GEŠTIN GIBIL *ŠA* 2-*a-an ḫu-up-pár*, ferner I. Singer, *StBoT* 27, 162 f.

[23] Die Bestimmung des DUG.KA.GAG als "Gefäß minderes Bier", "Gefäß mit geringer Bierart" (passim in der Literatur) scheint also unzureichend, und mit Recht läßt Ph.H.J. Houwink ten Cate, "Brief Comments on the Hittite Cult Calendar", in *FsOtten*² 192f., die Qualität des Inhalts dieser Gefäße unbestimmt. Eine verschiedene Qualität Bier enthält das Gefäß in S. Alp, *HKM* 113 Vs. 1: 1 DUG KAŠ 5 DUG*ḫu-pár-ra* GEŠTIN 6 DUG *PI-ḪU*.

[24] Vgl. F. Starke, *StBoT* 30, 306 ff.

[25] "Zum Trinken", vgl. A. Kammenhuber, *Materialien* 4, Nr. 5, 79.

gießt ein reines DUG.KA.GAG zum Trinken vor der Stele aus[26], steckt einen Trinkhalm ein und libiert dem Ištanu des Wettergottes von Ištanuwa und dem Wettergott von Ištanuwa in dem DUG.KA.GAG."

H.G. Güterbock, *RHA* 22 (1964) 104 streicht das erste DUG[27] nicht und interpretiert: "*dam-mi-i-li-in* belongs to a vessel of light beer (DUG DUG.KA.DÙ NAG) and may designate the drink as fresh or newly brewed." In diesem Zusammenhang von Bedeutung ist aber die Tatsache, daß das zweite Gußopfer in ein DUG.KA.GAG als (ausgeleertes) Gefäß gedacht gegossen wird; das DUG.KA.GAG also spielt hier die Rolle, die üblicherweise dem *ḫuppar*-Gefäß, gelegentlich auch anderen Gefäßen, zugewiesen wird[28], eine Libation zu empfangen. Das aus dem DUG.KA.GAG gegossene Getränk bleibt entweder ungenannt (wie hier nahegelegt), oder war eine Art Bier (Güterbock); das ins leere DUG.KA.GAG gegossene ist KAŠ-Bier. Ein ähnliches Gußopfer mit Wein (GEŠTIN) in eines DUG.KA.GAG wird im Totenritual KUB XXXIX 17 Vs. iii 5'-6'...11'-12'[29] bezeugt: EGIR-*pa-ma A-NA* ZI-*ŠU a-ku-w*[*a-an-na*] *pí-ia-an-zi nu* GEŠTIN 3-*šu e-*[*ku-zi*] ... *ma-aḫ-ḫa-an-ma-aš-ši I-NA* 3 KASKAL*ni* *A-NA* DUG.KA. GAG GUL-*an-ti a-ku-wa-an-*[*na pí-ia-an-zi*] "Dann gibt man seiner Seele (mit einer Libation) [zu] trinken; er tr[inkt] dreimal Wein ... Wenn er aber zum dritten Mal in das ... DUG.KA.GAG ihr [zu] trinken [gegeben hat ...]."

Wenn die Schreibweise DUG.KAB.KA.GAG in KUB I 17 (CTH 691, 3A) Vs. iii 36 nur als Schreibvariante für dasselbe Gefäß angenommen werden darf, haben wir ein Beispiel eines *walḫi*-Bier enthaltenden DUG.KA.GAG-Gefäßes: *ták-kán wa-al-aḫ-ḫi-i̯a-aš* DUG.KAB.KA.GAG-*an an-da ú-da-an-zi ša-an A-NA* GIŠ. dINANNAḪI.A *ta-pu-uš-za ti-an-zi* / *nu wa-al-ḫi A-NA* DUMUMEŠ É.GAL *ME-ŠE-DI* ḪI.A *ḫu-u-ma-an-da-a-aš a-še-eš-ni-i̯a hu-u-ma-an-ti šar-ra-an-zi* "Man bringt ein DUG.KAB.KA.GAG-Gefäß *walḫi*-Bier herein und legt es neben die INANNA-Instrumente. Man teilt das *walḫi*-Bier den Palastangestellten, den Leibgarden allen und der ganzen Versammlung zu." Ferner, wenn es erlaubt ist, in der Schreibweise KAB?.KA.GA in der oben angeführten Stelle KBo XX 33+ Vs. 8 eine weitere Schreibvariante anzunehmen, dann gab es auch DUG.KA.GAG-

[26] Wörtlich: "man gießt." Übersetzung aus dem Zusammenhang nach *CHD* L-N 14b sub 2. "to empty a container (acc.) by pouring its contents out."

[27] F. Starke, *StBoT* 30, 311, streicht es. Es ist möglich, daß der Schreiber in dieser Zeile an die übertragene Bedeutung ("ein Getränk") des Logogramms DUG.KA.GAG dachte und deshalb ein zweites Zeichen DUG voransetzte. Darauf hätte er aber in Zeile 45 verzichtet; deshalb, und weil es ein Einzelfall bleibt, scheint uns die Vermutung einer Dittographie wahrscheinlicher. Die ganze Stelle allerdings ist in diesem Textexemplar offensichtlich verderbt.

[28] Vgl. A. Goetze, *JCS* 23 (1970) 80; A. Kammenhuber, *SMEA* 14 (1971) 147 ff. ; A. Archi - A. Kammenhuber, *Materialien* 6, Nr. 5, 302 ff.; 7, Nr. 5, 351 ff.

[29] H. Otten, *HTR* 86. Über *akuwanna pai-* in diesem Zusammenhang vgl. A. Archi, *Materialien* 6, Nr. 5, 252 f.; A. Archi - A. Kammenhuber, *Materialien* 7, Nr. 5, 339.

Gefäße aus Silber deren Inhalt wurde KAŠ.LÁL.[30] In KUB XXXIV 88 (CTH 677,2): 3' begegnen wir ein [DUG.K]A.GAG NAG aus Kupfer.

Mit dieser kurzen Festgabe möchten wir nur auf die Fragen hinweisen, die ein hethitischer und allgemein ein altvorderasiatischer Text uns stellt, wenn wir über die wörtliche Übersetzung hinausgehen sollen: wenn wir mit einem der vorher genannten hethitischen Getränke zutrinken sollten, werden wir ganz bestimmt Gefahr laufen, *fischi per fiaschi* in den Händen zu haben! .Deshalb wollen wir Philo Houwink ten Cate zum 65. Geburtstag mit einem Becher nicht zweideutigen, echten tuskanischen Chiantis zutrinken!

[30] Das dritte Zeichen GA kann von einem Hörfehler abhängen; die wahrscheinlichere Lesung des ersten Zeichens ist KAB. Allenfalls handelt es sich um ein Gefäß. Der Vorschlag von E. Neu, *HZL* 115, KIN.DUG4.GA zu lesen, bleibt uns unverständlich: das sumerische k i n - d u g4 kann tatsächlich nur "Arbeit leisten" bedeuten, vgl. H. Steible, *Die neusumerischen Bau- und Weihinschriften* (= *FAOS* 9), Teil 1, 160, Teil 2, 13; A. Falkenstein, *Grammatik der Sprache Gudeas von Lagaš*, 1 (Roma 1949), 128 Anm. 1.

GRAMMATISCHE SKIZZE ZUM TEXT DER ALTHETHITISCHEN 'PALASTCHRONIK' (CTH 8)

ERICH NEU

Einleitung

0.1 Von den verschiedenen Exemplaren, in denen uns die sogenannte Palastchronik[1] überliefert ist, stellt nur das kleine Textfragment KUB XXXVI 104 eine althethitische Niederschrift dar. Bei allen anderen der zu CTH 8 gehörigen Exemplare handelt es sich um junge Abschriften (13. Jh. v.Chr.).[2] Unsere Kenntnis der althethitischen Grammatik beruht vornehmlich auf zeitgenössischen Texten, also auf Niederschriften, die durch ihren Schriftduktus eindeutig als althethitisch ausgewiesen sind. Nun gibt es aber bekanntlich eine stattliche Anzahl von Texten, die auf Grund ihrer Sprachform mehr oder weniger als althethitisch zu gelten haben, die sich jedoch wegen ihrer paläographischen Merkmale zweifelsfrei als Abschriften mittel- oder junghethitischen Alters erweisen. Hat man sich an Hand von althethitischen Originalen eine Vorstellung von dem, was althethitische Sprache ist, erworben, wird man mit großer Umsicht versuchen dürfen, aus Abschriften althethitischer Vorlagen, die vom Kopisten mitunter starke Veränderungen erfahren haben, die typisch althethitischen Sprachelemente herauszupräparieren, um auf diese Weise die Textbasis für eine althethitische Grammatik zu erweitern. Ohne jeden Zweifel muß eine Grammatik des Althethitischen auf Texten aus jener Zeit aufbauen, es hieße aber angesichts des nicht gerade sehr umfangreichen original althethitischen Textbestandes, kostbares Sprachmaterial gleichsam brach und unverwertet liegen lassen, wenn man Informationen, die man bei entsprechend sauberer

[1] Die nicht ganz unumstrittene Bezeichnung 'Palastchronik' behalten wir hier etikettartig bei.

[2] Aus der Textgruppe CTH 9 werden lediglich im Anmerkungsteil einige Wortformen ergänzend zitiert. Die Keilschriftzeichen des Editionsbandes weisen für CTH 9.1 (KUB XXXVI 105) auf eine mittelhethitische Niederschrift, während das unter CTH 9.5 gebuchte Fragment KBo VIII 42 paläographisch althethitischen Alters ist (vgl. F. Starke, *StBoT* 23, 1977, 10).

Methode aus Abschriften unterschiedlicher Güte über die althethitische Sprachform gewinnen könnte, von vornherein gänzlich ausklammern wollte.[3]

Methodisch empfiehlt es sich, die beiden Textkorpora, das uneingeschränkt althethitische zeitgenössischer Niederschriften und das aus Abschriften gewonnene, getrennt zu halten und auch bei einer deskriptiven Zusammenschau eigens zu kennzeichnen.[4]

0.2 Der weitaus größte Teil unserer Kenntnis der althethitischen 'Palastchronik' entstammt jungen Abschriften. Das alte Textfragment KUB XXXVI 104 bietet uns nur einen kleinen Ausschnitt dieses kulturgeschichtlich bedeutsamen Textes, der u.a. mit seinen 'juristischen' Casus-Sammlungen Einblick in das alltägliche Leben am Königshof und in dessen unmittelbares Umfeld gewährt. Der Sprachstil wirkt im positiven Sinne schlicht, die Knappheit des Ausdrucks mutet archaisch an. Entsprechend ist die Syntax gestaltet, die in ihrer Kargheit noch weit entfernt ist von der satzperiodenreichen Sprachform des sogenannten klassischen Hethitischen, wo vor allem die Satzanfänge durch reichhaltige Partikelketten charakterisiert sind.[5] Auch wenn im Einzelfall, mitbedingt durch die ungünstige Überlieferungssituation, noch Verständnisschwierigkeiten hinsichtlich des Inhalts bleiben, wird man die verhältnismäßig einfache, gedrängte, mitunter allzu verkürzend wirkende, etwas urtümlich anmutende Darstellungsweise insgesamt als eine weitgehend unkompli-zierte Sprachform bezeichnen dürfen.

0.3 Da die Abschriften unterschiedlicher Qualität sind und in die grammatische Skizze auch das bisher einzige alte Textfragment Aufnahme findet, wird die hier gebotene sprachliche Dokumentation notwendigerweise in bestimmten Grammatikbereichen Inhomogenität aufweisen. Einen pluralischen Akkusativ auf *-uš* in Nominativfunktion z.B. wird man dem Abschreiber anlasten dürfen, wie überhaupt eine Reihe graphischer und sprachlicher Phänomene auf das Konto des Kopisten geht. Dennoch ergeben sich genügend Spracheigentümlichkeiten, um die Textkomposition in ihrer sprachlichen Ausgestaltung für althethitisch zu halten, was ja auch durch die Existenz eines paläographisch althethitischen Textfragments bestätigt wird. Schon aus Raumgründen beschränken wir uns auf die bloße Dokumentation und bringen nur in den Anmerkungen einige Interpretationshinweise.

3 So hat etwa auch S. Luraghi in ihrer Untersuchung *Old Hittite Sentence Structure* (London/New York 1990) die jungen Abschriften der 'Palace Chronicles' mitberücksichtigt (Seiten 7, 8, 89f. et passim); vgl. M. Marazzi, *Or* 62 (1993) 432.

4 Vgl. F. Starke, a.a.O. 11; N. Oettinger, *Stammbildung* xi. – Als bound transcription gebrauchen wir in diesem Beitrag eine graphie- bzw. transliterationsnahe Umschrift.

5 Manche Sätze der Textgruppe CTH 8 bestehen aus nur zwei Wörtern; vgl. ^{DUG}*ša-ak-ka$_4$-a-an da-a-ir* A I 10, LUGAL-*i te-et* II 4, *mān luktat* D (orig.) Vs. 17′.

0.4 Im Anschluß an CTH 8 bezeichnen wir die einzelnen Exemplare abkürzend mit Großbuchstaben, fügen jedoch bei D, dem althethitischen Fragment, in Klammern noch “orig.” hinzu, um der Kennzeichnung der beiden unterschiedlichen Textkorpora Rechnung zu tragen. Folgende Siglen finden demnach Verwendung: A = KBo III 34; B = KBo III 35; C = KBo III 36; D (orig.) = KUB XXXVI 104; E = KUB XXXI 38; F = KBo XIII 44+44a(+) KBo XII 10; G = KBo XII 11; H = KBo XIII 45; I = KUB XLVIII 77.

Die vorliegende Untersuchung widmen wir mit den besten Wünschen dem verehrten Jubilar, der in seiner für die mittelhethitische Sprachstufe grundlegenden Monographie *The Records of the Early Hittite Empire*[6] im Zusammenhang mit der Erschließung und Gewinnung genuin mittelhethitischer Textkompositionen ebenfalls mit dem Verhältnis von Original und Abschrift und dabei gleich mit mehreren unterschiedlichen Textkorpora konfrontiert war.

1. *Nominalflexion*

Nom.Sing.c. -*š*: vgl. ^{m}*Pa-ap-pa-aš* (*a*-St.) A I 5, ^{LÚ}*ḫu-up-ra-la-aš* (*a*-St.) A II 15, ^{m}*A-aš-ga-li-i̯a-aš* (*i̯a*-St.) A II 8, ^{LÚ}*u-ri-an-ni-iš* (*i*-St.) A I 5, LÚ-*iš* (*i*-St.) C Vs. 16’, 18’, *za-ḫur-ti-iš-ši* (*i*-St.; -*ši* “ihm”) D (orig.) Rs. 5’, LUGAL-*uš* (*u*-St.) A II 5, ^{GIŠ}BANŠUR-*uš-še* (*u*-St.; -*še* “ihm”); III 21’, *šar-ku-uš* (*u*-St.; Adj.) A II 11.[7]

-*s*: vgl. *mar-ša-an-za-u̯a* (*t*-St., -*u̯a* Redepartikel) A II 20 (°*ant*+ -*s* > °*anz*), *né-ku-ma-an-za* (*t*-St.) A II 35, ^{m}*Na*$^{!}$*-ki-li-az* (*t*-St.) H 6’.

-ø: ^{m}*Šu-up-pí-u-ma-an* (*n*-St.) A II 22.[8]

Gelegentlich stehen Personennamen, denen Subjektfunktion zukommt, in der bloßen Stammform; vgl. [^{m}*Am-*]*mu-na* DUMU (Var. LÚ) ^{URU}*Šu-uk-z*[*i-i̯a* A III 15’, KUR *Ar-za-ú-i-i̯a* ^{m}*Nu-un-nu* LÚ ^{URU}*Ḫu-ur-m*[(*a*)] ⌈*e*⌉*-eš-ta* D (orig.) Vs. 9’ (= A I 11; F (KBo XIII 44a) I 3’), ^{m}*Pí-im-pí-ri-it* [DUMU UR]U*Ni-na-aš-ša* A III 16’, *UM-MA Šar-ma-aš-šu* A I 22. In der Überlieferung begegnet auch der Wechsel zwischen Stammform und Nominativ an der gleichen Textstelle: ^{m}*Zi-di* ^{LÚ}ZABAR.DIB *e-eš-ta* A II 1 gegenüber

[6] Philo H.J. Houwink ten Cate, *The Records of the Early Hittite Empire (C. 1450-1380 B.C.)*, İstanbul 1970. Zur Würdigung dieser wichtigen Untersuchung s. H. Otten, *BiOr* 27 (1970) 234f.; Verf., *IF* 77 (1972 [1974]) 279ff.; J. Klinger - E. Neu, *Hethitica* 10 (1990) 135ff.

[7] Zur Frage nach der Aussprache von <š> s. H. Eichner, in M. Mayrhofer - M. Peters - O. E. Pfeiffer (Edd.), *Lautgeschichte und Etymologie* (Wiesbaden 1980), 134 mit Anm. 51.

[8] Vgl. zur Bildungsweise F. Starke, *WO* 24 (1993) 24[12](sub 2.)

^{m}*Zi-di-iš* C Vs. 11'. Ob dafür akkadischer Einfluß geltend zu machen ist[9] oder sich darin alte Gebrauchsweisen eines indogermanischen Kommemorativus widerspiegeln[10], soll hier schon aus Raumgründen nicht weiter erörtert werden.

Akk.Sing.c. -*n*: vgl. ^{LÚ}*ma-ni-aḫ-ḫa-tal-la-an* (*a*-St.) A II 16, ^{LÚ}*u-ri-an-ni-in* (*i*-St.) A I 7, *šal-li-in* (*i*-St.; Adjektiv) A I 3, ^{m}*Nu-un-nu-un* (*u*-St.) A II 40.[11]

-*an*: vgl. SIG$_5$-*an-ta-an* (*t*-St., Adj./Partizip) A II 3.

Nom.-Akk.Sing. n. -*n*: vgl. den neutralen *a*-Stamm *mar-nu-an-na* (*marnuann=a*) A I 6 (*marnuu̯ann=a* Exemplar I 2').

-ø: vgl. GAL-*ri* (= *zeri*; *i*-St.) A II 34[12], *še-ku-nu-uš-me-et* (*šeknu=šmet*; *u*-St.) A I 21, *i-da-lu* (*u*-St.) G 4' (vgl. A III 14'), ^{TÚG}*iš-ḫi-al-še-me-et-ta* (*išḫial=šemett=a*, *l*-St.) A I 20, *ḫé-en-kán* (*n*-St.) A III 14', *e-eš-ḫar* (*r*-St.) A I 22, *ne-e-an* (< **nēant*, *t*-St., Partizip) A I 21.[13]

Gen.Sing. -*aš*: vgl. *a-ru-na-aš* (?; *a*-St.) A III 7'[14], *ú-*⌈*ba*⌉*-ti-i̯a-aš* (*i*-St.) A II 25, 26, LUGAL-*u̯a-aš* (*ḫaššuu̯aš*, *u*-St.) A II 33, *kat-ta-u̯a-an-na-aš* (*r/n*-St.) C Vs. 10', [(*m*)*ar-nu-a*]*n-da-aš* (*t*-St.) A I 7 (vgl. Exemplar I 4').

-*š*: ^{m}*Nu-un-nu-uš-ša* (*Nunnušš=a*, *u*-St.) A I 16.[15]

9 Vgl. etwa *UM-MA* ^{m}*Pu-ul-li* HKM 65 Vs. 1 (Briefformular).

10 Vgl. Verf., *IBS* 25 (1979) 180ff., 185.

11 Zwei Gefäßbezeichnungen zeigen vor der Akkusativendung Pleneschreibung des Stammvokals: ^{DUG}*ḫar-ḫa-ra-a-an* A II 1, ^{DUG}*ša-ak-ka*$_4$*-ra-a-an* I 10.

12 Wie im althethitischen Ritual für das Königspaar (*StBoT* 8) werden auch im Text der 'Palastchronik' die beiden Ausdrücke *zeri-* (GAL-*ri*) n. und *teššummi-* c. für "Becher" gebraucht, letzteres mit der auffallenden Anlautschreibung *di-* D (orig.) Vs. 6', Exemplar I 4' (vgl. H. Eichner, a.a.O. 149[72]).

13 Zum Partizip *anda ne-e-an* (sic) und zur Deutung der betreffenden Textstelle s. H. Eichner, *Sprache* 21 (1975) 162.

14 Zu dem Versuch einer indogermanischen Etymologie für heth. *aruna-* "Meer" s. M. Furlan, *Linguistica* 33 (1993) 49ff.

15 Möglicherweise aus **Nunnuu̯ašš=a* 'verkürzt'; vgl. J. Friedrich, *HE* I^2 § 58. Bei einem ablautenden *u*-Stamm erwartet man im Gen. Sing. bekanntlich bloßes -*s* als indogermanische Endung; vgl. altind. *śatroḥ* "des Feindes", got. *sunaus* "des Sohnes". Nunnu ist Fremdname und folglich nicht stammablautend.

Dat.-Lok.Sing. -*i*: vgl. *at-ti-mi* (*atti*=*mi*, *a*-St.) A II 9[16], *pí-di-iš-ši-ma* (*pidi*=*šši*=*ma*, *a*-St.) D (orig.) Vs. 12' (= A I 14), ᵐ*A-aš-ka-li* (*-*i̯a*+*ī* > -*ī*; *i̯a*-St.) A II 18, ᵐ*Ḫu-uz-zi-i* (*i̯a*-St.) A II 31,[17] ᴳᴵŠ*za-lu*[-*u̯a-n*]*i* (*i*-St.) A III 19', ᴸᵁ*u-ri-an-ni-ma* (*i*-St.) D (orig.) Rs. 8', ᵐ*Šar-ma-aš-šu-ú-i* (*u*-St.) A I 17, ᵐ*Šu-up-pí-um-ni* (*n*-St.) A II 24, *ḫi-kán-ni* (*n*-St.) C Vs. 9', *te-ep-ša-u-u̯a-an-ni* (*r*/*n*-St.) A II 12, *iš-pa-an-ti* (*t*-St.) A II 23, 27. ᵁᴿᵁ!*An-ku-u̯a* A II 13 fehlerhaft für ᵁᴿᵁ*An-ku-i* ibid. II 10, 11.

-*e*: *eš-ḫé* "(zu) dem Herrn" (*išḫa*-, *a*-St.) A I 25.[18]

Allativ Sing. -*a*: *tu-uz-zi-i̯a* (*i*-St.) A II 37, 42,[19] [(*pá*)*r*-]*na-aš-ša* (*parna*=*šša*; *r*/*n*-St.) A I 12. Später in Dat.-Lokativ-Funktion bei *i*-Stämmen; vgl. KUR *Ar-za-ú-i-i̯a* "in A." A I 11 (*i*-Stamm ᵁᴿᵁ*Ar-za-u̯i*$_5$ KBo XI 12 I 1).

Ablat. 'Sing.' nicht belegt; doch vgl. in CTH 9.2, 6' ᵁᴿ]ᵁ*Ḫu-ur-ma-az*.

Instrum. 'Sing.' -*it*: GEŠTIN-⌈*it*⌉ (*u̯ii̯anit*, *a*-St.) A II 1, GI-*it* (*natit*, *a*-St.) C Vs. 8'.[20]

Nom.Plur.c. -*eš*: *ka-ak-ka*$_4$*-pé-eš*$_{15}$ (*a*-St.) A II 13 (= *ka-ka-pu-uš* C Vs. 20'), *ma-ak-la-an-te-eš* (*t*-St.) A II 14.

-*uš*: *ka-ka-pu-uš* (*a*-St.) C Vs. 20' (= *ka-ak-ka*$_4$*-pé-eš*$_{15}$ A II 13).[21]

Akk.Plur.c. -*uš*: vgl. *ḫa-p*[*a-a*]*š-šu-uš* (*a*-St.) D (orig.) Rs. 9' = *ḫa-ap-pa-aš-š*[*u-uš*] G 9' = *ḫa-pa-šu-uš* A III 19'; *ka-ak-ka*$_4$*-pu-uš* (*a*-St.) A II 13 = *ka-ak-ka*-° C Vs. 19'; *la-aḫ-ḫé-mu-uš* (*a*-St.) A II 23,[22] *pár-ḫu-uš-šu-uš* (*parḫuš*=*šuš*, *a*-St.) B I 8', *u̯a-aš-ta-uš* (*i*-St.) A II 24, *a-am-mi-i̯a-an-tu-uš-mu-uš* (°*i̯antuš*=(*š*)*muš*, *t*-St.) A II 28.

16 Zu *atti*=*mi* s. auch CTH 9.3 A (KBo III 29) I 20', 21'.

17 Von dem auf -*i̯a* auslautenden Bergnamen ḪUR.SAG*Ta-ḫa-i̯a* findet sich der Dat.-Lok. ḪUR.SAG*Ta-ḫa-i̯a-i* D (orig.) Vs. 14' (= A I 16). Dieser Wortausgang versteht sich wohl wie ᵈ*U̯a-šu-ma-i* oder luw. ᵈ*Kamrušepai* (*IBS* 25, 188). - In der Verbindung *A-NA Na-ak-ki-li-it* A II 30 liegt die bloße Stammform vor.

18 Die Graphie *eš-ḫé* ist dem Kopisten anzulasten, erwartet man doch im Althethitischen die Form *iš-ḫi-i* (vgl. KBo VII 14 +KUB XXXVI 100 Rs. 10').

19 Zum *i*-stämmigen Lokativ *ut-ni-i*(*m-mu*) s. CTH 9.4 (KBo III 33) II 3'.

20 Die heth. Casus Ablativ und Instrumental sind bezüglich ihrer Endung numerusindifferent.

21 Wie schon oben in der Einleitung (0.3) erwähnt, folgt die Verwendung des pluralischen Akkusativs als Nominativ jungem Sprachgebrauch, geht also auf das Konto des Abschreibers. Zu *kakkapa*- s. auch J. Klinger, *N.A.B.U.* 1994 (nº 2 - Juin), 31.

22 Zu *la-aḫ-ḫé-mu-uš* vgl. *CHD* L-N, 10b.

Nom.-Akk.Plur.n. -*a*: *eš-ḫa*[*-aš-*]*kán-ta* (*t*-St.) A I 20.

Dehnungsplural -*ār*: *ud-da-a-ar* A II 18 (Kollektiv).

Gen.Plur. -*an* nicht belegt.

Dat.-Lok.Plur. -*aš*: vgl. *ḫur-la-aš-ša* (*ḫurlašš=a, a*-St.) A I 24, *ša-ku-u̯a-aš-ma-* <*aš*> (*šakuu̯aš=*(*š*)*maš*, zu *šakuu̯a*) A I 18 (vgl. F (KBo XII 10) I 7’),[23] ANŠE.KUR.RA-*aš* (mit -*šan*) A II 27, ÉRIN^{MEŠ}-*aš* D (orig.) Vs. 7’.

2. *Pronomina*

a. Personalpronomina

Betonte Formen: [*ú-*]*uk* “ich” (B I 9’), *zi-ik* “du” (A II 20, B I 5’).

Enklitische Dative:

-*še* “ihm”: ^{GIŠ}BANŠUR-*uš=še* A III 21’, 24’.

-*šše* “ihm”: *nu-uš-še* (*nu=šše*) A II 33, 34, D (orig.) Rs. 2’.

-*ši* “ihm”: *zaḫurtiš=ši* D (orig.) Rs. 5’, ^{GIŠ}*zaluu̯aniš=ši* A III 25’.[24]

-*šši* “ihm” *nu-uš-š*[*i*] (*nu=šši*) G 11’.

Die altheth. Niederschrift zeigt also -*šše* und -*ši*.[25]

-*šmaš* “ihnen”: *nu-uš-ma-aš* (*nu=šmaš*) A II 39, III 17’.

-(*š*)*maš* “ihnen”: G[(^{IŠ}BANŠU)]R-*uš-ma-aš* (°-*uš=*(*š*)*maš*) A III 18’ (mit Dupl. G 8’).

b. Enklitisch -*a*- “er, sie, es”

-*aš* “er”: *na-aš* (*n=aš*) A II 37, *ša-aš* (*š=aš*) A II 7, 19, III 9’, *a-ki-iš-ma-aš* (*akiš=ma=aš*) A II 12, *pa-iz-zi-ma-aš* (*paizzi=ma=aš*) A I 14.

[23] Doch s. auch H.M.Kümmel, *StBoT* 3, 162 mit Anm. 41.

[24] Vgl. Verf., *StBoT* 12, 73ff.

[25] Zu erwarten ist die Lautentwicklung *-*soi* > heth. -*še* > -*ši*.

-an "ihn": *ša-an* (*š⸗an*) A I 4 (2x), 13 (= D (orig.) Vs. 11'), 17, 25, II 10, 11, 15,16, 17, *ša-na-aš-ta* (*š⸗an⸗ašta*) A I 8, II 6, 9, 19, *a-pé-e-ma-an* (*ape⸗ma⸗an*) A II 38, *ma-na-an-kán* (*man⸗an⸗kan*) A II 17 = *ma-a-na-an-kán* (*mān⸗an⸗kan*) C Vs. 22'.

-e(**-oi*) "sie" (Nom.Pl.c.): *še* (*š⸗e*) A I 2, 3.[26]

-uš "sie, eos" (Akk.Pl.c.): *nu-uš* (*n⸗uš*) A I 16 (= D (orig.) Vs. 14'), II 28, 29, *šu-uš* (*š⸗uš*) A II 32.

Möglicherweise liegt in *e-az* A II 34 nicht-enklitisches *e* (**oi*) vor.[27]

c. Possessivpronomina

1. Pers. Sg.:

-man "meinen" (Akk.Sg.c.): ⸢NINDA⸣-*ma-an* E Vs.$^{?}$ 29' (zu erg. in VBoT 33, 2').

-mi "meinem"(Dat.Sg.): *at-ti-mi* (*atti⸗mi*) A II 9.

-met "mein" (Nom.Sg.n.): ^{d}UTU-*me-et* (**Ištanu⸗met*) "Meine Sonne!".[28]

3. Pers.Sg.:

-šiš "sein" (Nom.Sg.c.): *ga-i-na-aš-ši-iš* (*gainaš⸗šiš*) A III 20'.

-šan "seinen" (Akk.Sg.c.): ^{LÚ}*ga-i-na-aš-ša-an* (**gainan⸗šan*) D (orig.) Vs. 15' = ^{LÚ}*ka-i-na-aš-ša-an* (**kainan⸗šan*) A I 17, DUMU-*aš-ša-an* (**DUMU-an⸗šan*) B I 10'.

[26] Im Junghethitischen ist die Pronominalform *-e* durch *-at* verdrängt worden; vgl. J. Friedrich, *HE* I^2 § 102b.

[27] Sehr fraglich. Eigentlich wäre dann **e-ez* (*e⸗z*) zu erwarten gewesen. Graphie *e-az* etwa fehlerhalft für *e-uk*$^{!}$-<*zi*> "er trinkt"? A. Kammenhuber, HW^2 A 41: *e* + *-za*.

[28] Als Vokativ verstanden. Lesung mit H.G. Güterbock bei Ph.H.J. Houwink ten Cate, *RHA* XXIV/79 (1966) 125^3. Der Vokativ hätte richtig ^{d}UTU-*mi* (**Ištanui⸗mi*) oder ^{d}UTU-*miš* (**Ištanuš⸗miš*; Nominativus pro Vocativo) heißen sollen; vgl. *ú-uš-ki* ^{d}UTU-*uš* "Schau, Sonnengottheit!" CTH 9.3 A (KBo III 29) I 6'.

-ša-aš "seines" (Gen.Sg.): *ú-*⌈*ba*⌉*-ti-i̯a-aš-ša-aš* (*ubatii̯aš⸗šaš*) A II 25, *ták-ka-ni-aš-ša-aš* (*takkaniaš⸗šaš*) B I 8' *kar-di-i̯*[*a-aš-ša-a*]*š* (*kardii̯aš ⸗šaš*) A III 17'.

-šši "seinem" (Dativ.Sg.): *pí-di-iš-ši-ma* (*pidi⸗šši⸗ma*) D (orig.) Vs. 12' = A I 14 = F (KBo XIII 44a, 6').[29]

-šša "zu seinem" (Allativ): [(*pá*)*r-*]*na-aš-ša* (*parna⸗šša*) A I 12.

-šet "sein"(Nom.-Akk.Sg.n.): *ḫa-ad-da-tar-še-*⌈*et*⌉(*ḫaddatar⸗šet*) H 9'.[30]

-šuš "seine" (Akk. Pl.c.): *pár-ḫu-uš-šu-uš* (*parḫuš⸗šuš*) B I 8'.

3. Pers.Pl.:

-šaman bzw. *-šman* "ihren" (Akk.Sg.c.): LÚ*u-ra-al-la-aš-ša-ma-an* (**urallan⸗šman*) A II 23.[31]

-šmit "ihr" (Nom.-Akk.Sg.n.): *pí-ra-aš-mi-it* (**piran⸗šmit* "vor ihnen") D (orig.) Rs.7'.

-šmet "ihr" (Nom.-Akk.Sg.n.): *še-ku-nu-uš-me-et* (*šeknu⸗šmet*) A I 21.[32]

-š(e)met "ihr" (Nom.-Akk.Sg.n.): TÚG*iš-ḫi-al-še-me-et-ta* (*išḫial⸗šemett⸗a*) A I 20.

-šmuš "ihre" (Akk.Pl.c.): *a-am-mi-i̯a-an-tu-uš-mu-uš* (*ammii̯antuš⸗(š)muš*) A II 28.

-šumuš "ihre?" (Akk.Pl.c.): *a-ru-uš-šu-mu-uš* (*aruš⸗šumuš*) A III 14'.[33]

29 Auf die Fragen, ob *pí-di* oder *pé-di* zu transliterieren ist und ob man bei einem Ansatz *pidi* mit *i*-Umlaut zu rechnen hat (dazu H. Eichner, in: *Lautgeschichte und Etymologie* [s. oben Anm. 7], 144[65]), braucht hier nicht eingegangen zu werden.

30 Unter Beibehaltung des auslautenden *-r* von *ḫattatar*. Zur Verbindung von *ḫ*. mit Possessivpronomina s. Verf., *IBS* 40, 212.

31 Wohl nur graphisch bedingtes *-a-* in *-ša-ma-an*, also /-sman/.

32 Zu den unterschiedlichen Schreibungen *-šmet*, *-šmit* vgl. H.Otten -Vl. Souček, *StBoT* 8, 72f.

33 Die Graphie *-šu-* in *-šu-mu-uš* weist eher auf die 1. Pers. Plur. ("unsere"), doch wäre dann auch Doppelschreibung des Nasals zu erwarten (vgl. altheth. *né-e-ku-šum-mu-uš*; H. Otten, *StBoT* 17, 76; Verf., *StBoT* 18, 65f.). Eine Deutung als "unsere Gefährten" (Akk.) würde direkte Rede nahelegen. Der Kontext ist bruchstückhaft. In der vorhergehenden Zeile (A III 13') steht allerdings die Redepartikel *-u̯a*.

-*šmaš* "ihren"(Dat.-Lok.Pl.): *ša-ku-u̯a-aš-ma<-aš>* (*šakuu̯aš*=(*š*)*maš*) A I 18.[34]

d. Demonstrativpronomina

ka- "dieser":

ku-u-un "diesen" (Akk.Sg.c.): A II 30.

ki "dies(es)" (Nom.-Akk.Sg.n.) *ki-ma-az* (*ki*=*ma*=*z*) A I 23.

ki-i "dies(es)" (Nom.-Akk.Sg.n.): A III 17' (= *ke-e* Nom.Pl. c., G 7').[35]

ke-e "diese"(Nom.Pl.c.): G 7' (= *ki-i* A III 17').

ku-u-uš "diese" (Akk.Pl.c.): A I 19, II 31, 32, *ku-u-uš-ša* (*kūšš*=*a*) A II 30.

apa- "jener":

a-pa-a-aš "jener" (Nom.Sg.c.): A II 29,30, [(*a-pa-*)]⌈*a*⌉*-ša* (*apāš*=*a* "jener aber") D (orig.) Vs. 10' (= *a-pa-aš-ša*; *apašš*=*a* A I 12), *a-pa-a-aš-ša* (*apāšš*=*a*) ... *a-pa-a-aš-ša* (*apāšš*=*a*) "sowohl dieser ... als auch jener" A II 4, 6, *a-pa-aš-ša* (*apašš*=*a* "und jener") C Vs. 10', 16' (= *a-pa-a-aš-ša*, *apāšš*=*a* A II 8).

a-pu-u-un "jenen" (Akk.Sg.c.): A II 5, 25, *a-pu-u-un-na* (*apūnn*=*a* "und jenen") A II 26, *a-pu-u-na* (*apūn*=*a* "jenen aber") A II 22 (= *a-pu-na* C Vs. 26').

a-pé-el "jenes" (Gen.Sg.): *a-pé-el-la a-p*[*é-e*]*l-la* (*apell*=*a apell*=*a*) D (orig.) Rs. 6'.

a-pé-e "jene" (Nom.Pl.c.): *a-pé-e-ma-an* (*ape*=*ma*=*an*) A II 38.

a-pé-e-da-aš "jenen" (Dat.Plur.): *a-pé-e-da-aš-ša* (*apedašš*=*a* "und jenen") A II 3.

e. "Reflexiv"-Partikel

[34] S. schon oben Anm. 23.

[35] Der engere Kontext legt *ke-e* Nom.Pl.c. als die zu erwartende Pronominalform nahe: " . . . diese waren die Söhne seines Herzens". Vgl. altheth. *ke-e* . . . *e-šir* CTH 9.5 (KBo VIII 42) IV 6'.

-*z*: *ki-ma-az* (*ki=ma=z*) A I 23, LUGAL-*un-ua-az* (*ḫaššun=ua=z*) A II 21, *e-az*(?) A II 34.[36]

f. Fragepronomen

ku-it (Nom.-Akk.Sg.n.): "Warum?" A I 20 (im Satzinnern)

g. Relativpronomen

ku-iš (Nom.Sg.c.): A I 19, II 33, 34.

ku-in (Akk.Sg.c.): A II 5.

ku-it (Nom.-Akk.Sg.n.): A I 12 = D (orig.) Vs. 10', *ku-i-da* (*kuid=a* "was aber das betrifft . . . ") A I 3, II 24, 27.

ku-i-[-*e*-]*eš* (Nom.Pl.c.): A III 15'.

h. Indefinitpronomen

ku-iš-ki (Nom.Sg.c.): C Vs. 8'.

Adverbiell: *ku-ua-at-ta ku-ua-at-ta* "in welcher Hinsicht auch immer; in jeder Beziehung" A II 9 (vgl. *ku-ua-ad-da* C Vs. 16').

i. Pronominaladjektiv

tamaiš "anderer":
ta-ma-in (Akk.Sg.c.) A II 4 = ⸢*dam*⸣-*ma-in* C Vs. 13'.

3. *Verbalflexion*

Indikativ des Präsens, Aktiv

-*mi*-Konjugation

[36] Doch s. auch schon oben Anm. 27.

Sg. 1. *-mi*: *e-et-mi* A III 9’, *pa-i-mi* A I 23,[37] *ti-iš-ši-ki-mi* (*-šk-*) A III 4’.[38]

2. *-ši*: *u*]*š*?*-ki-ši* (*-šk-*) A I 30.[39]

3. *-zi*: vgl. *e-eš-zi* “sitzt“ D (orig.) Rs. 8’, *ḫa-az-zi-iz-zi* “trifft” A II 33, 34, *ḫu-eš-ki-iz-zi* (*-šk-*) A II 23, *ku-i-en-zi* A II 17, *ma-ni-i̯a-aḫ-ḫe-eš-ki-iz-zi* (*-ḫḫ-*, *-šk-*) A II 28, ⸢*pa*⸣*-iz-zi* A I 14, *pí-it-ta-iz-zi* A I 12, II 35, *ú-e-mi-iz-zi* D (orig.) Vs. 10’ (= *ú-e-mi-i̯a-*⸢*zi*⸣ F (KBo XIII 44a) I 4’), *ú-e-mi-i̯a-az*[*-zi* C Vs. 26’ (= *ú-e-mi-ir* A II 24).[40]

Pl. 3. *-(a)nzi*: vgl. *a-ša-an-zi* “sitzen” D (orig.) Rs. 7’, *ši-eš-kán-zi* (*-šk-*) “schießen (jeweils)” A II 33[41], *zi-kán-zi* (*-šk-*) A III 19’.

-ḫi-Konjugation

Sg. 1. *-ḫi*: *pí-iḫ-ḫi* A I 28, *u-uḫ-ḫi* A I 23.[42]

2. *-ti*: *ḫa-li-iḫ-la-at-ti* A II 21.[43]

3. *-i*: *ú-da-i* D (orig.) Vs. 10’ (= A I 12).

[37] Die in Verbindung mit dem Adverb *nāu̯i* “noch nicht” auftretenden Präsensformen wie *pa-i-mi na-a-ú-i u-uḫ-ḫi na-a-ú-i* A I 23, *-m(i n)*]*a-a-ú-i e-et-mi n*[*a-a-ú-i* III 8′f. und *pa-iz-zi-ma-aš na-a-ú-i* A I 14 sind im Deutschen wohl durch Ausdrücke der Vergangenheit wiederzugeben; vgl. mit Bezug auf das Englische *CHD* L-N, 421 (sub a) und zuvor schon Ph. H.J. Houwink ten Cate, a.a.O. 125[3]. – Auch gilt es, innerhalb der hier behandelten Textgruppe dem Phänomen des Praesens historicum Rechnung zu tragen.

[38] Die Schreibung °*-ši-ki-mi* wird man mit den von H. Otten (*StMed* I/2, 439ff.) behandelten *-šk*-Bildungen wie *tar-ši-ki-* oder *a-an-ši-ki-* in Verbindung zu bringen haben; vgl. *tar-ši-kán-zi* CTH 9.3 A (KBo III 29) I 20′.

[39] Möglich erscheint auch ⸢*ú-uš*⸣*-ki-ši*; vgl. CTH 9.3 A (KBo III 29) I 6′ *ú-uš-ki* (2. Pers. Imperativ); CTH 9.5 (KBo VIII 42) Vs. 2′ *ú-uš-ki-iz-zi* (altheth.).

[40] Fragen der verbalen Stammbildung, die teilweise ebenso das hohe Alter der Textkomposition CTH 8 zu stützen vermögen, haben wir hier aus Raumgründen beiseite gelassen. So weisen vor allem die Formen *ḫazzizzi* (zu *ḫazzii̯a-*; s. *StBoT* 18, 82ff.) und *u̯emizzi* auf höheres Alter; vgl. *ti-iz-zi* (zu *tii̯a-* “hintreten”) CTH 9.3 A (KBo III 29) I 13′.

[41] Nicht *šeškanzi*, sondern *šieškanzi* muß es auch in bound transcription heißen. Dies zu R. Uvira (in: R. Thieroff-J. Ballweg (Edd.), *Tense Systems in European Languages*. Tübingen 1994, 312), der auch irrtümlich den Text KBo III 34 zu den hethitischen Gesetzen stellt; auch muß in seiner Umschrift statt GEŠTIN-*aš* (Gen.) richtig GEŠTIN-*an* (Akk.) geschrieben werden. – Bei athematischem Verbum hat man die Pluralendung als *-anzi*, bei thematischem Verbum aber als *-nzi* anzusetzen.

[42] In Verbindung mit *nāu̯i*; s. schon oben Anm. 37.

[43] Vgl. Verf., *StBoT* 5, 33f.

Pl. 3. -(*a*)*nzi*: *ḫal-zi-iš-ša-an-zi* (-*šš*-) A II 27, *i-iš-ša-an-zi* (-*šš*-) D (orig.) Rs. 9'[44], *pí-an-zi* A II 33, 34.

Indikativ des Präteritums, Aktiv

-*mi*-Konjugation

Sg. 1. -*un*: *e-šu-un* B I 9'.

2. -*t*: *a-uš-ta* (oder mit sprachwirklichem -*a* der -*ḫi*-Konj.?)[45]

3. -*t*: vgl. *an-na-nu-ut* (-*nu*-) A II 29, 30, *ar-nu-ut* (-*nu*-) A II 10, *a-uš-ta* A I 22, ⌈*e*⌉-*eš-ta* D (orig.) Vs. 9', *e-uk-ta* "trank" D (orig.) Vs. 6' (= Exemplar I 4')[46], *ḫar-ta* A I 26, *ḫa-at-ra-it* A I 14, *ḫa-zi-it* "traf" C Vs. 8'[47], *ḫi-in-kat-ta* A II 3, *ḫu-e-ek-ta* D (orig.) Vs. 16' (= A I 18)[48], *ḫu*-⌈*iš*⌉-*nu-ut* (-*nu*-) C Vs. 9', *i-e-et* A II 11, 16 (= *i-i̯a-at* C Vs. 22'), 23, *ma-ra-ak-ta* A I 6, 10 (= D (orig.) Vs. 7', erg.), 1̂3, *n*[*a*-]*aḫ-ta* (+ Dativ) A I 25[49], *pa-it* A II 37, *pí-ḫu-te-et* A I 19[50], *te-et* "sprach" A II

44 Zum Alter der *i*-haltigen Anlautschreibung dieses halbthematisch flektierenden Verbums s. Verf. *KZ* 93 (1979) 70f.

45 Die Ansetzung dieser Verbalform als 2. Pers. Sing. Prät. beruht auf folgendem Textzusammenhang (A II 5f.): *na-at-ta a-pu-u-un* GEŠTIN-*an pí-i-e-er* LUGAL-*uš ku-in a-uš-ta* "nicht gaben sie jenen Wein, den du, der König, gesehen hast" (vgl. S.Luraghi, a.a.O. 90). Da die beiden Betrogenen unmittelbar bei dem König vorstellig werden, ist diese Interpretation plausibler als: "... den der König gesehen hat". Bei der zuvor gebotenen Deutung als 2. Person ließe sich der Nominativ funktional auch als Vokativ "König!" verstehen (statt LUGAL-*u-i*). Die Form *a-uš-ta* /aust/ (endungsmäßig 3. Pers., *mi*-Konj.) fungiert auch im mittelheth. Ḫukkana-Vertrag wie in IBoT I 36 als 2. Pers. (A. Kammenhuber, *HW*[2] A 578a). Als genuine 2. Pers. Prät. der *ḫi*-Konj. wäre vielleicht **a-ut-ta* zu erwarten. - Der Relativsatz ist wegen des emphatischen Hauptsatzes nachgestellt.

46 Zu *e-uk-ta* mit Labiovelar im Wurzelauslaut vgl. J. Puhvel, *HED* 2, 263, 267f., Verf., *IF* 85 (1980 [1981]) 84[16].

47 Zu altertümlichem *ḫa-zi-it* (s. oben *ḫazzizzi*) vgl. altheth. *ḫa*[-*a*]*z-zi-e-et*; Verf., *StBoT* 18, 82.

48 Für *ḫu-e-ek-ta*, die betreffende Textstelle sowie für das Verhältnis *ḫuek-/ḫunik-* sei auf K. Strunk, *IBS* 25, 237ff., 244 und G. Meiser, *IBS* 72, 289f., 310f. verwiesen; vgl. H.M. Kümmel, a.a.O. 162.

49 Zu *n*[*a*-]*aḫ-ta* wie überhaupt zum Verbum *naḫ*(*ḫ*)- vgl. J. Friedrich, *HE* II 56; J. Catsanicos, *BSL* 75/1 (1980) 167ff.; H.G. Güterbock - H.A. Hoffner, *CHD* L-N, 338ff.

50 Zur Graphie *pí-ḫu-te-* vgl. Verf., a.a.O. 39.

4, C Vs. 14', *ti-i-it* "trat hin" C Vs. 24' (= *ti-e-et* A II 19), *ú-it* "kam" A II 6.[51]

Pl. 3. *-ir*: vgl. *a-še-šir* A II 25, 26, *e-ep-pir* D (orig.) Vs. 15' (= A I 17), *e-šir* A II 22, *e-eš-ši-kir* (*-šk-*) A II 7 (= *e-eš-ši-iš-kir* C Vs. 15'),[52] *ḫa-a-li-ir* A III 12', *ḫu-u-up-pí-ir* A I 3, *ku-en-nir* B I 12', *ku-uk-ku-re-eš-ki-ir* (*-šk-*) A I 25, *°-re-eš-kir* B I 5' *pa-a-ir* "gingen" A I 2, *pa-ak-nu-ir* (*-nu-*) A II 10, *pí-i-ir* "schickten" A II 18 (= [*p*]*í-e-er* C Vs. 24'), *ša-mi*[*-nu-ir*] (*-nu-*) A I 4, *šar-ti-ir* Exemplar I 3' (= *š*[*ar-*]⌈*te*⌉*-er* D (orig.) Vs. 5'), *taḫ-iš-kir* (*-šk-*) A III 14', *tu-ri-ir* A I 16, *ú-e-mi-ir* A II 24 (= *ú-e-mi-i̯a-az*[*-zi* C Vs. 26').

-er: vgl. *e-še-er* A III 17' (neben *e-šir* A II 22), *i-e-er* A II 25, *š*[*ar-*]*te-er* (*šartai-*) D (orig.) Vs. 5' (= *šar-t*[*e-* F I 7, *šar-ti-ir* Exemplar I 3'), [*p*]*í-e-er* "schickten" C Vs. 24' (= *pí-i-ir* A II 18), *pí-ḫu-te-er* D (orig.) Vs. 14' (= A I 16), *ú-u̯a-te-er* D (orig.) Vs. 12' (= A I 14), A II 39.

-*ḫi*-Konjugation

Sg. 3. *-š*: vgl. *a-ki-iš* "starb" A II 12 (= C Vs. 18')[53], *a-ra-a-iš* A II 18 (= *a-ra-iš* C Vs. 23'), *ḫal-za-iš* A I 19, *i-ši-aḫ-ḫi-iš* (*-ḫḫ-*) D (orig.) Vs. 11' (= A I 13), *ma-ni-i̯a-aḫ-ḫi-iš* (*-ḫḫ*) A II 2, III 9', LÚAGRIG-*iš* C Vs. 10', *pa-iš* "gab" A II 31, 32, *pa-a-iš* C Vs. 7', *pé-en-ni-iš* A I 25, *da-a-aš* "nahm" A II 16, 21, 38, *da-iš* "legte" A II 17 (= *da-a-iš* C Vs. 23'), *da-i-iš* (mit *-šan*) A II 27.

Pl. 3. *-ir*: vgl. *a-ú-ir* A II 38, *ḫa-at-ta-an-ni-ir* (*-annai-*) A I 4, *na-i-ir* A I 22, *pa-ri-ir* A I 3, *šu-uḫ-ḫa-ir* D (orig.) Vs. 6' (= *šu-uḫ-ḫa-a-ir* A I 8, Ex. I 4'), *da-a-ir* "nahmen" D (orig.) Vs. 8', *tar-ni-ir* A II 19 (= *tar-n*[*ir*] C Vs. 24'), *tu-u̯a-ar-ni-ir* D (orig.) Vs. 7' (= A I 9), *ul-ke-eš-ša-ra-aḫ-ḫi-ir* (*-ḫḫ-*) A II 32, *up-pí*[(*-ir*)] A III 14'.

-er: vgl. *pí-i-e-er* "gaben" A II 4, 5.

[51] Liegt in *-i*]*š-*⌈*šu*⌉*-u-e-en* H 11′ eine Präteritalform (1. Pers.Plur.) vor? Etwa *i-i*]*š-*⌈*šu*⌉*-u-e-en* (zu *iššalešša-*) ? Vgl. *i-iš-ša-an-zi* D (orig.) Rs. 9′.

[52] In C sekundäre verdeutlichende *-šk*-Markierung.

[53] Bei Verbalformen wie *a-ki-iš, i-ši-aḫ-ḫi-iš* oder *ma-ni-i̯a-aḫ-ḫi-iš* vielleicht mit morphologischer Anaptyxe vor *-š* (vgl. N. Oettinger, *Linguistica* 33 (1993) 155).

Mediopassiv, Präsens:

Sg. 3. *-ta*: *ar-ta* A II 36, *a-ar-ta* B I 13', H 4', *ki-it-ta* D (orig.) Rs. 5', A III 18', 19', 21', 22', 24'.

Pl. 3. *-(a)nta*: *e-eš-kán-ta*[54] A III 15'.

Präteritum:

Sg. 1. *-ḫat*: *-ḫ]a-at* B I 10'.[55]

3. *-ati*: *ḫal-zi-i̯a-ti-u̯[a* A III 13'.[56]

-at: *ki-ša-at* B I 16'.

-tat: *iš-tar-ni-ik-ta-at* A II 39[57], *lu-uk-ta-at* D (orig.) Vs. 17' (= A I 19).

Pl. 3. *-andati*: *a-ra-an-da-ti* B I 7'.

Imperativ

Sg. 2. *-t* (aktiv): *i-it* A I 23, III 1'.

-i (aktiv): *na-a-ḫi* A III 3'.[58]

3. *-aru* (mediopassiv): [*ma*]*r-ki-i̯a-ru* A II 41.[59]

Partizip auf *-ant-*: vgl. *mar-ša-an-za* (Nom. Sing.c.) A II 20, *anda ne-e-an* (Nom. -Akk.n., zu *nāi-*) A I 21.

Infinitiv auf *-anna*: *a-ku-u̯a-an-na* A II 33 (zu ablautendem *eku-*).

[54] Als *-šk-*Ableitung zu *eš-* "sitzen" gehörig (*StBoT* 5, 27).
[55] Vgl. *ar-ḫa-ti* CTH 9.3 A (KBo III 29) I 18'.
[56] Vgl. Verf., *StBoT* 5, 37[3].
[57] Vgl. Verf., a.a.O. 78; zum syntaktischen Verhalten der Krankheitsverben s. *StBoT* 6, 101f.
[58] Zur grammatischen Bestimmung vgl. *CHD* L-N, 338b. Man denkt hier an das Vorliegen der Wendung *lē=ta*] *nāḫi* "fürchte dich nicht"; dazu ibid. 340b; J. Catsanicos, a.a.O. 168ff. (der in *nāḫi* eine Nominalform sieht); Verf., *StBoT* 18, 105f.
[59] Zur Endung *-taru* s. *ḫu-la-da-ru* CTH 9.3 B (KBo VIII 41), 5' (= 3 A I 15').

Verbalsubstantiva: *-u̯ar* (*ḫa-aš-ḫa-aš-šu-ar* A II 29),[60] *-tar* (*ap-pa-a-tar* A II 29).

4. *Syntax* (*Auswahl*)

a. Ortsbezugspartikeln

-ašta: *ša-na-aš-ta* (*š=an=ašta*) *IŠ-TU* É.EN.NU.UN *tar-ni-ir* A II 19 " und ihn ließ man aus dem Gefängnis heraus", *ša-na-aš-ta*! *ar-ḫa pé-e-ḫu-te-er* A II 6 " und man brachte ihn weg"; *ša-na-aš-ta e-uk-ta* D (orig.) Vs. 6' " und ihn (den Becher) trank er aus" (vgl. Exemplar I 4'); *ša-na-aš-ta at-ti-mi pa-ak-nu-ir* A II 9f. "und ihn verleumdete man bei meinem Vater".

-šan: *a-ki-iš-ša-an* (*akiš=šan*) [(*te-e*)]*p-ša-u̯a-an-ni* C Vs. 18' f. " er starb in Armut" (A II 12: *akiš=ma=aš* "er starb aber ..."); *da-i-iš-ša-an* (*daiš=šan*) ANŠE.KUR.RA-*aš* A II 27 "gelegt hat er (sie) auf die Pferde" (oder "auf den Wagen"?).

-kan: URU*Ḫa-at-tu-ši-ma-kán* (URU*Ḫattuši=ma=kan*) ÉRINMEŠ-*aš u̯a-al-ḫi ma-ra-a*[(*k-ta*)] D (orig.) Vs. 7' "in Hattuša aber gab er an die Truppen das *u̯alḫi*-Getränk aus"; *ma-na-an-kán* (*man=an=kan*) m*A-aš-ka-li-i̯a-aš ku-i-en-zi* A II 17 (*ma-a-na-kán* C Vs. 22') "Aškalija beabsichtigt, ihn zu töten".

b. Partikel der direkten Rede

-u̯a: *zi-ik-u̯a* (*zik=u̯a*) B I 5', *mar-ša-an-za-u̯a zi-ik* (*maršanz=u̯a zik*) A II 20, *ḫal-zi-i̯a-ti-u̯*[*a* (*ḫalzii̯ati=u̯a*) A III 13', LUGAL-*un-u̯a-az* (*ḫaššun=u̯a=z*) A II 21.

Der Beginn berichteter Rede wird auch durch akkadographisches *UMMA*(*-MA*) gekennzeichnet (vgl. A I 1, 21, 22, 23).

c. Modalpartikel *man*

ma-na-an-kán (*man=an=kan*) m*A-aš-ka-li-i̯a-aš ku-i-en-zi* A II 17 (*ma-a-na-kán* C Vs. 22') "Aškalija beabsichtigt, ihn zu töten" [s. schon oben unter *-kan*].[61]

[60] Als Genitiv eines Verbalnomens auf *-numar* (mit *-u-* zu *-m-* nach *-u-*) fraglich bleibt -]*i̯a-ru-nu-ma-aš* E Rs.? 8′ (einzuordnen in A III 10′).

[61] Vgl. H.A. Hoffner, *GsKronasser* 39.

d. Konjunktionen

Beiordnende Konjunktionen:

šu *ša-aš* (*š=aš*) A II 7, 19, III 9', *ša-an* (*š=an*) A I 4 (2x), 13 (= D (orig.) Vs. 11'), 17, 25, II 7, 10, 11, 15, 16, 17, C Vs. 9', 10', *ša-na-aš-ta* (*š=an=ašta*) A I 8, II 6, 9, 19, *še* (*š=e*) A I 2, 3, *šu-us* (*š=uš*) A II 32.

nu A I 10 (= D (orig.) Vs. 8'), 19 (= D (orig.) Vs. 17'), 21, 22, 25, III 12', H 10', *na-aš* (*n=aš*) A II 37, *nu-uš-še* (*nu=šše*) A II 33, 34, D (orig.) Rs. 2', *nu-uš* (*n=uš*) A I 16 (= D (orig.) Vs. 14'), II 28, 29, *nu-uš-ma-aš* (*nu=šmaš*) II 39 (ergänzt), III 17'.

ta A II 24, 27, D (orig.) Rs. 9'.

-a (nach Doppelkonsonanz) "und; auch":[62] *a-pa-a-aš-ša* (*apāšš=a*) A II 8 (= *a-pa-aš-ša, apašš=a* C Vs. 16'), *a-pa-aš-ša* (*apašš=a*) A I 12 (= [(*a-pa-*)]*a-ša* D (orig.) Vs. 10', C Vs. 10'), *a-pé-e-da-aš-ša* (*apedašš=a*) A II 3, *ku-u-uš-ša* (*kūšš=a*) A II 30, *a-ap-pa-an-na* (*appann=a*) A III 16', 23', *a*<*-ap*>*-pa-an-na* (*appann=a*) G 10', [*ap-p*]*í-iz-zi-an̯-na* (*appizziann=a*) H 7', *ḫur-la-aš-ša* (*ḫurlašš=a* Dat.Pl.) A I 24, TÚG*iš-ḫi-al-še-me-et-ta* (*išḫial=šemett=a*) A I 20, m*Ḫa-ap-ru-uz-zi-iš-ša* (°*uzzišš=a*) B I 14', m*Ma-ra-aš-ša-an-na* (*Maraššann=a*) A II 22, *mar-nu-an-na* (*marnuann=a*) A I 6 (*marnuu̯ann=a* Exemplar I 2'), m*Nu-un-nu-un-na* (*Nunnunn=a*) A I 15, m*Nu-un-nu-uš-ša* (*Nunnušš=a*) A I 16, [(LUGAL-*uš-š*)]*a* (*ḫaššušš=a*) A I 28.

-a ... -a "sowohl ... als auch": *a-pa-a-aš-ša ... a-pa-a-aš-ša* A II 4, 6 *a-pé-el-la a-p*[*é-e*]*l-la* D (orig.) Rs. 6'.

-i̯a (nach Vokal und Sumerogramm) "und; auch": m*Nu-un-nu-ú-i-i̯a* (*Nunnui=i̯a*) A I 18, m*Ma-ra-aš-ša-i̯a* (**Maraššai=i̯a*,?) A II 24, KÙ.BABBAR-*i̯*[*a*] A I 11.

-a (nach Einfachkonsonanz) "aber": [(*a-pa-*)]⌈*a*⌉*-ša* (*apāš=a*) D (orig.) Vs. 10' (= *a-pa-aš-ša, apašš=a* A I 12), *a-pu-u-na* (*apūn=a*) A II 22 (= *a-pu-na* C Vs. 26'), *ku-i-da* (*kuid=a*) A I 3, II 24, 27, [(m*E-u̯a*$_a$*-ri-š*)]*a-tu-ni-ša*

[62] Zur Partikel *-a* s. Ph.H.J. Houwink ten Cate, *FsOtten* 119ff.; *Acta Orientalia Neerlandica*, Leiden 1971, 39ff. Wie Textvarianten des Typs *a-pa-aš-ša/a-pa-a-ša* zeigen, ist in den jungen Niederschriften der Textgruppe CTH 8 das Prinzip der Verteilung von Einfach- und Doppelkonsonanz (mit bedeutungsunterscheidender Funktion: "aber" gegenüber "und, auch") nicht mehr konsequent beibehalten worden.

(°*tuniš=a*) A I 26, ^{m}*Ḫa-ki-pu-i-li-na* (°*lin=a*) C Vs. 9', ^{m}*Ḫu-ur-ri-li-ša* (°*liš=a*) H 8', ^{m}*Pa-ap-pa-na* (°*pan=a*) A I 7, *di-iš-šu-um-*⌈*mi-na*⌉ (°*ummin=a*) D (orig.) Vs. 6' (= *di-iš-šu-me-e*[*n-na*?] Exemplar I 4'), *pí-ra-a-na* (*pirān=a*) D (orig.) Rs. 3'.

-*ma* "aber": *a-ap-pa-ma* (*appa=ma*) B I 9', 10', *na-at-ta-ma* (*natta=ma*) A II 34 (am zweiten Wort des Satzes), ^{m}*A-aš-ka-li-ma* (°*kali=ma*) A II 18, ^{m}*Iš-pu-ta-aš-i-na-ri-ma* (°*inari=ma*) A II 18, [^{URU}*D*(*ur-mi-it-t*)]*i-ma* (°*itti=ma*) A III 6' (mit E Rs.? 8'), *a-ri-i̯a-al-li-ma* (°*alli=ma*) D (orig.) Rs. 6', *pí-di-iš-ši-ma* (*pidi=šši=ma*) ibid. Vs. 12' (= A I 14), ^{LÚ}*u-ri-an-ni-ma* (°*anni=ma*) D (orig.) Rs. 8', LUGAL-*i-ma* (*ḫaššui=ma*) B I 7', *pa-iz-zi-ma-aš* (*paizzi=ma=aš*) A I 14, *a-ki-iš-ma-aš* (*akiš=ma=aš*) A II 13, *a-pé-e-ma-an* (*ape=ma=an*) A II 38, ^{URU}*Ḫattuši=ma=kan* D (orig.) Vs. 7', *ki-ma-az* (*ki=ma=z*) A I 23.

Untergeordnete Konjunktion *mān* "als" (temporal):

ma-a-an lu-uk-ta-at D (orig.) Vs. 17' (= A I 19) "als es hell wurde"; *ma-a-an A-BI* LUGAL *IŠ-ME* A I 27 (= B I 3') "als der Vater des Königs hörte".

e. Σχῆμα Ἀττικόν

Die für das Ṛgvedische, Gāthā-Avestische und Griechische nachgewiesene Konstruktion, wonach sich ein aus einem pluralischen Neutrum (eigentlich Kollektivum) bestehendes Subjekt mit einem Prädikatsverbum im Singular verbindet, findet sich bekanntlich auch im Hethitischen.[63] Aus dem hier behandelten Textkorpus läßt sich dafür folgender Satz anführen: ^{m}*A-aš-ka-li-ma ud-da-a-ar a-ra-a-iš* A II 18 "gegen Aškalija aber erhob sich Gerede".

f. Doppelter Akkusativ

Die Wendung "jem.n zu etwas machen" wird durch das Verbum *i̯a-* "machen" mit dem doppelten Akkusativ zum Ausdruck gebracht:[64] *ša-an* ^{URU}*Ân-ku-i-pát* ^{LÚ}AGRIG-*an i-e-et* A II 11 "und ihn machte er eben in Ankuu̯a zum Verwalter"; *ša-an I-NA* ^{URU}*U-taḫ-zu-mi* (Var. ^{URU}*Ul-lam-ma*) ^{LÚ}*ma-ni-aḫ-ḫa-tal-la-an* (Var. *ma-ni-i̯a-aḫ-ḫi-iš-kat-tal-la-an*) *i-e-et* (Var. *i-i̯a-at*) A II 11 (Var.: C Vs. 22') "und ihn machte er in U. zum Verwalter"; *a-pu-(-u)-na* ^{LÚ}*u-ra-al-la-aš-ša-ma-an i-e-et* A II 23 (mit C Vs. 26') "jenen aber machte er zu ihrem (3. Pers.

63 Vgl. J.Friedrich, *HE* I² § 196a.
64 Vgl. Th.P.J. van den Hout, *StMed* 7, 275ff.

Plur.) *ural(l)aš*." – Im Passiv mit *kiš-* und doppeltem Nominativ (vgl. B I 15'f. mit Dupl. H 6').

g. Possessivsyntagma

Das typisch altheth. Possessivsyntagma enthält neben dem vorangestellten Genitivattribut auch noch ein dem Regens angefügtes Possessivsuffix: ^m^*Nu-un-nu-uš-ša* ^LÚ^*ka-i-na-aš-šan* A I 16f. (Var. ^LÚ^*ga-i-na-aš-ša-an* D (orig.) Vs. 15' "und des Nunnu seinen Verwandten".

h. Allativsyntagma

Beachtung verdient das für das Althethitische typische Allativsyntagma, das aus einem allativischen Adverb und einem substantivischen Allativ besteht.[65] Hierher gehören [*a*]*nda tuzzii̯a* und E]GIR-*pa tu*[*z*]*zii̯a* in Verbindung mit folgenden Prädikatsverben: *na-aš* [*a*]*n-da tu-uz-zi-i̯a pa-it* A II 37 "und hin(ein) zum Heer ging er"; bruchstückhaft E]GIR-*pa tu-*[*uz-*]*zi-i̯a pí-ḫu-te-er* A II 42 "]zurück zum Heer brachte man".

i. Position des adjektivischen Attributs

Im Textkorpus von CTH 8 finden sich sowohl Syntagmen, bei denen das Adjektiv seinem Bezugswort folgt, als auch solche mit Voranstellung des adjektivischen Attributs.

Voranstellung: [(*i-d*)]*a-lu ḫé-en-kán* A III 14' (mit graphischer Variante in G 4') "schlimme Seuche", *šar-ku-uš* LÚ-(*me*)-*eš* A II 11 (mit Var. LÚ-*eš* bzw. LÚ-*iš* C Vs. 18') "ein angesehener/erhabener Herr", SIG$_5$-*an-ta-an* GEŠTIN-*an* (Akk.) A II 3 "(qualitätsmäßig) guten Wein". Die Voranstellung des Attributs entspricht der des Pronomens bzw. eines Pronominaladjektivs; vgl. *a-pu-u-un* GEŠTIN-*an* A II 5 "jenen Wein", *ta-ma-in* GEŠTIN-*an* A II 4 "einen anderen Wein".

Nachstellung: [*pa-aš-ši-*]⌈*la*⌉*-an šal-li-in* (Akk.) A I 3 "einen großen Kieselstein", ḪUR.SAG-*i š*[*a-an-na-pí-l*]*i* (Lok.) A I 2 "im einsamen/öden Gebirge". Bei der Nachstellung scheint ein größerer Nachdruck auf dem Adjektiv zu liegen (unterscheidende Funktion). Demgegenüber ist *ḫenkan* immer auch *idalu* bzw. ist Wein normalerweise gut; in den altheth. Texten kommt einem LÚ auch ohne adjektivischen Zusatz beinahe schon fürstliches Flair zu. Vielleicht darf man bei der Voranstellung im weitesten Sinne von "schmückender" Funktion des Adjektivs sprechen.

65 Vgl. F. Starke, *StBoT* 23, 151.

j. Nachstellung des Relativsatzes

Normalerweise geht im Hethitischen der Relativsatz als Attributivsatz dem regierenden und übergeordneten Satz voraus (vgl. A I 12 = D (orig.) Vs. 10', A II 33, 34). Der Text der 'Palastchronik' bietet jedoch zwei bemerkenswerte Beispiele für Nachstellung: *na-at-ta* (Var. *Ú-UL*) *a-pu-u-un* GEŠTIN-*an pí-i-e-er* LUGAL-*uš ku-in a-uš-ta* A II 5f. "nicht gaben sie jenen Wein, den du, der König, gesehen hast", *ma-a-an lu-uk-ta-at nu A-BI* LUGAL *ḫal-za-iš ku-u-uš ar-ḫa ku-iš pí-ḫu-te-et* A I 19 "als es hell wurde, rief der Vater des Königs (denjenigen), der diese weggebracht hatte".

5. *Graphisches -Lautliches*

Abschließend sei anhangsweise in Auswahl auf einige Phänomene hingewiesen, die für die Frage nach dem sprachlichen Alter bedeutsam sein können:

a. Gleitlaute: -*i̯*-, -*u̯*-[66]

i-ši-aḫ-ḫi-iš D (orig.) Vs. 11' (= A I 13) - *i-ši-i̯a-aḫ-ḫi*[- F (KBo XIII 44a) I 5'; [LÚ]*ma-ni-aḫ-ḫa-tal-la-an* A II 16 - *ma-ni-i̯a-aḫ-ḫi-iš-kat-tal-la-an* C Vs. 22' (vgl. *ma-ni-i̯a-aḫ-ḫe-eš-ki-iz-zi* A II 28, [*ma-ni-*]*i̯a-aḫ-ḫi-iš* III 9'); [LÚ]*u-ri-an-ni-in* A I 7 - [([LÚ]*u-ri-*)*i̯*]*a-ni-in* Exemplar I 3' (vgl. im altheth. Exemplar [LÚ]*u-ri-an-ni-iš* D Vs. 3', [LÚ]*u-ri-an-ni* Rs. 8').

ḫa-aš-ḫa-aš-šu-ar A II 29 (nicht °-*šu-u̯a-ar*); *mar-nu-an-na* D (orig.) Vs. 4' (= A I 6) - *mar-nu-u̯a-an-na* Ex. I 2'.

b. Assimilation[67]

[LÚ]*ga-i-na-aš-ša-an* (< **gainan*=*šan*) D (orig.) Vs. 15'= [LÚ]*ka-i-na-aš-ša-an* A I 17; DUMU-*aš-ša-an* (< *°*lan*=*šan*) B I 10'.

[66] Vgl. Verf., *StBoT* 12, 53, 64.

[67] Vgl. H. Otten -Vl. Souček, a.a.O. 57f. – In C Vs. 26′ scheint der späte Kopist die Assimilation in [LÚ]*u-ra-al-la-aš-ša-ma-an* (so in A II 23) rückgängig gemacht zu haben: [LÚ]*u-ra-la-a*[*n*-.

c. Tenuis-/Media-Zeichen: *k/g, t/d*[68]

[^{m}*Aš-k*]*a-li-i̯a-aš* C Vs. 16' - ^{m}*A-aš-ga-*° A II 8; *ḫi-in-kat-ta* A II 3 - *ḫi-in-g*[*a-* C Vs. 12'; *ta-ma-in* A II 4 - ⸢*dam*⸣*-ma-in* C Vs. 13', ^{URU}*Ḫu-un-ta-ra-a* A I 13 - °*-un-da-ra-a* D (orig.) Vs. 11' (wie in F (KBo XIII 44a) I 5'); ^{m}*Iš-pu-ta-aš-i-na-ra-aš* C Vs. 21' - °*-pu-da-aš-*° A II 15 (ibid. II 18 *-ta-*); *ku-u̯a-at-ta ku-u̯a-at-ta* A II 9 - *ku-u̯a-ad-da* C Vs. 16'

Schluß

6. Mit diesen wenigen Hinweisen zum Graphischen/Lautlichen brechen wir unsere grammatische Skizze zum Text der althethitischen 'Palastchronik' ab. Die Zusammenstellung bietet ein objektives Bild dessen, was uns die einzelnen Exemplare an Wortformen und grammatischen Elementen überliefern. Wer mit der althethitischen Sprachform, soweit sie sich aus zeitgenössischen Texten, also an Hand paläographisch alter Tontafeln, gewinnen läßt, einigermaßen vertraut ist, erkennt, welche Phänomene problemlos auch in einer deskriptiven Grammatik des Althethitischen Aufnahme finden können. Auch andere Bereiche, die hier ausgeklammert wurden (z.B. Stammbildung des Verbums und Nomens), enthalten althethitische Charakteristika. Daß sich in der Bewertung bestimmter Sprachformen auch Zweifelsfälle ergeben, ist angesichts unserer noch lückenhaften Kenntnis des Althethitischen nicht ungewöhnlich. Markiert man eigens das aus jungen Abschriften aufgenommene Sprachmaterial, brächte ein vereinzelter Irrläufer oder 'Blender', der sich trotz sorgfältigen Abwägens in eine grammatische Darstellung des Althethitischen eingeschlichen hätte, noch lange nicht das gesamte Konzept zu Fall.

68 Zum graphischen Wechsel Tenuis/Media vgl. E. Neu - Chr. Rüster, *FsOtten* 227, 230, 232. - Beachtung verdienen die Graphien *ú-u̯a-a-tar* "Wasser" A II 35 und *ú-u̯a-aš-ta-i* "er sündigt" CTH 9.6 (KBo III 28) II 10'. - Zu akkadograph. *I-NA QA-TI A-B*[*I* LUGAL A III 10' vgl. ⸢*I-NA*⸣⸢*QA-TI*⸣⸢*A*⸣*-BI-I̯A* CTH 9.5 (KBo VIII 42) Vs.$^{?}$ I 8'. – Gelegentlich ist vor einem Personennamen kein Determinativ gesetzt (A I 22, II 30).

DAS SIEGEL B 229 VON ḪATTUŠILI III.- PUDUḪEPA

HEINRICH OTTEN

I. In meinem Vortrag auf dem II. *Congresso Internazionale di Hittitologia* in Pavia im Sommer 1993 hatte ich das Augenmerk auf einige ausgewählte Siegelabdrücke aus dem neuen Archivfund in Boğazköy gelenkt. In Hinsicht auf seine besondere Stellung in der Geschichte des hethitischen Herrscherhauses gehörten zu dieser Auswahl auch Siegel, die lediglich den Namen des Großkönigs Ḫattušili allein führen – ohne Gemahlin. Es waren nicht allzuviele Stücke dieser Art, und so schien es nützlich, die Vorstellung der rezenten Funde anzuknüpfen an einen schon lange bekannten Abdruck, gefunden 1933 auf Büyükkale, Gebäude A, Raum 5 (= *SBo* I 45 = B 184).[1]

Der im oberen Teil gut erhaltene innere Keilschriftring bietet noch die Legende:

UR.SAG *na-ra-a[m . . . . .* ^{U}]^{RU}*Ša-mu-ḫa*

(s. Pl. 27a), die nunmehr mit Hilfe eines Duplikat-Abdruckes (Bo 90/491) vollständig wiederherzustellen war:

UR.SAG *na-r⌈a-a⌉m* ^{d}U ^{URU}*Ni-ri-ik na-ra-a⌈m* ^{d}IN⌉ANNA ^{URU}*Ša-mu-ḫa* (s. Pl. 27b).

Die hh Schreibung des Königsnamens im eigentlichen Siegelbild verläuft von rechts nach links. Der Inschriftring weist mit den Köpfen der Keilschrift-Senkrechten nach außen. Ein zweiter, äußerer Keilschriftring ist nicht erhalten, angesichts des Wortlautes aber vorauszusetzen. – Soweit meine Ausführungen in der Mainzer Akademie-Abhandlung 1993 S. 29ff. mit Abb. 23 und 24 (erweiterte Fassung des oben erwähnten Vortrages).

II. Die Weiterarbeit konnte dabei von der Besonderheit ausgehen, daß die Legende bei der Nennung der persönlichen Götter zweimal den Begriff *narām*

[1] *SBo* = Siegel aus Boğazköy (I. Teil) von H.G. Güterbock = *AfO* Beih. 5 (1940) – B = Beran, Thomas, *Die Hethitische Glyptik von Boğazköy* (I. Teil) = *BoHa* V.

"Geliebter" verwendet – nicht, wie sonst üblich, diesen nur einmal nennt, dafür aber die Namen der Gottheiten mit *ù* "und" zusammenfaßt. – Weiterhin war die auffällige Nennung der Göttin unter dem Namen INANNA neben Wettergott von Nerik (in der Graphie *Ni-ri-ik*)[2] ein wichtiges Indiz für das Suchen nach etwaigen weiteren (Teil-)Abdrücken dieses Siegels.

III. Einen parallelen Beleg schien B 229a (s. Pl. 27c) zu bieten, der Abdruck eines mit B 184 etwa gleichgroßen Siegels in ähnlicher glyptischer Gestaltung: Die Flügelsonne mit langen, waagerecht ausgebreiteten, stark gefiederten Schwingen, die sich zeichnerisch klar von der Mitte absetzen, die durch eine Sonnenscheibe im Strahlenkranz gefüllt wird. – Das runde Mittelfeld wird umsäumt von einer dicken Ringleiste und bietet in hethitischen Hieroglyphen die Namen von Ḫattušili zusammen mit Puduḫepa.

Die Köpfe des (einzig erhaltenen) Schriftringes, weisen – ebenfalls abweichend von B 184 – nach innen. Die Legende bietet im unteren Teil des Abdruckes die Lesung ^{d}IN]ANNA ⌈^{URU}*Ša-mu-ḫ*⌉*a* UR.SAG x[[3], scheint also inhaltlich weitgehend mit B 184 – nach dessen Vervollständigung durch Bo 90/491 – übereinzustimmen.

Der neue Archivfund bietet nunmehr an die dreißig weitere Bullen mit Abdrücken wohl des gleichen Siegels, z.B. Bo 90/979 (s. Pl. 28a), das wegen seiner klar lesbaren Legende im einzigen abgedrückten Innenring hier vorgelegt sei: *na-ra-a*]*m* ^{d}INANNA ^{URU}*Ša-mu-u-ḫa* UR.S[AG – oder Bo 90/1042 (s. Pl. 28b) mit gut erhaltenem Innenbild und seiner klaren Zeichnung der Flügelsonne sowie dem fortlaufenden Text des Innenringes: UR.SAG *na-ra-a*[*m*] ^{d}U ^{URU}*Ni-ri-i*⌈*k*⌉ *na-ra-am* ^{d}INANNA ^{URU}*Ša-mu-u-ḫa*.[4]

IV. Fast vollständig auf uns gekommen ist Bo 90/1018 (s. Pl. 29a), das sich als Duplikat erweist[5], eine schlanke kegelförmige Tonbulle mit 2 Schnurlöchern an der Spitze; Höhe 6.6 cm, Durchmesser des Abdruckes 6.2 cm. Wie die beiden vorher genannten Stücke (Bo 90/979 und 1042) stammt auch dieses aus dem

[2] Auch diese Schreibung mit *Ni-* ist in den Texten ausgesprochen selten, vgl. G. del Monte (– J. Tischler), *RGTC* 6, 286ff. und 6/2, 113ff. – Es wurde die kürzere Zeichenform NI auf den Siegeln vielleicht aus Raumgründen gewählt.

[3] Die Transkription ^{URU}*Ša-mu-ḫa* bei Beran, auch *Boğazköy* III 44, entspricht dem beigegebenen Photo. Die Zeile ist in ihrem unteren Teil allerdings nicht vollständig erhalten; dieser Hinweis scheint wegen der folgenden Diskussion angebracht.

[4] Ein weiterer Abdruck mit fast vollständig erhaltenem Innenring: Bo 90/232 findet sich bei P. Neve, *AA* 1991, 329 Abb. 31c.

[5] Der Abdruck wirkt "größer" als andere Stücke (so Fundkartei), was sich objektiv beim Nachmessen aber nicht bestätigt.

Sammelfund im Archivgebäude (L/12) Raum 3. Die Legende beginnt rechts unten und lautet (s. Pl. 29b):

Äußerer Ring:

$^{\text{NA4}}$KIŠIB *ta-⸢ba⸣-ar-na* ^{m}*Ḫa-at-tu-ši-li* LUGAL.GAL LUGAL KUR[^{URU}]*Ḫa-at-ti*

Innerer Ring:

[U]R.SAG *na-ra-am* ^{d}U ^{URU}*Ni-ri-ik na-ra-am* ^{d}INANNA ^{URU}*Ša-mu-u-ḫa*

"Siegel des Tabarna Ḫattušili, des Großkönigs, Königs von Ḫatti, des Helden, Geliebter des Wettergottes von Nerik und der INANNA von Šamuḫa".

V. Ohne auf die weiteren Abdrücke im einzelnen einzugehen, können wir zusammenfassen:

Die von Th. Beran seinerzeit unter Nr. 229 vorgelegten Fragmente stammen alle von Büyükkale (t/12-13 und v/16) und sind als Einzelfunde anzusehen. Die neuen Stücke fanden sich im westlichen Trakt des Archivgebäudes L/12, gehäuft in Raum 3.

Das Innenrund zeigt nebeneinander die Namen von Ḫattušili (links) und Puduḫepa (rechts) in hethitischen Hieroglyphen. – Die beiden Keilschriftringe nennen dagegen nur den Namen des Großkönigs mit ausführlicher Titulatur, worin er sich als "Geliebter des Wettergottes von Nerik und der INANNA von Šamuḫa"[6] bezeichnet.

Die Schreibung des Namens der Göttin mit dem Sumerogramm INANNA ist in den Boğazköytexten ungewöhnlich.[7] Es ist aber in Verbindung mit dem Ortsnamen Šamuḫa hier nur an eine Schreibvariante gegenüber häufigem ^{d}*IŠTAR* ^{URU}*Šamuḫa*, ^{d}GAŠAN, ^{d}LIŠ ^{URU}*Šamuḫa*, zu denken.[8]

Diese "*IŠTAR* von Šamuḫa und der Wettergott von Nerik" werden als persönliche Schutzgottheiten von Ḫattušili III. nicht nur auf den beiden Siegelgruppen B 184 und B 229 herausgestellt, sondern auch die gleichzeitigen Texte nennen sie[9], bisweilen auch in Verbindung mit anderen Gottheiten, so

6 Eine Pleneschreibung ^{URU}*Ša-mu*[*-u*]*-ḫa* ist m.E. auch bei B 229 - vgl. Anm. 3 – ohne weiteres zu akzeptieren.

7 Als einzigen Beleg könnte ich im Augenblick nur das fragmentarische KBo XXVI 137 nennen (Z. 2′]^{d}INANNA-*aš ḫa-lu-kán*). Denn trotz Ähnlichkeit beider Zeichen (HZL 41/42) ist KUB XXX 55 Rs. 6′ mit *CHD* L-N 445 (und Lit.) ^{d}ŠUR-/AN.ŠUR- zu lesen.

8 Vgl. G. del Monte, *RGTC* 6, 340, und V. Haas, *Gesch. d. heth. Religion* 339, 349f.

9 S. seine Apologie III 71 (*StBoT* 24, 22f.).

KBo VI 28 Vs. 1f. “Sonnengöttin von Arinna, Wettergott von Nerik und *IŠTAR* von Šamuḫa”.

VI. Auf ein weiteres Siegel mit Nennung von Ḫattušili und Puduḫepa im Innenrund macht H.G. Güterbock in *BoHa* XIV 124 aufmerksam. Das Siegel ist von kleinerem Format und hat nur einen einzigen Keilschriftring, wobei die Köpfe der Senkrechten nach außen weisen. Die konkaven Abdrücke Nr. 257A-C, unter Wiederholung von B 230a und b (= 342/n, 341/n, Unterstadtgrabung), zeigen einen einzigen Keilschriftring mit der Legende:

^{NA4}KIŠIB *ta-ba-ar-na* ^{m}*Ḫa-at-tu-ši-*⌈*li*⌉ LUGAL.GAL (s. Pl. 29c)

Zurecht verweist dabei H.G. Güterbock darauf, “daß hier die Königin zwar in den Hieroglyphen, nicht aber in dem Keilschriftring genannt ist. Da sonst bei gemeinsamen Siegeln eines Königspaares der Name der Königin regelmäßig im inneren, d.i. zweiten Ring steht, wird man kaum annehmen wollen, daß er hier in einem nicht mit abgedrückten äußeren Ring gestanden hätte.” – Die Parallelität zu B 229 ist offensichtlich. Somit hat es mehrere Siegel des Großkönigspaares gegeben, wo im Keilschriftring bzw. in den beiden Keilschriftringen nur der Name des Großkönigs erscheint. Darauf hatte für Ugarit bereits Cl.F.-A. Schaeffer, *Ugaritica* 3 (1956) 12f. bei einer dritten Siegelgruppe dieser Art aufmerksam gemacht mit dem Hinweis 'Les empreintes <RS> 17.130 et 18.03 sont identiques ... La légende en cunéiforme signifie: “Sceau du tabarna Hattusili, grand roi, héros”. Le nom de la reine n'apparaît que dans la moitié gauche du cartouche hieroglyphique.'[10]

Ein Grund für diese vielfältige unterschiedliche Gestaltung der einzelnen Königssiegel ist nicht ersichtlich, wäre aber bei diesem Königspaar angesichts der langen und gut bezeugten Regierungszeit als Tatsache verständlich. Das Gleiche gilt hinsichtlich der Verwendung der einzelnen offiziellen Siegel jeweils durch König oder/und Königin. So führt die Königin Puduḫepa auch ein eigenes Siegel, wobei jedoch auf einem in Ugarit gefundenen Schreiben (RS 17.133) die Königin offensichtlich eine Entscheidung des Königs über die Schadensregelung bei einer Schiffshavarie beglaubigt, und zwar mit ihrem Siegel allein. Der Text (gekürzt) lautet: “So Meine Majestät zu Amistamri sprich: Als der Mann aus Ugarit und Šukku vor Meiner Majestät zum Gericht erschienen ... , da hat Meine Majestät folgendermaßen ihre (von Kläger und Beklagtem) Rechtssache entschieden.”[11]

[10] E. Laroche, ibid. S. 108 erkennt diese Besonderheit nicht, weil er irrtümlich den einzigen Keilschriftring von RS 18.03 (und 17.130) als “cercle extérieur cun.” bezeichnet; auch in der Angabe der Titulatur scheint einiges korrekturbedürftig.

[11] Vgl. H. Otten, *Puduḫepa* 26.

Die Aussagen dieses Aufsatzes seien abschließend tabellenartig kurz zusammengefaßt; nach der Aufarbeitung des neuen Archivfundes wird das Bild sich jedoch weitaus differenzierter darstellen, als es heute für den Jubilar als Geburtstagsgabe gezeichnet werden kann.

Siegelabdrücke von	*Ḫattušili*	*Ḫattušili-Puduḫepa*	*Puduḫepa*
König links		B 229	
		Bo 90/1018	
		B 230	
König rechts		RS 17.130	
KS nach außen	B 184	B 230	RS 17.133
	Bo 90/491	RS 17.130	
KS nach innen		B 229	
		Bo 90/1018	
1 KS-Ring		B 230	RS 17.133
		RS 17.130	
2 KS-Ringe	B 184	B 229	
	Bo 90/491	Bo 90/1018	
nur König genannt	B 184	B 229	
	Bo 90/491	Bo 90/1018	
		B 230	
		RS 17.130	
nur Königin genannt			RS 17.133

Plate 27a. Siegelabdruck B 184, Umzeichnung.
b. Siegelabdruck Bo 90/491.
c. Siegelabdruck B 229, Umzeichnung.

Plate 28a. Siegelabdruck Bo 90/979.
b. Siegelabdruck Bo 90/1042.

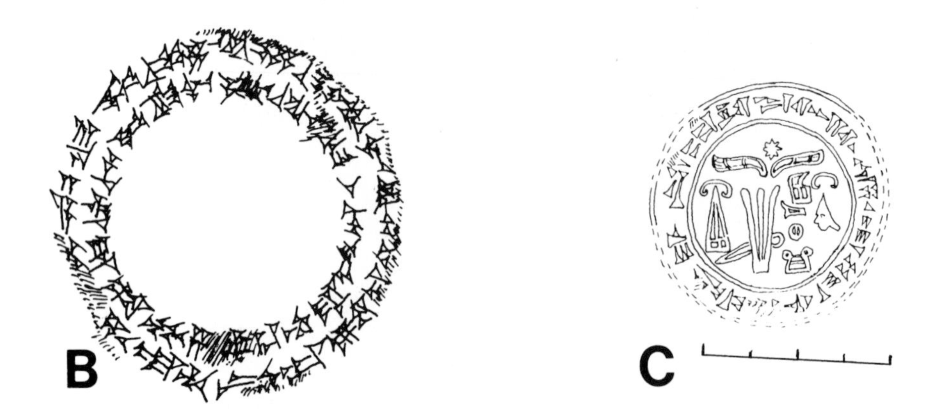

Plate 29a. Siegelabdruck Bo 90/1018.
b. Rohumzeichnung der Keilschriftringe von a. Bo 90/1018.
c. Siegelabdruck in kombinierter Umzeichnung (R.M. Boehmer - H.G. Güterbock, *BoHa* XIV Nr. 257).

ZUR GEOGRAPHIE DES NÖRDLICHEN ZENTRALANATOLIENS IN DER HETHITERZEIT

MACIEJ POPKO

In den letzten Jahren ist in unserer Kenntnis der hethitischen Geographie ein gewisser Fortschritt zu notieren, den wir vor allem neuentdeckten Urkunden verdanken wie die Briefe von Maşathöyük bzw. die Bronzetafel aus der Oberstadt von Ḫattuša. Trotzdem bleiben manche Probleme weiterhin ungeklärt. Um mindestens einige von ihnen beantworten zu versuchen, lohnt es sich, auf die schon lange bekannten Texte nochmals zurückzukommen. Dieser bescheidene Beitrag ist den ausgewählten Fragen der Topographie des Gebiets nordwärts von der hethitischen Hauptstadt gewidmet. Ich hoffe, damit das Interesse des hochverehrten Jubilars zu finden, der selbst so viel zur Erforschung der altkleinasiatischen Geographie beigetragen hat.

Im zweiten Teil meiner Arbeit, deren Gegenstand Zippalanda ist[1], werden die zum Kult in dieser heiligen Stadt gehörigen Texte in Umschrift und Übersetzung geboten. Sie zeigen in ihrer Gesamtheit eine inhaltliche Zusammengehörigkeit, was sowohl bei der Ausarbeitung der Einordnungskriterien als auch bei der Bearbeitung einzelner Text-fragmente hilfreich war. Folglich können wir mehrere Urkunden besser als vorher verstehen. In der Monographie wurde das Textmaterial vor allem vom philologischen Gesichtspunkt behandelt. Wie es aber leicht zu bemerken ist, sind einige Zippalanda-Texte von Bedeutung auch für die hethitische Geographie.

1. *Noch zur Identifizierung von Zippalanda mit Alacahöyük*

In meiner Arbeit wird Zippalanda mit dem modernen Ort Alacahöyük, und der heilige Berg Daḫa(ja) mit dem ca. 4 Kilometer NNO von Alacahöyük gelegenen Kalehisar/Karahisar vorläufig gleichgesetzt; s. *Zippalanda* 13, 29ff., 90f. Für diese Hypothese sprechen Argumente geographischer, topographischer und ikonographischer Natur, auch wenn ihre Beweiskraft noch nicht genügend

1 *Zippalanda, ein Kultzentrum im hethitischen Kleinasien* (Heidelberg 1994 = *THeth* 21) [ferner: *Zippalanda*].

ist, um die vorgeschlagene Lokalisierung von Zippalanda als sicher zu betrachten.

Auf der Suche nach weiteren Beweisen sei hier wieder auf KBo XVI 78 aufmerksam gemacht.[2] Dieses Textstück zählt jetzt zum Kult von Zippalanda (vgl. *Zippalanda* 142ff.). Die Vs. i beschreibt Lieferungen für ein Fest, das höchstwahrscheinlich in Zippalanda gefeiert wurde, wovon Analogien im großen althethitischen Ritual KBo XVI 71+ Vs. i x+1ff. zeugen (zu dieser Texteinheit vgl. *Zippalanda* 94ff.).[3] Die Rs. iv (teilweise parallel läuft KBo XVI 49 Rs. iv, vgl. *Zippalanda* 146ff.) nennt außer den typischen Vertretern des örtlichen Kultpersonals (vgl. *Zippalanda* 72ff.) auch den Gott Taḫa, der aufgrund anderer Texte mit dem Berggott Daḫa(ja) gleichzusetzen ist (vgl. *Zippalanda* 26ff.).

In KBo XVI 78 Vs. i werden sieben Städte aufgezählt, deren Verwalter ($^{LÚ.MEŠ}$AGRIG) für die erwähnten Kultlieferungen verantwortlich sind. Diese Ortsliste wurde schon in den Kreis der Betrachtungen zur hethitischen Geographie gezogen[4], jedoch blieb ihr Zusammenhang mit Zippalanda unbeachtet. In Hinblick auf die Paläographie ist KBo XVI 78 ins 14. Jh. v. Chr. zu datieren, inhaltlich aber bezieht es sich offensichtlich auf eine frühere Periode. Unter den AGRIG-Städten wird dort u.a. Takašta genannt; in altheth. Zeit gehörte jene Stadt wohl zum hethitischen Reich, später jedoch wurde sie von den Kaškäern erobert.[5] Die in KBo XVI 78 geschilderte Situation geht also auf die Zeiten vor der Regierung Arnuwandas I. zurück, denn damals wurde Takašta achon kaškäisch.[6]

Die Ortsliste dieser Urkunde umfaßt außer Takašta auch Šanaḫḫuitta, Tapikka, Taptiga, Katapa, Karaḫna und Ḫattuša. In den bisherigen Untersuchungen wurden diese Städte (außer Ḫattuša) gewöhnlich nördlich bzw. nordöstlich von der Hauptstadt in Richtung der Kaškäer-Zone lokalisiert[7]. Es ist anzunehmen, daß aus praktischen Gründen mit Lieferungen für Zippalanda Verwalter der umliegenden Orte belastet wurden. Wahrscheinlich erwähnte dieses unvollständig erhaltene Textfragment ursprünglich die Verwalter noch

[2] In meiner Arbeit (*Zippalanda* 11) wurde KBo XVI 78 in geographischer Hinsicht schon teilweise ausgewertet, wobei ich annahm, daß die von S. Alp vorgeschlagene Identifizierung von Maşathöyük mit Tapikka gesichert ist. Jedoch bezweifeln andere Forscher diese These; vgl. auch unten S. 259.

[3] Vgl. KBo XVI 78 Vs. i 18'f. ... *ša-a-la-aš-tu*!*-r*[*i*] (19') [III-*ŠU ḫar-pa-an-*]*te-eš* ... und KBo XVI 71+ Vs. i (erg. nach jh. Duplikaten) x+1f. . . . (*ŠA* KISLAḪ V) $^{G]IŠ}$*ša-a-la-aš*[*-tu-u-ri*] (2') [(III-*ŠU ḫar-pa-an-te-eš*)] ... Auch bunte Behälter (*kurtali* GÙN.A) und bunte Platten (*wera* GÙN.A) KBo XVI 78 Vs. i 9'f. findet man wieder in KBo XVI 71+ Vs. i 2'.

[4] I. Singer, *AnSt* 34 (1984) 115ff.

[5] Vgl. dazu E. von Schuler, *Kaškäer* 156ff.

[6] Zur Datierung von KBo XVI 78 vgl. auch H. Otten - Vl. Souček, *StBoT* 8, 104 und E. Neu, *FsNeumann* 208.

[7] Zur Literatur vgl. Anm. 24.

anderer Orte, z.B. jenen von Ankuwa, der in den Zippalanda-Texten gut belegt ist.[8] Alle diesen AGRIG-Städte, zu denen auch Ḫattuša gehörte, dürften folglich etwa einen Ring um Zippalanda herum gebildet haben.

Weitere Anhaltspunkte zur Lokalisierung dieser Städte ergeben sich aus den Briefen von Maşathöyük.[9] Die in dieser Textgruppe belegten Ortsnamen beziehen sich auf ein bestimmtes Gebiet nordöstlich von Ḫattuša, das u.a. einen Teil des Oberen Landes umfaßt. Die Grenze dieses Gebiets wird nur selten überschritten; die Nennung der hethitischen Hauptstadt ist eine Ausnahme, die keines Kommentars bedarf. In den Texten von Maşathöyük treten auch einige Ortsnamen aus der Ortsliste von KBo XVI 78 auf; bemerkenswert ist aber, daß weder Katapa noch Zippalanda dort belegt sind. Daraus ist zu folgern, daß diese zwei Städte außerhalb des erwähnten Gebiets, und zwar westwärts von ihm und nordwärts von Ḫattuša gelegt haben müssen. Somit zeigt KBo XVI 78 eine allgemeine Richtung, wo Zippalanda gesucht werden muß.

In meiner Monographie versuche ich, die Stadttopographie von Zippalanda in allgemeine Umrissen zu rekonstruieren (*Zippalanda* 18ff.). Die Texte lassen nämlich eine Lagebeziehung zwischen einzelnen Kultanlagen und andere Gebäuden der Stadt näher bestimmen, wobei die Orts- und Richtungsadverbien von Bedeutung sind.[10] Eine Analyse der Urkunden führt zum Schluß, daß Zippalanda in eine Oberstadt mit dem Tempel des örtlichen Wettergottes und dem der Sonnengöttin der Erde und eine Unterstadt eingeteilt wurde. Allerdings bot ein Vergleich des auf diese Weise rekonstruierten Stadtplans mit den Bebauungsresten auf dem "Höyük" Schwierigkeiten, und deswegen werden Schlußfolgerungen in meinem Buch mit aller Vorsicht formuliert. So lokalisiere ich den Tempelkomplex "auf einer Erhöhung", im Gegensatz zur königlichen Residenz, die sich "unten", d.h. niedriger als der Tempelkomplex befand.

Während des II. Hethitologischen Kongresses in Pavia (28.6. - 2.7.1993) hat P. Neve im Beitrag " Zur Datierung des Sphinxtores in Alaca Höyük" einzelne Fragen der Topographie dieses Ausgrabungsortes aufs neue erörtert und ist zu wichtigen Schlüssen gekommen. Dieser Beitrag war mir vor der Drucklegung meiner Monographie unbekannt, und erst vor kurzem konnte ich ihn studieren.[11] P. Neve macht auf die Reste eines mit Löwen flankierten Stadttores und einer Außenmauer südwärts vom Sphinxtor aufmerksam. Diese Bebauungsspuren erlauben es uns anzunehmen, daß die großreichszeitliche Stadtanlage "aus einer Oberstadt ... und einer südwärts vorgelagerten Unterstadt"

[8] KBo XVI 71+ Rs. iv 3 (ah.), KBo XI 50 Vs. ii 5' (erg.), KUB XLI 46 Vs. ii 9' (erg.), Bo 2689 Rs.v 17'.

[9] S. Alp, *HKM*, und ders., *HBM*.

[10] Vgl. dazu bereits I. Singer, *StBoT* 27, 25 Anm. 10.

[11] Dem Verfasser für die Zusendung des Aufsatzes noch vor der Veröffentlichung möchte ich an dieser Stelle herzlich danken.

bestand.[12] Diese Feststellung ist für die vorgeschlagene Identifizierung von Zippalanda mit Alacahöyük von wesentlicher Bedeutung. Erst jetzt kann meine Formulierung “die rekonstruierte Stadttopographie von Zippalanda steht zu derjenigen von Alacahöyük nicht im Widerspruch” (*Zippalanda* 91) als korrekt gelten.

Zur Klärung dieser Frage könnten neue Ausgrabungen beitragen, und in diesem Zusammenhang seien Fragmente aus einem Brief von P. Neve zitiert: “Der Ort verspricht noch viele wichtige Ergebnisse und vielleicht auch Überraschungen ... Es sollte dort weiter geforscht werden – sowohl im Hinblick auf das Löwentor und die möglicherweise damit verbundene Unterstadt, als auch in der Oberstadt, d.h. auf dem Höyük, wo noch längst nicht alles untersucht ist.”[13]

Erwies sich die vorgeschlagene Lokalisierung von Zippalanda als richtig, so hätten wir bei der Erforschung des nord-zentralen Gebiets des Hethiterreiches einen Fixpunkt, an den eine Reihe von Ortsnamen anhängt. In Frage kommt hier ein wichtiger Teil des hethitischen Kernlandes, an den die Kaškäer-Zone stieß. Die bisherigen Bemühungen, die historische Geographie dieses Gebiets zu klären und systematisch darzustellen, haben zu voneinander abweichenden Resultaten geführt.

2. *Zur Lage von Ankuwa*

Die Zippalanda-Texte erwähnen oft Ankuwa (s. *Zippalanda*, Indices S. 327)[14] und lassen die Lage dieser Stadt näher bestimmen. Nach KUB XX 96 Vs. iii x+1ff. (*Zippalanda* 192ff.) nimmt der König an Kulthandlungen in Zippalanda teil, dann besucht er noch den Berg Daḫa und fährt am selben Tag mit dem Streitwagen nach Ankuwa. Zu vergleichen ist KBo XIII 214 Rs. iv? x+1ff.(*Zippalanda* 182ff.): es folgen Opfer bei einer Kultstele, dann verläßt der König Zippalanda und fährt mit dem Streitwagen, je nach Jahreszeit, entweder nach Katapa oder nach Ankuwa. Die beiden Textfragmente lassen denken, daß Ankuwa nahe Zippalanda lag. Andere Texte, und zwar KUB XX 25 + KUB X 78 und KBo XXX 155 (*Zippalanda* 304ff.), beschreiben eine kultische Reise in südliche Richtung, die sicherlich in Zippalanda anfängt.[15] Einzelheiten dieser

[12] Theoretisch könnte man dieses Stadttor wegen der phrygischen Inschrift auf dem westlichen Löwen in die phrygische Zeit datieren, jedoch sind sowohl R.O. Arık, *Les fouilles d'Alaca Höyük* (Ankara 1937), 16ff. als auch P. Neve, loc. cit. der Meinung, daß es sich hier um eine ältere, scil. hethitische Bebauung handelt. Doch sind Nachgrabungen am Orte vorzunehmen, um diesbezüglich eindeutige Ergebnisse zu erhalten.

[13] Der Brief vom 24.1.1994.

[14] Zu dieser Stadt s. vor allem A. Ünal, *SMEA* 24 (1984) 87ff. ferner auch G.F. del Monte - J. Tischler, *RGTC* 6, 19ff. und P. Cornil, *Hethitica* 10 (1990) 11f.

[15] Vgl. auch H.G. Güterbock, *JNES* 20 (1961) 92.

Reise sind unklar (die Texte sind fragmentarisch erhalten); es scheint aber, daß sie nicht lange (nur einen Tag?) dauerte und daß es sich hier um eine Prozession zu Fuß handelt. Als einzige besuchte Stadt wird dabei Ankuwa genannt. Somit wird die Vermutung verstärkt, daß sich Ankuwa unweit von Zippalanda befand, überdies noch wissen wir jetzt, daß Ankuwa südlich von dieser Stadt zu suchen ist. Unter den in Frage kommenden Ausgrabungsorten in dieser Gegend ist vor allem Eskiyapar zu nennen (vgl. schon *Zippalanda* 31 mit Anm. 4), obgleich es nicht südlich, sondern südöstlich von Alacahöyük liegt.[16]

Früher wurde Ankuwa in Alişar lokalisiert[17], und diese Hypothese hat immerfort ihre Anhänger.[18] Die dort gefundenen altassyrischen Texte erwähnen häufig die Stadt A(m)ku(w)a, und in diesem Ortsnamen liegt vermutlich der alte Name von Alişar vor. Was Ankuwa betrifft, so haben A. Goetze und E. Laroche wegen des Wechsels Ankuwa/ Ḫanikkuil in KBo X 24 Rs. iv 22, 30 die Urform dieses Ortsnamens als *Ḫanikku(wa) rekonstruiert, wofür auch weitere Argumente sprechen.[19] Höchstwahrscheinlich sind also die Ortsnamensformen Ankuwa und A(m)ku(w)a voneinander zu trennen. Zu noch anderen Lokalisierungsansätzen für die Lage Ankuwas vgl. A. Ünal, *SMEA* 24 (1984) 105.

3. *Zur Lage von Katapa*

Auch eine nähere Lagebestimmung von Katapa ist jetzt möglich. Diese Stadt ist als Verwaltungsort und zugleich als Kultzentrum bekannt.[20] Der Ortsname taucht in den Zippalanda-Texte sehr oft auf; für Belege vgl. *Zippalanda*, Indices S. 327. Wie schon oben aufgrund von KBo XVI 78 angedeutet, ist diese Stadt unweit von Zippalanda und nordwärts von Ḫattuša zu suchen. Daß die Stadt nahe Zippalanda lag, wird auch durch andere Urkunden bestätigt. Wie wir in KBo XIII 214 lesen, verläßt der König Zippalanda und fährt nach Katapa (Rs. iv$^?$ 18'ff.), wo noch am selben Tag weitere Kulthandlungen vollzogen werden (Rs. v$^?$). Von Bedeutung ist hier auch ein Fragment des großen althethitischen Kultrituals (*Zippalanda* 94ff.). Im Haupttextfragment

16 Die Ergebnisse der türkischen Ausgrabungen in Eskiyapar werden von R. Temizer bei T. Özgüç, *İnandıktepe*, S. XXVIIIf. resümiert.

17 Als erster schlug diese Lokalisierung Ankuwas I. Gelb, *OIP* 27, 9f. vor.

18 Vgl. zuletzt R.L. Gorny, *Alişar Höyük in the Second Millennium B.C.*, (Ph.D. Diss. University of Chicago 1990), 395ff.; ders. *AnSt* 43 (1993) 163 mit Anm. 2 und 191, und noch *Newsletter for Anatolian Studies* 9/2 (1993) 8f.

19 A. Goetze, *JCS* 16 (1962) 29; E. Laroche, *OLZ* 57 (1962) 29, *RHA* 31 (1973) 89. Ḫanikku als ON ist wahrscheinlich im altheth. Text KBo XVII 21+ Vs. 36 (E. Neu, *StBoT* 25, 55 mit Anm. 198) belegt.

20 Vgl. A. Ünal, *THeth.* 3, 195f. und H. Otten, *RlA* V 486.

KBo XVI 71+ (ergänzt nach jh. Duplikaten) Vs. i 5'ff. ist die Rede vom Schlachten der für eine Kultzeremonie in Zippalanda bestimmten und aus Katapa, Šalampa, Kartapaḫa und Ulušna gelieferten Opfertiere. Vgl. insbesondere Z. 14' "Wenn die *ḫapi*-Leute und die Wolfsleute (von Šalampa, Kadapa und Kardabaḫa) i h r e Schweine töten, ..." Aus verschiedenen, vor allem praktischen Gründen erscheint es kaum wahrscheinlich, daß die besagten Opfertiere aus entfernten Orten getrieben wurden. Es folgt daraus, daß nicht nur Katapa, sondern auch Šalampa, Kartapaḫa und Ulušna nahe Zippalanda gesucht werden müssen.

Eine örtliche Lagebeziehung zwischen Zippalanda und Katapa kann auch anhand der Texte erschlossen werden, die diese Städte im Zusammenhang mit anderen in Umgebung von Zippalanda gelegenen Ortschaften erwähnen. Vor allem ist hier KUB LVII 71 zu nennen, das die geographische Verbindung von Ziplanda, Katapa, Š[alampa], Kartapaḫa und Ḫal[iputta] bestätigt; s. *Zippalanda* 136f. Die Beziehung von Ḫaliputta zu Kartapaḫa und zu anderen Orten in Umgebung von Zippalanda ist auch den Texten KUB XI 33 (*Zippalanda* 312ff.) und KBo X 10 zu entnehmen. Überdies ist Ḫaliputta in KUB XL 106 Rs. iii 6' belegt, also in der Urkunde, in welcher Katapa als Station eines Feldzuges gegen die Kaškäer auftritt (iii 3').[21] Es sei hier daran erinnert, daß in den Muršili-Annalen Katapa als Winterquartier nach einem Feldzug gegen eine kaškäische Stadt genannt wird.[22] Man kann daraus schließen, daß Katapa etwa nördlich von Zippalanda, in Richtung der kaškäischen Grenze gesucht werden muß, obgleich keine direkten Zeugnisse von seiner Bedrohung mit dem feindlichen Angriff vorliegen.

Für eine nördliche Lage spricht auch eine Opferzeremonie für den Wettergott von Nerik während des königlichen Aufenthaltes in Katapa; vgl. das schon erwähnte jh. Textfragment KBo XIII 214 Rs. v?, das wohl auf die Zeiten vor dem König Ḫattušili III. zu datieren ist, als der Zugang zu Nerik den Hethitern verschlossen war. Die erwähnte Opferhandlung in Katapa ist als Substitut einer Zeremonie in Nerik zu verstehen. Man kann also annehmen, daß Katapa die letzte wichtige hethitische Stadt vor der kaškäischen Grenze auf dem Weg von Ḫattuša nach Nerik, d.h. in nördliche Richtung gewesen ist[23], daher wurde es als Ort der Opferzeremonie für den Wettergott von Nerik ausgewählt.

Die hier vorgelegten Argumente scheinen für eine Lokalisierung Katapas etwa NNW von Alacahöyük, ungefähr halbwegs von Sungurlu nach Çorum zu sprechen.

21 Dupl. KUB XIX 19 Rs. Zu diesen Texten vgl. H. Klengel, *MIO* 8 (1961) 15ff.

22 E. von Schuler, *Kaškäer* 28 mit Anm. 124.

23 Zur Lokalisierung von Nerik s. H.G. Güterbock, *JNES* 20 (1961) 93f. (nahe Kargı), J. Yakar - A. Dinçol, *Belleten* 38 (1974) 573ff. (nördlich von der Linie Boyabat-Durağan-Vezirköprü). Vgl. auch Ph.H.J. Houwink ten Cate, *FsLaroche* 160f.

4. *Die übrigen Ortsnamen in KBo XVI 78*

Im Gegensatz zu Zippalanda und Katapa gehören Takašta, Šanaḫḫuitta, Tapikka, Taptiga und Karaḫna zum geographischen Kreis der Urkunden von Maşathöyük und sind folglich nordöstlich bzw. östlich von Alacahöyük zu suchen.[24] Weder die Briefe von Maşathöyük noch die Texte von Ḫattuša enthalten ausreichende Angaben, um die Lage dieser Orte genauer zu bestimmen. Trotz allen Bemühungen bietet auch eine identifizierung von Maşathöyük selbst Schwierigkeiten. Wie schon oben bemerkt (s. Anm. 2), wird die von S. Alp vorgeschlagene Gleichsetzung dieses Ortes mit Tapikka[25] von J. Yakar und Ph.H.J. Houwink ten Cate in Zweifel gezogen.[26]

Infolge der Zuordnung von KBo XVI 78 dem Zippalanda-Textkorpus und der evtl. Gleichsetzung von Zippalanda mit Alacahöyük bedürfen bisherige Vorschläge zur Lokalisierung der besagten Orten einer Korrektur, deren Wert übrigens eher gering ist. Vor allem sind jene Städte in einer gemäßigten, d.h. nicht zu großen Entfernung von Alacahöyük zu suchen. So lag Takašta wohl nicht auf der Ebene von Merzifon[27], sondern etwa nordöstlich von Çorum oder in der Gegend von Mecitözü. Zur Lokalisierung von Šanaḫḫuitta gibt es evtl. einen neuen Anhaltspunkt, und zwar ist es bemerkenswert, daß im Kult von Zippalanda der Verwalter von Šanaḫḫuitta neben dem Verwalter von Ankuwa gelegentlich auftritt.[28] Unter der Voraussetzung, daß Ankuwa südlich von Zippalanda scil. von Alacahöyük lag, erscheint es möglich, Šanaḫḫuitta in entgegengesetzter Richtung, also ungefähr nördlich oder NNO von Alacahöyük, in der Gegend südwärts von Çorum zu lokalisieren.

Karaḫna muß wohl südwestlich von Ortaköy gesucht werden. Was Taptiga betrifft, so geben die bisher bekannten Belegstellen für die Lage dieser Stadt nichts Handgreifliches her.

[24] S. zu einzelnen Städten A. Ünal, *THeth* 3, Kap. VIII s.v., G.F. del Monte - J. Tischler, *RGTC* 6, s.v., und S. Alp, *HBM* 17f. (Karaḫna), 36 (Šanaḫḫuitta), 40ff. (Takašta), 42f. (Tapikka) und 43f. (Taptiga). Zu Karaḫna s. noch H. Otten - W. Röllig, *RlA* V 403 und S. Alp, *FsBittel* 43ff.

[25] S. Alp, *Belleten* 41 (1977) 637ff. und *FsLaroche* 29ff.; vgl. auch ders., *HBM* 42f.

[26] J. Yakar, *MDOG* 112 (1980) 75ff.; Ph.H.J. Houwink ten Cate, in D.J.W. Meijer (Hrsg.), *Natural Phenomena*, Anm. 17 auf S. 133ff.

[27] Vgl. dazu A. Ünal, *THeth* 3, 213f. (mit Literatur), ferner auch S. Alp, *HBM* 40ff., wo eine südlichere Lage dieser Stadt erwägt wird.

[28] KBo XI 50 Vs. ii 6' (erg.), KUB XLI 46 Vs. ii 10', Bo 2689 Rs. v 18'.

EARLY TRAVELLERS TO BOĞAZKÖY

JOHAN DE ROOS

It is perhaps not generally known that my highly esteemed teacher Philo Houwink ten Cate, to whom I owe so much, is a great lover of the history of Hittitology. It is for this reason that my modest contribution on the occasion of his sixty-fifth birthday will be devoted to this subject.

We know that the study of the then unknown Hittite culture began with Charles Texier's discovery on July 28, 1834 of the architectural and artistic remains of 'Pteria', the city that would later come to be known as the Hittite capital Ḫattuša. His three-volume account[1] of various journeys to the area was published four years after William J. Hamilton's 1835 visit to Ḫattuša ('Tavium'). Hamilton's account of his own travels appeared in 1842.[2]

Both travellers also visited and described Yazılıkaya. It is no secret that in later years Texier was widely criticized for the lack of precision displayed by his drawings.[3] However, that does not alter the fact that for many years those drawings were considered the most authoritative representation of what was to be seen there. G. Perrot is also mild in his judgement of the work of his countryman:[4] "Voulant donner tout au moins une idée approximative de certains aspects et de certains détails que ne fourniraient ni nos esquisses ni nos clichés, nous devons donc recourir quelquefois aux planches de Texier, le premier voyageur qui ait visité Boghaz-Keui et le seul qui jusqu'à nous ait entrepris d'en représenter les monuments." But this is immediately followed by criticism: "Le malheur c'est qu'il n'avait pas le respect du vrai, la sainte passion de l'exactitude." Hamilton also comes in for criticism from Perrot, but this takes quite a different form: "Hamilton parcourait l'Asie Mineure en même temps que Texier en 1835 et 1836. Il était plus soigneux et plus exact,

[1] Ch. Texier, Description de l'Asie Mineure I-III, 1839-1842.

[2] William J. Hamilton, *Researches in Asia Minor, Pontus and Armenia. With some account of their Antiquities and Geology*. In two volumes, 1842 (1984^2).

[3] For example, E. Meyer (*Reich und Kultur der Chetiter* (Berlin 1914), 127): "... mit prächtigen Tafeln, die aber in einzeln sehr unzuverlässig sind ..." and "... auch in der Zeichnung der Monumente nicht selten die Phantasie ganz frei schalten lassen." Meyer himself provides one of the most comprehensive historical surveys of the discovery of the Hittites up until the appearance in 1975 of the magnificent work *Das Hethitische Felsheiligtum Yazılıkaya* (K. Bittel, ed.), a highly accurate history of the rocky sanctuary.

[4] G. Perrot/Ch. Chipiez, *Histoire de l'Art dans l'Antiquité IV, Judée, Sardaigne, Syrie, Cappadoce*, 1887, 597.

comme le prouvent les copies qu'il a données de 435 inscriptions, mais il ne savait pas dessiner."[5]

It is a little-known fact that another Englishman, James Brant, the consul at Erzurum, visited Boğazköy in the same year as Hamilton, though independent of him. Brant was apparently acquainted with Texier's drawings as far back as 1836, since he mentions them in the *Journal of the Royal Geographical Society* (July 1836, 218): "Monsieur Texier has made some beautiful drawings from these interesting remains, but they give you an idea of a greater degree of preservation than the figures are in."

We may also assume that Brant knew of the lecture which Texier delivered in 1835, during which the drawings were exhibited, and which was published in the *Journal des Savants* Année 1835, 368-376.[6] As early as 1837 Hamilton himself responded to Texier's discoveries in the above mentioned journal, in een article in which he defended the identification of Ḫattuša with ancient Tavium.[7] It is clear from the two books that the authors were regularly in touch with one another. On the basis of the details of their journeys, it is unlikely that either Hamilton or Brant was prompted to set off on his quest by the discoveries of Texier, a suggestion which has recently been put forward by E. Masson.[8] Each of the nineteenth-century travellers had his own reasons for visiting Anatolia, alongside their shared hope of discovering Greek and Roman antiquities. In the case of Hamilton, an amateur geographer and geologist, these branches of science clearly took pride of place. Texier, an architect by profession, was acting on behalf of the French government, who hoped he would return with written documents of scientific interest, particularly for the history of the region. Brant, as we know, was the British consul in Erzurum.

Quite different motives were entertained, some thirty years after Texier, by another traveller to the interior of Anatolia, one whose name is often undeservedly absent in the later literature. I am referring to the Turkish-born English Protestant missionary Henry J. van Lennep, who worked in the Levant from 1840 on. He subsequently spent 10 years in Constantinople, seven years in the interior, and a total of 13 years in Smyrna. It is obvious from the composition of the party – which consisted of his 10-year-old son, a cousin with his wife, an American friend who was travelling for his health, and an Armenian Protestant from Tocat – that Mr. van Lennep's journey in 1864 was not prompted by any urge to serve the world of science. After a detailed

[5] O.c. 598 note 1.

[6] See K. Bittel (ed.), *Yazılıkaya*[2] 13 with note 8.

[7] "Observations on the position of Tavium." This information, and the material on James Brant were provided by Ms. M. van der Waal, who in 1992 dedicated her thesis at Utrecht University to the rediscovery of the Hittites.

[8] "Alertés par les fruits de ces explorations, d'autres érudits-voyageurs ne tardèrent pas à prendre leur bâton de pélerin avec l'espoir de déceler quelques vestiges antiques dans le sol anatolien. C'est ainsi que la chance allait sourire au brittannique William John Hamilton dès 1836, avec la découverte des ruines de Alaca Höyük" etc. (*Les Hittites. Les dossiers d'archéologie* 193 (1994) 4).

description of the route from Yozgat to Boğazköy, which made a deep impression on him, Van Lennep gives us this account of his first view of ancient Ḫattuša: "As we came out of the Boghaz we landed upon a plateau occupying the left bank of the stream, where lie the remains of the Great Temple[9] described by Texier and of which Hamilton has given a very good plan.[10] A minute examination enabled us to find only unimportant errors, referring solely to the internal communications existing between the different apartments. It must have been a grand edifice, and its high position, with a slightly inclined and extensive square in front, must have greatly heightened the effect.[11]

It is a pity that a combination of modesty and lack of time prevented Van Lennep from describing and depicting the rest of the city with the same degree of accuracy that he bestowed on Yazılıkaya. "But they (i.e., the ruins. J. de R.) have been faithfully described by others, and particularly by Mr. Texier, who has thrown into the inquiry so much learning and acuteness, that I feel incapable of adding anything to what has already been published upon the subject. I shall, therefore, merely state such items as have been omitted by my learned predecessors; for these remains are, perhaps, the most remarkable and important that occur in the whole Peninsula of Asia Minor."[12] Because Van Lennep's visit to Boğazköy lasted only from the afternoon of August 3 to the following afternoon, when he departed for Alaca, he spent no more than half a day at Yazılıkaya. Nonetheless, the drawings that he did there are quite faithful representations, while his interpretation is remarkable.

Texier originally saw the main representation in the present Chamber A as the portrayal of a meeting between Amazons and Paphlagonians. In a

[9] Correctly identified by Texier and Hamilton as a temple, this later Temple I was for many years referred to as a palace. This designation was first employed in 1860 by Barth (see note 10) on p. 48: "Zuerst will ich bemerken, dass es wohl unzweifelhaft ein Palast ist oder vielmehr ein Palast-Tempel, wie wir solche Gebäude in Theben mehrfach finden. Aber im Ganzen hat diess Gebäude die grösste Ähnlichkeit im Grundplan mit dem Nordwest-Palast im Nimrod, während es auch nicht die geringste Ähnlichkeit mit einem Tempel hat." Elsewhere, Barth is highly critical of Texier. While Perrot reproduces Texier's drawing (Pl. VI) in his 1887 work *L'Histoire de l'art* (see note 4), the caption reads: "Vue des restes du palais de Boghaz-Keui." On p. 699 he, like Barth, also includes Barth's plan, which he designates as "Plan du Palais, according to Barth." Texier himself employed the caption: "Temple d'Anaïtis à Pterium." In *The Land of the Hittites* (London 1910) 207 J. Garstang continues to refer to the Lower Palace, although he adds: " ... and whether to be identified as palace or as a temple it presents an interesting study ... ", etc. In 1914 E. Meyer was emphatic in his use of the designation 'palace': "Diese Bauten sind wohl nicht Tempel, wie Puchstein meinte, sondern Paläste, die auch einen Kultraum enthielten, wie in Assyrien, auf Kreta und sonst." (*Reich und Kuiltur der Chetiter*, 20, 21. With fig. 8: "Grundriß des größten Palastes von Boghazkiöi").

[10] This remark shows that Van Lennep was not acquainted with the travel account of H. Barth, who in 1860 published a much more accurate plan: Dr. H. Barth's *Reise von Trapezunt durch die nördliche Hälfte Klein-Asiens nach Skutari im Herbst 1858*, 48. Barth described Yazılıkaya separately in the Monatsbericht der Berliner Akademie der Wissenschaften in February 1859.

[11] Rev. Henry J. van Lennep, *Travels in Little-Known Parts of Asia Minor in Two Volumes*, 1870. This passage appears in Vol. II, Ch. XIX, 109).

[12] O.c. 110-111.

summary of the original edition which appeared in 1862 (together with alterations and additions[13]), Texier leaves it to his readers to decide whether the event was primarily of historical, political or religious significance, but says that in any case it is not the work of the peoples who inhabited Western Asia. He asks himself whether it might be the goddess Anaïtis who is portrayed here, arriving from the East upon the back of a lion, and accepting gifts from the Cappadocians.[14] Hamilton saw in the representation a peace treaty between the kings of Persia and Lydia, while Barth, who visited the place on November 23, 1858 (when, due to the cold, he was unable to execute more than a few drawings), judged it to be the peace and marriage treaty between Cyaxares and Alyattes. Van Lennep's description of Yazılıkaya comes closest to the true meaning of the reliefs, and his observations concerning the execution of the reliefs are in general extremely detailed and precise. For example, he describes the central scene in Chamber A as follows: "It evidently represents the meeting of a man and a woman, each of whom is followed by a long train of attendants, mostly of his or her own sex, the chief figures are represented larger than the rest, which is in accordance with both Assyrian and Egyptian custom. The King stands on what seem to be men with pointed caps, bending their heads forward while he stands upon their necks; the Queen and her son (?) stand upon panthers or leopards. Texier has figured a unicorn by the side of each; I did not succeed in making out what it was ... It is also the converging point toward which all the other figures turn their faces."[15]

It is worth noting that Texier, Hamilton and Barth were actually at a disadvantage here: being better acquainted with the history of the Near East than Van Lennep, they erroneously interpreted the reliefs as the portrayal of an historical event.

As regards the other reliefs, Van Lennep displays a similar attention to detail. He notes that after Texier's visit the twelve-god relief was excavated: "I have reproduced with great care a sculpture which appears to have been uncovered since Texier's visit, occupying the left side of the passage, and nearly opposite to the last figures. It is by far the best preserved of these bas-reliefs, and quite uninjured, having apparently been but recently uncovered from the earth which hid it, being very low down. I was informed by our guide that it was uncovered by a Frank, who was taking photographs, and whom I suppose to be Mr. Perrot, a young Orientalist of great merit."[16] Perrot was

[13] *Asie Mineure. Description géographique, historique et archéologique des provinces et des villes de la Chersonèse d'Asie* par Charles Texier, de l' Institut, 1862.

[14] O.c. 614. In this later edition, too, Texier is further away from fact in his descriptions on pp. 611-616 than Van Lennep.

[15] Van Lennep. *Travels II*, 119.

[16] O.c. 123. The excavation and the photography were carried out on the eight-month journey through Turkey which Perrot undertook in 1861 at the request of the French Ministry of State. The photographer was Jules Delbet, "docteur en médicine de la Faculté de Paris." As soon as the plans for the trip began to take definite shape, he took responsibility for all the photography and, in Perrot's words, "s'improvisait, en trois semaines, l'émule des Baldus et des Bisson."

indeed in Boğazköy from November 7-15, 1861, and spent each morning in Yazılıkaya, " ... les mystérieux sanctuaires des cultes évanouis sans laisser de trace dans l'histoire."[17] The reason Van Lennep decided to publish the photographs was that Texier's drawings were, in his words, more perfect than the originals, which were quite severely damaged and created quite a different impression. Van Lennep's interpretation of the main relief is also quite close to the truth, as noted above, even though he sees Cupid following his mother Venus or Astarte, having mistakenly identified an embryo in the hieroglyph of Sarruma. It is surprising that the self-effacing Van Lennep supported Texier's ingenious hypothesis – the scene represents the introduction into Phrygia of the veneration of Astarte – as this is only one of a number of possible explanations which Texier puts forward, one which, moreover, takes the form of a question. Van Lennep then journeyed on to Eyuk[18], which he describes in considerable detail.

As we have seen, Van Lennep receives very little mention in the older literature. Perrot does refer to him back in 1864 (before Van Lennep's journey) in connection with the latter's view that there is nothing Christian about the 'kisil-bachi' and their leader Hadji Bektach, and that they are rather the heirs to an ancient pagan cult [19].

In the *Histoire de l'Art* [20] Van Lennep is mentioned by Perrot/Chipiez in relation to Aladja Euiuk:[21] "Nous ne ferons donc guère ici que résumer les résultats de nos propres recherches que reproduire les images données par nous de ces sculptures qui, jusqu'au moment où a paru notre ouvrage, étaient, à vrai dire, tout à fait inconnues." Note 1 reads: "Les bas-reliefs d'Euiuk ont été décrits d'une manière assez satisfaisante dans un ouvrage postérieur au nôtre[22], mais qui mérite d'être lu, quoique l'auteur ne fût pas archéologue de profession. Il a pour titre: "Travels in little-known Parts of Asia Minor", etc., par H. J. van Lennep, 1870. Les chapitres XIX et XX du second volume sont consacrés à Boghaz-Keui et Euiuk. Ils renferment plusieurs croquis, ceux-ci, quoique à petite échelle, donnant une idée assez exacte des monuments." But where Perrot refers to Yazılıkaya, on p. 596 of the *Histoire de l'Art*, and where he

The third member of the company was the architect E. Guillaume (Georges Perrot, *Souvenirs d'un voyage en Asie Mineure*, 1864, 2). The scientific account of the journey appeared in 1872 in two volumes: *Exploration archéologique de la Galatie et de la Bithynie, d'une partie de la Mysie, de la Phrygie, de la Cappadoce et du Pont exécutée en 1861 et publiée sous les auspices du Ministère de l'institution publique par Messrs. G. Perrot, E. Guillaume, et J. Delbet.*

[17] G. Perrot, *Souvenirs*, 404.

[18] The spelling employed by the various authors has been respected.

[19] *Souvenirs*, 429: "La curiosité de M. Van Lennep, missionaire protestant établi bien des années à Siwas, avait été piquée par cet énigme."

[20] See note 4.

[21] Page 659. From now on, I will refer to Perrot as the author.

[22] In the English translation of 1890, this enigmatic reference was altered to read "in a recent work." In his *Souvenirs* of 1864 (p. 420) Perrot says with reference to the remains: "... les ruines intéressantes, à peine entrevues par MM. Hamilton et Barth." At that time, of course, no mention of Van Lennep's name could have been made.

makes mention of the fact that he was able to add a great many details which his predecessors Texier, Hamilton and Barth had not noticed, Van Lennep could and should have been mentioned.

Similarly, it is remarkable that J. Garstang refers to Van Lennep exclusively in connection with Eyuk[23] and that, although he deals with Yazılıkaya in great detail, he does not mention Van Lennep's name alongside those of Perrot/Chipiez, Ramsay, and Hamilton [24]. Nationality cannot have played a role here, as both Garstang and Van Lennep were British.

There is, however, some indication of a degree of rivalry among the French, German and English scholars, reflected in a remark by Perrot about A.H. Sayce. He refers to the latter's oft-repeated claim – later invariably quoted by others – that he was the first to actually identify the Hittites as the makers of the artistic works discovered in Syria and Anatolia.[25] The story is as follows.

On May 2, 1876 Sayce delivered a lecture for the Society of Biblical Archaeology on The Hamathite Inscriptions[26], in the course of which he acknowledged that Dr. Ward had demonstrated that the inscriptions must be read from the direction in which the characters are looking, i.e., the first line from right to left and the rest in boustrophedonic fashion.[27] On p. 25 he says that he believes he has identified certain characters as either the name of Hamath or that of the Hittites. There follows, on p. 27, an interesting remark: "The probability then is that the North-Syrian inventors of these Hamathite characters did not speak a Semitic or inflectional tongue. Who the inventors were it is of course impossible to determine with certainty, but it is extremely likely that they belonged to the great Hittite race." Four years later, in a second lecture for that same Society on July 6, 1880, Sayce said that thanks to the discovery of the "capital of the ancient Hittites, Carchemish", three statements proved to be correct[28]:

1. The 'Hamathite' inscriptions are Hittite.
2. Hieroglyphics were invented by the Hittites.
3. There was an early link between Hama and the Hittites.

[23] *The Land of the Hittites* (1910) 243: "Here the ruins which we now know to be Hittite were lighted upon by Hamilton 'the prince of travellers" in 1835; subsequently they were visited by Barth and Van Lennep. The account of them given by the last-named, who was for thirty years a missionary in Turkey, was the first attempt to hand down a reliable and complete description, accompanied by a rough plan of a building and sketches of the sculptures which adorned its portico."

[24] O.c. 229[3].

[25] For Perrot's remark, see the conclusion of this article.

[26] Published in the Transactions of this Society (*TSBA*) V - 1, 1876(-1877), 22-32.

[27] Thus not Sayce's discovery, as maintained by L. Delaporte, *Les Hittites*, 1936, 6.

[28] "The Monuments of the Hittites" in *TSBA* VII, 1880-1882.

One of these conclusions was launched independent of Sayce by the Rev. W. Wright, as Sayce recounts.[29] In 1872 Wright attributed the texts to the Hittites, as he himself says: "It was only in 1872 that I drew attention to the Hamah inscriptions and forenamed them the Hittite remains. My conclusions received no support at first, but they are now generally admitted."[30]

As regards Sayce's discovery, Wright says:[31] "In 1872 when sending casts of the Hamah inscriptions to England, I suggested that they were Hittite remains. As Captain Burton[32] says, my theory was received, when first suggested, "magno cum risu". The theory is now accepted by most scholars who have a claim to be heard on such subjects. Prof. Sayce ... arrived subsequently at the same conclusion without having seen my article." As regards the question of whether Sayce was indeed unaware of Wright's article, which appeared in 1874, A. E. Cowley does not take a stand:[33] "Wright claims to have been the first (in the *British and Foreign Evangelian Review* 1874) to apply the name, but it was Sayce who first (in *TSBA*) 1876) gave it currency. It did not meet with immediate acceptance and even to-day one uses it with a half-apology." And a little later: "Wright's or Sayce's conjecture was thus amply confirmed."[34]

In 1888 Sayce himself describes his discovery in *The Hittites. The Story of a Forgotten Empire*, a work that would later be reprinted many times over. In the foreword we read: "Already a large and increasing literature has been devoted to them. The foundation stone, which was laid by my paper 'On the Monuments of the Hittites' in 1880,[35] has been crowned with a stately edifice in Dr. Wright's *Empire of the Hittites*, the second edition of which appeared in 1886, and in the fourth volume of the magnificent work of Prof. Perrot and M. Chipiez, *L'Histoire de l'Art dans l'Antiquité*, published at Paris a year ago." And further on: "What was the origin of this art, or who were the people it commemorated, was a matter of uncertainty. A few weeks, however, before my visit to the Pass of Karabel, I announced (note: in the *Academy* of Aug. 18th. 1879) that I had come to the conclusion that the art was Hittite, and that the hieroglyphics accompanying the figure at Karabel would turn out, when carefully examined, to be Hittite also. Let us now see how I had arrived at it."[36] And on p. 59: "Dr. Wright at once suggested that they (the stones from Hama. J. de R.) were the work of the Hittites, and that they were memorials of

29 Page 248: "Among these suggestions was one which I have since learned had been independently started by the Rev. William Wright and which was confirmed almost immediately afterwards by the discovery of the site of Carchemish, the capital of the ancient Hittites, by Messrs Skene and George Smith."

30 Preface of the first edition of W. Wright's *The Empire of the Hittites*, 1884.

31 O.c., 2nd edition, 1886, 124.

32 In 1872 Burton, consul in Damascus, published the stones from Hama in *Unexplored Syria I*, 335, figs. 3 and 4.

33 1918 *Schweich Lectures*, 'The Hittites' [1920], 5.

34 O.c. 7.

35 According to the original, the correct title is "The Monuments of the Hittites."

36 *The Hittites*, 56.

Hittite writing. But his suggestion was buried in the pages of a periodical better known to theologians than to Orientalists, and the world agreed to call the writing by the name of Hamathite ..." And further on: "In 1876, two years after the publication of Dr. Wright's article, of which I had never heard at the time, I read a Paper on the Hamathite inscriptions before the Society of Biblical Archaeology." There, as we have seen, Sayce attributes the system of writing to the Hittites.

Making no further mention of Perrot, although he does refer to Ward, Ritter and Davis, Sayce launches on pp. 62 and 65 the following statement: "Suddenly the truth flashed upon me (i.e., in the summer of 1879. J. de R.). This peculiar kind of dress was the same as that which distinguished the sculptures of Karabel, of Ghiaur-kalesi and of Kappadokia. In all alike we had the same characteristic features, the same head-dresses and shoes, the same tunics, the same clumsy massiveness of design and characteristic attitude. The figures carved upon the rocks of Karabel and Kappadokia must be memorials of Hittite art."

Thus it is precisely in the field of art that Perrot is sold short, although Sayce is, of course, to be credited with the discovery that the combination of writing and art was Hittite. Sayce acknowledges that Perrot spotted the remarkable resemblance between, for example, the Karabel sculptures and Cappadocian rock sculptures.[37] But the fact that this resemblance had been oberved by Perrot some 18 years earlier was either unknown to Sayce or was omitted because he considered it unimportant. It does not seem likely that he was unaware of Perrot's statements, since in a combined review of Sayce's *Monuments of the Hittites* (*TSBA* VII, 1880-1882) and Wright's *The Empire of the Hittites* (2nd ed., 1886) Perrot places special emphasis on his own observations. [38] He asks himself why it had not been suggested much earlier that the works of art could be explained by the significant role which one of those peoples had played in Asia Minor, a people whose influence – thanks to the superiority of its culture – extended well beyond its own borders. It is on the day after his return from a journey through Asia Minor, where the best-preserved monuments are to be found, that he asked himself that question – the first person, as he himself says, to do so. In 1870 he drew up a list of the rock reliefs in Asia Minor, together with the characteristics which they had in common, thus sketching the outlines of an art "which is typical of the peninsula and far removed from the accomplishments of Greek genius."[39]

Without explicitly mentioning Sayce, who, as we know in 1880 had named Carchemish as the capital of the ancient Hittites, Perrot refutes this

[37] Idem.

[38] G. Perrot, "Une civilisation retrouvée. Les Hétéens, leur écriture et leur art." In: *Revue des deux mondes*, Tome LXXVI (1886) 303-342. The following on pp. 304 and 305.

[39] Recorded in "L'Art de l'Asie Mineure, ses origines, son influence" (Mémoire lu à l'Académie des inscriptions le 4 avril 1873), 1875.

possibility and in two magnificent sentences bestows the honour on Boğazköy[40]: "Ce n'est pas de Gargamich que l'on a jamais pu gouverner l'Asie Mineure qui en est séparée par toute l'épaisseur de l'Amanus et du Taurus, mais il ne répugne point d'admettre que, pendant deux ou trois siècles, la ville la plus importante de cette contrée, la seule même qui meritât ce nom, ait été celle dont la vaste et puissante enceinte couronne encore les hauteurs voisines du village de Boghaz-Keui. La Troie de M. Schliemann n'est en comparaison, qu'une pauvre bourgade; à Boghaz-Keui, devant ces murs massifs qui ont plusieurs kilomètres de développement, en face de ces grands bas-reliefs où figurent les dieux et les rois de la cité, ses prêtres et ses défenseurs, on devine une vraie capitale."

Thus it was Perrot, who had concentrated his attention on Anatolia - rather than Sayce, who in the light of the early discoveries and the Biblical references to the Hittites, focused on Syria – who discovered the site of the capital of the Hittites. It was understandably galling to Perrot that Sayce also claimed for himself the discovery of the uniformity of the works of art, and this even surfaces in the odd veiled allusion. In the *Histoire de l'Art Tome III, Phénicie-Cypre*, 1885, 448, note 2, Perrot says somewhat cautiously what he would later repeat in more explicit terms: "J'ai peut-être été le premier à essayer d'indiquer les caractères communs qui distinguent les monuments que l'on appelle aujourd'hui Hittites." And in 1887 he says, with considerably more conviction:[41] "Sous cette réserve, nous persistons à croire que nous ne nous sommes pas trompé quand, il y a vingt ans, au retour de notre voyage d'Asie Mineure, nous avons, pour la première fois, rapprochés les uns des autres ces monuments que séparent de si grandes distances. La comparaison que nous avions instituée, d'autres l'ont reprise et poursuivie;" etc.

Contrary to the views generally expressed in the literature, it was Georges Perrot who gave the Hittites their rightful place in art history.

In conclusion, I would like to address to Philo Houwink ten Cate, on the occasion of his sixty-fifth birthday, the wish originally intended for the 'Lord of the offering': *ANA* EN SÍSKUR EGIR-*pa* TI-*tar ḫaddulātar innarau̯u̯atar* MU.ḪI.A GÍD.DA IGI.ḪI.A-*u̯aš uškii̯au̯u̯ar* GÚ-*tar šarā appātarra ŠA* EGIR UD-*MI pīški* (KBo 15.25 + ABoT 20 Obv. 10f.).

[40] On p. 339 of the work given in note 38.
[41] *Histoire de l'Art, Tome IV, Judée etc.*, 775 f.

THE TOPONYMS TIWA AND TAWA

ITAMAR SINGER

Within the broad spectrum of his interests, one of Professor Houwink ten Cate's favorite subjects of study has been the Hittite Royal Prayers. In a seminal article[1] he delineated the main characteristics and the basic spirit of this literary genre, tracing its development from the Early Hittite Empire[2] to the age of Ḫattušili and Puduḫepa.[3] More specifically, he dealt with two prayers of king Muwatalli, which are considered to be among the finest of their kind. Together with Folke Josephson he presented a full edition of CTH 382, centered on the Storm-god and the gods of Kummanni.[4] In the same year he devoted a concise article to the redactional history of CTH 381, a prayer addressed to the Stormgod *piḫaššašši-*.[5] A few years later, as a young Hittitology student of Professor Otten in Marburg, I had the rewarding opportunity of first meeting Philo in Amsterdam. I enjoyed his renowned hospitality and discussed with him this exceptional prayer, one of the first texts to arouse my interest in Hittite religion and Anatolian historical geography.[6] I dedicate these preliminary remarks on an intriguing geographical variant in CTH 381 to our continuing friendship and shared interest in the prayers of Muwatalli.

CTH 381 has come down to us in two main manuscripts (A = KUB VI 45+ and B = KUB VI 46) and a small fragment of a third copy (C = KUB XII 35) which is closer to A. As convincingly demonstrated by Professor Houwink ten Cate, B is probably a dictated first draft, while A is a corrected and revised

[1] "Hittite Royal Prayers", *Numen* 16 (1969) 81-98.

[2] An apt term referring to the generations immediately preceding Šuppiluliuma I, that was introduced by Professor Houwink ten Cate in his paradigmatic monograph *The Records of the Early Hittite Empire* (c. 1450-1380 B.C.), Istanbul 1970.

[3] Presently, there are no prayers conclusively attributed to the successors of Ḫattušili, although some fragments of prayers dedicated to the Sun-goddess of Arinna (such as KBo XII 58) may have been composed in the age of Tutḫaliya IV. See R. Lebrun, *Hymnes* 422.

[4] "Muwatallis' Prayer to the Storm-god of Kummanni (KBo XI 1)", *RHA* 25 (1968) 101-140.

[5] "Muwatallis' 'Prayer to be Spoken in an Emergency,' An Essay in Textual Criticism,", *JNES* 27 (1968) 204-208.

[6] I studied the list of gods in this prayer in my M.A. thesis, the essence of which was published as "Hittites and Hattians in Anatolia at the Beginning of the Second Millennium B.C.", *JIES* 9 (1981) 119-134.

edition of the prayer.[7] The editorial contribution of A consists of the correction of many errors, a few stylistic changes, and the translation of a Luwian gloss into Hittite.[8] As often happens in such cases, the scribe, while correcting the flaws of the first draft, introduced a few errors of his own. In addition to these revisions of linguistic character, the scribe of A also introduced a major emendation in the general layout of the text; namely, he moved the long list of gods and their cult centres from the end of the text (after the bread offerings) to immediately after the invocation of the great gods of Ḫatti and the supplication to Šeri, the sacred bull of the Stormgod, to transmit truthfully the words of the prayer (B ii 2-iii 40 = A i 37-iii 3).

Except for spelling variants, differing division lines and the correction of a few errors,[9] the list of deities is identical in both versions. There is one notable exception, however, which has received almost no attention in treatments of the list to date. In the second entry, immediately following the deities of Arinna, B ii 7 ^{URU}*Ti-wa* is replaced in A i 40 by ^{URU}*Ša-mu-ḫa*.[10] The full section reads:

> ^{d}U ḪI.ḪI ^{d}*Ḫé-pát* ^{URU}*Ša-mu-ḫa* (written over correction in B)
> DINGIR.LÚ^{MEŠ} DINGIR.MUNUS^{MEŠ} ḪUR.SAG^{MEŠ} ÍD^{MEŠ} *ŠA* ^{URU}*Ti-wa* (A: *Ša-mu-ḫa*)
> Stormgod *piḫaššašši-* (ḪI.ḪI), Ḫebat of Šamuḫa, gods (and) goddesses, mountains (and) rivers of (the city) Tiwa (A: Šamuḫa)

Logically, A, the "revised edition", should have the more accurate version, and the section should enumerate deities of Šamuḫa. However, the two names are entirely different, and this cannot be regarded merely as a correction of an error in B. Besides, the scribe of B also seems to have hesitated with the city of Ḫebat, finally deciding in favour of the more familiar Šamuḫa. Perhaps here too he originally wrote Tiwa and then corrected it to the more familiar Šamuḫa.

A look at the following entries may show that, in fact, the draft version B fits better the general context. The next section, following a division line, lists the divinities of the "Palace of the Grandfather" (É.GAL *ḫuḫḫaš*). And then we are again confronted, after a division line, with the gods of Šamuḫa, only this

7 *JNES* 27 (1968) 208. I still cannot explain why -AT in ^{d}*BE-E-LA-AT A-IA-*(*AK-*)*KI* is in both versions inserted above the line (A i 44 = B ii 10). Did the scribe of A repeat the mistake of B, or was the text corrected in both versions after their completion? The second possibility would imply that the "revised edition" A was written immediately after the draft B.

8 B iv 53 :*ḫu-u-wa-ia-al-li* ^{d}UTU-*i* is replaced by *ku-ut-ru-i* ^{d}UTU-*i*, "witnessing Sungod".

9 B ii 63 ^{URU}Šuwanzipa is corrected in A ii 23 to ^{URU}Šuwanzana. On the other hand, A repeats the erroneous form *La-u-wa-an-a*$^{!}$*-ti-ia* , with A instead of ZA (A i 76 = B ii 41).

10 J. Garstang and O. R. Gurney, *Geogr.* 116, ignores the variant; Lebrun, *Hymnes* 259, notes the variant (correct *Té* into *Ti*) with no commentary. The place-name Tiwa is not recorded in G. F. del Monte, *RGTC* 6 and *RGTC* 6/2 (*Supplément*).

time the two versions agree on the name of the city. This section does indeed include some prominent deities of the well-known cult centre of Šamuḫa, such as Ištar of the Fields and Apara.[11]

Unless we assume that the deities of Šamuḫa cover three consecutive entries divided by separation lines, including the middle section of the "Palace of the Grandfather", we must conclude that the second section originally listed the deities of an otherwise unknown city of Tiwa. This seems to be a case where, as customary in biblical textual criticism, the *lectio difficilior* should be preferred. Why would the scribe of A change the name of this city into Šamuḫa? I suggest that this is due to the influence of Ḫebat of Šamuḫa mentioned at the beginning of the line. At any rate, I would not exclude the possibility that Tiwa, which had a cult of Ḫebat of Šamuḫa, was located in the region of Šamuḫa, and this may have increased the confusion. Šamuḫa rose to a very prominent position in the New Kingdom, and its local Ištar climbed to the zenith of the national pantheon, especially from the reign of Muršili II on.[12]

Judging by its prominent position in the list, second only to Arinna, Tiwa must have been an important place, despite its anonymity. One could question the significance of order in the list, but it is unlikely that such a solemn appeal to all the gods of the kingdom would be compiled at random in both the draft and the revised version. Gurney observed that "the order in which the cities occur evidently depends partly on the status of the deities worshipped in them and partly on their geographical situation, and it is not easy in any given instance to determine which of these considerations has been decisive."[13]

That the seat of the Sungoddess of Arinna should open the list is to be expected. In their clerical role the Hittite kings are first and foremost priests of this great goddess who provides legitimacy to their rule. It would be logical to assume that the second entry in the list, that of Tiwa, would be connected somehow to the person of the ruling king. This may be supported by the third entry in the list, the "Palace of the Grandfather", which in this context can only refer to Šuppiluliuma, the great figure of the ruling dynasty. Next follow Šamuḫa and Katapa, with Ḫatti/Ḫattuša occupying a mere sixth place. This may already reflect the transfer of the political centre of gravity to the south.

As indicated above, the place name Tiwa is *hapax legomenon*, although the names of several places begin with *Tiwa-*: Tiwaliya, Tiwalwaliya, Tiwanzana, Tiwara, Tiwataša.[14] A connection may be suggested between Tiwa and another isolated name, which has recently turned up in the Bronze Tablet, iv 30: ^{URU}*Ta-a-wa*.[15] This is the place where the treaty between Tuthaliya and Kurunta of Tarḫuntašša was ratified, in the presence of the

[11] For the deities of Šamuḫa, see R. Lebrun, *Samuha* 15ff.

[12] Lebrun, *Samuha* 20; I. Wegner, *AOAT* 36, 160ff.

[13] *Geogr.* 116.

[14] *RGTC* 6, 431f.; *RGTC* 6/2, 171. The last name, and perhaps others as well, may be related to the name of the Luwian Sungod Tiwat. See E. Laroche, *NH* 283.

[15] H. Otten, *StBoT Beih.* 1, 26f.

cream of Hittite aristocracy. Certainly, this must have been a prominent place, despite its absence from other documentation.[16]

Could Tiwa of the Muwatalli Prayer and Tawa of the Bronze Tablet be one and the same place? Phonetically there is hardly any obstacle; *i/e/a* alternations are quite widespread in Anatolian toponomy, in particular in the first syllable: Aštanuwa/Ištanuwa, Kaššiya/Kiššiya, Ka[š]kilušša/Kiškilušša, Liḫzina/Laḫzan, Šapiduwa/Šipiduwa, Tagarama/ Tegarama, Zapišḫuna/ Zipišḫuna, etc.[17] Geographical evidence is lacking since we have no information on the location of either place.

Tiwa/Tawa, if indeed the equation is valid, did not have to be a large town, which would explain its absence from other texts. It could have been some sort of royal estate used for festive occasions. Tiwa is followed in the Muwatalli Prayer by the "Palace of the Grandfather", and towards the end of the list we encounter the gods of the father, the grandfather and the grandmother of His Majesty in connection with the "house/palace of (the city) Gazzimara".[18] This last entry is also a place which occurs in texts only in connection with its palace.[19] Palaces of the Grandfather are also known to have existed in Šamuḫa[20] and in Katapa,[21] two cities which appear in the list considered here as the fourth and the fifth entries, just before Ḫatti/Ḫattuša. The matter deserves more research,[22] but it would seem that the underlying principle dictating the composition of the list, at least its beginning, is the location of leading royal edifices, some of them connected with the dynastic cult. Until further evidence on Tiwa/Tawa turns up we can say nothing on its whereabouts. That it was the venue of the ceremony of signing the treaty with Tarḫuntašša does not necessarily prove a location within the boundaries of that kingdom.[23] A prestigious locality associated with the dynastic tradition would have served ideally the purpose of sanctioning this delicate political accord between two rival branches of the Hittite royal family.[24]

16 *StBoT Beih.* 1, 53; a connection with Tawana/Tawiniya seems improbable.

17 See *RGTC* 6, 563.

18 In B iii 24-28 the deities of the ancestors are included within the entry of the "house of Gazzimara", whereas in A ii 56-59 they are listed as four entries separated by division lines.

19 *RGTC* 6, 205.

20 KUB XII 5 iv 17f.: *INA* URU*Šamuḫa* É *ABI ABI* dUTU*ŠI*; J. Danmanville, *RHA* 70 (1962) 51ff.

21 HT 2 i 2: É.GAL dUTU*ŠI*; i 3: É.GAL *ḫuḫḫaš*. For further references to the Palace of the Grandfather, see A. Archi, *OA* 12 (1973) 211, n. 12, 222.

22 I intend to prepare a full edition of the text, with special emphasis on the list of deities and cult places.

23 There is not much direct evidence on the location where Hittite state treaties were signed. One documented case is the accord between Šuppiluliuma and Niqmaddu of Ugarit which was signed at Alalaḫ (*PRU* IV 50).

24 For the feud between the royal houses of Ḫattuša and Tarḫuntašša and its consequences, see P. Neve, "Ausgrabungen in Boğazköy-Ḫattuša 1986", *AA* 1987, 403f.; Otten, *StBoT Beih.* 1, 4 f.; J.D. Hawkins (forthcoming), The Hieroglyphic Inscription of Chamber 2 of the Sacred Pool Complex (*StBoT Beih.*)("Südburg evidence for Šuppiluliuma II").

THREE TABLETS FROM TELL HAMMĀM ET-TURKMĀN

WILFRED H. VAN SOLDT

The three tablets presented here were found in 1986 during the first season at Tell Hammām et-Turkmān. Since the texts are all of special interest I offer them in a separate article rather than in a comprehensive excavation report where they may escape the attention of philologists.[1] It is with pleasure that I dedicate this paper to my teacher Professor Houwink ten Cate.

1. *A letter from the Old Babylonian period*

HMM 86 - O8[2] (s. Pl. 30) is a letter from the Old Babylonian period which shows many similarities with the letters known from the Mari archives (note, for example, the Amorite personal name Bunuma-Addu, lines 7 and 22) and the Old Assyrian texts (see the commentary). Unfortunately, the tablet is not very well preserved and the text cannot be reconstructed in its entirety.

Excavator's note: "Found in square K 22, on the floor of area 18 level 8. K 22 is a sizeable room in the 'administrative complex'; HMM 86 - O6 was found in a side room of this complex (see below). The context of O8 is earlier than that of O6 by one subphase, but it is also MB II. The text itself may of course be earlier, and may have been forgotten during cleaning-out operations (see also O6, below). The findspot probably does not reflect the original location of the object."

The tablet measures 5 x 3.5 x 2 cm.

Transliteration:

O.1. *a-na* [x x]x-*an-na*
qí-[*b*]*í*-[*ma*]
um-ma ⌈*iq*⌉-*bi*–^{d}⌈i š k u r⌉-*ma*
šum-ma k ù . b a b b a r *a-na* ì . g i š

[1] The character before the 8 is the letter O, not a zero. The excavation report is in preparation by Dr. D.J.W. Meijer and his staff, and will appear in the near future. I thank Dr. Meijer for his information on the find circumstances.

[2] All three tablets were studied by me on the site in June 1986. When I had left the tablets were baked in an oven built by Mr. L.F.H.C. Jacobs of the department of Archaeology of Leiden University. New photos were then prepared which I have used in the preparation of this edition. Unfortunately, no photo was taken of the left edge of this tablet.

5. *ú-ul i-ba-aš-ši šum-ma* 3 A PA N[I$^{?}$ o]
a-na 1 g í n k ù . b a b b a r ì . g i š *iz-za-az* [o]
1 a n š e ^{p}*bu-*[*n*]*u-ma–*^{d}[i š k u r]
ì . g i š *li-*[*ma-al-l*]*i-*⌈*ma*⌉
Lo.E. *ar-ḫi-iš li-ik-š*[*u-dam*]
10. *a-na-ku a-*[*d*]*i re-eš* i [t i$^{?}$]
R. *lu-up-pu-ta-k*[*u*]
ù šum-ma ma-ḫi-ir ì .[g i š ...]
⌈x x-*al*⌉ k ù . b a b b a r *i-ba-aš-š*[*i*]
⌈x⌉[x x]x 1,0 š e-*im*
15. ⌈x⌉ *šu-*[o]-⌈x⌉-ZI-KI-*šu*
[x]⌈x x⌉-*ma* ⌈*li-ri*⌉-*šu-ma*
[..........................]
⌈x x x x⌉ *a-na* u d u . ⌈ḫ i⌉. a
a-ḫa-am la i-na-ad-di
UE.20. *ù at-ti a-na* é-*ki*
⌈*a-aḫ-ki la*⌉ *ta-na-*[*d*]*i-i*
Le.E. *šum-ma bu-nu-ma–*^{d}i š k u r
la wa-⌈*ši-ib*⌉ GI NA
⌈x x⌉[......]⌈*i*⌉*-re-eḫ*

Translation:

"[2]Speak [1]to ... anna: [3]Thus says ʿIqbi-Addu. [4,5]If there is no silver (in exchange for) the oil [5,6](and the price of) oil stands at one shekel of silver per *three* ..., [7,8]let Bunuma-ilu load one donkey with the oil and [9]let him arrive here soon. [10,11]I myself am held up till the end of the month. [12]But if the price of oil [*is* ... *and*] [13]*payment* of silver takes place, [14]... one kor of barley [15]... *prepare it.* [16][*Let them* ...] and cultivate and ... (break) [18,19][...] must not neglect the sheep, [20,21]and as for you, do not neglect the family. [22]If Bunuma-Addu is not there, ..." (rest too fragmentary)

Commentary:

1. The addressee is a woman, see lines 15, 20, 21. She may be the writer's wife, see line 20f. Possible candidates for her name are [^{f}*ḫa-n*]*a-an-na* and [^{f}*me-n*]*a-an-na*, see I.J. Gelb, *AS* 21, 585, no. 2167 and 623, no. 4653, respectively. Note, however, that the sign after the break looks more like BA.

3. For the name ʿIqbi-Addu, see Gelb e.a., *AS* 21, 609, no. 3743 (Kisurra).

4-5. See for similar expressions in Old Assyrian, K.R. Veenhof, *AOATT* 375f. and especially 380f.

5-6. The same expression with the verbal form *izzaz* is attested in Old Assyrian, see Veenhof, *AOATT* 381 and 415. In view of lines 12-13, where the alternative is presented, the writer of the letter wants to prevent the merchant from selling the oil on credit or at too low a price. As long as the end of line 5 is not clear, the minimum price for the oil required by the writer remains obscure. According to *CAD* s.v. *šamnu* mng. o, the price of oil could fluctuate between four and twenty liters of oil (of various qualities) per shekel of silver. According to Farber, *JESHO* 21, 1978, 22f., sesame oil cost half a shekel per *sūtu* in the time of Samsuiluna, but about one shekel per *sūtu* during the reign of Ammiṣaduqa (figures for North Babylonia).

At the end of line 5 one expects a measure and, if one skips 3 A, 0,0.2 ⸢ì⸣.[g i š] would make good sense. It would give the same price as that for sesame oil in the time of Samsuiluna (see above). However, I can offer no explanation for the signs 3 A. One could also think of a hitherto unattested container *apānum*.

8. The terms for loading in Old Assyrian have been treated by Veenhof, *AOATT* 8f. The most common verb, *sarādum*, is attested outside Old Assyrian, but not with the meaning "to load (a pack animal)", see *CAD* s.v. mng. 2. The only time oil is mentioned as a load for a donkey, the D-stem of *malûm* is used, see Veenhof, ibid., 12. The verb conveys the meaning "to provide with a full load", which would fit our context. See in general, *CAD* s.v. *malû* 7f., and add Mari A1153:7, *Voix de l'opposition* 181 (ref. K.R. Veenhof).

10. The term *rēš warḫim* has most recently been discussed by Whiting, *Tell Asmar*, 62f.

12-13. These two lines seem to give the alternatives for lines 4-6, namely, that both the price is good and silver is available for payment. At the end of line 12 one expects a verb with the meaning "high, satisfactory", or the like. Note, however, that no such verb is so far attested with the word *maḫīrum*. Although the traces are not exactly in agreement with this reading, I tentatively restore ⸢*ša-qá-al*⸣ at the beginning of line 13. The expression *šaqāl kaspim ibašši* has a good parallel in Old Assyrian, see Veenhof, *AOATT* 380.

15. The sign marked x between ŠU and ZI can be TA or UZ. Theoretically, one could restore *šu-*[*u*]*s-sí-ki-šu*, "remove him/it!"; however, *šussukum* hardly ever occurs outside Standard Babylonian texts. One could also read *šu-*[*u*]*z-zi-qí-šu*, "pester him", which occurs regularly in Old Babylonian letters, or *šu-*[*t*]*a-sí-qí-šu*, "prepare it", for which I have tentatively opted here. The following line seems to point to agricultural activities.

2. *A letter from the Mittanni(?) period*

HMM 86 - O14 (s. Pl. 31) dates to a time somewhat later than the previous letter. The date is based mainly on the archeological context; according to the script this little text is Old Babylonian or slightly later. On the reverse the tablet has a cylinder seal impression, for which see *Akkadica* 52 (1987) 9, fig. 13.

Excavator's note: "Found in square M 23 area 45 level 22, incorporated in the mud bricks of a wall. The wall belongs to the second subphase of the first phase of the Late Bronze palace, for whose general plan see D.J.W. Meijer in M.N. van Loon (ed.), *Hammam et-Turkman* I (Leiden 1988), 119 pl. 43. The tablet is thus to be dated earlier. There may have been little time between the end of the MB II occupation and the beginning of the LB Age at the site of Hammam. Although the orientation of the walls of the LB palace is different, the MB II administrative complex's ruins were partly incorporated, and were apparently still standing at the time of the construction of the LB building. A round date is difficult to give. However, the analysis of the seal impression favors a date at the beginning of the Late Bronze Age, presumably shortly before 1500 B.C."

The tablet measures 4.2 x 3.9 x 1.8 cm.

Transliteration:

O.1. *a-na ša-tu-wa-at-ri*
qí-bí-ma
um-ma [l u]g a l-*ma*
p*ka-ru-uk-ka-ma*
5. *ar-ḫi-iš li-il-li-kam*
R. (anepigraphic seal)

Translation:

"1,2Speak to Šatuwatri: Thus says the king. 4,5Let Karukka(ma) come quickly."

Commentary:

1. The name Šatuwatri is so far not attested. The first element could be Hurrian (*šat-* or *šatt-*, see *NPN* 252), Anatolian (*šattuwa*, see *NH* 161) or even Indo-Aryan (*šatta-*, see *NPN* 252, Kammenhuber, *Die Arier im Vorderen Orient* (Heidelberg 1968), 161). A name which is reminiscent of Šatuwatri is Šattumarti, which is attested at Nuzi (*NPN* 127; for parallels to the metathesis of a consonant plus *-r-*, see Speiser, *Intr.* 68). However, the element *-marti* is so far unexplained (see *NPN* 233).

2. Although the "king" could theoretically be the local ruler who writes to one of his subjects in the city, the letter is more likely to have come from outside Hammām et-Turkmān. Therefore, the king is probably the overlord of the city ruler. If the letter has indeed to be dated to the Mittanni period this king could very well be the Mittannian king himself.

3. It is unclear whether the *-ma* at the end of the name is part of it or has to be regarded as the enclitic. As for the name Karukka(ma), there is as yet no clear parallel. The only possible candidate is Kurruka attested at Nuzi (*NPN* 92, cf. also Šurukka, ibid., 140?).

3. *A lexical text*

HMM 86 - O6 (s. Pl. 32-34) is an originally cube-shaped object of unbaked clay of which only three sides are preserved. The center of the cube shows a cylindrical hole, which allowed a stick to be fastened and the text to be turned 'page by page'. The prism contains a bilingual version of Proto-Ea and has the format of Proto-Aa.[3]

Excavator's note: "Found fragmented in square K 22, area 17 level 6, a side room in the 'administrative complex', penultimate phase (MB II, ca. 1650-1600 B.C.?), on a flimsy floor representing a minor rebuilding phase. The tablet was probably dropped and subsequently forgotten when the building was cleaned out in preparation for the rebuilding. Although no traces of archival shelves have been found, the object's findspot may very well represent its original context."

The tablet measures 10 x 8.5 x 7.5 cm, the bottom is broken.

[In the columns listing corresponding line numbers of Ea and Aa, [a] stands for "Identical pronunciation glosse", and [b] stand for "Identical Akkadian equivalent".]

Side A.

		Proto-Ea/Aa	Ea	Aa
i.1.	[¶ KU(?)]	10f.	I:132f.	
	[ ]			
	[ ]⸢x⸣			
	[-*u*]*m*			
5.	[x (x)]-*mu-ú*			
	[KA].KA.SI.GA			
	[¶ ŠÈ *a*]-⸢*ga*⸣-*rum*	58	I:176	
	[ḫu-un] *nu-úḫ-ḫu*		I:175	
	[*na*]-*pa-al-sú-ḫu*[4]			
10.	[ ]⸢*i*⸣-*tap-la-sú-ḫu*			
	[¶ ŠÈ *r*]*u-bu-ú*		I:177	
	[ge-e]*ru-ba-a-tum*			
	[¶ ŠÈ]*ru-bu-ú*	60		
	[e-gi]*ru-ba-a-tum*		I:178	
15.	[¶ Š]È *i*-⸢*na*⸣	61?		
	[e-eš(?)] *a*-⸢*na*⸣		I:180	
	[¶ Š]È *i*-⸢*na*⸣	61?		

[3] *MSL* 14, 88f.

[4] See *CAD* s.v.: KU = dúr = *napalsuḫu*.

	[še-e(?)[5]]		*a*-⸢*na*⸣		I:(181[a])[6]	
	[¶	?	*e*]*b*?-*bu*			
20.	[		x]⸢x-*ak*?⸣-*tum*			
	[		-B]I?-*ḫu*			
	[		]-*gu-ú*			
	[		]-*mu-um*			
	[		]-*kum*			
25.	[		]-*wu*?			
	[		]-AB/AT?-*tum*			
	[		]⸢x⸣-*rum*			
	[		]-*um*			
	(break)					
ii.1.	[¶] ze-el	NUN	*qá-la-pu-um*	392		V/3:8
			ne-sú-ú[7]			
			nu-us-sú-ú			
			na-sa-ḫu[8]			
5.			*ša-la-tum*		V:131	V/3:[1]
			an-zi-il-lum[9]			
	¶ nu-un	NUN	*nu-nu-um*	391		V/3:33
			ṣi-rum			V/3:30
			ᵈ*é-a*			V/3:28
10.			*ru-bu-ú*		V:134	V/3:25
	¶ ne-er	NIR	*e-te-el-lum*	395	V:138	V/3:[37]
			ta-ka-lum[10]			
			tu-ku-ul-tum			
	¶ a	AK	*e-pé-šum*	524	VIII:23	
15.	¶ na	AK	*e-pé-šum*	525	VIII:(22[a])	VIII/1:52
	¶ ša	AK	*e-pé-šum*	526	VIII:(21[a])	VIII/1:(49[a])
	¶ ki	AK	*e-pé-šum*	527	VIII:24	VIII/1:53

[5] Cf. secondary branch no. 9:588 ¾ 587, *MSL* 14, 124.
[6] The Akkadian column has *kîma*.
[7] Cf. Nabnitu XVII (J) 354 (*MSL* 16, 165).
[8] See *CAD* s.v.: zé & zi = *nasāḫu*.
[9] Possibly from an.zil.
[10] Possibly from nir.gál.

	¶ ak	AK	KA.KA.SI.GA	528	VIII:(25^{a})	VIII/1:(54^{a})
	¶	AK	*e-pé-šum*	528		
20.	a-ki		*na-bu-ú*		VIII:(22^{b})	VIII/1:(51^{b})
	¶	IŠ	*ba-ṣú*	247	IV:(82^{a})	IV/2:(121^{a})
	iš		*na-ás-pa-an-tum*		IV:(83^{b})	
	¶	IŠ	*ku-uk-ku-šu*	249	IV:87	
	me-el		*ši-ba-ḫu*[11]			
25.			*ta-ba-aš-ta-nu*[12]			
	¶ ⌈sa⌉-ḫar	IŠ	*e-pé-ru*!(ŠU)	250	IV:84	IV/2:127
	¶ ku-um	IŠ	*tar-bu-úḫ-tu*[*m*]	250a	IV:85	IV/2:131
			ši-ba-ḫu-um[13]			
	¶ še-⌈en⌉	⌈IŠ⌉	*šu-úḫ-tum*	—[14]	—[15]	
	(break)					

Side B.

i.1.	¶	UL	*ba-nu-*[*ú*?[16]]	281		
	du-ú		*ba-nu-*⌈*ú-um*⌉			
			it-ku-pu		IV:151	IV/3:57’
			šu-uk-lu-lum[17]			
5.			*ṭú-úḫ-ḫu-du*[18]			
			wa-ás-mu		IV:151a	
	¶ na-gá	KUM	*e-si-it-tu*[*m*]	607		
	¶ gu[19]	KUM	KA.KA.SI.GA			
	¶	KUM	*ḫa-ša-lu*[*m*]	606		
10.	gu-um		*ḫe-su-ú*			
			da-kum			

[11] Cf. *CAD* s.v. *šabīḫu* and *šibḫu*, and cf. line 28.
[12] Normally equated with LUM.
[13] Cf. line 24.
[14] Cf. line 192 (URUDU).
[15] Cf. Ea III:202 (DUB).
[16] Or possibly *-tum.*
[17] From šu.du_7.
[18] From du_8.
[19] Read qù?

	¶	GAZ	*da-kum*	608		
	ga-az		*ma-ḫa-ṣum*			
			ḫa-ṣa-ṣu[m][20]			
15.			*pa-la-q[um]*			
	¶ i-pí-ig	SIG	*ma-[aš?]-qú-ú*[21]	725		
	¶	SIG	⌈*qá*⌉-[*at-nu*]	723		
	si-ig		*qú?-[ut-(tu)-nu*[22]]			
			x[			
20.			x[			
			š[u?-			
	¶	TUR	*ṣe-eḫ-rum*	467		
	tu-ur		*ṣú-úḫ-ḫu-rum*			
			i-ṣú-um			
25.	¶	TUR	*ma-ru-um*	469		
	du-um		*ma-ar-tum*			
	⌈¶⌉[	]⌈x⌉	⌈*tu?-di?-tum*⌉[23]			
	(break)					
ii.1.	[¶ ku-ú	TAR]	*p[a]-ra-sú-um*	195	III:213b	III/5:53
			pa-⌈*ra*⌉*-ás di-nim*			
	¶	TAR	*na-ka-súm*	194a	III/5:70	
	ku-ud		*na-ka-ás qá-qá-di*			
5.			*e-re-rum*[24]			
	[	]	*pa-ra-súm*		III/5:71	
	[	]	*pa-ra-ás da-mi*			
	[	]	*pa-ra-ás di-nim*			
	[¶	TAR	*s]u-qum*	198	III:[218]	III/5:170
10.	[si-la		*r]i-bi-tum*			III/5:171
	[		*su]-qá-aq-qụ-ú*			
	[¶	UR	*b]a-aš-tum*	646		VII/2:81
	[te-eš		*i]š-ti-ni-iš*			VII/2:83
	[		*mi]-it-ḫa-ri-iš*			

[20] Normally equated with ḫaš.
[21] From dug.a.sig?
[22] Restored after the next paragraph: *ṣeḫrum* - *ṣuḫḫurum*.
[23] Highly dubious.
[24] Either *arārum*, "to curse" or *erûm*, "to cut (wood)". For the latter, see Aa III/5:61.

15.	[		*š*]*u-ud-du-lum*[25]			
	[		*r*]*u-up-pu-šum*[26]			
	[¶]	UR	*kal-ba-tum*			
	ni-ig		*ne-eš-tum*			
	⸢¶⸣	UR	KA.KA.SI.GA	648		VII/2:102?
20.	ka-la-ab					
	⸢¶⸣	UR	*kal-bu-um*	645		VII/2:91
	ur		*ne-šum*			VII/2:95
			[*a*]*-wi-lum*			VII/2:93
			[*wa*]*-ar-du*			
25.	[¶	ZÉ/ZI(?)[27]]*ba-qá-mu*		287/452	IV:(168[a])	III/1:84(ZI)[28]
	[		]*ba-ra-šum*		/III:(24[a])	III/1:85(ZI)
	[		*n*]*a-sa-ḫu*			III/1:82(ZI)
	[¶ ?		]⸢x⸣-KUM			
	[		x (x)-*d*]*u-um*[29]			
	[		x (x)-*d*]*u*?*-um*			
	(break)					

Side C

i.1.	¶	TA	*i-*[*na*]	535	
	ta		*a-*[*na*]		IV:224
			iš-[*tu*]		IV:223
			mi-iš-[*šum*[30]]		
5.			*mi-*[*num*]		
			mi-⸢*nam*⸣*-m*[*i*?]		
			a-na mi-⸢*nim*⸣		
	¶ pé-e	PI	KA.KA.SI.GA		
	¶ e	PI	KA.KA.SI.GA		

25 See the next note.

26 The two equations *šuddulum* and *ruppušum*, both "to widen", are unusual. For *ruppušum*, a connection teš - tál could be proposed, see side C, i:11f.

27 T. Krispijn suggests BU for this and the following paragraphs. For ZÉ/ZI, see Sjöberg, *ZA* 83 (1993) 14.

28 The corresponding section of ZÉ is broken.

29 This line was possibly followed by a ruling.

30 Suggested by T. Krispijn.

10.	¶ wa-a	PI	KA.KA.SI.GA	603		
	¶	PI	*ra-ap-⸢šum⸣*	604		
	ta-al		*ra-pa-[šum]*			
			šu-ud-du-lum			
			ru-up-pu-⸢šum⸣			
15.			*šu-te-ṣú-⸢ú⸣*[31]			
			šu-zu-bu-[um][32]			
			šu-ta-AG-x[x][33]			
			šu-tam-ḫ[u-rum[34]]			
			šu-tam-ḫ[u-ṣum[35]]			
20.			*šu-us-sú-[kum]*			
			šu-um-sú-[kum[36]]			
	¶ ba-lu?[37]-⸢x⸣	PI	*ba-ás-⸢ki-il⸣-tum*[38]			
	¶	PI	*uz-[nu]-um*	605		
	ge_6-eš-tu-nu		*ḫa-[si-s]úm*[39]			
25.	¶ ⸢ir-sag⸣	KASKAL	*u[r-ša-nu]*	—	I:276	I/6:51
	¶ eš	KASKAL	KI-[[40]	—	I:(274[a])	I/6:(47[a])
	¶ [ ]	KASKAL	x[			
	(break)					
ii.1'		[				
		[				
	¶ ⸢gá-ra⸣	GAR	[	209	III/6:30	
	¶ ⸢ni-ig⸣	GAR	[	208	III:[220]	III/6:[1f.]
5'	¶	PAD	[	212	III:228	

31 Or perhaps *šu-te-zu-⸢bu⸣*, see the next line.

32 From tak_4?

33 Perhaps *šu-ta-ak-ṣ[ú-rum]*.

34 From RI = tal.

35 From RI = tal. The last two lines can be interchanged.

36 The last two entries from RI = tal.

37 Read perhaps zu-lu-u[g] which, however, belongs to LUL. The second sign should perhaps be read -ra!?-.

38 See Nougayrol, *RA* 66 (1972) 191 and *CAD* s.v. **maskiltu*.

39 One could also think of *ḫa-[as-s]úm*.

40 Possibly a mistake for *karašu* or *kaeššu*, or for *giršānu*.

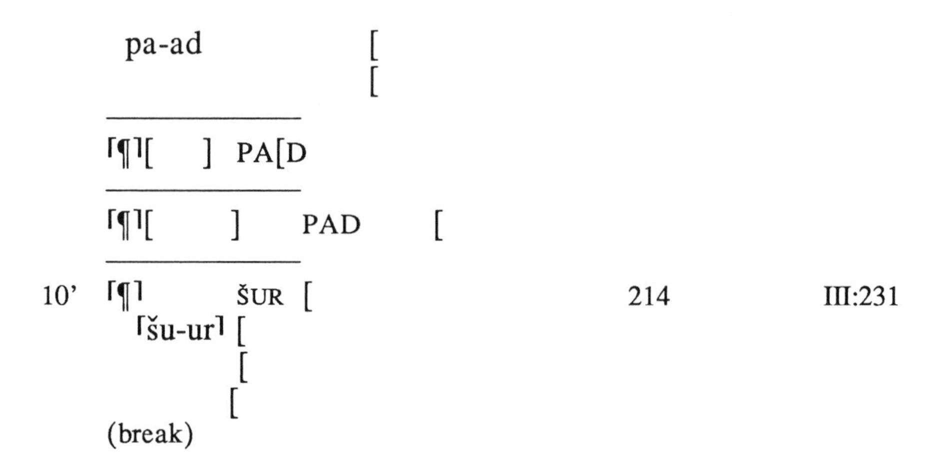

pa-ad [
[

⸢¶⸣[ ] PA[D

⸢¶⸣[ ] PAD [

10' ⸢¶⸣ ŠUR [214 III:231
⸢šu-ur⸣ [
[
[
(break)

(On the upper edge parts of three lines are preserved. Since these lines could only be read after baking and cleaning I was unable to prepare a copy. The text differs in its format from the rest of the text:

(unknown number of lines lost)
¶ AN [
¶ AN.x[
¶ AN.ḪA.x[
(break)

The exact nature of this small piece of text escapes me, perhaps an excerpt from a god list?)

The orthography of this tablet accords well with the date deduced on archaeological grounds, the second half of the 17th century (note, for example, the regular lack of mimation). It also points to North-Babylonia as the place of origin (note in particular the spellings with S-signs, especially the use of ÁŠ for /as/, AŠ is used to write /aš/, note also the use of TU for /ṭu/).

As to the format, it has already been said that the tablet is a version of the Old Babylonian Proto-Ea Vocabulary or Proto-Aa. However, as can be seen from the columns which list corresponding entries in (Proto-)Ea and Aa, the order of the signs is quite different from that of the Nippur version.[41] Even within a single column the order can be different. What exactly the principle behind the scribe's sign order may have been remains obscure. The order followed by the students at Nippur apparently had a didactical background[42] which helped to memorize the text. There are, however, so-called secondary branches of Proto-Aa.[43] As observed by Civil, "there was no widespread

[41] Note that according to Civil, *MSL* 14, 109, deviating recensions of Proto-Aa also existed in Nippur itself.

[42] Edzard, *FsDiakonoff* 42f.

[43] *MSL* 14, 107f.

established way of ordering the signs and each school followed its own."[44] Thus HMM 86 - O6 appears to have been written by a scribe who was writing in the tradition of North Babylonia during the latter half of the Old Babylonian period and whose sign sequence was different from the one used at Nippur. That this scribe probably was a student can be gathered from his mistakes in the Akkadian column.[45].

Unfortunately, we have no clue whether the text was written at Ḥammām or was brought in from outside the city. As long as the tell has not produced more texts of this genre, it would seem safer to seek its origin elsewhere.

[44] *MSL* 14, 109.

[45] For example, the equivalents for PI = tál taken from RI = tal (C i 18f.).

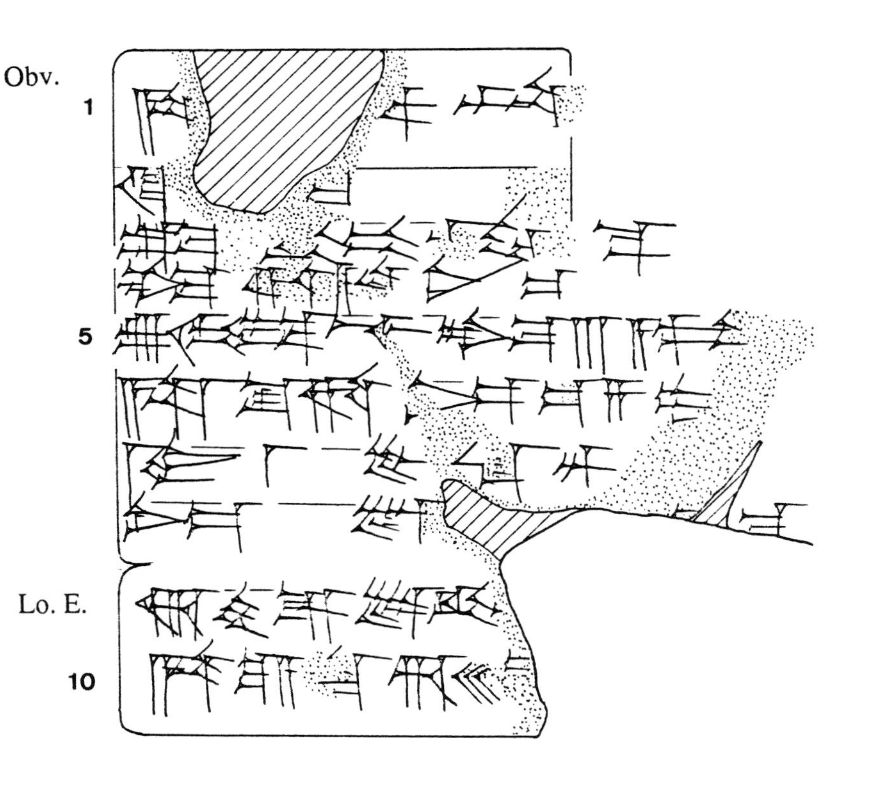

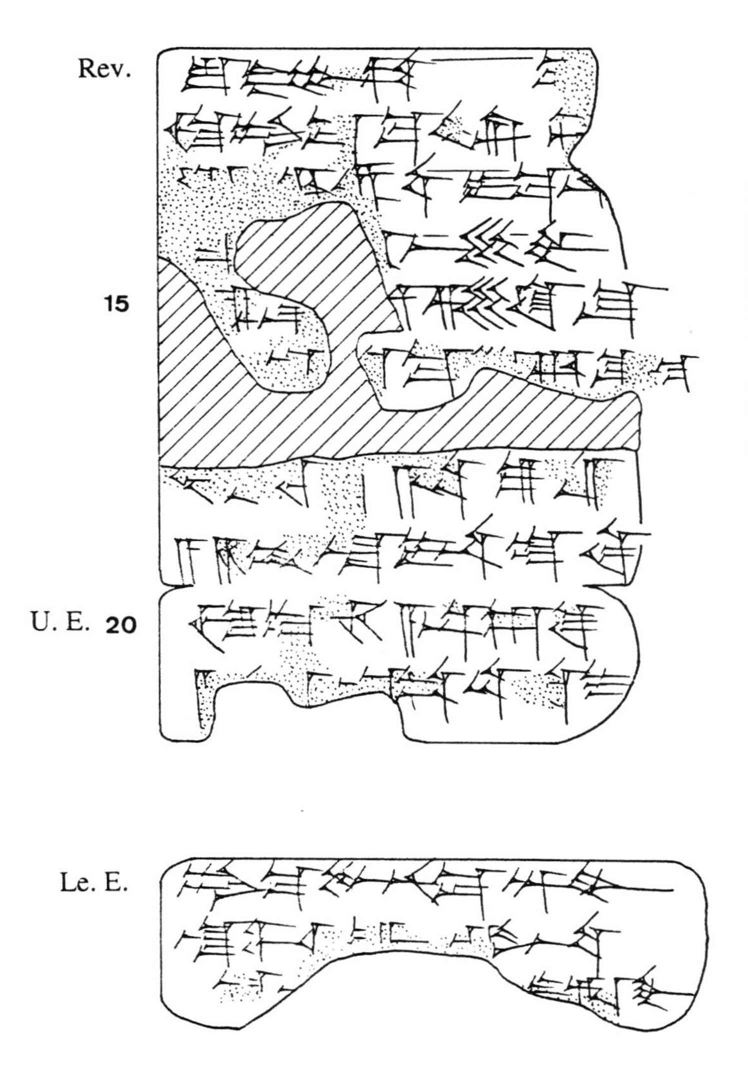

HMM 86 - O 8

Plate 30. HMM 86 - O8.

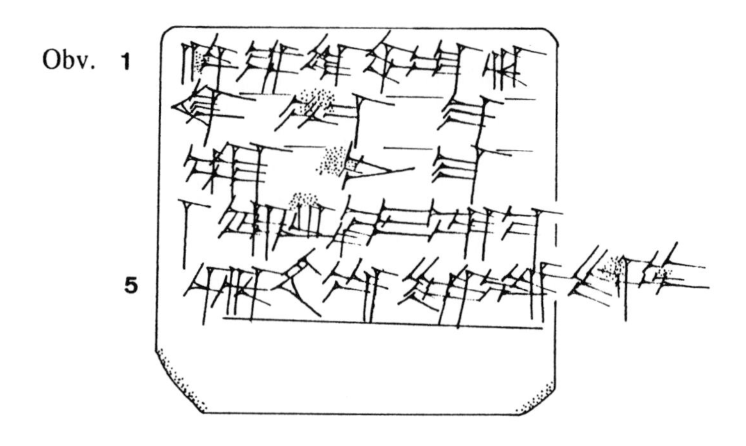

HMM 86 - O 14

Plate 31. HMM 86 - O14.

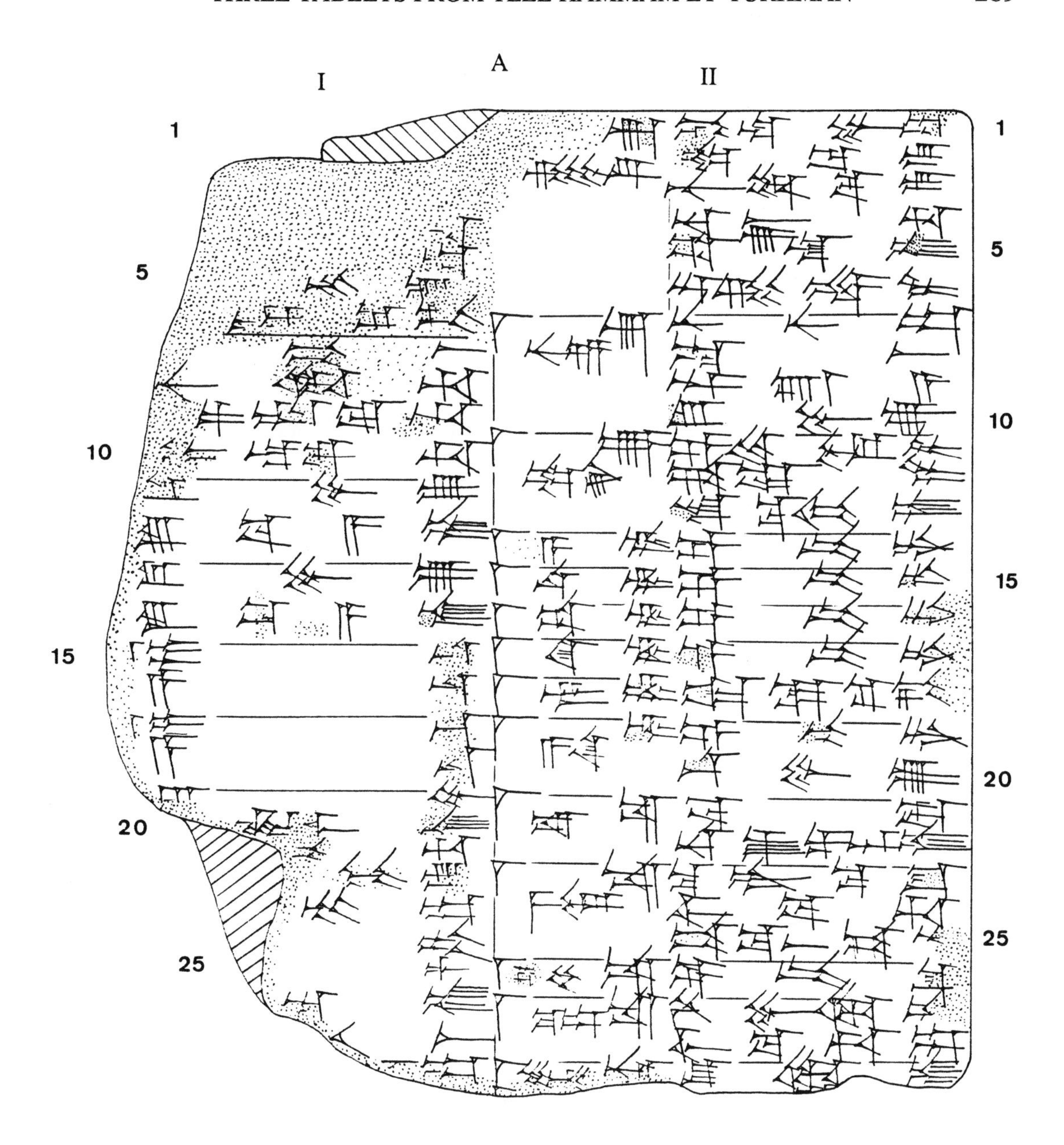

HMM 86 - O 6

Plate 32. HMM 86 - O6 side A.

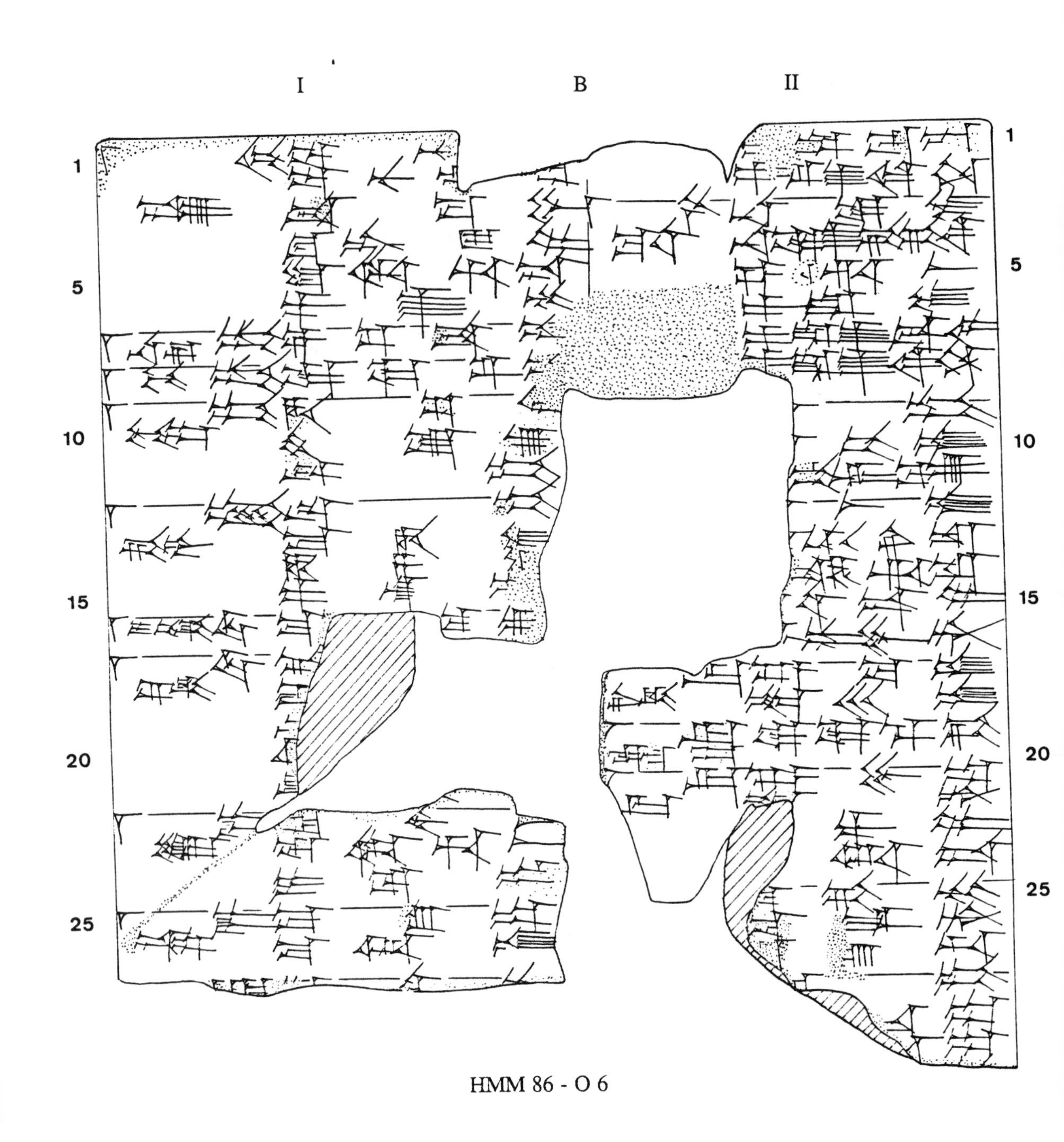

Plate 33. HMM 86 - O6 side B.

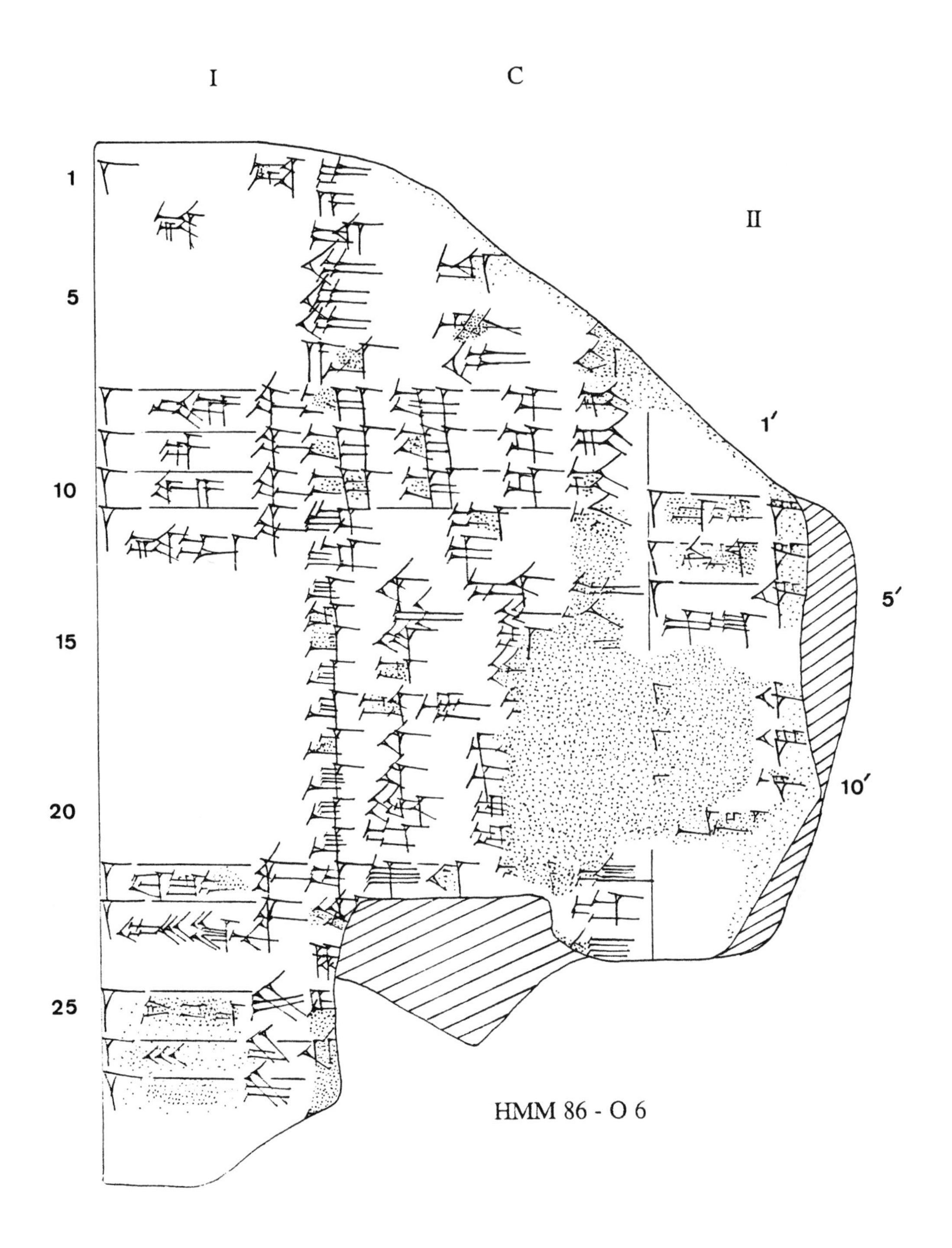

Plate 34. HMM 86 - O6 side C.

OLD BABYLONIAN CORVÉE (*tupšikkum*)

MARTEN STOL

In Mesopotamia, free people could be called up to do forced labour. Some kings boasted that they had freed their subjects from these work assignments. Cities had privileges which protected them from compulsory labour. It is remarkable that so little has been written on this institution.[1] This article wishes to remedy this to some extent for the Old Babylonian period. From the group of relevant terms *dekûtum*, *ḫarrānum*, *ilkum*, and *tupšikkum* we have singled out *tupšikkum* and for convenience's sake we will translate it as "corvée." A full study of *ilkum* is needed but would require no thing less than a book. This kind of "service" was tied to the family and was passed down through the generations.

The word

Not much will be said here on the Sumerian word, d u s u (written GI.ÍL), in Akkadian *tupšikkum* (in the Atramḫasīs myth *šupšikkum*).[2] It primarily denotes a basket used for carrying goods: when made of wood, for fruits (third millennium Sumerian g i š. ÍL), when made of reed, for carrying earth.[3] The latter led to its secondary meaning, "corvée work."[4] Gudea claims to have freed a high cult official from, among other obligations, "the basket of earth" (ÍL s a ḫ a r . r a).[5] Some Sumerologists tend to see in it a predecessor to Old

[1] A notable exception is the book by J.N. Postgate, *Taxation and Conscription in the Assyrian Empire* (1974). Also G. Evans, "The incidence of labour-service in the Old babylonian period", *JAOS* 83 (1963) 20-26; R. Frankena, *SLB* IV (1978) 85-87.

[2] The *t* is not emphatic; see W. von Soden, *BiOr* 36 (1979) 330.

[3] A.L. Oppenheim, *AOS* 32 (1948) 64; M. Civil, *OIC* 22 (1975) 125; J.N. Postgate, *BSA* 3 (1987) 123-4, g; J.A. Peat, *JCS* 28 (1976) 213 no. 17. – Etymology: Th. Jacobsen, *Essays in Memory of J.J. Finkelstein* (1977) 116, d u b . s í g "wool pad." Cf. S.J. Lieberman, *The Sumerian Loanwords in Old-Babylonian Akkadian* (1977) 194, d a b s i g "hod"; W.G. Lambert, CRRAI XXXVIII (1992) 133 (z u b . s ì g; lex. *tu-ub-ši-ig*). See also the article by A. Salonen, *BiOr* 27 (1970) 176-7.

[4] In early Sumerian texts: refs. collected by J.N. Postgate, *Early Mesopotamia* (1992) 324 note 417. Imposed on conquered peoples: UET 1 275 II 20, with *RIME* 2 (1993) 133 (Narām-Sîn) – In literary texts z i . g a, "Aufgebot"; A. Falkenstein, *ZA* 57 (1965) 93-4; A.W. Sjöberg, *HSAO* 205 n. 7.

[5] E.Sollberger, *JCS* 10 (1956) 12, 25 no. 1 II 5; now H. Steible, *FAOS* 9/1 (1991) 242 (Statue R).

Babylonian (and later) *ilkum* – perhaps rightly so.[6] The Sumerograms vary in the Old Babylonian texts, as will be seen in the examples that will be cited. The reading is d u s u in Sumerian; it is sometimes preceded by e r é n "workmen." This does not necessarily mean that it always referred to workers. However, some passages show that d u s u is the work force: it "stands up" (*tebûm*) to go to work (CT 48 64:19-20; see below).

In literary texts, this basket is often mentioned together with the hoe (a l) when compulsory work is meant.[7] Administrative and other Old Babylonian texts more often combine it with the shovel, *marrum*.[8]

A recently published letter from Mari offers a new word derived from it, *tupšikkānum*, obviously a military occupation. It occurs in the row "élite troops, *t.* troops, (trustworthy) slaves" (*ṣābaka beḫram ṣāb tu-up-ši-ik-ka-nim ù* ì r-*di.* m e š-*ka (taklūtim)*) and has been translated by J.-M. Durand as "la troupe du génie."[9] This translation was inspired by the use of the *tupšikkum* as a basket to carry earth. We add to this that the personal name *Tupšikkānu* is known from a Diyāla text (*JCS* 24 [1972] 62 no. 54:16). If it means "a man doing corvée work", we are reminded of the name *Andakullum*: Kienast found this name as a word in a few letters, which he translates, without argumentation, as "(etwa) Fronarbeiter."[10]

The "carrying" of the basket is conveyed by the Akkadian verbs *našûm* and *zabālum*.[11] As to corvée work, assigning a person this kind of work is called *šakānum*, relieving him from it is called *nasāḫum*.[12] Summoning people to do

[6] P. Michalowski, *JNES* 45 (1986) 327b (on NATN 258, in Nippur); P. Steinkeller, *JNES* 52 (1993) 143a (in Nippur, the Enlilemaba archive, d u s u a d . d a, "paternal corvée obligation").

[7] See the Dictionaries under *allu* and *tupšikku*. Also in Sumerian texts: Sum. Proverbs 2.140; Lugale 337-8, with Römer, *TUAT* III/3 (1993) 445 (named é š . g à r, "work assignment").

[8] D. Arnaud, *Larsa et 'Oueili. Travaux de 1978-1981* (1983) 274, 275 no. 1, 288 no.1 (u r u d u. m a r – g i š . m a r – g i š . ÍL); AbB 9 158:3-7; TIM 1 5:11, 13; B. Kienast, FAOS 2/II no. 155 (house building); OB Atramḫasīs I 65-66. In an obscure clause in a field sale: YOS 14 111:16. SB incantation: BAM 5 480 III 67 with B.R. Foster, *Before the Muses* (1993) 875 (making a dam in the canal). – It is striking that the word *allum* "hoe" is hardly attested in OB texts: perhaps in YOS 13 49, 229 (a l . u r u d u, but used for harvesting!).

[9] Apud D. Charpin, *AEM* 1/2 (1988) 164, on no. 362:6, 19. – Now the *tu-up-ši-k[i]-nim* in AbB 12 36:18 needs collation.

[10] The names: UET 5 p. 43 s.v. "Ilum-da-ak-ku-ul(-lum)"; D. Charpin, *Archives familiales ...* (1980) 302-3; D. Arnaud, ARV 14:4. The word: B. Kienast, *FAOS* 2/II (1978) p. 143.– Not in the Dictionaries.

[11] *našûm*: UET 1 275 II 20-23 (= *FAOS* 7 [1990] 256 Naram-Sin C 5:52-55; *RIME* 2 (1993) 133); Kienast, *FAOS* 2/II no. 155:5, 10 (*nāši tupšikkim*); OB Atramḫasīs I 191, 197; contrast *zabālum*, I 2; also DCS 98:4. – For kings carrying the basket, see B.N. Porter, *Images, Power and Politics. Figurative aspects of Esarhaddon's Babylonian Policy* (1993), 82-94.

[12] Both in Arnaud, ARV 174:8, 10 (the work is *iškarum*, 13). *Šakānum* alone: AbB 11 133:10, "there is not one corvée worker (e r é n d u s u) with me; they even put merchants to the corvée work (d u s u)." Mobilising merchants is exceptional; see D. Charpin on this passage, *RA* 83 (1989) 95. *Nasāḫum*: *CAD* N/2 8-9; cf. *ina dikūt awil Šatlaš ana* X *na-ás-*[*ḫu*], CT 48 83:7, with M. Gallery, *JAOS* 99 (1979) 74-5. Note g i š . d u s u . t a z i in Isin royal inscriptions (see below).

forced labour is *šasûm* in Akkadian, literally "to call", when pressure is exerted, the verb *dabābum* D is used, "to harrass."[13].

tupšikkum and ilkum

One of our questions is, how this corvée (*tupšikkum*) relates to the *ilkum* obligation.[14] A number of letters shed light on this. In the first, we read: "Now you are taking away a soldier from his *ilkum* and enlist him for *tupšikkum* (...) Why do you enlist him for corvée? To you it is that he should be released (*wuššur*)! The soldier should not carry out another *ilkum*; let him return to his own *ilkum*" (AbB 3 26). The final remark suggests that *tupšikkum* was a kind of *ilkum*. In another letter, the people of the city Ḫabbuz complain: "They have summoned us for corvée (e r é n d u s u), not our *ilkum*, and they harrass us." The king decides that they should not be harrassed because it had been found in (the records of) the "House of the Accounts" that the corvée is not "their old (obligation)" (*labirtum*) (AbB 10 13). Note that the king is involved in this matter. Elsewhere we read that another man of Ḫabbuz, a singer of dirges, was already burdened by five *ilkum*'s and two taxes to be paid in silver (*igisûm*); he complains that he is now called up by the Head of the District (*šāpir mātim*) to do "carrying work" (*babbilūtum*). His chief writes to the Head that this is indeed too much: "Nobody shall summon his house" (AbB 10 1). In another letter, the Head of Kish seizes and detains a person for carrying (*babbilūtum*) sesame (AbB 13 156). The obligation "to carry" in both letters must be comparable to the *tupšikkum*. It could be a form of *ilkum*; for the poor man the sixth. In another letter, we see that the *tupšikkum* workers were led by the Head of the District, as here (AbB 2 27:5).

One letter begins with the remark "As to the jesters whom they summoned (!) for corvée (*a-na* e r é n . d u s u *i-sú-nim*): as to me, the king spoke as follows: this young man here who is with me, I certainly know him. I do not know those other people. Perhaps they will equal themselves to him (?) in respect to the *ilkum* (*mi-id-de a-na il-ki-im i-ša-an-na-nu-ú-šu*)" (AbB 8 109). We assume that the young man is the jester and that his forced labour is his *ilkum*.

A number of passages speaking of "summoning" or "harrassing" a house make clear that the *tupšikkum* is the obligation of a family ("house").[15] The *ilkum* is also a matter of the family.

13 *CAD* Š/2 155-6; F.R.Kraus, *Ein Edikt* ... (1958) 54-9. More: CT 48 64:18 (*ilkum*), AbB 8 9:12; 109:4 (!) (corvée). Followed by *dabābum* D: AbB 10 13:9-10. Cf. AbB 12 40:13, *piqat ana tupšikkim bītam udabbabū*; AbB 11 43:8 (*la tašassi*), 10 (*bītam la tubazzaḫ*), 17-8 (*bītam la tudabbab*).

14 R. Frankena, *SLB* IV (1978) 87, concludes: "Der Unterschied zwischen *ilkum* und *tupšikkum* ist also wohl, daß die *tupšikkum*-Leistung von jedem Bürger gefordert werden konnte, während die *ilkum*-Leistungen nur bestimmten Leuten oblagen, die dafür aber durch Zuteilung eines Feldes entschädigt wurden."

15 AbB 12 40:13; AbB 11 43:8. See the preceding note.

Corvée and the City Ward

J.J.Finkelstein discovered a legal text in the British Museum, in which *tupšikkum* and *ilkum* occur side by side, again suggesting their identity. He published the text as CT 48 64; so far, no attention has been given to it in Assyriology. The text is difficult but we will attempt a first step towards its interpretation here.

obv.
(1) 1 s a g . ì r *Ša–*^{d}u t u*–dam-q[á* m u .]n i .[i m]
(2) *ša* ^{d}*Na-bi-um–ma-lik* d u m u ^{d}I š k u r*–n[a*(?)*-ṣi-ir*]
(3) *a-na mi-ši-il* d u s u*-šu ša-n[i-im]*(?)
(4) *šu-ul-lu-mi-im*
(5) *a-na Gi-mil–*^{d}M a r d u k PA d a g_4. g i_4. a
(6) *id-di-iš-šu*
(7) *i-na* k á . d i n g i r . r a^{ki} s a g . ì r *a-na ši-pí-ir aš-la-ku-ti-šu*
(8) *a-na ki-iṣ-ri* ^{p}*Gi-mil–*^{d}M a r d u k
(9) *ú-um-ma-as-sú-ma*
(10) 4 g í n k ù . b a b b a r *ki-ṣi-ir* s a g . ì r
(11) ^{p}*Gi-mil–*^{d}M a r d u k *i-le-qé-e-ma*
(12) l ú . ḫ u n . g á *ša mi-ši-il* d u s u
(13) *ša* ^{d}*N[a-bi-um–m]a-lik ù* x x [o]
(14) *i-g[a-ru* .....]
(15) *i-li-[ik šar-ri-im il-la-ak*] (?)
rev.
(16) š à . b i 4 g í [n k] ù . b a b b a r *ša* ^{d}*Na-bi-um–m]a-lik* (?)
(17) *aš-šum i-li-ik š[ar-ri-i]m* (?)
(18) *a-na* é ^{d}*Na-bi-um–ma-lik ú-ul i-ša-si*
(19) u_4*-um* d u s u k á . d i n g i r . r a^{ki}
(20) *a-na ši-ip-ri-šu* (!) *i-te-eb-bu-ú*
(21) ^{p}*Ša–*^{d}u t u*–dam-qá* k á . g a l k á . d i n g i r . r a^{ki} *ú-ul uṣ-ṣí*
(22) *ši-pí-ir qa-ti-šu-ma i-ip-pé-eš*
(23) *a-na ši-pí-ir* d u s u *ú-ul i-sa-an-ni-iq*
(24) *šum-ma Gi-mil–*^{d}Marduk
(25) ^{p}*Ša–*^{d}u t u*–dam-qá ši-pí-ir aš-la-ku-ti-šu*
(26) *uš-ta-ad-di-šu-ma a-n[a*] [*ši*]*-p[í*]*-i[r*]
(27) d u s u *ut-te-d[i* (??) ... *-ma*]
(28) *im-tu-ut* ^{p}*Gi-mi[l–*^{d}M a r d u k]
(29) s a g . ì r *ki-ma* s a g . ì[r *i-ri-a-ab*]
(30) i g i ^{d}I š k u r*–sú-p[é-e-*x x ..] (?)
(31) i g i ^{d}u t u*–l[i-*x (x) ...]
(32) i g i ^{d}N a n n a*-tum* d u m u *Bur-*[30]
(33) i g i *Ḫa-ap-pa-tum* d u m u ^{d}I š k u r-⌜*i*⌝-[*din-nam*]
(34) i t u g a n . g a n . è u_4.10.k a m
(35) m u è š . n u n . n a^{ki} a g a l . g a l . l a
(36) m u . u n . g u l . l a

Translation:

(1-6) One male slave, Ša-Šamaš-damqā is his name, of Nabium-mālik, the son of Adad-n[aṣir] (?), he gave to Gimil-Marduk, the Overseer of the Ward, for completing the second (?) half of his *tupšikkum*: (7-15) in Babylon, the male slave to (do) his laundry work, for hire, Gimil-Marduk shall impose on (?) him and Gimil-Marduk shall take the four shekels of silver, the hire of the male slave, and a hireling for half of the *tupšikkum* whom Nabium-mālik and ... will hire (?), shall serve the *ilkum* of the king (?). (16) Four shekels of silver from it [belong to Nabium-m]ālik (?).
(17-23) He shall not summon the house of Nabium-mālik for the *ilkum* of the king (?). On the day that the *tupšikkum* of Babylon "stands up" to do its work, Ša-Šamaš-damqā shall not go out from the city gate of Babylon; he shall do his own work alone; he shall not come to the work of *tupšikkum*. (24-29) If Gimil-Marduk makes Ša-Šamaš-damqā neglect his laundry work and assigns him (?) to the work of *tupšikkum* [... and] he dies, Gimil-Marduk shall replace a male slave for the male slave.
(Four witnesses; dated 10.IX Hammurabi, year 38).

Our text comes from Sippar. Two witnesses are known from Sippar: Nannatum, son of Bur-Sîn (32) in Arnaud, ARV 130:19 (Hammurabi 23) and in CT 2 15:21 (Samsuiluna 3); Ḫappatum, son of Adad-iddinam (33) in CT 8 43b:17 (Hammurabi 41).

R.Harris wrote that the two main persons, Nabium-mālik and Gimil-Marduk, are not Sipparians [16]. Elsewhere in Sippar texts, Nabium-mālik, son of Adad-nāṣir, buys from his brother (?) and wife a slave girl and a child , in CT 8 22c (= VAB 5 79; Hammurabi 35). Harris assumes that this text originates in Babylon. Here, Nabium-mālik, son of Adad-n[āṣir] (?) owns a male slave. Was slave trading his business? The text itself suggests that the Overseer of the Ward Gimil-Marduk lives in Babylon. In Appendix A to this contribution, I will give a survey of all Overseers known to me; not a single one is attested in the rich material from Sippar. A legal text from Mari, however, speaks of "Overseers of the Ward (PA *ba-ba-a-tim*. m e š) of your cities Babylon and Sippar."[17] Such an Overseer was known in Mari.[18] But what did people in Mari know of the local organisation in other cities, like Sippar?

What is the story in the text? An overseer of a ward in Babylon takes it upon him to set the slave to do laundry work[19] and is expected to cash 4 shekels

[16] *Ancient Sippar* (1975) 58 note 4.

[17] D. Charpin, *NABU* 1992/122, A. 3357:10-11.

[18] ARM 6 43:18, with J.-M. Durand, *MARI* 5 (1987) 664, [l]ú PA *ba-ba-tim*.

[19] It is possible that this is a prebend owned by Gimil-Marduk. The only other text on *ašlakūtum* is BE 6/2 126: "*x* shekels of silver, in the weight stone of Šamaš, the laundry man Abi-lu-dari has borrowed from Iddin-Ea, the judge, in order to do the laundry work (*ana šipir ašlakūtim epēši*). [... l]aundry work" (broken). Reverse 1, first witness: Šumum-libši, the s a n≠ g a. Does Iddin-Ea own this prebend and is, therefore, the head of the temple a witness? On this text: R. Harris, *Ancient Sippar* (1975) 272 (correct her *sukkallu*); K. van Lerberghe, MHET I 27:8-10, with note.

of silver as hire. Nabium-mālik hires a hireling who fulfils the (second) half of his *tupšikkum* obligation, possibly called "the *ilkum* of the king" (thus, the restoration by Finkelstein in his description of the text; cf. line 17). We are indeed in Babylon. Line 16 seems to say that the 4 shekels are in fact for Nabium-mālik. The first lines of the text indicate that giving the slave to the Overseer of the Ward is for this purpose: "for completing the second (?) half of his corvée." But the slave is *not* supposed to carry out the corvée, as lines 19-27 show. The four shekels of silver, his hire, are meant for another man, a hireling, who will actually do that. The second half of the text states in various ways that "the house of Nabium-mālik" has thus fulfilled its obligation (by hiring a person, we suppose) and that one should not take its slave away from the laundry work in order to carry out the corvée outside Babylon.[20]

The role of Gimil-Marduk, Overseer of the Ward, is intriguing. He could be the man under whose authority Nabium-mālik is placed and who is responsible for summoning for corvée the "houses" in his ward; actually, he promises in line 18 not to do so. The arrangement between the two men is complicated. It appears that Gimil-Marduk wished to have a safeguard: one man of Nabium-mālik was now in Babylon, under his supervision, and if something went wrong with the "hireling", he could still have the slave Ša-Šamaš-damqā do the corvée work.

At the end of the next section, we will discuss the role played by the city ward in the harvest season.

Hiring contracts

As always in Babylonia, one could avoid the hard physical work of compulsory labour by making a payment in silver or by hiring a substitute. "Should they harrass the house because of the corvée, give one shekel of silver wherever T. tells you (to do)" (AbB 12 40:13-18). "We are being harrassed about the (construction of) the wall of Dūr-Sin-muballiṭ; they made us give two shekels of silver for the corvée" (AbB 9 2:16-18). Paying these amounts could be the alternative of one or two months of corvée work, as the instances of hiring substitutes suggest (see below).

One could hire a person to do *tupšikkum* work. An agreement from Ur shows that three persons had their corvée (construction work) carried out by hiring one (!) hireling among the soldiers (1 lú.ḫun.gá *i-na* aga.ús *agurma*).[21] A letter from the Kish region contains this remark: "Corvée workers, hirelings, and extra soldiers (dusu.meš *ag*(!)*-ru-um ù wa-at-ta-ar*

[20] As suggested by the negatively phrased end of line 21: "He shall not go out from the city gate of Babylon." Note that the verb "to go out" is used again for corvée work in YOS 12 140:6, *a-na u*$_4$*-<<um>>-ma-at uṣ-ṣú-ú* "for the (number) of days that he will go out" (he has paid him).

[21] UET 5 268, with D. Charpin, *Le clergé d'Ur* (1986) 155-7.

a g a . ú s), who(ever) are available in Ḫarbidum, shall build his house (?)."[22] A badly preserved passage in a letter on corvée suggests that soldiers help.[23]

Fortunately, we have three hiring contracts in which people take it upon themselves to do the corvée work.

Pirḫum hires a free man, Eriša, to do this work for a period of 30 days (n a m d u b-*ši-ik-ki* n a m u4 .30. k a m) and has already paid his wages "as those on the right and the left", i.e., at the current price. "His (Eriša's) heart is satified; if he quits service, (Pirḫum) has to account to the Palace (*ipaṭṭarma* é . g a l *ippal)*" (YOS 12 146; dated 3.VII, Samsuiluna 5). A witnessed receipt, dated the same day, runs: "2 kor (= 600 litres) of barley; 110 litres of [flour] (?), ... litres of oil: received by Eriša, from Pirḫum, his hirer (*āgirānum*)" (YOS 12 145). Clearly, these are the wages agreed upon in the other text.

In a second contract, Pirḫum hires a man from his brother "for the *tupšikkum* of the Palace" (*a-na* GI.DUB.ÍL é . g a l-*lim*). "For the days that he will go out[24], his heart is satisfied as[25] those on the right and the left" (YOS 12 140; dated 25.V, Samsuiluna 5). Pirḫum is known to us from a number of texts; most probably he is a merchant.[26]

The third text is D. Charpin, J.-M. Durand, DCS 98. A man hires a son from his father "for carrying the *tupšikkum* for one month" (*ana* i t u .1. k a m GI.DUB.ÍL *zabālim*). The monthly hire consists of one (?) shekel of silver; and in addition rations of flour, a barley-made beverage and ointment. Son and father have already received everything. The last clause seems to read: "On the days that he quits service, he shall account to the king" (*i-na u4-ma-ti-šu* (!) *i-pa-aṭ-<ṭa>-ra-a*[*m*] l u g a l *i-ip-pa-al*) (15-16).

The three texts have several points in common.

1. One month is the standard duration of *tupšikkum* work. We read in another contract: "He shall do his corvée one month (i t u .1. k a m e r é n . d u s u-*šu illak*)."[27] This is confirmed by the following from a letter: "You and PN will go for GI.SAG.ÍL for one month."[28] Another letter speaks of food rations for one month (AbB 2 27:10). In an obscure fragment of a letter, "two months, her assignment", is mentioned in connection with corvée workers.[29] In the Middle Assyrian Laws, the royal corvée lasts one month (A §21, B §8; etc.). Note that one month is in the Old Testament the time labour brigades have to work (1 Kings 5:14; 1 Chronicles 27:1).

22 M. Birot, *RA* 62 (1968) 21 HE. 191:28-29, cf. tr.lat.

23 AbB 8 109:11-13.

24 On the meaning of "to go out", see note 20, on CT 48 64:21. For the syntax of *ūmmāt* (sic) *uṣṣû*, cf. *u4-ma-at i-la-kum* (sic), YOS 12 333:7.

25 *qá-ti imitti ù šumēlim* (7). For this meaning of *qāti*, see AbB 11 153:17, with note b.

26 D. Charpin, *BiOr* 38 (1981) 530-1, Archives E (Larsa).

27 E.Szlechter, TJAUB (1963) 49 UMM H 26:22. Also possible is: "He shall make the *t.* workmen serve one month"; cf. C. Wilcke, *RA* 73 (1979) 94 (not: "1 Tag").

28 AbB 6 100:5; archive from Lower Yaḫrurum; see D. Charpin, *BiOr* 38 (1991) 519-529, Archives A and B. The same correpondents in TCL 18 145 (transportation of earth by ship).

29 OECT 13 176 rev., [x] e r é n d u s u x x x Ḫ u r . s a g . k a l a m . m a *ša* i t u .2. k a m *i-si-iḫ-ta-ša* ⌜*e*⌝*-mi-id-ma*.

2. The technical word *paṭārum* "to quit service" is used.[30]
3. The wages are paid in advance. They are not low. The official remuneration for work was 10 litres of barley, or 6 grains (š e) of silver per day; this is quite a lot.[31] One of our contracts stipulates 600 litres barley for one month = 12 grains daily, plus extra allocations (YOS 12 145). Another has the standard amount, 1 (?) shekel (= 180 grains) of silver for one month = 6 grains daily, plus extra allocations (DCS 98). This one shekel per month – a minimum – made me assume that the payment in silver instead of corvée worth the same amount (see above) was for one month.
4. The phrase "as those on the right and the left" is rare in hires of persons; actually, it is attested almost exclusively in contracts on hiring persons who have to carry out *tupšikkum* and *ḫarrān šarrim* work.[32] I think that this phrase does not refer to some local fixed standard but to unpredictable prices determined by market mechanisms. As we will see in the discussion on corvée and harvesting, prices went up when there was a great demand for workers.

Corvée and ḫarrān šarrim

The observation under (4) leads us to a comparison between *tupšikkum* and *ḫarrān šarrim* "the expedition of the king", another type of compulsory work. In both cases, persons could be hired to carry out corvée. We have four contracts.[33] The first thing that strikes us is that here, again, one or two months is the normal duration.[34] Furthermore, the wages are paid in advance. Moreover, in two texts, they are 1 shekel silver per month. In the third, the wages are higher: 30 grains of silver per day. This text has the additional remark: "one *rigimtum*-garment (?) has been received."[35] This reminds us of the food rations for one month (z í d . k a s k a l i t u .1. k [a m]) and a *rigimtum* in case of corvée (AbB 2 27:10). In a text on *ḫarrānum*, a man guarantees the presence of another man who is apparently his colleague (they are each other's *ālik ḫarrānišu*): "Should he not present him, he shall give 1

[30] M. Birot, *ARM* 27 (1993) 252, note c. Also in AUCT IV 44:6, *i-na pa-ṭa-ar* (sic !) *ma-za-az-ti*. Now in AbB 13 10:6.

[31] M. Stol, "Miete", in *RlA* VIII/3-4, 171 §3.4 and compare the examples given in §3.9.

[32] YOS 12 138 (*ḫarrān šarrim*), 140, 146; otherwise: only TLB 1 21. See M. Stol, "Miete", in *RlA* VIII/3-4, 171f., §3.4, end; §3.9, end.

[33] Texts and contents: see the survey by Stol, "Miete", in *RlA* VIII/3-4, §3.9, end, "Frondienst"; and the next note. Add VS 8 37 (VAB 5 239): fifty hirelings had been hired "for the expedition of the king."

[34] One month: Th. Friedrich, *BA* 5 (1906) 496 no. 19; C. Wilcke, *ZA* 73 (1983) 54 no. 2 (both 1 shekel per month). Two months: VS 7 47 (10 shekels). The time is not indicated but the wages are at least 2 kor = 600 litres: YOS 12 138.

[35] VS 7 47, cf. H. Klengel, *AoF* 4 (1976) 91-2. Ten shekels for two months. Lines 10-11: *ù* 1 t ú g *ri-gi-im-tu*[*m*] *ma-ḫi-ir* (*AHw*: "1 g í n"). Can we relate this word to the Semitic root *rqm* "mit bunten Farben weben, sticken"?

shekel of silver."[36] This would be the standard amount for one month of *ḫarrān šarrim* service.[37]

What is *ḫarrān šarrim*? We cannot investigate this problem in detail here. There is a broad definition: "umfaßt wohl alle Arten staatlicher Dienstverpflichtung" (C. Wilcke); and a more restrictive qualification, "military service" (B. Landsberger).[38] For *ḫarrān šarrim*, we prefer the second definition for the time being. Support for this comes from literary phrases of kings of Isin. Hymn A of Išme-Dagan says that he freed the workmen (e r é n) from the corvée (g i š . d u s u ; verb z i = *nasāḫum*), and the troops (u g n i m) from the weapon(s) (g i š . t u k u l ; verb g á . a r).[39] Does "the weapon(s)" refer to what is later called *ḫarrān šarrim* ? Other inscriptions of king Išme-Dagan speak of freeing (z i . g) the citizens (d u m u, or e r é n) of Nippur from the k a s k a l (= *ḫarrānum*).[40] This k a s k a l may have had the more general meaning which C. Wilcke adopted.

We have seen that in CT 48 64 the Overseer of the Ward was responsible for the corvée. It is interesting to compare this with the duties of the burgomaster (*rabiānum*).

In YOS 12 60, a burgomaster has the duty to "show" a man. Our translation of the text is: "As to Aplum, son of ..., whom they told Awil-ili, the burgomaster, to show to Šūnuḫ-Šamaš: if Awil-ili does not give a substitute (?) (*kallimum* lit. "showman") to Šūnuḫ-Šamaš within five days from now, (or) if he (himself) does not show Aplum, Awil-ili has to carry out the *ḫarrānum* of Aplum (*ul ukallamma A. ḫarrān Aplum illak*)."[41] Clearly, the burgomaster is fully responsible. We note that he takes care of the *ḫarrānum*, whereas the Overseer of the Ward does so for the *tupšikkum*. A letter shows that a burgomaster is unjustly harrassing a land steward (e n s í) carrying out his *ilkum* (AbB 10 151). This means that ultimately the *ilkum* is a burgomaster's responsibility, and we know that the *ilkum* is closely related to *ḫarrānum* (*ḫarrānam ilkam illak*, YOS 12 253;11-12, cf. 5). In another letter, the burgomaster of Kish is told "Do not summon the house of the land steward; also, they shall not summon him for the harvest" (AbB 5 134). The vague "*they* shall not summon him" shows that this corvée is not the burgomaster's direct responsibility.

36 BIN 2 81 (HG 6 1492). The obscure signs in line 1, after š u . d ù, can only be a PN (Elamite?). We suggest for line 6, *ú-ul ú-<uš>-za-sú-ma*, the form *ušzaz* followed by *-šu*.

37 As in the texts published by Friedrich (1, hardly ⌜10⌝ shekel) and Wilcke.

38 Wilcke, *ZA* 73 (1983) 55; Landsberger, *JCS* 9 (1955) 128a ("war service"), cf. 10 (1955) 39b.

39 Lines 188-189; A. Falkenstein, *BiOr* 23 (1965) 283; F.R. Kraus, *Kön. Verfügungen* (1984) 18-9.

40 Edzard, ZZB 81; Kraus, *Kön. Verfüg.* 17; now *RIME* 4 (1990) 32-3.

41 Otherwise *CAD* K 82b, 521b, where full transliterations and translations will be found. We do not know what the "showman" means. Contrary to the fanciful "compensation (?)" in *CAD* K, we are thinking of a (temporary) occupation like *kannikum, zabbilum*; *GAG* §55m (*parris*). Probably a substitute. Note the new word *mukallimum* in AbB 13 63:18, in a letter on the dispatch of two house builders to the king in Babylon. A soldier and the *m.* will accompany them. Can we emend *kallimam* in our text to *mukallimam*, or is this *obscurius per obscurum*?

If it is true that the corvée/military service of an individual lasted one month, it is interesting to compare this with the 4 days of service (g u b) per month king Enlil-bani of Isin imposed on his subjects (*muškēnum*).[42] This is more than one month per year (one twelfth). It is not clear what is meant by the figures "70" and "10 per month" in the prologue to Lipit-Ištar's law code. Edzard's latest translation is literal: "Ich ließ im 'Vaterhause', im Haus mit (mehreren) Brüdern, 70 antreten; im Haus des Junggesellen ließ ich [mon]atlich 10 antreten."[43] The traditional interpretation is: 70 days of forced labour per year, 10 days per month. A Sumerian proverb informs us that "the hoe and the basket" (g i š . a l g i š . d u s u) were indeed the duty of that "Junggesellenhaus" (é . g u r u š) (Proverbs 2.140).

Ur III scholars inform us that the population had to carry out the corvée for a number of months per year.[44] It was a family business among the foresters at Umma and they received subsistence fields as compensation.[45] They worked in the forests for no less than six months. We know from a much-discussed document from Nippur that a subsistence field was indeed linked to corvée: a widow (?) asks a man "Take upon you my subsistence (field), its corvée" (š u k u . g á ÍL.b i í l . b a . a b). He pays 5 shekels of silver for the 9 iku of land.[46] This is one of the rare cases where ÍL means "corvée." Also consider this passage in an Ur-Nammu hymn, "I made its citizens (d u m u - g i_7) return into their houses, I ... its corvée (ÍL.b i m u . u n . g i_4)."[47]

Old Babylonian texts show that corvée workers received food rations[48] but there is one text that relates corvée to the possession of a field. A herdsman says that he has received a field (*ṣibtum)* of 2 i k u in exchange for the corvée service of two men in the countryside of Sippar (2 e r é n d u s u *nawê Sippar allak*; AbB 7 46). The field has been given to other people and those now have to carry out the corvée. One should harrass the herdsman about the corvée no longer, writes the king. Two texts speak of "the corvée field." In one, a rented field in Dilbat is described as being situated "adjacent to the corvée field of Babylon" (a . š à *tu-up-ši-ik* k á . d i n g i r . r a^{ki}).[49] In the other, princess

42 Kraus, *Kön. Verfüg.* 29-30. Cf. G. Evans, *JAOS* 83 (1963) 21-22.

43 Edzard, *Acta Antiqua Academiae Scientiarum Hungaricae* 22 (1974) 150. Earlier in *ZZB* 96-7. Kraus, *Kön. Verfüg.* 23, skipped this. Cf. G. Evans, *JAOS* 83 (1963) 21-22.

44 A. Uchitel, *ASJ* 6 (1984) 85-87; 14 (1992) 326; K. Maekawa in: M.A. Powell, *Labor in the Ancient Near East* (1987) 65 ("at least sixty days per year"); P. Steinkeller, ibid., 86 (six months).

45 P. Steinkeller, "The foresters of Umma: towards a definition of Ur III labor", ibid., 73-115, esp. 87-8

46 D.I. Owen, NATN 258, with H. Neumann, *JAOS* 105 (1985) 153, and in J. Zablocka - S. Zawadzki, *Šulmu IV. Everyday life in Ancient Near East* (1993) 226, 232; H. Limet, *BiOr* 41 (1984) 410; P. Michalowski, *JNES* 45 (1986) 327b (identifies it with *ilkum*); P. Steinkeller - J.N. Postgate, *Third millennium legal and administrative texts in the Iraq Museum, Baghdad* (1992) 99-100.

47 TCL 15 12:89, with A. Falkenstein, *NSGU* 1 (1956) 94 note 2; G. Castellino, *ZA* 53 (1959) 120.

48 AbB 2 27:10; 6 162; 8 109:15 ff.

49 YOS 13 294:3, with F. Pomponio, *I contratti di affitto dei campi* (1978) 66-8.

Iltani rents from a number of authorities of Kār-Šamaš "the field of Ilī-imguranni (situated) within the corvée of the troops (?) of ..."[50] There is a number of texts where Kār-Šamaš acts as a city, represented by those authorities, the burgomaster and the elders; we cannot go into that here. Are these fields *ṣibtum* fields?

Two brief remarks on *tupšikkum* and *ḫarrānum* (not that of the king):
– We have seen Pirḫum hiring persons for corvée (two texts): he also hires someone from his father and mother "for the *ḫarrānum*, the *ilkum*" (*a-na* k a s≠ k a l *i-il-ki-im* (?)) for an indeterminate period [51].
– A letter speaks of three named persons, *a-we-lu-ú* d u s u *i-na qá-ti-ja aš-šum* k ù . b a b b a r *ma-aḫ-ri-ka k*[*i*]*-a-*[*am*] (?) [*i*]*q-qá-bu-ú.* The reverse has this syntacticaly isolated line: *a-we-lu-ú* 3 *ḫar-ra-na-tum.*[52] It is impossible to understand this letter.

Corvée and harvesting

The high wages in YOS 12 145 remind us of those in contracts in which individuals are hired to harvest: 30 litres (a child), 18 grains, 15 litres, 20 litres.[53] In one case, a third party guarantees that the harvester will be there; a similar phrase is found in a *ḫarrān šarrim* contract.[54] The harvest season must have required the energies of large parts of the population. Long before the season, "harvest labour contracts" on the delivery of harvesters were concluded with middlemen; the high wages show that during the harvest period the "market" must have determined the prices. We interpreted the phrase "as those on the right and the left" in the same light; the phrase is attested in one "harvest labour contract."[55] Texts show that outsiders like carpenters or gardeners were engaged in harvesting.[56] It will not come as a surprise that corvée was one way of mobilising the population during this period; the letter published by P. Villard, *MARI* 6 (1990) 573f., shows this. Whatever §22 of the Edict of Ammi-ṣaduqa exactly means, it shows that harvesting is singled out as

50 YOS 13 490:2-3, with Pomponio, 87-8: š à GI.ÍL e r é n *um(!)-ma-an x (x) tim.* Inspired by e r é n *um-ma-an* D i l . b a t[ki], YOS 13 156:4. We admit, however, that Hunger's b à d in: B à d [d][Ḫ]a-ià, is not bad: construction work on a fortress (H. Hunger, *WO* 8 (1976) 328)?

51 YOS 12 253. "He has to perform the *ḫarrānum*, the *ilkum*" (k a s k a l *il-k*[*a*]*-am i-la-ak*), 11-12. Wages: 712 litres of barley.

52 Jean, ŠA CXCVII:195, lines 6-10 and rev. 6. Note that again 3 persons had a corvée in UET 5 268 (see above).

53 Refs. in Stol, "Miete", in *RlA* VIII/3-4, 172b §3.9, "Erntearbeit."

54 BAP 57:17-18 (VAB 5 157) and Th. Friedrich, *BA* 5 (1906) 496 no.19:13-14 (VAB 5 159).

55 VAT 805, in J.G. Lautner, *Altbabylonische Personenmiete und Erntearbeiterverträge* (1936), frontispiece and p. 152-3. Unpublished harvest labour contracts offer "as his colleague", *ki-ma a-li-ik i-di-šu* harvesters *i-la-ak*, BM 97085 and 97862 (courtesy Bram Jagersma and Els Woestenburg).

56 Pinches, *Berens Coll.* 96, ARMT 13 40:7-9 (verb *lapātum*) and YOS 12 399; cf. E. Sollberger, TCS 1 no. 173 (š i t i m).

the most important job to be done: "for harvesting or doing a work."[57] A letter, discussing the harvest, opens: "As you know, it is harvest (time); who shall give whom his due right now (*ina kima inanna mannum mannam ippal*)?" Everybody is too busy, is the implication. Then, the burgomaster of Kār-Šamaš states: "that field has been assigned to the corvée workers (*eqlum šû ana* e r é n . d u s u . m e š *esḫam*)" (AbB 7 110:16). From this perspective, we can interpret the meaning of the short text published here as Appendix B: "Nobody shall summon the corvée workers of the Gate for harvesting." The text was written one or two months before the harvest and sealed by a high-ranking "scribe." Unfortunately, corvée workers of the Gate are not attested elsewhere. They were probably watchmen at the city gate.[58] This order has a fine parallel in the letter to the burgomaster of Kish quoted above: "they shall not summon him for the harvest" (AbB 5 134).

In an Old Babylonian letter we see how various groups have been recruited to do the harvest; among them are "workmen, Amorites" and "workmen, army of the king." We are interested in the "workmen, city ward" (e r é n d a g4. g i4. a) in this letter. They have to "produce" the barley; the same verb was used in the Kār-Šamaš letter on corvée.[59] We will remember that in CT 48 64, studied above, it is the Overseer of the Ward who levies his people for corvée (*tupšikkum*).[60] So probably the harvesters from the ward in our letter are carrying out this corvée.

A letter published recently by W.H. van Soldt gives us a new perspective on the arrangements made during this hectic period: their "Head" (probably Sin-iddinam) gave barley to the burgomaster and elders of Atašum which they gave to/for hirelings (AbB 13 44). It later became clear, however, that the burgomaster and elders "had been given" to two other persons, not their Head; they have to harvest and collect the barley of the *biltum* fields of those other men. Clearly, the city elite had to carry out a corvée for which they used hirelings.[61]

[57] Kraus, *Kön. Verfüg.* 182.

[58] Cf. "(the men) e r é n k á é . g a l . m e š who at the order of the Palace are stationed in the gates (k á . g a l . m e š) of Sippar and check the gate (k á *usannaqū*)", AbB 12 9:7-10. – F.R. Kraus has suggested the meaning "Komplex von Feldern vor einem Stadtore (*abullum*)" for the Gate and compares this with *bābtum* "Stadtviertel am Tore (*bābum*); see his *Vom mesopotamischen Menschen der altbabylonischen Zeit und seiner Welt* (1973) 75. If this is true, we cannot rule out that the corvée workers of our text were taken from the "sons of the Gate" discussed by Kraus.

[59] AbB 11 186 (*elûm* Š); cf. AbB 2 66:10, 21 (Š; "harvest and produce"), 7 110:21 (G). For the verb *elûm* in this meaning, see now ARM 27 4:21 (G); 37:33, 44; 100:9, 11; 102:8, 12 (Š).

[60] Note the house situated between "Broad Street" and "the House of the Soldiers, workmen of the ward" (e g i r . b i é a g a . ú s . m e š e r é n d a g4. g i4. a), YOS 13 94:8 (Wilcke, *FsKraus* 454). Another link between ward and soldiers: rental of a field "at the order of the soldier of the ward", CT 8 10b:6 (VAB 5 123).

[61] Was the barley given to them payment for hiring harvesters? We know that barley was used for that purpose (AbB 13 78). During the reigns of Ammi-ditana and Ammi-ṣaduqa, the burgomaster and elders of Dilbat acted as middlemen in harvest labour contracts. It would be interesting to have a fresh look at those texts. See M.Stol, *Studies in Old Babylonian History* (1976) 90 ff.

Other aspects

We have discussed corvée and harvest in some detail. It might be useful to add here that *tupšikkum* can also involve (brick) construction work (AbB 9 2, 264; UET 5 268). The only explicit evidence for *tupšikkum* as "digging canals" is found in mathematical texts.[62]

This passage in an inscription of Hammurabi poses a problem: "Sippar, the ancient city of Šamaš: I relieved its workmen from the corvée, for Šamaš (e r é n . b i d u s u . t a ^{d}u t u . r a ḫ é . b í . z i / e r é n-*šu in* d u s u *a-na* ^{d}u t u *lu as-sú-uḫ*)."[63] F.R. Kraus was of the opinion that "for Šamaš" means that Hammurabi abolished the royal corvée so that the men could now work for the Šamaš temple.[64] This or a similar phrase may have been imitated by the author of the Cruciform Monument, a Neo-Babylonian forgery from Sippar situating itself in the reign of the Old Akkadian king Maništusu: "38 cities have been released to Šamaš, I did not covet their corvée (*ana Šamaš lū uššurū ilikšunu la aḫšiḫu*), they did not summon them (*šisīta la issūšunuti*); they shall do the corvée of Ebabbar only (*ilik Ebabbarim-ma lū illakū*)."[65] This more elaborate wording corroborates Kraus' interpretation.

Two related letters written by king Hammurabi indicate that the size of one corvée crew was ten men in Larsa (n a m .10).[66] Crews of this size were not uncommon and had an overseer.[67] According to the first text, they are to be at hand on 1.III (harvest time). We can extract more information from these letters when we succeed in identifying the persons who are expected to deliver the crews. They are, according to the second letter, Sin-iddinam, head of the Lower District, the recipient of many letters from Hammurabi[68]; Šamaš-mušallim, whom we can equate with the unnamed "Head of the District" (*šāpir mātim*) in the parallel passage of the first letter[69]; and Nannatum of Bad-Tibira, Nabium-mālik of Larsa, Zimru-Akšak of [...]. They probably are the

62 MCT (1945) 88, Text L, "work at lower levels in the excavation of a canal."

63 I.J. Gelb, *JNES* 7 (1948) 269 II 13-16 with note 16; *RIME* 4 (1990) 33-6 E.4.3.6.2, lines 56-60.

64 Kraus, *Kön. Verfüg.* 55 note 119. Cf. M. Gallery, *JAOS* 99 (1979) 79 note 8.

65 E. Sollberger, *JEOL* 20 (1967-68) 57, 127-138.

66 AbB 2 27:11 and AbB 13 30. – The pertinent phrase in AbB 2 27:10-11, studied above (z í d. k a s k a l i t u .1. k a m *rigimtam ù* n a m .10. e 1 m á .10. g u r *lilqiam*), is rather similar to one in a Sippar text belonging to a group where the middleman Ipqatum, son of Paḫallum, is active: z í d . k a s k a l i t u .1.k a m n a m .10 (K. van Lerberghe, OLA 21 no. 66:9-10; cf. n a m .10 *Ipqatum* in no. 60:9). Again food provisions for one month, for a crew of ten men. But there is no sign that corvée work is involved in Sippar. Moreover, other texts show that this Ipqatum could be in charge of 12 or 16 men (n a m .12; BE 6/1 29:7-8; n a m .16, van Lerberghe no. 66:8). Ten men with food (š u k u) for one month in AbB 13 110:34.

67 W. von Soden, *AHw* s.v. *ušurtum.*

68 W.H. van Soldt, note (a) to AbB 13 8.

69 AbB 2 27:5. Confirmed by AbB 13 44:10. The Head of the District ranks below Sin-iddinam: AbB 2 27; AbB 13 8, 19.

"heads" (*šāpirum*) of these cities because Nabium-mālik is the head of Larsa [70]. This is in accordance with the letters on "carrying work" mentioned above: the Head of the District and the Head of Kish seized the people and had them to carry out this corvée. We learn from all this that the highest authorities were responsible for delivering corvée workers.

Scholars consider the u n . í l workers of the Ur III period to be people with a lower status than the prebend-holding corvée workers (e r é n), although they do the same work; they are "menials."[71] If the Akkadian equivalent of this Sumerian word is indeed *kinattûm (*thus a lexical text), we can be sure that the u n . í l were indeed menials in the following Old Babylonian period.[72] Texts speak of "keeping under guard" (*naṣārum*) the e r é n u n . í l and the *kinattûm*.[73] The numbers of u n . í l workmen are larger than those of corvée workers and multiples of thirty, as far as we can tell: 90, 180, 720 [74].

[70] Nabium-mālik *šāpir Larsam*: AbB 4 14:8-9, Birot, TEBA 23:9, with M. Gallery, *AfO* 27 (1980) 19 n. 86. – In the Larsa texts, Nabium-mālik has no title and it is not easy to identify a man with this name as the Head of Larsa. We assume that he is referred to in the following passages: AbB 2 15:15 (with colleagues); AbB 4 14:8-9 (*šāpir Larsam*, as in TEBA 23:9), 65:6 (in charge of ensí's, as in AbB 2 38:7, 10); AbB 13 30:7 (corvée), 48:6 (*namriātum ša Larsam* n í g . š u *Nabium-mālik),* 119:7 (shares field with Nannatum); W.H. van Soldt, *JEOL* 25 (1977-78) 46:3,5 (judicial capacities; cf. YOS 12 192:7); M. Anbar - M. Stol, *RA* 85 (1991) 19 no. 8:10, 18 and seal, "servant of Hammurabi" (responsible for the quays of a canal and those "of the land"; cf. AbB 13 109:3). Perhaps also in Arnaud, *Larsa et 'Oueili* (1983) 267 no. 3:15 (Ubalani-namḫe follows).

[71] Steinkeller, in: M.A. Powell, *Labor in the Ancient Near East* (1967) 98.

[72] Latest discussion by Joan G. Westenholz, *JNES* 42 (1983) 227, who sees in them the "nomadic laborers, unskilled tribesmen" in M. Rowton's dimorphic state. The passages from letters given by her are not enough to prove this.

[73] AbB 2 77:9; 9 24:9 (u n . í l) and B. Kienast, *Kisurra* 153:15. In ARM 10 150, the *kinattûm* escape from prison.

[74] BIN 2 97:2, TCL 1 3 (VAB 6 45), Kienast, *Kisurra* 154:27.– The few refs. for OB u n . í l have been given in CAD Z 9a, under *zābilu*. Add YOS 5 12:2 (70 kor of dates as š e . b a e r é n . u n . í l . m e š), M. Krebernik, *Isin-Išān Bahrīyāt* IV (1992) 119 IB 1722:8 (barley *ni-šu/i* . d i b u n . í l), Kienast, *Kisurra* 154:27, 33; AbB 12 172:26, 29.

APPENDIX A: List of Overseers of the Ward, PA d a g$_{4}$. g i$_{(4)}$. a (or *rabi(ān) bābtim*)

Nippur

Tarībum, BE 6/2 30:2 (-, IV Si 11)
I-bi-ja, ARN 86 rev. 5 (1.XI Si 11)
I-bi-i, S. Langdon, *Babyl.* 7 (1914) 71 rev. 3 (Si 12)
Ninurta-mansum, Stone-Owen, *Adoption* (1991) 62 no. 26 IV 3 (Si [..]).
Dingir-mansum, Stone, *Nippur Neighborhoods* (1987) Text 40:1 (collated).

Larsa

⸢Ip⸣qu-Ištar, VS 13 82 rev. 4 (RS 44)
Ilum-tajjār, VS 18 1:29, cf. 5 (RS 55)
Luštammar, Anbar, *RA* 72 (1978) 116 no. 3:17 (Hamm 31)
Ṣilli-Šamaš, TCL 1 174 rev. 39 (Hamm 40); YOS 12 557:33 (Si); H. Limet, *FsKupper* (1990) 52 no. 9 rev. 12 (Si 3).
Muḫaddûm, YOS 12 214:29 (10. II Si 7)
Awil-ili, YOS 12 227:38 (7.VI Si 7)
Awil-Adad, Anbar-Stol, *RA* 85 (1991) 35 no. 23:13 (Si 11)
Warad-Sebetti, ARV 26:2, 11 (Si 12) (Larsa?)
x-a, Boyer, CHJ 2 HE 120:27 (Si ..)

Other cities

Dumuq-Šamaš, SCT 42:25 (Si 5; Ur?)
Erība-Sin, UET 5 214:4-5 (RS II; Ur)
Ga/Bi-ni/ir-ma-bi-de-e *ra-bi-an ba-ab-ti-šu*, RIME 4 659 E.4.9.1 (Mutalu?)
Gimil-Marduk, CT 48 64:5 (Hamm 38; Babylon?)
Ḫilalum *ra-bi ba-ab-ti-šu*, D. Collon, *BM Cylinder Seals* III no. 76:3
Inbi-ilišu, in: d a g$_{4}$. g i$_{4}$. a Inbi-ilišu, OECT 13 78:2 (Si 26)
Sin-erībam PA *ba-ab*(!)-*tum*, OECT 13 8 rev. 5 (Kish)
Ṣilli-Ištar, Anbar-Stol, *RA* 85 (1991) 29 no. 19:25 (Hamm 32; Uruk?)
[....] (?) Speleers, *Receuil* 246, edge

Note PA d a g$_{4}$. g i$_{4}$. a in UET 7 73 II 5 (lexical; after l ú . g e$_{6}$. DU.DU "nightwatch").

APPENDIX B

YBC 10986 (s. Pl. 35), published by courtesy of Dr. William W. Hallo, Curator of the Babylonian Collection, Yale University.
Dimensions: 3,8 cm high; 3,6 cm wide; 2,2 cm thick. The rims of the cylinder seal run over the tablet.
Date: 4. XII, Samsuiluna year 5.

obv. e r é n GI.ÍL k á . g a l
a-na š e . g u r_{10}. k u d
ma-am-ma-a[*n*]
la i-š[*a*]-*ás-si*
(blank)
rev. i t u . š e . g u r_{10}. k u d u_4. 4 .k a m
m u g u . z a b i z e m . a

Inscription on seal impression:

mu-ḫa-ad-du-[*um*]
[d]u b . s[a r]
d u m u *li-pí-it–Iš*[*tar*] (?)
ì r *sa-am-su–i-lu-n*[*a*]

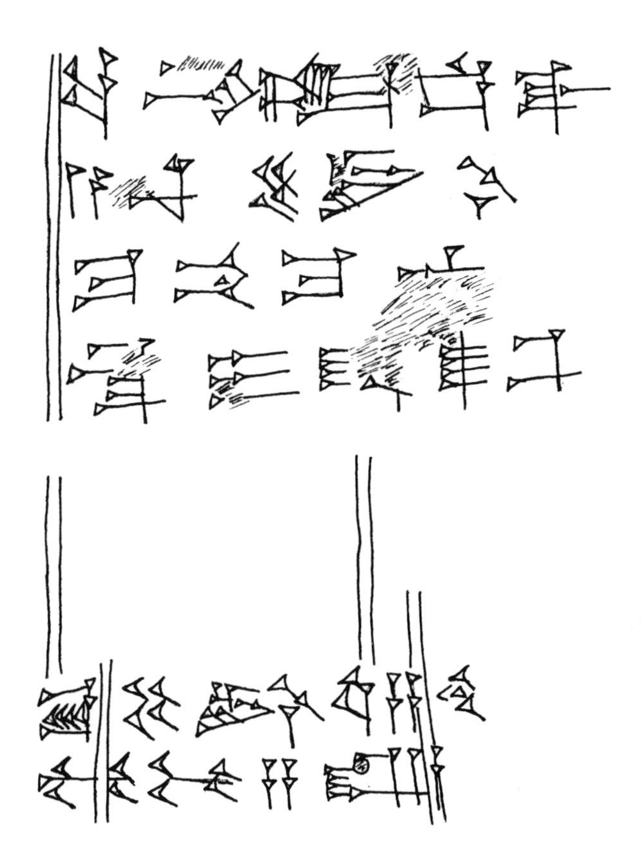

Plate 35. YBC 10986.

OLD ASSYRIAN *IṢURTUM*, AKKADIAN *EṢĒRUM* AND HITTITE GIŠ.ḪUR

KLAAS R. VEENHOF

Written documents play a vital role in Old Assyrian trade and no other corpus of texts probably contains so many references to them as the so-called Kültepe texts. Letters were essential for communication between Assur and Anatolia and inside Anatolia between the various trading stations. Contracts and judicial records of every kind recorded and validated a variety of legal transactions of which they served as written evidence, also in lawsuits. Many lists, notes and memorandums enabled the traders to keep track of their goods and transactions, especially lists of outstanding claims which were used for collecting debts and for the periodic settling of accounts (*nikkassū*) arranged by the organization of the traders, the *kārum*.

The terminology reflects this state of affairs. The use of the all-embracing word *ṭuppum*, "(inscribed clay) tablet", is ubiquitous, often with a reference to it being sealed- i.e. encased in a clay envelope on which the seals are impressed - which lends its legal, evidentiary force (*ṭuppum harmum*, with or without added *ša kunukkim*). A variety of genitival adjuncts helps to specify the nature, contents or function of a tablet: *ša šībē,* "of witnesses", a recorded testimony or deposition validated by seal impressions; *ša naruqqim*, "of a money bag", a record of a capital investment in a firm; *ša šabā'ē*, "of satisfaction", a quittance issued when the original debt-note could not be returned to the debtor upon payment; *ša mamītim*, "of an oath" sworn in the "gate of the god" in the context of a lawsuit; *ša šiamātim*, "of purchases", a letter specifying purchases made and expenses paid for equipping a caravan in Assur; *ša be'ūlātim*, "of a working capital", recording an interest free loan granted to caravan personnel instead of a fixed wage in exchange for their service; etc. Duplicates (*mehrum*) of tablets occur time and again, written as archive copies, for sharing essential information with partners and associates, or drawn up for reasons of security, when valuable original deeds had to be sent overland. Other frequently mentioned types of documents are *našpertum*, "document sent (overland)", often under seals and with the legal force of an authorized statement or order[1], and *tahsistum*, "memorandum", in particular lists of outstanding debts without legal force but as

[1] See M.T. Larsen, in: M. Gibson - R.D. Biggs (eds.), *Seals and Sealing in the Ancient Near East* (*Bibl. Mes.* 6, Malibu 1977), 97f., with *CAD* N s.v.

aid to memory[2]. Rare and less well defined are *dannutum*, "strong, valid document", probably not a specific type of text but a designation stressing its binding and final character[3], and *nudu'um*, "booking", derived from the use of the verb *nadā'um*, "to note down", especially in the expression *tahsistam nadā'um*, "to draw up a note", "to put to writing", as aid to memory[4].

Less frequent and still rather enigmatic is *iṣurtum*, of which some twenty occurrences are known to me. In EL no. 320:14 Julius Lewy translated "Aufzeichnungen" and in footnote h) he argued for his translation by referring to CCT 1, 37b:2f. (below no.4), where the word is the direct object of the verb *eṣārum*, "to draw", assuming that the OA term is a dialectical variant of the well-known *uṣurtum*, "drawing", attested in Assyrian and Babylonian in most other periods.

The occurrence of records called "drawing" during the Old Assyrian period in Anatolia (roughly the 19th century B.C.) soon caught the attention of Hittitologists, not surprising since the Boğazköy tablets had acquainted them with the existence of a type of document designated by the sumerogram GIŠ.HUR, which in Akkadian has the equivalent *uṣurtum*, "drawing", probably the same word as *iṣurtum*. Among the Hittites the word was used to refer to a type of "wooden tablets", presumably a wooden writing board coated with wax. H.G. Güterbock was the first to refer to OA *iṣurtum* in his discussion of GIŠ.HUR and "wooden tablets". While for the latter he hesitated between the meanings record, list and catalogue, OA *iṣurtum*, in his opinion, could only be a kind of record ("Urkunde")[5]. B. Landsberger[6], in 1948, believed that *iṣurtam eṣārum* was used for the drawing up of a debt-note or quittance, not in cuneiform writing, but as a "prägrafische Urkundenform", whose nature, however, he did not define. H.Th. Bossert deduced from the occurrence of *iṣurtam eṣārum* in the framework of commercial contacts between Assyrians and native, Anatolian palaces "dass die einheimische anatolische Bevölkerung ihre Schriftstücke in Bilderschrift anfertigte, also wirklich "eine Zeichnung zeichnete", denn um diese Zeit müssen die einzelne Zeichen der hethitischen Hieroglyphenschrift noch in grösseren

[2] See K.R. Veenhof, Observations on Old Assyrian memorandums ...., *JEOL* 28 (1983-4) 10-23.

[3] See *CAD* D, 90, 8 and 91a, 2, with *JNES* 16 (1957) 164: 35ff. and Larsen-Møller, *Festschrift Garelli* (Paris 1991) 229 no. 2:14 (*ana mala dannitišu*). See for its character the expression *ṭuppum ša dannātim* (BIN 6, 162:4') and the use of *dannum* and the verb *dannunum* used of tablets, both binding orders and records containing valid testimonies. See for the MA occurrences and meaning J.N. Postgate, *AoF* 13 (1986), 17f. and for NA also *SAAB* 5 (1991) 85f. no. 38.

[4] See *CAD* N s.v. with Adana 237B (Donbaz, *AfO* 31 (1984) 23f.): 48 (plural); cf. for *tahsistam nadā'um* i.a. CCT 5, 17c: 8ff.

[5] In *Festschrift P. Koschaker* (Leiden 1939), 35f. His reference to *uṣurtum* (GIŠ.HUR) in UM 2/2 no. 81:33 (MBab.), also found in *AHw* 1440 a s.v. 3), is better ignored, since the reading most probably has to be GIŠ.KÍN, to be equated with *kiškanû*, a type of tree and wood, cf. also *NABU* 1987 no. 2.

[6] *Sam'al* I (Ankara 1948), 107f.

Ausmasse erkennbare Bilder gewesen sein"[7]. His ideas may have influenced Julius Lewy, who observed in 1954[8] that OA *iṣurtum* referred to "documents relating to goods sold by Assyrians to non-Assyrian princes and their servants, thus strongly suggesting that *iṣurtum* was used as a technical term for *"records written in a foreign language and script"* (italics mine, K.R.V.). But Lewy did not try to identify these nor did he suggest they were Hittite hieroglyphs, although this would have been the most likely identification given the time and place of their occurrence. Bossert's conviction, that the so-called Hittite hieroglyphs represented the older "genuine Hittite" script (based on his belief that the "real Hittites" were the ones using that script) and that the introduction of cuneiform only came later, was soon refuted by H.G. Güterbock, who also argued that the oldest evidence for the existence of the hieroglyphic script was not really earlier than the middle of the second mill. B.C.[9]

In 1964 H. Otten conceded: "das früheste Vorkommen der Hieroglyphen, wohl mit symbolhaften Charakter, schon zur Zeit der altassyrischen Handelsniederlassungen, scheint unbestreitbar", but he too did not refer to OA *iṣurtum* nor did he speak of the hieroglyphic script[10]. Subsequently many Hittitologists have dealt with the Hittite "wooden tablets", GIŠ.HUR, their shape, nature, function and implications[11], recently also using a few occurrences outside the Boğazköy corpus, in texts from Ugarit and Emar.[12] The present writer, notwithstanding the references kindly supplied by J. de Roos, also on the problems of identification of other types of Hittite administrative records[13], does not feel competent to enter this discussion, which is better left to specialists[14], which now can draw on the admirable summary and analysis by D. Symington.[15] It is also

[7] *BiOr* 9 (1952) 172f.; cf. his contributions in *WO* 1 (1952) 480ff. and in *Minoica. Festschrift J. Sundwall* (1958) 67ff.

[8] *HUCA* 25 (1954) 196 with note 108.

[9] *OLZ* 1956 Sp. 513ff.

[10] *NHF* 7.

[11] Bossert's views were accepted by J. Friedrich, *HW* 274: GIŠ.HUR is "Holztafel (Urkunde) mit hethitischer Hieroglyphenschrift", but in his *Geschichte der Schrift* (1966) 63, he did not repeat this identification, merely stating that this type of script "kann ein selbständiges Produkt des alten Kleinasien sein, das neben (oder sogar vor?) der aus der Fremde importierten Keilschrift in vielleicht zunächst primitiver Gestalt erfunden wurde".

[12] Cf. D. Arnaud, *Hethitica* 8 (1987) 13f. with note 43; in *Emar* VI no. 261:20f. we meet a d u b . s a r . g i š living in Šatappi. See for Ugarit, PRU VI no. 19 (*ṭuppa ša iškuri*, a wax coated tablet, to serve as quittance); RSO VII no. 7: 23 and no. 8: 22, both letters of the king of Karkemish.

[13] Such as *dušdumi-*, *lalami*, and *parzaki-*.

[14] See, most recently, the observations by Ph.H.J. Houwink ten Cate, *BiOr* 51 (1994) 235f. on the nature and contents of wooden tablets in connection with the discovery of deposits of royal bullae at Boğazköy.

[15] Late Bronze Age Writing Boards and their Uses. Textual Evidence from Anatolia and Syria, *AnSt* 41 (1991) 111-123, with pls. xvii-xix.

not necessary, since in these recent discussions OA *iṣurtum* no longer plays a role. Short remarks by some Old Assyrian specialists[16] may have convinced Hittitologists that this word, notwithstanding Lewy's statement quoted above, is not a document drawn (up) in Hittite hieroglyphs, hence is not relevant for the meaning of GIŠ.HUR. Moreover, the more recent consensus[17] that, even when isolated symbols incorporated in the hieroglyphic script may have occurred earlier, the script as such, as a fully developed system, is not attested before the end of the 16th century B.C. (hence at least three hundred years later than the occurrences of *iṣurtum*) may have discouraged them of considering a possible link.

But the question what exactly an *iṣurtum* is, also found in *AHw* ("von einheimischen Fürsten (nichtassyrisch?) ausgestellte Urkunde"[18]), still has to be answered. The last clear answer was given by Balkan in 1965[19], who stated on the basis of ten occurrences, that *iṣurtam eṣārum* means "das Herstellen einer speziell für die einheimische Bevölkerung in Bilderschrift gezeichnete (hölzerne) Schuldurkunde", a statement reviving the ideas of Landsberger, Bossert and Lewy. This conviction should give Hittitologists cause for concern, the more so since both Garelli and Laroche[20] have shown that the bulk of the population of Anatolia in Old Assyrian times was already "Neshite", i.e. culturally and linguistically the direct ancestors of the Hittites. Since also students of Old Assyrian trade are still not certain what an *iṣurtum* is, a fresh investigation seems useful. It might be of interest to the jubilarian too, who in the Netherlands embodies the scholarly interest in the cultural history of Anatolia.

The verb eṣērum

Isurtum is derived from *eṣērum*, which means "to draw, to make a drawing". The references quoted in *CAD* E s.v. show that this can be done by means of paint, paste or flour upon the ground, on walls and other surfaces, but also by simply drawing lines in the soil, the clay (of a tablet), the wax of a writing-board. But it can also be done by engraving on metal or stone. It may even refer to the making of reliefs in stone and metal, such as the war scenes on

[16] B. Kienast, *ATHE* (1960) ad no.12:1 ("Urkunde" not "Aufzeichnung", with a reference to Landsberger quoted above note 6), and P. Garelli, *AC* 227 note 1, *RHA* XVIII/66 39:14, and *RA* 59 46f. ad MAH 19613:2, where he always translates *iṣurtum* with "relevé".
[17] Cf. E. Laroche in *RlA* 4, 399, §5, 2, and J.D. Hawkins, Writing in Anatolia: imported and indigenious systems, *World Archaeology* 17/3 (1986) 363-76, esp. 371.
[18] *AHw* 391b s.v. 2, with reference to J. Lewy (as quoted in note 8 above).
[19] *OLZ* 1965 Sp. 157f. ad ICK 2, 292.
[20] E. Laroche, *NH* 364, and P. Garelli, *AC* 133ff., notably 150 and 167: "Les Assyriens se sont établis dans un milieu hétérogène, mais où les éléments hittitisants prédominent."

sculptured stone slabs in Assyrian palaces or the bronze plaques picturing Ishtar while she is driving a lion.[21] It is also used for describing the reliefs on boundary stones, depicting the "seats" or symbol socles, the weapons and the "images" of the gods.[22]

The verb is common in extispicy texts to designate various grooves and linear marks observed by diviners on the intestines, both the "standard features" (the "presence", *manzāzum*; the "path", *padānum*; the "yoke", *nīrum*[23]) and some "fortuitous marks"[24], such as the "split" (*piṭrum*), the "foot" (*šēpum*), and the "cross" (*pillurtum*). They may appear as straight (*išāriš*), curved (like a *gamlum*), long, short or crossed (*parkiš*) lines. "Drawings" are also observed in the sky and identified as stars and features related to the halo.[25]

Since OA *iṣurtum* must be some kind of inscribed document, the question arises whether the meaning "to draw" could have developed into "to write", and that at a fairly early moment in view of the date of OA *iṣurtum*. It is known that in extispicy some marks or grooves, belonging to the "fortuitous marks", already in the Old Babylonian period were considered so similar to certain cuneiform signs that they were actually given their names. There is a mark called *kakkum*, not primarily because it looks like a weapon, (the meaning of the Akkadian word *kakkum*), but because it exhibits the typical shape of the cuneiform sign KAK (in the shape of the capital V turned 90 degrees to the left). Other signs or sign names used in this way are AŠ, BAD, PAP, LÁ, DINGIR, HAL and IDIM.[26] In describing them, however, the texts never state that such a sign/mark is "drawn" (*eṣir*), let alone "written" (*šaṭir*), but simply state its presence (*ibašši, šakin*). Lieberman is probably right in assuming that it was the similarity of some of them with cuneiform signs which gave rise to the idea that the gods Shamash and Adad wrote their message or verdict on the liver, and not the idea of or belief in divine writing which led to the recognition of cuneiform signs on the surface of

[21] Cf. *CAD* Ṣ 84b, b), 4', 1 and Winckler, *Sargon* pl. 48:18.

[22] *MDP* 2 pl. 23 VII:34, and cf. *ZA* 65 (1975) 58:76ff., with some variation, though in both texts pictorial representations (for which the verbs *uddûm* or *bašāmum*, *kullumum* and *uṣṣurum* are used) are distinguished from verbal renderings ("whose names are mentioned", with *zakārum*). See also U. Seidl, *BaMitt.* 4 (1968) 113f.

[23] According to J.W.Meyer, *Untersuchungen zu den Tonlebermodellen aus dem Alten Orient* (*AOAT* 39; Neukirchen 1987) 69f., 81f., these "normal drawings" (*uṣurātu kajjānātu*) usually are impressions on the surface of the liver made by neighbouring organs.

[24] They are anomalous and refer to changes in the parts of the liver which are the result of diseases, worms etc. Cf. J.W. Meyer, op.cit. 72f., and U. Jeyes, *Old Babylonian Extispicy* (Leiden 1989) 180 note 7.

[25] Cf. *CAD* E 348a, a, 1', end and see also *SAA* VIII (1992) nos. 19 rev:6f., 55:4, 124:6 and 530:4. In no. 19 "stars should be drawn on an Akkadian writing-board (*le'u*) of the king". See for actual drawings E. Weidner, *Gestirndarstellungen auf babylonischen Tontafeln* (Wien 1967).

[26] See S.J. Lieberman, in: M. de Jong Ellis (ed.), *Essays on the Ancient Near East in Memory of Jacob Joel Finkelstein* (Hamden 1977) 147-154.

the liver.[27] The idea of linking "drawing" and "writing" might have arisen much earlier, from the technique of "drawing" the earliest pictographs on tablets. But the technique of writing in the Old Babylonian period – impressing the tip or edge of a stylus in the wet clay, for which the verbs *lapātum*, *šaṭārum* and *mahāṣum* are used – apparently was considered different from that of making a drawing, drawing lines in clay.

There are even a few (late) references which actually contrast writing and drawing. Sennacherib in OIP 2, 140:9 distinguishes the god Assur, whose image (*ṣalmum*) is drawn (*eṣir*) on a gate, from other gods "not drawn" but "whose names (only) are written down". And the Lamashtu text LKU 33 rev.:19 mentions a tablet to be written (*šaṭārum*), on which also a crescent and a sun-disc are to be drawn (*eṣērum*).[28]

Occasionally the verb has the meaning "to notch, to score". The demon Lamashtu counts the days of the pregnant women by "scoring" them on a wall.[29] And Utnapishtim's wife used the same device to convince Gilgamesh that he had slept through seven days (Gilgamesh XI:212). This seems to be the nearest approach to a meaning "to register, to book", conceived as a simple, primitive bookkeeping system.

uṣurtum and g i š . h u r

A development "drawing" > "writing" also cannot be argued for from the meaning of the noun *uṣurtum* and its Sumerian counterpart g i š . h u r, borrowed into Akkadian as *gišhurrum*. The primary meaning is "drawing", "groundplan". According to Gudea Cyl. A V:2ff. the king, in his dream saw a hero holding a lapis lazuli plaque (*le'um*) with the "drawing" of the temple to be built, possibly its groundplan, as shown on Gudea's statue B (AO 2, "l'architecte au plan"). The hero is identified in VI:5ff. as the god Nin.dub, "who put on it the drawing of the house" (é . a g i š . h u r . b a i m . m i . s è . s è . g e). g i š . h u r is interpreted by D.O. Edzard[30] as "holz einritzen", referring to the action itself and to its result: the drawing/engraving of or the engraved wood(en board). The term

27 Ibidem 150 note 43.

28 According to LKA 137:16 "seven gods should be drawn upon the ground" (*iṣir ina qaqqari*), which *CAD* E 347a, 1' renders by "draw seven (names of) gods ...", an interpretation accepted by W. Horowitz - V. Hurowitz in *JANESCU* 21 (1922) 103f. with note 32, though they mention S. Paul's view, that actually divine symbols were drawn. Line 4 on the rev. of the text presents the names of the seven gods to be drawn in vertical position with irregular interspace. This layout, though writing the names, is clearly intended to show the position of the drawings upon the ground and does not mean that cuneiform signs should be written on the soil. Images or symbols have to be drawn.

29 LKU 33: 15'// KAR 239 I:4', where *eṣērum* D is used in parallelism with *manû*, "to count".

30 *ZA* 62 (1962) 8.

is very frequent in literary texts with the meaning "plan, regulation", referring to divine or meta-divine plans or rules, frequently also rites of temples and cults, once "drawn" and hence fixed, which are at the basis of phenomena and ritual acts and determine how they should be and should function.[31] They must not be changed, turned over or be forsaken (k ú r, b a l, ḫ a l a m), but be maintained and kept in correct state (s i . s á). The use of g i š . h u r seems to stress the notion that such rules have been drawn, fixed from old and hence cannot be changed. There is, again, no reference to writing but rather to a design, a groundplan, a pattern laid down. The terminology is that of an architect, surveyor or accountant rather than that of a scribe. Hendursanga is the "accountant" (ŠITA$_5$.DÙ) of Nindar, "for whom Nanše made the stick and staff grow for (drawing?) the g i š . h u r."[32] According to Šulgi Hymn C:46 the king was trained in "counting and accounting the g i š . h u r of the land" and this can be connected with the statement that Lipit-Ishtar was granted both the art of writing (with a golden stylus on a (clay) tablet, d u b) and the art of surveying, "the measuring rod (lustrous) like lapis lazuli, the *aslum*-cubit and the wooden tablet (*le'um*) which bestows wisdom".[33] Surveying implied calculations and drawing a groundplan on a writing board, the g i š . h u r of Gudea.

The same is true of Akkadian *uṣurtum*, originally "drawing, design" (ARMT 18, 12:20; *AbB* 5, 229:5', an oath in the temple court *ina* GIŠ.HUR-*tim* / *uṣurtim*; cf. *uṣurāt qātim* in MSL 9, 69:28), but more frequently metaphorically "plan, regulation, rule". Such *uṣurātum* rest in the hand of Marduk[34] and according to a bilingual text from Ugarit it is by the god Ea that the *uṣurātum* are drawn (parallel:*himmātum*), "regulations" which, like those of heaven and earth, cannot be changed (CT 17, 34:5f.). The best known examples of *uṣurātum* produced by a human being are to be found in Hammurapi's Code. In his epilogue he tries to secure the survival of and regard for his stela and its wise verdicts by means of prayers, blessings and curses: his words should not be distorted, his verdicts not be rejected (*šussukum*) or blotted out (*pussusum*), his *uṣurātum* not be changed/discarded (*nukkurum*) nor his written name erased

[31] See the analysis in G. Farber-Flügge, *Der Mythos "Inanna und Enki"* ... (Rome 1973) 181ff.

[32] In *Festschrift S.N. Kramer* (*AOAT* 25; Neukirchen-Vluyn 1976) 144:15ff.

[33] See for the texts and their interpretation A. Sjöberg, *Festschrift T. Jacobsen* (*AS* 20; Chicago 1975) 173ff. Note that Šulgi Hymn B: 45 also mentions a lapis lazuli tablet, cf. Gudea Cyl. A V:3. In Šulgi B: 161 the verb g i š . ḫ u r is used in connection with music, for the tuning of the lyre (Th. Krispijn, *Akkadica* 70 (1990) 1, with commentary: "Ich habe die Schemata ... aufgestellt"). See for the verb also *TCS* 3 (1969) 176:5', "the temple which sketches the outlines of heaven and earth".

[34] F.N. al-Rawi, *RA* 86 (1992) 79:11. I see no reason to parse the plural of *uṣurtum* in OB, with Reschid - Wilcke (*ZA* 65, 1975, 62), as *uṣṣurātum*. The indeed "irregular" plural is also attested with *nukurtum* - *nukurātum* and I assume the insertion of an epenthetic vowel to resolve the cluster VCV*rtum*. It may not be a coincidence that the alternation between *u* and *i* as first vowels is also attested in *ni/ukurtum*.

(*pašāṭum*; col.xlix:2ff.). In col. xl:92 and xli:74 he also uses *šussukum* with *uṣurātum* as object, and *CAD* N/2, 19,5a translates "removes what I engraved/my reliefs". The various verbs used for describing the harm to be done to monuments and inscriptions in OB show a measure of free variation and overlap in meaning, but neither *nukkurum* nor *šussukum* demand an inscription, a written text as object. They primarily refer to the (inscribed) object itself. As a rule only *pussusum* and *pašaṭum* are used when the erasing, the blotting out of an inscription is meant. The *CAD* could be right in taking *uṣurātum* as "what I engraved", which could mean both the relief at the top of the stela and the engraved text. One could adduce the bilingual inscription of Šulgi, no doubt originally also engraved on a stone monument, TIM 9, 35:13: *ša uṣurāt narēja ašar uṣṣaru upaššaṭu*, where exceptionally the verb *pašāṭum* D is used, which suggests an inscription, a written text, as object. Still, it remains possible that Hammurapi was not primarily referring to the signs he had engraved, but metaphorically to the rules and regulations which his stela embodied. We need more proof before we can posit a meaning "(lapidary) inscription" for *uṣurtum.*

Specific uses of eṣērum in Old Babylonian

In some OB letters and administrative texts we meet *eṣērum* with a meaning which cannot simply be "to draw". Twice the verb is used with a fine or punishment as object. In *BaMi* 2 (1963) 79f., W 20472/102:22f. a man, charged with the task of guarding prisoners, is made responsible to the king. For any prisoner which escapes *aran mūtim ina ramanišu i-ṣi-ir*. And in *AbB* 1, 14:26 people guilty of having instituted unfounded claims against a woman[35] for her inheritance, "in conformity with the tablet of the (royal) decree, because they have claimed what is not theirs [25] *šērtam* [26] *i-ṣi-ru-šu-nu-ši-im*".

Falkenstein translates in the first text "zieht sich selbst die Todesstrafe zu", which is more or less what the text means, but his derivation of the verbal form from *zerûm,* "to hate > "to disregard", is not acceptable. With Kraus and von Soden[36] we have to take the verb as *eṣērum.* Von Soden proposes "(Strafe) verhängen", which he adds as a fifth meaning of *eṣērum* G.[37] Kraus translates

[35] The wronged party is a *nadītum*, with the name Ibbi-Šamaš, cf. O.R. Gurney, *WZKM* 77 (1987) 197f.

[36] See *BiOr* 22 (1965) 290a, *ad loc.*, and *AHw* 1554b. *CAD* Š/2 324, 2, a writes *i-*ṢI-*ru* and translates "exacted a penalty" in *AbB* 1, 14.

[37] For a D-stem of this verb *AHw* 1554b s.v. (*w*)*uṣṣurum* refers to CT 48, 10:15, a text edited by Kümmel in *AfO* 25, 79. In front of a series of witnesses lady H [25] *rittam issuh* [26] *u šībūša ú-wa-ṣi-ru*. Assuming that *rittam nasāhum* is a symbolic gesture, presumably marking the end of some link or involvement, the role of the witnesses must have been to certify this fact, which should be what the verb (*w*)*uṣṣurum* must mean, "to establish, ascertain". The document CT 48, 10 probably is the concrete result of this action: it is recorded, fastened down, on a tablet.

"hat sich selbst die Todesstrafe eintatowiert", referring to *AbB* 1, 14:25f., adding "bildlich gebraucht". Such a figurative use of the verb is not impossible, especially in view of the added *ina ramanišu* and it evokes the scene of a culprit who is not simply branded, but in whose skin words revealing his crime are "engraved" as a tattoo. Such a custom is indeed attested in *ana ittišu*, with a fugitive slave, but the verb used here is not *eṣērum* but *naqārum*.[38] Therefore, I prefer another interpretation, which derives support from the use of the verb to denote the result of an administrative action, whereby certain data are "drawn", i.e. "fixed, determined".

In *AbB* 3, 38 the addressee is blamed for having spent much more barley than the ration (ŠUKU) assigned for three months, which was 6 kor. The writer adds: DUMU.É. DUB.BA [28] ŠUKU *e-ṣi-ra-ku-um*, "the administrator has "drawn" the ration for you", and warns him that he will have to answer for his waste. He has with him a tablet with the figures of what was available to him (SAG.NÍG.GA-*ka našiāku*) and wants to meet him to settle accounts. Lines 27f. mean, either that the ration had been "fixed" for him - hence he knew he was spending too much – or that the amount actually spent had been "drawn", "booked" – hence there was no way of denying his waste. The continuation makes me favor the second interpretation, but it is anyhow clear that *eṣērum* means "to fix, to book": the figures were known, black upon white. The same meaning fits well for the two occurrences dealing with a fine or punishment: by their deeds the culprits have passed their own verdict, fixed their own predictable penalty. In *BaMi* 2:69 the penalty for negligence is stated in advance, in the very order to guard the prisoners. In *AbB* 1, 14 a standard punishment apparently is meted out "in accordance with the text of the (royal) decree" (*ana pī ṣimdatim*), which had already fixed the penalty for the presumably not infrequent cases of unfounded claims.[39]

"Drawing", whether by means of actual drawings, by notching, by marking something in a list or ledger, or by booking it on a tablet yields clear data, tangible evidence which cannot be disputed. At times it is impossible to decide which method was used. In *AbB* 3, 12:10 the writer is asked "to draw the

The form *uwanṣir* in *AEM* I/2, 437:28, perhaps from the same verb, could mean "to establish, to inform, to warn".

[38] See *ana ittišu* II, iv:14. The words "a runaway, seize him" are to be "engraved" in his face, on his forehead. Cf. *CAD* N/1 332, d) for a similar use of *naqārum* in *AbB* 2, 46:21 and 3, 22:9, both times with *ṣalmum*, "picture", as object, and ibid. 4, for examples with the D-stem (i.a. a figure in metal). The verb is also used for the scratching of a bird in the soil and the hollowing out of a bowl by a stonecutter, and also has the notion of mutilation, scarification (Middle Assyrian Laws). But note the occurrence of *uṣṣuru*, "marked", said of a slave in *Cambyses* 290:3 (ref. M. Stol).

[39] See F.R. Kraus, *SD* 11 (1984) 9, 5 for this letter and a possible relation to CH § 179. Claiming without title earns the plaintiff a penalty also in *AbB* 4, 67:16ff. Cf. CT 8, 24b:4-8 and 47, 63:49 (cases of *ragāmum*) and *AbB* 6, 6:23ff. (*dabābum*).

area/surface (*qaqqarum*) on his tablet".[40] Does the writer expect a clear description with exact data and figures of the garden plot in question[41] or a groundplan with added figures?

An even more specific use of *eṣērum* is attested in the unpublished legal document YBC 11041, made available to me by M. Stol. The record deals with a large amount of barley, the delivery of which had been assigned ("given") to a military unit in Babylonia in the year Samsuiluna 12. Since it had not been duly delivered (line 7: MU.TÚM *lā iršû*), when the accounts were settled, four years later, the old sealed record "was drawn" (*kanīkum labirum in-ne-ṣi-ir-ma*, 1.9), whereupon those responsible for the delivery "issued a (new) sealed record" (*kanīkam īzibū*, 1.15), which acknowledged their duty to pay the barley to the palace, when it would issue them a call ([16] *ūm ekallum išassūšunūšim* [17] *še'am ekallam ippalū)*. The context leaves no doubt that "drawing" here means "to strike, to scratch out", apparently by drawing lines over the tablet, a practice actually attested for the OB period. In *MARI* 3 (1984) 258f., D. Charpin observed that small account tablets were marked by drawing red stripes over their full length, to indicate that they had been filed and digested and could be discarded, apparently without being "broken". An even better example is CT 6,6, a judicial record, stating that when a field was sold the old title deeds (*ṭuppāt ummātim u serdē*), to be handed over to the new owner, could not be found. It states that the sellers will search for them and that they belong to the new owner when they turn up. By drawing a large X over both sides of the tablet, it was "crossed out", invalidated, "wohl weil die vermissten Urkunden wieder auftauchten".[42] Another tablet "crossed out" is CT 45, 46 (Ad 6), which records a large sum of silver, "the remainder of an *ilkum* obligation", to be delivered to the palace by the overseer of the traders in Sippar, when it is asked for (lines 15-20). The tablet may have been "crossed out" for reasons similar to those mentioned in YBS 11041. The tablets in question were not destroyed ("broken"), presumably because one wished to keep them as archival records, but they had to be cancelled in another way.

Finally there is the statement in the letter *AbB* 1 142:26ff.: "Two sealed records [27] of 10 shekels of silver of B. [28] *e-ṣi-ra-am-ma uštābilakkum*; [29] give (them) to him [30] and his sealed record (of) 1 1/3 shekel of silver ... [32] let him collect (it)". Kraus translates: "Zwei Quittungen ... habe ich gesiegelt und schicke ich dir hiermit", a translation which seems to assume that "to draw" can be used for applying a seal to a tablet, perhaps because of the pictorial nature of

[40] See for this letter and the closely related TIM 2/*AbB* 8, 152, R. Frankena, *SLB* 4 (1968) 133 *ad loc.*

[41] Cf. *AbB* 3, 11:38ff. and *AbB* 2, 90, where in view of a problem with fields (to be) assigned to service-men, the writer has consulted "the tablet of allotments to (service-men now) dead" and has booked in a list (*mudasû*) where they hold fields and their plots/surfaces (*qaqqarātum*, 1.19-23), probably by noting the *ugārum*, the neighbours, and the size.

[42] C. Wilcke, *Zikir šumim, Festschrift Kraus* (1982) 467.

the scene engraved on the seal. But one wonders why *kanākum* was not used or why the verb was not simply omitted since *kanīkum* implies sealing. Were the two tablets shipped in a sealed bag? It seems better to understand this text in the light of YBS 11041 and CT 6,6. This means that *kanīkum* is not a quittance, as proof of payment , but the original sealed debt-note, which the creditor has to return to the debtor upon payment. Since the debtor lived elsewhere they had to be sent overland and this entailed the risk that they might fall into other people's hands. Before sending them off they were "crossed out", invalidated. The debtor, having received them, would destroy or discard them (this could be the reason why so few crossed out tablets have come to light). The creditor himself was not allowed to do that, since the debt-note was considered the tablet of the debtor; he had sealed it and he was entitled to receive it back upon payment, as we know from numerous OA examples.

eṣārum and iṣurtum in Old Assyrian

The last discussed meaning of *eṣērum* in OB is very specific and rare, but the one first mentioned, where "to draw" acquires the meaning "to decide, to fix", also by booking something, perhaps comparable to our " to put down in black and white", may help us to understand the OA occurrences. I present them in groups, in a sequential numbering.

In support of Balkan's opinion, quoted above, that *iṣurtum* (henceforth *i.*) was a debt-note drawn up for native Anatolians, several texts can be adduced. **No. 1**, CCT 1, 33b: 1-10, lists various items, "all owed by the Anatolian Tarmana".[43] It starts with: "8 minas 21$\frac{3}{4}$ shekels of [2] silver of his *i.* *(ša iṣurtišu)*, [3-4] the price of *kusītu*-textiles", followed by some silver paid for copper, an amount of wheat and one fattened ox (the text continues by listing claims on three other Anatolians (the last one the *alahhinnum*). It is closely linked to **no. 2**, ATHE 12. "(As for) the *i.* of Tarmana, [2] to the amount of 8 minas 21$\frac{3}{4}$ shekels [3] of silver with the interest on it, [4] it has mounted up to 12 minas". Next it is mentioned that this is claimed by "me" (Buzazu) and Puzur-Aššur. The structure of no.1 is comparable to that of

no. 3, *RHA* XVIII/66, 39. After listing in lines 1-12 claims on a certain Dudu and Nakiahšu, lines 13-22 record debts due from (*išti*) the ruler of Tišima. This listing starts with: [13] "6 minas 3 shekels of silver [14] of his *i.*" (*ša iṣurtišu*),

[43] Tarmana figures as customer and supplier in records and letters of B(uzāzu) and P(uzur-Aššur), to which our texts nos. 1-3 belong. In BIN 6, 62:26f. B. tells P. that Tarmana should not be without goods; he has to be granted whatever he asks. In KTS 32:6 he delivers an ox (cf. no. 1:8f.), in CCT 3, 48b:7 he supplies grain, payments of silver by him are recorded in KTS 29a:6 and TC 3, 16:3ff. (interest). B. is asked to collect silver from him in TC 3, 13:19f., VS 26, 136:11 mentions the sale of a textile to his wife, and 124:11ff. lists a claim on him for grain, flour and oil. Cf. also TuM I, 27a:3.

followed by items given to him, promised by him, or due from him. Nakiahšu (lines 7 and 12) recurs in text

no. 4, CCT 1, 37b. "15 shekels of silver [2-3] I gave him on the day he drew (up) for me an/the *i.*" (*iṣurtam e-ṣí-ra-ni*). The text continues by listing silver and textiles owed by him (*illibbišu*), items paid to the man of Mamma, metals taken by Nassuhum, and two expensive textiles "which I gave to him". The "him" is identified in the last line (16): "memorandum (*tahsista*) of /about Nakiahšu". An *i.* alongside a memorandum (*tahsistum*) also occurs in the unpublished document

no. 5, kt n/k 126 (courtesy S. Bayram). Its heavily damaged obv. lists claims, to all appearances in copper, on native Anatolians, concluding with: "all this they will pay in springtime" (1-18). The rev. adds: "Separately, 65 minas, [20] one *i.*, [21] one talent, a second [22-3] *i.*, due from T. [24] In the memorandum [25] of outstanding claims [26] which [27] I. left behind [28] it is not written" (1 GÚ 5 *mana ahamma* [20] *ištēt iṣurtam* [21] *šanītum* 1 GÚ [22] *iṣurtum* [23] *išti T.* [24] *ina tahsistim* [25] *ša bābtim* [26] *ša I.* [27] *ēzibu* [28] *ulā lapit*). Two additional claims, not entered in the memorandum, are substantiated by mentioning the existence of *i.*'s in which they are recorded.

No. 6, KTS 57c (parallel to *RA* 59, 47f., MAH 19613, no. 21). "4 minas 13½ shekels of silver [2-3] of the previous *i.* of /concerning small wares". The note continues by listing additional, new deliveries made to Dalaš (8), a smith (10) and Tamišed, all of which result in claims.

No. 7, ICK 2, 296. "170 minas (of copper) [2] of the *i.*, which you drew (up) for me" (*ša iṣurtim ša jāti te-ṣu-ra-ni*), followed by other items which "you took" (3b-6) and "[7-8] 20 minas (of copper which) have not been entered in/added to the *i.*" (*ana iṣurtim lā ṭahhūni*[44]). Summary: "In all 300[+x] minas of copper due from (*iští*) Alāhum". We may compare the unpublished text (courtesy J.G. Dercksen):

No. 8, kt a/k 488b (cf. Balkan, *OLZ* 1965, 157). A letter written by an Assyrian to the *alahhinnum* of the town of Ninašša: "2 *kutānu*-textiles, a ruler's wear (*lubūš rubā'im*) and 12 shekels of *husārum* I gave to your escort (*rādium*), which you sent along with my transport and he brought it to you. [10] And over there my partner has entered it in his *i.* (*ana iṣurtišu uṭahhi*). Here I took the price of the textiles and of my *husārum* from the silver of my partner. [19] Give him his silver over there!".

These texts, personal memorandums without legal force (cf. 4:16), list debts due from and deliveries made to various Anatolians. They distinguish between older, existing claims, already recorded in an *i.*, and later deliveries, at times specified with their value in silver, apparently not yet entered in an *i.* Note that no. 6:3 speaks of a "previous *i.*" and that no.7 distinguishes items for which an *i.* had been drawn (up) from those "not (yet) entered in an *i.*" The verb used

[44] Cf. Balkan, *OLZ* 1965, 1958, who quotes the unpubl. text b/k 36: *ana iṣurtim* [5] *lā ṭaḫḫū*.

here, *ṭahhu'um ana*[45] is known as a bookkeeping term and its exact translation depends on our idea about the writing material used. If an *i.* was a wax coated writing-board, one could enter new items in an existing *i.* If it was a clay tablet, one would have to draw up a new *i.* for every new item. The data of such individual *i.*'s in due time could be digested in a "memorandum" (*tahsistum*), as mentioned in no. 4, and no. 5 distinguishes data about individual claims booked in a memorandum from those not (yet) booked, but for which individual *i.*'s are available as proof. No. 7 speaks of "entering in an/the *i.*", which could mean the drawing (up) of a (new) *i.*, but no.8 speaks of entering something "in his *i.*", which might suggest an existing *i.*, to which data were added.

An *i.*, as is clear from nos. 4:3 and 7:3 (both with personal dative after the verb), was drawn (up) for the creditor. But "his *i.*", according to Old Assyrian parlance, refers to the debtor. His seal (in the case of clay tablets) was impressed on the debt-note and when he paid his debt he received *his* tablet back in order to "kill" it.[46] The fact that some texts simply speak of "an *i.* of x. silver" is also in accordance with Old Assyrian custom. For merchandise sold on credit or given on commission the recipient had to seal a valid bond (*ṭuppum harmum*), which as a rule only mentioned the amount of silver due, the term of payment and the rate of default interest, but not the merchandise taken. The way our texts speak of or perhaps quote *i.*'s suggests that they were functionally similar to debt-notes. This is confirmed by no. 2, where there is question of interest on a debt recorded in an *i.*, apparently on fixed terms (rate, date), which allows the writer to calculate how much interest in the mean time has accrued (more than 40 percent of the capital). No. 8 seems to present a problem. It informs the Anatolian official, to whom this letter was addressed by his Assyrian creditor, that his debt had been entered by the latter's partner "in his *i.*" (not: "in *your i.*"). But note that the writer of the letter[47] had already indemnified himself by taking the price of the goods, his claim, from his partner's silver(14 f.), whereupon the latter had booked it "in his *i.*". Now the Anatolian recipient and debtor is asked to refund the partner, who seems to have lived in the same place as the Anatolian ("there", lines 10, 19), which explains the complications. But we have to retain that the Assyrian partner kept an *i.* of his claims. Who "drew (up) the *i.* for me",

[45] See for *ṭahhu'um ana*, "to add to an account", expressions like *kaspam ana nikkassī ana qāt* PN *ṭaḫḫu'um*, KTS 4a, :7f., 14; BIN 4, 42:39f. (to add to an existing debt), BIN 6, 183:24 (to "add" gold to somebody's tablet), *TTAED* 4 (1940) 12 no. 2:12-15 (*ana ša ṭuppišu*). Cf. in OB TCL 10, 96:8-13 and YOS 8, 154:16f.

[46] See my remarks in E. Mindlin e.a. (eds.), *Figurative Language in the Ancient Near East* (London, 1987) 46ff.

[47] The sender, Irišum, son of Amur-Šamaš, was a business associate, perhaps even partner of Adad-ṣululī, whose archives are registered under kt a/k. Since this letter was found in a sealed envelope in Adad-ṣululī's house, it may have been an archive copy or duplicate, passed on to Irišum's partner to inform him about his request to the *alahhinnum* to pay back to Adad-ṣululī.

in no. 7, is not clear; not necessarily the Assyrian debtor, mentioned in the summary, since it uses the third person.

A clear link between *i.* and Anatolians is also attested in a few texts where an *i.* is a document issued by a local palace, which has bought Assyrian merchandise on credit. The situation in principle is not different from that in the first set of references, where private Anatolians appear, since some of the latter may have acted for a palace. I quote three new texts:

No. 9, VS 26, 146. A memorandum on the acquisition of merchandise by a local palace. First 62 textiles are "taken" in the temple of the weathergod (É ᵈIŠKUR) by the "head of the storage" (*rabi huršātim*, lines 1-8a), next some tin and 2 donkeys. "All this the palace bought, [15] its (price in) silver is owed by the palace. [17] I have an *i.* of the textiles, but not one of the tin" (verb: *ka'ulum*).

No. 10, VS 26, 56. Suejja reports to have been forced by a local *kārum* to bring all his textiles up to the palace, where he must "reach an agreement" (*išti ekallim mitgar*, 18f.). He has brought them up, "but the palace has not yet given me an *i.*" He now wants to go to the palace together with the representatives of the *kārum*, in order "to remind (it) personally (of his claim)" (*raminī lūhassis*), so that the palace will speak/negociate (*dabābum*, 28) with him.

No. 11, I 507 (unpubl., courtesy K. Hecker). Two Assyrians report that [15] "copper has not yet become freely available" (*zakā'um*). Ask Š. over there [17] how much copper in/from the palace is yours and how much belongs to D., [20] and seize D. since I left the *i.* to him [24] and let him make the copper available to you."

The situation in nos. 9 and 10 is clear. The palace has bought merchandise without paying cash and has issued/should issue an *i.* to its creditor/supplier. Such an *i.* is not simply a list of goods taken (the merchants themselves certainly kept such lists), but an acknowledgement of its debt, hence a legal document and presumably sealed. It must have stated how much and presumably also when it would pay. In no. 10 the owner of the merchandise is still waiting for such a document and that it is more than just a receipt can be gathered from the fact that he is told by the *kārum* "to reach an agreement with the palace". When reporting that he complied he does not mention the agreement and its absence probably explains why no *i.* has yet been issued to him. The palace is contractually entitled to levy fixed taxes and preempt part of the textiles. The agreement hence must have concerned an additional purchase or, more likely, the price of the textiles, conditioned their quality and the market situation. Suejja intends to discuss the matter personally with the palace.

The background of no. 11 is similar, but since OA does not know *ezābum* in the meaning "to issue a (legal) document", lines 21f. must mean that the *i.*, previously issued by the palace, has been left to/with Š., when the (main) writer of the letter had to depart. Since Š. had failed to collect the copper on the basis of the *i.* and had not notified its owners, he has to be seized by the addressee in order to force him to make the copper available (*balluṭum*). The text mentions

that two traders are entitled to receive their share of the copper in the palace and this could mean that they had taken part in a collective transaction organized by the *kārum*. The *kārum* also plays a role in the difficult text
no. 12, EL 320 + CCT 6, 17a (perfect join, which yields a complete record). B. states that, when he had to leave, he had left to I. *i.*'s which *kārum* Wahšušana had put at his disposal as pledges (*šapartum*). B. wants to know whether I. has used them to collect copper in his name. We cannot go into details,[48] but it is clear that possession of an *i.* made collection of a claim possible. We may assume that the *i.*'s here embody claims by the *kārum* on the palace, which it had, for unknown reason, ceded to B. An alternative interpretation is that the *kārum* had acted as court-of-law and had assigned somebody else's *i.*'s (perhaps entitling him to a share in a transaction as assumed for no. 11) to B., his creditor, as security. This latter interpretation is supported by EL no. 316, where the assumption is that I. has collected claims of B., i.a. amounts of copper from two native Anatolians. The Anatolians in question could have issued these *i.*'s to an Assyrian trader (perhaps Šū-Ištar), who had had to yield them to B.

The *Kārum* is also involved in:
No. 13, kt c/k 459:12-17. (cf. Balkan, *OLZ* 1965, 158). In this memorandum we read: "216 minas (of copper) in the first/previous tablet, the big (*rabium*) *i.*, 45½ shekels of silver I will collect in the *kārum* office". The anonymous writer registers how much silver he will acquire in exchange for copper he had sold or was entitled to (ca. 1 shekel of silver for ca. 28,5 shekels of copper). The mention of a "big *i.*" may have served, simply, to make its identification easy. But it is not clear why for a modest claim of copper a big *i.* was needed. It may also have meant that it contained a list of a number of assets. In that case a comparison with the few occurrences of "big tablets" (BIN 6, 156:7; KUG 18:7f.; VS 26, 46:4f.) may be in order, since they invariably refer to bookkeeping in the *kārum*-office, which played an important role in the copper trade.

Other references are less specific:
No. 14, kt n/k 516 (courtesy C. Günbattı). Its writer, Lāqīp, accuses Nab-Suen of having taken silver belonging to "our father", without having sent him any "to save his life". "Fine, you did not take anything of what is (recorded) in the *i.* (*ina ša iṣurtim*)!". An *i.* recorded a claim which could be collected and something similar is the case in

48 Read in lines 13f.: [*ina*] *W šazzuztī* 14 *ušāzizka u iṣurātim* 15 *ša kārum W.* 16 *ana šapartim iddianni* 17 *ēzibakkum ina erīm šuāti* 18 *kīma jāti mimma talqe*. See for the transactions and background of this text also MP 1 (*RA* 60, 121f.) and EL no. 321, according to which Šū-Ištar was a debtor of B., while P. – whose death is at the base of our lawsuit – had been his guarantor. The *i.*'s, being Š.'s bonds, might have been given as pledges first to P. (his guarantor) and after the latter's death to B., whose claim on Š. was finally settled by the agreement recorded in EL no 321. It entailed that B. ultimately would "release" (*waššurum*) "his tablets to Š.", which could mean the release of the bonds handed over as security (cf. EL II p. 53).

no. 15, CTMMA I no. 84. Lines 32-38 of this protocol, which lists the contents of an archive of which a trader was robbed, mention: "one tablet (stating) that I. and A. have been paid in full the 35 talents of good copper being the price of/ for *i.*'s (*ša šīm iṣurātim*) ... [35] One tablet (stating) that I. and A. gave me 30 talents of good copper of *i.*'s (copper *iṣurātim*) and that I will (now) be responsible for the debt of 30 talents of good copper which I_2. owes to the *alahhinnum* Dašušu". The first tablet is a quittance, either for the purchase price paid for some *i.*'s (Larsen's translation) or for the amount of copper recorded in some *i.*'s as the price to be paid by an (Anatolian?) debtor who had bought Assyrian import goods at credit in exchange for copper (I favor this interpretation because the text writes *ša šīm* and not simply *šīm*). The second is a legal document whereby S. assumed responsibility for (*izēzum ana*) paying a debt in copper to an *alahhinnum*, after I. and A. had paid him the amount in question, an amount recorded in some *i.*'s. Perhaps the two transactions recorded in these tablets were complimentary and part of a general settlement of accounts (an attorney was involved according to lines 34f.). Whatever the details, the specified list of records missing only speaks of "tablets" (*ṭuppū*). It is therefore remarkable that the summary in lines 58ff. states: "*ṭuppū'a iṣurātū'a lū tahsisātū'a* of much copper, all this under seals in two coffers" and hence includes *i.*'s. The settlement of lines 32ff. implies that *i.*'s changed hands and they may have ended up in the coffers in question, but the list of lines 10-47 does not mention them. Judging from the use of *lu* in OA in enumerations (see my *AOATT* 18 note 35), the Assyrian phrase quoted does not mean: "tablets, as well as *i.*'s and memorandums" (listing three categories), but most probably: "tablets, both *i.*'s and memorandums". The general category "(clay) tablets", to which all records listed in lines 10-47 belong, is distinguished in two groups: legal documents as proof of claims and memorandums without legal force but serving as aids to memory. This would mean that *i.*'s are indeed clay tablets of a specific kind, a conclusion also to be drawn from text no. 13, lines 13-15, *ina ṭuppim panīm iṣurtim rabītim*, where *i.* is in apposition to *ṭuppum.* It is possible, but not certain that the term was used here because among the tablets missing there was quite a number of promissory notes recording debts in copper.

We also note that in both occurrences in this text *i.* occurs in the plural. The transactions recorded apparently referred to a number of claims in copper, each of them booked in a separate *i.* For administrative purposes and when accounts were settled, a number of claims could be added and booked as one single asset. It is possible that the "big *i.*", mentioned in source no. 13, meant such a record, the information on its size being added in order to facilitate its identification among the many documents in the archive.

In almost all examples quoted an *i.* must be a legal document made out to an Assyrian supplier or creditor by an Anatolian person or palace, in which the latter acknowledges a debt and, at least in some cases, promises to pay at a certain date on the penalty of default interest. Only in no. 6 we do not know who wrote the *i.* for the creditor and in no. 7 an Assyrian trader entered a payment due "in his *i.*" As a legal document an *i.* must have been sealed by the debtor who accepted the liability recorded.

If that is true, why did they not simply designate such debt-notes or bonds as *ṭuppum harmum* (*ša kunukkišu*)? This becomes a serious question in **no. 16**, ICK 1, 13. In this letter by Aššur-mālik to five persons, among which two Anatolians, we read:"5 12½ minas of silver and 100 bags of barley Happuala, the shepherd of the queen, owes me. 8 I have his valid tablet with his seal (*ṭuppušu harmam ša kunukkišu*). 10 Since 4 years it is accumulating interest for his account according to the word (rule) of Kanish. 12 Please, my fathers, my lords, 14 try as best as you can to make him pay the capital, silver and barley, 16 and charge him the interest on silver and barley 19 and make him pay in annual instalments (*šattišamma*). 20 Please ... take care to collect my capital of silver and barley 24 and draw up his *i.* (*iṣurtušu eṣrā*) for the interest on the silver and the barley". Why a *ṭuppum harmum* for the capital loan and *i.* for the contract recording the accumulated interest? Could the latter, notwithstanding the functual similarity or even identity, have been a record of a native type, perhaps a tablet with a native Anatolian seal impression on it, not encased in a sealed envelope? But sealed tablets do not occur during level II of the *kārum* and only start to appear during the younger level IB. The alternative, a wooden writing board (comparable to the Hittite GIŠ.ḪUR), is also very unlikely. It might have disintegrated without trace, but since *i.*'s must have been sealed, one would have found the sealed clay bullae once attached to them, as was the case in Hattuša, according to the convincing explanation for the discovery of hoards of bullae with royal seals.[49] But this has not been the case in *kārum* Kanish and the bullae discovered in many houses seem to have served transport and storage of merchandise, silver and also clay tablets.[50] Moreover, as we have seen, the native hieroglyphic script, as a fully developed writing system, which would be required to draw up records of the *i.*-type, only came into existence much later. In the absence of any other native Anatolian candidate, a clay tablet, inscribed in cuneiform, is the only possible candidate for a record listing a debt, a date and /or term of payment, an interest clause and the names of the debtor and creditor.

Our difficulty in identifying such *i.*'s among the clay tablets excavated may simply be due to the fact that it was not really different from a *ṭuppum harmum.* There is, as far as I know, not a single debt-note with an Anatolian palace as debtor. But no. 9 shows that the palace acted through its officials: the *rabi huršātim* "takes" textiles, but later it is stated that they were actually bought by the palace, which owed their price in silver. Hence debt-notes sealed by Anatolians may very well be the *i.*'s we are looking for. On the other hand it is

[49] See the reference mentioned in note 14, above, and see also P. Neve, *Hattuša, Stadt der Götter und Tempel* (Mainz 1993) 55.
[50] See my remarks on such bullae in *FsN. Özgüç,* 645ff.

remarkable that the number of contracts recording debts/credits in copper, granted by Assyrians to Anatolians is very small; Garelli *AC* p. 384 lists only two small amounts and p. 389f. only one large amount. Since there was much trade in copper, and certainly not all payments were cash, we have to assume that the nature of or the way these transactions were administered was different. Trade in copper in most cases was bulk trade in a product mined in Anatolia, which perhaps made it less suited for transactions with private Anatolians. On the Assyrian side, there is clear evidence for active involvement of the *kārum* organization, even though Garelli's statement (*AC* p. 294.4, cf. p. 176, 1, a) "le commerce du cuivre faisait l'object d'un contrôle strict de l'office des marchands qui centralisait des achats et le produit des ventes" goes too far.[51] Anyhow, this may have resulted in many indirect transactions in copper between the *kārums* and the palaces, in which individual traders could take a share, the administration of which probably was kept in the *kārum* office (cf. the role of the *kārum* in text no. 12). *I.*'s dealing with copper hence may (also) have been issued by or kept by that office, and text no. 13 may reflect that situation. This may also be the case in text

no. 17, kt u/k 2 (photo in T. Özgüç, *Kültepe-Kaniş* II, 1986, pl. 60, 2; collated). This letter by Ahšalim in lines 20-30 states: "If the affair of I. has been settled (or: set down for trial? *awutum ittaškan*), you and A_1. must retort (or: raise it again, *ta'erā*). And B. and A_2 ... have knowledge (of the facts). [27] Let them open their mouths there, before the *kārum*, (and declare) that one has made a deduction from my *i.*'s."[52] The plaintiff considers himself the victim of an administrative measure (penalty?), whereby his claim, recorded on an *i.*, probably kept in the *kārum*, was reduced.

These observations suggest that the designation *i.* was used for a clay tablet recording a claim, a debt or an acknowledgement, in order to stress a particular aspect. This idea is supported by the highly interesting new reference

no. 18, kt 79/k 101 (H. Sever, *DTCFD* 34, 1990, 260-3). The beginning of this letter by the ruler (*waklum*) of Assur to *kārum* Kanish reads as follows: "The tablet [5] with the verdict of the City (of Assur), [6] which concerned the sale of gold, [7] which we sent you – [8] that tablet is invalid (cancelled; *akkuš*). [9] Concerning gold we "have not drawn an *i.*" (*iṣurtam* [10] *ulā né-ṣú-ur*). The rules (*awātum*) for gold are (still) [12] the previous (*paniātum*) ones." The text then spells them out: gold may be sold between Assyrians, but not, "according to the stipulation of the stela" (*kīma awāt naru'āim*, 16f.), to Akkadians, Amorites or Subaraeans, under penalty of death.

[51] The problems connected with the trade of copper will be treated in the dissertation by J.G. Dercksen.

[52] The verb, *ṣahhurum*, is typical for administrative operations, whereby accounts are settled, taxes paid, not by cash payment but by balancing assets and debts.

I interpret this fascinating incident as follows. The City of Assur, the highest judicial authority, presumably at the request of a trader who had made an appeal or of *kārum* Kanish (where the case must have started), had passed a verdict which forbade or approved the sale of gold by an Assyrian to a non-Assyrian in a particular case. *Kārum* Kanish had been informed about this verdict by an official letter. Soon, however, the authorities in Assur realized that their verdict was liable to misunderstanding, since it could be interpreted as a change of a hitherto valid regulation, "published" by being carved on a stela. By means of our letter the *kārum* was informed that the verdict was cancelled, revoked and that the previous regulation was still valid. In order to exclude any doubts the letter added: "We have not made an *i.* concerning gold". This must mean: "We did not draw up/decide on/ draft a (new) rule" and the verb *eṣārum* is used with a meaning akin to that deduced for some OB references quoted above. The *i.* is the result of taking a decision, fixing a rule.

The reference to the stela is intriguing, since it was an official stone monument, on which the text of regulations were engraved (cf. the words of Hammurapi and Šulgi about their *uṣurātum* embodied in stelae). But I doubt whether this aspect is responsible for the use of verb and noun in our text. The focus is on the fact that no new regulation has been fixed, irrespective of where it was inscribed and how it was "published". The words in question can be interpreted as "we never really intended to change the rules", or as "the cancellation of the verdict means that no new rule has been fixed". The move seems understandable if the verdict – as some verdicts were – was formulated in a rather general way. Such a permission to sell gold would undermine the regulation of the stela, since gold could not be sold to Akkadians, Amorites and Subaraeans, hence to Mesopotamian people/traders. But a generally formulated prohibition would harm the trading activities in Anatolia, where in particular cases gold might have to be sold to Anatolians. The Anatolian trade was not to suffer, but the Assyrian monopoly on the trade in gold inside Mesopotamia was maintained: all gold had to be concentrated in the city of Assur.[53]

We may conclude that the medium of writing and the language were irrelevant. What mattered was the decision taken. It is understandable that in the context of the Assyrian trade, where bookkeeping and recording, especially of liabilities, played such an important role and was so useful, in practice *i.* in many cases may have come to denote a record, a bond. But the element of deciding is not absent. In commenting on text no. 10 we observed that the

53 The frequent expression "gold for the journey to the City" (*hurāṣum ša harrān ālim*) now acquires a new dimension. The fact that all gold acquired in Anatolia was shipped to Assur was not just the goal of the traders, it was a commercial policy of the city-state, even embodied in a regulation carved in a stela. This also explains why, whenever gold arrived from Anatolia, it was not used to buy merchandise for a next caravan, but was first converted into silver, which was used as "money" for making purchases.

absence of an agreement with the palace, apparently on the number and the price of the textiles to be bought, explained the absence of an *i.* fixing the liability.

The use of *eṣārum* with the meaning "to decide, to fix", is attested a few more times in Old Assyrian:

No. 19, kt 89/k 252 (courtesy Y. Kawasaki). The letter informs I. that the palace needs (*hašāhum*) textiles which are stored with Z. Z. had told the writer of the letter that the palace keeps pressing him and that the ruler had told him: [13] "Fix their price (*šīmšina e-ṣir-ma*), so that I can take them". "But since I. has not (yet) fixed their price (*e-ṣí-ru-ni*), I refused to give them. Write to him, that he may fix their price for me (*le-ṣí-ra-ma*) and we may give them" (15-21).

No. 20, I 439 (courtesy K. Hecker). A verdict of *Kārum* Kaniš stipulates that I. and E. shall take three impartial traders to inspect (*amārum*) a lot of disputed textiles and "they will fix their price" (*šīmšunu e-ṣí-ru-ma*, [22]), whereupon I. and E. will take them.

No. 21, C 43 (Collection Holzmeister, transliteration Landsberger). Atata writes to Innāja: [3] "Even when your instruction does not come to me, [5] for you, what I wrote to you concerning your copper of good quality, I will fix (it) for you!".[54] I assume that the writer means he will stick to what he had promised on the price and quantity of copper. He uses *eṣārum* to assure that his promise will be fixed, in writing, so that simple *eṣārum* may have the meaning of "to draw up an *iṣurtum*", to put down in black and white. The same meaning of the verb is attested in the OB record YOS 5, 186:8, listing capital goods delivered to merchants in Larsa (by the palace) consisting of sesame, wool and sheep, of which it is said: *ša adīni* KAR.BI *lā*! *eṣ-ru*, "whose exchange value has not yet been fixed". The same fact is registered in the comparable text YOS 5, 153:4 by means of the words KAR.BI NU.GAR (referring to sesame and wool).

The idea of deciding, fixing something is also present in

no. 22, CCT 4, 1a: 7ff. As in other letters, Aššur-idī urges his son to "heed the words of the god(s)" and to stick to his promise. He warns him: *ana nikištim* [8] *ša ilum i-ṣí-ra-ku-ni* [9] *lā tatu'ar*. Thusfar the meaning of *nikištum*, the object of *eṣārum*, was not very clear,[55] but a new reference suggests that it is something like a warning, a prohibition as the result of a decision. In kt 91/k 297 the writer states that certain textiles and an amount of oil have not been sold and are still in stock. Lines 10ff. explain why: "Here, by *nikištum* of the *kārum*, nobody shall

54 [3] *u šumma ana jāti* [4] *tērtaka lā illakam* [5] *ana kuātima* [6] *ša adi* URUDU-*ika* SIG5 [7] *ašpurakkunni le-ṣú-ra-kum.*

55 The letters where *nikištum* occurs were discussed by H. Hirsch in *UAR*² 1, §1 and in Nachträge 5f. Derivation from *nakāsum* seems excluded, but the meaning of *nkš* is not quite clear. Hirsch proposes "etwa Abgabeverpflichtung", echoed in *CAD* N/2, 222f. "contribution(?)". The new reference in kt 91/k 297 does not support these interpretations. It reads: [10] *annakam ni-ki-iš-tám* [11] *ša kārim* [12] *ša kīma ana* [13] *nuā'im mimma* [14] *šīmim mamman* [15] *lā iddunu. Nikištam* must be an adverbial accusative, while *ša kīma* introduces the contents of the decision, as it is used after terms for written documents, orders etc.

sell anything to the Anatolian". The *kārum* apparently had issued a prohibition of commercial dealings with an Anatolian, presumably because he had refused to meet his obligations vis-à-vis the Assyrians. We know other cases where the *kārum* authorities issued such prohibitions, which could be made known by letter or as verdicts.[56] Something similar must have been the case here, and the use of the verb *eṣārum* with *nikištum* as object in our text indicates that the god had made it (painfully?) clear to Aššur-nādā (in comparable cases we read about relatives being visited by demons and evil spirits or being plagued by illness[57]) that a limit had been reached. The god had made known his will, issued a strong warning.

The examples quoted reveal the semantic range of the verb, "to draw, to make a drawing, to design, to fix, to decide". Perhaps one may even add "to shape, to fashion", if our verb is indeed attested in the expression *dūram i*-ZI-*ir*, twice used in OA royal inscriptions, both in the first and in the third pers. sing.[58]. *AHw* 252b, 4 lists them under "gestalten", together with the first line of Etana, *ālam iṣirū*, but *CAD* E 349a, which translates with "to construct", has doubts. One could translate "to design", but the rulers in question no doubt also meant the realization of their building projects.[59] Another problem of the verb is the remarkable variation of the stem vowel. We have a preterit with *-i-* (texts nos. 4, 19 and 21; cf. the imperative *eṣir* in no. 19:13) and with *-u-* (texts nos. 18 and 20). I cannot explain it - it is perhaps free variation or conditioned by the final stem consonant *-r-* but it does not affect the meaning of the verb.

Summing up, we may conclude that an *i.* was a clay tablet in the nature of a valid legal document written in cuneiform, which recorded a liability of the same kind as a promissory note called *ṭuppum harmum*. Most *i.*'s were records of liabilities by Anatolians or Anatolian palaces, but in rare cases they were also said to be drawn up by Assyrians. It embodies the obligation or promise to pay a certain amount of money/goods (frequently copper), which presupposes a commercial decision. But such a decision was never a matter of one party only and every commercial transaction implied such decisions, whereby both parties agreed (*namgurum*) on the conditions, both quantities and prices, because there were no fixed prices. In no. 19 the Assyrian trader had to fix the price of his textiles which the palace wished to buy, and in nos. 20 and 21 prices were

[56] Cf. the order of the *kārum* communicated by letter in kt c/k 1055 and the *kārum* verdict edited as EL 273. See for both texts Larsen, *OACC* 263 and 327.

[57] Cf. MAH 19612 (*RA* 59, 1965, 165f., no. 28), KTS 24 and 25. See my discussion of these texts in K.R. Veenhof (ed.), *Schrijvend Verleden* (Leiden/Zutphen 1983) 86ff.

[58] See for the text and context *RIMA* 1 17:28 and 23:40.

[59] The root *jṣr* is well attested in West-Semitic, where it means "to shape, to fashion". In the Old Testament it is used i.a. for the work of the potter and for the creation of man. B. Otzen, in *ThWAT* III 1981 830, adduces Akkadian *eṣērum*, but obscures the semantic facts by giving "formen" as its first meaning. His mention of the noun *ēṣirum*, "potter" is a mistake, since it is only attested as "seal cutter, carver of reliefs" (*CAD* E 350).

decided upon and fixed between Assyrians. Hence I am reluctant to explain the use of *i.* from the fact that it implied a decision. I would rather assume that its use reflects the importance attached to the fact that the seller/creditor finally got into his hands a valid bond, recording the amount he was entitled to in writing, secured by the debtor's seal. But this does not explain why the term was used by preference in describing dealings in copper with Anatolians. The fact that Anatolians usually made use of stamp seals hardly can have made the difference. And if *i.* was preferred because it was a convenient one-word equivalent of the rather cumbrous *ṭuppum harmum ša kunuk* ..., it would not have been so rare in purely Assyrian commercial contexts. It is unsatisfactory that we cannot identify even one single *i.* among the bonds sealed by native Anatolians, but perhaps more references within a well defined archival context will allow such identifications in the future. And a better knowledge of the still imperfectly understood administrative procedures of the *kārum* office, whose discovery remains a serious desideratum, may turn out to be helpful. With so many thousands of texts still unpublished and with the excavations of *kārum* Kanish bringing to light hundreds of new texts every year, there is no reason to be pessimistic about the possibility of solving old and new riddles of the Kültepe texts and the techniques of Old Assyrian trade.

SIGMATIZATION AND THEMATIZATION IN HITTITE

JOS J.S. WEITENBERG

It is with feelings of respect and of immense gratitude that I dedicate this paper to Professor Houwink ten Cate, who guided my steps in Hittite Studies, and whose profound scholarship and truely humanistic attitude I admire. I hope that these lines reflect a part of what he gave to me, though it is hardly more than a footnote to his teaching.

0. In the course of its history, Hittite tended to give formal expression to gender distinction in the nominative singular. With a few (very important) exceptions, commune nouns show a nominative singular in *-s*; asigmatic nominatives are considered to be of neuter gender. This dualism is of relevance for the behaviour of inherited non-neuter nouns with an original asigmatic nominative (*-eH*$_2$, *-n, -r, -l* stems). Adjustments took place in such words: either the inherited form prevailed over the inherited gender, or, conversely, gender prevailed over the form. In the first case, inherited non-neuter nouns changed their gender, becoming neuters in Hittite (as PIE **dheg´hm* "earth", feminine, Hitt. *tēkan*, neuter). In the latter case, the form of the nominative singular was changed to express the inherited gender. Hittite employed two procedures to change the form of an inherited non-sigmatic nominative singular: sigmatization (as in *ḫaššā-š* "hearth" or *ḫašter-za* "star") and thematization (as in the suffix *-ttar-a-š*). In the following I shall argue that thematization is fundamentally different from sigmatization and that the distribution of these two devices reflects inherited gender divisions.

1. The discovery of the NomSg. *ḫašterza* "star" and the discussions around the interpretation of the *n*-stems of the type (NomSg.) *šummanza* "rope" have drawn renewed attention to the feature of "sigmatization." Sigmatization is the addition of *-s* to an inherited asigmatic non-neuter NomSg. Two types of sigmatization may be distinguished: the first is represented by the NomSg.c. of the inherited *eH*$_2$-stem *ḫaššā-š* "hearth"; it is also found with *n*-stems of the type *ḫarāš* (GenSg. *ḫaranaš* "eagle". The second type of sigmatization shows the outcome *-nz* (NomSg. *šummanza* next to PIE **suH*$_1$*mēn*) or *-rz* (in the NomSg. *ḫašterza* next to PIE **H*$_2$*stēr*); it is found in non-neuter consonant-stems (especially *-n, -r* stems).

Thematization at first sight is a mere subtype of sigmatization: an original asigmatic nominative (as the agent noun suffixes *-*te*/*or*-, *-*te*/*ol*-, Hittite NomSg. *-*ttar*, *-*ttal*) is incorporated into the thematic flexion under the influence of other endings (e.g. AccSg. **te*/*olm* > Hittite -*ttalan*) and quite naturally received a sigmatic nominative (Hittite -*ttalaš*). I shall argue below, that thematization rather is a subtype of non-sigmatization.

On this basis, it has been generally accepted until relatively recently that in Hittite there do not occur asigmatic nominatives with nouns of commune gender. A summary of this approach is available in E. Neu, *FsMeriggi*[2](1979).

1.1 There are a few exceptions to this precise binary system, which, however, without the availability of additional data did not permit unequivocal interpretations. Thus, the noun *keššar* "hand" has an asigmatic commune nominative in the Hittite Laws: *keššar-šiš*, I §3 text B, but the form could be interpreted as erroneous in the light of ŠU-*aššet* (Laws §II, in the young parallel text) that seems to preserve the required neuter gender. Likewise the asigmatic NomSg. forms *kurur* "enemy" and *takšul* "friend" were interpreted as a secondary specialization of original neuter abstract nouns ("enmity" and "peace"; see especially Neu, *FsMeriggi*[2] (1979)).

2. Shortly after the publication of the form *ḫašterza* (H. Otten-W. von Soden, *StBoT* 7 (1968), 40-41), J. Friedrich, *Athenaeum* NS 47 (1969) 118, suggested by way of "kühne Hypothese" that the form constitutes the sigmatic nominative of a non-neuter ("geschlechtig") noun. Friedrich cautiously added that such an hypothesis was contradicted by the fact that a sigmatic nominative was absent in the likewise non-neuter *keššar* "hand". In retrospect, the"bold" aspect of Friedrich's paper is not formed by his proposal to find asigmatized non-neuter *r*-stem. Such a proposal was in line with the generally accepted idea that Hittite does not possess asigmatic nominative singular forms in commune nouns. The real impact came from the realization, by Friedrich and others (O. Carruba - V. Souček - R. Sternemann, *ArOr* 33 (1965) 4-5) that the form *keššar-šiš* in the Hittite Laws indeed attests the existenceof a non-neuter *r*-stem with an asigmatic nominative. But Friedrich immediately formulated a main consequence of this new insight: in front of both *keššar* and *ḫašterza* the assumption of a general, uniform, distribution of sigmatization could not be upheld any more.

2.1 A new impetus was added by H. Eichner , *MSS* 31 (1973) 98 n. 78, who analyzed stems of the type (NomSg.) *šummanza* "rope", *ištanza* "soul" as inherited *n*-stems with secondary sigmatization in the NomSg. This immediately raised the question how the sigmatization in *šummanza* relates to commune *n*-stems of the type *ḫarāš*. Since then, the discussion has been focused on attempts to solve this particular problem. The broader issue, *i.e.* the fact that sigmatization does not seem to be uniform, the problem of how to explain the relation of *ḫašterza* and *keššar*, has attracted less explicit attention.

3. The relevant material has been discussed several times. E. Neu, *FsIvânescu* (1982-1983), 129 n. 19, is most explicit in his voicing of the consequences of the interpretation of *keššar* as an asigmatic nominative commune: it opens the way to reinterpret other words as non-sigmatic non-neuter nominatives. For a recent discussion on the sigmatization of *n*-stems I refer to O. Carruba, *StMed* 7 (1992), 73-76.

3.1 *R-stems*

Outside of the *n*-stems a non-neuter consonant stem with sigmatization is provided only in the *r*-stems, where we find sigmatized *ḫašterza* "star".

Sigmatization in *ḫašterza* stands in opposition to the behaviour of other non-neuter *r*-stems, especially *keššar* (NomSg.c. *keššar-šiš* Laws I §3, text B): *[ki]ššeran* (*StBoT* 25, 141, 5; E. Neu, *FsIvânescu* (1982-1983), 127) "hand". Neu (*FsIvânescu*) has adduced new material to establish the paradigm of non-neuter *r*-stems. He pointed out that the words *ḫuppar* "(a kind of) vessel" and *išpanduzziyaššar* "(libation) bowl" require a commune paradigm like *keššar* with an asigmatic NomSg.c.: **ḫuppar*, Acc.Sg.c. *ḫupparan*.[1]

The two procedures which Hittite employed to eliminate the inconsistency between form and gender are attested in this inflectional type: the asigmatic nominative was either interpreted secondarily as a neuter form and also received the function of a neuter accusative (*ḫuppar*) or, alternatively, a new nominative was created on the basis of the accusative. The latter procedure resulted in thematization: NomSg.c. *ḫupparaš* next to AccSg.c. *ḫupparan*. Both ways of reorganizing the paradigm can be witnessed in Old Hittite texts. From this, Neu rightly concludes that the thematization is a "junge Erscheinung" (*FsIvânescu* (1982-1983), 127), recent in the sense of taking place in the historical period, in the Old Hittite texts. A dating possibility is provided by the existence of the female proper names *Ḫašušar, Ḫašušar-niga* in Cappadocian texts next to *ḫaššuššara-š* in Old Hittite. Thus, thematization is not a pre-anatolic feature (as assumed by O. Carruba, *StMed* 7 (1992), 79).

To this group also belongs the thematized suffix *-ttara* (as in *akuttara-*, *weštara-*), which can be compared to the Greek *-τωρ, -τηρ* suffixes (H. Kronasser *EHS* (1966), 175). Also, there now are no a priori objections any

[1] Ms. A. Prins kindly draws my attention to the varying gender of *šuppiwašḫar* in KUB XXIX 7 rev. 27 (*ka-a-aš- ... šu-up-pi-wa-aš-ḫar*) ff.; cf. H.A. Hoffner, *AlHeth.* 108-109 on the gender of this word.

more to accepting *kurur* "enemy(/inimical)" (and *takšul*) as an asigmatic commune NomSg.

3.2 *N-stems*

Among the nasal stems, *tekan* "earth" is a non-neuter noun in which the form prevailed upon the inherited gender. PIE **dheg'hm*, a feminine, resulted into Hittite *tekan*, a neuter noun.

Sigmatization in *n*-stems shows two outcomes; it results into the type *ḫarāš* (GenSg. *ḫaranaš*) "eagle" or the type *šummanza* (GenSg. *šummanzanaš*) "cord".[2] The commune *n*-stems of the type *ḫarāš* represent a PIE (hysterodynamic) type with lengthened grade in the NomSg. One generally assumes that the suffix shows *o*-degree (**-ōn*) in the nominative. As N. Oettinger, *GsKronasser* (1982), 162-177, and H.C. Melchert, *Sprache* 29 (1983) 1-26, confirmed, this type is attested in words like *ḫarāš* "eagle": *ḫaranan, išḫimāš* "cord": *išḫimenan*, and also in derivations with the suffix *-uman* (NomSg.c. *-u(m)maš* as in *Zalpumaš* "person originating from Zalpa"). In the traditional view (e.g. H. Pedersen, *Hitt.* 41), rejected by Oettinger but rightly accepted again by Melchert, *Sprache* 29 (1983) 1-26, and J.A. Harδarsson, *MSS* 48 (1987) 115-137, this type (PIE **-ōn*) had lost its final *-n* already in PIE times and had adopted a sigmatic nominative subsequently (*harā + s*); the nominative *-s* was added to what was synchronically considered as a vocalic stem. In this view, the sigmatization in *ḫarāš* may be compared with the sigmatization of the inherited vocalic (*-eH*$_2$) stem *ḫaššā-*: *ḫaššā + s*. The sigmatization of *ḫarāš* is Common Anatolian, as is proven by Palaic *ḫaraš* (Melchert, *Sprache* 29 (1983) 9; F. Starke, *StBoT* 31 (1990), 76).

As N. Oettinger, *KZ* 94 (1980) 44-63, following H. Eichner, *MSS* 31 (1973) 53-107, showed in his fundamental discussion, the type Nom.Sg. *šummanza* represents an original *n*-stem. An earlier explanation considered the type as to be formed with a suffix *-tiyōn* (H. Pedersen, *Hitt.* 43-44, following Milewski); this explanation cannot be uphold in view of a word like *ḫantezzi(ya)-* which shows that, in Hittite, **-tiyo-* does not develop into *-za(n)-* (Oettinger, *KZ* 94 (1980) 44-63, 50). It is also difficult to accept that a suffix **-tiyon-* was added to a nominal n-stem (Carruba, *StMed* 7 (1992), 79).

From the words which belong to this type, only *šummanza* can be shown to be inherited as an *n*-stem: **suH*$_1$*men* (gr. *ὑμήν*). In addition, the word *ištanza*

[2] With the acceptance of asigmatic commune nominatives in the *r*-stems, there now emerges a possibility that such a paradigm (which would have the form NomSg.c. -*Can*, AccSg.c. -*Canan*) may also have been present among the *n*-stems. Maybe such words are among the material which Oettinger, *KZ* 94 (1980) 52-53, mentions as having secondary *n*-inflection, like *ewa(n)-* , *eya(n)-* or *memiya(n)-*.

"soul", originating from a PIE root noun *(*p*)*sten-* "(female) breast", was incorporated into this type by virtue of its ending in *-n*. No etymological certainty consists on *alanza* ("some wood"), *laḫanza* "(some bird)".

Words of the type *šummanza* show the inflexion NomSg. *šummanza* : AccSg.c. *šummanzanan*. The details of the formation of this (certainly secondary) inflexional type remain obscure (cf. Harδarsson, *MSS* 48 (1987) 122). It seems probable that the AccSg. *šummanzanan* was created to diminish the chance that the type was incorporated in the *nt*-stems.

3.2.1 *"woman"*

The NomSg. MUNUS-*an-za* was immediately connected to the type *šummanza* (Oettinger, *KZ* 94 (1980) 59-60; Starke, ibid. 85-86) but remains difficult to interpret. The possible identification of a Hittite *kuinna-* "woman" by Neu, *HS* 103 (1990) 208-217 (in an AccSg.c. form *kuinna*(*n*)*-ššan*), seriously doubted by Güterbock, *HS* 105 (1992) 1-3, does not solve the problem of this NomSg. There can hardly be any doubt, that the form MUNUS-*an-za* represents a nominative singular ending *-s*, added to a base in *-n*. Oettinger, *KZ* 94 (1980) 59, and Starke, ibid. 85, are in favor of a complete identification with the *šummanza* type. They consider MUNUS-*anza* as representing an *n*-derivation from the root (**gwén-ōn + s*: *gwenanza*) and even interpret the casus obliqui (AccSg.c. MUNUS-*nan*, GenSg. MUNUS-*naš*, DLSg. MUNUS-*ni*) according to the *šummanza* paradigm: **gwenanzan* etc. Such an analysis is not cogent. Already Harδarsson, *MSS* 48 (1987) 121-122, pointed out that, as a root noun, the nominative MUNUS-*za* is comparable to *ištanza* (**pstēn + s*) and therefore might be interpreted as **gwantsa*; but on the strength of the inflexional type *šummanza* : *šummanzanan* he probably is correct in accepting the identification of MUNUS-*nan* as **gwentsanan*. Of course, one might go one step further, and propose a paradigm on the basis of an inherited consonantal type; this is done by Carruba, *FsPolomé* (1991), 160-167) who proposes to depart from PIE **g^{w}en-s*, GenSg. **g^{w}en-os* etc., in Hittite **g*(*u*)*wanz*, **g*(*u*)*wanan* etc. Such a consonantal paradigm is attested in the Luwian dative form *wani*. At the current stage of our knowledge one can only speculate about the Hittite form of the casus obliqui. But on the basis of the data which we possess, it seems safe to consider at least the Nom.Sg. MUNUS-*anza* as typologically identical to the Nom.Sg. *šummanza*, i.e. as a secondarily sigmatized non-neuter consonant stem. I follow Jasanoff, *Ériu* 40 (1989) 135-141, (different opinion in Neu, *HS* 103 (1990) 214-215) in his view that it is not necessary to accept two roots, **g^{w}en-* next to **g^{w}enH$_2$-* in PIE, and that the Anatolian NomSg of PIE **g^{w}enH$_2$* originally ended in *-n*. This form was then secondarily sigmatized like *šummanza*.

3.3 *L-stems*

To my knowledge, there are no examples of sigmatized nominatives of non-neuter *l*-stems in Hittite.

On the other hand, as Kronasser, *EHS* (1966), 339, pointed out, the existence itself of the agent noun suffix *-ttalla-* (just like its counterpart *-ttara-*) may be indicative for the existence of non-sigmatized non-neuter *l*-stems next to the type *keššar*. Maybe, too, a thematization like *šuppala-* "cattle" reflects a non-neuter asigmatic singular form. On *takšul* see above.

3.4 *Other stemclasses*

Inherited *-eH*$_2$ stems (*ḫaššā-* "hearth", *ḫišša-* "cover") always show asigmatic nominative; they simply add *-s* to the inherited non-sigmatic form. This procedure is Common Anatolian. As will be explained below, the addition of *-s* to a nominative ending in a vowel is older than the sigmatization of the NomSg. in consonant stems.

4. *Luwian*

J. Friedrich, *Athenaeum* NS 47 (1969) 118, compared the Luwian nominal case in *-ša*/*-za* (as in *adduwalz*/*ša*, to the sigmatized NomSg. *ḫašterza*. This view was most recently discussed by O. Carruba, *StMed* 7(1992), 76-78 with reference to earlier literature, who, apart from other arguments, pointed out that the functions of *-š*/*za* in Hittite *šummanza* (explicitation of gender) and of Luwian *-ša*/*za* (according to Carruba: transferring a neuter to the function of an animate agens) are incompatible. I agree with Carruba that Luwian neuters in *-ša* have no direct link with sigmatization of the *ḫašterza* type. It might be worthwhile to reexamine the function of Luwian *-ša*/*za* at the background of the possibility that it derives from **-ga* and might be related to the Palaic derivations in *-ga-* (on this suffix see Starke, *StBoT* 31 (1990), 71-76).

In Luwian, the type *šummanza* does not exist. Also, according to Starke, *StBoT* 31, 62, inherited non-neuter consonant-stems generally received a thematic "Motionssuffix" *-i-* in the nominative and accusative commune of both singular and plural. The spread of the "Motionssuffix" over nouns is a secondary feature; Starke, *KZ* 100 (1987) 264, discovered that inherited non-neuter consonant stems preserved their consonantal character in the individual Luwian languages. So it would seem that Luwian went other ways than Hittite did, to characterize commune gender of inherited non-neuter nouns.

In his study on the stem-formation of the correspondents of PIE **dhugH*$_2$*tḗr* "daughter" (*duwattri-* etc.) in the Luwian languages, Starke, loc.cit., showed that these behave differently from other inherited non-neuter consonant-stems (such as the inherited non-neuter *iššr*(*i*)-"hand") in that they are thematized and do not preserve the original consonantal inflection. Starke ascribes this deviant development of the words for "daughter" in the individual languages to analogy. In the current context it may be of interest to retain that Luwian shows traces of a divergent treatment within the group of inherited non-neuter nouns (*duwattri*-, an *i*/*ya*-stem, against *iššr*(*i*)-, *tiyamm*(*i*)-, two semi-consonantal stems, Starke, *KZ* 100 (1987) 262 ff.; *StBoT* 31, 346-347) as Hittite does (*ḫašterza* vs. *keššar*, *tekan*).

5. N. Oettinger, *KZ* 94 (1980) 51, still acts on the assumption of a "reguläre Sigmatisierung uranatolischer geschlechtiger Nominative"; he states (ibid. n. 25) that "geschlechtige Nominative werden im Uranat. stets sigmatisch", adducing the cases of *ḫašterza* and lyd. *kaveś* "priest". His statement is repeated by Harδarsson, *MSS* 48 (1987) 120. However, Oettinger, *GsKronasser* (1982), 175 (still maintaining that "im Uranatolischen ... alle geschlechtigen Stämme" show sigmatization of the NomSg.) is aware of the contradicting evidence of *keššar*. As pointed out already by Friedrich and later again by Melchert, *Sprache* 29 (1983) 8 n. 20, the material does not allow such a generalizing approach.

The data indicate that non-neuter consonant stems are divided into sigmatizing and non-sigmatizing nouns. Non-sigmatizing nouns are subsequently thematized in historical times. Sigmatization shows two phonetic outcomes, the type *ḫarāš* and the type *šummanza*, *ḫašterza*. The type *ḫarāš* is Common Anatolian. The first question is, whether the two types of sigmatization belong to the same chronological level. Because we find co-occurrence of the two types of sigmatization in the *n*-stems only, the answer will be provided by the interpretation of the much debated type *ḫarāš* versus *šummanza*. The second question then will be, what precisely is the relation of sigmatization and thematization.

5.1. *Sigmatization*

As is well known, Oettinger, *KZ* 94 (1980) 44-63, provides an explanation which assumes that the two types (*ḫarāš* : *šummanza*) belong to the same chronological ("(vor)uranatolisch)') level and are the outcome of *-n+s* under different accent conditions. In doing so he gave up the earlier explanation (e.g. Pedersen, *Hitt.* 41) according to which the type *ḫarāš* (PIE -**ōn*) had lost its final *-n* already in PIE times and had adopted a sigmatic nominative subsequently. Harδarsson, *MSS* 48 (1987) 118 ff., while accepting Oettingers accent rule and chronology, proposed a way to combine both views by assuming that the outcome of the sigmatization depends on the form of suffix: PIE *-*ōn* had developed into PIE *-*ō* and Hittite simply added an *-s* to the vocalic ending (*ḫarāš*); PIE *-*ēn* had been preserved into Anatolian; addition of *-s* resulted in a group *-nz* (*šummanza*). This approach had been proposed already by Melchert, *Sprache* 29 (1983) 3-10); it is also accepted by Carruba, *StMed* 7 (1992), 78. Like Oettinger and Harδarsson, Carruba dates the sigmatization of the type *šummanza* explicitly to a "fase protoanatolica" (*StMed.* 79).

I follow the traditional view, taken up again by Melchert and Harδarsson, that some *n*-stems reached the Common Anatolian period with an asigmatic NomSg. ending in a vowel (PIE **-ōn* > **-ō*, **ḫarā*), and that others had preserved a final nasal. The reason for this result may well have been the form of the suffix (maybe **-ēn* as in **summan*: Gk. *ὑμήν*, -CN as in **dheg'hm* : *tēkan*). The type **ḫarā* was sigmatized in the Common Anatolian period. But **ḫarā* was sigmatized because it synchronically was conceived of as a vocalic stem, along with the inherited *-eH*$_2$ stem *ḫaššā*. If this is the case, the sigmatization of the type *šummanza* is not necessarily related and may well represent another (younger) chronological level.

A chronology of the sigmatization in the type *šummanza* is possible only by dating the development of -N+*s* into Hittite *-nz*. The development of the sequence nasal + *s* has been intensely debated since Oettingers, *KZ* 94 (1980), paper. For an overview I refer to O. Carruba, *StMed* 7 (1992), 74-79. In my opinion (as expressed in J. Weitenberg, *U-Stämme* (1984), 159-162), it is crucial to separate the development of Nasal+*s* in intervocalic position (where one should reckon with different outcomes for *-ms-* and *-ns-*; cf. also Melchert, *Sprache* 29 (1983) 7-8, *HS* 101 (1988) 211-212) from the result of nasal + *s* in final position. As for Hittite, the material shows, in my opinion beyond doubt, that the oldest groups Nasal+*s* in final position assimilated into *-s*:

- The GenSg. *-waš* of the verbal substantive in *-war* represents a proterodynamic (and improductive) **-we/ons*.
- The Accusative plural ending -C*uš* derives from -CN*s*, i.e from either -C*ns* or -C*ms*; for the latter see Starke, *StBoT* 31 (1990), 44 n. 72).
- The form *anzaš* "us" from **ns* does not speak against this development, as the element *-aš* may have been added to it before the development of *ns* into *nz* in Hittite (cf. Melchert, *Sprache* 29 (1983) 7-8). It would follow that the outcome *nz* of *n+s* is valid only for new groups of *n+s* in final position.

In Luwian, an original group Nasal+*s* in final position did not change, as is shown by *anz* "us" and the AccPlural forms in *-nz*+Vowel.

It follows, that the type *šummanza* cannot be dated to Pre-Anatolian times. Also, though this does not follow with unrestricted certainty from the material which I presented, the type is probably not Common Anatolian; it originated after at least some of the differences between the Hittite and Luwian branch had been developed. In contrast, sigmatization of the type *ḫarāš*, being already Common Anatolian, belongs to a different chronological layer. The motivation for the sigmatization of *šummanza* therefore is different from the motivation of the sigmatization in the type *ḫarāš*. One may suppose that at the Common Anatolian stage, a non-neuter NomSg. ending in a vowel generally was unacceptable. The coexistence of *keššar* and *ḫašterza* / *šummanza* indicates that subsequently, in late Common Anatolian or early Hittite, a non-neuter asigmatic nominative came to be unacceptable in a number of cases only.

5.2. *Thematization*

From now on, the sigmatization of *ḫarāš* will be left out of consideration and I shall concentrate on the younger sigmatization of the type *ḫašterza* and *šummanza*. At the beginning of the Old Hittite period we now may distinguish the following groups: inherited non-neuter consonant-stems with "younger" sigmatization (*ḫašterza*, *šummanza*), inherited non-neuter consonant-stems with an asigmatic NomSg. (*keššar*), inherited non-neuter consonant stems in thematized form (suffix *-ttalla-*). The thematized forms develop from non-sigmatic stems before our very eyes (as in *ḫuppar*(*a*)-). Thematization, therefore, is a property of such non-neuter consonant stems that were not subject to sigmatization. Thematization in Hittite is indicative of a non-sigmatized noun.

5.3. *Summing up:*

Non-neuter consonant stems are treated in two ways with respect to their Nom.Sg.: some receive a sigmatic ending, but some do not. The latter may be subsequently thematized in Hittite (from the Old Hittite texts onwards); in Luwian there are traces of a similarly differentiated treatment. It would seem that Hittite and Luwian both distinguish two groups of non-neuter *n*- and *r*-stems, though they seem to differ in the means through which they express these groups: Hittite sigmatizes, Luwian thematizes.

Is it possible to find a reason for these two ways of treating inherited asigmatic non-neuter nominatives?

6. This again is the question which Friedrich posed. An answer has been provided by Neu, *FsIvânescu* (1982-1983), within the context of PIE gender. I shall go into that aspect below; but there also is a formal aspect to consider. As explained above, it has been proposed (Melchert, Harðarsson) that asigmatic animate *n*-stems which retained an *-n* in the NomSg.c were of the form **ēn* (*šumman+za* : gr. ὑμήν). I agree that the form of the suffix may be the reason for the preservation of final *-n* in the NomSg.; but, of course, the form of the suffix at the synchronic level does not give a direct explanation for the lack of a uniform sigmatization in the group of non-neuter consonant stems as a whole.

A formal distribution may suggest itself in an historic approach. When we draw up a listing of the (very few) relevant words which have a reliable etymology, we immediately see that the sigmatization may be related to full degree of the suffix in the NomSg., whereas asigmatic forms occur with a zero degree suffix. The thematization in Luwian goes paralell with the Hittite sigmatized forms:

šummanza	_*suH$_1$mén_	Gk. ὑμήν m.
ištanza	_*pstén_	Skr. _stána-_ m.
ḫašterza	_*H$_2$stér_	Gk. ἀστήρ m.
	*dhugH$_2$tér (feminine)	Luw. _duttari-_
MUNUS-_za_	_*g^{w}énH$_2$_ (feminine)	
tekan	_*dhég'hm_ (feminine)	Luw. _tiyamm(i)-_
keššar	_*g'hésr_ (feminine)	Luw. _iššr(i)-_

One might draw a provisional conclusion from this listing: if the suffix does not show full grade at the prehistoric level, no sigmatization occurs.

7. As the table shows, apart from the purely formal distribution which emerges, based on the form of the suffix, it is also possible to relate the sigmatization (as well as the form of the suffix) to the distribution of PIE gender. If we make abstraction for a moment of the suffix derivations (_-ttara-, -ttalla-_) we find a distribution as follows:
- sigmatization occurs with words which in PIE are unmotivated masculines and animate beings.
- no sigmatization occurs with words which in PIE are unmotivated feminines.

These results show a remarkable agreement with the conclusions which I reached in a previous study (_MSS_ 48 (1987) 213-230) and which I briefly summarize here. On the basis of Starke's study on the "dimensional" cases (directive, dative, locative), I concluded that it is possible to find a threefold distinction as to nominal classification in Hittite. Starke pointed out that the use of the dimensional cases was dependent on animacy; non-animates may be used with (among others) a directive, animates may not. By combining the elements of animacy and gender in Hittite with the restrictions on the use of the dimensional cases, a threefold distribution emerges in the Old Hittite nominal system. There are neuter nouns - these always allow the use of a directive case; next to these there are two types of commune nouns: some commune nouns may occur with a "directive" case - from the etymological point of view these are unmotivated feminines in other PIE languages; other commune nouns may not occur with a "directive" case - from the etymological point of view they correspond with unmotivated masculines and natural animate beings (both male and female) in other PIE languages. This distinction goes parallel with, and originates from, the threefold gender division in PIE. It seems to me that combination of data of Hittite and of the other IE languages enables us to reach back one step into the development of PIE gender. In that particular stage, the PIE gender system was a three member system; its motivation was to a high degree already automatic, not clearly semantically motivated. The Hittite facts now enable us to be slightly more precise about the semantic contents of the PIE gender system: in my view, it turns out that in PIE (before the split of Hittite) the natural animates belong to the masculine gender. For that reason I coined the terms proto-masculine, proto-feminine, which exist together with the neuter. Proto-masculine comprises semantically unmotivated members (like **ped-* "foot") and a group of semantically motivated members, viz. all natural animate beings ("man", "woman"); proto-feminine comprises unmotivated members (like *keššar*). In my 1987 paper I refrained from discussing the gender of collective formations; also I did not discuss the way in which the semantic category of natural female beings migrated from the formal category of proto-masculine to feminine.

With the exception of the derived nouns (on which see below), the distribution of the sigmatization in non-neuter consonant stems corresponds to the results of my 1987 paper and I consider my view that the gender system of Hittite has developed on the basis of an inherited three member nominal classification system in PIE as confirmed by this distribution.

7.1 According to this line of thought, agent nouns with the suffix *-ttalla-/-ttara-* do not belong to the category of natural animates. In my terminology they are "proto-feminines". Such a qualification would apply not only to inner-Hittite derivations (like *aku-ttara* "one who gives to drink") but also to (probably) inherited formations like *weštara-*"shepherd" (next to av. *vāstar-*). This situation may be of importance to get a firmer grip on the implementation of the concept of "animacy" both in Hittite and in PIE. A tentative formulation might be that derivations, even when denoting natural animates, are not necessarily considered to be animate nouns in the formal sense. In the particular case of derived agent nouns, they are treated as adjuncts showing an adjectival character; it is the expression of an activity (*akuttara-* "giving to drink"etc.) which prevails upon the fact that the activity is normally performed by a natural animate being ("drink-giver").

8. The sigmatization of non-neuter consonant stems has been brought into relation with Anatolian and PIE nominal gender by Carruba and by Neu.

According to Carruba (most recently *StMed* 7 (1992), 79-80), both sigmatization and thematization belong to a first, pre-anatolian, stage of "animatization", of development into a binary system characterized by the morphological expression of the semantic contrast animate : inanimate. In that stage, animacy finds explicit expression through either direct sigmatization (*ḫarāš, šummanza*) or thematization, considered as a mere variant form of sigmatization. Apart from the (in my opinion incorrect) chronology, I reject Carruba's approach because it does not take into account the fundamental difference between sigmatizion and thematization (which, as I explained above, is not a special kind of sigmatization but a reflection of the absence of sigmatization).

Like Carruba, Neu, *FsIvânescu* (1982-1983), 128-129, places the development of the non-neuter nouns in the perspective of the opposition animate : inanimate. Neu, too, does not make a fundamental distinction between sigmatization and thematization which he ranges among other means (*-ant*-suffixation, con-gruence) which allow to make extra-linguistic animacy formally explicit in Hittite. Neu discusses the Hittite tendency to formalize the distinction animate : inanimate against the background of an inherited binary PIE gender system.

On the basis of my interpretation of the Hittite material as given here and in my 1987 paper I do not follow the opinion that there is an immediate link between the Hittite and PIE binary systems. There are Hittite facts which in Hittite receive a meaningful explanation on the basis of an inherited PIE three-member system. Hittite does not possess a three gender system, but it shows traces of an earlier, prehistoric three member nominal classification system. Late Common IE therefore possessed a three member system. Internal reconstruction strongly indicates that such a three member system derived from an earlier PIE binary system. But the Hittite facts, and especially the Hittite formal opposition commune : neutrum cannot be used as a direct witness for the semantic motivation (animate : inanimate) of the PIE binary system. Rather, Hittite should be studied with respect to its contribution to our understanding of the nature and origin of the Common IE three member system.